Introduction to Business

Introduction to Business

Jeff Madura
Florida Atlantic
University

SOUTH-WESTERN College Publishing

An International Thomson Publishing Company

PRODUCTION CREDITS

Art
Edward M. Rose/Visual
Graphic Systems, Ltd.

Composition
Parkwood Composition Inc.

Copyediting
Joan Torkildson

Cover Photo
Mark Segal/Tony Stone
Images

Indexing
Sandi Schroeder

*Interior Design and
Page Makeup*
David Farr/ImageSmythe

Photo Research
Dallas Chang

*Table, figure, feature, and
photo credits follow the index.*

Library of Congress Cataloging-in-Publication Data

Madura, Jeff.
        Introduction to business / Jeff Madura
                p. cm.
        Includes bibliographical references and index.
        ISBN 0-538-87883-5 (Student version; hardcover: alk. paper)
        ISBN 0-538-87884-3 (Looseleaf version: alk. paper)
        1. Industrial management. 2. Business. I. Title
HD31.M2815 1998   96-26938
658—dc20   CIP

    2 3 4 5 6 7 8 9   WST   6 5 4 3 2 1 0 9 8

Printed in the United States of America

I⒯P®

International Thomson Publishing
South-Western College Publishing is an ITP Company. The ITP trademark is
used under license.

v

PART V

Marketing 375

PART VI

Financial Management 469

PART VII

Special Topics 555

CONTENTS

PART I

CHAPTER 1

APPENDIX 1

vii

CHAPTER 2

CHAPTER 3

Summary of Part I 99

Business Environment 101

Economic Environment 102

PART II

CHAPTER 4

CHAPTER 6

Global Environment 160

APPENDIX 6

The Foreign Exchange Market 194

Summary of Part II 197

PART III

Management 199

CHAPTER 7

Fundamentals of Effective Management 200

CHAPTER 8

Organizational Structure 230

CHAPTER 9

Production Management 256

CHAPTER 10

Improving Production Quality and Efficiency 284

Summary of Part III 310

PART IV

CHAPTER 11

Managing Employees 311

Motivating Employees 312

PART V

CHAPTER 13

CHAPTER 14

Distribution Strategies 410

CHAPTER 15

Promotion Strategies 438

Summary of Part V 467

PART VI

CHAPTER 16

Financial Management 469

Accounting and Financial Analysis 470

CHAPTER 17

Financing 494

CHAPTER 18

Business Investment 522

CHAPTER 20

Risk Management 586

CHAPTER 21

Synthesis of Business Functions 612

APPENDIX A

APPENDIX B

APPENDIX C

A course on the Introduction to Business can be one of the most important courses for students. It provides the foundation of business knowledge and may steer the student's future academic and professional career into business. This text is written and organized in a manner that prepares students for careers in business. The text is organized into seven parts. Part I of the text explains how to establish a business, how to choose a type of business organization, and how to establish ethics guidelines for the business. Part II describes how a business can be affected by the business environment (economic, industry, and global conditions). Parts III and IV focus on the management of a business, while Part V focuses on the marketing, and Part VI explains the financial management of the business. Part VII discusses other business topics.

Focus on Key Business Concepts

This textbook is designed to prepare students for the business world by focusing on business concepts, without dwelling only on definitions. It uses a unique approach to place students in positions as decision-makers so that they can truly understand the dilemmas faced by businesses. Here are some examples of key business concepts that are discussed in this text:

➤ What are the objectives of managers, and what potential conflicts of interest can occur?
➤ How does the level of competition within an industry affect a firm's performance?
➤ How can firms benefit by expanding overseas? How can they be adversely affected by expanding overseas?
➤ Why do firms restructure their operations?
➤ How can firms motivate their employees?
➤ How should firms promote their products?
➤ How does the Federal Reserve System (the Fed) affect a firm's performance?
➤ How are the roles of different business departments integrated?
➤ How can a firm use the Internet to enhance its performance?

The concepts in this text are intended to make students think, rather than just rely on memory. This enables students to understand business strategy, so that they can not only survive but be successful in the business world. This text also emphasizes the types of concepts that have been identified by the American Assembly of Collegiate Schools of Business (AACSB), including teamwork, ethics, and cultural diversity.

Special Features That Distinguish This Text From Others

This text is loaded with features that help students learn concepts. In particular, there are six special features that differentiate this text from other texts:

VALUE CREATION FIRST, DEFINITIONS SECOND

Introduction to Business provides complete and thorough definitions to the hundreds of terms this course requires. Key terms are highlighted in four different ways:

➤ Bold-faced within the text
➤ Placed in the margin with full definitions
➤ Listed at the end of the chapter where they first appear
➤ Assembled in a glossary at the end of the text and page-referenced to where the definition appears.

But this isn't a dictionary of business terms. It emphasizes business concepts and strategy, which are much more important to your students' success in understanding business than memorizing a list of terms.

Introduction to Business reaches students through a variety of vignettes, exercises, and projects. In addition, end-of-chapter material reinforces this practical application through four distinct elements for each chapter: **Review Questions** that emphasize the review of basic chapter concepts; **Discussion Questions** that ask students to apply chapter concepts to business situations; **Case Applications** that present real-world scenarios for students to analyze and make decisions about the direction of a business; and **Video Cases** that allow you to bring a real business into the classroom, where students can discuss the situation faced by the business and the results of the action the business decided to take.

THE *Coca-Cola* COMPANY ANNUAL REPORT PROJECT

Introduction to Business can be packaged with the Coca-Cola™ Company Annual Report at no additional cost. This unique feature gives your students an inside look at how "America's Most Admired Corporation"[1] operates on a daily basis, helping them grasp business concepts by seeing those concepts at work in the real world, in a company they instantly recognize.

Discussion and exercises after each chapter specifically reference the annual report and show practical applications of chapter topics. This stimulating hands-on look at the Coca-Cola Company gives your students first-hand, real-life exposure to how all functional areas of a company work together to propel one of the world's most recognizable products into the 21st century.

[1.] SOURCE: *Fortune* magazine 1996 poll of leading executives.

PRACTICAL, REAL-WORLD APPLICATIONS AND TEAM-BUILDING PROJECTS

➤Global Business

Global Business boxes in each chapter show how global realities impact every area of business and emphasize how international opportunities and dilemmas affect the value-creation ability of the firm. For example, see *Global Quality Standards* on p. 292 in Chapter 10 and *Promoting Products Across Countries* on p. 452 in Chapter 15.

➤Self-Scoring Exercises

Self-Scoring Exercises scattered throughout the text prepare students for the business world by helping them understand their strengths and weaknesses and how those characteristics can successfully fit into a business setting. Questions posed include *Assessing Whether Specific Situations Are Ethical* (Chapter 3, p. 84), *Are You an Empowered Employee?* (Chapter 11, p. 327), and *How Much Risk Can You Take?* (Appendix A, p. 648).

➤Cross-Functional Teamwork

Cross-Functional Teamwork boxes emphasize the need for managers of different functional areas to work as a team in order to maximize profits, focusing on planning errors that occur when individual units are NOT working together towards the same goal.

➤ *Investing in the Stock of a Business* Project

Students acquire the annual report of a company in which they want to invest, then track that company's stock price throughout the semester. Students also investigate how their company finances their business operations, analyze how it markets products, and generally learn how it conducts business. An appendix after Chapter 1 provides information (including WWW addresses) on how to contact many of the leading businesses in the United States.

►Integration of Business Concepts

The text integrates business concepts throughout. There is a Part Introduction at the beginning of each part that introduces the chapters in that part and explains how those chapters are related. At the end of the part, a Part Summary summarizes how various concepts covered within the part are integrated.

As previously mentioned, the "Cross-Functional Team-work" feature in each chapter explains how various business strategies discussed within the chapter require team-work and interaction among employees of different departments. The final chapter of the text (Chapter 21) summarizes the entire text and integrates many of the key business functions that were described throughout the text.

EMPHASIS ON TECHNOLOGY

►Surfing the Net

The Internet has quickly become a critical ingredient in the formula for business success. **Surfing the Net** provides a background about what the Internet is, how to access important material, and what tools can make using the net more productive. Later chapters include a web site that ties into the chapter, like the General Motors web site on p. 466 in Chapter 15 and how it ties in with promotion. While students are encouraged to "surf the Net," this feature offers in-text graphical exposure to the World Wide Web. Featured sites include The Dilbert Zone on p. 228 in Chapter 7 and the Online Career Center on p. 669 in the Careers Appendix.

►Spotlight on Technology

The role technology plays in business continues to grow. **Spotlight on Technology** explores the integration of technology in business, both now and in the future, and develops the relationship between technology resources and each functional area of business. Examples include *American Airline's SABRE System: When Does Tough Competition Become Unethical?* on p. 82 in Chapter 3, *Using Information Technology to Improve Product Quality* on p. 299 in Chapter 10, and *Electronic Shopping Offered by Firms* on p. 444 in Chapter 15.

SMALL BUSINESS APPLICATIONS

Examples from Fortune 500 companies are beneficial, but it's also important to recognize issues facing smaller businesses. This text gives you many flexible options to do just that.

►College Health Club: Small Business Dilemma

This on-going simulation tracks the dilemmas of Sue Kramer's new business, College Health Club, from start-up through the growth phase. The *Small Business Dilemma* is tied closely to specific issues in individual chapters as students encounter the problems and opportunities faced by Sue and her business.

►Small Business Survey

Who are the board members of small firms? Do employees want more influence in business decisions? How do CEOs allocate their time when managing employees? Answers to these and similar questions are discussed in this feature, providing your students with a reality-based picture of how small business managers conduct day-to-day business.

►Running Your Own Business Project

This project takes students step-by-step through issues and decisions they would face in running their own business. Students choose their own business and develop a business plan as they go through the chapters of the text. Questions guide them through the issues they would face. At the end of the project, students can convert their accumulated answers into a formal business plan.

COST-SAVING FEATURES

➤ In-Text Study Guide

Found at the end of each chapter, the **In-Text Study Guide** questions essentially serve as an in-text study guide without the additional cost. Segments focus on test preparation, with 10 true/false and 25 multiple-choice questions per chapter. Answers to these questions are provided in Appendix C in the text. **In-Text Study Guide** questions are repeated in a separate section of the test bank for instructors who want to provide an incentive for students to work through the questions.

➤ Loose-Leaf Version of *Introduction to Business*

If you're concerned about keeping costs down for your students, or if you prefer to teach the topics in a different order, you should look into the loose-leaf version of *Introduction to Business.*

REINFORCEMENT OF KEY CONCEPTS

Many of the features just described reinforce the key concepts in each chapter. This leads to better understanding on the part of the student. In turn, instructors have more flexibility to focus on current events and class discussion exercises. To illustrate how this text can ensure a clear understanding through reinforcement, consider the concept of making a decision on how to promote a product, which is discussed in Chapter 15. The Small Business Survey section in that chapter discusses the opinions of small businesses about the skills that are necessary to be successful in selling products. The Global Business section in that chapter explains why promotion strategies need to be adjusted to appeal to customers in foreign countries. The Small Business Dilemma section in that chapter explains the dilemma of a health club that is considering various strategies to promote its services. The Coca-Cola Company Project in that chapter enables students to determine the ways in which The Coca-Cola Company promotes its

products. The "Running Your Own Business" exercise in that chapter asks students to determine how they would promote the products that they would sell if they could start their own business. The "Investing in the Stock of a Business" exercise in that chapter asks students to determine how the firm that they decided to invest in at the beginning of the term promotes its products. The cases in that chapter illustrate potential advantages and disadvantages of various promotion strategies. Finally, the in-text study guide in that chapter allows students to test their understanding of promotion strategies. Students are consistently empowered to make decisions as if they were managers of a firm.

Every key concept in the text can be reinforced with one or more of the text features just described. While instructors may vary in their emphasis of features in this text to reinforce each concept, they have a wide variety of features available to them.

THE SUPPLEMENT PACKAGE

We know how vital the supplement package is to the success of your Introduction to Business course, so we're pleased to provide an extensive package to accompany *Introduction to Business.*

➤ The **Instructor's Manual** prepared by Jeff Madura, James McGowen and Dennis Shannon (both of Belleville Area College), and Thomas Lloyd of Westmoreland County (PA) Community College includes chapter outlines, end-of-chapter answers, case solutions, suggestions for guest speakers, additional examples and exercises, and information on obtaining annual reports.

➤ The **Test Bank,** prepared by Thomas Lloyd, includes over 2,000 true/false, multiple-choice, and essay questions. Each question notes the learning objective, page references, and difficulty. Questions from the in-text study guide are included in a separate section.

➤ **WESTEST 3.2 Computerized Testing** allows you to create, edit, store, and print exams directly to work processor format. This version of WESTEST is more intuitive and less demanding of technical computer skills. New questions may be added and existing questions edited directly on-screen, similar to a word processor. Exam questions can be arranged automatically by type, randomly, or directly on-screen using the drag and drop feature. Available in Windows format to qualified adopters.

➤ **PowerPoint® Presentation Files** prepared by Susan Peterson of Western International are available in Windows format to qualified adopters. If you have access to Power-Point software, you can edit the custom presentations to create your own original presentations that include text, graphics, animation, and sound. The package that accompanies *Introduction to Business* includes custom presentations that contain chapter outlines and key exhibits from the text.

➤ **Video Case Segments:** Qualified adopters can choose from 21 selections from the Blue Chip Enterprise Initiative series. Additional videos include *How Wall Street Works,* This is *Internet: Roadmap for the Information Superhighway, Lee Jeans Marketing* and *The Minnesota Twins.*

➤ For instructors that go beyond the in-text coverage of the Internet, **Understanding and Using the Internet, Second Edition** by Bruce McLaren of Indiana State University can be packaged with the text at a reduced price.

➤ **Electronic Templates** are tied to both the *Running Your Own Business* and *Investing in the Stock of a Business* end-of-chapter projects.

➤ **Internet Updates** provide information on the text as well as marketing information and hot links to Web sites discussed in the text. These updates are available through the South-Western College Publishing home page on the Internet at **http://www.swcollege.com.**

For more information about supplement availability and qualifications, contact your local South-Western College Publishing representative.

Acknowledgments

Several reviewers reviewed drafts of chapters and helped improve the final product. They are acknowledged here in alphabetical order.

Dina Adler	Moorpark College
John Anstey	Univ. of Nebraska–Omaha
Jill Austin	Middle Tennessee State
Harold Babson	Columbus State CC
Todd Baker	Salt Lake City CC
Mary Jo Boehms	Jackson State CC
John Bowdidge	Southwest Missouri St.
Ernest Cooke	Loyola College MD
Donna Cooke	Florida Atlantic University
Robert Cox	Salt Lake City CC
Nancy D'Albergaria	Univ. of Northern Colorado
Bruce Erickson	Univ. of Minnesota
Jud Faurer	Metro State–Denver
Jan Feldbauer	Austin Community College
Jacque Foust	U of Wisconsin–River Falls
Richard Grover	Univ. of Southern Maine
Pola Gupta	Univ. of Northern Iowa
Douglas Heeter	Ferris State University
Craig Hollingshead	Marshall University
Raj Javalgi	Cleveland State University
Cheryl Johnson	Red Rocks CC
Melinda Jones	Morehead State University
Carol Jones	Cuyahoga CC
John Knappenberger	Mesa State University

Kenneth Lacho	Univ. of New Orleans
Thomas Lloyd	Westmoreland Co. CC
Trudi Manuel	Aims CC
John Mastriani	El Paso CC
James McGowen	Belleville Area College
Rusty Mitchell	Inver Hills CC
Bob Mitchum	Arkansas State at Beebe
Theresa Palmer	Illinois State Univ.
Susan Peterson	Western International
Lana Podolak	CC of Beaver County
John Porter	West Virginia Univ.
Richard Randall	Nassau CC
Andy Saucedo	Dona Ana CC
Robert Schramm	U Wisc–Whitewater
Dennis Shannon	Belleville Area College
Dawn Sheffler	Central Michigan
Cindy Simerly	Lakeland CC
Dennis Smith	The CC of Western Kentucky
Louise Stephens	Volunteer State CC
Ted Valvoda	Lakeland CC
John Warner	Univ. of New Mexico
W. J. Waters Jr.	Central Piedmont CC
Lewis Welshofer	Miami Univ (Ohio)
Tim Wright	Lakeland CC

In addition, many others offered insight and suggestions on particular business concepts, including Carol Annunziato, John Bernardin, Ed Diarias, Bob Duever, Dick Fenton, Dan Hartnett, Joan Hedges, Victor Kalafa, Dave Lynde, Randy Rudecki, Mike Suerth, Tom Vogl, Rachel Zera, and Peter Zutty. In addition, Grandon Gill contributed to the parts of the text that were focused on technology and management information systems. The Coca-Cola Company deserves recognition for its cooperation in developing The Coca-Cola Annual Report Project for this text. Special thanks go to John Szilagyi and Alex von Rosenberg (acquisitions editors) for their editing and creative ideas, to Laura Mezner Nelson (production editor) for ensuring a quality final product, and to John Tuvey (marketing manager) for his promotional and marketing efforts. Finally, I wish to thank my wife Mary and my parents for their moral support.

A business is created to provide products or services to customers. The first step in understanding how businesses operate is to recognize the most important functions and how a business is initially organized. Part I, which contains Chapters 1 through 3, provides this background. Chapter 1 describes key business functions and explains how to develop a plan for a new business. Chapter 2 describes the possible forms of business ownership that can be selected by creators of new businesses. It also describes how business owners are exposed to risk when they establish a business. Chapter 3 describes the ethical and social responsibilities of owners who establish a business and of employees who are hired to manage the business. This chapter is contained in Part I because a business should recognize ethical and social responsibilities as soon as it is established. Overall, Part I explains the main decisions that owners consider when they create a new business. These decisions serve as a foundation for other decisions that are made by employees as the business is developed. Consequently, they affect the performance of the firm and ultimately the value of the firm.

1

Planning A Business

A business (or firm) is an enterprise that provides products or services that customers desire. According to the U.S. Labor Department, more than eight hundred thousand businesses are created in the United States every year. Many businesses, such as Kodak and Ford Motor Company, develop products for customers. Others, such as American Airlines and Hilton Hotels, provide services rather than products. Common types of service organizations include travel agencies, and health care, law, and accounting firms. Managing a business that provides services can be as challenging and rewarding as managing a business that provides products.

The Learning Goals of this chapter are to:

1 Identify the key participants that are involved in a business.

2 Describe the key functions of business.

3 Explain how to develop a business plan.

KEY PARTICIPANTS IN A BUSINESS

1 **Identify the key participants that are involved in a business.**

Four types of participants are involved in a business:

➤ Owners
➤ Creditors
➤ Employees
➤ Customers

Each type of participant plays a critical role for firms, as explained next.

Owners

entrepreneurs people who organize, manage, and assume the risk of starting a business

Every business begins as a result of ideas about a product or service by one or more people, called **entrepreneurs,** who organize, manage, and assume the risk of starting a business. More than 8 million people in the United States are entrepreneurs.

In 1995 Allen Breed was selected as Entrepreneur of the Year by Inc. magazine. Breed focused on producing air bags in the 1980s. By 1990, all automobiles were required to have driver's side air bags. Automobile manufacturers were satisfied with the quality of Breed's air bags and steadily increased their demand for them.

An entrepreneur who creates a business initially serves as the sole owner. However, as a business grows, it may need more funding than the amount that can be provided only by the entrepreneur. As Allen Breed's business expanded, he raised $67 million by allowing investors to invest in the firm and become co-owners in 1992.

When the ownership of the firm is shared, the proportion of the firm owned by existing owners is reduced. Consider a bakery that two people created with a $100,000 investment each. Each person owns one-half of the firm. More funds could be obtained by allowing a third person to invest in the firm. If the third person were asked to invest $100,000, each of the three people would own one-third of the firm. Any profits (or earnings) of the firm that are distributed to owners would be shared among three owners. However, when the firm accepts investment from more owners, it should be able to increase its earnings so that the original owners can benefit despite their decreased share of ownership.

stock certificates of ownership of a business

stockholders investors who wish to become partial owners of firms

Many large firms periodically sell **stock** (certificates of ownership of a business) to investors who wish to become partial owners (called **stockholders**) of those firms. Large firms such as Exxon, IBM, and General Motors have millions of stockholders. Their stock can be sold to other investors who wish to invest in these firms.

Creditors

creditors financial institutions or individuals who provide loans

Firms typically require financial support beyond that provided by their owners. When a firm is initially created, it incurs expenses before it sells a single product or service. Therefore, it cannot rely on cash from sales to cover its expenses. Even firms that have existed for a long time, such as Little Caesars Pizza, Disney, and Nike, need financial support as they attempt to expand. A fast-growing business such as Little Caesars Pizza would not generate sufficient earnings to cover new investment in equipment or buildings.

Many firms that need funds borrow from financial institutions or individuals called **creditors,** who provide loans. Citicorp, NationsBank, and thousands of other

After selling his Book Stop chain to Barnes & Noble for $1.2 million, entrepreneur Gary Hoover moved on to his next business venture, TravelFest. The travel superstore opened in 1994 and features books, maps, luggage, and reservation and ticketing services.

commercial banks commonly serve as creditors for firms. Firms that borrow from creditors pay interest on their loans. The amount borrowed represents the debt of the firm, which must be paid back to the creditors along with interest payments over time. Large firms such as General Motors and DuPont have billions of dollars in debt.

Creditors will lend funds to a firm only if they believe the firm will perform well enough to pay the interest on the loans and the principal (amount borrowed) in the future. The firm must convince the creditors that it will be sufficiently profitable to make the interest and principal payments.

Employees

Employees of a firm are hired to conduct the business operations. Some firms have only a few employees; others, such as General Motors and IBM, have more than two hundred thousand. Those employees who are responsible for managing job assignments of other employees and making key business decisions are called **managers.** The performance of a firm is highly dependent on the decisions of its managers. While managers' good decisions can help a firm succeed, their bad decisions may cause a firm to fail.

managers employees who are responsible for managing job assignments of other employees and making key business decisions

GOALS OF MANAGERS　The goal of a firm's managers is to maximize the firm's value. Maximizing firm value is an obvious goal for many small businesses since the owner and manager are often the same. Firms such as McDonald's have publicly traded stock that can be purchased by individuals who are called stockholders or shareholders. For these firms, managers attempt to maximize the firm's value, which will maximize the value of stock held by stockholders (in which most of the stock is typically owned by investors who are not employees of the firm). The goal of maximizing shareholder value is confirmed by the following statements from recent annual reports:

> *We are not promising miracles, just hard work with a total focus on why we're in business: to enhance stockholder value.*
> — Zenith Electronics

> *Our objectives are well defined—to increase stockholder value, to have partnerships among employees, and to be good citizens.*
> — Bethlehem Steel Corporation

> *Our prime purpose is to reward risk-bearers [shareholders] by building long-term shareholder wealth.*　— Campbell's Soup

> *We create value for our share owners, and that remains our true bottom line.*
> — Coca-Cola Company

Maximizing the firm's value encourages prospective investors to become shareholders of firms.

To illustrate how managers can enhance the value of the firm, consider the case of Compaq Computers, a highly successful computer firm. Compaq's managers created a competitive advantage with an efficient system for producing computers. This resulted in low costs and allowed Compaq to provide high-quality computers at low prices. In this way, Compaq's sales increased substantially over time, as did its profits. The ability of Compaq's managers to control costs and sell computers at low prices satisfied not only the customers but also the owners (shareholders).

Customers

Firms cannot survive without customers. A firm must provide a desired product or service at a reasonable price. It must also ensure that the products or services produced are of adequate quality so that customers are satisfied. If a firm cannot provide a product or service at the quality and price that customers desire, customers will switch to the firm's competitors. Procter & Gamble and Saturn (a division of

Saturn pays particular attention to its customers. The photos shown are from the 1994 Saturn homecoming attended by 44,000 Saturn owners. Any Saturn owner is invited to an all-day picnic held at their Spring Hill, Tennessee factory.

General Motors) attribute some of their recent success to recognizing the types of products that consumers want. These firms also have a commitment to quality, and price their products in a manner that is acceptable to customers.

Summary of Key Participants

Firms rely on entrepreneurs (owners) to create business ideas and possibly to provide some financial support. They rely on other owners and creditors to provide additional financial support. They rely on employees (including managers) to produce and sell their products or services. They rely on customers to purchase the products or services they produce.

INTERACTION AMONG PARTICIPANTS   The interaction among a firm's owners, employees, customers, and creditors is illustrated in Exhibit 1.1. Managers decide how the funds obtained from owners, creditors, or from sales to customers should be utilized. They use funds to pay for the resources (including employees and machinery) needed to produce and promote their products. They also use funds to repay creditors. The money left over is profit. Some of the profit (or earnings) is retained and reinvested by the firm. Any remaining profit is distributed as **dividends** or income that the firm provides to its owners.

dividends income that the firm provides to its owners

Exhibit 1.1
Interaction among Owners,
Employees, Customers, and
Creditors

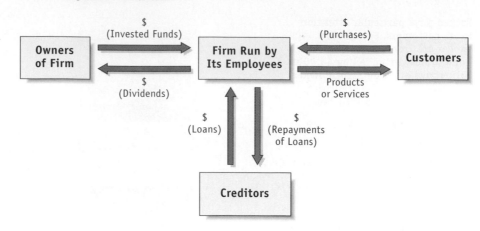

KEY FUNCTIONS OF BUSINESS

2 Describe the key functions of business.

The five key functions involved in operating a business are management, marketing, finance, accounting, and information systems. These five functions are the focus of this text because they must be conducted properly to make a business successful. Each of the functions is briefly introduced here and will be thoroughly discussed in other chapters.

management means by which employees and other resources (such as machinery) are used by the firm

marketing means by which products (or services) are developed, priced, distributed, and promoted to customers

finance means by which firms obtain and use funds for their business operations

accounting summary and analysis of the firm's financial condition

information systems include information technology, people, and procedures that work together to provide appropriate information to the firm's employees so they can make business decisions

Management is the means by which employees and other resources (such as machinery) are used by the firm. **Marketing** is the means by which products (or services) are developed, priced, distributed, and promoted to customers. **Finance** represents the means by which firms obtain and use funds for their business operations. **Accounting** is the summary and analysis of the firm's financial condition and is used to make various business decisions. **Information systems** include information technology, people, and procedures that work together to provide appropriate information to the firm's employees so they can make business decisions.

Interaction among Business Functions

Most business decisions can be classified as management, marketing, or finance decisions. Examples of these types of decisions are provided in Exhibit 1.2. Notice from this exhibit that management decisions focus on the use of resources, marketing decisions focus on the products, and finance decisions focus on obtaining or using funds.

A firm's earnings (or profits) are equal to its revenue minus its expenses. The manner by which each type of business decision affects a firm's earnings is illustrated in Exhibit 1.3. Since management decisions focus on the utilization of employees and other resources, they affect the amount of production expenses incurred. Since marketing decisions focus on strategies that will make the product appealing to customers, they affect the firm's revenue. Marketing decisions also influence the amount of expenses incurred as a result of distributing and promoting products. Since finance decisions focus on how funds are obtained (borrowing money versus issuing stock), they influence the amount of interest expense incurred. As the management, marketing, and finance decisions affect either a firm's revenue or expenses, they affect the earnings and value of the firm.

Much interaction takes place between management, marketing, and finance in making decisions. For example, production managers of Compaq Computer receive

Exhibit 1.2
Common Business Decisions

Management Decisions
1. What equipment is needed to produce the product?
2. How many employees should be hired to produce the product?
3. How can employees be motivated to perform well?

Marketing Decisions
1. What price should be charged for the product?
2. Should the product be changed to be more appealing to customers?
3. Should the firm use advertising or some other strategy to promote its product?

Finance Decisions
1. Should financial support come from the sale of stock or from borrowing money? Or a combination of both?
2. Should the firm attempt to obtain borrowed funds for a short-term period (such as one year) or a long-term period?
3. Should the firm invest funds in a new business project that has recently been proposed (such as expansion of its existing business or development of a new product), or should it use these funds to repay debt?

sales projections from the marketing managers to determine how much of a product to produce. The finance managers must receive the planned production volume from production managers to determine how much funding is needed.

How Some Business Functions Enhance Decision Making

Proper business decisions rely on accounting and information systems.

ACCOUNTING   Managers of firms use accounting to monitor their operations and to report their financial condition to their owners or employees. They can also assess the performance of previous production, marketing, and finance decisions. They may even rely on accounting to detect inefficient uses of business resources that can be eliminated. Consequently, a firm's accounting function can be used to eliminate waste, thereby generating higher earnings.

Exhibit 1.3
How Business Decisions Affect a
Firm's Earnings

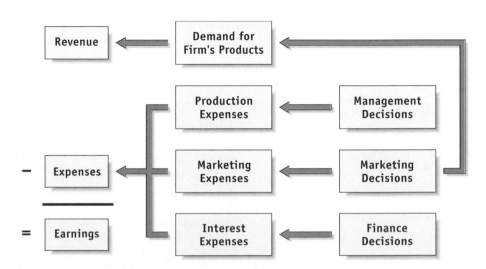

INFORMATION SYSTEMS   Firms use information systems to continually update and analyze information about their operations. This information can be used by the firm's managers to make business decisions. In addition, the information can be used by any employee within the firm who has access to a personal computer. For example, FedEx uses information on its computer system to track deliveries and determine when packages will arrive at their destination.

CREATING A BUSINESS IDEA

People will be willing to create a business only if they expect to be rewarded for their efforts. The rewards of owning a business come in various forms. Some people are motivated by the chance to earn a large income. Others desire to be their own boss rather than work for someone else. Many people enjoy the challenge or the prestige associated with owning a business. Most business owners would agree that all of these characteristics motivated them to start their own business.

A recent survey by the Center for Entrepreneurial Leadership found that 69 percent of high school students were interested in starting their own business. Yet, about 86 percent of the students rated themselves as very poor to fair on their business knowledge. People need to learn how a business operates before they consider creating a business.

Examples of highly successful firms that were created recently are listed in Exhibit 1.4. Notice the wide variety of successful businesses that have been created by entrepreneurs. Even though these firms are different, they all created a **competitive advantage** over their competitors.

competitive advantage an organization's unique qualities that allow it to compete successfully with other organizations offering similar products or services

Many firms have been successful as a result of quick response to a change in consumer preferences. For example, when running and rollerblading became popular, Nike and In-Line Skating produced more running shoes and rollerblades, respectively. Firms monitor consumer behavior trends to anticipate how consumer demand for products may change.

Examples of Successful Business Ideas

Many of the successful businesses identified in Exhibit 1.4 require a high degree of technology, a large amount of funds, or both. Yet, numerous business ideas can be implemented without relying on technology or much funding. A classic example is

Exhibit 1.4
Recent Examples of Successful Firms

Newly Established Business	Description of Business
Grand Casinos	Casinos in the Midwest and Gulf Coast
Netscape	Computer software
Sports Authority	Clothes and sports equipment store
Outback Steakhouse	Restaurant chain
Mesa Airlines	Airline
Papa Johns Int'l	Pizza chain
Regal Cinemas	Movie theaters
Petsmart	Pet stores

Rollerblades went from being a summer training product for ice skaters to becoming one of the most popular recreational products in the country in just a few years.

Domino's Pizza, which was established when Tom Monaghan (a college dropout) and his brother bought a bankrupt pizza parlor in 1960. Tom had to borrow the $500 that he needed to invest in the firm. Later, he bought his brother's interest in the business. Domino's Pizza now generates sales of about $1 billion per year.

Along with such classic examples, many other success stories have not received as much attention. Here are some examples:

1 *Roofing after a Hurricane* After Hurricane Andrew hit south Florida during the fall of 1992, many homes were left without roofs. There were not enough roofers in the area to repair all the roofs that were destroyed. Many people from other parts of the country with some background in roofing moved to south Florida and began roofing businesses. Some people had limited roofing experience but decided to quickly learn the business. Most of these roofers did not have a place of business but simply advertised in local newspapers.

Many of these new roofing businesses were successful because they provided a much-needed service. Screened-in porches were also destroyed during the hurricane, which generated many new screening businesses.

2 *Office Lunch Deliveries* When office workers in many cities were unable to find convenient, uncrowded restaurants for lunch, delivery service businesses were established to pick up food at various restaurants and deliver to offices. This type of business, which requires only a car and a car phone, has been successful because it provides a service that many people desire.

3 *Bed and Breakfast Rooms* Some households in popular tourist areas have created a bed and breakfast service for tourists. The room rates at bed and breakfasts are typically lower than that of hotels. This type of business has become popular over time, as some tourists are more comfortable staying in a home than in a hotel.

The three business ideas described here are quite different, but all were created in response to a perceived need or desire by potential customers. Entrepreneurs recognize customer needs and establish businesses that accommodate those needs.

Steps for Creating a Business Idea

Two steps for creating business ideas within a particular industry are to (1) identify consumer needs and (2) assess the business environment.

IDENTIFY CONSUMER NEEDS   A successful business idea usually begins by identifying what a customer needs or wants. Many firms conduct surveys to identify specific needs or preferences of consumers. A survey is most useful when focused on a particular type of product or service. For example, if Nike decided to produce rollerblades, the survey might focus on determining whether customers are satisfied with the rollerblades being sold by other firms.

ASSESS THE BUSINESS ENVIRONMENT   A second step when creating a business is to assess the business environment, which includes the industry environment, the economic environment, and the global environment. The industry environment is assessed to determine the degree of competition. If a market for a specific product is

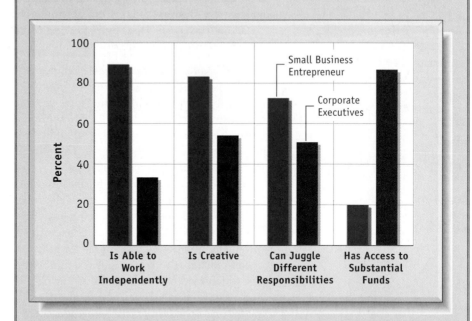

SMALL BUSINESS SURVEY

Characteristics of Business Entrepreneurs

A recent survey asked adults whether specific business characteristics described here describe small business entrepreneurs, corporate executives, or both. The perceptions of the adults who responded to the survey are shown in the following graphic.

In general, the entrepreneur is perceived favorably in terms of various business characteristics. However, the one characteristic in which the entrepreneur is rated lower than corporate executives is access to funds. A high percentage of respondents thought that entrepreneurs do not have access to substantial funds. This one possible deficiency cannot necessarily be controlled by entrepreneurs, as they must rely on investors and creditors for funds.

served by only one or a few firms, a new firm may be able to capture a significant portion of the market.

One must also ask whether a similar product could be produced and sold at a lower price, while still providing reasonable earnings. A related question is whether the new business would be able to produce a higher-quality product than the competitors. A new business idea is more likely to be successful if it has either a price or quality advantage over its competitors.

The economic environment is assessed to determine how demand for the product may change in response to future economic conditions. The demand for a product can be highly sensitive to the strength of the economy. Therefore, the feasibility of a new business may be influenced by the economic environment.

The global environment is assessed to determine how the demand for the product may change in response to future global conditions. The global demand for a product can be highly sensitive to changes in foreign economies, the number of foreign competitors, exchange rates, and international trade regulations.

DEVELOPING THE BUSINESS PLAN

3 **Explain how to develop a business plan.**

business plan a detailed description of the proposed business, including a description of the business, the types of customers it would attract, the competition, and the facilities needed for production

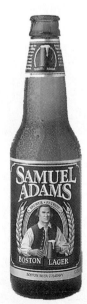

Samuel Adams is a leading product in the specialty beer market. The company's high product standards helped them become the first American beer to receive a prestigious quality designation from the German beer council.

Once entrepreneurs create a business idea, they can fully assess the potential profitability of that idea by developing a **business plan.** A business plan is a detailed description of the proposed business, including a description of the business, the types of customers it would attract, the competition, and the facilities needed for production.

The business plan is not only for the entrepreneur but also for any investors or creditors who may provide financial support. Entrepreneurs commonly provide their plan to those investors who may be willing to serve as partial owners. They also provide their plan to creditors (such as commercial banks) that may be willing to provide business loans. Thus, the business plan should be clear and must convince others that the business will be profitable. If investors do not believe in the business plan, they will be unwilling to invest funds in the business. If creditors do not believe in the plan, they will not provide any loans. In this case, entrepreneurs would have to rely completely on their own funds, which may not be sufficient to support the business.

In 1985, Jim Koch developed a business plan for Boston Beer Company to produce Samuel Adams beer. He invested $100,000 of his own money and raised $140,000 in additional funds to begin his business. He focused on the specialty beer market and focused on selling the beer within four months from when it was bottled, since beer could become stale over time. This was the first application of freshness dating to beer. Samuel Adams beer developed a reputation for its quality. By 1995, the Boston Beer Company generated $14 million in profits. The success of this business was partially attributed to an excellent business plan.

The business plan can demonstrate that the entrepreneur has conducted a comprehensive review of all business aspects. The plan should stay focused on all aspects that have some impact on potential profitability. Many business plans are between eight and twelve pages long. A complete business plan normally includes a management plan, a marketing plan, and a financial plan, as explained in more detail next.

Management Plan

A management plan focuses on the proposed organizational structure and production of the firm.

ORGANIZATIONAL STRUCTURE   An organizational structure identifies the roles and responsibilities of the employees hired by the firm. The organizational structure of a new factory is more complicated than that of a pizza delivery shop. If the owner plans to manage most of the operations, the organizational structure is simple. Some businesses begin with the owner assuming most responsibilities, but growth requires the hiring of managers. Even if owners initially run the business, they should develop plans for the future organizational structure. The job descriptions of each employee should be identified, along with the estimated salary to be paid to each employee.

PRODUCTION   Various decisions must be made about the production process, such as the site (location) of the production facilities and the design and layout of the facilities. The location decision can have a major effect on a firm's performance because it influences both the price of renting space in a building and the revenue generated by the business.

 The proposed design and layout of the facilities should maximize the efficiency of the space available. This proposal should contain cost estimates on any machinery or equipment purchased. The cost estimates for factories are normally more complicated than those for retail stores.

Marketing Plan

A marketing plan focuses on the target market, as well as product characteristics, pricing, distribution, and promotion.

customer profile characteristics of the typical customer (based on gender, age, hobbies, and so on)

TARGET MARKET   The **customer profile,** or characteristics of the typical customer (based on gender, age, hobbies, and so on), should be identified. This helps to deter-

High performance motorcycles, such as the Triumph Daytona, are targeted primarily to long term motorcycle enthusiasts.

target market market of customers that fit the customer profile

mine the **target market,** which represents the market of customers that fit the customer profile. A paperback book of fiction for adults has a much larger target market than one for young children.

PRODUCT CHARACTERISTICS   The characteristics of the product should be described, with an emphasis on how the product is more desirable than similar products offered by competitors. A product may be desirable because it is easier to use, is more effective, or lasts longer. Any competitive advantage of this product over similar products should be identified.

PRICING   The proposed price of the product should be stated. Prices of similar products sold by competitors should also be mentioned. The price will influence the demand for the product.

DISTRIBUTION   The means by which the product will be distributed to the customers should be described. Some products are sold to customers directly, while others are distributed through retail outlets.

PROMOTION   The means by which the product will be promoted should be stated. The promotion strategy should be consistent with the customer profile. For example, products that appeal to college students may be advertised in student newspapers.

Financial Plan

The financial plan should demonstrate why the business is feasible and should propose how the business will be financed. That is, how much of the funds will come from owners and how much from creditors?

FEASIBILITY   The benefits and costs of a business must be estimated to determine whether the business is feasible (whether the benefits exceed the costs). The business must be judged as feasible by the owner and by any creditors who will provide financial support.

The details of the business plan can be used to create forecasts of expected revenue and expenses of the business over time. Forecasts of the sales volume and product price could be used to forecast periodic revenue. The proposed organizational structure, location, design, and layout can be used to estimate the expenses involved in the proposed business.

The estimated revenue and expenses (including payments to creditors) can be used to forecast periodic earnings. These earnings can be evaluated to determine whether they provide an acceptable profit to the owners. In addition, the risk of the business should be assessed by measuring the uncertainty of future earnings. If the risk is high, owners should be willing to implement the project only if the potential profits adequately compensate for the risk involved.

FINANCING THE BUSINESS   The business must be financially supported. Most businesses require a large initial outlay to cover purchases of machinery, equipment, and possibly a building. While the owners of the business normally use some of their own funds to support the business, they may need additional financing. If they decide to request financing from a financial institution (such as a commercial bank), they will need to disclose a detailed business plan. Then the lending institution can determine whether the proposed business deserves a loan. If the lending institution

---

SPOTLIGHT ON TECHNOLOGY

Business Planning Software

A good business plan is a complex document. It must be well organized so that the reader can grasp the nature of the company, the marketplace, and the entrepreneur's vision of the future. It usually offers sophisticated financial analysis, to demonstrate the bottom-line implications of the plan. To aid readers in digesting the analysis, high-quality graphics are often desirable, both numeric (such as financial and market information) and qualitative (such as organization charts). In the past, the mechanics of putting such a plan together were both time-consuming and expensive. Today, business plan software can be used to make the process of creating such a plan much easier.

Many examples of business plan software are available on the market. Most of the packages contain a collection of tools which, together, can be used to create a complete business plan. The best packages incorporate many of the following capabilities:

➤ *Business Plan Outlines:* Packages normally offer one or more outlines of business plans, which the manager can use as a starting point for creating the plan. Some packages take managers through a series of questions in order to select the most appropriate outline for the specific business.

➤ *Text Generation:* Much of the information that goes into a business plan is relatively standardized, sometimes referred to as "boilerplate." Business plan software can often insert such text directly into the plan, making appropriate substi-

tutions for company names and products. Once in place, managers should be able to edit the text.

➤ *Forecasting:* The ability to create consistent projections is a must in business plan software. Packages should allow managers to predict sales and costs in a variety of ways (for example, using percentage growth models, market share models, or values that are individually specified by the planner) and should ensure that wherever data interrelates, it is consistent. For example, when the planner changes values in a table of projected market shares, forecasted sales in other parts of the document should automatically be updated.

➤ *Graphics:* Business plan software should, at a minimum, offer the ability to create charts of several different types (bar charts, pie charts, line charts) and should also allow users to draw other common charts, such as organizational charts.

➤ *Word Processing:* The best business plan software comes with a built-in word processor. The planner can then use the word processor to edit the final plan, spell-check it, and automatically generate a table of contents. Some business planning software, in the future, may also be sold as an add-on to existing word processors or office suites, such as Microsoft's Office.

➤ *Supplementary Documents:* A number of business plan packages offer supplementary documents, such as disclosure agreements, which are often used in conjunction with business plans, although not necessarily part of the document.

Today, business plan software does little to help the manager formulate the ideas behind the business plan. It can be invaluable, however, in organizing and constructing the plan itself.

---

believes that the projections of revenue are overestimated or projections of expenses are underestimated, it may decide not to provide financing.

An alternative source of funds is to issue stock to the public. However, most firms rely heavily on funding from the entrepreneurs who established them, and from loans when they are initially created. They may consider issuing stock only after demonstrating adequate performance for several years. Recently, firms such as Netscape (producer of computer software) and Red Hook Ale (producer of beer) have issued stock to obtain additional funds.

Summary of a Business Plan

The key parts of a business plan are summarized in Exhibit 1.5. Notice that the business plan is based on key business functions: management, marketing, and finance.

Exhibit 1.5
Contents of a Typical Business Plan

1. *DESCRIPTION OF PROPOSED BUSINESS* Describe the product (or service) provided by the proposed business.
2. *MANAGEMENT PLAN*

➤ Organizational structure: Describe the organizational structure and show the relationships among the employee positions. This structure should also identify the responsibilities of each position in overseeing other positions, and describe the specific tasks and salaries of managers and other employees.
➤ Production Process: Describe the production process, including the site, design, and the layout of the facilities needed to create a product. Also describe the planned amount of production per month or year.

3. *MARKETING PLAN*

➤ Target Market: Describe the profile (such as the typical age and income level) of the customers that would purchase the product and therefore make up the target market. (Who will buy the product?)
➤ Product Characteristics: Explain desirable features of the product. (Why will customers buy the product?)
➤ Pricing: Describe how the product will be priced relative to other competitors. (How much will customers pay for the product?)
➤ Distribution: Describe how the product will be distributed to customers. (How will customers have access to the product?)
➤ Promotion: Describe how the product will be promoted to those potential customers. (How will customers be informed about the product?)

4. *FINANCIAL PLAN*

➤ Feasibility: Estimate the revenue, expenses, and earnings of the proposed business over the next five years. Consider how the estimates of revenue, expenses, and earnings of the proposed business may change under various possible economic or industry conditions.
➤ Funds Needed: Estimate the amount of funds needed to establish the business and to support operations over a five-year period.

ASSESSING A BUSINESS PLAN

Many business ideas may seem reasonable but may not be undertaken because of various concerns by the entrepreneur after developing the business plan. Some concerns may relate to the potential revenue to be generated by the business. Perhaps the potential demand for the product or service is highly uncertain. Other concerns may relate to the expense of producing the product or service. For example, the entrepreneur may believe that the costs of production may be too high. Any concerns about the revenue or the expenses cause concerns about the potential profitability. If the business idea does not have much potential for profit, the entrepreneur may decide to search for alternative business ideas.

If the estimated costs of the business are too high, this does not necessarily mean that the business idea should be completely eliminated. Perhaps one or more aspects of the proposed business needs to be changed to make the idea feasible. For example, a new Blockbuster Video store may not be feasible in a business district because of the high costs of renting space in that location. An alternative location may significantly reduce the cost of renting a facility. Yet, the firm's revenue may also be affected by a different location. An entirely new cost-benefit analysis should be conducted after revising the proposed location or any other part of the business plan for a specific business.

Developing A New Health Club Business

In every chapter of this text, some of the key concepts are illustrated with an application to a small health club business. The "Business Dilemma" section in each chapter allows students to recognize the dilemmas and business decisions that they may face in the future. For this chapter, the application is on the development of a business plan for the health club.

BACKGROUND   Sue Kramer is a business major in her senior year. Although she has limited funding, she has always wanted to own a business. Throughout her college years, she has belonged to a health club that is a thirty-minute drive from campus. This club has all types of weight and exercise machines but does not offer any aerobics classes. Sue's informal discussions with several other students who also use the club have revealed that they would prefer a health club that not only has weight and exercise machines but also offers aerobics classes. The students would also prefer a health club that is inexpensive and more convenient to the college campus.

Sue begins to seriously consider establishing her own business, a health club that would serve the needs of other students at the college. She hands out a brief questionnaire to two hundred students on campus to determine whether they might be interested in joining a new health club and what types of club facilities they desire. She then checks a local yellow pages directory and other sources to identify any other health clubs that would be considered competitors within the local area.

Next Sue inquires about the price of renting space at a small shopping mall across the street from the college campus. She also starts pricing weight and exercise machines that she would need to purchase or rent to start this business. To reduce the initial outlay necessary for the business, she plans to rent the machines rather than purchase them.

Dilemma

Sue cannot establish the health club until she determines that the idea is feasible and obtains financial support. Suggest a business plan that Sue could use to establish her business.

Solution

Sue develops a business plan and determines that she would need a $40,000 loan; her plan is summarized in Exhibit 1.6, although an actual business plan may contain more details. Review this business plan before continuing.

The business plan summarized in Exhibit 1.6 can help Sue (the owner) estimate the revenue and expenses resulting from the business. While these estimates are normally completed for a five-year period, they are provided for only the first year in Exhibit 1.7.

ESTIMATION OF REVENUE   The estimated number of memberships per period can be multiplied by the price to derive an estimate of revenue. In our example, the estimated demand in the first year is 300 memberships, while the price per membership

Exhibit 1.6
Summary of Business Plan for College Health Club (CHC)

Description of Proposed Business

The proposed business is a health club called College Health Club (CHC) that would be located at the corner of 1st Street and Bell Avenue. Space for the health club would be obtained by leasing (renting) four connected units within the shopping mall. The health club would offer weight machines, exercise machines, and aerobics classes.

Management Plan

➤ Production Process: This business would produce health club services. The facilities needed to provide the health club services are (1) four connected units in the shopping mall across from the campus, (2) numerous weight machines and exercise machines, (3) a small locker room with showers, and (4) miscellaneous items. The units can be leased for a total of $40,000 per year. The weight and exercise machines would be rented for a total of $10,000 per year. The insurance and utility expenses are included within the rent expense.

  The facilities should be able to handle five hundred memberships. If the memberships increase beyond that amount, the facilities would be expanded.

➤ Organizational Structure: Sue Kramer would be the sole owner and president of CHC, and would oversee all policies established by CHC. Sue would earn a salary of $20,000. Her salary is intended to only cover her general living expenses. Since she is the sole owner, she will earn most of her return on the business from the business earnings. These earnings will be reinvested into the firm to support any growth in the business. Initially, Sue will be the only full-time employee. She will spend much of her time on marketing tasks, in order to boost memberships.

  Lisa Lane (friend of Sue's and a senior at the college) would work at the firm on a part-time basis. She would be an aerobics instructor for some of the classes. Lisa will be paid $10 per hour for her work. She will probably be paid about $10,000 in the first year (based on one thousand hours of work), but will receive a higher salary as the club's memberships increase.

  Given the small size of the proposed business, the organizational structure is very basic. Lisa reports to Sue. If the business grows, the organizational structure will have to be revised.

Marketing Plan

➤ Target Market: CHC would target students and employees of the college.

➤ Product (or Service) Characteristics: This health club would offer benefits over existing competitors. It would offer weight machines, exercise machines, aerobics classes, convenience, and affordability. Two competing health clubs are in the area. One is thirty minutes away by car; it does not offer aerobics classes at the present time. The other is ten minutes away by car; it offers a wide variety of exercise and weight machines and aerobics. However, the membership fee is much higher than that of the first club.

➤ Pricing: CHC would charge an annual membership fee of $250 to customers. This price is much lower than the other competitor health club that is 10 minutes away by car.

➤ Distribution: CHC would distribute its health club services on its own facilities. The distribution strategy tends to be simplified for firms like CHC that provide services instead of products.

➤ Promotion: CHC would advertise regularly in the college's newspaper. Its promotion efforts would focus on college students and employees. It would attempt to develop a close relationship with the college and would create promotions for college students. The total promotion expense would be about $10,000 per year.

Financial Plan

➤ Funds Needed: Various expenses must be paid before any revenue is generated by CHC. Sue Kramer desires to have $50,000 to start the business. Part of this amount would be needed to pay the lease expense over the first few months. Also, the equipment and miscellaneous items would need to be purchased immediately. Sue has $10,000 that she has saved over the years. She plans to invest that amount and would like to borrow the remaining $40,000 from the commercial bank. She believes she would be able to pay off the loan in three years, based on her expectations of revenue and expenses. If she decides to expand the business in the future, she may need to borrow additional funds to support the expansion.

➤ Feasibility: The earnings of the health club are forecasted as the estimated revenue minus estimated expenses. The source of revenue is annual memberships, and the key factor affecting revenue is the number of people who will sign up for membership each year. The membership level is expected to grow each year. The main expenses are the cost of leasing the space, the cost of renting the weight and exercise machines, and salaries paid to the two employees.

  The revenue is expected to be $21,000 less than the business expenses in the first year (negative earnings). In the second year, the revenue is expected to equal business expenses (zero earnings). In the next three years, the revenue is expected to exceed expenses, resulting in positive earnings. Specifically, the firm's earnings are expected to be $40,000 in Year 3, $80,000 in Year 4, and $90,000 in Year 5.

Exhibit 1.7
Estimates of Revenue and
Expenses of CHC in First Year

(1)	Estimated Demand for the Service	300
(2)	Price of the Service (Membership Fee)	$250
(3)	**Revenue = (1) × (2)**	**$75,000**
(4)	Salary Expense (Sue and Lisa's Salaries)	$30,000
(5)	Rent Expense (Leasing Space)	$40,000
(6)	Machine Rental Expense	$10,000
(7)	Marketing Expense	$10,000
(8)	Interest Expense	$6,000
(9)	**Total Expenses = (4) + (5) + (6) + (7) + (8)**	**$96,000**
(10)	**Earnings = (3) − (9)**	**−$21,000**

is $250. Thus, the estimated revenue is $75,000 (300 × $250 per membership) as shown in row (3) of Exhibit 1.7.

ESTIMATION OF EXPENSES The total expenses can be estimated by deriving an estimate of each type of expense, as shown in rows (4) through (9) of Exhibit 1.7. The estimated salary expense of $30,000 is the combination of Sue and Lisa's salaries specified in the business plan. The rent, machine rental expenses, and marketing expenses are stated in the business plan. The interest expense is based on the $40,000 Sue wishes to borrow at an annual interest rate of 15 percent (15% × $40,000 = $6,000).

ESTIMATION OF EARNINGS The business earnings are estimated as the difference between the estimated revenue and estimated expenses. To simplify the example, taxes are not considered here. While the earnings are expected to be negative in the first year, the firm's performance should improve if memberships increase over time. It is not unusual for a firm to incur a loss in its first year.

Given that the salary, lease, and machine rental expenses are somewhat predictable, much of the uncertainty about this firm's earnings involves the firm's revenue; that is, the demand for CHC's services is uncertain. If the revenue is overestimated, the earnings will likely be overestimated as well. Even if the health club has zero memberships (resulting in zero revenue), it will still incur the expenses just described.

While Sue recognizes this uncertainty, she is confident that the health club would generate her predicted earnings. She decides to submit her plan to her local commercial bank.

Additional Issues for Discussion

1 Why would Sue attempt to obtain the $40,000 from a creditor rather than from a second owner?

2 Assume that the enrollment at the college is expected to grow by 10 percent each year. How would this affect the estimated earnings for CHC?

3 Sue would need four connected units in the shopping mall to create CHC.

Assume that there are two more connected units that Sue could lease as well. What would be an advantage of leasing more space? What is the main disadvantage of leasing more space?

SUMMARY

1 The key participants involved in business are owners, creditors, employees, and customers. The owners invest in the firm, while creditors lend money to the firm. Employees are hired to conduct the firm's business operations efficiently, in order to satisfy the owners. The firm's revenue is generated by selling products or services to customers.

2 The key functions in operating a business are management, marketing, finance, accounting, and information systems. Management

decisions determine how the firm's resources are allocated. Marketing decisions determine the product to be sold, along with the pricing, distribution, and promotion of that product. Finance decisions determine how the firm obtains funds and invests funds.

Business decisions are improved as a result of accounting and information systems. Accounting is used to monitor performance and detect inefficient uses of resources in order to improve business decisions. Information systems are used to provide the

firm's employees with information in order to improve business decisions.

3 A business plan forces an owner of a proposed business to specify all the key plans for the business. The business plan normally consists of (1) a management plan that explains how the firm's resources are to be used, (2) a marketing plan that explains the product pricing, distribution, and promotion plans, and (3) a financial plan that demonstrates the feasibility of the business and explains how the business will be financed.

KEY TERMS

accounting
business plan
competitive advantage
creditors
customer profile

dividends
entrepreneurs
finance
information systems
management

managers
marketing
stock
stockholders
target market

REVIEW QUESTIONS

1 Identify the four key participants in a business and explain their roles.

2 If you were to start your own business, discuss the key functions needed to operate the business. Discuss some decisions made by each function.

3 Identify the steps involved in creating a business idea within a particular industry.

4 Discuss the environmental factors

that may impact the success of a business.

5 Why should a business plan be clear and precise? Explain what is included in a business plan.

6 How can the three major decisions made within a business plan be classified?

7 Explain how business plans become working documents for practicing

managers in their daily operations.

8 What is included in a marketing plan? Give a brief explanation of the elements.

9 Give a brief description of a typical financial plan in starting a new business.

10 Explain the concerns an entrepreneur would have in launching a business.

DISCUSSION QUESTIONS

1 Assume you are in a rock band that performs at the college you attend. Is a product or a service being provided? Is the management function more important or less important than the marketing function for your band?

2 You are planning to open your own record store in a local mall. Discuss this statement: "The customer is king."

3 Assume that you have just bought stock in an existing corporation. Discuss what you would look for in the corporation's performance.

4 You are thinking about starting a pizza business in your hometown. How important would information systems be in your decision to launch this type of business?

5 Wal-Mart is planning to open a new store in your local area. Since Wal-Mart is nationally known, is it necessary for this store to have a marketing plan designed for this particular location?

RUNNING YOUR OWN BUSINESS

The following exercise allows you to apply the key concepts covered in each chapter to a business that you would like to create for yourself. The application of these concepts to a business in which you are interested enables you to recognize how these concepts are used in the business world. Since this chapter focused on the creation of a business idea, you will be asked to create your own business idea. Give this some serious thought, since you will be developing specific details about your business idea at the end of each chapter. In this chapter, you learned how a college student developed a health club business. One could develop numerous types of small businesses without necessarily being a business expert. If you do not have any ideas initially, consider the types of businesses that are in a shopping mall. Or consider the firms that produce and sell products to those businesses. You might look through the yellow pages to recognize the types of small businesses that exist.

The "Running Your Own Business" exercise at the end of each chapter will apply the key concepts contained in that chapter to the business that you create here. By developing a business idea, you may actually implement it someday. Alternatively, you may realize from developing your idea why such a business could fail, which may lead you to alternative business ideas.

When developing your business idea, you should try to create a business that will require the hiring of at least a few employees in the future. This allows for easier application of those chapters that focus on managing employees.

1 Describe in general terms the type of business that you would like to create.

2 Explain in general terms how your business would offer some advantage over competitive firms.

INVESTING IN THE STOCK OF A BUSINESS

The following exercise allows you to apply the key concepts covered in each chapter to a firm in which you are interested.

If you had funds available right now to purchase the stock of a firm, which stock would you purchase? Record the stock price of that firm by reviewing today's stock quotations in your local paper or in the *Wall Street Journal.* Your instructor may explain how to find these quotes. If the stock was issued by a large U.S. firm, it is probably listed on the New York Stock Exchange (NYSE). Otherwise it may be on the American Stock Exchange (AMEX) or on the Over-the-Counter Exchange (NASDAQ).

Record the following information:

➤ Name of the Stock _____
➤ Today's Date _____
➤ Present Stock Price per Share _____
➤ Annual Dividend per Share _____
➤ Standard & Poor's (S&P) 500 Index _____

The price and dividend information is provided for each stock within the stock quotations.

The S&P 500 index is based on the stock prices of five hundred large firms. It indicates the general level of stock prices and is quoted in the section of the newspaper that provides stock price quotations. It also serves as a benchmark with which you can compare your stock's performance at the end of the term.

At the end of each chapter, the section "Investing in the Stock of a Business" will allow you to determine how the chapter's key concepts apply to that firm. You will need the annual report of the firm, which can be ordered by calling or writing to the firm's shareholder relations department. Addresses of many firms are available at your local library. Addresses for some well-known firms are disclosed in Appendix 1, which is at the end of this chapter. For your information, Appendix A (near the end of this text) provides a background on investing in stocks.

You should also monitor how the price of your stock moves over time in response to specific conditions. This will help you recognize the factors that can affect the firm's stock price (and therefore its value). At the end of the school term, the "Investing in the Stock of a Business" project at the end of the last chapter will help you determine the performance on your investment. An investment disk is also available for you to keep your comments on this project in one place. This disk allows you to easily monitor the performance of the stock you selected. It also allows you to select two other stocks that you would like to invest in, so that you can gain experience in monitoring stocks of business.

CASE 1 Starting a New Business

Joe Shott is planning to launch a small business of footwear production in his hometown. He recently graduated from a local community college. He perceives himself as a risk taker and high achiever who wants instantaneous feedback of results. These skills are much different from what he expects are needed to manage the operation once the business is started. As a practicing manager, he knows he must make decisions and work with people to achieve objectives. Joe recognizes the need for a business plan to present to his local bank. He believes this can be a working document to start his business, and he will use this proposal as an operating plan once the business is up and running. He is ahead of the game because he has already conducted marketing research and has a small market niche he envisions for the production of athletic shoes. His target market will be teenagers who participate in athletics. He plans to use high-profile athletes to promote his merchandise.

Joe recognizes an inherent part of a business plan is the financing of a business. He will need $120,000 to launch this business. He has $40,000 in savings and needs an $80,000 loan from the bank. He forecasts the business to be profitable and economically feasible during the first six months of operation.

The organization will be structured as follows: Joe will be the president, his wife, Ann, will handle the accounting function, and Joe's brother-in-law, David, will handle all the sales and marketing activities. He plans to hire eight to ten shop employees who will be accountable directly to Joe.

Questions
1 Is Joe an entrepreneur or a practicing manager? Distinguish one term from the other.
2 Does Joe have a business plan? If so, what are its major components?
3 In your opinion, does Joe have a financial plan to present to the bank? Explain.
4 Who are the creditors of Joe's business plan, and how do you distinguish owners from creditors?

CASE 2 Organizing a Business

Sarah Ashley owns and operates Patches Ltd. Restaurant. Sales of the business are declining. She believes that if radio advertising were increased by 10 percent, sales would increase by more than 10 percent. A management consultant is brought in and suggests that employees do not take pride in their jobs because of a morale problem. He recommends that employees be retrained and made to fully understand the responsibilities of their jobs. Sarah's advertising idea and the consultant's recommendation are both instituted, yet sales do not increase and the morale problems continue.

Sarah, a marketing major in college, decides to poll her customers through a market research survey to identify their concerns. She discovers that her customers perceive that prices are too high for the quality and portion of food they are getting. She assesses this information, hires a new cook, and changes the menu. Sales increase dramatically.

Her marketing plan is to develop new products reflecting customers' health-conscious desire for low-fat, low-calorie foods. She develops new supply sources, buying fresh inventory every day from local wholesalers. She changes her local newspaper advertising, running ads every weekend. Finally, her pricing strategy concentrates on running daily specials to bring in new customers.

Questions

1 What types of decisions were made initially to try to improve revenue for Sarah's business? Were they the right decisions?

2 Who are the key participants in this business?

3 Discuss the key functions that are being performed in Sarah's business.

4 What is Sarah's marketing plan?

VIDEO CASE Creation of a Successful Business

How does a small company introduce to world markets a product that no one has been able to make before, taking it from the idea stage through development to manufacturing in a few years? It helps if the company is led by someone who knows what to do to get crucial technical and financial help. GS Technologies, Inc., of Fairfield, Iowa, had that someone in its founder and president, Ralph Grosswald. Its product, a revolutionary pharmaceutical capsule, is his brainchild.

Unlike other such capsules, VEGICAPS are not made from gelatin, a byproduct of animal slaughter, but from a vegetable cellulose developed by Dow Chemical and licensed exclusively to GS Technologies. The two-piece capsules are filled with medicines or food supplements by GS Technologies' customers—pharmaceutical firms and supplement companies—and the pieces are joined as a single hard shell.

To understand the significance of making a pharmaceutical capsule from vegetable matter, recognize that there are a lot of vegetarians in the world—hundreds of millions in India, alone. Also, cellulose stands up better than gelatin to extreme heat or cold.

Grosswald outlined a path to success: Determine the market for a vegetarian capsule; do research on previous efforts to make one and where to get materials and technical support for a new effort; develop a business plan; get a license from Dow; secure funds.

In raising money, the company was meticulous in doing its homework and presenting its case coherently. After making a good impression in four hours of exhaustive questioning on its first visit, GS Technologies snagged its largest financial backer, a supplement producer. The backer's prestige swayed Dow into licensing the technology.

Today more than 30 employees in GS Technologies' factory—located in Orem, Utah—are turning out millions of capsules for markets in the Americas, Europe, and Asia. Demand is rising, and the company is looking into licensing manufacturers abroad. Its "simple product," says Grosswald, "will affect the lives of millions of people worldwide."

Questions

1 What makes the product of GS Technologies different from the other related products sold by other firms?

2 Why would the marketing function be critical to the success of GS Technologies? Explain how the financing function was critical to the success of GS Technologies.

3 Describe some possible conditions that could cause the demand for the product produced by GS Technologies to decline in the future.

THE *Coca-Cola* COMPANY ANNUAL REPORT PROJECT

You are probably familiar with the product Coke. The producer of that product is The Coca-Cola Company. Throughout this book there are questions related to The Coca-Cola Company's annual report. *Fortune* magazine recently conducted a survey of leading executives and named The Coca-Cola Company as America's most admired corporation. This exercise will provide you with some insights about the operations of one of the world's most successful business organizations.

The following questions apply concepts learned in this chapter to The Coca-Cola Company. Read from page 2 up to Reality #1 (on page 3) of The Coca-Cola Company annual report before answering these questions.

1 **a.** What three-step planning process does The Coca-Cola Company use to earn the trust of their investors?

   b. What are the benefits to The Coca-Cola Company of using this process?

2 What did a major business publication point out

about The Coca-Cola Company in 1938? How do such comments relate to The Coca-Cola Company's growth potential today?

3 **a.** Why does The Coca-Cola Company exist today? (See page 41).

b. Why do you think its main goal is to satisfy stockholders?

c. What are the four key objectives of The Coca-Cola Company?

IN-TEXT STUDY GUIDE

Answers are in an appendix at the back of the book.

True or False

1 Creditors organize, manage, and assume the risks of the business.

2 A firm's earnings (or profits) are equal to its revenue plus its expenses.

3 If the estimated costs of the business are too high, the business idea should always be completely eliminated.

4 The business plan is only for the entrepreneur, not for any investors or creditors who may provide financial support.

5 Firms make dividend payments to pay off expenses from ordering supplies.

6 A marketing plan focuses on various decisions that must be made about the production process, such as site location and design and layout of the facilities.

7 Firms use information systems primarily to determine how to finance their business.

8 The goal of a firm's managers is to maximize the firm's value, which is in the best interests of the firm's owners.

9 Assessing the business environment includes the industry of concern, the economic environment, and the global environment.

10 A firm must satisfy its customers by providing the products or services that customers desire at a reasonable price.

Multiple Choice

11 An enterprise that provides products or services that customers desire is a(n):
a) institution.
b) philanthropy.
c) market.
d) agency.
e) business.

12 The four types of participants involved in a business include the following except for:
a) owners.
b) creditors.
c) couriers.
d) employees.
e) customers.

13 A key function of business by which employees and other resources (such as machinery) are used by the firm is:
a) finance.
b) accounting.
c) management.
d) information systems.
e) marketing.

14 When an entrepreneur allows other investors to invest in the business, they become:
a) agents.
b) brokers.
c) employees.
d) sponsors.
e) co-owners.

15 A certificate of ownership of a business is a:
a) bond.
b) stock.
c) mutual fund.
d) co-article.
e) contract.

16 Many firms that need funds borrow from financial institutions or individuals called:
a) debtors.
b) creditors.
c) collateral.
d) joint ventures.
e) investors.

17 The act of gathering information about the firm and providing it to the firm's employees to make business decisions is the function of business known as:
a) management.
b) information systems.
c) accounting.
d) finance.
e) marketing.

18 Firms must ensure that the products or services produced are the following except for:
a) myopic markets.
b) reasonably priced.
c) what customers want.
d) properly designed.
e) adequate quality.

19 Every business begins as a result of ideas about a product or service by one or more people called:
a) entrepreneurs.
b) purchasing agents.
c) change agents.
d) franchisees.
e) business agents.

20 The business environment assesses the industry of concern to determine the degree of:
a) competition.
b) ownership.
c) debt.
d) inventory.
e) collateral.

21 Management, marketing, and finance are key parts of a(n):
a) accounting plan.
b) production strategy.
c) inventory plan.
d) business plan.
e) information systems plan.

22 A business plan is a detailed description of the proposed business that includes the following except for:
a) description of the business.
b) types of customers it would attract.
c) competition.
d) facilities needed for production.
e) monetary and fiscal policy.

23 Employees responsible for making key business decisions are:
a) stockholders.
b) rank and file.
c) managers.
d) business agents.
e) creditors.

24 The type of decision that focuses on strategies that will make the product appealing to customers and that will also affect the firm's revenue is:
a) production.
b) marketing.
c) manufacturing.
d) personnel.
e) financial.

25 Most business owners would agree that the following characteristics motivated them to start their own business except for:
a) earning large incomes.
b) being their own boss.
c) independence of ownership from management activities.
d) prestige associated with owning a business.
e) risk.

26 Firms anticipate how the consumer demand for products changes by:
a) production control.
b) accounting.
c) empowering management.
d) incorporating.
e) monitoring consumer behavior.

27 The function of business that summarizes the firm's financial condition and is used to make various business decisions is:
a) accounting.
b) information systems.
c) production.
d) marketing.
e) management.

28 The management action that identifies the roles and responsibilities of the employees hired by the firm is the:
a) unity of command.
b) division of work.
c) degree of specialization.
d) organizational structure.
e) standardization concept.

29 A marketing plan focuses on the following except for:
a) financing the business.
b) a profile of typical customers.
c) product characteristics.
d) pricing of the product.
e) distribution of the product.

30 Characteristics of the typical customer are identified through a:
a) stockholders' report.
b) customer profile.
c) Dun & Bradstreet report.
d) credit report.
e) production schedule.

31 A plan that demonstrates why the business is feasible and proposes how the business should be financed is the:
a) production report.
b) marketing plan.
c) financial plan.
d) human resource plan.
e) bottom-up plan.

32 The function of business that represents the means by which firms obtain funds to finance their business operations and invest funds among business projects is:
a) finance.
b) marketing.
c) accounting.
d) information systems.
e) management.

33 The key participants of a firm are the following except for:
a) entrepreneurs.
b) creditors.
c) employees.
d) customers.
e) government officials.

34 To detect some inefficient use of business resources that can be eliminated, managers rely on:
a) owners.
b) creditors.
c) marketing research.

d) marketing mix studies.

e) accounting data.

35 The function of business by which products are created, priced, distributed, and promoted to customers is:

a) finance.

b) information systems.

c) accounting.

d) management.

e) marketing.

WHAT IS THE INTERNET?   Perhaps the most important commercial use of information technology to emerge in the past decade is the Internet. Originally established in the late 1960s as an experimental communications network intended to survive a nuclear war, the Internet was designed to establish connections between computer networks at different universities and government agencies. Until the early 1990s, interest in the Internet was largely limited to these universities and research institutions. Suddenly, other potential users began to recognize two of the Internet's most attractive characteristics: (1) huge amounts of information could be accessed through it, and (2) it was free. Because of the development of new Internet applications, such as the World Wide Web, and user-friendly Internet software, such as Mosaic and Netscape, the user base of the Internet began to explode—growing at rates of up to 10 percent per month. For a list of Internet-access providers, see Exhibit 1.8.

At the present time, the Internet offers major advantages to managers in three areas:

➤ *Research:* With its huge access to university and government information, the Internet affords companies a tremendous potential resource for performing market and economic research.

➤ *Marketing/Public Relations:* The typical Internet user has demographic characteristics that most companies dream of: affluent, well educated, willing to try new things. To "meet" these users, many companies have established an Internet presence. For example, many companies now provide Internet addresses in their print and televised advertising.

➤ *Communications:* As a network whose presence is truly global, and whose usage is free, the Internet represents an excellent carrier for communications. The most

Exhibit 1.8
Commercial Internet-access Providers

PROVIDER	PHONE NUMBER	E-MAIL ADDRESS FOR MORE INFORMATION
America Online	(800) 827-6364	
CompuServe	(800) 487-9197	7006.101@compuserve.com
Delphi	(800) 695-4005	info@delphi.com
I-Link	(800) ILINK99	info@I-link.net
ImagiNation Network	(800) 462-4461	www.Ingames.com
InterRamp	(800) PSI-0852	interramp-info@psi.com
IQuest	(800) 844-8649	info@iquest.net
Netcom	(800) 353-6600	info@netcom.com
Prodigy	(800) 776-3449	info99a@prodigy.com
Your Personal Network	(800) NET-1133	www.YPN.com

commonly used communications method is electronic mail (e-mail), which allows individuals to send and receive electronic messages in a fraction of the time required for traditional letters or interoffice mail. Many companies are subscribing to the Internet primarily to take advantage of such e-mail for communications between branches. Beyond e-mail, software and hardware are now available that allow users to literally talk back and forth across Internet connections.

Using the Internet for commercial purposes also has a number of drawbacks:

➤ *Accessibility:* Only a small fraction of the U.S. population (under 10 percent) has full access to the Internet. While that fraction has impressive demographics, with far higher average income and education than the general population, it nonetheless does not represent the entire market for many products.

➤ *Reliability:* The Internet's performance can vary significantly from day to day, and even from minute to minute. Sometimes entire portions of the Net go down. As a result, managers cannot count on the same level of reliability as they can for other services, such as the phone company.

➤ *Security:* When financial data passes between two Internet users, it is often routed through many intermediate networks. Unethical hackers could intercept that information and use it for illegal purposes.

➤ *Quality Control:* Because no one "owns" the Internet, the materials that pass over it are not policed. As a consequence, Internet scams are possible and the opportunity exists for illegal materials, such as child pornography, to be distributed. Such quality control issues could tarnish the reputation of the entire medium. When gathering information from the net, users should remember that the source of the information may have a bias toward a particular product or service. The information contained on any one web site may or may not be accurate.

These concerns are currently being addressed by participants in the Internet, and possible solutions are constantly being advanced. As a result, in the foreseeable future the Internet is likely to be as common as cable TV. When that happens, it will revolutionize the way we buy and sell products in a way that has not been seen since the introduction of television in the 1950s.

Business Addresses

Listed here are mailing addresses, phone numbers, and website addresses of many well-known firms. Also listed is the primary type of business conducted by the company. To obtain an annual report of any specific firm, send a brief letter to the firm of your choice or call them. Detailed information about some companies can also be obtained by using a computer and looking up their website address.

A

Abbott Laboratories   Drugs
100 Abbott Park Road, Abbott Park, IL 60064-3500
847-937-6100

Adobe Systems   Computer software
PO Box 7900, Mountain View, CA 94039-7900
415-961-4400
http://www.adobe.com

Advanced Micro Devices Computer peripherals
PO Box 3453, Sunnyvale, CA 94088-3453
408-732-2400
http://www.amd.com/

Aetna Life & Casualty   Diversified insurance
151 Farmington Avenue, Hartford, CT 06156-3224
203-273-0123
http.://www.aetna.com

Albertson's   Supermarkets & convenience
PO Box 20, Boise, ID 83726   208-385-6200

AlliedSignal   Aerospace & defense
PO Box 2245, Morristown, NJ 07962-2245
201-455-2000
http://www.alliedsignal.com

Allstate   Property & casualty ins
2775 Sanders Road, Northbrook, IL 60062-6127
847-402-5000
http://www.allstate.com/

Aluminum Co of America   Nonferrous metals
425 Sixth Avenue, Pittsburgh, PA 15219-1850
412-553-4545
http://www.alcoa.com/

America Online   Computer software
8619 Westwood Center Drive, Vienna, VA 22182-2285
703-448-8700
http://www.aol.com/

American Brands   Tobacco
PO Box 811, Old Greenwich, CT 06870-0811
203-698-5000
http://www.ambrands.com/

American Express   Lease & finance
American Express Tower, New York, NY 10285-4814
212-640-2000
http://www.americanexpress.com

American Home Products   Drugs
Five Giralda Farms, Madison, NJ 07940
201-660-5000

American International Group Diversified ins
70 Pine Street, New York, NY 10270
212-770-7000
http://www.aig.com

American Stores   Supermarkets & convenience
PO Box 27447, Salt Lake City, UT 84127-0447
801-539-0112

Ameritech   Telecommunications
30 South Wacker Drive, Chicago, IL 60606
312-750-5000
http://www.ameritech.com

Amoco   International oil
PO Box 87703, Chicago, IL 60680-0703
312-856-6111
http://www.amoco.com

AMR   Airline
PO Box 619616, DFW Airport, TX 75261-9616
817-963-1234
http://www.amrcorp.com/

Anheuser-Busch Cos   Beverages
One Busch Place, St. Louis, MO 63118-1852
314-577-2000
http://www.budweiser.com

Apple Computer   Computer systems
1 Infinite Loop, Cupertino, CA 95014
408-996-1010
http://www.apple.com

Applebee's International   Restaurants
4551 West 107th Street, Overland Park, KS 66207
913-967-4000
http://www.applebees.com/

Ashland   Miscellaneous energy
PO Box 391, Ashland, KY 41114   606-329-3333
http://www.ashland.com/

AT&T   Telecommunications
32 Avenue of the Americas, New York, NY 10013-2412
212-387-5400
http://www.att.com

Atlantic Richfield   Miscellaneous energy
515 South Flower Street, Los Angeles, CA 90071-2201
213-486-3708
http://www.arco.com

Automatic Data Processing   Business services
One ADP Boulevard, Roseland, NJ 07068-1728
201-994-5000
http://www.adp.com/

AutoZone   Specialty stores
PO Box 2198, Memphis, TN 38101
901-495-6500
http://www.autozone.com/

Avery Dennison   Business supplies
PO Box 7090, Pasadena, CA 91109-7090
818-304-2000

Avon Products   Personal products
9 West 57th Street, New York, NY 10019-2683
212-546-6015
http://www.avon.com/

B

Ball   Packaging
PO Box 2407, Muncie, IN 47307-0407
317-747-6100
http://www.ball.com

Banc One   Regional bank
100 East Broad Street, Columbus, OH 43271
614-248-5944
http://www.bankone.com

Bank of New York   Regional bank
48 Wall Street, New York, NY 10286
212-495-1784

BankAmerica   Multinational bank
PO Box 37000, San Francisco, CA 94137
415-622-3456
http://www.bankamerica.com

Baxter International   Medical supplies
One Baxter Pkway, Deerfield, IL 60015
708-948-2000
http://www.fete.com

Bell Atlantic   Telecommunications
1717 Arch Street, Philadelphia, PA 19103
215-963-6000
http://www.ba.com

BellSouth   Telecommunications
1155 Peachtree Street NE, Atlanta, GA 30309-3610
404-249-2000
http://www.bellsouth.com

Best Buy   Electronics Stores
PO Box 9312, Minneapolis, MN 55440-9312
612-947-2000
http://www.bestbuy.com/

Bethlehem Steel   Steel
1170 Eighth Avenue, Bethlehem, PA 18016-7699
610-694-2424
http://www.bethsteel.com

BET Holdings   Cable TV
1900 W Place, NE, Washington, DC 20018
202-608-2000
http://www.betnetworks.com/

Beverly Enterprises   Health Care services
5111 Rogers Avenue, Fort Smith, AR 72919
501-484-8412

Black & Decker   Appliances
701 East Joppa Road, Towson, MD 21286
410-716-3900
http://www.blackanddecker.com/

Blimpie International   Restaurants
740 Broadway, New York, NY 10003   212-673-5900
http://www.blimpie.com/

H&R Block   Business services
4400 Main Street, Kansas City, MO 64111
816-753-6900
http://www.hrblock.com/

Boeing   Aerospace & defense
PO Box 3707, Seattle, WA 98124-2207   206-655-2608
http://www.boeing.com

Boise Cascade   Paper & lumber
PO Box 50, Boise, ID 83728-0001   208-384-6161
http://www.bc.com

Bristol-Myers Squibb   Drugs
345 Park Avenue, New York, NY 10154-0037
212-546-4000
http://www.bms.com

Brown-Forman   Beverages
PO Box 1080, Louisville, KY 40201-1080
502-585-1100
http://www.brown-forman.com

C

Campbell Soup   Food processor
Campbell Place, Camden, NJ 08103-1799
609-342-4800
http:www.campbellsoup.com/

Case   Heavy equipment
700 State Street, Racine, WI 53404
414-636-6011

Caterpillar   Heavy equipment
100 Northeast Adams Street, Peoria, IL 61629-1425
309-675-1000
http://www.caterpillar.com/

Centex   Builder
PO Box 19000, Dallas, TX 75219
214-559-6500
http://www.centex.com/

Cheesecake Factory   Restaurants
26950 Agoura Road, Calabasas Hills, CA 91301
818-880-9323

Chevron   International oil
225 Bush Street, San Francisco, CA 94104-4289
415-894-7700
http://www.chevron.com

Cheyenne Software   Computer network software
3 Expressway Plaza, Roslyn Heights, NY 11577
516-484-5110
http://www.cheyenne.com/

Chiquita Brands International   Food processor
250 East Fifth Street, Cincinnati, OH 45202
513-784-8011
http://www.chiquita.com/

Chrysler   Autos & trucks
1000 Chrysler Drive, Auburn Hills, MI 48326-2766
810-576-5741
http://www.chryslercorp.com

Circle K   Supermarkets & convenience
PO Box 52084, Phoenix, AZ 85072-2084
602-437-0600

Circuit City Stores   Electronics stores
9950 Mayland Drive, Richmond, VA 23233
804-527-4000
http://www.circuitcity.com/

Circus Circus Enterprises   Hotels & gaming
PO Box 14967, Las Vegas, NV 89114-4967
702-734-0410
http://www.circuscircus.com/

Cisco Systems   Computer peripherals
170 West Tasman Drive, San Jose, CA 95134-1706
408-526-4000
http://www.cisco.com

Citicorp   Multinational bank
399 Park Avenue, New York, NY 10043
212-559-1000
http://www.citicorp.com/

Clorox   Personal products
1221 Broadway, Oakland, CA 94612-1888
510-271-7000
http:/www.clorox.com

Cobra Golf   Leisure products
1812 Aston Avenue, Carlsbad, CA 92008
619-929-0377
http:www.cobragolf.com/

The Coca-Cola Company   Beverages
PO Drawer 1734, Atlanta, GA 30301   404-676-2121
http://www.cocacola.com

Colgate-Palmolive   Personal products
300 Park Avenue, New York, NY 10022-7499
212-310-2000
http://www.colgate.com

Columbia/HCA Healthcare   Health care services
One Park Plaza, Nashville, TN 37203   615-327-9551
http://www.columbia.net

Comcast   Broadcasting & movies
1500 Market Street, Philadelphia, PA 19102-2148
215-665-1700
http://www.comcast.com

Compaq Computer   Computer systems
PO Box 692000, Houston, TX 77269-2000
713-370-0670
http://www.compaq.com

ConAgra   Food processor
One ConAgra Drive, Omaha, NE 68102-5001
402-595-4000
http://www.omaha.org/con-pr.ntm

Conrail   Railroad
PO Box 41417, Philadelphia, PA 19101-1417
215-209-2000
http://www.conrail.com/

Consolidated Edison   Electric util-NE
4 Irving Place, New York, NY 10003   212-460-4600
http://www.coned.com/

Continental Airlines   Airline
PO Box 4607, Houston, TX 77210-4607
713-834-5000
http://www.flycontinental.com/

Cummins Engine   Auto parts
Box 3005, Columbus, IN 47202-3005   812-377-5000
http://www.cummins.com

D

Day Runner   Office supplies
15295 Alton Parkway, Irvine, CA 92718
714-680-3500
http://www.dayrunner.com/

Dayton Hudson   Department stores
777 Nicollet Mall, Minneapolis, MN 55402
612-370-6948

Dean Witter, Discover & Co   Lease & finance
Two World Trade Center, New York, NY 10048
212-392-2222

Deere & Co   Heavy equipment
John Deere Road, Moline, IL 61265-8098
309-765-8000
http://www.90.deere.com

Dell Computer   Computer systems
2214 West Braker Lane, Austin, TX 78758
512-338-4400
http://www.dell.com

Delta Air Lines   Airline
PO Box 20706, Atlanta, GA 30320-6001
404-715-2600
http://www.delta-air.com/index.html

Deluxe   Business supplies
PO Box 64235, St. Paul, MN 55164-0235
612-483-7111
http://www.deluxe.com/

Dial   Personal products
Dial Tower, Phoenix, AZ 85077   602-207-4000
http://www.dialcorp.com

Digital Equipment   Computer systems
111 Powdermill Road, Maynard, MA 01754-2571
508-493-7182
http://www.digital.com

Dillard Department Stores   Department stores
PO Box 486, Little Rock, AR 72203   501-376-5200

Discount Auto Parts   Specialty retail
4900 Frontage Road South, Lakeland, FL 33801
941-687-9226

Walt Disney   Broadcasting & movies
500 South Buena Vista Street, Burbank, CA 91521-0301
818-560-1000
http://www.disney.com/

RR Donnelley & Sons   Advertising & publishing
77 West Wacker Drive, Chicago, IL 60601-1696
312-326-8000
http://www.donnelley.com/

Dow Chemical   Diversified chemicals
2030 Dow Center, Midland, MI 48674   517-636-1000
http://www.dow.com

Dow Jones   Advertising & publishing
200 Liberty Street, New York, NY 10281
212-416-2000
http://www.dowjones.com/

El du Pont de Nemours   Diversified chemicals
1007 Market Street, Wilmington, DE 19898
302-774-1000
http://www.dupont.com

Dun & Bradstreet   Advertising & publishing
187 Danbury Road, Wilton, CT 06897   203-834-4200
http://www.dnb.com

Duracell International   Personal products
Berkshire Corporate Park, Bethel, CT 06801
203-796-4000
http://www.duracell.com

E

Eastman Kodak   Photography
343 State Street, Rochester, NY 14650-0910
716-724-4000
http://www.kodak.com/

Eckerd   Drug & discount stores
PO Box 4689, Clearwater, FL 34618   813-399-6000
http://www.eckerd.com/

Estee Lauder Cos   Personal products
767 Fifth Avenue, New York, NY 10153
212-572-4200
http://www.clinique.com/

Exxon   International oil
5959 Las Colinas Boulevard, Irving, TX 75039-2298
214-444-1000

F

Federal Express   Airline
2005 Corporate Avenue, Memphis, TN 38132
901-369-3600
http://www.fedex.com/

Federated Dept Stores   Department stores
7 West Seventh Street, Cincinnati, OH 45202
513-579-7000

First Bank System   Regional bank
601 Second Avenue South, Minneapolis, NM 55402-4302
612-973-1111
http://www.fbs.com

First Team Sports   Apparel
2274 Woodale Drive, Mounds View, MN 55112
612-780-4454
http://www.teamsports.com/

First Union   Regional bank
One First Union Center, Charlotte, NC 28288-0013
704-374-6161
http://www.firstunion.com

Fluor   Builder
3333 Michelson Drive, Irvine, CA 92730
714-975-2000
http://www.fluor.com/

Food Lion   Supermarkets & convenience
PO Box 1330, Salisbury, NC 28145-1330
704-633-8250

Ford Motor   Autos & trucks
PO Box 1899, Dearborn, MI 48121-1899
313-322-3000
http://www.ford.com/

Foster Wheeler   Builder
Perryville Corporate Park, Clinton, NJ 08809-4000
908-730-4000

Fruit of the Loom   Wearing apparel
233 South Wacker Drive, Chicago, IL 60606
312-876-1724
http://www.fruit.com/

G

Gannett   Advertising & publishing
1100 Wilson Boulevard, Arlington, VA 22234
703-284-6000
http://www.gannett.com

Gap   Apparel stores
One Harrison Street, San Francisco, CA 94105
415-952-4400

Gateway 2000   Computer systems
PO Box 2000, North Sioux City, SD 57049-2000
605-232-2000
http://www.gw2k.com

Gaylord Entertainment   Broadcasting & movies
One Gaylord Drive, Nashville, TN 37214
615-316-6000

General Dynamics   Aerospace & defense
3190 Fairview Park Drive, Falls Church, VA 22042-4523
703-876-3000

General Electric   Electrical equipment
3135 Easton Turnpike, Fairfield, CT 06431-0001
203-373-2211
http://www.ge.com

General Mills   Food processor
PO Box 1113, Minneapolis, MN 55440
612-540-2311
http://www.genmills.com/

General Motors   Autos & trucks
3044 West Grand Boulevard, Detroit, MI 48202-3091
313-556-5000
http://www.gm.com/

General Nutrition Cos   Specialty stores
921 Penn Avenue, Pittsburgh, PA 15222
412-288-4600

Genuine Parts   Auto parts
2999 Circle 75 Parkway, Atlanta, GA 30339
770-952-1700

Georgia-Pacific   Paper & lumber
PO Box 105605, Atlanta, GA 30348-5605
404-652-4000
http://www.gwol.org/companies/comp0025.html

Gillette   Personal products
Prudential Tower Building, Boston, MA 02199
617-421-7000

BF Goodrich   Specialty chemicals
3925 Embassy Parkway, Akron, OH 44333-1799
330-374-2000

Goodyear Tire & Rubber   Auto parts
1144 East Market Street, Akron, OH 44316-0001
330-796-2121
http://www.goodyear.com/

WR Grace   Specialty chemicals
One Town Center Road, Boca Raton, FL 33486-1010
407-362-2000

Grand Casinos   Leisure-gaming
13705 First Avenue North, Minneapolis, MN 55441
612-449-9092
http://www.grandcasinos.com/

Gymboree   Specialty retail
700 Airport Boulevard, Suite 200, Burlingame, CA 94010
415-579-0600
http://www.service.com/Gymboree/home.html

H

Harley-Davidson   Recreation equipment
PO Box 653, Milwaukee, WI 53201   414-342-4680

Harrah's Entertainment   Hotels & gaming
1023 Cherry Road, Memphis, TN 38117-5423
901-762-8600

Hasbro   Toys
1027 Newport Avenue, Pawtucket, RI 02862-0200
401-431-8697
http://www2.hasbrotoys.com/hasbro/

HJ Heinz   Food processor
PO Box 57, Pittsburgh, PA 15230-0057   412-456-5700

Hershey Foods   Food processor
PO Box 810, Hershey, PA 17033-0810   717-534-6799
http://www.hersheys.com

Hewlett-Packard   Computer systems
3000 Hanover Street, Palo Alto, CA 94304
415-857-2030
http://www.hp.com

Hilton Hotels   Hotels & gaming
9336 Civic Center Drive, Beverly Hills, CA 90210
310-278-4321
http://www.hilton.com/

Home Depot   Home improvement stores
2455 Paces Ferry Road, Atlanta, GA 30339-4024
770-433-8211
http://www.homedepot.com/

Honeywell   Electrical equipment
PO Box 524, Minneapolis, MN 55440-0524
612-951-1000
http://www.honeywell.com

Hormel Foods   Food processor
1 Hormel Place, Austin, MN 55912-3680
507-437-5611
http://spam.co.net/spamgift/index.html/

Host Marriott   Hotels & gaming
10400 Fernwood Road, Bethesda, MD 20817-1109
301-380-9000
http://www.hostmarriot.com/

I

Inland Steel Industries   Steel
30 West Monroe Street, Chicago, IL 60603
312-346-0300
http://www.inland.com

Intel   Computer peripherals
2200 Mission College Boulevard, Santa Clara, CA
95052-8119   408-765-8080
http://www.intel.com

Intl Business Machines   Computer systems
Old Orchard Road, Armonk, NY 10504
914-765-1900
http://www.ibm.com/

International Paper   Paper & lumber
Two Manhattanville Road, Purchase, NY 10577
914-397-1500

Intuit   Computer software
2535 Garcia Avenue, Mountain View, CA 94043
415-944-6000
http://www.qfn.com

ITT   Hotels & gaming
1330 Avenue of the Americas, New York, NY
10019-5490   212-258-1000
http://www.ittinfo.com/

J

Jefferson-Pilot   Life & health insurance
PO Box 21008, Greensboro, NC 27420   910-691-3000
http://www.ipc.com

Johnson & Johnson   Medical supplies
One Johnson & Johnson Plaza, New Brunswick, NJ
08933 908-524-0400
http://www.jnj.com

K

Kellogg   Food processor
PO Box 3599, Battle Creek, MI 49016-3599
616-961-2000
http://www.kelloggs.com/

Kelly Services   Business services
999 West Big Beaver Road, Troy, MI 48084
810-362-4444
http://www.kellyservices.com

Kimberly-Clark   Personal products
PO Box 619100, Dallas, TX 75261-9100
214-281-1200

King World Productions Broadcasting & movies
1700 Broadway, New York, NY 10019-5963
212-315-4000
http://www.kingworld.com/

Kmart   Drug & discount stores
3100 West Big Beaver Road, Troy, MI 48084-3163
810-643-1000
http://www.kmart.com/

Kroger   Supermarkets & convenience
1014 Vine Street, Cincinnati, OH 45202-1100
513-762-4000
http://www.foodcoop.corn/Kroger/

L

Landry's Seafood Restaurants   Restaurants
1400 Post Oak Boulevard Suite 1010, Houston, TX
77056   713-850-1010

Eli Lilly   Drugs
Lilly Corporate Center, Indianapolis, IN 46285
317-276-2000
http://www.lilly.com

Limited   Apparel stores
PO Box 16000, Columbus, OH 43216
614-479-7000

Litton Industries   Aerospace & defense
21240 Burbank Boulevard, Woodland Hills, CA
91367-6675   818-598-5000
http://www.littoncorp.com

Liz Claiborne   Wearing apparel
1441 Broadway, New York, NY 10018   212-354-4900
http://www.lizclaiborne.com/

Lockheed Martin   Aerospace & defense
6801 Rockledge Drive, Bethesda, MD 20817
301-897-6000
http://www.lmco.com/

Lone Star Steakhouse & Saloon   Restaurants
224 East Douglas, Suite 700, Wichita, KS 67202
316-264-8899
http://www.centernet.com/comm/retailer/food//star/
main.html

Lowe's Cos   Home improvement stores
Box 1111, No Wilkesboro, NC 28656-0001
910-651-4000
http://www.lowes.com

M

Manpower   Business services
PO Box 2053, Milwaukee, WI 53201   414-961-1000
http://www.manpower.com/

Marriott International   Hotels & gaming
Marriott Drive, Washington, DC 20058   301-380-3000
http://www.marriott.com/

Mattel Sports   Toys
333 Continental Boulevard, El Segundo, CA
90245-5012   310-252-2000
http://www2.thegallery.com/mattel.html

May Department Stores   Department stores
611 Olive Street, St. Louis, MO 63101   314-342-6300
http://maycompany.com

Maytag   Appliances
403 West Fourth Street North, Newton, IA 50208
515-792-8000
http://www.maytag.com/

MBNA   Lease & finance
Wilmington, DE 19884-0786
302-453-9930

McDonald's   Restaurant chain
One Kroc Drive, Oak Brook, IL 60521-2278
708-575-3000
http://www.mcdonalds.com/

McDonnell Douglas   Aerospace & defense
PO Box 516, St. Louis, MO 63166-0516
314-232-0232
http://www.mdc.com

Merck   Drugs
PO Box 100, Whitehouse Station, NJ 08889 0100
908-423-1000
http://www.merck.com/

Micron Technology   Computer peripherals
PO Box 6, Boise, ID 83707-0006
208-368-4000
http://www.micron.com/

Microsoft   Computer software
One Microsoft Way, Redmond, WA 98052-6399
206-882-8080
http://www.microsoft.com

Minnesota Mining & Mfg.   Business supplies
3M Center, St. Paul, MN 55144-1000   612-733-1110
http://www.mmm.com

Mirage Resorts   Hotels & gaming
PO Box 7777, Las Vegas, NV 89177-0777
702-791-7111
http://www.themirage.com/

Mobil   International oil
3225 Gallows Road, Fairfax, VA 22037-0001
703-846-3000
http://www.mobil.com

Monsanto   Diversified chemicals
800 North Lindbergh Blvd, St. Louis, MO 63167
314-694-1000
http://www.monsanto.com

Morton International   Specialty chemicals
100 North Riverside Plaza, Chicago, IL 60606-1596
312-807-2000

Motorola   Telecommunications
1303 East Algonquin Road, Schaumburg, IL 60196
847-576-5000
http://www.motorola.com/

Motorcar Parts & Accessories   Auto parts
2727 Manicopa Street, Torrance, CA 90503
310-212-7910

N

National Steel   Steel
4100 Edison Lakes Parkway, Mishawaka, IN 46545-3440
219-273-7000

NationsBank   Regional bank
Corporate Center, Charlotte, NC 28255
704-386-5000
http://www.nationsbank.com

Navistar International   Autos & trucks
455 North Cityfront Plaza Dr, Chicago, IL 60611
312-836-2000

NetManage   Software
10725 North De Anza Boulevard, Cupertino, CA 95014
408-973-7171
http://www.netmanage.com/

Netscape Communications Computer software
501 East Middlefield Road, Mountain View, CA 94043
415-254-1900
http://home.netscape.com

New York Times   Advertising & publishing
229 West 43rd Street, New York, NY 10036-3959
212-556-1234
http://www.nytimes.com/

NIKE   Wearing apparel
One Bowerman Drive, Beaverton, OR 97005-6453
503-671-6453
http://www.nike.com/

Northwest Airlines   Airline
101 Northwest Drive, St. Paul, MN 55111-3034
612-726-2111
http://www.nwa.com/

Novell   Computer software
1555 North Technology Way, Orem, UT 84057
801-429-7000
http://www.novell.com/

Nynex   Telecommunications
1095 Avenue of the Americas, New York, NY 10036
212-370-7400
http://www.nynex.com

O

Office Depot   Specialty stores
2200 Old Germantown Road, Delray Beach, FL 33445
407-278-4800

OfficeMax   Specialty stores
PO Box 228070, Shaker Heights, OH 44122-8070
216-921-6900
http://www.officemax.com

O'Reilly Automotive   Specialty retail
233 South Patterson, Springfield, MO 65802
417-862-6708

Owens Corning   Building materials
Fiberglass Tower, Toledo, OH 43659   419-248-8000
http://www.owens-corning.com

P

Paging Network   Telecommunications
4965 Preston Park Boulevard, Plano, TX 75093
214-985-4100
http://www.pagenet.com

Papa John's International   Restaurants
11492 Bluegrass Parkway, Suite 175, Louisville, KY 40299
502-266-5200

Paychex   Business services
911 Panorama Trail South, Rochester, NY 14625
716-385-6666
http://www.paychex.com/

Payless Cashways   Home improvement stores
PO Box 419466, Kansas City, MO 64141-0466
816-234-6000
http://www.paylesscashways.com/

JC Penney   Department stores
6501 Legacy Drive, Plano, TX 75024-3698
214-431-1000
http://www.jcpenney.com

Pennzoil   Miscellaneous energy
PO Box 2967, Houston, TX 77252-2967
713-546-4000
http://www.pennzoil.com/

PeopleSoft   Computer software
4440 Rosewood Drive, Pleasanton, CA 94588
510-225-3000
http://www.peoplesoft.com

PepsiCo   Beverages
700 Anderson Hill Road, Purchase, NY 10577
914-253-2000
http://www.pepsico.com/

Pfizer   Drugs
235 East 42nd Street, New York, NY 10017-5755
212-573-2323
http://www.fdncenter.org/pfizer

Phillips Petroleum   Miscellaneous energy
Phillips Building, Bartlesville, OK 74004
918-661-6600

Pitney Bowes   Business supplies
1 Elmcroft Road, Stamford, CT 06926-0700
203-356-5000
http://www.pitneybowes.com

Price/Costco   Specialty stores
999 Lake Drive, Issaquah, WA 98027   206-313-8100
http://www.pricecostco.com

Procter & Gamble   Personal products
One Procter & Gamble Plaza, Cincinnati, OH 45202
513-983-1100
http://www.pg.com/

Q-R

Quaker Oats   Food processor
PO Box 049001, Chicago, IL 60604-9001
312-222-7111
http://www.quakeroats.com/

Quantum   Computer peripherals
500 McCarthy Boulevard, Milpitas, CA 95035
408-894-4000
http://www.quantum.com

Quick & Reilly Group   Brokerage
230 South County Road, Palm Beach, FL 33480
407-655-8000
http://www.quick-reilly.com

Ralston Purina   Food processor
Checkerboard Square, St. Louis, MO 63164
314-982-1000
http://www.ralston.com/

Reader's Digest   Advertising & publishing
Reader's Digest Road, Pleasantville, NY 10570-7000
914-238-1000

Reebok International   Wearing apparel
100 Technology Center Drive, Stoughton, MA 02072
617-341-5000
http://www.planetreebok.com/

Regal Cinemas   Movie theaters
7132 Commercial Park Drive, Knoxville, TN 37918
615-922-1123

Revco DS   Drug & discount stores
1925 Enterprise Parkway, Twinsburg, OH 44087
216-425-9811
http://www.revco.com/

Reynolds Metals   Nonferrous metals
PO Box 27003, Richmond, VA 23261-7003
804-281-2000
http://www.rme.com

Rite Aid   Drug & discount stores
PO Box 3165, Harrisburg, PA 17105-0042
717-761-2633
http://www.riteaid.com

RJR Nabisco   Tobacco
1301 Avenue of the Americas, New York, NY
10019 6013   212 258 5600

Roadway Express   Shipping
PO Box 471, Akron, OH 44309-0471   216-384-1717
http://www.roadway.com

Rockwell International   Electrical equipment
2201 Seal Beach Boulevard, Seal Beach, CA 90740-8250
310-797-3311
http://www.rockwell.com

Rubbermaid   Home furnishings & recreation
1147 Akron Road, Wooster, OH 44691   216-264-6464
http://www.rubbermaid.com

Ryder System   Shipping
3600 Northwest 82nd Avenue, Miami, FL 33166
305-593-3726
http://www.ryder.com

S

Safeway   Supermarkets & convenience
Fourth & Jackson Streets, Oakland, CA 94660
510-891-3000

SBC Communications   Telecommunications
PO Box 2933, San Antonio, TX 78299-2933
210-821-4105
http://www.sbc.com/

Charles Schwab   Brokerage
101 Montgomery Street, San Francisco, CA 94104
415-627-7000
http://www.schwab.com

Seagate Technology   Computer peripherals
920 Disc Drive, Scotts Valley, CA 95066
408-438-6550
http://www.seagate.com

Sears, Roebuck   Department stores
3333 Beverly Road, Hoffman Estates, IL 60179
847-286-2500

Sherwin-Williams   Specialty chemicals
101 Prospect Avenue NW, Cleveland, OH 44115-1075
216-566-2000

Silicon Graphics   Computer systems
2011 North Shoreline Boulevard, Mountain View, CA
94043-1389   415-933-1980
http://www.sgi.com

Sodak Gaming   Leisure products
5301 South Highway 16, Rapid City, SD 57701
605-341-5400

Sonic   Restaurants
101 Park Avenue, Oklahoma City, OK 73102
405-280-7654

Southland   Supermarkets & convenience
PO Box 711, Dallas, TX 75221-0711
214-828-7011

Southwest Airlines   Airline
PO Box 36611, Dallas, TX 75235-1611   214-904-4000
http://www.iflyswa.com

Spiegel   Home shipping
3500 Lacey Road, Downers Grove, IL 60515
708-986-8800
http://www.spiegel.com/

Sprint   Telecommunications
PO Box 11315, Kansas City, MO 64112   913-624-3000
http://www.sprint.com

Stanley Works   Misc industrial equip
100 Stanley Drive, New Britain, CT 06053
203-225-5111
http://www.stanleyworks.com/

Staples   Specialty stores
PO Box 9328, Framingham, MA 01701-9328
508-370-8500
http://www.staples.com

Stone Container   Packaging
150 North Michigan Avenue, Chicago, IL 60601-7568
312-346-6600

Sun Microsystems   Computer systems
2550 Garcia Avenue, Mountain View, CA 94043-1100
415-960-1300
http://www.sun.com

SunTrust Banks   Regional bank
PO Box 4418, Atlanta, GA 30302   404-588-7711
http://www.suntrust.com/

T

Tandem Computers   Computer systems
19333 Vallco Parkway, Cupertino, CA 95014-2599
408-285-6000
http://www.tandem.com

Tandy   Electronics stores
PO Box 17180, Fort Worth, TX 76102   817-390-3700
http://www.tandy.com

Tenneco   Heavy equipment
1275 King Street, Greenwich, CT 06831-2946
203-863-1000
http://www.tenneco.com/

Texaco   International oil
2000 Westchester Avenue, White Plains, NY 10650
914-253-4000
http://www.texaco.com

Texas Instruments   Computer peripherals
PO Box 655474, Dallas, TX 75265   214-995-2011
http://www.ti.com/

Time Warner   Broadcasting & movies
75 Rockefeller Plaza, New York, NY 10019
212-484-8000
http://pathfinder.com/Corp

Toys 'R' Us   Specialty stores
461 From Road, Paramus, NJ 07652   201-262-7800
http://www.toyrus.com/

Trans World Airlines   Airline
515 North Sixth Street, St. Louis, MO 63101
314-589-3000
http://www.twa.com/

Tribune   Advertising & publishing
435 North Michigan Avenue, Chicago, IL 60611
312-222-9100
http://www.tribune.com

TRW   Auto parts
1900 Richmond Road, Cleveland, OH 44124-3760
216-291-7000
http://www.trw.com

Turner Broadcasting   Broadcasting & movies
One CNN Center, Atlanta, GA 30303
404-827-1700
http://www.turner.com/

Tyson Foods   Food processor
PO Box 2020, Springdale, AR 72765-2020
501-290-4000

U

UAL   Airline
PO Box 66919, Chicago, IL 60666   847-952-4000
http://www.ual.com

Union Camp   Paper & lumber
1600 Valley Road, Wayne, NJ 07470
201-628-2000
http://www.uccden.com/

Union Carbide   Diversified chemicals
39 Old Ridgebury Road, Danbury, CT 06817-0001
203-794-2000

Union Pacific   Railroad
Eighth & Eaton Avenues, Bethlehem, PA 18018
610-861-3200
http://www.up.com/

Unisys   Computer systems
PO Box 500, Blue Bell, PA 19424-0001   215-986-4011
http://www.unisys.com

US Robotics   Computer peripherals
8100 North McCormick Boulevard, Skokie, IL 60076
847-982-5010
http://www.usr.com

United Technologies   Aerospace & defense
One Financial Plaza, Hartford, CT 06101
203-728-7000
http://www.utc.com

USAir Group   Airline
2345 Crystal Drive, Arlington, VA 2227
703-418-7000
http://www.usair.com/

USX-Marathon   Miscellaneous energy
600 Grant Street, Pittsburgh, PA 15219-4776
412-433-1121

USX-US Steel   Steel
600 Grant Street, Pittsburgh, PA 15219-4776
412-433-1121

V

Viacom   Broadcasting & movies
1515 Broadway, New York, NY 10036
212-258-6000
http://www.viacom.com/

W

Wackenhut Corrections   Correctional facilities
1500 San Remo Avenue, Coral Gables, FL 33146
305-666-5656

Wal-Mart Stores   Drug & discount stores
702 Southwest 8th Street, Bentonville, AR 72716-8001
501-273-4000
http://www.wal-mart.com/

Walgreen   Drug & discount stores
200 Wilmot Road, Deerfield, IL 60015 708-940-2500
http://www.walgreens.com

Warner-Lambert   Drugs
201 Tabor Road, Morris Plains, NJ 07950 201-540-2000
http://www.warner-lambert.com/

Western Digital   Computer peripherals
8105 Irvine Center Drive, Irvine, CA 92718
714-932-5000
http://www.wdc.com

Westinghouse Electric   Electric equipment
11 Stanwix Street, Pittsburgh, PA 15222-1384
412-244-2000
http://www.westinghouse.com/

Whirlpool   Appliances
2000 M-63, Benton Harbor, MI 49022-2692
616-923-5000
http://www.whirlpool.com/

Winn-Dixie Stores   Supermarkets & convenience
PO Box B, Jacksonville, FL 32203-0297
904-783-5000

WMX Technologies   Environmental & waste
3003 Butterfield Road, Oak Brook, IL 60521
708-572-8800
http://www.wmx.com

Woolworth   Drug & discount stores
233 Broadway, New York, NY 10279-0003
212-553-2000

Wm Wrigley Jr   Food processor
410 North Michigan Avenue, Chicago, IL 60611-4287
312-644-2121

X-Z

Xerox   Business supplies
PO Box 1600, Stamford, CT 06904   203-968-3000
http://www.xerox.com

Yellow   Shipping
PO Box 7563, Overland Park, KS 66207-0563
913-967-4300
http://www.yellowcorp.com/

Zilog   Semiconductors
210 East Hacienda Avenue, Campbell, CA 95008
408-370-8000
http://www.zilog.com/

CHAPTER 2

Selecting a Form of Business Ownership

When entrepreneurs establish a business, they must decide on the form of business ownership. The choice of a specific form of business ownership can affect various business characteristics, which influence the firm's value.

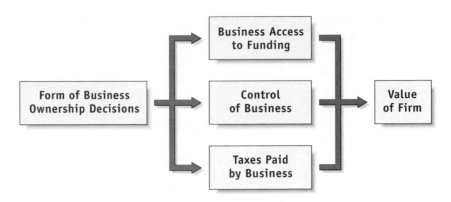

Consider the case of Outback Steakhouse, which has more than 235 restaurants spread from California to New Jersey. Outback's sales have recently grown at an annual rate of 114 percent. What is the ideal form of business ownership for Outback? What factors did Outback consider when it selected a form of business ownership? What are the risks of Outback from the perspective of its owners? This chapter provides a background on business ownership, which can be used to address these questions.

The **Learning Goals** of this chapter are to:

1 Explain how business owners select a form of business ownership.

2 Describe methods of owning existing businesses.

3 Explain how business owners can measure their business performance.

POSSIBLE FORMS OF BUSINESS OWNERSHIP

1 Explain how business owners select a form of business ownership.

Entrepreneurs choose one of three possible forms of business ownership:

➤ Sole proprietorship
➤ Partnership
➤ Corporation

Sole Proprietorship

sole proprietorship a business owned by a single owner

sole proprietor the owner of a sole proprietorship

A business owned by a single owner is referred to as a **sole proprietorship.** The owner of a sole proprietorship is called the **sole proprietor.** A sole proprietor may obtain loans from creditors to help finance the firm's operations, but these loans do not represent ownership. The sole proprietor is obligated to cover any payments resulting from the loans, but does not need to share the business profits with creditors.

Typical examples of sole proprietorships include a local restaurant, a local construction firm, a barber shop, a laundry service, and a local clothing store. About 70 percent of all firms in the United States are sole proprietorships. But because these firms are relatively small, they generate less than 10 percent of all business revenue. The earnings generated by a sole proprietorship are considered as personal income received by the proprietor and are subject to personal income taxes imposed by the Internal Revenue Service (IRS).

CHARACTERISTICS OF SUCCESSFUL SOLE PROPRIETORS   Sole proprietors must be willing to accept full responsibility for the firm's performance. The pressure of this responsibility can be much greater than any employee's responsibility. Sole proprietors must also be willing to work flexible hours. They are on call at all times and may even have to substitute for a sick employee. Their responsibility for the success of the business encourages them to continually monitor business operations. They must exhibit strong leadership skills, be well organized, and communicate well with employees.

Many successful sole proprietors had previous work experience in the market in which they are competing, perhaps as an employee in a competitor's firm. For example, restaurant managers commonly establish their own restaurants. Experience is critical to understanding the competition and behavior of customers in a particular market.

ADVANTAGES OF A SOLE PROPRIETORSHIP   The sole proprietor form of ownership has the following advantages over other forms of business ownership:

1 *All Earnings Go to the Sole Proprietor* The sole proprietor (owner) does not have to share the firm's earnings with other owners. Thus, the rewards of establishing a successful firm come back to the owner.

2 *Easy Organization* Establishing a sole proprietorship is relatively easy. The legal requirements are minimal. A sole proprietorship need not establish a separate legal entity. The owner must register the firm with the state, which can normally be done by mail. The owner may also need to apply for an occupational license to conduct a particular type of business. The specific license requirements vary with the state and even the city where the business is located.

3 *Complete Control* Having only one owner with complete control of the firm eliminates the chance of conflicts during the decision-making process. For example, an owner of a restaurant can decide on the menu, the prices, and the salaries paid to employees.

4 *Lower Taxes* The earnings in a proprietorship are considered as personal income, and may be subject to lower taxes than some other forms of business ownership, as will be explained later in this chapter.

DISADVANTAGES OF A SOLE PROPRIETORSHIP   Along with its advantages, the sole proprietorship has the following disadvantages:

1 *The Sole Proprietor Incurs All Losses* Just as sole proprietors do not have to share the profits, they are unable to share any losses that the firm incurs. For example, assume you invested $10,000 of your funds in a lawn service and borrowed an additional $8,000 that was invested in the business. Assume that the revenue was barely sufficient to pay salaries to your employees, which caused you to terminate the firm. You not only lost all of your $10,000 investment in the firm but also are liable for the $8,000 that you borrowed. Since you are the sole proprietor, no other owners are available to help cover the losses.

unlimited liability no limit on the debts for which the owner is liable

2 *Unlimited Liability* A sole proprietor is subject to **unlimited liability**, which means there is no limit on the debts for which the owner is liable. If a sole proprietorship is sued, the sole proprietor is personally liable for any judgment against that firm.

3 *Limited Funds* A sole proprietor may have limited funds available to invest in the firm. Thus, sole proprietors have difficulty engaging in airplane manufacturing, shipbuilding, computer manufacturing, and other businesses that require substantial funds. Sole proprietors have limited funds to support the firm's expansion or to absorb temporary losses. A poorly performing firm may improve if given sufficient time. But if this firm cannot obtain additional funds to make up for its losses, it may not be able to continue in business long enough to recover.

4 *Limited Skills* A sole proprietor has limited skills and may be unable to control all parts of the business. For example, a sole proprietor may have difficulty running a large medical practice because different types of expertise may be needed.

Partnership

partnership a business that is co-owned by two or more people

partners co-owners of a business

A business that is co-owned by two or more people is referred to as a **partnership.** The co-owners of a business are called **partners.** The co-owners must register the partnership with the state and may need to apply for an occupational license. About 10 percent of all firms are partnerships.

general partnership all partners have unlimited liability

limited partnership a firm that has some limited partners

limited partners partners whose liability is limited

general partners partners who manage the business, receive a salary, share the profits or losses of the business, and have unlimited liability

In a **general partnership,** all partners have unlimited liability. That is, these partners are personally liable for all obligations of the firm. Conversely, a **limited partnership** is a firm that has some **limited partners,** or partners whose liability is limited to the cash or property they contributed to the partnership. Limited partners are only investors in the partnership and do not participate in the management of the business. Yet, because they invested in the business, they share the profits or losses of the business. A limited partnership has one or more **general partners,** or partners who manage the business, receive a salary, share the profits or losses of the business, and have unlimited liability. The earnings distributed to each partner represent personal income and are subject to personal income taxes imposed by the IRS.

ADVANTAGES OF A PARTNERSHIP   The partnership form of ownership has three main advantages:

While most of the work of a physician is done on an individual basis, physicians commonly form partnerships to share the basic administrative responsibilities and expenses of running an office.

1 *Additional Funding* An obvious advantage of a partnership over sole proprietorships is the additional funding that one or more partners can provide. Therefore, more money may be available to finance the business operations.

2 *Losses Are Shared* Any business losses that the partnership incurs do not have to be absorbed by a single person. Each owner will absorb only a portion of the loss.

3 *More Specialization* A partnership can allow partners to focus on their respective specializations and serve a wide variety of customers. For example, an accounting firm may have one accountant who specializes in personal taxes for individuals and another who specializes in business taxes for firms. A medical practice partnership may have doctors with various types of expertise.

DISADVANTAGES OF A PARTNERSHIP   Along with its advantages, the partnership has the following disadvantages:

1 *Control Is Shared* The decision making in a partnership must be shared. Partners may disagree about how a business should be run, which may destroy business and personal relationships. For example, about 53 percent of Kiwi International Air Lines was owned by employees (primarily pilots). Many of the owners were good pilots but poor managers. Kiwi experienced major financial problems in 1995 because of poor management.

2 *Unlimited Liability* General partners in a partnership are subject to unlimited liability, just like sole proprietors.

3 *Profits Are Shared* Any profits that the partnership generates must be shared among all partners.

S-CORPORATIONS   A partnership that has thirty-five owners or less and satisfies other criteria may choose to be a so-called **S-corporation.** The earnings of an S-corporation are distributed to the owners and taxed at the respective personal income tax rate of each owner. Thus, the owners are only subject to limited liability (like owners of corporations), but are taxed as if the firm was a partnership. Some state governments impose a corporate tax on S-corporations.

S-corporation a partnership that has thirty-five owners or less and satisfies other criteria. The earnings are distributed to the owners and taxed at the respective personal income tax rate of each owner

limited liability company (LLC) a firm that has all the favorable features of a typical general partnership but also offers limited liability for the partners

LIMITED LIABILITY COMPANY (LLC)   A type of general partnership called a **limited liability company (LLC)** has become popular in recent years. An LLC is a firm that has all the favorable features of a typical general partnership but also offers limited liability for the partners. It typically protects a partner's personal assets from the negligence of other partners in the firm. This type of protection is highly desirable for partners, given the high frequency of liability lawsuits. The assets of the company (such as the property or machinery owned by the company) are not protected. While S-corporations may also provide liability protection, various rules may restrict some partners of S-corporations from limited liability. The LLC does not impose such stringent rules.

The LLC must be created according to the laws of the state where the business is located. The precise rules on liability protection vary among states. Most states either allow for the creation of LLCs or have enacted legislation to allow them in the future. Numerous general partnerships (including many accounting firms) have converted to LLCs to capitalize on the advantages of a partnership, while limiting liability for their owners.

COMPARISON OF A PROPRIETORSHIP WITH A PARTNERSHIP   A general comparison of a proprietorship with a partnership can be illustrated by considering how your earnings and losses would be affected by the form of business you choose. Exhibit 2.1 shows the earnings of your business over four years if you were the sole proprietor, versus those if you were a co-owner (partner) in a partnership. In the first two years when the business incurred losses, your loss would be larger if you were the sole owner of the business rather than a co-owner. However, in the next two years when the business generated positive earnings, your gain would be larger if you were the sole owner of the business. The comparison illustrates the relative advantage of being the sole owner when the business performs well, but the relative disadvantage when the business incurs losses.

Corporation

corporation a state chartered entity that pays taxes and is legally distinct from its owners

A third form of business is a **corporation,** which is a state-chartered entity that pays taxes and is legally distinct from its owners. About 20 percent of all firms are corporations. Yet, corporations generate almost 90 percent of all business revenue. Exhibit 2.2 compares the relative contributions of sole proprietorships, partnerships, and corporations.

charter a document to incorporate a business; the charter describes important aspects of the corporation

An individual or group must adopt a corporate **charter,** or a document to incorporate a business, and file it with the state government. The charter describes important aspects of the corporation such as the name of the firm, information about the stock issued, and a description of the firm's operations. The people who organize the corporation must also establish **bylaws,** which are general guidelines for managing the firm.

bylaws general guidelines for managing the firm

Since the shareholders of the corporation are legally separated from the entity, they have limited liability, meaning they are not held personally responsible for the firm's actions. The most that the stockholders of a corporation can lose is the amount of money they invested.

The stockholders of a corporation elect the members of the board of directors, who are responsible for establishing the general policies of the firm. One of the board's responsibilities is to elect the president and other key officers (such as vice-presidents), who are then given the responsibility of running the business on a day-to-day basis.

Exhibit 2.1
Your Portion of Earnings (or
Losses) on a Proprietorship
Versus a Partnership

Year	Total Business Earnings (or Loss)	Earnings to a Sole Owner	Earnings to One Partner
1	−$40,000	−$40,000	−$20,000
2	−$20,000	−$20,000	−$10,000
3	+$40,000	+$40,000	+$20,000
4	+$80,000	+$80,000	+$40,000

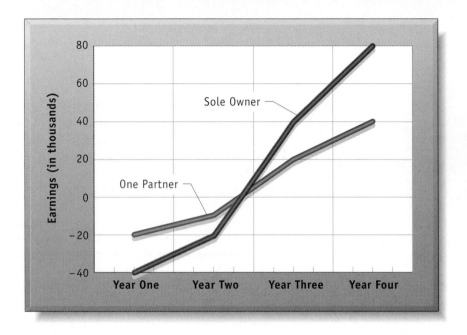

If the board of directors becomes displeased with the performance of the key officers, the board has the power to replace them. Similarly, if the stockholders become displeased with the performance of members of the board, the stockholders can replace the directors in the next scheduled election. In some corporations, one or a few individuals may serve as a stockholder, as a member of the board of directors, and as a key officer of the firm. For example, Louis Gerstner is the chief executive officer of IBM, is the chairman of the board, and holds more than eighty thousand shares of IBM stock.

HOW STOCKHOLDERS EARN A RETURN ON THEIR INVESTMENT   Stockholders can earn a return on their investment in a firm in two different ways. First, they may receive dividends from the firm, which represent a portion of recent earnings of the firm over the last three months that are distributed to stockholders. Second, the stock they hold may increase in value. When the firm becomes more profitable, the value of its stock tends to rise, meaning the value of stock maintained by owners has increased. Thus, they can benefit by selling that stock for a much higher price than they paid for it. In the 1994–1996 period, stock prices of many well-known firms such as the Coca-Cola Company, Eastman Kodak, IBM, and PepsiCo more than doubled. The stock price of Netscape increased by more than 500 percent during 1995.

Lou Gerstner, chief executive officer and chairman of the board, speaks at IBM's annual meeting of shareowners.

Exhibit 2.2
Relative Contributions of Sole
Proprietorships, Partnerships,
and Corporations

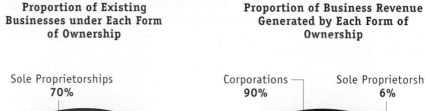

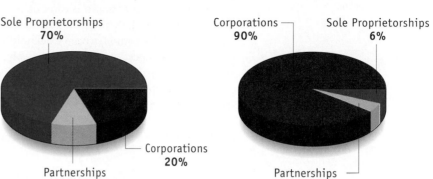

**Proportion of Existing
Businesses under Each Form
of Ownership**

Sole Proprietorships
70%

Corporations
20%

Partnerships
10%

**Proportion of Business Revenue
Generated by Each Form of
Ownership**

Corporations
90%

Sole Proprietorships
6%

Partnerships
4%

privately held ownership is restricted
to a small group of investors

publicly held shares can be easily
purchased or sold by investors

PRIVATELY HELD VERSUS PUBLICLY HELD CORPORATIONS   People become owners
of a corporation by purchasing shares of stock. Many small corporations are **privately held,** meaning that ownership is restricted to a small group of investors. Some
of the more well-known privately held firms include L L Bean, Enterprise Rent-A-
Car, Polo Ralph Lauren, Rand McNally and Company, and United Parcel Service.
Most large corporations are **publicly held,** meaning that shares can be easily purchased or sold by investors.

Stockholders of publicly held corporations can sell their shares of stock when
they need money, are disappointed with the performance of the corporation, or simply expect that the stock price will not rise in the future. Their stock can be sold
(with the help of a stockbroker) to some other investor who would like to invest in
that corporation.

Netscape founder Marc
Andreessen helped make
Netscape one of the hottest pub-
lic stock offerings of 1995.

While virtually all firms (even Ford Motor Company) were privately held when they were created, some of these firms became publicly held when they needed funds to support large expansion. The act of initially issuing stock to the public is called **going public.**

going public the act of initially issuing stock to the public

Publicly held corporations can obtain additional funds by issuing new common stock. This means that either their existing stockholders could purchase more stock, or other investors could become stockholders by purchasing the corporation's stock. By issuing new stock, corporations may obtain whatever funds are needed to support any business expansion. Corporations that wish to issue new stock must be able to convince investors that the funds will be utilized properly, resulting in a reasonable return for the investors.

ADVANTAGES OF A CORPORATION   A corporate form of ownership has the following advantages:

1 *Limited Liability* Owners of a corporation have limited liability (as explained earlier), whereas sole proprietors and general partners typically have unlimited liability.
2 *Access to Funds* A corporation can easily obtain funds by issuing new stock (as explained earlier). This allows corporations the flexibility to grow and to engage in new business ventures. Sole proprietorships and partnerships have less access to funding when they wish to finance expansion. To obtain more funds, they may have to rely on their existing owners or on loans from creditors.
3 *Transfer of Ownership* Investors in large, publicly traded companies can normally sell their stock in minutes by calling their stockbrokers. Conversely, owners of sole proprietorships or partnerships may have some difficulty in selling their share of ownership in the business.

DISADVANTAGES OF A CORPORATION   Along with its advantages, the corporate form of ownership has the following disadvantages:

1 *High Organizational Expense* The expense of organizing a business normally is greater for the corporate form of business than for the other forms. The higher expense results from the necessity of creating a corporate charter and filing it with the state. Some expense also may be incurred in establishing bylaws.
2 *Financial Disclosure* When the stock of a corporation is traded publicly, the investing public has the right to inspect the company's financial data, within certain limits. As a result, firms may be obligated to publicly disclose more about their business operations and employee salaries than they would like. Privately held firms are not forced to disclose financial information to the public.
3 *Agency Problems* Publicly held corporations are normally run by managers who are responsible for making decisions for the business that will serve the interests of the owners. Managers may not always act in the best interests of stockholders. For example, managers may attempt to take expensive business trips that are not necessary to manage the business. These types of actions may increase the expenses of running a business, reduce business profits, and therefore reduce the returns to stockholders. When managers do not act as responsible agents for the shareholders who own the business, this results in a so-called **agency problem.** Such a problem does not normally occur with proprietorships, because the sole owner may also serve as the sole manager and make most or all business decisions.

agency problem when managers do not act as responsible agents for the shareholders who own the business

4 *High Taxes* Since the corporation is a separate entity, it is taxed separately. The annual taxes paid by a corporation are determined by applying the corporate tax rate to the annual earnings. The corporate tax rate is different from the personal tax rate.

Consider a corporation that earns $10 million in earnings this year. Assume that the corporate tax rate applied to earnings of corporations is 30 percent this year (the corporate tax rates can be changed by law over time). Thus, the taxes and after-tax earnings of the corporation are shown here:

Earnings before Tax = $10,000,000
Corporate Tax = $ 3,000,000 (computed as 30% of $10,000,000)
Earnings after Tax = $ 7,000,000

If any of the after-tax earnings are paid to owners as dividends, the dividends represent personal income to stockholders. Thus, the stockholders will pay personal income taxes on the dividends. Continuing with our example, assume that all of the $7 million in after-tax earnings is distributed to the stockholders as dividends. Assume that the personal tax rate is 20 percent for all owners who will receive dividends (personal tax rates depend on the person's income level and can be changed by law over time). The actual dividend income received by stockholders after paying income taxes is as follows:

Dividends Received = $7,000,000
Taxes Paid on Dividends = $1,400,000 (computed as 20% of $7,000,000)
Earnings after Tax = $5,600,000

Since the corporate tax was $3,000,000 and the personal tax was $1,400,000, the total tax paid as a result of the corporation's profits was $4,400,000. This total tax amount represents 44 percent of the $10,000,000 profit that was earned by the corporation.

This example shows how owners of corporations are subject to double taxation, because the corporation's entire profits from their investment are first subject to corporate taxes. Then, any profits distributed as dividends to individual owners are subject to personal income taxes. Exhibit 2.3 shows the flow of funds between owners and the corporation to illustrate how owners are subject to double taxation.

To recognize the disadvantage of double taxation, consider what the taxes would have been for this business if it was a sole proprietorship or partnership rather than a

Corporations, just like individuals, have to pay taxes. PepsiCo pays hundreds of millions of dollars in taxes each year.

Exhibit 2.3
Illustration of Double Taxation

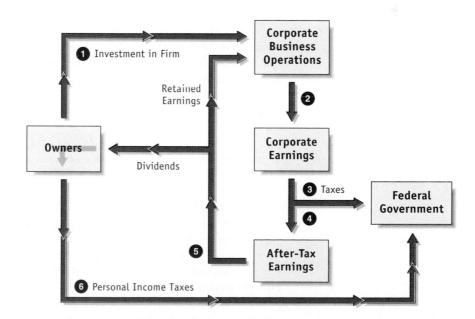

Exhibit 2.4
Comparison of Tax Effects between Corporations and Sole Proprietorships

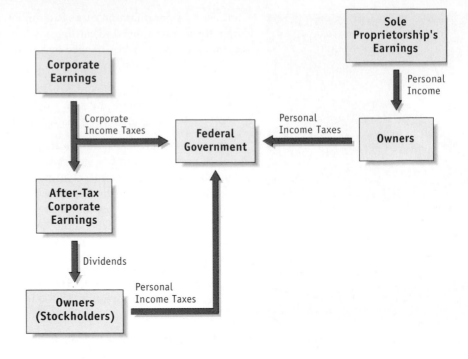

corporation. The $10,000,000 profit would have been considered personal income to a sole proprietor or to partners, which would be subject to personal taxes. If the personal tax rate was 20 percent, the total tax amount would be $2,000,000 (computed as 20 percent of $10,000,000). This tax amount is less than half of what would be paid out by a corporation that earned the same profit. Even if the personal income tax rate of a sole proprietor or a partner was higher than 20 percent, the taxes paid by a corporation would probably still be higher. A comparison of the tax effects between corporations and sole proprietorships is provided in Exhibit 2.4.

One way in which the corporation may reduce the taxes paid by owners is to reinvest its earnings (called "retained earnings") rather than pay the earnings out as dividends. If owners do not receive dividends from a corporation, they would not be subject to personal taxes on the profits earned by the corporation. This strategy makes sense only if the corporation can put the retained earnings to good use.

When stockholders of a corporation sell their stocks for more than they paid for them, they earn a **capital gain,** which represents the price received from the sale of stock minus the price they paid for the stock. The stockholders would pay a so-called capital gains tax on the capital gain. Whether stockholders receive income from selling the stock at a gain or from receiving dividend payments, they are subject to taxes.

capital gain the price received from the sale of stock minus the price paid for the stock

Comparing Forms of Business Ownership
No single form of business ownership is ideal for all business owners. An individual setting up a small business may choose a sole proprietorship. Some people who decide to co-own a small business may choose a partnership. However, if they would prefer to limit their liability, they may decide to establish a privately held corporation. If this corporation grows substantially over time and needs millions of dollars to support additional business expansion, it may convert to a publicly held corporation so that it can obtain funds from stockholders.

SMALL BUSINESS SURVEY

Key Concerns about Business Ownership

A survey by the consulting firm Arthur Andersen and Company and a lobbying group (National Business United) asked business owners their main concerns about their businesses. Multiple answers were allowed. Some of the key results are summarized in the following table:

Concerns about Business Ownership	Percentage of Respondents
Identifying a successor	35%
Handling nonfamily key employees	32%
Management training for family members	31%
Financing	28%
Estate-tax problems	27%
Employee morale	9%

These results suggest that owners have a wide variety of concerns, most of which are related to management or to financing.

METHODS OF OWNING EXISTING BUSINESSES

2 | **Describe methods of owning existing businesses.**

Many people become sole owners of businesses by starting their own business. However, some people become the sole owners without starting the business. The following are common methods by which people become owners of existing businesses:

➤ Assuming ownership of a family business
➤ Purchasing an existing business
➤ Franchising

Assuming Ownership of a Family Business

Many people work in a family business and after a period of time assume the ownership of it. This can be an ideal way to own a business because its performance may be somewhat predictable as long as the key employees continue to work there. Major decisions regarding the production process and other operations of the firm have been predetermined. If the business has historically been successful, a new owner's main function may be to ensure that the existing operations continue to run efficiently. Alternatively, if the business is experiencing poor performance, the new owner may have to revise management, marketing, and financing policies.

Purchasing an Existing Business

Businesses are for sale on any given day in any city. They are often advertised in the classified ads section of local newspapers. Businesses are sold for various reasons, including financial difficulties and death or retirement of an owner.

People who consider purchasing an existing business must determine whether they have the expertise to run the business or at least properly monitor the managers. Then they must compare the expected benefits of the business with the initial outlay that would be required to purchase it. Historical sales volume may be provided by the seller of a business and can be used to estimate the future sales volume. However, the prospective buyer must be cautious when using these figures. In some businesses such as dentistry and hair styling, personal relationships between the owner and customers are critical. Many customers may switch to competitors if the ownership changes. For these types of businesses, the historical sales volume may substantially overestimate future sales. For some other less personalized businesses such as grocery stores, a change of ownership is not likely to have a significant effect on customer preferences (and therefore on sales volume).

Franchising

franchise arrangement whereby a business owner allows others to use its trademark, trade name or copyright, under specific conditions

franchisor firm that allows others to use its trade name of copyright, under specified conditions

franchisee firm that is allowed to use the trade name or copyright of a franchise

A **franchise** is an arrangement whereby a business owner (called a **franchisor**) allows others (the **franchisee**) to use its trademark, trade name or copyright, under specified conditions. Each individual franchise operates as an independent business and is typically owned by a sole proprietor.

Franchises in the United States number over five hundred thousand, and they generate more than $800 billion in annual revenue. Some of the more well-known franchises include Hardees, Thrifty Rent-a-Car System, Mail Boxes Etc., Dairy Queen, Super 8 Motels Inc., TGI Fridays, Pearle Vision Inc., and Baskin-Robbins. The ten fastest growing franchises are identified on Exhibit 2.5.

To gain more insight on the costs and potential benefits of franchising, consider the following examples. A franchise called Kid to Kid Franchise System sells used clothing for children. This franchise can be purchased for about $90,000. A Wendy's restaurant franchise can be purchased for $25,000, but the building costs over $500,000 and the equipment costs about $200,000. The costs of purchasing a franchise can vary significantly, depending on the specific trademarks, technology, and services provided to the franchises.

McDonald's is probably the most successful franchise in the world. Starting at this original location in DesPlaines, Illinois, McDonalds has 18,000 locations in more than 90 countries.

Exhibit 2.5
Fastest Growing Franchises

Firm	Number of Franchises	Percentage of Growth in Franchises over 1991–1994
Snap on Tools	2,922	1,298%
GNC Franchising	608	533%
Play It Again Sports	495	450%
Tower Cleaning Systems	1,095	213%
Jackson Hewitt Tax	916	125%
Mail Boxes Etc.	2,441	69%
Coverall North America	3,083	66%
Blimpie	691	63%
O.P.E.N. Cleaning	807	59%
Miracle Ear	963	58%

TYPES OF FRANCHISES   Most franchises can be classified as a distributorship, a chain-style business, or a manufacturing arrangement.

A **distributorship** is a firm in which a dealer is allowed to sell a product produced by a manufacturer. For example, Chrysler and Ford dealers are distributorships.

A **chain-style business** is a firm that is allowed to use the trade name of a company and follows guidelines related to the pricing and sales of the product. Some examples are Dunkin' Donuts, CD Warehouse, Holiday Inn, Subway, and Pizza Hut.

A **manufacturing arrangement** is a firm that is allowed to manufacture a product using the formula provided by another company. For example, Microsoft may allow a foreign company to produce its software, as long as the software is sold only in that country. Microsoft would receive a portion of the revenue generated by that firm.

distributorship a firm in which a dealer is allowed to sell a product produced by a manufacturer

chain-style business a firm that is allowed to use the trade name of a company and follows guidelines related to the pricing and sales of the product

manufacturing arrangement a firm that is allowed to manufacture a product using the formula provided by another company

ADVANTAGES OF A FRANCHISE   The typical advantages of a franchise are as follows:

1 *Proven Management Style* Franchisees look to the franchisors for guidance in production and management. McDonald's provides extensive training to its franchisees. The management style of a franchise is already a proven success. A franchise's main goal is to duplicate a proven business in a particular location. Thus, the franchise is a less risky venture than a new type of business, as verified by a much higher failure rate for new businesses.

2 *Name Recognition* Many franchises are nationally known because of advertising by the franchisor. This provides the franchisee with name recognition, which can significantly increase the demand for the product. Therefore, owners of Holiday Inn, Pizza Hut, and other franchises may not need to spend money on advertising because the franchises are already popular with consumers.

3 *Financial Support* Some franchisees receive some financial support from the franchisor, which can ensure sufficient start-up funds for the franchisee. For example, some McDonald's franchisees can receive funding from McDonald's. Alternatively, franchisees can purchase materials and supplies from the franchisor on credit, which represents a form of short-term financing.

DISADVANTAGES OF A FRANCHISE   Two common disadvantages of franchising are as follows:

SPOTLIGHT ON TECHNOLOGY

Organizing Your Business by Using the Internet

The decision on the form of business ownership can have long-term implications for taxes, liability, and control of the business. For these reasons, it should not be made lightly and will usually require a lawyer. Unfortunately, good legal advice does not come cheap. Therefore, entrepreneurs should familiarize themselves with the issues involved in organizing their businesses prior to retaining legal counsel. In recent years, the Internet has become an excellent place for finding out about such issues.

Perhaps the best starting point for learning more about business organization is the Small Business Administration (SBA). The SBA's home page (http://www.sbaonline.sba.gov/), pictured in Exhibit 2.6, represents an excellent starting point for further research. Among the resources offered:

➤ Information on local SBA offices.
➤ Access to the Service Corps of Retired Executives (SCORE), consisting of over ten thousand retired businesspeople who have volunteered to help small businesses for free.
➤ SBA publications. As illustrated (Exhibit 2.7), the range of topics covered by the publications is enormous, and each can be copied directly to the entrepreneur's computer at no charge.

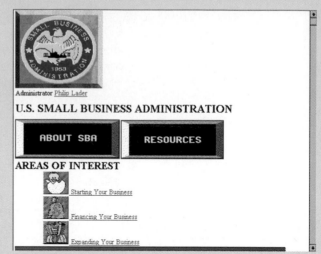

Exhibit 2.6 The Small Business Administration's Home Page

While all of these services are also available through local SBA offices, the entrepreneur can reach them far more quickly over the Internet.

In addition to government agencies, such as the SBA, many private organizations provide information and services to small businesses just getting set up. Many of these, such as the Company Corporation (Exhibit 2.8), allow corporations and other forms of businesses to be set up entirely over the Internet. Such services are made particularly attractive by their low cost—often hundreds or thousands of dollars less than using a lawyer. The entrepreneur is cautioned, however, that "undoing" the wrong form of ownership can often be expensive. Therefore, unless the entrepreneur has extensive knowledge of various forms of ownership, establishing a long-term relationship with a local attorney is generally prudent.

Exhibit 2.7 List of SBA Publications on the Internet

Exhibit 2.8 The Company Corporation Home Page

1 *Sharing Profits* In return for services provided by the franchisor, the franchisee must share profits with the franchisor. Annual fees paid by the franchisee may be 8 percent or more of the annual revenue generated by the franchise.

2 *Less Control* The franchisee must abide by guidelines regarding product production and pricing, and possibly other guidelines as well. Consequently, the franchisee's performance is dependent on these guidelines. Owners are not allowed to revise some of the guidelines.

While decision making is limited, owners of a franchise still make some critical decisions. They must decide whether a particular franchise can be successful in a particular location. In addition, even though the production and marketing policies are somewhat predetermined, the owners are responsible for managing their employees. They must provide leadership and motivation to maximize production efficiency. Thus, a franchise's performance is partially dependent on its owners and managers.

RECEIVING ASSISTANCE AS A NEW BUSINESS

When new businesses are established, they are relatively small. These businesses may be assisted by the Small Business Administration (SBA), which was established by Congress in 1953 to encourage entrepreneurship. The SBA attempts to enhance the managerial capabilities of small business owners through counseling, workshops, and free brochures. In addition, retired business executives offer free assistance to business owners through the SBA. These executives have varied backgrounds and periodically conduct workshops in local communities for people planning to begin their own businesses.

In recognition of the relatively small proportion of minority-owned businesses, the SBA has offered much assistance to minorities that considered establishing their own businesses. Special financing assistance has also been available. Some universities maintain small business development centers that can help small business owners or people planning to start a business.

The degree of government assistance offered to small businesses frequently changes in response to the funds allocated for this purpose in the federal budget. When pressure to reduce government spending exists, the funding for small business assistance may be reduced.

HOW OWNERS MEASURE BUSINESS PERFORMANCE

 3

Explain how business owners can measure their business performance.

Owners who invest in a firm focus on two key criteria to measure a firm's performance: (1) return on their investment and (2) risk of their investment. These two criteria are discussed now, because the business strategies that managers implement should be intended to satisfy the business owners. Managers must determine how various business strategies will affect the firm's return on investment and risk.

Return on Investment

The return on investment in a firm is derived from the firm's profits (also called "earnings" or "income"). As a firm produces income, a portion of these earnings is paid to the Internal Revenue Service as income taxes. The remaining (after-tax) earnings represent the return (in dollars) to the business owners. However, dollar value of a firm's after-tax earnings is not necessarily a useful measure of the firm's perfor-

equity the total investment by the firm's stockholders

return on equity (ROE) earnings as a proportion of the equity

mance unless it is adjusted for the amount of firm's **equity**, which is the total investment by the firm's stockholders. For this reason, business owners prefer to measure the firm's profitability by computing its **return on equity (ROE)**, which is the earnings as a proportion of the equity:

$$\text{Return on Equity} = \frac{\text{Earnings after Tax}}{\text{Equity}}$$

For example, if a firm was provided with $1,000,000 by stockholders, and if its after-tax earnings last year were $150,000, its return on equity last year was:

$$\text{ROE} = \frac{\$150,000}{\$1,000,000}$$

$$= .15, \text{ or } 15\%.$$

Thus, the firm generated a return equal to 15 percent of the owner's investment in the firm.

To recognize why a "return" measurement such as ROE is more useful than the dollar value of profits, consider the following situation for Firms A and B in a particular industry:

	Firm A	Firm B
Earnings after Tax Last Year	$15 million	$15 million
Stockholders' Equity	$100 million	$300 million
Return on Equity	15%	5%

Notice that each firm had the same dollar value of earnings after taxes. However, it took three times the investment in Firm B to achieve the same level of annual profit. Therefore, the return on equity (measured as earnings after taxes divided by stockholders' equity) is much higher for Firm A than for Firm B. Thus, Firm A is apparently making better use of the funds invested by stockholders.

As a realistic application, the return on investment for Campbell Soup Company last year is derived in Exhibit 2.9. Notice that Campbell generated an earnings before taxes of $1,042 million. Of this amount, $344 million was used to pay corporate taxes. The remaining $698 million represents after-tax earnings. Given the total investment (equity) of $2,468 million, the after-tax earnings represent a return of 28 percent (computed as $698 million divided by $2,468 million).

Risk

risk the degree of uncertainty about the firm's future earnings

The **risk** of a firm represents the degree of uncertainty about the firm's future earnings, which reflects an uncertain return to the owners. A firm's future earnings are dependent on its future revenue and its expenses. Firms could experience losses if the revenue is less than expected, or if the expenses are more than expected. Some firms that experience severe losses ultimately fail. In these cases, the owners may lose most or all of the funds they invested in the firms. Also, creditors may not be repaid for the loans that they provided to the firms.

To illustrate the risk of a business, consider the uncertainty of the future revenue and expenses of a lawn service firm. Revenue generated by the firm could be less than expected if unusually cold weather prevents grass and shrubs from growing. In addition, other lawn service firms may be created, which will compete for any avail-

Exhibit 2.9
Annual Profits for Campbell Soup Company

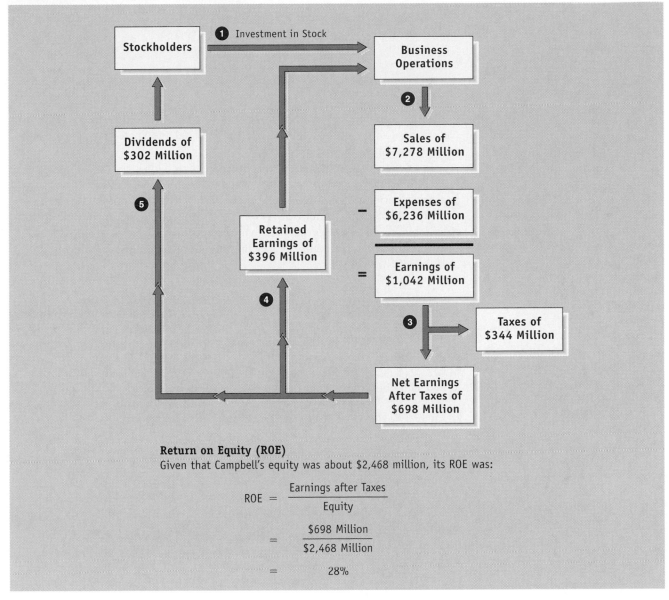

Return on Equity (ROE)

Given that Campbell's equity was about $2,468 million, its ROE was:

$$ROE = \frac{\text{Earnings after Taxes}}{\text{Equity}}$$

$$= \frac{\$698 \text{ Million}}{\$2,468 \text{ Million}}$$

$$= 28\%$$

able business. Given a limited number of lawns in a community, any lawn jobs done by new lawn service firms take away the business that was previously provided by this firm. The expenses of a lawn service may be higher than expected if lawn mowers break down or if the cost of hiring employees rises.

Exhibit 2.10 illustrates how business risk applies to the lawn service. This exhibit shows that the owner of the lawn service anticipated the firm's earnings to be $30,000 in one year. However, since actual revenue was $40,000 less than expected, and expenses were $4,000 more than expected, the firm incurred a loss of $14,000. Large firms such as KMart and Smith Corona (typewriters) have experienced losses following a decline in the demand for their products.

Firms cannot control some factors that may affect their revenue or expenses. However, firms should recognize how possible adverse conditions can affect demand,

Exhibit 2.10
Example of Business Risk

	Expected	Actual
Revenue	$90,000	$50,000
Expenses	60,000	64,000
Earnings	$30,000	−$14,000

so that they can develop a realistic forecast of revenue. In addition, to create a more realistic expectation of the total expenses, they should anticipate that some repairs on their machinery may be needed.

To prepare for potential problems, the risks of each business should be recognized. While many success stories are created in business, many failures occur as well. Some new businesses fail simply because the entrepreneur did not recognize the risks. The Self-Scoring Exercise offers a self-test for assessing your own skills to succeed in business. However, recognize that some people may be successful as managers but not as entrepreneurs because they do not recognize the risks involved in establishing a new business.

SELF-SCORING EXERCISE

Do You Have Necessary Skills to Succeed in Business?

According to the U.S. Department of Labor, achieving success in the workplace, now and in the future, will require that a person possess three enabling skills as a foundation for the five functional skills required in the business environment. Answer each of these three basic questions.

1. Do you believe you possess the basic reading, speaking, listening, and mathematics skills required for future learning?
2. Do you believe you possess the intellectual skills for effective-decision making and problem solving?
3. Do you believe you possess the affective skills required for you to cooperate with others and achieve effective sociability?

If you answered each question yes, you have the needed basic skills to enable you to master five functional skills in the business environment. How do you rate yourself now in each of these five functional skill areas? In the blank before each skill, place the number from 1 (very good) to 5 (needs improvement) that reflects your self-rating.

_____ 1. Resource management skills, such as human resource management, time management, and financial resources management.
_____ 2. Information management skills, such as identifying and interpreting information.
_____ 3. Personal interaction skills, such as teamwork, negotiation, and working with customers.
_____ 4. Systems behavior and performance skills, such as anticipating consequences of behavior and cause-effect relationships.
_____ 5. Technology utilization skills, such as selecting, using, maintaining, and/or troubleshooting technology.

If you rated yourself a 4 or 5 on any one of the five functional skills, you may want to talk with your instructor or the university's career and counseling office about specific opportunities that will enable you to strengthen those skills.

CROSS-FUNCTIONAL TEAMWORK

Sources of Risk Across Business Functions

 A firm relies on the management of resources (including human resources and other resources such as machinery), marketing, and finance functions to perform well. Poor performance can normally be attributed to poor management of resources, poor marketing, or poor financing, as explained next.

If resources are not properly managed, the firm will incur excessive expenses. The following are typical mistakes that can cause excessive production expenses:

1 Hiring more employees than necessary, which results in high operating expenses
2 Hiring fewer employees than necessary, which prevents the firm from achieving the desired volume or quality of products
3 Hiring employees who lack proper skills or training
4 Investing in more equipment or machinery than necessary, which results in high operating expenses
5 Investing in less equipment or machinery than necessary, which prevents the firm from achieving the desired volume or quality of products

The following are typical marketing mistakes that can cause poor performance:

1 Excessive spending on marketing programs
2 Ineffective marketing programs, which do not enhance the firm's revenue

The following are typical finance mistakes that can cause poor performance:

1 Borrowing too much money, which results in a high level of interest expenses incurred per year
2 Not borrowing enough money, which prevents a firm from investing the necessary amount of funds to be successful

Since business decisions are related, a poor decision in one department can affect other departments. For example, Compaq Computer's production volume is based on the forecasted demand for computers by the marketing department. When the marketing department underestimates the demand, Compaq experiences shortages.

RELATIONSHIP BETWEEN RISK AND RETURN   Some firms have a much higher degree of risk than others when the demand for their products is highly uncertain. Potential owners will support these high-risk firms only if they are expected to provide a higher return. For example, people may be willing to become owners of an exotic jewelry store only if they expect the store to generate high profits. The people could have used their money to invest in a less risky business, such as a retail bookstore or a grocery store, but investing in the exotic jewelry store offers the possibility of earning a higher return on their investment.

Like business investors, creditors will provide funds to a risky firm only if they have the potential to earn a relatively high return on the funds provided. The return to creditors is the interest rate charged on the loans they provide. To compensate for the higher risk, creditors charge a higher rate of interest when lending funds to a risky business.

RISK OF SMALL BUSINESSES   Small businesses tend to be riskier than larger businesses because small businesses have neither the managerial expertise nor the funds to diversify into other businesses. Thus, if their single line of business experiences problems, they are highly susceptible to failure. Any event that affects the single industry they have entered (such as a workers' strike in a supplier firm or reduced demand for the type of products they produce) can result in failure. In addition, the death or retirement of a key manager can have a greater impact on a small business. Larger businesses typically employ several employees for high-level positions to make key decisions, so that no one person is irreplaceable.

Investors recognize the higher risk of small businesses and will invest in them only if the potential for high profitability outweighs the risk involved. Creditors will lend to small businesses only if they will receive a higher return (higher interest rate) that properly reflects the risk. Consequently, the cost of financing for a small business is generally higher than for a large corporation.

Ownership of Foreign Businesses

Opportunities in foreign countries have encouraged many entrepreneurs in the United States to establish foreign businesses in recent years. A common method for an entrepreneur to establish a foreign business is to purchase a franchise created by a U.S. firm in a foreign country. For example, McDonald's, Pizza Hut, and KFC have franchises in numerous foreign countries. The potential return on these franchises may be higher than in the United States if there is less competition.

Another popular method for U.S. entrepreneurs to own a foreign business is to purchase a business that is being sold by the foreign government. During the 1990s, many foreign governments in Eastern Europe and Latin America sold a large number of businesses that they had owned. They also encouraged more competition among firms in each industry. Entrepreneurs recognized that many businesses previously owned by the government were not efficiently managed. Consequently, many businesses were perceived as having relatively low values, thus enabling some entrepreneurs to purchase the businesses at low prices. However, these businesses were subject to a high degree of risk because the foreign environment was so uncertain. Since most of the businesses in these countries had been managed by their respective governments, the rules for privately owned businesses were not completely established. The tax rates that would be imposed on private businesses were uncertain. The degree of competition was also uncertain, as firms were now allowed to enter most industries.

Given the uncertainty for businesses that were just established in these foreign countries, some entrepreneurs made agreements with existing foreign firms rather than establishing their own business. For example, an entrepreneur may recognize that various household products would be popular in some Latin American countries, but may prefer not to establish a firm there because of uncertainty about tax rates and other government policies. The entrepreneur may make an agreement with an existing firm that distributes related products to retail stores throughout Latin America. This firm would earn a fee for selling the household products produced by the entrepreneur. This example is just one of many possible arrangements that allow U.S. entrepreneurs to capitalize on situations in a foreign country without owning a business there.

COLLEGE
HEALTH CLUB

BUSINESS DILEMMA

Ownership Decision at College Health Club

Sue Kramer has completed her business plan for College Health Club (CHC), as explained in Chapter 1, in which she would be sole proprietor. She believes that she is well prepared to run her own health club. She submits the plan along with a request for a business loan from her local bank. Shortly after submitting her plan, she notices that a national health club chain is planning to establish a health club franchise near a huge corporate office complex at the other end of town. This franchise is not perceived as a competitor to CHC because it is far away from the campus and is targeted at employees who work in the office complex. However, the franchise is of interest to Sue because it is searching for someone to purchase it. Sue decides to consider purchasing the franchise. The franchisee would be trained by the national chain on how to run the health club and would receive a fraction of the revenue earned by the franchise. While similar types of health clubs are in the area, the national chain believes that room exists for at least one more competitor.

Dilemma

Sue has to decide whether to purchase the franchise or establish CHC. For this reason, she needs to consider the advantages of purchasing the franchise health club versus establishing CHC. What are the advantages of each alternative? Which alternative should Sue select?

Solution

One advantage of the franchise health club is that it would offer training. Second, it has a well-established plan for managing health clubs. Third, the club has a national name that potential customers recognize.

However, an advantage of owning CHC is that it would be less expensive than the franchise health club. Second, CHC would allow Sue to capitalize on her specific idea of targeting college students. Third, Sue would be able to manage CHC without any interference, whereas the franchise would need to be managed in a manner dictated by the national chain. Fourth, Sue would not have to pay any fraction of her revenue to the national chain if she establishes her own health club.

Given the balanced advantages of each alternative business opportunity, the choice is dependent on personal preferences and abilities. Since Sue feels that she has the skills to run her own health club, she decides to do it on her own rather than purchase a franchise.

Additional Issues for Discussion

1 Sue could also have considered purchasing one of the existing health clubs that are for sale in the area. What do you think is an advantage of purchasing an existing health club? What is a disadvantage?

2 One advantage of a partnership is that it allows partners to focus on their respective specializations. Should this advantage cause Sue to search for a partner for her health club business?

3 How will CHC be taxed given that Sue plans to be the sole owner?

SUMMARY

1 When starting a new business, entrepreneurs must select from among three forms of ownership:

➤ a sole proprietorship, owned by a single person who often manages the firm as well.

➤ a partnership, composed of two or more co-owners who may manage the firm as well. A partnership can allow for more financial support by owners than a sole proprietorship, but it also requires that control and profits be shared among owners.

➤ a corporation, which is an entity that is viewed as separate from its owners. Owners of a corporation have limited liability, while owners of sole proprietorships and partnerships have unlimited liability.

2 The common methods by which people become owners of existing businesses are as follows:

➤ assuming ownership of a family business

➤ purchasing an existing business

➤ franchising

Assuming the ownership of a family business is desirable because a person can normally learn much about that business before assuming ownership. Yet, many people are not in a position to assume the family business. To purchase an existing business, one must estimate future sales and expenses to determine whether making the investment is feasible. Franchising may be desirable for people who will need some guidance in running the firm. However, the franchisee must pay annual fees to the franchisor.

3 A firm's performance is measured by its owners using two criteria: return on the owner's investment (equity) and risk. Owners of a business commonly assess the return on their investment by measuring the firm's return on equity (ROE), which represents a firm's after-tax earnings as a percentage of the total investment by owners.

The risk of a business represents the uncertainty about its future earnings. Firms that have more uncertain revenue or expenses will have more uncertain earnings, and therefore higher risk. The owners and creditors require a higher return when providing funds to firms whose future earnings are more uncertain.

KEY TERMS

agency problem
bylaws
capital gain
chain-style business
charter
corporation
distributorship
equity
franchise
franchisee

franchisor
general partners
general partnership
going public
limited liability company (LLC)
limited partners
limited partnership
manufacturing arrangement
partners
partnership

privately held
publicly held
return on equity (ROE)
risk
S-corporation
sole proprietor
sole proprietorship
unlimited liability

REVIEW QUESTIONS

1 Compare a sole proprietorship with a partnership and a corporation.
2 Discuss the advantages and disadvantages of a sole proprietorship.
3 Distinguish between a general partnership and a limited partnership.
4 Identify and explain the differences between an S-corporation and a limited liability company.
5 How can stockholders earn a return on their investment?
6 Identify and explain the differences between privately held and publicly held corporations.
7 Identify the advantages of an S-corporation.

8 Explain why stockholders are concerned that managers do not always act in their best interests.
9 Identify and explain the advantages and disadvantages of a franchise.
10 Explain the difference between the corporate tax rate and the personal tax rate.

DISCUSSION QUESTIONS

1 For the following situations, recommend an appropriate form of business ownership:

a. Four physicians wish to start a practice together, and each wants to have limited liability.

b. A friend wants to start her own convenience store.

c. An entrepreneur wants to

acquire a large U.S. steel business.

d. Five friends want to build an apartment complex and are not concerned about limited liability.

2 Discuss the basic steps that should be undertaken to organize a corpora-tion in your state.

3 Discuss and give examples of what you believe is the most common form of business ownership in your hometown.

4 Assume you are creating your own business. What decisions have to be made for you to consider the type of ownership and control of your business?

5 Identify a fast-food franchise that experienced growth in the 1970s and compare it with a fast-food franchise that experienced growth in the 1990s.

RUNNING YOUR OWN BUSINESS

1 Describe whether your business will be a sole propri-etorship, a partnership, or a corporation. Why did you make this decision?

2 Describe the risk of your business. That is, explain what conditions could result in lower revenue than what you expect or in higher expenses than what you expect.

INVESTING IN THE STOCK OF A BUSINESS

Using the annual report of the firm in which you would like to invest, complete the following:

1 Each annual report contains an income statement, which discloses the firm's earnings before taxes, its taxes, and its earnings after taxes over the most recent year. Search for the table called "Income Statement" and deter-mine your firm's earnings before taxes, taxes paid, and earnings after taxes last year. What proportion of your firm's earnings were eventually paid as tax expense?

2 Is your firm involved in franchising? If so, describe the details on its franchises. Write the company and ask for information on opening a franchise.

3 Describe any conditions mentioned in the annual report that expose the firm to risk.

CASE 1 Deciding the Type of Business Ownership

Paul Bazzano and Mary Ann Boone are lifelong friends and have decided to go into business. They are not sure of the form of business ownership and control. Paul has stated he would like to invest his savings of $25,000, but does not want to take an active role in managing the day-to-day operations of the business. Mary Ann, on the other hand, is a self-starter, enjoys cooking and baking, and has a vast number of pizza recipes. An existing pizza business is for sale for $50,000. Paul and Mary Ann both like the idea of getting into a business investment. Mary Ann has $5,000 she would like to contribute and believes that buy-ing an existing business has certain advantages. She likes the idea that Paul will not be an active owner and that she will have full control of the pizza operation.

The existing business has sales of $150,000 and gener-ates earnings after taxes of $32,500. Mary Ann believes the business can be expanded and foresees future growth to expand into different locations throughout the Boston area. She projects two more stores in the next five years. The only problem is that she and Paul would take out of the business any profits that are made.

Questions
1 What form of business ownership would you recom-mend for this business?

2 Would Mary Ann's form of ownership be any differ-ent from Paul's?

3 As the business expands, what recommendations would you give Mary Ann?

CASE 2 The Franchising Decision

In recent years the growth of franchises in the United States has slowed. Many franchises are shutting their doors because of saturation in business communities and neighborhoods around the country. Franchisees are also concerned about new economic development, such as food courts appearing in shopping malls.

The franchise contract, an agreement between the franchisor and the franchisee, must detail the exact conditions under which the franchise will operate. Franchise contracts are often lengthy, with few obligations placed on the franchisor. The franchisee must heed the warning "Let the buyer beware." Franchisees must also be acutely aware of everything that is put into writing because the contract generally favors the franchisor's rights. "Franchise contracts are inordinately one-sided. I'd never sign one again unless I could make major revisions," says Greg Johns, a franchisee with American Fastsigns.

The initial costs to get into a franchise are high, often ranging from $5,000 to $35,000. An exception is McDonald's, which costs $500,000 or more. When franchisees open for business, they often pay monthly royalties (from 2 percent to 8 percent of gross sales), plus another 1 or 2 percent for advertising. In addition to advertising fees and royalties, the costs of getting into a franchise are often initially higher than starting a small business. However, the profits and success rate for the franchise are still higher than they are for small businesses.

Questions

1 Distinguish a franchisor from a franchisee.
2 Discuss some of the problems confronting franchisees.
3 What is the meaning of the statement "Let the buyer beware"?
4 Are the costs of getting into a franchise higher than starting a small business? Explain.

VIDEO CASE A Business Ownership Dilemma

 Douglas Bagley's moving company called A-1 Pioneer of Salt Lake City, Utah, lost so much ground years ago that it almost failed. But Bagley reversed its direction quickly. It has been moving forward ever since.

The business piled up debt in 1988, and the debt load became heavier when a tractor-trailer carrying $150,000 worth of furniture was lost in a fire. Insurance didn't cover all the loss.

In April, 1988, the partner died. His widow struggled to run the business until the life insurance proceeds were paid; that took six months. And A-1 Pioneer's debt was so heavy that it couldn't meet all its obligations on time.

Bagley filed for bankruptcy protection in January, 1989. The company recovered in less than 12 months.

What made that rapid recovery possible? The key was to obtain funds, or at least retain the funds previously borrowed from creditors. While Bagley may have been able to obtain funds by taking on a new partner, he decided to focus on working with his creditors. First, Bagley assured creditors that they would be paid and gained their confidence by outlining plans for his company. Then he visited his longtime clients and pledged that A-1 Pioneer would do a good job for them. Although some clients took their business elsewhere, most did not.

Today, Bagley has 37 employees—up from eight in 1989. He also has the revenue to justify the rise in payroll. Annual sales have increased year by year and now exceed $1.5 million.

Questions

1 When Douglas Bagley, owner of A-1 Pioneer Moving & Storage, needed to improve the firm's financial condition, he decided to negotiate with his existing creditors. What is an advantage of this strategy over finding a partner who would be willing to invest in the firm:? What is a disadvantage?
2 Assume that Bagley needs about $100,000 of additional support for his firm. Do you think that his firm is in a position to offer stock to the public and become a publicly traded corporation?
3 Assume that Bagley expects that he will earn a return of 20 percent annually on his investment in his moving and storage firm. He based this estimate on the firm's earnings in the last few years. Given the recent population growth in the local area, he expects that the demand for his firm's moving and storage services will increase. Gasoline expenses incurred in the moving business have not risen much because gasoline prices have been stable. Furthermore, wages in the moving business have not risen much, so that the labor expenses incurred by the firm have been stable. Offer some reasons why the return on investment may not be as high as expected.

THE *Coca-Cola* COMPANY ANNUAL REPORT PROJECT

The following questions apply concepts learned in this chapter to The Coca-Cola Company. Read from Reality #1 on page 3 up to Reality #4 (on page 6) in The Coca-Cola Company annual report before answering these questions.

1 Why do you think The Coca-Cola Company is orga-nized as a corporation rather than a sole proprietorship or a partnership?

2 The annual report suggests that The Coca-Cola Company's economic values added (EVA) influences the return on the investment by shareholders. What does this mean?

3 What challenges does The Coca-Cola Company face?

IN-TEXT STUDY GUIDE

Answers are in an appendix at the back of the book.

True or False

1 A sole proprietor may obtain loans from creditors to help finance the firm's operations, which constitutes ownership.

2 The legal requirements for establishing a sole proprietorship are very difficult.

3 When stockholders of a corporation sell their stocks for more than what they paid for them, they can be subject to a capital gain.

4 If the board of directors becomes displeased with the performance of the key officers, the board has the power to replace them.

5 Publicly held corporations can obtain additional funds by issuing new common stock.

6 Publicly held corporations are not obligated to periodically disclose financial information to the public.

7 To incorporate a business, one must adopt a corporate charter and file it with the state government where it is to be located.

8 The limited liability feature is an advantage in owning a sole proprietorship.

9 A limited liability company must be created according to the laws of the state where the business is located.

10 Limited partners are investors in the partnership and participate in the management of the business.

Multiple Choice

11 People become owners of a corporation by purchasing:
a) shares of stock.
b) corporate bonds.
c) retained earnings.
d) inventory.
e) accounts receivable.

12 The following are possible forms of business owner-ship except for a:
a) sole proprietorship.
b) partnership.
c) bureaucracy
d) corporation.

13 The return on investment in a firm is derived from the firm's ability to earn:
a) assets.
b) liabilities.
c) profits.
d) expenses.

14 What percentage of all firms in the United States are sole proprietorships?
a) 10 percent
b) 20 percent
c) 30 percent
d) 50 percent
e) 70 percent

15 A partnership that has thirty-five owners or less and meets other criteria may choose to be a so-called:
a) cooperative.
b) proprietorship.
c) joint venture.
d) S-corporation.
e) bureaucracy.

16 A sole proprietorship has the following disadvantages except for:
a) unlimited liability.
b) complete control.
c) limited skills.
d) limited funds.

17 Sharing profits and less control of the business ownership are two common disadvantages of:
a) sole proprietorships.
b) downsizing.
c) divestiture.
d) franchising.

18 Partners have unlimited liability in a:
a) general partnership.
b) corporation.
c) limited partnership.
d) cooperative.

19 An arrangement whereby business owners allow others to use their trademark, trade name, or copyright under specified conditions is a:
a) franchise.
b) labor union.
c) bureau.
d) joint venture.
e) cartel.

20 The degree of uncertainty about future earnings, which reflects an uncertain return to the owners, is known as:
a) certainty.
b) profits.
c) risk.
d) equity.
e) dividends.

21 Stockholders of a corporation elect the members of the:
a) organization.
b) labor union.
c) business trust.
d) board of directors.
e) project team.

22 Stockholders can earn a return on their investment if the stock they hold increases in value over time or through:
a) interest payments.
b) divestiture.
c) dividends.
d) bank notes.
e) conservation.

23 A business that is allowed to use the trade name of a company and follows guidelines related to the pricing and sales of the products is a:
a) joint venture.
b) monopoly.
c) chain-style business.
d) sole proprietorship.

24 General guidelines for the management of a company are called:
a) rules.
b) bylaws.
c) procedures.
d) standards.
e) controls.

25 A general partnership that protects a partner's per-sonal assets from the firm is a:
a) limited liability company.
b) sole proprietorship.
c) cooperative.
d) nonprofit institution.

26 A state-chartered entity that is legally distinct from its owners and pays taxes is a:
a) sole proprietorship.
b) corporation.
c) partnership.
d) limited partnership.
e) joint venture.

27 When ownership of a small corporation is restricted to a small group of investors, it is:
a) publicly held.
b) government owned.
c) bureaucratic.
d) privately held.
e) perfectly competitive.

28 Most franchises can be classified as the following except for:
a) business agent.
b) chain-style business.
c) manufacturing arrangement.
d) distributorship.

29 Small businesses are riskier than larger businesses because small businesses lack :
a) enthusiasm.
b) managerial expertise.
c) better service.
d) creativity.
e) innovativeness.

30 A business owned by a single owner is referred to as a:
a) partnership.
b) sole proprietorship.
c) limited partnership.
d) corporation.
e) subchapter S-corporation.

31 The following are disadvantages of a partnership except for:
a) control is shared.
b) losses are shared.
c) unlimited liability.
d) profits are shared.

32 When a corporation's shares can be easily purchased or sold by investors, it is:
a) publicly held.
b) privately held.
c) institutionalized.
d) monopolized.
e) franchised.

33 Important aspects of the corporation, such as the name of the firm, information about the stock issued, and a description of the firm's operations, are contained in a:
a) mission.
b) policy.
c) charter.
d) plan.
e) venture.

34 When two or more people, having complementary skills, agree to co-own a business, this agreement is referred to as a:

a) partnership.
b) sole proprietorship.
c) cooperative.
d) corporation.
e) joint venture.

35 When entrepreneurs establish a business, they must first decide on the form of:
a) divestiture.
b) global expansion.
c) joint ventures.
d) ownership.

What is the World Wide Web?

The Internet evolved primarily as a U.S. network. It became more popular to established and new businesses as a result of a new application, referred to as the World Wide Web (WWW). Today, the WWW has become nearly synonymous with the Internet in the minds of most users.

What makes the WWW different from other Internet applications is its user-friendly graphic interface. Organizations and individuals create web pages, such as the University of Central Arkansas' web page (Exhibit 2.11), using a document format called hypertext markup language (HTML). Web pages can incorporate both

Exhibit 2.11

The University of Central Arkansas' Web Page

http://www.sbaer.uca.edu/

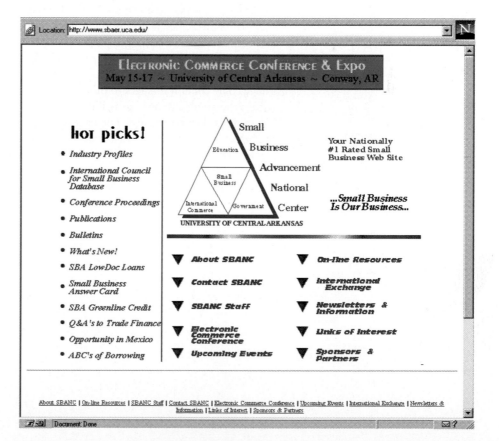

Exhibit 2.12
Popular Web Browsers

	e-mail
Netscape Navigator	http://home.netscape.com/
Microsoft Explorer	http://www.inet.fi/microsoft/
NCSA Mosaic	webdev@ncsa.uiuc.edu
Lynx (text-based only)	grobe@ukans.edu
America On-Line	info@aol.com

text and graphics. Features such as on-line questionnaires, polls, and even product ordering screens can also be incorporated into HTML documents. Today's most advanced web pages go even further, and are now delivering multimedia effects including sound and animation.

Once a web page has been developed, it is then placed on a web server, a computer running special software that is directly connected to the Internet. Each server has its own Uniform Resource Locator (URL), which normally begins with http: (for example, http://www.sbaer.uca.edu/). The web page that is called up when the site is accessed is sometimes referred to as the site's home page. To access web pages, a user needs a connection to the Internet and a program called a web browser. Examples of such browsers include Mosaic, Netscape, and America Online (Exhibit 2.12). The purpose of the browser is to take a copy of the web page sent by the web server and display it on the user's screen. The site featured above is one of the top resources for small business information on the web. Through this site an entrepeneur can gather information on many topics related to starting and running a small business, including advice on selecting a form of business ownership.

Probably the key factor in the rapid acceptance of the WWW is the ability to establish linkages between web pages. Using URLs and HTML document file names makes it possible to reference any other WWW site in the world. On the user's screen, these linkages typically appear as underlined text, although buttons and images may contain linkages to other sites as well (such as the <u>Links of Interest icon</u> within the graphic image in the illustration). To jump to these references, all the user has to do is click on the text. The page from the new site is then automatically sent to the browser, where it is displayed on the user's screen. Conceptually, then, the WWW can be viewed as a giant web of connected documents, and "surfing the net" is the process of jumping from site to site using these connections.

For an explanation of the language commonly used in reference to the World Wide Web, see Exhibit 2.13: "The Lingo to Know".

Exhibit 2.13
"The Lingo to Know"

By Leslie Miller
USA TODAY

Business conversation—even cocktail chatter—is getting tough these days without a grasp of cyberspeak. Webs, home pages, on line, long strings of codes beginning with h-t-t-p-colon-slash-slash. . . . Language skills suddenly fail you.

Here's a concise phrasebook to help you talk like a local.

➤ **Bulletin board system (BBS).** A computer service similar to an on-line service, usually smaller (and cheaper) with fewer users, fewer features and a narrow focus. A bulletin board is also any on-line or Internet area for posting messages.

➤ **Bits per second (bps).** How fast modems send and receive data. A 14.4 modem moves 14,400 bits per second; a 28.8 modem, also known as a V.34 (say it V-dot-three-four) is twice as fast. An earlier term, baud, is considered archaic.

➤ **Browser.** Software to view the graphical "pages" on the World Wide Web.

➤ **Chat rooms.** Areas on an on-line service, BBS or the Internet that allow real-time, typed-in communication with other people.

➤ **Cyberspace.** The metaphoric space where electronic communication takes place. Everything in cyberspace is "virtual"—not physically real perhaps but a shared experience nonetheless.

➤ **Download.** To electronically copy a file to your computer from another computer.

➤ **E-mail.** Electronic mail, messages from one user to another (or to a group).

➤ **Emoticons,** also called smileys or winkies, are little punctuation faces to add body language to cybercommunication. A smiley looks like this :) or, with a nose, like this :^) and a winky is this ;).

➤ **Flame.** Noun or verb; a nasty on-line message or personal attack, often sent in response to a posting the flamer disagrees with.

➤ **Forum.** An on-line area on a particular topic; the new-age forum on CompuServe has bulletin boards, a chat room and a library.

➤ **FTP.** File transfer protocol. A way to download remote files over the Internet.

➤ **GIF** (pronounced *jif*). A format for transmitting photos. A newer photo format: JPEG (say it *JAY-peg*).

➤ **Gopher.** A way to search for information on the 'Net with a program that lets you burrow into a remote computer's files through on-screen menus. Also the mascot at University of Minnesota, where the program was born.

➤ **Home page.** A main page on the Web. Companies and organizations have home pages that serve as virtual brochures; individual home pages often share personal passions.

➤ **Hypertext.** Hidden codes that let users click on a highlighted word or phrase to automatically access a related site. Hypertext markup language (HTML) is the language in which Web pages are written and linked; hypertext transfer protocol (http) is how information is sent over the Web.

➤ **IMHO.** In my humble opinion. Often appended to opinionated posted views.

➤ **Snail mail.** U.S. Postal Service, disparagingly.

➤ **Surfing the 'Net.** Navigating the Internet, usually random Web browsing.

➤ **Sysop.** The system operator of a BBS, a forum or area on an on-line service (pronounced *SIS-op*).

➤ **Upload.** To send a copy of a file from your computer to another computer.

➤ **Usenet newsgroups.** More than 15,000 Internet bulletin boards on a huge variety of topics. Each line of discussion is called a thread.

➤ **URL.** Uniform Resource Locator (pronounced *you-are-el,* not *earl*) is the address of an Internet site; all Web URLs start with http://.

➤ **World Wide Web.** the fastest-growing part of the 'Net. It's multimedia-capable, intricately interlinked and set up for viewing in colorful magazine-style "pages" containing text, photos and sounds.

CHAPTER 3

Business Ethics and Social Responsibility

A firm's employees should practice business ethics, which is a set of principles that should be followed when conducting business. Each firm has a social responsibility, which is the firm's recognition of how its business decisions can affect society. The term *social responsibility* is sometimes used to describe the firm's responsibility to its community and to the environment. However, it may also be more broadly used to include the firm's responsibility to its customers, employees, and creditors. While a firm makes business decisions that are intended to increase its value, its decisions must not violate its ethics and social responsibilities.

To illustrate how business ethics can affect the value of a business, consider the case of Homestake Mining Company, which focuses on gold mining in the United States, Canada, and other countries. What responsibilities does Homestake have toward its employees who are involved in mining? What responsibilities does Homestake have toward the environment in which it conducts mining operations? What responsibilities does Homestake have toward the stockholders who have invested their funds in the firm? Can Homestake satisfy all of these responsibilities simultaneously? This chapter provides a background on a firm's social responsibilities, which can be used to address these questions.

The **Learning Goals** of this chapter are to:

1 Describe the responsibilities of firms to their customers.

2 Describe the responsibilities of firms to their employees.

3 Describe the responsibilities of firms to their stockholders and creditors.

4 Describe the responsibilities of firms to the environment.

5 Describe the responsibilities of firms to their communities.

6 Explain the costs that firms incur in achieving their social responsibilities.

RESPONSIBILITY TO CUSTOMERS

1 **Describe the responsibilities of firms to their customers.**

social responsibility firm's recognition of how its business decisions can affect society

A firm's responsibility to customers goes beyond the provision of products or services. Firms have a **social responsibility** when producing and selling their products, as discussed next.

Responsible Production Practices

Products should be produced to ensure customer safety. Proper warning labels should be attached to products to prevent accidents that could result from misuse. For some products, proper information on possible side effects should be provided. For example, Tylenol gelcaps, Nyquil cough syrup, and Coors beer all have warning labels about possible adverse effects.

Responsible Sales Practices

When employees are hired to sell a firm's products, they usually receive a commission or bonus based on sales volume. Employees of some firms may attempt to maximize their product sales, even when they recognize that the product is not appropriate for particular customers. For example, to increase commissions some insurance salespeople sell more insurance than customers need. Furthermore, some firms falsely advertise their products. Firms need guidelines that discourage employees from using overly aggressive sales strategies or deceptive advertising.

How Firms Ensure Responsibility toward Customers

A firm can ensure responsibility toward its customers by following these steps:

business ethics a set of principles that should be followed when conducting business

1 *Establish a Code of Ethics* Firms can establish a code of **business ethics** that sets guidelines for product quality, as well as guidelines for how employees, customers, and owners should be treated. The pledge (from an annual report) by Bristol-Myers Squibb Company in Exhibit 3.1 is an example of a code of ethics. Many firms have a booklet on ethics that is distributed to all employees.

2 *Monitor Complaints* Firms should make sure that customers have a phone number that they can call if they have any complaints about the quality of the product or about how they were treated by employees. The firm can attempt to determine the source of the complaint and ensure that such a complaint does not occur again. Many firms have a department that receives the complaints and attempts to resolve them. This step may involve assessing different parts of the production process to ensure that the product is produced properly. Or it may require an assessment of particular employees who may be violating the firm's code of responsibility to its customers.

3 *Customer Feedback* Firms can ask customers for feedback on the products or services they recently purchased, even if the customers did not call in to complain. This process may detect some other problems with the product's quality or with the way customers were treated. For example, automobile dealers such as Saturn send a questionnaire to customers to determine how they were treated by salespeople. They may also be asked whether they have any complaints about the automobile they recently purchased. Once the firm is informed of problems with either production defects or customer treatment, it should take action to correct these problems.

Exhibit 3.1
Excerpts from a Pledge of Ethics
and Responsibility by Bristol-
Myers Squibb Company

THE BRISTOL-MYERS SQUIBB PLEDGE

TO THOSE WHO USE OUR PRODUCTS . . .
We affirm Bristol-Myers Squibb's commitment to the highest standards of excellence, safety and reliability in everything we make. We pledge to offer products of
the highest quality and to work diligently to keep improving them.

TO OUR EMPLOYEES AND THOSE WHO MAY JOIN US . . .
We pledge personal respect, fair competition and equal treatment. We acknowledge
our obligation to provide able and humane leadership throughout the organization, within a clean and safe working environment. To all who qualify for advancement, we will make every effort to provide opportunity.

TO OUR SUPPLIERS AND CUSTOMERS . . .
We pledge an open door, courteous, efficient and ethical dealing, and appreciation
of their right to a fair profit.

TO OUR SHAREHOLDERS . . .
We pledge a companywide dedication to continued profitable growth, sustained
by strong finances, a high level of research and development, and facilities second to none.

TO THE COMMUNITIES WHERE WE HAVE PLANTS AND OFFICES . . .
We pledge conscientious citizenship, a helping hand for worthwhile causes, and
constructive action in support of civic and environmental progress.

TO THE COUNTRIES WHERE WE DO BUSINESS . . .
We pledge ourselves to be a good citizen and to show full consideration for the
rights of others while reserving the right to stand up for our own.

ABOVE ALL, TO THE WORLD WE LIVE IN . . .
We pledge Bristol-Myers Squibb to policies and practices which fully embody the
responsibility, integrity and decency required of free enterprise if it is to merit and
maintain the confidence of our society.

How Consumerism Ensures Responsibility toward Customers

The responsibility of firms toward customers may be enforced not only by the firms
but also by specific groups of consumers. **Consumerism** represents the collective
demand by consumers that businesses satisfy their needs. Consumer groups became
popular in the 1960s and have become increasingly effective as a result of their growth.

consumerism the collective demand
by consumers that businesses satisfy their
needs

How the Government Ensures Responsibility toward Customers

In addition to the codes of responsibility by firms and the wave of consumerism, the
government attempts to ensure responsibility to customers with various laws on
product safety, advertising, and industry competition.

GOVERNMENT REGULATION OF PRODUCT SAFETY   The government protects consumers by regulating the quality of some products produced by firms. For example,
the Food and Drug Administration (FDA) is responsible for testing food products to
determine whether they meet specific requirements. The FDA also examines new
drugs that firms have recently manufactured. Because the potential side effects may
not be known immediately, some drugs are continually tested by the FDA for several
years.

GOVERNMENT REGULATION OF ADVERTISING   The federal government also has established laws against deceptive advertising. Yet, it may not be able to prevent all unethical business practices. Numerous examples of advertising could be called deceptive. It is difficult to know if a product is "new and improved." In addition, the use of a term such as "lowest price" may have different meanings or interpretations.

GOVERNMENT REGULATION OF INDUSTRY COMPETITION   Another way in which the government ensures that consumers are treated properly is to promote competition in most industries. Competition between firms is beneficial to consumers, because firms that charge excessive prices or whose goods are of unacceptable quality will not survive in a competitive environment. Because of competition, consumers can avoid a firm that is using deceptive sales tactics.

monopoly sole provider of goods or services

A firm has a **monopoly** if it is the sole provider of goods or services. It can set prices without concern about competition. However, the government regulates those firms that have a monopoly. For example, it regulates utility firms that have monopolies in specific locations and can control the pricing policies of these firms.

In some industries, firms created various agreements to set their prices and avoid competing with each other. The federal government has attempted to prevent such activity by enforcing antitrust laws. Some of the more well-known antitrust acts are summarized in Exhibit 3.2. All of these acts share the objective of promoting competition. Yet, each act focuses on particular aspects that can influence the degree of competition within the industry.

The trucking, railroad, airlines, and telecommunications industry have been deregulated, allowing more firms to enter the industry. In addition, banks and other financial institutions have been deregulated since 1980 and now have more

Exhibit 3.2
Key Antitrust Laws

Sherman Antitrust Act (1890)	Encouraged competition and prevented monopolies.
Clayton Act (1914)	Reinforced the rules of the Sherman Antitrust Act and specifically prohibited the following activities because they reduced competition: *Tying agreements* Forced firms to purchase additional products as a condition to purchase the products desired. *Binding contracts* Prevented firms from purchasing products from a supplier's competitors. *Interlocking directorates* Prohibited the same person from serving on the board of directors of two competing firms.
Federal Trade Commission Act (1914)	Prohibited unfair methods of competition; also called for the establishment of the Federal Trade Commission (FTC) to enforce antitrust laws.
Robinson-Patman Act (1936)	Prohibited price policies or promotional allowances that reduce competition within an industry.
Celler-Kefauver Act (1950)	Prohibited mergers between firms that reduce competition within an industry.

flexibility on the types of deposits and interest rates to offer. They also have more freedom to expand across state lines. In general, deregulation results in lower prices for consumers.

RESPONSIBLITY TO EMPLOYEES

2 | Describe the responsibilities of firms to their employees.

Firms also have a responsibility toward their employees to ensure safety, proper treatment by other employees, and equal opportunity.

Employee Safety

Firms ensure that the workplace is safe for employees by closely monitoring the production process. Some obvious safety precautions are to check machinery and equipment for proper working conditions, require safety glasses or any other equipment that can prevent injury, and emphasize any special safety precautions in training seminars.

Firms that create a safe working environment prevent injuries and improve the morale of their employees. Many firms, such as Allied Signal, now identify workplace safety as one of their main goals. Levi Strauss and Company imposes safety guidelines not only on its U.S. facilities but also on Asian factories where some of its clothes are made. Starbucks Coffee Company has developed a code of conduct in an attempt to improve the quality of life in coffee-producing countries.

Proper Treatment by Other Employees

Firms are responsible for ensuring that employees are treated properly by other employees. Two of the key issues regarding the treatment of employees are diversity and the prevention of sexual harassment, which are discussed next.

DIVERSITY   In recent years, the work force has become much more diverse. More women have entered the job market, and more minorities now have the necessary

In Bangladesh, garment factories were forced to respond to the Levi Strauss Company's demand to stop employing child labor. In a deal to keep the children from being put out on the street, Levi's pays their full salary while they attend school.

Starbuck's has been proactive in monitoring working conditions in coffee-producing countries. A portion of their statement of beliefs reads, "We respect human rights and dignity. We believe that people should work because they want or need to, but not because they are forced to do so. We believe that people have the right to freely associate with whichever organizations or individuals they choose. We believe that children should not be unlawfully employed as laborers."

sexual harassment unwelcome comments or actions of a sexual nature

skills and education to qualify for high-level jobs. Exhibit 3.3 discloses the proportions of various job categories held by women, Blacks, and Hispanics.

Many firms have responded to the increased diversity among employees by offering diversity seminars. These seminars are normally intended to inform employees about cultural diversity. Such information can help employees recognize that certain statements or behavior may be offensive to other employees.

The following statement from a recent annual report of General Motors reflects the efforts that have been made by many firms to encourage diversity:

❚❚ *Internally, we are working to create an environment where diversity thrives. We are trying to remove barriers that separate people and find new ways to engage teams to maximize productivity and profitability. This is being done through communication, teamwork, mutual support, and pulling together to achieve common objectives. Our challenge is to seek a diverse population in leadership roles with a wide range of backgrounds, views, and experiences to ensure we capture diverse perspectives to meet and exceed customer expectations.* ❚❚

Firms such as Johnson and Johnson, MCI, the Coca-Cola Company, IBM, Merrill Lynch, Sara Lee Corporation and many other firms have made major efforts to promote diversity. Rockwell International has a diversity task team that developed guidelines for work force diversity planning in each of its businesses. Xerox has improved its workplace diversity in recent years. About 32 percent of its employees are women, and 26 percent of its employees are minorities.

PREVENTION OF SEXUAL HARASSMENT   In addition to diversity in the workplace, another issue is **sexual harassment,** which represents unwelcome comments or actions of a sexual nature. For example, one employee might make unwelcome sexual advances toward another and use personal power within the firm to threaten the

Exhibit 3.3
Proportion of Women and Minorities in Various Occupations

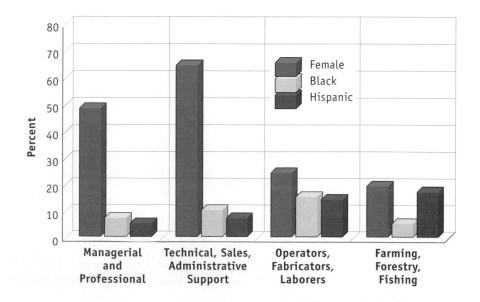

Denny's has taken many positive steps to overcome claims of racial bias in their restaurant operation.

other employee's job status. Firms attempt to prevent sexual harassment by offering seminars on the subject. Like the diversity seminars, these seminars can help employees recognize how some statements or behavior may be offensive to other employees. These seminars are not only an act of responsibility to employees but also can improve a firm's productivity by helping employees get along.

Equal Opportunity

Employees who apply for a position at a firm should not be subjected to discrimination because of their national origin, race, gender, or religion. The Civil Rights Act of 1964 prohibits such forms of discrimination. The act is enforced by a federal agency known as the Equal Employment Opportunity Commission (EEOC). Beyond the federal guidelines, many firms attempt to ensure equal treatment among applicants for a position by assigning someone to monitor the hiring process. The concept of equal treatment applies not only to the initial hiring of an employee but also to annual raises and promotions within the firm.

affirmative action a set of activities intended to increase opportunities for minorities and women

Many firms and government agencies implement **affirmative action** programs. Some people expect affirmative action programs to ensure equal treatment among prospective and existing employees. Other people expect these programs to establish quotas, which would designate specific positions for minorities or women. Most people would agree that affirmative action programs have good intentions, but quotas may be viewed as a form of reverse discrimination.

Denny's (a restaurant business) was charged with racial discrimination in 1993. In 1993, it began implementing a program to promote diversity. It increased minority management from 18 percent in 1993 to 24 percent in 1996. It also increased African-American owned franchises from one in 1993 to twenty-seven in 1996.

How Firms Ensure Responsibility toward Employees

To ensure that employees receive proper treatment, many firms establish a grievance procedure for employees who believe they are not being given equal opportunity. A specific person or department is normally assigned to address such complaints. This method of addressing employee complaints is similar to that of addressing customer complaints. By recognizing the complaints, the firm attempts both to resolve them and to revise its procedures to prevent further complaints.

A good example of a firm's effort to resolve employee complaints is Marriott, which implemented three strategies. First, it created a mediation process, in which a neutral person outside the firm (called a mediator) assesses the employee complaint and suggests a solution. The mediator does not have the power to enforce a final judgement but may help the employee and the firm resolve the conflict.

Second, Marriott offers a toll-free number for employees to call if they believe they were subjected to discrimination, harassment, or improper firing. Marriott begins to investigate the complaint within three days of the call.

Third, Marriott allows the employee to voice complaints in front of a panel of other employees who determine whether the employee's complaints are valid, based on Marriott's existing guidelines.

Since Marriott began its procedure for resolving employee complaints, EEOC complaints against Marriott by its employees declined by 50 percent in the following year and by 83 percent in the year after. Since more employee complaints were resolved within the firm, employees were more satisfied with their jobs, which allowed them to focus on satisfying customers.

The cost to a firm that attempts to listen to every employee complaint can be substantial. Furthermore, some of the complaints may not be valid. Firms must attempt to distinguish between complaints that are valid and those that are not, and then focus on resolving the valid complaints.

Conflict with Employee Layoffs

Some business decisions are controversial because they may adversely affect employees in the local community despite their improving the firm's performance. Consider the following example, which reflects a common dilemma that many firms face. As your firm's business grew, you hired more employees. However, because of the recent decline in demand for your product, you no longer need twenty of the employees that you hired over the last two years. If you lay off twenty employees, you will reduce your expenses substantially and satisfy your stockholders. However, you may be criticized for not serving employee interests. This situation is unpleasant because the layoffs may be necessary (to cut expenses) for your firm to survive. If your firm fails, all your other employees will also be out of work as well.

This dilemma has no perfect solution. Many firms may do what's best for the business, while attempting to reduce the adverse effects on their employees. For example, they may help those employees find employment elsewhere, or may even attempt to retrain them for jobs that will be available within the firm.

GLOBAL BUSINESS

Global Ethics

U.S. firms typically have a code of ethics that provides guidelines to the employees. However, these guidelines may be much more restrictive than those generally used in some foreign countries. Consider a U.S. firm that sells supplies to manufacturers. The employees of this firm may be subject to rules that prevent them from providing payoffs ("kickbacks") to any employees of the manufacturing companies that order the firm's supplies. Yet, other competitors may provide payoffs to employees of the manufacturing companies ordering supplies from their company. In some countries, this type of behavior is acceptable. Thus, the U.S. supplier is at a disadvantage because its employees are required to follow a stricter code of ethics. This is a common ethical dilemma that U.S. firms face in a global environment. The employees of U.S. firms must either ignore their ethical guidelines or be at a disadvantage in specific foreign countries.

Another ethical dilemma that U.S. firms face in some foreign countries is their relationship with foreign governments. Firms that conduct business in foreign countries are subject to numerous rules enforced by the local government. Officials of some foreign governments commonly accept bribes from firms that need approval for various business activities. For example, a firm may need to have its products approved for safety purposes, or its local manufacturing plant may need to be approved for environmental purposes. The process of approving even minor activities could take months and prevent the firm from conducting business. Those firms that pay off government officials may receive prompt attention from the local governments. Employees of Lockheed were charged with bribing Egyptian government officials to win a contract to build new aircraft. Executives of IBM's Argentina subsidiary were charged with bribing Argentine government officials to generate business from the government.

A recent assessment of foreign countries by the U.S. Commerce Department and intelligence agencies detected more than one hundred deals in 1994 in which foreign firms used bribes to win business contracts over U.S. competitors. Many of these foreign firms are located in France, Germany, and Japan, as well as in some less-developed countries.

Many U.S. firms attempt to follow a worldwide code of ethics that is consistent across countries. This type of policy reduces the confusion that could result from using different ethical standards in different countries. While a worldwide code of ethics may place the U.S. firm at a disadvantage in some countries, it may also enhance the credibility of that firm.

RESPONSIBILITY TO STOCKHOLDERS

3 | **Describe the responsibilities of firms to their stockholders and creditors.**

Firms are responsible for satisfying their owners (or stockholders). Employees may be tempted to make decisions that satisfy their own interests rather than those of the owners. For example, some employees may use the firm's money to purchase personal computers for their personal use rather than for the firm.

How Firms Ensure Responsibility

Managers of a firm monitor employee decisions to ensure that they are made in the best interests of the owners. Employee salaries may be directly tied to the firm's performance. In this way, employees stay focused on maximizing the firm's value.

Owners of a firm recognize that the firm will incur costs in meeting responsibilities such as employee safety and prevention of pollution. The firm's efforts to provide a safe and pollution-free environment represent a necessary cost of doing business.

How Stockholders Ensure Responsibility

shareholder activism the active role that stockholders take to influence a firm's management policies

In recent years, there has been much **shareholder activism,** which represents the active role that stockholders take to influence a firm's management policies. Stock-

Ben and Jerry, shown here, have been recognized nationally for their focus on employees, the community in which they operate, and society as a whole. No employee of Ben & Jerry's can receive more than eight times the salary of the lowest paid employee.

institutional investors financial institutions that purchase large amounts of stock

holders have been especially active when they are dissatisfied with the firm's executive salaries or other policies.

The stockholders who have been most active are **institutional investors,** or financial institutions that purchase large amounts of stock. For example, insurance companies invest a large portion of the insurance premiums that they receive in stocks. If institutional investors invest a large amount of money in a particular stock, the return on their investment is highly dependent on how that firm performs. Since many institutional investors commonly invest $10 million or more in a single firm's stock, they pay close attention to the performance of any firm in which they invest.

If an institutional investor believes the firm is poorly managed, it may attempt to meet with the firm's executives and express its dissatisfaction. It may even attempt to team up with other institutional investors who also own a large proportion of the firm's stock. This gives them more negotiating power because the firm's executives are more likely to listen to institutional investors who collectively hold a large proportion of the firm's stock. The institutional investors do not attempt to dictate how the firm should be managed. Instead, they attempt to ensure that the firm's managers make decisions that are in the best interests of all stockholders.

Conflict with Excessive Executive Compensation

A firm's managers can attempt to satisfy its stockholders by ensuring that funds invested by the stockholders are put to good use. If these funds are used to cover unnecessary expenses, the firm's profits are reduced, which reduces the return that stockholders receive on their investment. A major concern of stockholders is the salaries provided to the firm's chief executive officer (CEO) and other executives. The potential effect of excessive executive salaries on a firm's performance (and therefore on the returns to stockholders) is illustrated with the following example.

Consider two firms called Firm C and Firm D, which are in the same industry and have similar revenue and expenses, as shown in Exhibit 3.4. Assume that the only difference is that Firm C pays its top five executives a total of $30 million in annual salary, while Firm D pays its top five executives a total of $5 million. As shown in Exhibit 3.4, the annual profits of Firm D are $25 million above those of

Exhibit 3.4
Impact of Executive Salaries on a
Firm's Performance

	Firm C	Firm D
Revenue	$200,000,000	$200,000,000
− Expenses (except executive salaries)	−$150,000,000	−$150,000,000
− Executive Salaries Expense	− $30,000,000	− $5,000,000
= Profits	= $20,000,000	= $45,000,000

Firm C. This difference is attributed to Firm C's higher executive salary expenses. Thus, the return to the stockholders of Firm C is smaller than the return to stockholders of Firm D.

Exhibit 3.5 discloses the salary, bonus, and other forms of long-term compensation of the top ten highest-paid CEOs in 1995. The total annual pay (including other compensation) exceeds $16 million for each of these CEOs. High compensation is also provided to other executives. Each of the top ten highest-paid executives who are not CEOs received more than $11 million during 1995.

Some customers and stockholders may argue that firms paying executives such high salaries are not meeting their social responsibilities. These firms may be serving the interests of the executives, and not the stockholders who own the firm. However, the counterargument is that these executives deserve high salaries because their contribution to the value of the firm exceeds the amount of their compensation.

RESPONSIBILITY TO CREDITORS

Firms are responsible for meeting their financial obligations to their creditors. If firms are experiencing financial problems and are unable to meet their obligations, they should inform creditors. Sometimes creditors are willing to extend payment deadlines and may even offer advice to firms on how to improve their financial condition. A

Exhibit 3.5
Highest Paid CEOs

CEO	Firm	Annual Salary (in thousands)	Other Compensation (in thousands)	Total Annual Compensation (in thousands)
Lawrence Coss	Green Tree Financial	$65,580	$0	$65,580
Sanford Weill	Travelers Group	5,607	44,233	49,840
John Welch Jr.	General Electric	5,321	16,741	22,060
Gordon Binder	Amgen	1,513	19,992	21,505
James Donald	DSC Communications	5,595	13,588	19,183
Casey Cowell	U.S. Robotics	2,799	15,770	18,569
Floyd English	Andrew Corp.	1,739	15,927	17,666
Howard Solomon	Forest Laboratories	611	16,416	17,026
Stanley Gault	Goodyear Tire & Rubber	2,207	14,343	16,550
Edward Brennan	Sears, Roebuck	3,098	13,252	16,350

Note: Amounts reflect compensation during 1995.

firm has a strong incentive to satisfy its responsibility to creditors. If the firm does not pay what is owed to creditors, it may be forced into bankruptcy by them.

RESPONSIBILITY TO THE ENVIRONMENT

4 Describe the responsibilities of firms to the environment.

The production processes that firms use, as well as the products they produce, can be harmful to the environment. The most common abuses to the environment are discussed next, along with recent actions that firms have taken to improve the environment.

Air Pollution

Some production processes cause air pollution, which is harmful to society because it inhibits breathing. For example, the production of fuel and steel, as well as automobile use, increases the amount of carbon dioxide in the air.

HOW FIRMS PREVENT AIR POLLUTION Automobile and steel firms have reduced air pollution by revising their production processes so that less carbon dioxide escapes into the air. For example, firms such as Allied Signal and Inland Steel spend substantial funds to prevent pollution.

HOW THE GOVERNMENT PREVENTS AIR POLLUTION The federal government has also become involved by enforcing specific guidelines for firms to limit the amount of carbon dioxide caused by the production process. In 1970, the Environmental

Don Laskowski (an engineer and farmer) and Dan Tekulve (a designer of motorized hospital beds) had no experience in the sawmill industry. That didn't stop them from designing a product that can extract 30% more useable lumber from trees, minimizing waste and pollution. The partners didn't stop there. They seeded the business by donations—10% of profits and 300 sawmills to third world countries. Sales at Wood-Mizer now top $50 million.

Inland Labs uses rare toxic substances from tropical rain forests (left) to produce a new cancer treatment called Ricin D (right). If these rain forests are destroyed, the promise of these treatments are lost forever.

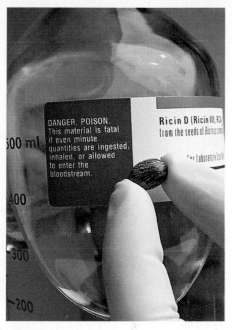

Protection Agency (EPA) was created to develop and enforce pollution standards. In recent years, pollution control laws have become more stringent.

Land Pollution

Land has been polluted by toxic waste resulting from some production processes. A related form of land pollution is solid waste, which does not deteriorate over time. As a result of waste, land not only looks less attractive but also may no longer be useful for other purposes, such as farming.

HOW FIRMS PREVENT LAND POLLUTION   Firms have revised their production and packaging processes to reduce the amount of waste. They now store toxic waste and deliver it to specified toxic waste storage sites. They also recycle plastic and limit their use of materials that would ultimately become solid waste.

Many firms have environmental programs that are designed to reduce damage to the environment. For example, Homestake Mining Company recognizes that its mining operations disturb the land, and it spends money to minimize any effect on the environment. PPG Industries restructured its production processes to generate about six thousand fewer tons of waste in a single year. Kodak recycles more than a half-billion pounds of material a year, and also supports a World Wildlife Fund environmental education program. IBM typically spends more than $30 million a year for environmental assessments and cleaning. Rockwell International has reduced its hazardous waste by more than 50 percent in recent years.

To appreciate the efforts that some firms have made to protect the environment and the costs of these efforts, consider the following statement from a recent annual report of DuPont:

❚❚ *The company operates about 150 manufacturing facilities, five petroleum refineries, 20 natural gas processing plants and numerous product-handling and distribution facilities around* *the world, all of which are significantly affected by a broad array of laws and regulations relating to the protection of the environment. It is the company's policy to comply fully with or exceed all legal requirements worldwide . . . About $400 million was spent for capital projects related to environmental requirements in 1994 . . . environmental expenses charged to current operations totalled about $950 million in 1994, as compared to $1 billion in 1993, and $900 million in 1992.*

Conflict with Environmental Responsibility

While most firms agree that a clean environment is desirable, they may disagree on how much responsibility they have in improving the environment. Consider two firms called Firm A and Firm B, which have similar revenue and expenses. Firm A, however, makes a much greater effort to clean up the environment; it spends $10 million, while Firm B spends $2 million. The profit of each firm is shown in Exhibit 3.6. Firm A has an annual profit of zero, while Firm B has an annual profit of $8 million. If you could invest in the stock of either Firm A or Firm B, where would you invest your money? Most investors desire to earn a high return on their money. While they recognize that a firm may have some environmental cleanup expenses, they would not want those expenses to be excessive. Therefore, most investors would prefer to invest in Firm B rather than Firm A.

Firm A could attempt to recapture its high environmental cleanup expenses by charging a higher price for its product. In this way, it may be able to spend heavily on the environment, while still generating a reasonable return to its stockholders. This strategy makes the customers pay for its extra environmental cleanup. However, if Firm A charges a higher price than Firm B, many customers would switch to Firm B in order to pay a lower price.

This example illustrates that there is a limit to which firms can use funds toward improving the environment. Firms have a responsibility to avoid damaging the environment. However, if they spend excessively on environmental improvement, they will not satisfy most of their customers or owners.

While firms have increased their efforts to clean up the environment, they do not necessarily agree with the guidelines enforced by the government. Oil refineries that are losing money remain open to avoid the cleanup that the EPA would enforce if they were closed down. Some refineries would pay about $1 billion for cleanup costs because of the EPA's strict guidelines. Firms have questioned many other environmental guidelines imposed by the EPA.

Exhibit 3.6
Effect of Environmental Expenses on Business Performance

	Firm A	Firm B
Revenue	$90,000,000	$90,000,000
Total Operating Expenses	−$80,000,000	−$80,000,000
Environmental Cleanup Expenses	−$10,000,000	− $2,000,000
Profit	0	$8,000,000

RESPONSIBILITY TO THE COMMUNITY

5 | **Describe the responsibilities of firms to their communities.**

When firms establish a base in a community, they become part of that community and rely on it for customers and employees. Firms demonstrate their concern for the community by sponsoring local events or donating to local charities. For example, SunTrust Bank, IBM, and many other firms have donated funds to universities. NationsBank has provided loans to low-income neighborhoods and minority communities.

Conflict with Maximizing Social Responsibility

The decisions of a firm's managers that maximize social responsibility could conflict with maximizing firm value. The costs involved in achieving such a goal would have to be passed on to consumers. Thus, the attempt to maximize responsibility to the community may reduce the firm's ability to provide products at a reasonable price to consumers.

Apple Computer invests substantially in local education programs. The investment is helpful to local communities but also helps increase sales to schools and individuals.

Many companies support charitable organizations that promote nutrition, education, performing and visual arts, and amateur athletics. Even though this social support requires a considerable financial commitment, the firm can gain from an enhanced image in the eye of the consumer to whom it sells its products. In a sense, the charitable support not only can help society but also can be a valuable marketing tool to create a desired image for the firm. Consequently, society and stockholders can benefit from the charitable support. If a company properly identifies a char-

When Does Tough Competition Become Unethical?

As more and more business is conducted over shared information networks, distinguishing between tough competition and unethical behavior frequently becomes difficult. The airline reservation systems are a case in point. Originally established in the mid-1960s as internal information systems, several of these systems (most notably American Airline's SABRE system and United Airline's Apollo system) were made available to travel agents in the mid-1970s. Using these systems, travel agents were able to book flights for their customers without calling the airlines. Early adoption of these systems by travel agents was slow, however. Because airline schedules and prices were regulated, there was no great benefit (aside from slightly greater convenience) to booking reservations electronically versus booking them by phone.

In the late 1970s, however, airline deregulation changed the situation dramatically. Suddenly, fares could change from minute to minute and routes could change in as little as thirty days. In addition, airlines were free to offer fares with complex restrictions. These changes made it necessary for travel agents to be on-line. They simply couldn't service their customers adequately with the paper-based schedules they had used in the past.

Deregulation proved to be a major boon for the airlines that had reservation systems in place, particularly American Airlines and United Airlines, which jointly accounted for about 75 percent of the reservation system market. Airlines that did not own their own reservation systems had to pay to become "co-hosts" on systems such as SABRE and Apollo. Even after paying to become co-hosts, however, these airlines argued they were being treated unfairly by system owners.

Among their complaints were the following:

➤ *Exclusion of carriers:* Where a carrier was in direct competition with a system owner, the carrier might be denied the right to become a co-host. Frontier Airlines, for example, claimed that United Airlines repeatedly refused to allow it to become a co-host because they were fierce competitors in Frontier's Denver hub.

➤ *Screen bias:* The reservation systems normally displayed flights on a separate screen page for each airline. Carriers directly competing with a system owner in a particular hub might find that their page was strategically placed at the end of all the pages, meaning that it could take the agent several minutes to reach the page. Such a delay was disastrous from a business standpoint, as 70 to 80 percent of all reservations were made from flights on the first page displayed by the system.

➤ *Unfair access to information:* The systems owners were instantly aware of any changes to routes or fares that their competitors made. The co-hosts did not have comparable access to such information from the reservation systems.

➤ *Unfair communications to agents:* The reservations systems provided a direct pipeline from owners to agents, which was sometimes used to send messages disparaging other airlines. For example, United Airlines was accused of making critical comments about a Frontier Airline rate reduction over Apollo. In Dallas, American Airlines was accused of sending messages to agents relating to the precarious financial state of Braniff Airlines over SABRE, and urging them to purchase tickets from American to protect their customers! (Both Frontier and Braniff ultimately went bankrupt).

➤ *Anticompetitive practice:* System owners employed a wide variety of techniques to ensure they were used exclusively by travel agents. Particular pressure was placed on agents located in competitive market areas. For example, in Denver, where United competed head-to-head with Frontier airlines, an estimated 75 percent of agents used United's Apollo system to book reservations.

One could easily argue that these techniques employed by system owners were simply tough competition, and ethics weren't really involved. However, system co-hosts such as Frontier and Braniff, had, in good faith, paid to be included on the systems. As a result, they were customers of the system owners, as well as being competitors. Was it ethical for the system owners to take money from their co-hosts while manipulating the systems to put them at a competitive disadvantage?

itable cause that is related to its business, it may be able to simultaneously contribute to society and maximize the firm's value. For example, a running shoe manufacturer may sponsor a race, or a tennis racket manufacturer may sponsor a tennis tournament.

Apple and IBM invest substantial funds in local education programs. This investment not only is helpful to the communities but also results in computer sales to schools. Home Depot donated $8 million to community programs in 1995. About 45 percent of the money was used for housing projects. Many Checkers restaurants have been targeted for locations in inner-city areas. They not only provide jobs to many minorities but also have been profitable.

SUMMARY OF BUSINESS RESPONSIBILITIES

Firms have many responsibilities toward customers, employees, the environment, the community, stockholders, and creditors that must be recognized when doing business. The general concern of firms about ethics and social responsibility can be illustrated with the quotations from recent annual reports on the next two pages.

SELF-SCORING EXERCISE

Assessing the Ethical Standards of the Firm Where You Work

Think about the organization you currently work for or one you know something about and complete the following Ethical Climate Questionnaire.

Please use the scale below and write the number that best represents your answer in the space next to each item.

To what extent are the following statements true about your company?

Completely false	Mostly false	Somewhat false	Somewhat true	Mostly true	Completely true
0	1	2	3	4	5

_____ 1. In this company, people are expected to follow their own personal and moral beliefs.

_____ 2. People are expected to do anything to further the company's interests.

_____ 3. In this company, people look out for each other's good.

_____ 4. It is very important here to follow strictly the company's rules and procedures.

_____ 5. In this company, people protect their own interests above other considerations.

_____ 6. The first consideration is whether a decision violates any law.

_____ 7. Everyone is expected to stick by company rules and procedures.

_____ 8. The most efficient way is always the right way in this company.

_____ 9. Our major consideration is what is best for everyone in the company.

_____ 10. In this company, the law or ethical code of the profession is the major consideration.

_____ 11. It is expected at this company that employees will always do what is right for the consumer and the public.

To score the questionnaire, first add up your responses to questions 1, 3, 6, 9, 10, and 11. This is subtotal number 1. Next, reverse the scores on questions 2, 4, 5, 7, and 8 (5 = 0, 4 = 1, 3 = 2, 2 = 3, 1 = 4, 0 = 5). Add the reverse scores to form subtotal number 2. Add subtotal number 1 to subtotal number 2 for an overall score.

Subtotal 1 _____ + Subtotal 2 _____ = Overall Score _____ .

Overall scores can range from 0 to 55. The higher the score, the more the organization's culture encourages ethical behavior.

SELF-SCORING EXERCISE

Assessing Whether Specific Situations Are Ethical

The purpose of this exercise is to explore your opinions about ethical issues faced in organizations. The class should be divided into twelve groups. Each group will randomly be assigned one of the following issues:

1. Is it ethical to take office supplies from work for home use? Make personal long-distance calls from the office? Use company time for personal business? Or do these behaviors constitute stealing?
2. If you exaggerate your credentials in an interview, is it lying? Is lying to protect a co-worker acceptable?
3. If you pretend to be more successful than you are to impress your boss, are you being deceitful?
4. How do you differentiate between a bribe and a gift?
5. If there are slight defects in a product you are selling, are you obligated to tell the buyer? If an advertised "sale" price is really the everyday price, should you divulge the information to the customer?
6. Suppose you have a friend who works at the ticket office for the convention center where Garth Brooks will be appearing. Is it cheating if you ask the friend to get you tickets so that you won't have to fight the crowd to get them? Is buying merchandise for your family at your company's cost cheating?
7. Is it immoral to do less than your best in work performance? Is it immoral to accept worker's compensation when you are fully capable of working?
8. What behaviors constitute emotional abuse at work? What would you consider an abuse of one's position of power?
9. Are high-stress jobs a breech of ethics? What about transfers that break up families?
10. Are all rule violations equally important? Do employees have an ethical obligation to follow company rules?
11. To what extent are you responsible for the ethical behavior of your co-workers? If you witness unethical behavior and don't report it, are you an accessory?
12. Is it ethical to help one work group at the expense of another group? For instance, suppose one group has excellent performance and you want to reward its members with an afternoon off. The other work group will have to pick up the slack and work harder if you do this. Is this ethical?

Once your group has been assigned its issue, you have two tasks:

1. First, formulate your group's answer to the ethical dilemmas.
2. After you have formulated your group's position, discuss the individual differences that may have contributed to your position. You will want to discuss the individual differences presented in this chapter as well as any others that you believe affected your position on the ethical dilemma.

Your instructor will lead the class in a discussion of how individual differences may have influenced your positions on these ethical dilemmas.

> ❚❚ *A comprehensive annual ethics training program heightens the awareness of our employees and provides guidelines to resolve issues responsibly.* ❚❚
>
> —Rockwell International

Ethical Responsibilities Across Business Functions

The perception of a firm's ethical standards is dependent on its team of managers. The ethical responsibilities of a firm's managers vary with their specific job assignments. Production managers are responsible for producing a product that is safe. They should also ensure that the production process satisfies environmental standards.

Marketing managers are responsible for marketing a product in a manner that neither misrepresents the product's characteristics nor misleads consumers or investors. Marketing managers must communicate with production managers to ensure that product marketing is consistent with the produc-

tion. Any product promotion by marketing managers that makes statements about quality should be assessed by production managers to ensure accuracy.

Financial managers are responsible for providing accurate financial reports to creditors or investors who may provide financial support to the firm. They rely on information from production and marketing managers when preparing their financial reports.

A firm earns a reputation for being ethical by ensuring that ethical standards are maintained in all business functions. If a part of the team of managers is unethical, the entire firm will be viewed as unethical.

> **Boise Cascade is committed to protecting the health and safety of our employees, being a responsible corporate citizen in the communities in which we operate, and providing active stewardship of the timberlands under our management.**
>
> —Boise Cascade

> **We . . . believe that to create long term value for shareholders, we must also create value in our relationships with customers, employees, suppliers and the communities in which we operate.**
>
> —Briggs & Stratton

Most firms have procedures in place to ensure that these social responsibilities are satisfied. They also enforce codes that specify their responsibilities. Prudential Securities has created a new position called "Corporate Values Officer," to ensure that its social responsibilities are satisfied.

Some firms may make more of an effort to follow ethical standards than others. The first Self-Scoring Exercise allows you to assess the ethical standards of the firm where you work. Employees may vary in their perception of what behavior is ethical. The second Self-Scoring Exercise provides a variety of situations which would probably be perceived as unethical behavior by some people but as acceptable behavior by others.

THE COST OF ENSURING SOCIAL RESPONSIBILITIES

6

Explain the costs that firms incur in achieving their social responsibilities.

A summary of possible expenses incurred as a result of social responsibilities is provided in Exhibit 3.7. Some firms incur large expenses in all areas of social responsibility. For example, automobile manufacturers such as Ford Motor Company and General Motors must ensure that their production of automobiles does not harm the environment. Second, they must ensure proper treatment of employees because of

Exhibit 3.7
Possible Expenses Incurred as a Result of Social Responsibilities

Responsibility to:	Expenses Incurred as a Result of:
Customers	Establishing program to receive and resolve complaints
	Conducting surveys to assess customer satisfaction
	Lawsuits by customers (product liability)
Employees	Establishing program to receive and resolve complaints
	Conducting surveys to assess employee satisfaction
	Lawsuits by employees based on allegations of discrimination
Stockholders	Disclosing financial information periodically
	Lawsuits by stockholders based on allegations that the firm's managers are not fulfilling their obligations to stockholders
Environment	Complying with governmental regulations on environment
	Complying with self-imposed environmental guidelines
Community	Sponsoring community activities

their massive work force. Third, they must ensure that they deliver a safe and reliable product to their customers.

In recent years, many new government regulations have been imposed to create a cleaner environment and ensure other social responsibilities. Normally, all the firms in the industry will raise their prices to cover the expenses associated with following new government regulations. For example, restrictions on cutting down trees resulted in higher expenses for paper companies. These companies raised their prices to cover these higher expenses. Maintaining social responsibilities is necessary but costly, and customers indirectly pay the expenses involved.

Cost of Lawsuits

When assessing the expense involved in dealing with customer or employee complaints, firms will normally consider the cost of hiring people to resolve the complaints. However, they must also consider the cost of defending against possible lawsuits by customers and employees. Customers suing firms for product defects or deceptive advertising and employees suing their firms for discrimination are common practices today.

Some obvious expenses associated with a lawsuit are as follows. First, the court may fine a firm that is found guilty. Some fines imposed by the court have amounted to several million dollars. Second, some lawsuits are settled out-of-court but commonly require firms to make some payment to customers or employees. Third, a firm may incur substantial expenses when hiring an attorney. Many lawsuits continue for several years, and the expenses of the attorney (or a law firm) for a single case may exceed $1 million. Fourth, an indirect cost of a lawsuit is the decline in demand for a firm's product because of bad publicity associated with the lawsuit. This results in less revenue to the firm.

Even when firms establish and enforce a comprehensive code of social responsibility, they do not necessarily avoid lawsuits. They must recognize this when estimating the expenses involved in social responsibility. Consider the situation in June 1993, when the media announced that some customers had found syringes in their Pepsi cans. After this announcement, other customers reported similar findings. This

The cost of double hulling—creating a protective layer between the outside of the ship and the oil—leads to increased ship building costs, the increased cost of fueling a heavier vessel, and lost transport volume. This cost must be balanced against the costs of a spill to commercial fishermen, recreational fishermen, and beach visitors.

not only caused potential product liability lawsuits but also caused some consumers to switch to other soft drinks. Within two weeks of the first claim, several people were arrested for false tampering charges. One person placing a syringe in a Pepsi can was even caught on videotape. It became clear that the product was not defective but that people were claiming a defect to win large cash settlements through lawsuits. While the conclusion in this case was favorable, PepsiCo spent millions of dollars attempting to determine whether the claims were valid and then convincing the public that the claims were false.

Firms must recognize that they will incur some expenses arising out of customer or employee claims (whether the claims are valid or not). They may also incur expenses from purchasing product liability insurance to cover potential lawsuits. In some businesses (such as specific medical fields), a major expense to the firm is liability insurance. The threat of liability lawsuits may even discourage entrepreneurs from establishing some types of businesses.

BUSINESS DILEMMA

Social Responsibility At College Health Club

As a college student, Sue Kramer always had an interest in the social responsibility of businesses. Now that she is establishing the College Health Club (CHC), she can apply her beliefs about social responsibility to her own business.

Dilemma

Sue recognizes that being socially responsible might either reduce her firm's earnings or result in higher prices to her customers because expenses are incurred as a result of many social responsibilities. Sue's goal is to develop strategies for satisfying CHC's social responsibilities in a manner that could still maximize the value of CHC. What responsibilities should Sue have toward her customers? Employees? Community? Environment?

Solution

Sue identifies specific responsibilities of CHC to her customers, employees, and environment, as explained next:

➤ *Responsibility to Customers* Sue plans to spend some of her time talking with customers at the health club to determine whether the customers (members) are satisfied with the facilities that CHC offers. She also plans to send out a survey to all the members to obtain more feedback. Furthermore, she offers a money-back guarantee if the customers are not satisfied after a two-week trial period.

Sue's efforts are intended not only to fulfill a moral responsibility but also to increase the firm's memberships over time. In the health club business, the firm's reputation for satisfying the customer is important. Many customers choose a health club because of referrals by other customers. Therefore, Sue hopes that her efforts will identify ways in which she can make CHC more appealing to potential members. She also wants to show her interest in satisfying the existing members.

➤ *Responsibility to Employees* Sue started the business with herself as the only full-time employee. However, she has one part-time employee (Lisa Lane) and expects to hire more employees over time as the number of memberships increases. Sue plans to pay employees wages that are consistent with other health clubs in the area. She also plans to have employees that are diverse in gender and race. Her goal is not just to demonstrate her willingness to seek diversity but also to attract diversity among customers as well. For example, she wants her health club to have a somewhat even mix of males and females, and believes that an even mix of employees over time might attract an even mix of customers.

➤ *Responsibility to the Community* Sue feels a special allegiance to the local college she has attended over the last four years. She volunteers to offer a free seminar for the college students on health issues. She believes that this service would not only fulfill her moral responsibility but also allow her to promote her new health club located next to the college campus. Therefore, her community service could ultimately enhance the value of CHC.

➤ *Responsibility to the Environment* Since the health club is a service, no production process is involved that could damage the environment. However, Sue will establish recycling containers for cans of soft drinks consumed at CHC.

➤ *Summary of CHC's Social Responsibilities* In general, Sue develops strategies that not only would satisfy social responsibilities but also would retain existing customers and attract new customers.

Additional Issues for Discussion

1 Sue was recently asked if she wanted to sell aerobics clothing in her health club. A clothing firm has the clothing produced in Asia and would sell it to Sue at low prices. Sue could then sell it to her customers at reasonable prices and still earn a profit. This would be beneficial to the customers and to CHC. Sue has heard that the clothing in some Asian countries is sometimes produced by young children under poor working conditions. Should Sue purchase the clothing?

2 Based on the information in the previous question, what is Sue's social responsibility (if any) toward preventing improper treatment of employees in other countries?

3 Recently, several college students have asked Sue for jobs at CHC. While Sue would like to help the students out, she does not need any more employees at this time. Should she hire them anyway?

SUMMARY

1 The behavior of firms is molded by business ethics, which represent a set of moral values. Firms have a responsibility to produce safe products and to sell their products without misleading the customers. They ensure social responsibility toward customers by establishing a code of ethics, monitoring customer complaints, and asking customers for feedback on products they recently purchased.

2 Firms have a responsibility to safety, proper treatment, and equal opportunity for employees. They can ensure responsibility toward employees by enforcing safety guidelines, by offering seminars on diversity, and by establishing a grievance procedure that allows employees to state any complaints.

3 Firms have a responsibility to satisfy the owners (or stockholders) who provided funds. They attempt to ensure that managers make decisions that are in the best interests of stockholders.

4 Firms have a responsibility to maintain a clean environment when operating their businesses. However they incur expenses when attempting to fulfill their environmental responsibility.

5 Firms have a social responsibility to the local communities in which they attract customers and employees. They provide donations and other benefits to local communities.

6 When firms ensure their social responsibilities, they may incur substantial expenses. These expenses are ultimately incurred by the customers, since the prices of products charged by firms are influenced by the expenses incurred.

KEY TERMS

affirmative action
business ethics
consumerism

institutional investors
monopoly
sexual harassment

shareholder activism
social responsibility

REVIEW QUESTIONS

1 Define business ethics and describe an ethical situation in which you had to decide right from wrong.

2 Describe a firm's social responsibility to its community and the environment.

3 Identify and explain the major areas of social responsibility with which a business should be concerned.

4 Identify the steps a firm develops to ensure social responsibility to its customers.

5 How can a business ensure social responsibility to its customers and still have a right to earn a profit?

6 Explain how the government becomes socially responsible to consumers.

7 Describe the most common abuses to the environment and how businesses can prevent them.

8 How does a business's environmental responsibility impact product prices?

9 Identify and explain the conflicting objectives that often challenge a manager's responsibility.

10 Identify expenses that a firm may incur when assuming social responsibility for customers and employees.

DISCUSSION QUESTIONS

1 Assume you are a manager. How would your firm's business ethics and social responsibility impact your decision making, and what effect would these issues have on the organization's bottom line (earnings)?

2 Assume you are a manager. What are your ethical responsibilities to the following: (a) employees (b) stockholders (c) customers, and (d) suppliers.

3 Assume you are a salesperson on commission. How would you react if you just came out of a meeting in which the sales manager had stated: "Sales are down. I want you to sell at all costs"?

4 You are an advertising manager. You have just left a meeting having been made aware of truth in labeling laws. Would you be obligated to disclose the ingredients in your product, especially if that product has a potential side effect?

5 Discuss the pros and cons of affirmative action programs and how they impact business in their recruiting and selection efforts. Do they constrain or aid business?

RUNNING YOUR OWN BUSINESS

1 Describe the ethical dilemmas (if any) that you might face in your business. How do you plan to handle these situations?

2 What types of social responsibilities would your business have toward your employees, customers, or community? What, if any, special policies would you set to take better care of your employees, customers, or community?

INVESTING IN THE STOCK OF A BUSINESS

Using the annual report of the firm in which you would like to invest, complete the following:

1 Many firms disclose their policies on ethics and social responsibilities within their annual reports. Does your firm mention any specific policies that encourage employees' ethical behavior? Does the firm give any specific examples of how it accomplishes these goals?

2 Describe your firm's policies on its social responsibility toward its community and the environment. Does the firm give any specific examples of how it accomplishes these goals?

CASE 1 E-Mail and Ethics

The use of e-mail has become an ethical issue for many on-line computer services such as CompuServe, where fraud was committed by individuals who seized opportunities to sell illegal cellular phone devices to interested buyers. An engineer at AT&T Corporation's wireless unit was monitoring CompuServe's commercial on-line service when he came across an illegal advertisement, which permitted millions to view and purchase such equipment.

The illegal advertisements included a cellular phone that can eavesdrop on calls placed by other cellular phone users; a small, easily concealed device that steals legitimate users' phone numbers by taking them off the airwaves; and several phones that can be programmed with up to ninety-nine stolen phone numbers, instead of using a separate personal computer.

The wireless industry says it loses about $500 million in revenue each year to these individuals, but independent observers estimate the loss is closer to $1 billion. The industry must get a grip on this advancing technology. With the boom in wireless services expected to continue into the twenty-first century, current crimes are adding urgency to the industry's effort to crack down on fraud.

Questions

1 Explain whether e-mail is legal or illegal to advertise over telephone lines.

2 Do you believe there is an ethical issue in this case? If so, what is the issue?

3 Is fraud being committed over the airwaves?

4 Do sellers have a social responsibility in marketing cellular phones?

CASE 2 Social Responsibilities to Employees

David Thomas, a supervisor in the bearings department at the ABC Corporation, a rollerblade manufacturer, manages a nonunion plant where the work atmosphere appears to be a "good ol' boy" system. He desires to give preference to males by giving them the better jobs and newer equipment, and favoritism is often extended to them. Currently there are no females in management positions throughout the plant. Females tend to occupy token positions, often starting out as clerk-typists or file clerks, and few female employees advance into higher positions. Presently twenty people work in Mr. Thomas's department; only two are female. All perform the same job; skills, responsibility, and authority are the same. Males are paid $10.50 per hour; females with the same seniority earn $7.50 per hour. Working conditions throughout the department are often unsanitary, and neglect on the supervisor's part has made the department unsafe. Recently, many complaints have been made from Mr. Thomas's employees concerning the poor working conditions. Mr. Thomas is a profit maximizer with a bottom-line orientation and often ignores any safety policy directive that comes from top management.

In his office, Mr. Thomas has pinups on every wall. On his desk are sexually explicit slogans that some females have found offensive. His language tends to be off-color and is often upsetting to many people throughout the plant.

Mr. Thomas has just received a memo. He has been asked by the company president to attend a meeting on social responsibility. The memo reads, "The company is going in a new direction. We would like your input on social responsibility issues that this company should adopt." Mr. Thomas's immediate reaction is, "This company has always been a profit-maximizing firm and should not concern itself with any social issues because they constrain and impact the bottom line of the company's operations." Thus, he refuses to attend the meeting.

Questions

1 Is Mr. Thomas ignoring any social responsibility issues in his department operations?

2 Is Mr. Thomas correct in saying that the ABC Corporation should be a profit-maximizing firm at all costs?

3 Is Mr. Thomas discriminating against females and, if so, in what areas?

4 What are the potential costs to the firm as a result of Mr. Thomas's actions?

VIDEO CASE Payback for Social Responsibility

 One of a retailer's worst nightmares turned into reality for Alton Bankston when the principal supplier of his primary wares, paints, opened a company outlet a few blocks away and called on his customers, offering lower prices on the same paint he had been selling.

The big company thought Bankston might close up shop. But he wasn't going to give up a business he's put 10 years of his life into. He fought back.

The first thing Alton Bankston had to do to stay in business was choose a new paint line. He quickly got it in stock and informed his customers about it. (His new supplier didn't make marine paint, a necessity for a Gulf Coast paint retailer, so he found a supplier for that, too.)

To counter efforts to woo away his customers, he emphasized personalized treatment. He established a file of custom colors clients used. And customers began receiving Bankston's thank-you, get-well, and congratulations cards.

Believing that "people buy from people they know," he says, he and his staff became heavily involved in community affairs, joining civic, charitable, and service organizations. Bankston's sponsored Little League basketball, baseball, football, and soccer teams, and employees sometimes coached.

Paint sales increased 31 percent in a year. "We were a tired bunch of folks but very happy and thankful," Bankston says.

Then the street in front of the store was torn up in a major construction project, which was supposed to take six months but lasted 18.

If customers couldn't get to the store, it would go to them. It delivered and not just during normal business hours. "Each night our employees loaded up their cars and delivered on the way home and in the early morning," Bankston says.

The demand for Bankston's products increased over time in response to its efforts to satisfy the community. The community service not only was in the form of social responsibility, but also resulted in a continual demand by customers for its products.

Questions

1 Was it unethical for Bankston's supplier to open a paint store just a few blocks away and try to lure Bankston's customers to its new store?

2 Why might some firms benefit more than others as a result of social responsibility? To answer this question, consider whether a paint supplier that focuses on supply-ing paint to several paint stores around the country would benefit as much as Bankston's from serving the local community.

3 If you owned a store, how could you discourage one of your suppliers from opening a retail store nearby that would directly compete with your store?

THE *Coca-Cola* COMPANY ANNUAL REPORT PROJECT

 The following questions apply concepts learned in this chapter to The Coca-Cola Company. Read the section called "Environmental State-ment" on page 74 in The Coca-Cola Company annual report before answering these questions

1 Do you think The Coca-Cola Company has an advan-tage over other large companies with respect to its impact on the environment?

2 What is the focus of the Company's environmental efforts?

3 How can you obtain more information about The Coca-Cola Company's environmental efforts?

IN-TEXT STUDY GUIDE

Answers are in an appendix at the back of the book.

True or False

1 The responsibility of firms toward customers can be enforced by specific groups of consumers.

2 The government protects consumers by regulating the quality of some products that firms produce.

3 Deregulation results in lower prices for consumers.

4 Marketing managers are primarily responsible for providing accurate financial information to creditors or investors who may provide financial support to the firm.

5 In 1970, the Environmental Protection Agency was created to develop and enforce pollution standards.

6 Employees commonly sue firms for product defects or deceptive advertising.

7 Firms have a social responsibility when producing and selling their products.

8 An attempt by a firm to maximize social responsi-bility to the community may reduce the firm's ability to provide products at a reasonable price to consumers.

9 U.S. firms that conduct business in foreign coun-tries are not subject to the rules enforced by the local government.

10 The Clayton Act prevents competition.

Multiple Choice

11 The act that prohibits unfair methods of competition is the:
a) Humphrey Act.
b) Civil Rights Act of 1964.
c) Federal Trade Commission Act.
d) Garn Act.
e) Reagan Antitrust Act.

12 An active role by stockholders in influencing a firm's management policies is called:
a) empowerment.   b) reengineering.
c) self-managed teams.   d) quality circles.
e) shareholder activism.

13 Tying agreements, binding contracts, and interlock-ing directorates are prohibited by the:
a) Clayton Act.
b) Sherman Antitrust Act.
c) Robinson-Patman Act.
d) Celler-Kefauver Act.
e) Federal Trade Commission Act.

14 Many U.S. firms provide guidelines of behavior to employees through a code of:
a) reciprocity.
b) cartel arrangements.

c) kickback arrangements.

d) technical production manuals.

e) ethics.

15 Compensation that is based on the volume of an employee's sales of the firm's products is called:

a) share of stock.

b) stock certificate.

c) corporate bond.

d) promotion.

e) commission or bonus.

16 To ensure that employees receive proper treatment if they believe they are not being given equal opportunity, the firm's management establishes a:

a) labor contract.   b) strike.

c) grievance procedure.   d) walkout.

e) lockout.

17 _____ of a firm can monitor any employee decisions to ensure that the decisions are made in the best interests of the owners.

a) Unions   b) Customers

c) Creditors   d) Managers

e) Business agents

18 The act that prohibits mergers between firms that reduce competition within an industry is the:

a) Robinson-Patman Act.

b) Celler-Kefauver Act.

c) Federal Trade Commission Act.

d) Clayton Act.

e) Sherman Antitrust Act.

19 Programs intended to prevent discrimination against minorities and women are:

a) affirmative action.

b) American disability.

c) equal say.

d) minimum wage.

e) age discrimination and employment.

20 The recognition of how a firm's business decisions can affect society is its:

a) moral code.

b) social responsibility.

c) conservation policies.

d) recycling program.

e) consumer bill of rights.

21 The decisions of a firm's managers that maximize social responsibility could conflict with maximizing:

a) cartels.

b) union gains.

c) economic forecast.

d) firm value.

e) interest payments.

22 In some industries, firms created various agreements to set prices and avoid competition, which the federal government has attempted to prevent by enforcing:

a) business trust.

b) regulated monopolies.

c) antitrust laws.

d) consumerism.

e) conservationism.

23 If a firm is the sole provider of goods or services, it has a(n):

a) oligopoly.

b) monopsony.

c) partnership.

d) sole proprietorship.

e) monopoly.

24 Managers who are responsible for marketing a product in a manner that neither misrepresents the product's characteristics nor misleads consumers or investers are:

a) finance managers.

b) sales managers.

c) marketing managers.

d) human resource managers.

e) production managers.

25 Shareholder activism is most commonly practiced by:

a) customers.

b) chief executive officers.

c) institutional investors.

d) managers.

e) the government.

26 _____ represents the collective consumer demand that businesses satisfy their needs.

a) Conservationism

b) Consumerism

c) Social responsibility

d) Business ethics

e) Recycling

27 Managers responsible for producing a safe product are called:

a) marketing managers.

b) finance managers.

c) sales managers.

d) human resource managers.

e) production managers.

28 Most firms have procedures in place as well as codes to ensure individual employee accountability. This is a part of their:
a) program network.
b) division of work.
c) local area network.
d) social responsibility.
e) recycling program.

29 Firms are responsible to their creditors by meeting their:
a) dividend payments.
b) financial obligations.
c) retained earnings.
d) stockholder's equity.
e) treasury stock.

30 A set of principles that deal with the right and wrong issues pertaining to business decisions are:
a) business policies.
b) procedures.
c) rules.
d) business ethics.
e) work standards.

31 The act that prohibits discrimination due to national origin, race, gender, or religion is the:
a) Clayton Act.
b) Sherman Antitrust Act.
c) Federal Trade Commission Act.
d) Civil Rights Act of 1964.
e) Robinson-Patman Act.

32 The following industries have been deregulated, allowing more firms to enter the industry, except for:
a) trucking.   b) railroads.
c) airlines.   d) boating.
e) telecommunications.

33 The firm's management is responsible for satisfying their:
a) union demands.
b) owners or stockholders.
c) business agents.
d) competition.
e) friends.

34 The act that prohibits price differences on promotional allowances that reduce competition within an industry is the:
a) Celler-Kefauver Act.
b) Robinson-Patman Act.
c) Clayton Act.
d) Sherman Antitrust Act.
e) Federal Trade Commission Act.

35 The act that encourages competition and prevents monopolies is the:
a) Deregulation Act.
b) Federal Trade Commission Act.
c) Robinson-Patman Act.
d) Celler-Kefauver Act.
e) Sherman Antitrust Act.

Finding Information About Firms on the Internet

The Internet, particularly the World Wide Web (WWW), represents a tremendous source of firm and industry information. Tens of thousands of companies have placed information about themselves (including their social responsibilities and their products) on the WWW, information that is freely accessible to those who know where to look. Unfortunately, knowing where to look can be challenging. To aid users in that task, three different types of tools are available: directories, search engines, and metasearch engines.

DIRECTORIES In the past few years, a number of companies have undertaken the task of trying to catalog useful sites on the WWW. Yahoo! (Exhibit 3.8) whose mission is "To be the world's best guide for information and online discovery," is a prime example of a company that attempts to provide such a service. Using the service begins by accessing Yahoo!'s home page using a WWW browser such as Mosaic, Netscape, or the America Online browser (pictured). From that page, the search can then begin.

Suppose, for example, we are interested in finding out about participants in the brewery industry. We would begin by choosing "Business and Economy." A new win-

Exhibit 3.8
Yahoo! Home Page

http://www.yahoo.com/

dow appears, which displays a list of different topics to choose from (Exhibit 3.9). Since we are interested in brewery industry participants, the most appropriate selection would be "Companies."

The company page is then displayed, which organizes companies according to the industry in which they are located (Exhibit 3.10). By clicking the mouse on "Breweries," we are then presented with a list of breweries that have established WWW sites (Exhibit 3.11). By clicking on individual sites, access to the information provided by the company is then made visible.

Exhibit 3.9
Topics in Yahoo!'s "Business and Economy" Page

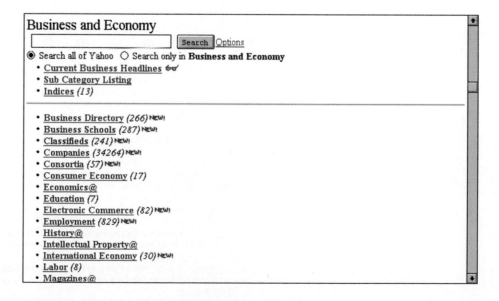

Exhibit 3.10
Yahoo! Links to Companies, by
Industry

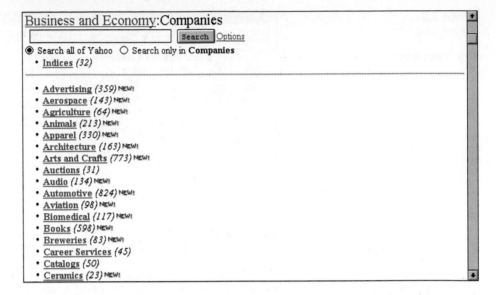

SEARCH ENGINES   In addition to searching by navigating through the menus, searching is also possible by using keywords (Exhibit 3.12). Yahoo! for example, offers keyword searches for sites contained in the Yahoo! system. Such searches are accompanied by entering the desired information in a search box, then pressing the search button (see figure). Other sites, such as Lycos and WebCrawler, continually search the web for new home pages and index them in a database that can then be searched. As of the end of 1995, both sites had over a million pages indexed. They are also easily accessible; for example, both are available for use in Yahoo! itself.

METASEARCH ENGINES   Metasearch engines are sites or software that automatically invoke other search engines to find user-specified keywords. In other words, when you type in your keyword, the metasearch site automatically contacts other search sites and returns the results of all searches. An example of such a site is SavvySearch (Exhibit 3.13). The advantage of such engines is that they free the user from worry-

Exhibit 3.11
Listing of Individual Breweries
with WWW Sites

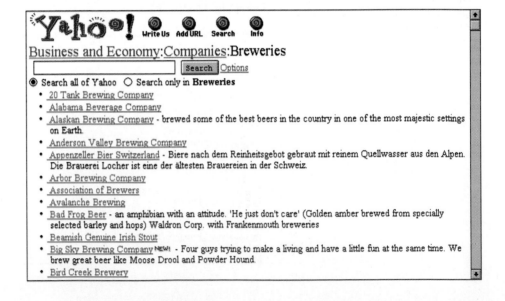

Exhibit 3.12
Major Search Resources

Search tools are accessed by plugging their address into a web browser. Below are the addresses for some of the most powerful search resources.

Search Engines

Open Text Index	http://www.opentext.com:8080/
Info Seek	http://www.infoseek.com/
Alta Vista (digital)	http://altavista.digital.com
Lycos	http://www.lycos.com/
Web Crawler	http://www.webcrawler.com/
World Wide Web Worm	http://wwww.cs.colorado.edu/wwww
Harvest	http://harvest.cs.colorado.edu/
Aliweb	http://www.nexor.co.uk/public/aliweb/aliweb.html
Deja News	http://www.dejanews.com/
Magellan	http://www.mckinley.com/
Yellow Pages	http://www.mcp.com/

Metasearch Engines

Search Savvy	http://guaraldi.cs.colostate.edu:2000/
Starting Point	http://www.stpt.com/

ing about the specifics of a search. PC-based software, such as Quarterdeck's Compass, is also capable of performing such searches. For an excellent review of using search engines for business purposes, see the Luckman Home Page (http://www.luckman.com).

Exhibit 3.13
Savvy Search

http://www.cs.colostate.edu/~dreiling/smartform.html

[**SAVVY SEARCH** : HOME | SEARCH | FEEDBACK | FAQ | HELP]

Keyword query:

[   ] [Start SavvySearch!]

- Sources and Types of Information:

☒ WWW Resources   ☐ Software
☐ People   ☐ Reference
☐ Commercial   ☐ Academic
☐ Technical Reports ☐ Images
☐ News   ☐ Entertainment

Query options:

▪ Search for documents containing [all query terms. ▾]
▪ Retrieve [10 ▾] results from each search engine.
▪ Display results in [○ Brief ● Normal ○ Verbose] format.
▪ ☐ Integrate results.

Business Environment

The success of a firm is partially dependent on its environment. While managers of a firm cannot control the business environment, they can attempt to make business decisions that benefit from that environment or that offer protection against adverse conditions. To do this, they need to understand how the business environment affects their firms.

A firm is exposed to three different parts of the business environment: (1) economic conditions, (2) industry conditions, and (3) global conditions. Chapter 4 describes how economic conditions affect a firm's performance. It also explains how government policies affect firms indirectly by influencing economic conditions. Chapter 5 explains how a firm's performance is affected by industry conditions, while Chapter 6 explains how it is affected by global conditions.

CHAPTER 4

Economic Environment

Economic conditions reflect the level of production and consumption for a particular country, area, or industry. **Macroeconomic conditions** reflect the overall U.S. economy, while **microeconomic conditions** are more focused on the business or industry of concern. This chapter focuses on the macroeconomic factors, while the following chapter focuses on microeconomic (industry) factors.

Economic conditions can affect the revenue or expenses of a business, and therefore can affect the value of that business.

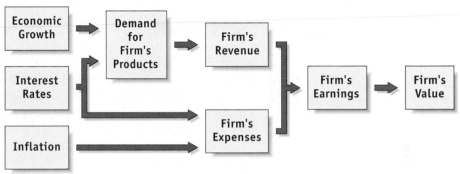

To illustrate how economic conditions can affect the performance and value of a business, consider the case of Inland Steel Industries, whose steel is purchased by Harley-Davidson, Ford Motor Company, and numerous other manufacturers. A change in the demand for motorcycles, automobiles, and other products produced with steel affects the demand for Inland's steel. How would weak economic conditions affect the demand for Inland's steel? How would inflation affect Inland's expenses? How would rising interest rates affect the demand for Inland's steel? How does the federal government influence Inland's performance? This chapter provides a background on the economic environment which can be used to answer these questions.

The **Learning Goals** of this chapter are to:

1 Identify the macroeconomic factors that affect business performance.

2 Explain how market prices are determined.

3 Explain how the government influences economic conditions.

MACROECONOMIC FACTORS THAT AFFECT BUSINESS PERFORMANCE

1 **Identify the macroeconomic factors that affect business performance.**

The performance of most firms is highly dependent on three macroeconomic factors:

➤ Economic growth
➤ Inflation
➤ Interest rates

Economic Growth

economic growth the change in the general level of economic activity

A critical macroeconomic factor that affects business performance is **economic growth,** or the change in the general level of economic activity. When U.S. economic growth is higher than normal, the total income level of all U.S. workers is relatively high, so that there is a higher volume of spending on products and services. Since the demand for products and services is high, firms that sell products and services should receive higher revenue.

To appreciate the impact of economic growth on a firm's performance, consider the following comments taken from annual reports after a period of strong economic growth in 1994:

> ❚❚ *1994 was a year of higher sales and earnings for International Paper. . . . Our 1994 results were driven by economic growth.* ❚❚
>
> — International Paper

> ❚❚ *To a great extent, it was a good year because of things beyond our control. The United States economy was strong.* ❚❚
>
> — Briggs & Stratton

While high economic growth enhances a firm's revenue, slow economic growth results in low demand for products and services, which can reduce a firm's revenue. General Motors and Ford Motor Company commonly shut down some factories in response to low economic growth.

aggregate expenditures the total amount of expenditures in the economy

INDICATORS OF ECONOMIC GROWTH   Two common measures of economic growth are the total production level of products and services in the economy, and the total amount of expenditures (also called **aggregate** expenditures). The total production level and total aggregate expenditures in the United States are closely related, because a high level of consumer spending represents a large demand for products and services. The total production level is dependent on the total demand for products and services.

gross domestic product (GDP) the total market value of all final products and services produced in the United States

Businesses can monitor the U.S. total production level by keeping track of the **gross domestic product (GDP),** which represents the total market value of all final products and services produced in the United States. The GDP is reported quarterly in the United States. The trend of GDP is shown in Exhibit 4.1. Notice that GDP typ-

Exhibit 4.1
Trend of Gross Domestic Product
(GDP) over Time

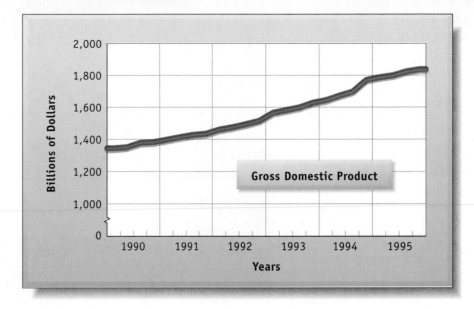

ically rises over time but was stagnant during a recession in the early 1990s. Economic growth is commonly interpreted as the percentage of change in the GDP from
one period (such as a quarter) to another. Businesses tend to monitor changes in
economic growth, which may signal a change in the demand for their products or
services.

An alternative indicator of economic growth is the unemployment level. Various
unemployment indicators may be monitored because they can indicate whether economic conditions are improving. The four different types of unemployment are as
follows:

frictional unemployment people
who are between jobs

➤ **Frictional unemployment** represents people who are between jobs. That is, their
unemployment status is temporary, as they are likely to find employment soon.
For example, a person with marketable job skills might quit her job before finding a new one because she believes she will find a new job before long.

seasonal unemployment people
whose services are needed only on a
seasonal basis

➤ **Seasonal unemployment** represents people whose services are needed only on a
seasonal basis. For example, ski instructors may be unemployed in the summer.

cyclical unemployment people who
are unemployed because of poor
economic conditions

➤ **Cyclical unemployment** represents people who are unemployed because of poor
economic conditions. When the level of economic activity declines, the demand
for products and services declines, which reduces the need for workers. For example, a firm may lay off factory workers if the demand for its product declines.

structural unemployment people
who are unemployed because they do not
have adequate skills

➤ **Structural unemployment** represents people who are unemployed because they do
not have adequate skills. For example, people who have limited education may be
structurally unemployed.

Of the types of unemployment just described, the cyclical unemployment level
is probably the best indicator of economic conditions. When economic growth
improves, businesses hire more people and the unemployment rate declines. Unfortunately, one difficulty is knowing how much of the unemployment level is cyclical.
Some people assume that when the unemployment rate changes, it is primarily
attributed to economic cycles. A reduced unemployment rate may be interpreted as
an indicator of increased economic growth. Conversely, an increased unemployment

Exhibit 4.2
Trend of U.S. Unemployment

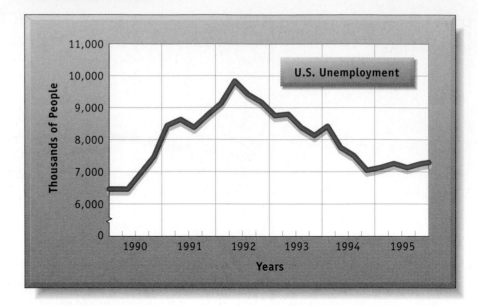

rate is commonly interpreted as a reduction in economic growth. The trend of U.S. unemployment is shown in Exhibit 4.2. Notice that the U.S. unemployment level was at its peak in 1992, when U.S. economic conditions were poor.

Many other indicators of economic growth, such as the industrial production index, new housing starts, and the personal income level, are compiled by divisions of the federal government and reported in business magazines and newspapers.

SENSITIVITY OF FIRM TO ECONOMIC GROWTH   Some firms are more sensitive than others to economic conditions because the demand for their product is more sensitive to such conditions. To illustrate this point, Exhibit 4.3 compares the perform-

Exhibit 4.3
Comparing the Sensitivity of Profits with Economic Conditions over Time

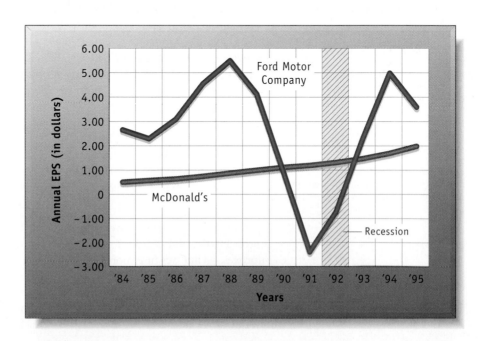

ance of McDonald's and Ford Motor Company. The profits in this exhibit are measured as the firm's earnings per share (EPS), which represents the annual earnings for each share of stock held by investors. The demand for the product (food) provided by McDonald's is not very sensitive to economic conditions because people still purchase McDonald's food even when the economy is weak. Notice from Exhibit 4.3 that the EPS of McDonald's increased every year at a somewhat steady rate.

Compare the EPS trend of McDonald's with that of Ford Motor Company in Exhibit 4.3. Ford's EPS is less stable because its profits are more sensitive to economic conditions. When the economy is weak, the demand for new automobiles declines. Ford Motor Company experienced negative profits during the 1991–92 period, when the United States experienced an economic recession.

Inflation

inflation the increase in the general level of prices of products and services over a specified period of time

Inflation represents the increase in the general level of prices of products and services over a specified period of time. The inflation rate can be estimated by measuring the percentage change in the consumer price index, which indicates the prices on a wide variety of consumer products such as grocery products, housing, gasoline, medical services, and electricity. The annual U.S. inflation rate is shown in Exhibit 4.4. Notice that in the 1970s the inflation rate was generally higher than it was in the 1980s and 1990s.

A firm's operating expenses from producing products can be influenced by inflation because the cost of supplies and materials may be affected by inflation. Wages can also be affected by inflation. A higher level of inflation will cause a larger increase in a firm's operating expenses. The revenue of firms may also be high during periods of high inflation because many firms charge higher prices to compensate for their higher expenses.

TYPES OF INFLATION   Inflation may result from a particular event that increases the costs of production. For example, when oil prices rise, gasoline prices increase and

Exhibit 4.4
U.S. Inflation Rates over Time

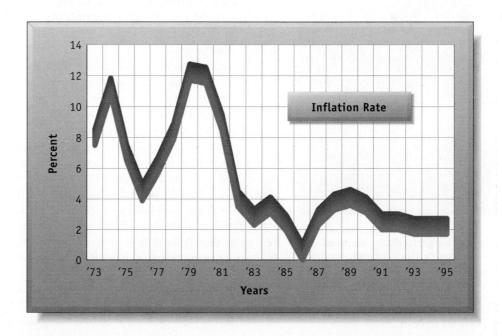

cost-push inflation higher prices charged by firms are caused by higher costs

the costs of transporting products increase. Firms that incur higher costs from transporting their products increase their prices to cover the higher costs. This situation is referred to as **cost-push inflation** whereby the higher prices charged by firms are caused by higher costs. For example, beverage producers such as PepsiCo and Anheuser-Busch raised prices in 1995 when the cost of aluminum (used to make the cans) increased. The same year, Procter and Gamble raised prices on paper towels following an increase in pulp (used in the production process).

Alternatively, inflation can be caused by strong consumer demand rather than higher costs. Consider an example in which consumers increase their demand for most products and services. Some firms may respond by increasing their prices. When prices of products and services are pulled up because of strong consumer demand, this is referred to as **demand-pull inflation.** In periods of strong economic growth, strong consumer demand can cause shortages in the production of some products. Firms that anticipate shortages may raise prices because they are confident they can sell the products anyway.

demand-pull inflation prices of products and services are pulled up because of strong consumer demand

Strong economic growth may place pressure not only on prices but also on wages. Strong economic growth may mean fewer unemployed people, so workers may negotiate for higher wages. Firms may be more willing to provide higher wages to retain their workers when no other qualified workers are available. As firms pay higher wages, production costs rise, and firms may attempt to increase their prices to recover the higher expenses.

Interest Rates

Interest rates represent the cost of borrowing money. They are closely monitored by businesses because they determine the amount of expense incurred by businesses that borrow money. If a business borrows $100,000 for one year at an interest rate of 8 percent, the interest expense is $8,000 (computed as .08 × $100,000). However, if the interest rate was 15 percent, the interest expense would have been $15,000 (computed as .15 × $100,000). Imagine how the interest rate level could affect firms such as Allied Signal or General Motors, who have borrowed more than $1 billion at any time. An interest rate increase of just 1 percent on $1 billion of borrowed funds results in an extra annual interest expense of $10,000,000.

Changes in market interest rates can influence a firm's interest expense, since the loan rates that commercial banks and other creditors charge on loans to firms are based on market interest rates. Even when a firm obtains a loan from a commercial bank over several years, the loan rate is typically adjusted periodically (every six months or year) based on the prevailing market interest rate at that time.

Exhibit 4.5 illustrates the annual interest expense for a reputable U.S. firm that borrows $1 million from a bank each year. The interest expenses are adjusted each year according to the interest rate that existed in the United States that year. This exhibit shows how interest rates can influence a firm's profit.

Notice that the interest expenses that the firm incurred in the early 1980s were much higher than they were in the mid-1990s. Because the interest rates in 1982 were more than twice as high as they were in 1994, the interest expense in 1982 would have been more than twice the expense incurred in 1994 for the same amount of funds borrowed.

Since interest rates affect the cost of financing, some possible projects considered by the firm that would be feasible during periods of low interest rates may not be feasible during periods of high interest rates. That is, the project may not generate an

Banks, such as Chase Manhattan, must be particularly aware of changes in the economic environment because they must accurately assess risk when making loans to companies. A bank must make sure a firm has addressed various growth possibilities.

Exhibit 4.5
Effect of Interest Rates on
Interest Expenses and Profits

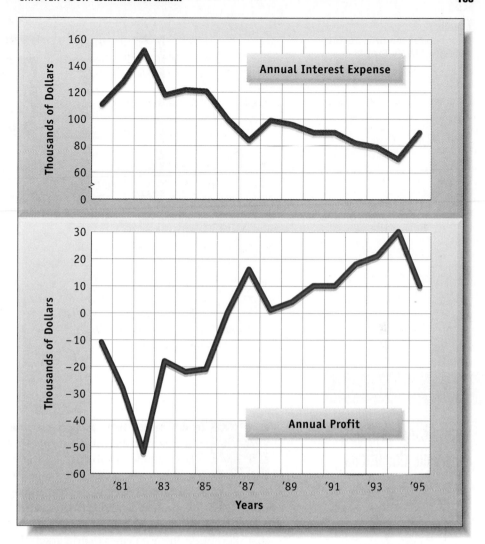

Note: Assume the firm's revenue equals $400,000 and its operating expenses equal $300,000.

adequate return to cover financing costs. Consequently, firms tend to reduce their degree of expansion when interest rates are high.

Interest rates affect the firm's interest expenses as well as its revenue. For example, when interest rates rise, the cost of financing the purchase of new homes increases. Therefore, the demand for new homes typically declines, and firms that build homes experience a decline in business. In addition, firms such as Caterpillar and Weyerhauser that produce construction products and equipment experience a decline in business. This explains why firms involved in the construction industry are highly influenced by interest rate movements.

Summary of Macroeconomic Factors that Affect a Firm's Performance

A summary of how the three macroeconomic factors affect a firm's performance is provided in Exhibit 4.6. The firm's revenue is affected by economic growth because of the influence of economic growth on the demand for products. Its revenue and

Exhibit 4.6
How Macroeconomic Factors
Affect a Firm's Profits

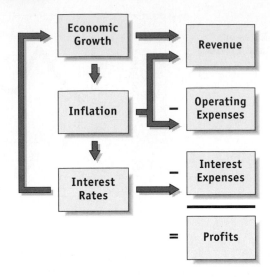

operating expenses are affected by inflation. Its interest expenses are affected by interest rate movements.

GLOBAL BUSINESS

Capitalizing on Global Economic Conditions

 The demand for a firm's products is dependent on the economic growth where the products are sold. Given the mature economy of the United States, there is limited potential for economic growth. However, economic growth in less-developed countries has much greater potential because they have not yet taken full advantage of existing technology. Furthermore, the governments of many less-developed countries have encouraged more business development by entrepreneurs, which accelerates economic growth. Many of these governments have also allowed U.S. firms to enter their markets. U.S. firms have attempted to capitalize on changes in economic and political conditions in less-developed countries by selling their products in those countries.

The Coca-Cola Company is among many U.S. firms that have targeted countries with high potential for economic growth. In 1995, its unit case sales increased by more than 34 percent in Brazil, and 16 percent in Chile. In this same period its sales increased by more than 25 percent in East Central Europe, by 16 percent in Northern Africa, and by 38 percent in China.

The Coca-Cola Company's increased sales in these countries can be attributed in part to economic growth, which increases the amount of consumer spending. It can also be attributed to reductions in government restrictions imposed on U.S. firms that desire to conduct business in these countries. Other U.S. firms are planning major expansion in less-developed countries to capitalize on the changes in economic and political conditions. General Motors plans to expand in various Asian markets, including China, India, and Indonesia, where the potential for economic growth is strong.

When U.S. firms attempt to capitalize on economic growth in foreign countries, they also can be adversely affected if these countries experience a recession. However, if a U.S. firm diversifies its business among several different countries, a recession in any single foreign country should not have a major effect on the firm's worldwide sales.

HOW MARKET PRICES ARE DETERMINED

2 **Explain how market prices are determined.**

The performance of firms is affected by changes in the prices they charge for products (which influence their revenue) and the prices they pay for supplies and materials (which influence their operating expenses). The prices of products and suppliers are influenced by demand and supply conditions.

The following framework uses demand and supply conditions to explain how prices of products change over time. The market price of a product is influenced by the total demand for that product by all customers. It is also affected by the supply of that product produced by firms. The interaction between demand and supply determines the price, as explained in detail next.

Demand Schedule for a Product

demand schedule a schedule that indicates the quantity of the product that would be demanded at each possible price

The demand for a product can be shown with a **demand schedule,** or a schedule that indicates the quantity of the product that would be demanded at each possible price. Consider personal computers as an example. Assume that the demand schedule for a particular type of personal computer is as shown in the first and second columns in Exhibit 4.7 for a given point in time. If the price is relatively high, the quantity demanded by consumers is relatively low. For example, if the price is $5,000, only 8,000 of these computers would be demanded (purchased) by consumers. At the other extreme, if the price is $3,000, a total of 25,000 of these computers would be demanded by customers. The quantity of personal computers demanded would be higher if the price is lower.

Exhibit 4.7
How the Equilibrium Price Is Determined by Demand and Supply

If the Price of a Particular Computer Is:	The Quantity of These Computers Demanded by Consumers Would Be:	The Quantity of These Computers Supplied (Produced) by Firms Would Be:
$5,000	8,000	30,000
$4,500	14,000	24,000
$4,000	18,000	18,000
$3,500	22,000	16,000
$3,000	25,000	10,000

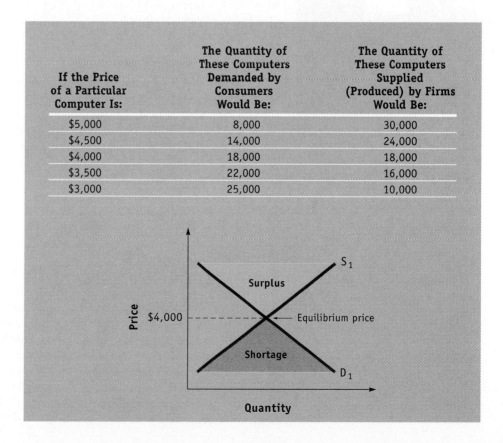

A graph accompanying Exhibit 4.7, based on the table, shows the relationship between the price of a computer and the quantity of computers demanded by consumers. The demand curve (labeled D_1) shows that as price decreases, the quantity demanded increases.

Supply Schedule for a Product

supply schedule a schedule that indicates the quantity of the product that would be supplied (produced) by firms at each possible price

The supply of a product can be shown with a **supply schedule,** or a schedule that indicates the quantity of the product that would be supplied (produced) by firms at each possible price. Assume that the supply schedule for the type of personal computer already discussed is as shown in the first and third columns of Exhibit 4.7 for a given point in time. If the price at which the personal computer could be sold is relatively high, a large supply of this computer would be produced by firms. For example, if the price is $5,000, 30,000 of these computers would be produced. Firms would be willing to produce the computers at this price because they would earn a high profit if they could sell the computers at such a high price.

At the other extreme, if the price of computers is only $3,000, only 10,000 of these computers would be produced. The quantity supplied is much smaller at a low price because some firms would be unwilling to produce the computers if they could sell them for only $3,000. If the actual cost for some firms to produce the computers is above this price of $3,000, these firms would be unwilling to produce the computers.

A graph accompanying Exhibit 4.7, based on the table, shows the relationship between the price of a computer and the quantity of computers supplied (produced) by firms. The supply curve (labeled S_1) shows that as price increases, the quantity of computers supplied increases.

Interaction of Demand and Supply

The interaction of the demand schedule and supply schedule determines the price. Notice from Exhibit 4.7 that at relatively high prices of computers (such as $5,000), the quantity supplied by firms exceeds the quantity demanded by customers, resulting in a so-called **surplus** of computers. For example, at the price of $5,000 the quantity supplied is 30,000 units and the quantity demanded is 8,000 units, resulting in a surplus of 22,000 units. This surplus occurs because consumers are unwilling to purchase computers when the price is excessive.

When the price of a computer is relatively low, the quantity supplied by firms will be less than the quantity demanded by customers, resulting in a so-called **shortage** of computers. For example, at a price of $3,000, the quantity demanded by customers is 25,000 units, while the quantity supplied by firms is only 10,000 units, causing a shortage of 15,000 units.

Notice from Exhibit 4.7 that at a price of $4,000, the quantity of computers supplied by firms is 18,000 units, and the quantity demanded by customers is also 18,000 units. At this price, there is no surplus and no shortage. The price of a product at which the quantity of the product supplied by firms equals the quantity of the product demanded by customers is called the **equilibrium price.** This is the price at which firms normally attempt to sell their products.

At any price above the equilibrium price, the firms will be unable to sell all the computers they produce, resulting in a surplus. Therefore, they would need to reduce their prices to eliminate the surplus. At any price below the equilibrium price, the firms will not produce a sufficient quantity of computers to satisfy all the customers

The supply of 7'2" basketball players of the caliber of David Robinson is very small. At the same time, every NBA team would love to have a player like him. This combination of low supply and high demand results in very high salaries for these players.

surplus the quantity supplied by firms exceeds the quantity demanded by customers

shortage the quantity supplied by firms is less than the quantity demanded by customers

equilibrium price the price of a product at which the quantity of the product supplied by firms equals the quantity of the product demanded by customers

willing to pay that price (resulting in a shortage). The firms could raise their price to correct the shortage.

The demand and supply concepts just applied to a particular type of computer can also be applied to every product or service that firms produce. Each product or service has its own demand schedule and supply schedule, which will determine its own equilibrium price.

Effect of a Change in the Demand Schedule

As time passes, conditions may change that can cause a demand schedule or a supply schedule for a specific product to change. Consequently, a change will occur in the equilibrium price of that product. Reconsider the previous example and assume that computers became more desirable to potential consumers. Assume that the demand schedule for the computer changed as shown at the top of Exhibit 4.8. At any given price, the quantity demanded is now 10,000 units higher than it was before the computer became more popular. The graph accompanying Exhibit 4.8 shows how the demand curve shifted outward from D_1 to D_2.

Now consider the effect of this change in the demand schedule on the equilibrium price of computers. Assuming that the supply schedule remains unchanged, the effect of the change in the demand schedule on the equilibrium price is shown in Exhibit 4.8. At the original equilibrium price of $4,000, the quantity of computers demanded is now 28,000, while the quantity of computers supplied is still 18,000. A shortage of computers occurs at that price. However, at a price of $4,500, the quantity of computers supplied by firms would equal the quantity of computers demanded

Exhibit 4.8
How the Equilibrium Price Is Affected by a Change in Demand

If the Price of a Particular Computer Is:	The Quantity of the Computers Demanded by Consumers Was:	But the Quantity of These Computers Demanded by Consumers Would Now Be:
$5,000	8,000	18,000
$4,500	14,000	24,000
$4,000	18,000	28,000
$3,500	22,000	32,000
$3,000	25,000	35,000

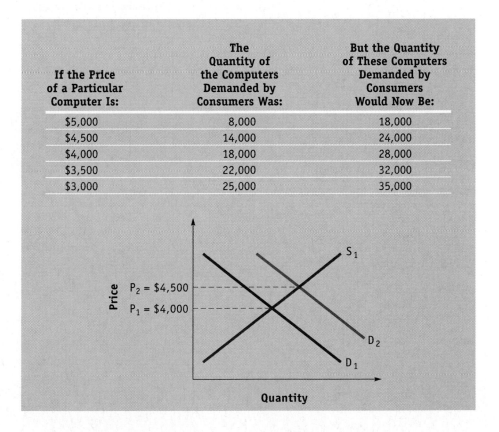

by customers. Therefore, the new equilibrium price is $4,500. The graph at the bottom of Exhibit 4.8 confirms that the shift in the demand schedule from D_1 to D_2 causes the new equilibrium price of computers to be $4,500.

The graph illustrating the effect of a shift in the demand schedule on the equilibrium price of a product can be supplemented with simple logic. When a product becomes more popular, the demand by consumers for that product increases, resulting in a shortage. Under these conditions, firms recognize that they can still sell whatever they produce at a higher price. Once the price is raised to the level at which the quantity supplied is equal to the quantity demanded, the shortage is corrected.

Effect of a Change in the Supply Schedule

Just as the demand for a product may change, so might the supply. A change in the supply can also affect the equilibrium price of the product. To illustrate this effect, reconsider the original example in which the equilibrium price of computers was $4,000. Now assume that improved technology allows firms to produce the computer at a lower cost. In this case, firms will be willing to produce a larger supply of computers at any given price, which reflects a change in the supply schedule.

Assume that as a result of the improved technology (lower production costs), the supply schedule changed as shown in Exhibit 4.9. At any given price, the quantity supplied is now 6,000 units higher than it was before the improved technology. The graph accompanying Exhibit 4.9 shows how the supply schedule shifted outward from S_1 to S_2.

Now consider the effect of this change in the supply schedule on the equilibrium price of computers. Assuming that the demand schedule remains unchanged, the effect of the change in the supply schedule on the equilibrium price is shown in Exhibit 4.9. At the original equilibrium price of $4,000, the quantity of computers demanded is 18,000, while the quantity of computers supplied (produced) is now 24,000. A surplus of computers occurs at that price. However, at a price of $3,500,

Michael Dell, CEO of Dell Computer. Dell Computer helped increase the supply of IBM compatible personal computers and was thus instrumental in sharp declines in computer prices over the last five years.

Exhibit 4.9
How the Equilibrium Price Is
Affected by a Change in Supply

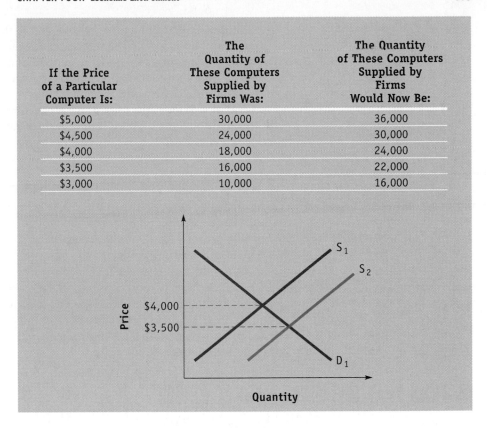

If the Price of a Particular Computer Is:	The Quantity of These Computers Supplied by Firms Was:	The Quantity of These Computers Supplied by Firms Would Now Be:
$5,000	30,000	36,000
$4,500	24,000	30,000
$4,000	18,000	24,000
$3,500	16,000	22,000
$3,000	10,000	16,000

the quantity of computers supplied by firms would equal the quantity of computers demanded by consumers. Therefore, the new equilibrium price is $3,500. The graph in the bottom of Exhibit 4.9 confirms that the shift in the supply schedule from S_1 to S_2 causes the new equilibrium price of computers to be $3,500.

This photo shows part of the United States' strategic oil reserves. These reserves hold billions of gallons of crude oil. Due to high gas prices in 1996, President Clinton ordered the sale of millions of these barrels in order to shift the supply schedule for crude oil and decrease gas prices.

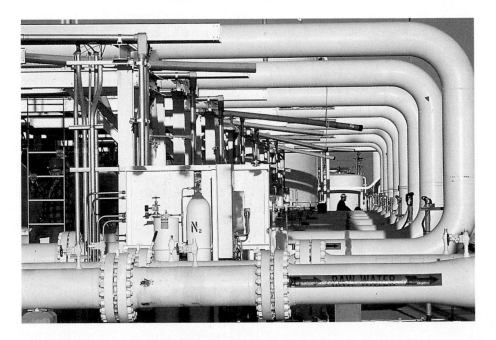

The graph illustrating the effect of a shift in the supply schedule on the equilibrium price of a product can be supplemented with simple logic. When improved technology allows firms to produce a product at a lower cost, more firms will be willing to produce the product. This results in a larger supply produced, which causes a surplus. Firms recognize that the only way they will be able to sell all that is supplied (produced) is to lower the price of the product. Once the price is lowered to the level at which the quantity supplied is once again equal to the quantity demanded, the surplus is eliminated.

Effect of Demand and Supply on the General Price Level

The discussion so far on demand and supply has focused on one product to determine how the equilibrium price of that product could change. Now consider how the general price level for all products may change. The general price level is an average of prices of all existing products and services. If the total (aggregate) demand by consumers for all or most products suddenly increases (perhaps because of an increase in the income level of most consumers), the general level of prices could rise. The general price level may also be affected by shifts in the supply schedules for all goods and services. If the supply schedule of all or most products suddenly decreases (perhaps because of increasing expenses when producing the products), the general level of prices should rise.

FACTORS THAT INFLUENCE MARKET PRICES

Examples have been given to illustrate how the demand by customers or the supply produced by firms can change, causing a new market price. Several factors can cause shifts in the demand schedule or a supply schedule, some of which are identified next.

Consumer Income

Consumer income determines the amount of products and services that individuals can purchase. A high level of economic growth results in more income for consumers. When the income of consumers rises, these consumers may demand a larger quantity of specific products and services. That is, the demand schedules for various products and services may shift out in response to higher income, which could result in higher prices.

Conversely, when the income level of consumers declines, the consumers may demand a smaller quantity of specific products. For example, in the early 1990s, the average income level in the United States declined substantially in specific areas where firms relied on government contracts (such as for building missiles and so on). The federal government's cutbacks for such expenditures resulted in less work for firms in specific regions of the country. As income declined, the demand for new homes in these areas declined, causing a surplus of new homes. The firms that were building new homes were forced to lower their prices because of the surplus.

Consumer Preferences

As consumer preferences (or tastes) for a particular product change, the quantity of that product demanded by consumers may change. There are numerous examples of products whose prices rose in response to increased demand. For example, in March of 1995, a scalped ticket for a Chicago Bulls basketball game in Chicago was selling for less than $50. In late March, Michael Jordan came back from retirement, and in his first game in Chicago, some scalped tickets were selling for $500.

When a product becomes less popular, the demand for the product declines. The resulting surplus may force firms to lower their prices to sell what they produce. For example, when specific clothes become unpopular, clothing manufacturers sell these clothes at discounted prices just to eliminate the surplus.

Production Expenses

Another factor that can affect equilibrium prices is a change in production expenses. When firms experience lower expenses, they are willing to supply (produce) more at any given price (as explained earlier). This results in a surplus of the product, forcing firms to lower their price to sell all that they have produced. For example, the prices of musical compact discs have declined every year since they were first introduced.

When expenses of firms increase, the opposite result occurs. For example, insurance companies that had insured south Florida homes in the early 1990s incurred high expenses in the aftermath of Hurricane Andrew. Some of these companies decided that they would no longer supply this insurance service in south Florida. Those companies that were still willing to provide insurance were able to raise their prices.

GOVERNMENT INFLUENCE ON ECONOMIC CONDITIONS

3 **Explain how the government influences economic conditions.**

The federal government can influence business by imposing regulations or by enacting policies that affect economic conditions. Since the regulations tend to vary by industry, they are discussed in the chapter on the industry environment. To influence economic conditions, the federal government implements monetary and fiscal policies, which are discussed next.

Monetary Policy

money supply demand deposits (checking accounts), currency held by the public, and travelers checks.

The term **money supply** is normally defined within the United States to represent demand deposits (checking accounts), currency held by the public, and travelers checks. This is a narrow definition, as there are broader measures of money supply that count other types of deposits as well. Regardless of the precise definition, any measure of money represents funds that financial institutions can lend to borrowers.

Federal Reserve System the central bank of the United States

monetary policy decisions on the money supply level in the United States

The U.S. money supply is controlled by the **Federal Reserve System** ("the Fed"), which is the central bank of the United States. The Fed sets the **monetary policy,** which represents decisions on the money supply level in the United States. The Fed can easily adjust the U.S. money supply by billions of dollars within a single day. As the Fed's monetary policy affects the money supply level, it affects interest rates.

HOW THE FED CAN REDUCE INTEREST RATES   The Fed maintains some funds outside of the banking system, which do not represent loanable funds. These funds are not available to firms or individuals who need to borrow. When the Fed increases the money supply, it places these funds in commercial banks and other financial institutions, which can be loaned out. In other words, the Fed's action increases the supply of loanable funds. Assuming that the demand for loanable funds remains unchanged, the increase in the supply of loanable funds should cause interest rates to decrease. The impact of the supply of loanable funds on interest rates is discussed in more detail in the appendix to this chapter.

Members of the finance community pay close attention to the comments of Fed Chairman Alan Greenspan.

HOW THE FED CAN INCREASE INTEREST RATES   When the Fed reduces the U.S. money supply, it pulls funds out of commercial banks and other financial institutions. This reduces the supply of funds that these financial institutions can lend to borrowers. Assuming that the demand for loanable funds remains unchanged, the decline in the supply of loanable funds should cause interest rates to rise.

When the Fed affects interest rates with its monetary policy, it directly affects a firm's interest expenses. Second, it can affect the demand for the firm's products if those products are commonly purchased with borrowed funds. The amount of expansion by firms is highly influenced by the interest rate they must pay on funds that must be borrowed to support the expansion.

Fiscal Policy

fiscal policy decisions on how the federal government should set tax rates and spend money

Fiscal policy represents decisions on how the federal government should set tax rates and spend money. These decisions are relevant to businesses because they affect economic growth and therefore can affect the demand for a firm's products or services.

REVISION OF PERSONAL INCOME TAX RATES   Consider a fiscal policy that reduces personal income taxes. This policy would give people a higher after-tax income, which may encourage them to spend more money. Such behavior reflects an increase in the aggregate demand for products and services produced by businesses, which can improve the performance of businesses.

REVISION OF CORPORATE TAXES   Fiscal policy affects a firm's after-tax earnings directly. For example, assume the corporate tax rate is adjusted from 30 percent to 25 percent for corporations. If a specific corporation's before-tax earnings are $10,000,000, its corporate taxes would have been $3,000,000 (computed as 30% $\times$ $10,000,000) at the old tax rate. However, at a corporate tax rate of 25 percent, its corporate taxes are now $2,500,000 (computed as 25% $\times$ $10,000,000). Therefore, the after-tax earnings of the corporation are now $500,000 higher, simply because the corporate taxes are now $500,000 lower.

SPOTLIGHT ON TECHNOLOGY

Monitoring the Economic Environment

In a world tied together by information technology, it has become increasingly important for companies to be aware of the economic environment. Mortgage brokers, for example, typically serve the financing needs of home buyers and home owners within their local region. They cannot, however, afford to be local in their outlook. The potential lenders they could use to provide money to borrowers are located across the U.S. Their business is also dramatically impacted by economic factors such as recession and interest rate fluctuations. For example, during periods of falling interest rates, much of their business comes from refinancing existing mortgages for homeowners. During periods of rising rates, however, that business virtually disappears. As a consequence, swings in loan volume of 50–60% are common from year to year.

Some of the most progressive mortgage brokers have recognized their dependence on information and have employed information technology to acquire it. Austin Kazinetz, President of the American Financial Network, Inc. in Boca Raton,

Florida, describes the systems he put in place as follows:

> Right now, we are hooked into every valuable source of data that we've been able to identify. The ISC system gives us on-line access to county tax roles, providing data on comparable sales, tax deeds and foreclosures. The Ready system hooks us into the local Board of Realtors, providing us with information on what's on the market and how it is being priced, based upon multiple listing service (MLS) listings. We can link directly to the tax collector's rolls. The Data Trace system allows us to perform on-line title searches. The Mortgage Banker's Association of America provides us with bulletin board system (BBS) access to various data, such as being able to identify FHA/VA case numbers and appraiser assignments. That BBS also allows us to exchange information with many lenders. We are tied into a number of providers of on-line credit information, so we can perform credit searches in-house. We have even installed a satellite dish, which allows us up-to-the-minute access to financial market news. . . . As a result, nobody has as much data as American Financial Network.

He believes these systems were instrumental in his company's ability to prepare for and weather a down market in the mortgage industry that occurred in 1994.

---

excise taxes imposed on the production of particular products by the federal government

REVISION IN EXCISE TAXES **Excise taxes** are imposed on the production of particular products by the federal government. These taxes raise the cost of producing these goods. Consequently, manufacturers tend to incorporate the tax in the price they charge for the products. Thus, consumers indirectly incur the tax. The tax may also discourage consumption of these goods by indirectly affecting the price. Excise taxes are imposed on various products, including alcohol, tobacco, and petroleum products.

REVISION IN THE BUDGET DEFICIT   The fiscal policy set by the federal government dictates the amount of tax revenue generated by the federal government and the amount of federal spending. The amount that federal government spending exceeds the amount of federal taxes, results in a so-called **federal budget deficit.**

federal budget deficit when the amount of federal government spending exceeds the amount of federal taxes and other revenue received by the federal government

When the federal government receives less revenue than it spends, it must borrow the difference. For example, if the federal government plans to spend $900 billion but receives only $700 billion in taxes (or other revenue), it has $200 billion less than it desires to spend. It must borrow $200 billion to have sufficient funds for making its expenditures (as shown in Exhibit 4.10). The federal government's excessive borrowing is a concern because it creates a high demand for loanable funds, which may result in higher interest rates (as explained earlier).

Summary of Government Influence on Economic Factors

A summary of how the federal government affects the performance of firms is illustrated in Exhibit 4.11. Fiscal policy can affect personal tax rates and therefore influ-

Exhibit 4.10
**Example of How a Budget
Deficit Occurs**

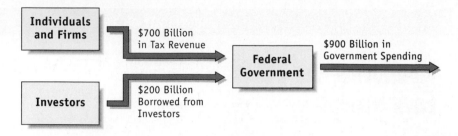

ences consumer spending behavior. It can also affect corporate tax rates, which influence the earnings of firms. Monetary policy can affect interest rates, which may influence the demand for a firm's product (if the purchases are sometimes paid for with borrowed funds). By influencing interest rates, monetary policy also affects the interest expenses that firms incur.

Dilemma of the Federal Government

The federal government faces a dilemma when attempting to influence economic growth. If it can maintain a low rate of economic growth, it can prevent inflationary pressure caused by an excessive demand for products. A restrictive monetary or fiscal policy may be used for this purpose. A restrictive monetary policy represents low growth in the money supply over time, which tends to place upward pressure on interest rates. This discourages borrowing and therefore can reduce total spending

Exhibit 4.11
**How Government Policies Affect
Business Performance**

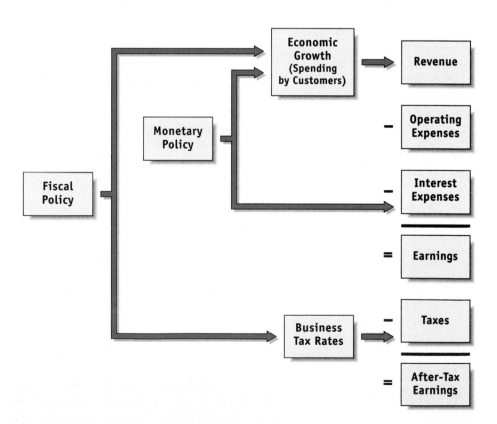

Economic Effects Across Business Functions

 Since managers of a firm have different responsi- bilities, they assess different aspects of the economic environment. Managers who focus on production monitor the changes in economic conditions that could affect the firm's production costs. They tend to monitor inflationary trends, or changes in the price levels of specific supplies or equipment that they purchase.

Marketing managers attempt to forecast sales of their products and assess economic conditions that affect the demand for the products, such as economic growth. They may also monitor interest rates if the products are commonly purchased with borrowed funds, since the demand for the products might increase in response to a reduction in interest rates. Since the firm's production volume is dependent on the forecasted demand for the product, it is influenced by economic conditions.

Marketing managers assess economic conditions because their marketing decisions can be affected by the strength of the economy. Some of a firm's products (such as necessities and relatively inexpensive products) may be marketed more heavily when economic conditions are weak because these products may be more popular when the economy is weak. Conversely,

the firm may market their expensive products more heavily when economic conditions are more favorable.

The firm's financial managers monitor the economic conditions that affect the cost of financing. They tend to focus on interest rates because the firm's financing expenses are directly affected by changes in interest rates.

When different types of managers forecast economic conditions so they can make business decisions, they should work as a team in developing economic forecasts. Otherwise, a forecast of some economic conditions may vary across managers, which may cause their business decisions to be different. For example, if the marketing managers of an automobile manufacturer expect low interest rates, they would expect a high sales volume, which would require a large production of automobiles. However, if the production managers expect high interest rates, they would expect a lower level of sales and would be concerned that a large production volume could cause excessive inventories.

Some firms assign one person or department to develop the forecasts of all economic conditions, which the managers use in all business functions. In this way, all managers make decisions according to the same forecasts of economic conditions.

---

within the economy. A restrictive fiscal policy represents high taxes and low government spending.

While restrictive monetary and fiscal policies may keep inflation low, a critical trade-off is involved. The unemployment rate may be higher when the economy is stagnant. The federal government can use a more stimulative policy (such as low tax rates or a monetary policy designed to reduce interest rates) to boost economic growth. While these policies increase economic growth, they may also cause higher inflation.

Rarely is consensus reached on whether the government should use a stimulative or restrictive policy at a given point in time. Some critics recommend that the government should not intervene at all.

Managers of firms commonly attempt to forecast how future fiscal and monetary policies will affect economic conditions. This information is then used to predict the demand for the firm's product, labor and material costs, and interest expenses. To illustrate, assume an automobile manufacturer forecasts that next year's interest rate on consumer loans will decrease by 2 percent. This forecast of interest rates will be used to forecast the demand for its automobiles. Lower interest rates will probably create higher demand, because more consumers will be willing to finance their purchases of new automobiles. Assume the firm believes that for every 1 percent decrease in interest rates, demand for its automobiles will increase by 3 percent. Thus, it anticipates a 6 percent increase in sales volume in one year.

Economic Effects on College Health Club

Sue Kramer, owner of College Health Club (CHC), is trying to estimate the performance of CHC over the next three years. The annual memberships of $250 are paid to CHC with cash. Many of the members are college students who work part-time.

CHC incurs interest expenses on its $40,000 loan. The loan has a variable rate that is based on the prevailing market interest rate. The annual interest paid is $6,000, based on a prevailing interest rate of 15 percent (15% × $40,000 = $6,000).

Sue reviews several business publications to find a consensus forecast of economic conditions:

1 The consensus forecast for the economy (including the local area) is strong economic growth over the next three years. Since many students at the local university rely on jobs to pay their tuition, the university enrollment was expected to increase due to the economic growth. Sue expects that this will result in about ten more annual memberships in each of the next three years.

2 The inflation rate will be about 3 percent in each of the next three years.

3 The Federal Reserve will raise interest rates by 2 percent over the next year, but interest rates are expected to remain steady for the following two years. This means that the interest rate that Sue paid on her business loan will rise to 17 percent next year and will remain at that level the following two years.

Dilemma

Sue is concerned about how economic conditions could affect CHC. She wants to forecast how CHC will be affected based on the forecasts of economic conditions. How will the change in economic conditions affect revenue? Expenses? Earnings (before taxes)?

Solution

A summary of Sue's analysis is provided next.

ECONOMIC GROWTH   The economic growth will result in more part-time work for the college students, and should cause an increase in the demand for annual memberships at CHC. Sue increases her forecast of annual memberships by ten over each of the next three years. At a membership fee of $250 per person, the extra ten memberships will generate an extra $2,500 per year.

INFLATION   The increase in inflation could result in higher prices for equipment. However, since CHC has a leasing agreement, the expense of leasing the equipment will not be affected. Wages may also rise nationwide as a result of inflation. At CHC, the effect will be minor, since CHC has only one employee besides Sue.

INTEREST RATES   The increase in interest rates will result in higher financing costs. CHC has a $40,000 loan with an interest rate that rises in response to higher market interest rates. The interest rate on CHC's loan will be 2 percentage points higher than it was, which results in extra annual interest payments of $800 (computed as 2% × $40,000).

The effects of changing economic conditions on CHC are as follows:

	Year		
	1	*2*	*3*
Change in Revenue	$2,500	$2,500	$2,500
− Change in Operating Expenses	$0	$0	$0
− Change in Financing Expenses	$800	$800	$800
= Change in Earnings	$1,700	$1,700	$1,700

The extra revenue resulting from economic growth exceeds the extra financing expenses resulting from higher interest rates. Overall, CHC should benefit from the forecasted economic conditions.

Additional Issues for Discussion

1 Which should Sue more closely monitor: economic growth in the United States or economic growth in her local area? Why?

2 Assume that the federal government is expected to raise income taxes for all people, regardless of income level. How could this change possibly affect CHC?

3 Which should Sue more closely monitor: inflation in the United States or inflation in her local area? How could Sue be affected by land and rental prices in the local area?

SUMMARY

1 A firm's performance is highly dependent on three macroeconomic factors: (1) economic growth, (2) inflation, and (3) interest rates. A high level of economic growth tends to increase the overall demand for a firm's products and services. Inflation affects the costs of supplies and wages, which represent the firm's operating expenses. Higher inflation tends to cause higher operating expenses. Interest rates affect the firm's interest expenses. An increase in interest rates will typically result in higher interest expenses for the firms.

2 Market prices are determined by demand and supply conditions. The demand for a product is influenced by consumer income and preferences. Higher consumer income generally results in a higher demand for products. The amount of a product produced is influenced by production expenses. Firms will supply products to the market only if the market price is sufficiently high to more than cover expenses.

3 The federal government influences macroeconomic conditions by enacting monetary or fiscal policies. Its monetary policy affects the amount of funds available at commercial banks and other financial institutions, and therefore affects interest rates. Its fiscal policy affects the taxes imposed on consumers, which can influence the amount of spending by consumers and therefore affects the performance of firms. Fiscal policy is also used to tax the earnings of firms.

KEY TERMS

aggregate expenditures
cost-push inflation
cyclical unemployment
demand schedule
demand-pull inflation
economic growth
equilibrium interest rate (chapter
    appendix)
equilibrium price

excise taxes
federal budget deficit
Federal Reserve System
fiscal policy
frictional unemployment
gross domestic product (GDP)
inflation
macroeconomic conditions
microeconomic conditions

monetary policy
money supply
seasonal unemployment
shortage
structural unemployment
supply schedule
surplus

REVIEW QUESTIONS

1 Explain a situation that would cause a supply curve to shift because of increased technology for a firm. What effect would this have on price?

2 Discuss the factors that will affect interest rate movements in our economy.

3 Distinguish macroeconomics from microeconomics. Which one of the two economic theories would apply when the government establishes a fiscal policy?

4 Describe the four different types of unemployment and which type a college graduate would face upon entering the job market.

5 Define monetary policy. Who is responsible for regulating monetary supply in the United States?

6 Discuss macroeconomic factors that affect business performance.

7 How are market prices determined?

8 Discuss the factors that will influence a shift in the demand curve for products or services.

9 Explain price equilibrium for businesses and consumers. What is the effect when there is a surplus?

10 Discuss the two primary responsibilities of the federal government in establishing economic policies. What does it mean to have a budget deficit?

DISCUSSION QUESTIONS

1 Assume you are a practicing manager in a plant that produces rollerblades. What factors would you consider in determining price for this product?

2 Take a trip to your local shopping mall and assess the degree of competition that businesses face. How do the businesses compete to market their goods and services?

3 Discuss the effect when the federal government spends more tax dollars than it takes in. Is this practice unhealthy for our economy?

4 In your community, do new businesses and housing starts show signs of economic growth or evidence of decay? What effect does this have on inflation and interest rates?

5 When college students are given federal grants (such as Pell Grants) that cover some education expenses, does this reflect a form of fiscal policy or monetary policy?

RUNNING YOUR OWN BUSINESS

1 How would the performance of your business be affected by economic conditions within the local area? How would it be affected by economic conditions across the United States? How could your company be affected by global economic events?

2 How would the performance of your business be affected by an increase in interest rates?

INVESTING IN THE STOCK OF A BUSINESS

Using the annual report of the firm in which you would like to invest, complete the following:

1 Was your firm's performance affected by economic growth last year? If so, how? Are these trends expected to continue? What does your firm plan to do about the economic conditions it faces?

2 Was your firm's performance affected by inflation or interest rates last year? If so, how?

CASE 1 How Economic Conditions Influence Business Decisions

Ron Krivda is considering opening a video store in Orlando, Florida. Several key decisions must be made before launching this business. He must decide whether to lease or buy a building. A second decision involves whether to lease or buy the equipment for the video store. Finally, he must decide whether to rent or buy the videos he plans to retail.

The level of interest rates will greatly influence Ron's decision to lease or purchase. He recognizes that he must assess important criteria, such as the cost of funds and the right time to request a loan from the bank.

Ron is inclined to lease rather than buy when interest rates are high, and to buy rather than lease when interest rates are low. Realizing that there is a proper time to either buy or lease, Ron is trying to decide which factors will influence interest rates. For instance, he knows that during times of economic growth, demand for money will increase, thus causing interest rates to climb.

Future prospects are bright, and Ron is optimistic. The time is right for him to go into business. Future economic growth forecasts indicate that his cost of obtaining funds is expected to rise because of an expected increase in interest rates.

Questions

1 Will interest rates affect Ron's decision to go into business at this time?

2 Will interest rate fluctuations impact Ron's decision to lease or buy?

3 Will the future economic climate have any effect on Ron's ability to make a decision today?

4 When should Ron purchase or lease assets of the business?

CASE 2 Supply and Demand for GM Automobiles

General Motors (GM) is transforming itself into the Wal-Mart of the automotive industry, by developing no-frills product lines and by offering customers value to increase market share. GM is supplying the marketplace with a simple, affordable car instead of a snazzy one packed with the latest gadgets.

GM's strategy is to increase its market share in the North American market and increase its profit without making any radical innovations. The car maker plans to redesign the Chevrolet Cavalier and the Pontiac Sunfire because the small sedans are outselling the competition. Since GM does not have any competition in the full-size, sport-utility vehicle line, it is selling all it can produce.

GM is planning to supply the market with twelve new automobiles and trucks within the next few years. It's striving to achieve a $100 billion sales volume. It has low-ered its production costs of refining existing engines and passed the savings on to customers in the form of lower prices. What customers are demanding is proven reliability, good value, and a good price. GM is striving to provide the most car for the customer's dollar, whereas the competition is striving to get the most performance for its customers.

Questions

1 Is this a microeconomic or macroeconomic issue for General Motors?

2 Is GM achieving growth?

3 What affects the supply and demand of GM automobiles?

4 What are GM's strategies to create a competitive edge in the automobile industry?

VIDEO CASE Exposure to Weak Economic Conditions

Linda Russell's CollectionCenter found itself in a can't-squeeze-blood-out-of-a-turnip situation. Major job sources in Wyoming—oil, gas, coal, uranium, and timber—were in trouble, a trouble especially deep in the area around Rawlins, location of Russell's collection and credit-reporting agency. Rawlins was experiencing a very weak economy which reduced the ability of customers to pay their bills.

Russell takes a gentle approach to debt collection, with a philosophy of helping people figure out ways to pay what they owe, rather than browbeat them. The approach had been working well.

However, CollectionCenter had strengths: a team of skilled, dedicated people and a reputation for outstanding service. The team included Russell's husband, Jerry, a lawyer with an outside practice who served as Collection-Center's executive vice president.

The Russells huddled with some of the team, the office, collection, and credit-reporting managers. It was agreed that CollectionCenter would shrink and die if its territory didn't expand. Input was solicited from everyone else on the team, and the company moved into Wyoming's two largest cities, Casper and Cheyenne, buying existing agencies there.

"We were off and running," says Linda Russell, "but we found we were in real need of more expertise in the rapidly changing world of computers with which we had to deal."

Since then, the company has expanded farther, to Ft. Collins and Grand Junction in Colorado and Salt Lake City, Utah. Its team has increased from 12 to 69.

Questions

1 Explain why the revenue generated by Linda Russell's CollectionCenter may decline when the local economy is weak, while the expenses of the CollectionCenter do not decline.

2 Explain how expansion of the CollectionCenter business into other locations can reduce the firm's exposure to the economic conditions of Rawlins, Wyoming. Would expansion into new locations where the economic conditions were similar to Rawlins, Wyoming, be a useful strategy for the CollectionCenter? Explain.

3 Assume that the one executive of the CollectionCenter suggested that the entire firm be moved to Salt Lake City, where the economic conditions are presently more favorable than all other regions. Is this an appropriate strategy to prevent any adverse effects of economic conditions over the next several years?

THE Coca-Cola COMPANY ANNUAL REPORT PROJECT

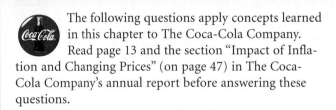

The following questions apply concepts learned in this chapter to The Coca-Cola Company. Read page 13 and the section "Impact of Inflation and Changing Prices" (on page 47) in The Coca-Cola Company's annual report before answering these questions.

1 a. How could inflation affect The Coca-Cola Company's future profitability?

b. Does it appear that inflation affected The Coca-Cola Company's profits in 1995?

2 Does the management of The Coca-Cola Company perceive any problems to be associated with doing business in so many different countries?

3 Given that it is impossible to predict future economic conditions, what might be a general strategy of a large firm such as The Coca-Cola Company to insulate against shifts in the economic environment of any particular country?

IN-TEXT STUDY GUIDE

Answers are in an appendix at the back of the book.

True or False

1 A higher level of inflation will cause a larger decrease in a firm's operating expenses.

2 A firm may be favorably affected by some economic conditions and unfavorably affected by others.

3 If the total (aggregate) demand by consumers for all or most products suddenly increases, the general level of prices should fall.

4 The Federal Reserve System sets the monetary policy that determines the money supply in the United States.

5 Macroeconomics are focused on a specific business or industry of concern.

6 A firm may lay off factory workers because of a decline in economic conditions over the last year, which is an example of seasonal unemployment.

7 The demand for a product can be shown with a demand schedule, which indicates the quantity of the product that would be demanded at each possible price.

8 A high rate of inflation can influence the performance of firms because it affects the operating expenses that firms incur.

9 When the U.S. economic growth is lower than normal, the total income level of all U.S. workers is relatively high.

10 Economic growth represents the change in the general level of economic activity.

Multiple Choice

11 The total market value of all final products and services produced in the United States is represented by:
a) gross domestic product.
b) demand side economics.
c) priming the pump.
d) multinational corporations.
e) international business.

12 The type of unemployment that represents people who are unemployed because of poor economic conditions is:
a) functional unemployment.
b) cyclical unemployment.
c) seasonal unemployment.
d) structural unemployment.
e) general unemployment.

13 A common measure of economic growth, represented by the total amount of expenditures, is called:
a) aggregate savings.
b) gross supply.
c) aggregate expenditures.
d) frictional income.
e) supply-side economics.

14 A corporation's profit, as measured by its annual earnings divided by its outstanding shares of stock, is called:
a) book value.   b) current ratio.
c) liquidity ratio.   d) earnings per share.
e) inventory turnover.

15 Taxes that the federal government imposes on the production of particular products are called:
a) excise taxes.   b) import taxes.
c) export taxes.   d) quotas.
e) embargoes.

16 Conditions reflecting the overall U.S. economy in aggregate form are:
a) microeconomic.
b) multinational corporations.
c) macroeconomic.
d) global markets.
e) consumer price indexes.

17 The type of inflation that requires firms to increase their prices to cover increased costs is referred to as:
a) demand-pull inflation.
b) stagflation.
c) cost-push inflation.
d) disequilibrium.
e) unemployment.

18 The type of unemployment that represents people who are between jobs is:
a) seasonal unemployment.
b) structural unemployment.
c) functional unemployment.
d) frictional unemployment.
e) cyclical unemployment.

19 The prices firms pay for supplies or materials directly influence their:
a) operating expenses.   b) operating revenue.
c) dividends.   d) stockholders' equity.
e) economic assets.

20 The type of inflation that occurs when prices of products and services are pulled up because of strong consumer demand is referred to as:
a) cost-push inflation.
b) demand-pull inflation.
c) consumer inflation.
d) supply-side inflation.
e) price equilibrium.

21 When the quantity of a relatively high-priced product supplied by a firm exceeds the product quantity demanded by customers, this creates a:
a) deficit.
b) price equilibrium.
c) demand-pull inflation.
d) cost-push inflation.
e) surplus.

22 The policy that affects personal tax rates and influences consumer spending behavior is called:

a) economic policy.
b) monetary policy.
c) fiscal policy.
d) gross domestic policy.
e) federal policy.

23 The price of a product at which the quantity of the product supplied by firms equals the quantity of the product demanded by consumers is called the:
a) disequilibrium price.
b) surplus.
c) production frontier.
d) equilibrium price.
e) opportunity costs.

24 The quantity of the product that would be supplied by firms at each possible price is shown on a:
a) demand schedule.
b) equilibrium schedule.
c) supply schedule.
d) consumer price index.
e) PERT diagram.

25 The amount of demand deposits, currency held by the public, and travelers checks in the United States is defined as the:
a) monetary policy.
b) fiscal policy.
c) surplus.
d) price equilibrium.
e) money supply.

26 When the price of a product is relatively low, the quantity of the product supplied will be less than the quantity of the product demanded, resulting in a:
a) surplus.   b) budget deficit.
c) shortage.   d) shift in supply.
e) shift in demand.

27 The central bank of the United States where the money supply is controlled and regulated, is the:
a) Federal Reserve System.
b) Senate.
c) Department of Congress.
d) Council of Economic Advisors.
e) Board of Directors.

28 The following are indicators of economic growth except for:
a) reduced unemployment.
b) increasing industrial production index.
c) higher cyclical employment.
d) new housing starts.
e) increasing personal income level.

29 When different types of managers forecast eco-nomic conditions so they can make business decisions, they should work as a team in developing:
a) labor unions.
b) production bottlenecks.
c) higher work standards.
d) production frontiers.
e) economic forecasts.

30 Decisions on how the federal government should set tax rates and spend money are represented by a:
a) fiscal policy.
b) monetary policy.
c) federal reserve system.
d) trade surplus.
e) balance of payments.

31 When the amount of federal government spending exceeds the amount of federal taxes, the result is a so-called:
a) trade deficit.
b) federal budget deficit.
c) balance of payments.
d) price equilibrium.
e) opportunity costs.

32 The type of government policy that is intended to influence interest rates is called:
a) fiscal policy.
b) corporate policy.
c) national policy.
d) monetary policy.
e) economic policy.

33 An increase in the general level of prices of products and services over a specified period of time is called:
a) inflation.
b) stagflation.
c) unemployment.
d) disinflation.
e) equilibrium.

34 Restrictive monetary and fiscal policies may keep inflation low, but the critical trade-off is that they may also cause:
a) disinflation.   b) environment problems
c) massive crime.   d) unemployment.
e) higher inflation.

35 The government can prevent inflationary pressure caused by an excessive demand for products by main-taining a low rate of:
a) fiscal policies.   b) economic growth.
c) monetary policies.   d) unemployment.
e) savings.

Surfing the Net

Exhibit 4.12
The U.S. Department of Commerce Home Page

http://www.doc.gov

Access to Economic Information on the World Wide Web

Extensive information on the economic environment is available over the Internet. A good starting point for accessing such information is the WWW home page for the U.S. Department of Commerce, which provides a number of tools for accessing information on virtually every subject of economic interest. This includes information on obtaining patents, current U.S. business statistics, and the budget of the United States.

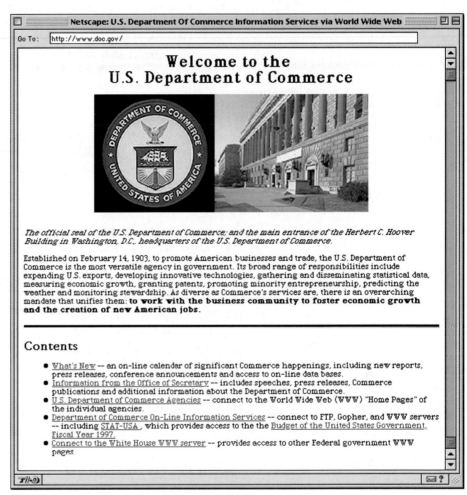

APPENDIX 4A

How Interest Rates Are Determined

Firms closely monitor interest rates because they affect the cost of borrowing money. The interest rate represents the price charged for borrowing money. Managers of firms should understand how interest rates change and should recognize the factors that can cause interest rates to change, as explained by this appendix.

HOW INTEREST RATES CHANGE

The interest rate on funds to be borrowed is influenced by the supply of loanable funds (provided by depositors) and the demand for those loanable funds by borrowers. The interaction between the demand and supply forces interest rates to change, as explained next.

Demand for Loanable Funds

To illustrate the effects of demand on interest rates, assume that the United States has only one commercial bank. The bank receives all deposits from depositors and uses all the funds to make loans to borrowers. Demand for loans by borrowers will vary with the interest rate the bank charges on loans. The higher the interest rate it charges, the lower the amount of loanable funds demanded (requested for loans). This is because some firms (and other borrowers) are unwilling to pay a high interest rate. If the interest rate is too high, firms may simply not borrow the funds they were hoping to use for expansion.

Consider the demand schedule for loanable funds shown in the second column of Exhibit 4A.1. The demand schedule for loanable funds is also shown on the graph accompanying Exhibit 4A.1 and is labeled D_1. This schedule shows the inverse relationship between the interest rate and the quantity of loanable funds demanded.

Supply of Loanable Funds

The quantity of funds supplied (by depositors) to the bank is also related to possible interest rate levels, but in a different manner. The higher the interest rate offered on deposits, the higher the quantity of loanable funds (in the form of deposits) that will be supplied by depositors to banks. The supply schedule for loanable funds to be supplied by depositors is shown in the third column of Exhibit 4A.1. It is also shown on the accompanying graph and is labeled S_1. This schedule shows the positive relationship between the interest rate and the quantity of funds supplied.

Combining Demand and Supply

Interest rates are determined by the interaction of the demand and supply schedules for loanable funds. Notice from Exhibit 4A.1 that at relatively high interest rates (such as 12 percent), the quantity of loanable funds supplied exceeds the quantity of loanable funds demanded, resulting in a surplus of loanable funds. When the interest

Exhibit 4A.1
How Demand and Supply of
Loanable Funds Affect
Interest Rates

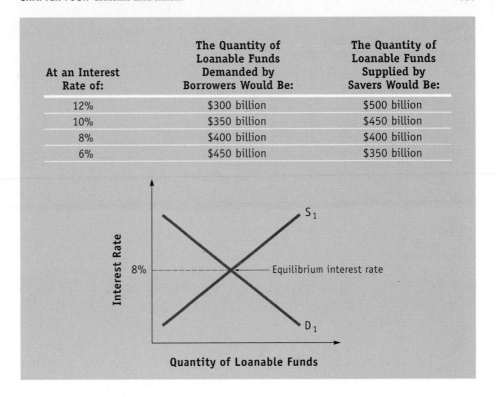

At an Interest Rate of:	The Quantity of Loanable Funds Demanded by Borrowers Would Be:	The Quantity of Loanable Funds Supplied by Savers Would Be:
12%	$300 billion	$500 billion
10%	$350 billion	$450 billion
8%	$400 billion	$400 billion
6%	$450 billion	$350 billion

rate is relatively low (such as 6 percent), the quantity of loanable funds supplied would be less than the quantity of loanable funds demanded, resulting in a shortage of funds.

Notice from Exhibit 4A.1 that at the interest rate of 8 percent, the quantity of loanable funds supplied by depositors is $400 billion, which is equal to the quantity of loanable funds demanded by borrowers. At this interest rate, there is no surplus or shortage of loanable funds. The interest rate at which the quantity of loanable funds supplied is equal to the quantity of loanable funds demanded is called the **equilibrium interest rate.**

equilibrium interest rate the interest rate at which the quantity of loanable funds supplied is equal to the quantity of loanable funds demanded

Effect of a Change in the Demand Schedule

As time passes, conditions may change that can cause the demand schedule of loanable funds to change. Consequently, a change will occur in the equilibrium interest rate. Reconsider the previous example and assume that most firms suddenly decide to expand their business operations. This decision may result from optimistic news about the economy. Those firms that decide to expand will need to borrow additional funds from the bank. Assume that the demand schedule for loanable funds changes, as shown in Exhibit 4A.2. The graph accompanying the exhibit shows how the demand curve shifted outward from D_1 to D_2.

Now consider the effect of this change in the demand for loanable funds on the equilibrium interest rate. Assuming that the supply schedule of loanable funds remains unchanged, the effect of the change in the demand schedule on the equilibrium interest rate is shown in Exhibit 4A.2. There is now a shortage of loanable funds at the equilibrium interest rate. However, at an interest rate of 10 percent, the quantity of loanable funds supplied by savers would once again equal the quantity of

Exhibit 4A.2
Effect of Change in Demand for
Loanable Funds on Interest Rates

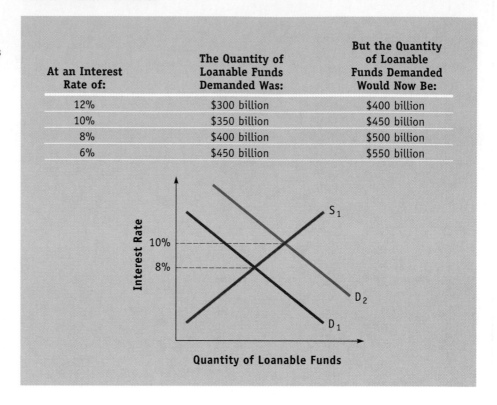

At an Interest Rate of:	The Quantity of Loanable Funds Demanded Was:	But the Quantity of Loanable Funds Demanded Would Now Be:
12%	$300 billion	$400 billion
10%	$350 billion	$450 billion
8%	$400 billion	$500 billion
6%	$450 billion	$550 billion

loanable funds demanded by borrowers. Therefore, the new equilibrium interest rate is 10 percent. The graph accompanying Exhibit 4A.2 confirms that the new equilibrium interest rate is 10 percent.

Effect of a Change in the Supply Schedule

Just as the demand schedule for loanable funds may change, so may the supply schedule. To illustrate how a change in the supply schedule can affect the interest rate, reconsider the original sample in which the equilibrium interest was 8 percent. Now assume that savers decide to save more funds than they did before, which results in a new supply schedule of loanable funds, as shown in Exhibit 4A.3. At any given interest rate, the quantity of loanable funds supplied is now higher than it was before. The graph accompanying Exhibit 4A.3 shows how the supply curve shifted out from S_1 to S_2.

Now consider the effect of the shift in the supply schedule on the equilibrium interest rate. Assuming that the demand schedule remains unchanged, the supply of loanable funds would exceed the demand for loanable funds at the previous equilibrium interest rate of 8 percent. However, at an equilibrium interest rate of 6 percent, the quantity of loanable funds supplied by savers would equal the quantity of loanable funds demanded by borrowers. The graph accompanying Exhibit 4A.3 confirms that the shift in the supply schedule from S_1 to S_2 causes a new equilibrium interest rate of 6 percent.

The discussion of interest rates has assumed just one single commercial bank that receives all deposits from savers and provides those funds as loans to borrowers. In reality, many commercial banks and other financial institutions provide this service. Yet, this does not affect the general discussion of interest rates. The equilibrium interest rate in the United States is determined by the interaction of the total demand

Exhibit 4A.3
Effect of Change in Supply of
Loanable Funds on Interest Rates

At an Interest Rate of:	The Quantity of Loanable Funds Supplied by Savers Was:	But the Quantity of Loanable Funds Supplied by Savers Would Now Be:
12%	$500 billion	$600 billion
10%	$450 billion	$550 billion
8%	$400 billion	$500 billion
6%	$350 billion	$450 billion

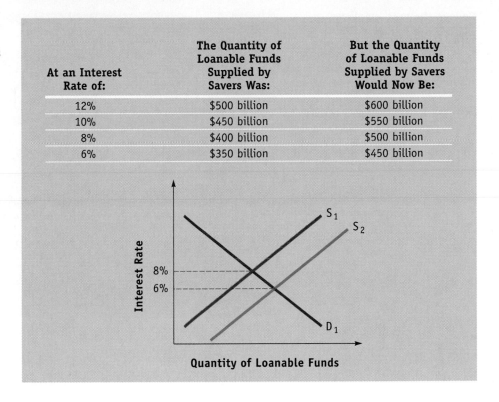

for loanable funds by all U.S. borrowers and the total supply of loanable funds provided by all U.S. savers.

FACTORS THAT CAN AFFECT INTEREST RATES

Several factors can cause shifts in the demand schedule or supply schedule of loanable funds, and therefore can cause shifts in equilibrium interest rates. Firms monitor these factors so that they can anticipate how interest rates may change in the future. In this way, firms can anticipate how their interest owed on borrowed funds may change.

Monetary Policy
Recall that the Federal Reserve System can affect interest rates by implementing monetary policy. As money supply is adjusted, so is the supply of funds that can be lent out by financial institutions. When the Fed increases the supply of funds, interest rates decrease (assuming no change in demand for funds). Conversely, when the Fed reduces the supply of funds, interest rates increase.

Economic Growth
When economic conditions become more favorable, firms tend to make more plans for expansion. They borrow more money, which reflects an increase in their demand for loanable funds. Assuming that the supply of loanable funds remains unchanged, the increased demand for loanable funds will result in a higher equilibrium interest rate.

College students' employee prospects are significantly impacted by economic growth. It is also important for students to understand economic factors when interviewing for a position.

To confirm the relationship just described, consider the effects of a strong economy during 1994. In that year, firms increased their demand for loans because of optimism about the future, and interest rates increased substantially.

The Wall Street Journal, Business Week, and other business sources frequently monitor the indicators of economic growth and suggest how interest rates may be affected. A common headline is something like this: "Economic Growth Increases; Higher Interest Rates Expected." When firms read this headline, they may interpret it as both good news and bad. The good news is higher economic growth, which may increase the demand for the firm's products, thereby increasing the firm's revenue. The bad news is that if the higher economic growth causes higher interest rates, it may also increase the annual interest expenses owed by the firm on its borrowed funds.

As a counterexample, a decline in economic growth can cause firms to reduce their plans for expansion. These firms may see no reason to expand if they expect poor economic conditions, because the demand for their products may decline. If firms demand (borrow) less loanable funds, and the supply of loanable funds remains unchanged, the equilibrium interest rate will decline.

Expected Inflation

When consumers and firms expect a high rate of inflation, they tend to borrow more money. To understand why, assume you plan to purchase a Ford Mustang in two years, once you have saved enough money to pay for it with cash. However, if you believe that the price of the Mustang you wish to purchase will rise substantially by then, you may decide to use borrowed funds to buy it now before the price rises. So when the rate of inflation in the United States is high (or is expected to be high in the near future), many consumers attempt to purchase automobiles, homes, or other products before the prices rise. Firms may also purchase machinery or buildings before the prices rise. These conditions cause an increase in the demand for loanable funds by consumers and firms, which results in higher interest rates. This explains why U.S. interest rates tend to be high when U.S. inflation is high.

Expectations of lower inflation can have the opposite effect. Consumers and firms may be more willing to defer making some purchases if they cannot afford them. They may wait until they are in a better financial situation. When planned purchases are put off until the future, consumers and firms do not need to borrow as much money. Given a lower demand for loanable funds, the interest rate should decline.

Changes in expected inflation could also affect the supply of loanable funds. However, the demand for loanable funds tends to be much more sensitive than the supply of loanable funds to changes in expected inflation.

Savings Behavior

As the savings behavior of people changes, so does the supply schedule of loanable funds, and so does the interest rate. For example, if people become more willing to save money, this increases the amount of money that will be deposited in banks at any possible interest rate. Since the amount of funds that can be loaned out by banks to borrowers has increased, a surplus of funds is available at the previous equilibrium interest rate. Therefore, the new equilibrium interest rate will decline to the level at which the quantity of funds supplied equals the quantity of funds demanded.

Summary of Factors that Affect Interest Rates

Four factors that influence interest rates have been identified and are illustrated in Exhibit 4A.4. The main effects of economic growth and inflation on interest rates occur as a result of influencing the demand for loanable funds. The main effects of savings behavior and monetary policy on interest rates occur as a result of influencing the supply of loanable funds.

The factors that affect interest rates can all be changed at the same time. One factor may be pushing interest rates up while the others are pushing interest rates down. The final effect on interest rates may depend on which factor had the biggest impact.

Exhibit 4A.4
Summary of Key Factors that Affect Interest Rates

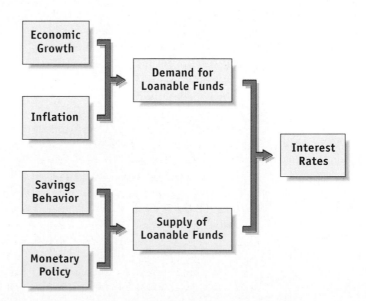

CHAPTER 5

Industry Environment

Just as a firm is affected by macroeconomic conditions, it is also affected by microeconomic conditions related to the firm and its respective industry.

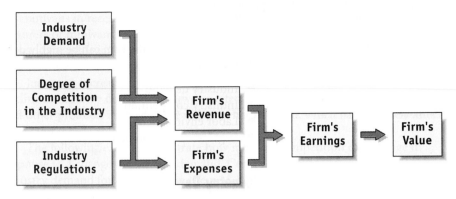

To illustrate how the industry environment can affect the value of a business, consider the case of Boeing, which produces airplanes for airlines and governments. Its earnings and value are strongly influenced by the demand for its airplanes. How would Boeing's value be affected by higher airplane fuel prices? By a war? By a cutback in government budgets? This chapter provides a background on the industry environment that can be used to answer these questions.

The **Learning Goals** of this chapter are to:

1 Identify the industry characteristics that influence business performance.

2 Explain why some firms are more exposed to industry conditions.

3 Explain how a firm can compete within its industry.

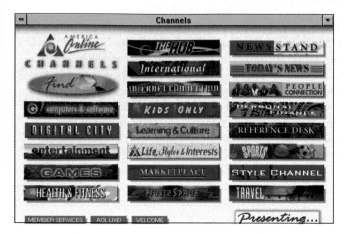
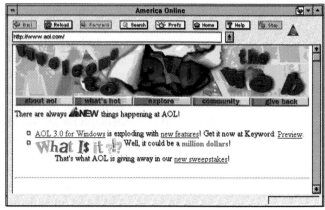

America On-Line is the leader in providing Internet access with over five million subscribers. But they face significant competition from AT&T, MCI, Microsoft, and many others.

may force each firm in the industry to lower its price to prevent competitors from taking away its business.

A classic example of intense industry competition is the fast-food industry. In the 1990s, many fast-food restaurants began offering value menus and low-priced "full-meal" deals. Taco Bell's 59¢, 79¢, and 99¢ menu propelled them from a small player to the fastest-growing firm in the industry. Consequently, fast-food companies have been forced to maintain low prices even when their operating expenses were increasing.

Labor Environment

Some industries have peculiar labor characteristics. The cost of labor is much higher in specific industries (such as health care) that require specialized skills. Unions may also affect the cost of labor. Some manufacturing industries, particularly those in the northern states, have labor unions, and labor costs in these industries are relatively high. Industries that have labor unions may also experience labor strikes. Understanding the labor environment within an industry can help a firm's managers estimate the labor expenses to be incurred from its business.

Regulatory Environment

The federal government may enforce environmental rules, or may prevent a firm from operating in particular locations or from engaging in particular types of business. All industries are subject to some form of government regulation.

In 1995, an effort was made to reduce federal regulations. President Clinton and Congress eliminated sixteen thousand pages of regulations. However, complying with existing regulations can still be very expensive. Many federal contracts involving businesses have more than one hundred pages of specifications.

Regulation is much more restrictive in some industries than others. Automobile and oil firms have been subject to increased environmental regulations. Firms in the banking, insurance, and utility industries have been subject to regulations on the types of services they can provide. An entrepreneur who wishes to enter any industry must recognize all the regulations that are imposed on that industry.

The Justice Department of the U.S. federal government attempts to prevent price-fixing, in which two or more firms in the same industry set prices. In the early 1990s U.S. airlines were forced to provide millions of dollars in discounts to passengers in order to settle a price fixing lawsuit.

SURGEON GENERAL'S WARNING: Cigarette Smoke Contains Carbon Monoxide.

Cigarette manufacturers, in particular, face tremendous government regulation when it comes to advertising, distributing, and packaging their products.

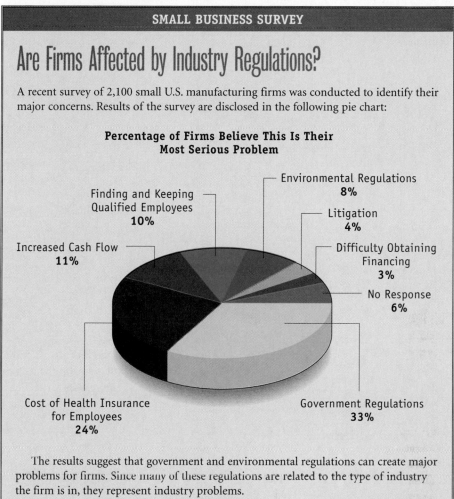

Are Firms Affected by Industry Regulations?

A recent survey of 2,100 small U.S. manufacturing firms was conducted to identify their major concerns. Results of the survey are disclosed in the following pie chart:

Percentage of Firms Believe This Is Their Most Serious Problem

- Environmental Regulations 8%
- Litigation 4%
- Difficulty Obtaining Financing 3%
- No Response 6%
- Government Regulations 33%
- Cost of Health Insurance for Employees 24%
- Increased Cash Flow 11%
- Finding and Keeping Qualified Employees 10%

The results suggest that government and environmental regulations can create major problems for firms. Since many of these regulations are related to the type of industry the firm is in, they represent industry problems.

Firms that have already been operating within an industry must also monitor industry regulations because regulations may change over time. For example, regulations have recently been reduced in the banking industry, which has allowed banks more freedom to engage in other types of business. Some banks have attempted to capitalize on the change in regulations by offering new services.

Summary of Industry Characteristics

All of the industry characteristics just identified must be considered to determine their impact on a firm's performance. The means by which these characteristics affect a firm's profits are shown in Exhibit 5.2. Changes in industry demand and competition affect the demand for a firm's products and therefore affect its revenue. Since these industry characteristics influence the quantity of products that the firm produces, they also affect operating costs, such as manufacturing and administrative expenses. Any changes in the labor and regulatory environments typically affect a firm's expenses. The overall effect on profits is dependent on the individual impact each characteristic has on either the firm's revenue or expenses.

The potential impact of industry demand and competition on a firm's performance can be confirmed by assessing any business periodical that discusses how a

Exhibit 5.2
Industry Effects on a Firm's
Performance

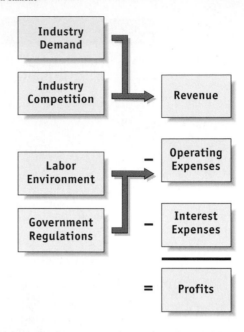

particular industry performed recently. Exhibit 5.3 discloses the performance of various industries, along with the reason for that performance. The industry demand or competition was cited as the reason for change in the performance of each industry.

INDUSTRY SOURCES

While a firm can attempt to monitor its industry's characteristics, it may also rely on other sources for industry information. The following sources provide useful information about the characteristics of each industry:

❶ *Value Line:* The *Value Line Investment Survey* provides valuable information about numerous publicly traded companies, including financial characteristics, forecasts of earnings, and general information about the respective industries.

Exhibit 5.3
Examples of How Industry
Conditions Affect
Business Performance

1995 Industry Performance	Reason
Railroad earnings increased	Increased demand for railroad shipments of coal and grain
Express mail earnings declined	Increased competition among firms
Homebuilders' earnings declined	Reduced demand for homes because of high interest rates
Lumber company earnings declined	Reduced demand for lumber because of a reduced demand for homes (due to high interest rates)
Electric utility earnings declined	Reduced demand for electricity because of mild weather

2 *Standard and Poor's:* The *Standard and Poor's Industry Outlook* provides industry data and assessments for several different industries. A firm can use this source to forecast the industry demand, competition, labor environment, and regulatory environment.

EXPOSURE TO INDUSTRY CONDITIONS

2 | **Explain why some firms are more exposed to industry conditions.**

The exposure of a firm to a given industry's conditions is dependent on its particular characteristics. Some firms are more exposed to industry conditions, which means that their performance is affected more by those conditions. Two of the key characteristics that affect a firm's exposure to industry conditions are the firm's market share and the firm's focus on its main industry.

Firm's Market Share

The degree to which a firm is affected by a change in industry conditions is dependent on its market share, or its share of total sales in the industry (or market). A firm that controls a larger share of the market will normally benefit more from an increase in industry demand. However, this firm would also be hurt more than other firms as a result of the decrease in industry demand.

Exhibit 5.4 illustrates how firms with a larger market share are affected more by changes in industry demand. It assumes that an industry has just two firms: Firm X with 80 percent market share and Firm Y with 20 percent market share. In Year 1, the total industry sales were just over 10,000,000 units. However, in Year 2, total industry sales declined to 5,000,000 units. Assuming that each firm's market share remained unchanged, Firm X's sales declined by about 4,000,000 units while Firm Y's sales declined by about 1,000,000 units.

A firm does not have much control over the industry demand. However, it may attempt to forecast industry demand, which may allow it to forecast the demand for its own product. For example, assume a firm expects industry demand to equal

Exhibit 5.4
Influence of Market Share on
Exposure to Industry Conditions

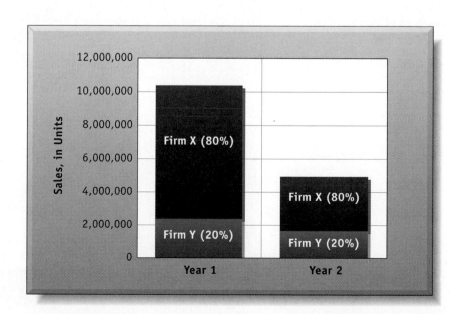

5,000,000 units over the next year. If its market share is 20 percent, its forecast of the demand for its product is as follows:

$$\begin{aligned}
\text{Demand for Firm's Product} &= \begin{array}{c}\text{Firm's Market} \\ \text{Share}\end{array} \times \begin{array}{c}\text{Industry} \\ \text{Demand}\end{array} \\
&= \qquad 20\% \qquad \times \quad 5{,}000{,}000 \text{ units} \\
&= 1{,}000{,}000 \text{ units}
\end{aligned}$$

If conditions change and cause industry demand to decline, the forecasted demand for the firm's product should be revised. For example, if the forecasted industry demand from the previous example was revised to be 4,000,000 units, the demand for the firm's product would only be 800,000 units (computed as 20% × 4,000,000 units).

Firm's Focus on Its Main Industry

Firms that focus all of their business in one industry are generally more exposed to the industry's conditions. For example, Smith Corona Corporation focused its business on producing typewriters and word processors, and was highly exposed to any changes in the total demand for these office machines. When the demand for these machines declined due to increased use of computers, Smith Corona filed for bankruptcy.

Exhibit 5.5 illustrates how the changes in industry earnings can vary substantially among industries. The aluminum and paper container industries experienced major improvement, while the performance of other industries such as retailing and broadcasting declined.

Exhibit 5.6 illustrates how return on equity varies among three different industries. It may be relatively high for one particular industry in a specific period but relatively low for that industry in another period. The exhibit confirms that the financial performance of any firm is subject to the performance of its respective industry.

Exhibit 5.5
Comparison of Performance across Industries

Note: The percentage change is based on the period from the second quarter of 1994 to the second quarter of 1995.

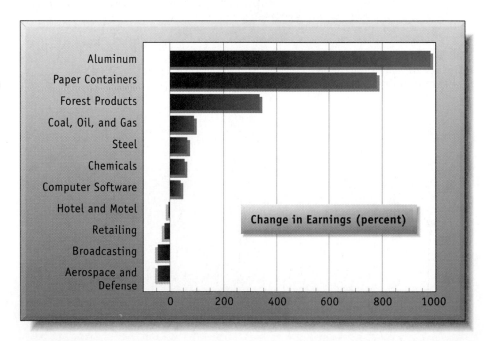

Exhibit 5.6
Return on Equity for Three Different Industries

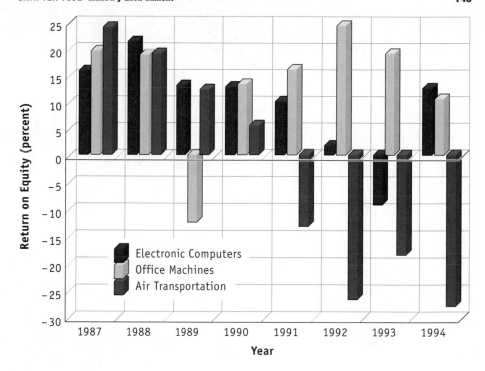

The Coca-Cola Company has been a world leader in diversifying into overseas markets. It is the leading seller of soft drinks in many countries including Prague, Czech Republic shown above.

REDUCING EXPOSURE THROUGH DIVERSIFICATION   A firm may desire to reduce its exposure to the possibility of poor conditions in its respective industry. One solution is to diversify its businesses across several different industries. Westinghouse Electric Corporation does business in electronics, real estate development, environmental cleaning services, and other industries. When a firm diversifies its business across different industries, it can attempt to switch its emphasis when industry demand shifts. For example, if Westinghouse anticipates a large decline in the demand for its real estate development services, it may adjust its operations to focus more on electronics and less on real estate development. In this way, it can reduce any adverse effects that could be caused by a decline in any particular industry. Ford Motor Company has diversification by producing a variety of trucks along with its cars. In 1995, demand for its cars was stagnant, but it benefited from a large increase in the demand for trucks and became the leading seller in the U.S. truck market.

Seagrams Company traditionally focused on sales of alcoholic beverages, but its performance was adversely affected by the decline in demand for alcoholic drinks. It has responded by producing nonalcoholic beverages to reduce its risk of poor performance because of exposure to a single industry.

The following comments from a recent annual report by Textron (a large diversified firm) confirm the potential benefits of diversification:

> *Textron's presence in diverse industries helps achieve balance and stability in a variety of economic environments by providing insulation from business and industry cycles. More specifically, we were able to maintain consistent growth . . . because the growth of our Aircraft, Automotive, Industrial and Finance businesses more than offset the downturns in the Systems and Components segment.*

Exhibit 5.7
How Diversification Can Influence the Return on Equity

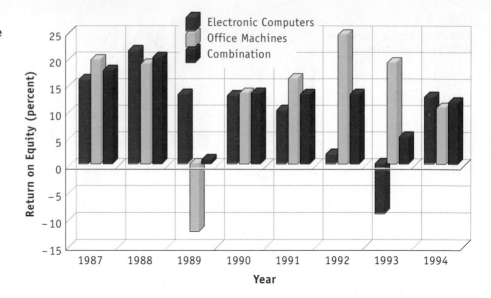

Exhibit 5.7 shows the average return on equity for two related industries and for a combination of those two industries. Notice how a diversified combination of the two industries creates a more stable return on investment over time. This occurs because the firm is not completely exposed to the general performance of a single industry. In a period when one industry performs poorly, the other industry may perform well. Exxon benefited from diversifying into petrochemical businesses because the performance of its oil business was highly exposed to changes in the market price of crude oil.

While diversification can effectively reduce a firm's exposure to one industry, firms should only diversify across industries in which they have sufficient expertise. During the 1980s, many firms diversified across industries completely unrelated to their expertise. Many of these unrelated businesses performed poorly and were sold by the firms during the 1990s. For example, Chrysler entered the corporate aircraft business, military defense business, and car rental business. It lost its focus by attempting to engage in too many different businesses, and incurred higher expenses than expected. W. R. Grace (producer of chemicals) engaged in health-care, coal mining, and numerous other businesses. In 1995, it sold many of these businesses so that it could focus on its core businesses.

COMPETING WITHIN AN INDUSTRY

3 Explain how a firm can compete within its industry.

Intense competition can separate the performance of the well-managed firms from the poorly managed firms in an industry. When the airlines industry became more competitive, some of the poorly managed airlines failed. The well-managed airlines captured some of the market share that was lost by those that failed. Similarly, when the banking industry became more competitive and many commercial banks failed, the well-run commercial banks were able to capture some of the market share that was lost by those that failed.

Given the influence of industry competition on a firm's performance, a firm should perform two tasks to assess the competition:

➤ Identify the competitors.
➤ Develop a competitive advantage.

Identify the Competitors

Every firm should be able to identify its competitors and measure the degree of competition. Each industry has **segments,** or subsets that reflect a specific type of business and the perceived quality. Thus, an industry can be narrowly defined by segmenting the industry according to type of business and quality. Segmenting the industry in this way helps identify the main competition.

segments subsets of the market that reflect a specific type of business and the perceived quality

SEGMENTING BY TYPE OF BUSINESS   Within an industry, some firms may focus on specific types of customers. For example, in the car rental industry, some firms (such as National Car Rental Systems) focus heavily on business customers, while others (such as Hertz) are more evenly split between businesses and individuals on vacation. The furniture industry has segments such as outdoor furniture, bedroom furniture, and office furniture. The degree of competition within each segment may vary. There may be heavy competition in bedroom furniture but little competition in outdoor furniture. A firm that focuses only on the production of outdoor furniture is not concerned with the demand for office furniture. Therefore, it is helpful for a firm to narrowly define its industry before assessing the degree of competition.

SEGMENTING BY PERCEIVED QUALITY   Once the firm defines the industry by the type of business, it should assess the different quality segments that exist. Exhibit 5.8 shows different quality segments (based on customer perceptions) in the market for small cars. Each type of car in this market is represented with a point. Some cars, such as the BMW 325 and the Corvette, are perceived to have high quality (measured according to engine size and other features that customers desire) and a relatively high price. Other small cars have a moderate quality level and a lower price, such as the Toyota Celica and the Firebird. The Ford Escort and the Cavalier represent cars in a lower quality and price segment. Because each consumer focuses only on one particular market segment, the key competitors are within that same segment. For example, the Escort and Cavalier are competitors within the low-priced segment. The Escort is not viewed as a competitor to the higher priced cars.

Many firms create products that are designed for different population segments. Firms commonly expand by producing different types of the same product, which are offered to various segments. General Motors produces the Cavalier for the low-priced, small-car segment, the Firebird for the moderate-priced segment, and the

Exhibit 5.8
Identifying Industry Segments

This BMW automobile is targeted at the high-priced segment in the automobile industry.

Corvette for the high-priced segment. They may produce a high-quality product for consumers who can afford to pay a high price, and a low-quality product for consumers who are less concerned about quality and more concerned about price. Tire companies such as Goodyear and Michelin produce tires that fit the high-priced and low-priced segments. Beer producers such as Anheuser-Busch and Miller Brewing produce different types of beer to satisfy high-priced and low-priced segments. Most airlines provide first-class (high-priced) and coach (low-priced) seats to satisfy different segments.

ANTICIPATING CHANGES IN COMPETITION   The competitors within an industry segment change over time. New firms may enter the market; others who were in the market but were unsuccessful may exit. Many competing firms in the same market attempt to expand. It is not unusual for every firm competing within a specific industry segment to share the same goal of increasing market share. Yet, all competitors within an industry segment cannot increase their market share at the same time. When some competitors gain market share, other competitors lose.

To understand how firms can be affected by changes in competition, consider the airline industry. In recent years, many new airlines began servicing specific routes. They attracted customers by offering low airfares. In response, some existing airlines reduced their airfares to discourage customers from switching to the new airlines. In general, the existing airlines were adversely affected by the new competition in two ways. First, their sales of airline tickets declined, as some customers switched to the new airlines. Second, the prices of many airline tickets were reduced to match the prices of new competitors. Both effects result in a decline in the revenue of the existing airlines, as well as a decline in their earnings. Recent annual reports by airlines, such as Delta Airlines, confirm the adverse effects of increased competition.

Firms in various other industries have also acknowledged that they have been adversely affected by more intense competition. Kellogg Company stated that it was adversely affected by increased competition in the cereal industry. Federal Express claimed that its earnings were hurt by fierce competition in the express mail industry.

How Information Technology Can Create a Competitive Advantage

When information technology is introduced by a firm, it may not only have a major impact on the firm, but on the entire industry. Consider the hospital supply firms that supply nearly all of the non-pharmaceutical products (such as bandages and casts), used by hospitals. In the 1960s, the industry was highly fragmented, with thousands of small suppliers competing for hospital business. The medical costs at the time were not as big an issue as they are today, so the entire purchasing process in hospitals was inefficient.

American Hospital Supply Co. (AHSC), one of the many players in the industry, perceived that information technology might provide a means to improve its market share. It began by placing computer cards in supply room stock bins, informing stock clerks that it was time to reorder. If they chose to reorder from AHSC, they simply mailed in the card to the sales representative. All the information they needed was already contained on the card, which was fed into their computer.

With the success of the stock cards, AHSC began to offer inventory tracking services to hospitals. Such services were viewed very positively by hospitals as few of them had computers, which were both expensive and hard to operate. AHSC began placing terminals in hospital supply rooms which could be used for convenient on-line ordering. The technology gave AHSC an advantage over other competitors.

By the late 1970s, the innovations introduced by AHSC had transformed the hospital supply industry. Rather than consisting of numerous small regional players, the industry became national in scope. And AHSC, the first company to recognize how technology could be employed, commanded a large share of the new market.

Develop a Competitive Advantage

Once a firm has identified and assessed its key competitors, it must search for ways to increase or at least maintain its market share. A firm must assess its specific industry segment to determine whether it has a competitive advantage. The following characteristics could create a competitive advantage for a firm:

➤ Low-cost production
➤ Better quality
➤ Product differentiation

In 1995, Miller debuted Miller Beer which is viewed as a direct competitor to Budweiser.

LOW-COST PRODUCTION   If a firm can produce a product of similar quality at a lower cost, it could price the product lower than its competitors. This should enable that firm to attain a larger market share. For example, assume that a firm can produce high-quality outdoor furniture at a lower price than the other firms in the high-priced segment. This may allow the firm to charge a lower price so that it can capture a larger share of the high-priced outdoor furniture market. The low production cost may result from efficient management of its employees (human resources) and its production process.

Some firms attempt to achieve a price advantage even when they do not have a cost advantage. For example, an entrepreneur may notice that the only gas station in a populated area has set high prices on its gasoline. The entrepreneur may consider establishing a new gas station in the area, with lower prices as its competitive advantage. However, the existing gas station may lower its gas prices in response to the new competitor. In this example, the entrepreneur's competitive advantage may be eliminated unless it has a cost advantage.

Airlines commonly attempt to achieve a price advantage over their competitors by advertising special fares on various routes over a particular period. The objective is to attract a higher demand by pulling customers away from other airlines. In

CROSS-FUNCTIONAL TEAMWORK

Industry Effects Across Business Functions

Managers of a firm have different responsibilities and therefore assess different aspects of the industry environment. Production managers monitor changes in labor costs in a particular industry when anticipating how their production costs may change. They monitor changes in the industry's technology, since their production costs will be influenced by the level of technology. They also monitor regulatory changes in the industry that could require revisions to the production process. Such revisions may also affect the cost of production. They may also monitor the level of industry demand so that they can determine the proper volume of products that their firm should produce.

Marketing managers monitor new competitors in the industry to become aware of the features of competing products. This industry information is considered when they search for strategies to make their product superior to those sold by competitors. Marketing managers must obtain production cost information from production managers when deciding how to make their product superior.

Financial managers monitor the industry environment to determine how much money they can afford to borrow. If the competition in the industry is intense, the firm may lose its market share to other competitors. Therefore, a firm should limit its debt so that it is capable of covering future interest payments on that debt. Financial managers should obtain information from the marketing managers about the intensity of competition in the industry so that they can determine the amount of funds that will be available (from sales) to cover future interest payments.

In general, the industry environment can affect a firm's production, marketing, and finance functions in different ways. The overall assessment of potential industry effects requires input from each function.

many cases, other airlines respond by lowering their airfares by the same amount. However, if some of the airlines are less efficient, they may not be able to continue the low fares for a long period of time (because their costs may exceed the fares charged). Thus, the more efficient firms may drive the inefficient competitors out of the industry.

BETTER QUALITY If a firm can produce a product of better quality without incurring excessive costs, it has a competitive advantage over other competitors in the same price range. For example, within the low-priced outdoor furniture market, one firm may be perceived to produce higher quality furniture than other firms. If its furniture is priced about the same as others in its segment, its superior quality creates a competitive advantage within the low-priced outdoor furniture segment.

Various characteristics may cause a product to be of better quality. It may be easier to use, may last longer, or may have better service. The specific characteristics that determine perceived quality vary among products. For soft drinks, quality may be measured by taste. For outdoor furniture, quality may be measured by durability. For computers, quality may be measured by ease of use, the service provided, and processing speed.

PRODUCT DIFFERENTIATION Firms commonly attempt to identify particular needs of some customers so that they can differentiate their product (or service) to satisfy those needs. For example, some contact lenses are made for permanent wear. Other lenses must be cleaned daily because some customers cannot wear lenses permanently. A third type of lens is disposable for those customers who are unable to keep the lenses clean and frequently need new lenses. Rarely can a particular product serve all customers, because customers desire different features for a given product.

Computer firms tend to differentiate their computers in ways to attract customers with specific preferences. Computers vary in power, size (some are portable), warranty, and service. They are also made to allow for replaceable components so that the product can precisely fit customers' needs.

Customer preferences for each particular type of service also vary, allowing firms in each service industry to differentiate their service. Some travel agencies specialize in cruise vacations. Others focus on international travel packages. The choice of a travel agent may be dependent on specific customer needs.

As time passes, customer preferences for a particular product's features can change. Firms must attempt to recognize these changes within the industry so that they can revise the products they offer. Failure to adapt can cause a reduction in the firm's market share. For several years, IBM conducted business without paying close attention to changes in industry conditions (such as a preference by many business customers for personal rather than mainframe computers). During that time their annual report stated that "IBM failed to keep pace with a significant change in the industry." General Motors was also slow to react to changes in customer preferences within the automobile industry. These firms improved their performance once they recognized the importance of responding to changes in customer preferences.

Assessing the Industry Environment from a Global Perspective

 When U.S. firms engage in international business, they must consider the segments within the foreign countries of concern. A specific product that is classified in a specific segment in the United States may be classified in a different segment in other countries. A product that is perceived as an inexpensive necessity in the United States may be perceived as an expensive luxury product in less-developed countries. U.S. firms may revise the quality and price of their products to satisfy a particular market segment. For example, Procter and Gamble produces a wide variety of household products that U.S. consumers may view as basic necessities. Yet, those products are not affordable to consumers in some less-developed countries. Rather than ignore those countries, Procter and Gamble has revised its product and pricing strategies to fit the country of concern. As stated in its recent annual report: "In some countries where incomes are low, striking this balance between quality and price requires us to market a diaper that offers more basic features, at a substantially lower price, than the premium diaper we sell in many countries." This example illustrates how a firm's assessment of market segment can vary across countries, and therefore how its product and pricing strategies may be revised in accordance with each foreign country's characteristics.

BUSINESS DILEMMA

Industry Effects On College Health Club

Sue Kramer, owner of College Health Club (CHC), is assessing the expected earnings of CHC. She expects that the two main industry characteristics that will affect CHC's future earnings are industry demand and industry competition, and summarizes her view of these two characteristics.

INDUSTRY DEMAND

The industry demand for health club services will continue to rise as people continue to focus on health and fitness. Sue is concerned about industry demand only within the local area, since the only potential customers live or work within thirty miles of CHC.

INDUSTRY COMPETITION

Presently, CHC has two competitors. One competitor is about twenty miles away and has prices similar to those of CHC, but only offers aerobics classes (no weight room facilities). The other competitor is a few miles from CHC but has not focused on college students. It has more facilities, but its annual membership fees are much higher than those of CHC.

Sue Kramer closely assessed these two competitors when she opened her health club across from the local college campus. The fact that no club was accommodating the college students motivated her to establish CHC. In the few months since its opening, CHC has been successful in attracting students. Sue still expects to achieve her initial goal of three hundred memberships in the first year, at an annual membership fee of $250.

Dilemma

Sue's main concern is that new competitors will be established and will pull away some of her customers. She expects that if a new competitor is established near the college campus, CHC may bring in only about two hundred annual memberships over the first year (assuming she does not lower CHC's membership fee). CHC's expenses (such as the lease expense and the equipment) would not be affected by the number of memberships. Sue wants to forecast how CHC's performance (specifically earnings) would be affected if a new competitor entered the industry. She also wants to forecast CHC's performance if she lowers the annual membership fee (to existing and potential members) to $200 as a way of competing against any new competitors. At such a low fee, Sue believes that CHC would attract 240 memberships if a new competitor did enter the industry.

Estimate the first year's revenue, total expenses, and earnings of CHC under Situation 1 (no new competition), Situation 2 (new competition and no change in CHC's membership fee), and Situation 3 (new competition and a reduction in CHC's membership fee).

Solution

Since CHC's expenses are generally fixed regardless of the quantity of memberships, Sue focuses on how the revenue of CHC is affected by the competition. Yet, to show how the profits would be affected, the forecasted operating expenses (of $90,000) and interest expenses (of $6,000) are also shown in Exhibit 5.9 (these estimates were initially developed in Chapter 1).

Based on the information provided, the expected impact on CHC's performance over its first year is shown in Exhibit 5.9. Situation 1 reflects the existing situation, in which no new competition enters the industry. Situation 2 reflects a new competitor, resulting in only two hundred memberships for CHC. This results in revenue of $50,000, which is $25,000 less than what was originally anticipated. Situation 3 reflects a lower membership price by CHC as a means of battling the new competition. This strategy can reduce the adverse effect of new competition on CHC memberships. However, it also means that CHC will receive less revenue from each member. Given Sue's expectations of 240 annual memberships at a membership price of $200, CHC's revenue would be $48,000.

Exhibit 5.9
Assessment of Profits of CHC Under Three Different Situations

	Situation 1: No New Competition	Situation 2: New Competition and No Change in Membership Fee	Situation 3: New Competition and a Reduced Membership Fee
Price of Membership	$250	$250	$200
× Quantity of Memberships	× 300	× 200	× 240
= Revenue	= $75,000	= $50,000	= $48,000
− Operating Expenses	− $90,000	− $90,000	− $90,000
− Interest Expenses	− $ 6,000	− $ 6,000	− $ 6,000
= Earnings	= − $21,000	= − $46,000	= − $48,000

Based on her assessment, Sue decides that she will not lower the membership price even if a new competitor does enter the industry. However, she recognizes that she may need to differentiate CHC's services in various ways to compete with any new competitors. CHC may incur some additional expenses when differentiating its services.

Additional Issues for Discussion

1 Explain how the increased popularity of exercise videos and portable weight machines could affect CHC's earnings.

2 How could Sue Kramer differentiate her services to maintain her customers (mostly college students) even if a new competitor enters the market?

3 Like other industries, the health club industry has segments that reflect a specific type of business and quality. Describe the characteristics of CHC that appeal to college students.

SUMMARY

1 The main industry characteristics that influence business performance are:

➤ industry demand,
➤ industry competition,
➤ labor environment, and
➤ regulatory environment.

Industry demand and the degree of industry competition affect the demand for a firm's products or services, and therefore affect the firm's revenue. The labor and regulatory environments typically affect the firm's expenses. Since a firm's profits equal its revenue minus its expenses, its profits are influenced by these industry factors.

2 A firm is more exposed to an industry's conditions when it has a large market share and focuses most of its business within that industry. As the industry's conditions change, most of its business will be affected. Firms can reduce their exposure to industry conditions by diversifying their business across industries.

3 A firm can battle the competition by identifying its main competitors and then attempting to develop a competitive advantage. To identify its main competitors, it must recognize the segment of the industry that it serves. It can develop a competitive advantage within that industry segment through efficient production (which allows it to charge a lower price), better quality, or product differentiation.

KEY TERMS

industry demand   market share   segments

REVIEW QUESTIONS

1 Identify and explain the main characteristics of the automobile industry that influence business performance.

2 While a firm's management can attempt to monitor its industry's characteristics, it may also rely on other sources for industry information. Comment.

3 Explain the production manager's responsibility in assessing the industry environment.

4 Discuss what happens to a firm that has a large market share in an industry in which demand suddenly increases.

5 How would a firm's management identify its competitors and measure the degree of competition?

6 When a firm is subject to less competition in an industry, why is it typically more profitable?

7 List some characteristics that could create a competitive advantage for a firm.

8 Give some examples of how firms can be affected by changes in competition.

9 Distinguish between the responsibilities of a marketing manager and a financial manager in monitoring a particular industry.

10 Explain why the cost of labor is so high in the health-care industry.

DISCUSSION QUESTIONS

1 Do you believe business enterprise should be regulated by the federal government, or should the marketplace determine price? Discuss.

2 A group is discussing how competitive forces must be preserved at all costs within the marketplace of a free enterprise system. What are your views?

3 Assume you are ready to start your own business. What business functions take precedence in launching your business? Is one more important than the other?

4 Assume you are a production manager in the automobile industry. Should your operation be labor intensive or capital (machinery) intensive? Discuss.

5 Consider a car that was typically classified in the low-price segment. Yet, it has been unable to compete there because it is priced higher than the other cars in that segment. What alternative strategies are possible for the car as it is redesigned for the next year?

RUNNING YOUR OWN BUSINESS

1 Describe the main competitors that would be competing against your business. Would it be easy for additional competitors to enter your market? Could you effectively expand your business?

2 How would the performance of your business be affected by industry conditions? Explain.

3 What competitive advantage can your business sustain compared with the competition?

INVESTING IN THE STOCK OF A BUSINESS

Using the annual report of the firm in which you would like to invest, complete the following:

1 Describe the competition within your firm's industry. If the annual report does not contain information, try to find a magazine or newspaper article that discusses the competitive environment within your firm's industry. How successful is your firm compared with its competitors?

2 Was your firm's performance affected by industry conditions last year? If so, how?

CASE 1 Exposure of Software Firms to Industry Conditions

The characteristics of the software industry are being reshaped to face new technological demands created by competitive forces within the industry. Industry demand has increased substantially. Most software manufacturers are experiencing record sales and profits, aided by new products and aggressive sales efforts.

High-tech products such as Windows 95 and Windows NT, manufactured and distributed by Microsoft, have become market leaders. Since its introduction in 1995, sales of Windows 95 have reached approximately $18 to $19 million. Other market leaders, such as Informix Corporation and Oracle Corporation, are extremely competitive and are planning to introduce new software applications to compete with Microsoft's best-selling products.

The market leaders' exposure to industry conditions is affected by two primary characteristics: increased market share and a single-industry focus. Despite escalating sales and profits, software manufacturers face a tremendous risk because they have not diversified away from the software applications industry. New competitors are entering this highly profitable industry every day, making it an extremely competitive market.

Questions

1 Is industry demand for software applications increasing or decreasing? Explain.

2 How can Microsoft develop a competitive edge within the software industry?

3 If new competitors enter the industry, how would prices and revenue of Microsoft be affected?

CASE 2 Impact of Industry Conditions on Pharmaceutical Firms

The pharmaceutical industry is characterized by three primary manufacturers who control 90 percent of the market share within this segment. The producers of insulin, used to treat diabetes, each have approximately 30 percent of the market share. The primary insulin industry characteristics that impact business performance are similar for each firm.

The industry is projected to grow 10 percent annually for the next five years because of an increase in the diabetic population. There are no apparent plans for new entrants in this health industry during the next five years. The increase in revenue should be divided equally among the three manufacturers, and profits should increase approximately the same for each of the producers.

The regulatory environment is another primary factor that impacts profits for all three firms. Recently the Food and Drug Administration (FDA) imposed strict guidelines on advertising and the labeling of Humulin insulin. The FDA's guidelines have affected the entire pharmaceutical industry and are expected to impact the earnings of the manufacturers who produce and distribute this drug.

Employment rates have also had an impact on the pharmaceutical industry. Employment has increased by 10 percent throughout the industry, and all three manufacturers have increased their payroll accordingly.

The three manufacturers of insulin are highly exposed to the industry's conditions, since they have a large market share. In the future, management will consider diversification because of the strong commitment these firms have given to the treatment of this disease. A cure for diabetes may be found soon, and these firms must plan accordingly.

Questions

1 What are the main industry characteristics that affect the demand for insulin produced by each firm?

2 Discuss any regulatory forces that have a positive or negative effect on profit.

3 Why are manufacturers of insulin exposed to much uncertainty regarding future earnings? How could these manufacturers reduce their risk in such a volatile industry?

VIDEO CASE　Exposure to Weak Industry Conditions

Choctaw—the name reflects the Indian ancestry of founder Gordon Gamble, now chairman emeritus—supplies industrial customers with valves, fittings, and other supplies and equipment. At the outset the customers were all in the oil business, and the outlook was bright. Plant construction and maintenance activity were flourishing.

But the oil-industry downturn of the early '80s smudged that outlook. East Texas—Galena Park is on the Houston ship channel—was full of suppliers like Choctaw. It was a challenge for the company just to stay alive.

Manufacturers of valves, fittings, etc., also faced stiff competition. That was when some of their prices were cut below Choctaw's inventory costs. The company managed to win price breaks that tided it over.

However, the oil-industry downturn created a greater problem, that of finding new markets. Choctaw, which is now run by Gordon Gamble's son, Bret, president, and his daughter, Zoe Gamble-Jones, vice president, thinks its original market is unlikely ever to return to former levels. So its sights were set on the aerospace industry, food and beverage plants, and municipalities. The company looked for ways to serve needs—consolidating orders to reduce the number of purchase orders, for example, or working out blanket arrangements for ordering miscellaneous items.

Choctaw, which has developed a quality procedure manual, improved quality with an effort that leaned heavily on outside training and idea exchanges between management and labor.

The company rewards its 11 employees with what it calls CROW money—"Choctaw Remembers Our Work." A share of profits is set aside at year-end, and employees get varying bonuses that depend on the company's performance.

Honors the company has won are evidence of the success of the effort to find new customers. Choctaw was nominated as Frito-Lay's 1991 "minority vendor of the year" and was the 1992 winner of an annual Boeing "small disadvantaged business supplier" award.

Sales last year were $2 million—a 20 percent rise in three years. Says Gordon Gamble: "Choctaw is alive and kicking."

Questions

1 Explain why Choctaw's performance was so sensitive to conditions in the oil industry. Explain how Choctaw reduced its exposure to these conditions.

2 Why doesn't every business follow Choctaw's example and diversify its business across industries?

3 Assume that the aerospace industry is booming, resulting in a substantial increase in the demand for Choctaw's supplies by aerospace firms. Should Choctaw discontinue offering supplies to other industries and devote all its attention to providing supplies to aerospace firms?

THE Coca-Cola COMPANY ANNUAL REPORT PROJECT

The following questions apply concepts learned in this chapter to The Coca-Cola Company. Read page 13 and the section "Bottling Partners" on page 40 of The Coca-Cola Company annual report before answering these questions.

1 Is The Coca-Cola Company directly in the soft drink bottling business?

2 Explain why the Company's competition varies by the specific products (Coca-Cola, Sprite, Minute Maid, etc.) that it sells. Why do you think The Coca-Cola Company views tap water as a major competitor?

3 What does The Coca-Cola Company consider to be its current share of sales?

IN-TEXT STUDY GUIDE

Answers are in an appendix at the back of the book.

True or False

1 Industries are never subject to some form of government regulation.

2 A firm that faces a high degree of competition can sell a low-quality product at a high price and therefore generate a high level of profit.

3 A firm's performance level can be measured by return on equity, which reflects annual earnings as a proportion of the investment by the firm's stockholders.

4 Firms that focus all of their business in one industry are generally less exposed to the industry's conditions.

5 Most competitors within an industry segment can increase their market share at the same time.

6 The main task of finance managers is to monitor new competitors in the industry to become aware of the features of competing products.

7 Industry demand and the degree of industry competition affect the demand for a firm's products or services.

8 A firm is normally more able to control a large proportion of the market when it has few competitors.

9 Improved product quality could create a competitive advantage for a firm.

10 A firm can safely conclude that it will perform well over the next year if there are favorable economic conditions in the United States.

Multiple Choice

11 Managers monitor changes in labor costs in a particular industry when anticipating how changes may occur in:
a) marketing costs.
b) macroeconomics.
c) production costs.
d) social responsibility.
e) industry demand.

12 The performance of a firm can be highly dependent on the following industry characteristics except for:
a) regulatory environment.
b) labor environment.
c) industry competition.
d) industry demand.
e) gross domestic product.

13 During the 1980s, many firms diversified across industries completely unrelated to their:
a) business ethics.
b) expertise.
c) management styles.
d) social responsibility.
e) goal of high performance.

14 The performance of the well-managed firm compared with the poorly managed firm in an industry can be highlighted by intense:
a) competition.
b) social responsibility.
c) ethics.
d) conservationism.
e) consumerism.

15 To determine how much money a business can borrow, financial managers monitor the:
a) bank's environment.
b) employee environment.
c) industry environment.
d) socialization process.
e) savings of employees.

16 Over a given time period, a specific industry can perform much better than others because the total demand for the product is high. This is called:
a) industry supply.
b) market share.
c) equilibrium price.
d) industry demand.
e) industry condition.

17 Labor costs are commonly higher in specific industries that have:
a) labor unions.
b) unemployment.
c) savings.
d) demand schedules.
e) interest expense.

18 Industry demand is commonly affected by changes in consumer preferences and:
a) ethics levels.
b) income levels.
c) gross domestic product.
d) supply schedules.
e) labor unions.

19 According to the text, industry regulations have recently been reduced in the:
a) automobile industry.
b) chemical industry.
c) oil industry.
d) banking industry.
e) steel industry.

20 A failure to recognize changes in the industry so that a firm can revise the products it offers can cause a reduction in the firm's:
a) technology schedule.
b) social responsibility.
c) business ethics.
d) market share.
e) equilibrium salary schedule.

21 Managers monitor changes in the following industry characteristics except for:
a) industry demand.
b) gross national product.
c) technology.
d) labor costs.
e) regulatory changes.

22 A firm's share of total sales in the industry is measured by its:
a) industry demand.
b) regulatory environment.
c) market share.
d) competition.
e) employee turnover.

23 The demand for a firm's product equals the firm's market share times:
a) industry demand.
b) gross national product.
c) gross domestic product.
d) inflation rate.
e) unemployment rate.

24 Even if a firm does not have a cost advantage, it may create a(n):
a) inflation advantage.
b) condition advantage.
c) monopoly advantage.
d) price advantage.
e) ethics advantage.

25 Once a firm has identified and assessed its key competitors, it must search for ways to increase or at least maintain its:
a) labor environment.
b) regulatory environment.
c) market share.
d) competition.
e) social costs.

26 Once a firm defines an industry by the type of business, it should assess the existing:
a) level of employees.
b) scrap reworked.

c) labor environment.
d) conservationism.
e) quality segments.

27 An industry characteristic that influences business performance is:
a) social responsibility.
b) competition.
c) machinery.
d) inflation throughout the U.S.
e) gross domestic product.

28 As industry demand changes, so does the _____ of firms in the industry.
a) performance
b) business ethics
c) consumerism
d) conservationism
e) regulatory environment

29 Another name for subsets in an industry that reflect a specific type of business and the perceived quality is:
a) demographics.
b) marketing.
c) sales.
d) segments.
e) economics.

30 A firm must assess its specific industry segment to determine whether it has a(n):
a) forecast.
b) competitive advantage.
c) industry condition.
d) cost differential.
e) shift in supply.

31 A firm can charge a higher price without losing its customers if it does not have much:
a) production.
b) competition.
c) marketing.
d) advertising.
e) industry demand.

32 To reduce its exposure to the possibility of poor conditions in its respective industry, a firm needs to:
a) diversify.
b) socialize.
c) privatize.
d) commercialize.
e) increase its size.

33 Changes in industry demand and competition affect both the demand for a firm's products and the firm's:
a) location.
b) customer service

c) revenue.

d) recycling.

e) segmentation.

34 Two of the key characteristics that affect a firm's exposure to industry conditions are the firm's market share and the firm's focus on its:

a) recycling.

b) downsizing.

c) main industry.

d) fringe market.

e) labor union.

35 A firm may attempt to conduct an industry forecast; however, it does not have much control over:

a) revenue.

b) production costs.

c) production schedules.

d) industry demand.

e) employee hiring.

Access to Industry Information on the World Wide Web

How do firms find out about their industry and their competitors? The Internet has many possible sources, including the home pages of the companies themselves. While many sources of information are free, some commercial services package together information on specific companies for a fee. Dun & Bradstreet Information Services (Exhibit 5.10), is an example of one of the best known of these services. A business manager trying to solve a crisis from a hotel room or home office could access up-to-the-minute news on virtually any topic.

Exhibit 5.10

Dun & Bradstreet Information Services

http://www.dbisna.com/

CHAPTER 6

Global Environment

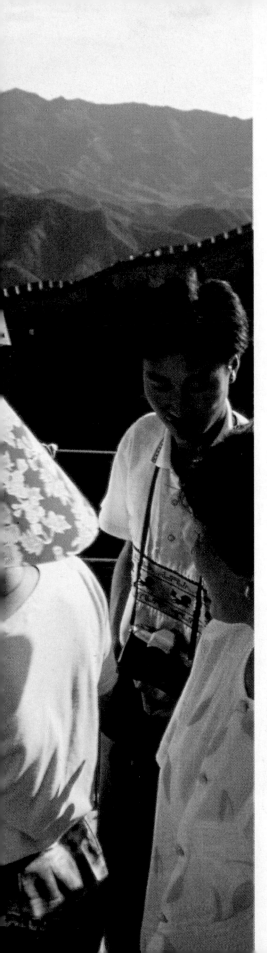

Many U.S. firms have capitalized on opportunities in foreign countries by engaging in international business. The amount of international business has grown in response to the removal of various international barriers. Even small U.S. firms are now engaging in international business by purchasing foreign supplies or by selling their products in foreign countries.

International economic conditions affect a firm's revenue and expenses, and therefore affect its value.

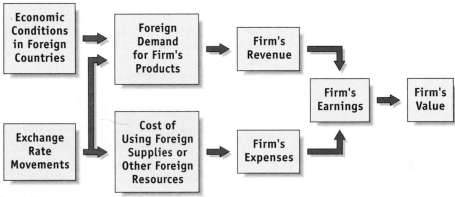

To illustrate how international economic conditions can affect the value of a business, consider the case of The Coca-Cola Company, which generates more than two-thirds of its revenue in foreign countries. In what ways can The Coca-Cola Company attempt to expand its business in China? What characteristics of China could influence its decision to expand there? How would The Coca-Cola Company's performance in China be affected by changes in the value of Chinese currency (the renminbi)? This chapter provides a background on the international environment, which can be used to address these questions.

The **Learning Goals** of this chapter are to:

1 Explain why U.S. firms engage in international business.

2 Describe how firms conduct international business.

3 Explain how foreign characteristics can influence a firm's international business.

4 Explain how exchange rate movements can affect a firm's performance.

WHY FIRMS ENGAGE IN INTERNATIONAL BUSINESS

1 **Explain why U.S. firms engage in international business.**

A firm may have several possible motives for engaging in international business. The following are some of the more common motives:

> ➤ Attract foreign demand
> ➤ Capitalize on technology
> ➤ Use inexpensive resources
> ➤ Diversify internationally

Attract Foreign Demand

Some firms are unable to increase their market share in the United States because of intense competition within their industry. Alternatively, the U.S. demand for the firm's product may decrease because of changes in consumer tastes. Under either of these conditions, a firm might consider foreign markets where potential demand may exist. Many firms, including DuPont, IBM, and PepsiCo, have successfully entered new foreign markets to attract new sources of demand. Wal-Mart Stores recently opened stores in numerous countries, including Mexico and Hong Kong. Boeing (a U.S. producer of aircraft) recently received an order for seventy-seven jets from Singapore Airlines. During the 1990s, Avon Products opened branches in twenty-six different countries, including Brazil, China, and Poland. McDonald's is now in eighty-one different countries and generates more than half of its total revenue from foreign countries. Blockbuster Entertainment has more than two hundred stores in Asia and plans to have about one thousand by the year 2000.

Exhibit 6.1 shows how The Coca-Cola Company's business has expanded globally over time and now has a significant presence in almost every country. It expanded throughout Latin America, Western Europe, Australia and most of Africa before 1984. Since then, it has expanded into Eastern Europe and most of Asia.

PepsiCo Inc. has been actively marketing in Russia for several years and holds a significant market share of the soft drink market. This PepsiCo snack bar in a Moscow subway station sells Pepsi soft drinks and Taco Bell burritos.

Exhibit 6.1
The Coca-Cola Company's Global Expansion

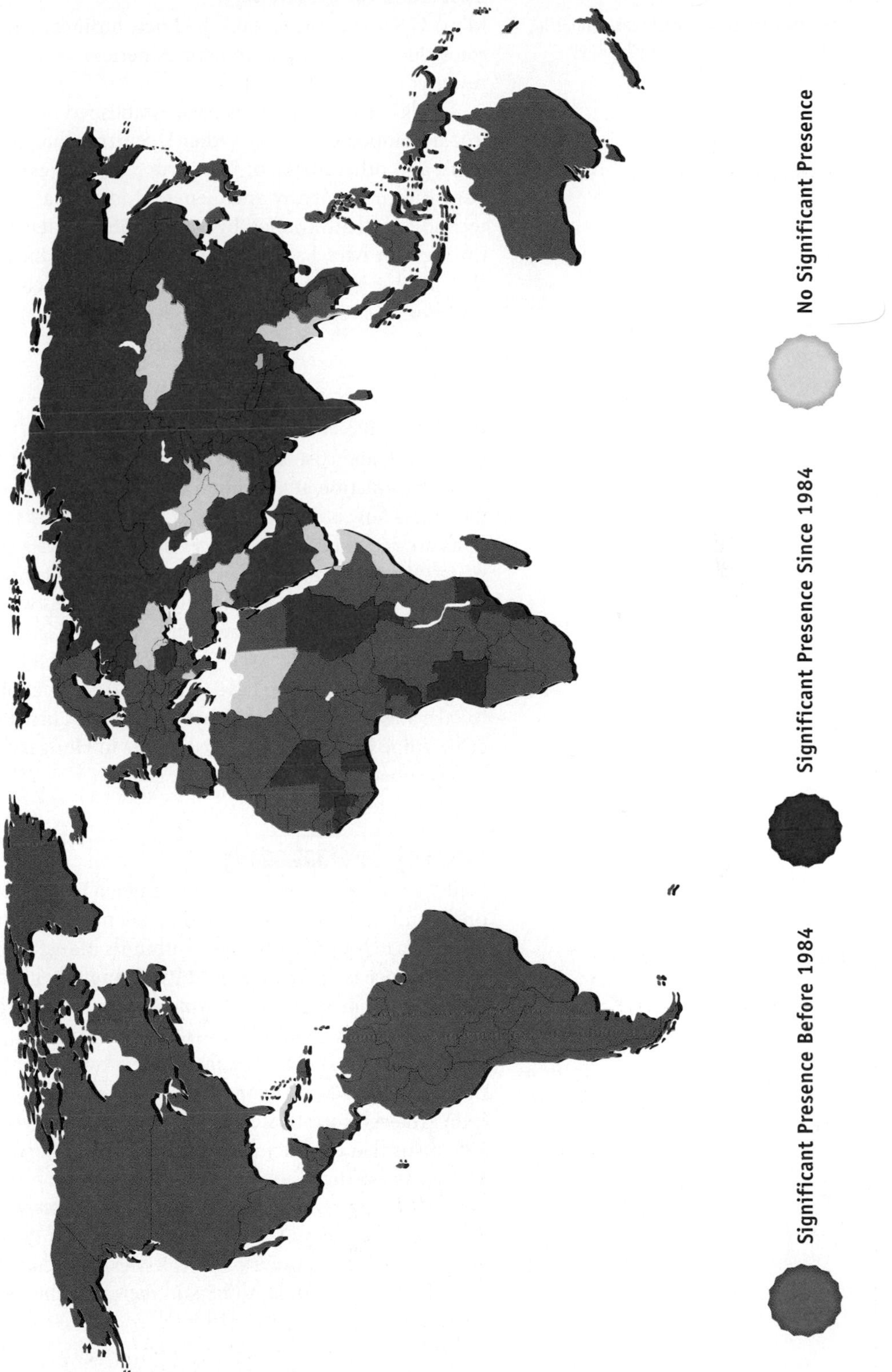

Significant Presence Before 1984

Significant Presence Since 1984

No Significant Presence

Capitalize on Technology

less-developed countries countries that have relatively low technology

Many U.S. firms have established new businesses in the so-called **less-developed countries** (such as those in Latin America), which have relatively low technology resources.

AT&T and other firms have established new telecommunications systems in less-developed countries. Other U.S. firms that create power generation, road systems, and other forms of infrastructure have extensive business in these countries. Ford Motor Company and General Motors have attempted to capitalize on their technological advantages by establishing plants in less-developed countries throughout Asia, Latin America, and Eastern Europe. IBM is doing business with the Chinese government to capitalize on its technology. Westinghouse Electric Corporation has established businesses in the Soviet Republic to capitalize on its technology.

Use Inexpensive Resources

Labor and land costs can vary significantly among countries. Firms often attempt to set up production at a location where land and labor are inexpensive. Exhibit 6.2 illustrates how hourly compensation (labor) costs can vary among countries. The costs are much higher in the developed countries (such as the United States and Germany) than they are in other countries (such as Mexico or Taiwan). Numerous U.S. firms have established subsidiaries in countries where labor costs are low. For example, Converse has shoes manufactured in Mexico. Dell Computer has disk drives and monitors produced in Asia. General Electric, Motorola, Texas Instruments, Dow Chemical, and Corning have established production plants in Singapore and Taiwan to take advantage of lower labor costs. Many firms from the United States and Western Europe have also developed plants in Hungary, Poland, and other parts of Eastern Europe, where labor costs are lower.

Diversify Internationally

When all the assets of a firm are designed to generate sales of a specific product in one country, the profits of the firm are normally unstable. This instability is due to the firm's exposure to changes within its industry or within the economy. The firm's performance is dependent on the demand for this one product, and on the conditions of the one economy in which it conducts business. The firm can reduce such risk by selling its product in various countries.

Exhibit 6.3 shows how economic growth rates can vary among countries. Notice how China and Malaysia have a much higher projected economic growth rate than industrialized countries (such as the United States and West European countries). U.S. firms that conduct international business are affected less by U.S. economic conditions. A U.S. firm's overall performance may be more stable if its product is sold in various countries, so that its business is not solely influenced by the economic conditions in a single country. For example, in 1995 the demand for PepsiCo's products in Mexico declined because of a weak Mexican economy, but economic growth in Brazil, the Netherlands, and Spain increased the overall demand for PepsiCo's products.

Combination of Motives

Many U.S. firms engage in international business because of a combination of motives that were just described. For example, when Digital Equipment Corporation engaged in international business, it attracted new demand from customers in for-

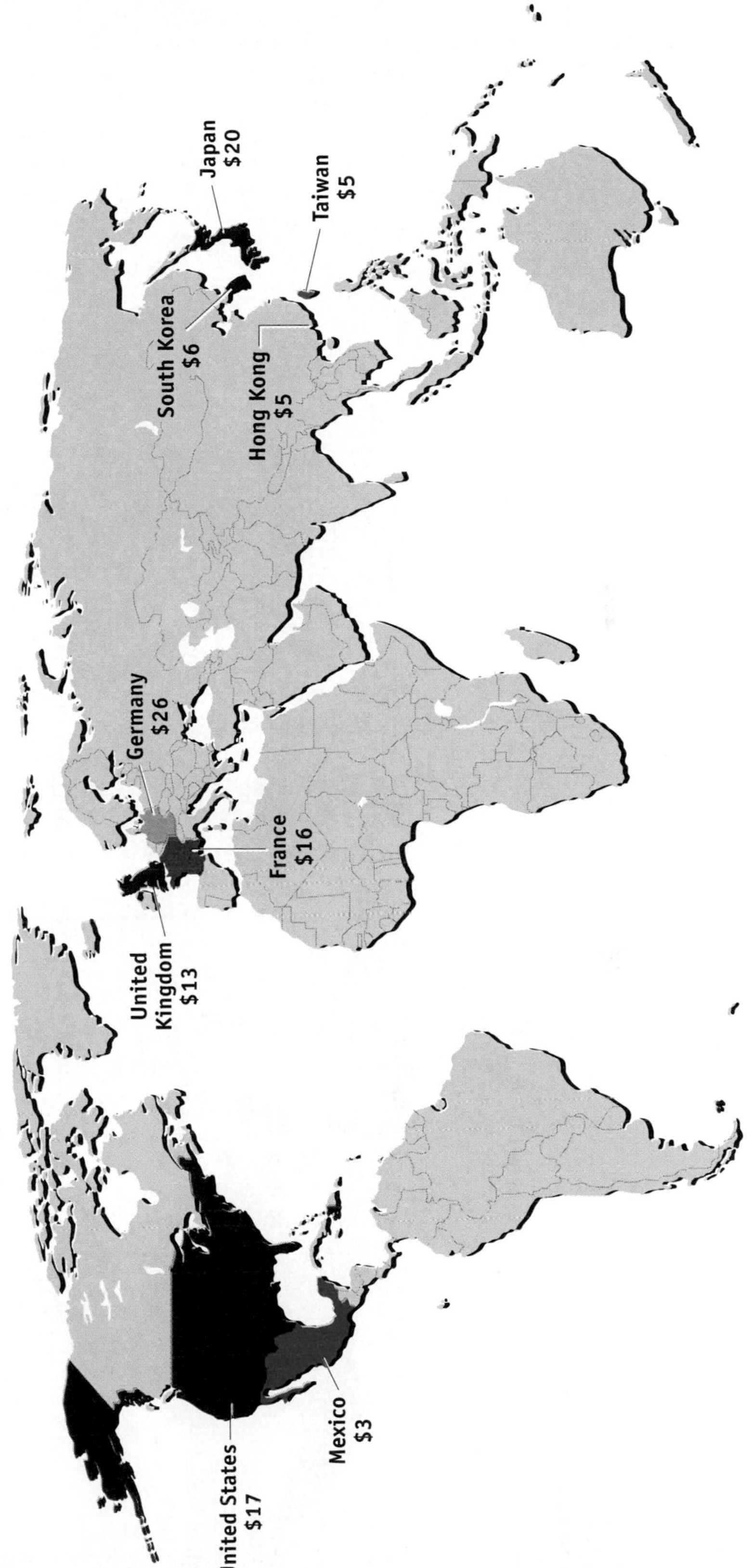

Exhibit 6.2
Hourly Compensation Costs for Manufacturing across Countries

United States
$17

Mexico
$3

United Kingdom
$13

Germany
$26

France
$16

Japan
$20

South Korea
$6

Taiwan
$5

Hong Kong
$5

Exhibit 6.3
Economic Growth Rates among Countries

Note: Percentages reflect the projected economic growth rates for 1996.

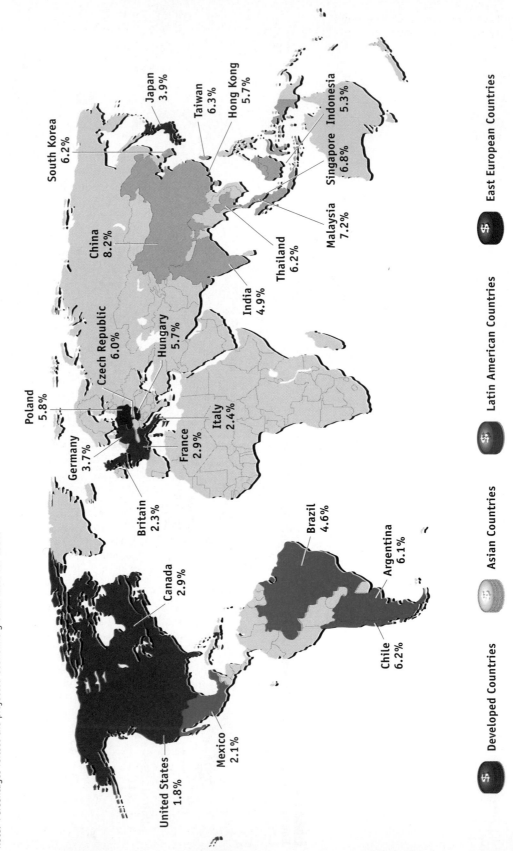

South Korea 6.2%

Japan 3.9%

Taiwan 6.3%

Hong Kong 5.7%

Indonesia 5.3%

Singapore 6.8%

Malaysia 7.2%

China 8.2%

Thailand 6.2%

India 4.9%

Poland 5.8%

Czech Republic 6.0%

Hungary 5.7%

Italy 2.4%

France 2.9%

Germany 3.7%

Britain 2.3%

Canada 2.9%

Brazil 4.6%

Argentina 6.1%

Chile 6.2%

Mexico 2.1%

United States 1.8%

Developed Countries

Asian Countries

Latin American Countries

East European Countries

Exhibit 6.4
Digital Equipment Corporation's
International Expansion

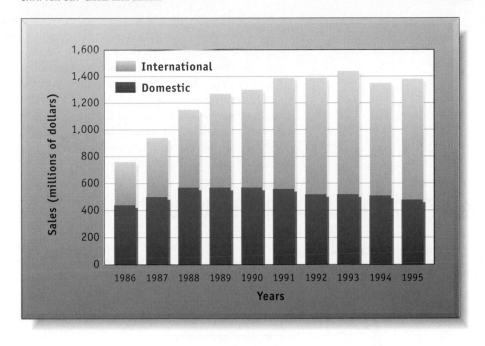

eign countries. Second, it was able to capitalize on its technology, since local firms in these countries did not have its technology. Third, it was able to use low-cost land and labor in some countries in Asia. Finally, it was able to diversify its business among countries. It also reduced its exposure to U.S. economic conditions by increasing its international business over time. Exhibit 6.4 shows that much of Digital's growth was attributed to international expansion. In 1986, 42 percent of Digital's sales were in foreign countries. By 1995, that figure had grown to 65 percent.

FOREIGN EXPANSION IN THE U.S.

Just as U.S. firms have expanded in foreign countries, foreign firms have expanded in the United States. Some foreign firms have established new subsidiaries (or branches) in the United States, such as Toyota (expanded its Kentucky plant), Mitsubishi Materials (built a silicon plant in Oregon), and Honda (expanded its Ohio plant). Other foreign firms such as Sony have acquired firms in the United States. Many foreign firms have spent hundreds of millions of dollars to develop or expand their U.S. business. Since foreign firms have expanded in the United States, even those U.S. firms that only sell their products domestically are subject to foreign competition.

Foreign Competition

Most industries in the United States are susceptible to foreign competition. Some foreign firms control a significant share of the U.S. market for the following reasons. Some countries, such as China, Mexico, and Thailand, have extremely low labor costs. The production costs of foreign firms in these countries can be especially low for labor-intensive industries, such as clothing. Competing in these industries is difficult for U.S. firms because the production expenses are higher in the United States.

A second reason why foreign firms are successful in the United States is that some foreign-made products may be perceived as having higher quality than U.S.-made products. For example, many U.S. consumers considered Japanese automobiles to be of higher quality than U.S. automobiles. While this general perception has changed in the automobile industry, some foreign products (such as furniture, watches, and wine) are still considered more desirable because of a quality perception.

In some industries, such as the automobile, camera, and clothing industries, many foreign firms offer their products to the United States. The U.S. firms in these industries must compete against the foreign firms for the U.S. market share. In industries that do not have much foreign competition, the U.S. firms compete only among themselves. For example, service industries such as accounting and hair-styling are not normally exposed to much foreign competition because foreign firms cannot easily offer these services.

HOW FIRMS CONDUCT INTERNATIONAL BUSINESS

2 | **Describe how firms conduct international business.**

Firms engage in various types of international business. Some of the more popular types are listed:

➤ Importing
➤ Exporting
➤ Direct foreign investment (DFI)
➤ Strategic alliances

Importing

importing represents the purchase of foreign products or services

Importing represents the purchase of foreign products or services. For example, some U.S. consumers purchase foreign automobiles, clothing, cameras, and other products from firms in foreign countries. Many U.S. firms import materials or supplies that are used to produce products. Even if these firms sell the products locally, they can benefit from international business. They import foreign supplies that are less expensive or of a higher quality than alternative U.S. supplies.

FACTORS THAT INFLUENCE THE DEGREE OF IMPORTING   The degree to which a firm imports supplies is influenced by government trade barriers. Governments can impose a **tariff** (or tax) on imported products. The tax is normally paid directly by the importer, who will typically pass the tax on to consumers by charging a higher price for the product. Thus, the product may be overpriced compared with products produced by firms based in that country. When foreign governments impose tariffs, the ability of foreign firms to compete in those countries is restricted.

tariff tax on imported products

quota limits the amounts of specific products that can be imported

Governments can also impose a **quota** on imported products, which limits the amounts of specific products that can be imported. This type of trade barrier may be even more restrictive than a tariff because it places an explicit limit on the amount of a specific product that can be imported.

In general, trade barriers tend to both discourage trade and protect specific industries from foreign competition. However, many trade barriers have been removed in recent years. In 1993 the North American Free Trade Agreement (NAFTA) was passed, which removed many restrictions on trade between Canada, Mexico, and the United States. Consequently, U.S. firms are more capable of expanding their business in Canada and Mexico. However, they are also more exposed to competition from foreign firms within the United States. Since NAFTA, other trade agreements have also occurred among the European countries and among countries in Southeast Asia.

The North America Free Trade Agreement (NAFTA) eliminated many tariffs and quotas on trade between the United States, Mexico, and Canada. This has led to a significant increase in the flow of goods between the two countries.

Exporting

exporting the sale of products or services (called exports) to purchasers residing in other countries

Exporting is the sale of products or services (called exports) to purchasers residing in other countries. Many firms such as DuPont, Kodak, Intel, and Zenith use exporting as a means of selling products in foreign markets. Many smaller firms in the United States also export to foreign countries.

TREND OF U.S. EXPORTS AND IMPORTS   The trend of U.S. exports and imports is shown in Exhibit 6.5. Notice that the amount of U.S. exports and imports in the mid-1990s has more than tripled since 1980, reflecting the increased importance of international trade.

balance of trade the level of exports minus the level of imports

trade deficit amount by which imports exceed exports

The U.S. **balance of trade** is equal to the level of U.S. exports minus the level of U.S. imports. A negative balance of trade is referred to as a **trade deficit** and means that the United States is importing (purchasing) more products and services from foreign countries than it is selling to foreign countries. The U.S. trade deficit has been consistently negative and reached its peak in the late 1980s.

Direct Foreign Investment (DFI)

direct foreign investment (DFI) means of acquiring or building subsidiaries in one or more foreign countries

Many firms engage in **direct foreign investment (DFI),** which is a means of acquiring or building subsidiaries in one or more foreign countries. For example, Ford Motor Company has facilities in various countries that produce automobiles and sell them in those locations. Blockbuster Video has stores in various countries that rent videos to customers in those countries. A U.S. firm may either build a subsidiary in a foreign country or acquire an existing foreign firm and convert that into its subsidiary. Many U.S. firms acquire foreign firms to expand internationally. They most commonly acquire firms in Canada and the United Kingdom, but have recently increased their acquisitions in countries such as Brazil, the Czech Republic, and Hungary. Direct foreign investment is feasible under a variety of situations, some of which are as follows:

Exhibit 6.5
Trend of U.S. Exports and Imports

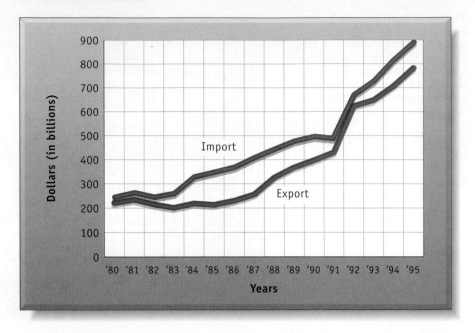

1 A firm that has successfully exported to a foreign country desires to reduce its transportation costs. It establishes a subsidiary in the foreign country that manufactures the product and sells it in that country. Kellogg Company uses this strategy and has production plants in nineteen different countries, including China and India.
2 A firm that has been exporting products is informed that the foreign government will impose trade barriers. Therefore, it establishes a subsidiary that can manufacture and sell products in that country. In this way, it avoids the trade barrier.
3 A foreign country is desperately in need of advanced technology and offers a U.S. firm incentives, such as free use of land, to establish a subsidiary in its country. The foreign country also expects that the firm will employ some local workers.
4 A U.S. firm believes that it could substantially reduce its labor costs by shifting its production facilities to a developing country where the labor and land are less expensive.

While direct foreign investment can often be feasible, firms should conduct a thorough analysis of its costs and benefits before implementing the idea. Once the funds are spent on direct foreign investment, the decision cannot be easily reversed because the foreign facilities would have to be sold at a loss in most cases.

Strategic Alliances

strategic alliance a business agreement between firms whereby resources are shared to pursue mutual interests

joint venture an agreement between two firms about a specific project

U.S. and foreign countries commonly engage in **strategic alliances,** which represent business agreements that are in the best interests of the firms involved. Various types of international alliances between U.S. firms and foreign firms can be made. One type is a **joint venture,** which involves an agreement between two firms about a specific project. Joint ventures between U.S. and non-U.S. firms are common. The U.S. firms may produce a product and send it to a non-U.S. firm, which sells the product in that country. The non-U.S. firm is involved because it knows the culture of that country and is more capable of selling the product there.

An alternative type of joint venture involves the participation of two firms in the production of a product. This type of joint venture is common in the automobile industry. The big three automakers in the United States are involved in a variety of ventures with foreign manufacturers. General Motors dealerships and Ford Motor Company dealerships sell cars manufactured by firms in France, Japan, and South Korea. RJR Nabisco has engaged in joint ventures with some food producers in the former Soviet Republics. This gives Nabisco access to local production facilities and skilled workers. These joint ventures represent a major change in attitude by companies about doing business in the Soviet Republic, which has resulted from improved commercial relations.

international licensing agreement
type of alliance in which a firm allows a foreign company (called the "licensee") to produce its products according to specific instructions

Another type of alliance is an **international licensing agreement,** in which a firm allows a foreign company (called the "licensee") to produce its products according to specific instructions. Many U.S. beer producers engage in licensing agreements with foreign firms. The foreign firm is given the technology to produce the products. As the foreign firm sells products, it channels a portion of revenue to the *licensing firm.* The advantage of licensing is that the firm is able to sell its product in foreign markets without the costs involved in exporting or direct foreign investment. One disadvantage, however, is that the foreign firm shares the profits from products sold in the foreign country.

GLOBAL BUSINESS

Nonverbal Communications in Different Cultures

Nonverbal behavior can only be interpreted within a specific cultural context. Here are five common nonverbal behaviors and how they are interpreted in different countries or geographic areas. Caution is always the better part of valor in using nonverbal behaviors outside your native land.

Withholding eye contact:
➤ In the United States, it indicates shyness or deception.
➤ In Libya, it is a compliment to a woman.
➤ In Japan, it is done in deference to authority.

Crossed legs when seated:
➤ In the United States, it is done for comfort.
➤ In Arab countries, it is an insult to show the soles of the feet.

Displaying the palm of the hand:
➤ In the United States, it is a form of greeting, such as a wave or handshake.
➤ In Greece, it is an insult.

Joining the index finger and thumb to make an O:
➤ In the United States, it means "okay."
➤ In Mediterranean countries, it means "zero" or "the pits."
➤ In Japan, it means money.
➤ In Tunisia, it means "I'll kill you."
➤ In Latin America, it is an obscene gesture.

Standing close to a person while talking:
➤ In the United States, it is an intrusion, and the speaker is viewed as pushy.
➤ In Latin America and southern Europe, it is the normal spatial distance for conversations.

HOW FOREIGN CHARACTERISTICS INFLUENCE INTERNATIONAL BUSINESS

3 **Explain how foreign characteristics can influence a firm's international business.**

When a firm engages in international business, it must consider the following characteristics of foreign countries:

➤ Culture
➤ Economic system
➤ Economic conditions
➤ Exchange rates
➤ Political risk

Culture

Because cultures vary, a firm must learn a foreign country's culture before it engages in international business. Poor decisions can result from an improper assessment of a country's tastes, habits, and customs. For example, a U.S. firm may decide to allocate millions of dollars toward promoting a program to export a product to a particular country. The business could fail if the people in that country do not desire that type of product. Many U.S. firms know that cultures vary, and adjust their products to fit the culture. For example, McDonald's sells vegetable burgers instead of beef hamburgers in India. PepsiCo (owner of Lay's snack foods) sells Cheetos without cheese in China because Chinese consumers dislike cheese, and has developed a shrimp-chip to satisfy consumers in Korea. Beer producers sell nonalcoholic beer in Saudi Arabia, where alcohol is not allowed.

Economic System

A firm must recognize the type of economic system used in any country where it considers doing business. A country's economic system reflects the degree of govern-

The 1997 Jeep Wrangler made its debut at the Tokyo Auto Show. Chrysler has been the most successful U.S. auto maker attempting to break into the Japanese market. Both left-hand-drive and right-hand-drive models will be produced.

ment ownership of businesses and intervention in business. A U.S. firm will normally prefer countries that do not have excessive government intervention.

While each country's government has its own unique policy on the ownership of businesses, most policies can be classified as capitalism, communism, or socialism.

capitalism an economic system which allows for private ownership of businesses

CAPITALISM   **Capitalism** allows for private ownership of businesses. Entrepreneurs have the freedom to create businesses that they believe will serve the people's needs. The U.S. is perceived as a capitalistic society because entrepreneurs are allowed to create businesses and compete against each other. In a capitalist society, entrepreneurs' desire to earn profits motivates them to produce products and services that satisfy customers. Competition allows efficient firms to increase their share of the market and forces inefficient firms out of the market.

U.S. firms can normally enter capitalist countries without any excessive restrictions by the governments of those countries. Yet, the level of competition there is typically high.

communism an economic system which involves public ownership of businesses

COMMUNISM   **Communism** is an economic system which involves public ownership of businesses. In a purely communist system, entrepreneurs are restricted from capitalizing on the perceived needs of the people. The government decides what products to produce and in what quantity. It may even assign jobs to people, regardless of their interests, and sets the wages to be paid to each worker. Wages may be somewhat similar, regardless of individual abilities or effort. Thus, workers do not have much incentive to excel because they will not be rewarded for abnormally high performance.

In a communist society, the government serves as a central planner. It may decide to produce more of some type of agricultural product if it recognizes a shortage. Since the government is not concerned about earning profits, it does not focus on satisfying consumers (determining what they want to purchase). So people are unable to obtain many types of products even if they can afford to buy them. In addition, most people do not have much money to spend because the government pays low wages.

Countries in Eastern Europe, such as Bulgaria, Poland, and Romania, were viewed as communist before 1990. However, government intervention in these countries declined during the 1990s. Prior to the 1990s, communist countries restricted most U.S. firms from entering. However, as they began to allow more private ownership of firms, they also allowed foreign firms to enter.

socialism an economic system that contains some features of both capitalism and communism

SOCIALISM   **Socialism** is an economic system that contains some features of both capitalism and communism. For example, governments in some so-called socialist countries allow people to own businesses and property and to select their own jobs. However, these governments are more involved in the provision of various services. Health-care services are run by many governments and are provided at a low cost. Also, the governments of socialist countries tend to offer high levels of benefits to unemployed people. Such services are indirectly paid for by the businesses and the workers who earn income. Socialist governments impose high tax rates on income so that they have sufficient funds to provide all their services.

Many businesses and workers in socialist countries would argue that the tax rates are excessive. Entrepreneurs have less incentive to establish businesses if the government taxes most of the income to be earned by the business. Entrepreneurs could establish businesses in other countries where taxes are lower.

Socialist countries face a trade-off when setting their tax policies. If the government wants to provide many services to the poor or unemployed, it must charge higher tax rates, which discourages entrepreneurs from starting new businesses. But

The lack of a true supply and demand relationship can lead to substantial misallocation of resources. These Russian citizens all want bananas; unfortunately there are few available.

if the government uses a low tax rate, it may not generate enough tax revenue to provide the services.

A socialist society may discourage not only the establishment of new businesses but also the desire to work. If the compensation provided by a socialist government to unemployed workers is almost as high as the wages earned by employed workers, unemployed people have little incentive to look for work. Employed people are typically subject to high tax rates in socialist countries, which also discourages people from looking for work.

COMPARISON OF SOCIALISM WITH CAPITALISM   In socialist countries the government has more influence because it imposes higher taxes and can spend that tax revenue as it chooses. In capitalistic countries, the government has less influence because it imposes fewer taxes and therefore has less funds to spend on the people. Businesses and highly skilled workers generally prefer capitalist countries because of less government interference.

Even if a capitalist county is preferred, people may disagree on the degree of government influence in that country. For example, some people in the United States believe that the government should provide fewer services to the unemployed and the poor, which would allow for lower taxes. Other people believe that taxes should be increased so that the government can allocate more services to the poor.

Many countries exhibit some degree of capitalism and socialism. For example, the governments of many developed countries in Europe (such as Sweden and Switzerland) allow firms to be privately owned, but control various services (such as health care) for the people. Even Germany's government provides child-care allowances, health care, and retirement pensions. The French government commonly intervenes when firms experience financial problems.

European countries have recently attempted to reduce their budget deficits as part of a treaty supporting closer European relations. This may result in less government control because the government will not be able to spend as much money.

PRIVATIZATION   Historically, the governments of many countries in Eastern Europe, Latin America, and the Soviet Bloc owned most businesses, but in recent

privatization government-owned businesses sold to private investors

years they have allowed for private business ownership. Many government-owned businesses have been sold to private investors. As a result of this so-called **privatization,** the governments are reducing their influence in numerous countries and allowing firms to compete in each industry. This allows firms to focus on providing the products and services that people desire and forces the firms to be more efficient to ensure survival. About one thousand businesses in the Soviet Bloc were privatized each month during 1994. Some U.S. firms have acquired businesses sold by the governments of the Soviet Republic and other countries. Privatization has provided an easy method for U.S. firms to own businesses in many foreign countries.

Privatization in many countries, such as in Brazil, Hungary, and the Soviet Bloc, is an abrupt shift from tradition. Most people in these countries were not experienced in owning and managing a business. Even those people who had managed government-owned businesses were not used to competition because the government had typically controlled each industry. Therefore, many people who wanted to own their own businesses were given some training by business professors and professionals from capitalist countries such as the United States. In particular, the MBA Enterprise Corps headquartered at the University of North Carolina—Chapel Hill, has sent thousands of business students to less-developed countries.

Even the industrialized countries have initiated privatization programs for some businesses that were previously owned by the government. The telephone company in Germany is being privatized, as are numerous large government-owned businesses in France.

Economic Conditions

To predict demand for its product, a firm must attempt to forecast the foreign country's economic conditions. The firm's performance in a foreign country is dependent on that country's economic growth and inflation, as explained next.

Cuban baseball star Osvaldo Fernandez defected to the U.S. in 1995 and signed a multimillion dollar contract with the San Francisco Giants. A free-enterprise system offers rewards for productivity. This attracts the best workers (players) in the world.

ECONOMIC GROWTH   When a foreign country experiences a high degree of economic growth, foreign demand for a U.S. firm's products may be high. Conversely, when the foreign country experiences weak economic conditions, foreign demand for the U.S. firm's products may be low. Many U.S. firms experienced lower revenue from their European business in 1993 when Europe's economy was weak. However, during the 1994–95 period, U.S. firms such as Alcoa, Dow Chemical, DuPont, Gillette, and Procter and Gamble experienced higher revenue in Europe because the European economy improved. PepsiCo experienced strong performance in this period as a result of the increased demand for its products in China, India, and Latin America. Hewlett-Packard experienced higher earnings as a result of the strong global demand for its computer products in 1995.

Many U.S. firms have recently expanded into smaller foreign markets because they expect that economic growth in these countries will be strong, resulting in a strong demand for their products. For example, Heinz has expanded its business throughout Asia. General Motors, Procter and Gamble, AT&T, Ford Motor Company, and Anheuser-Busch plan new direct foreign investment in Brazil. The Coca-Cola Company has expanded in China, India, and Eastern Europe.

The primary factor influencing the decision by many firms to expand in a particular foreign country is the country's expected economic growth, which affects the potential demand for their products. If firms overestimate the country's economic growth, they will normally overestimate the demand for their products in that country. Consequently, their revenue may not be sufficient to cover the expenses associated with the expansion.

The efforts of Commerce Secretary Ron Brown and many top business executives to investigate business opportunities in war-torn Bosnia unfortunately became headline news when their plane crashed on April 3, 1996.

INFLATION   For U.S. firms with production facilities in foreign countries, production expenses will be affected by inflation. For example, inflation in some Latin American countries has exceeded 100 percent annually, meaning that prices and wages more than doubled in a single year. Some facilities were established by U.S. firms in Latin American countries to produce products at a low cost; however, the production expenses turned out to be much higher than the U.S. firms anticipated.

A U.S. firm's exposure to a foreign country's economy is dependent on the firm's proportion of business conducted in that country. To illustrate, compare the influence of Canada's economy on two U.S. firms (Firm X and Firm Y), as shown in Exhibit 6.6. Assume that Firm X typically generates 20 percent of its total revenue from selling its products to Canada and 80 percent of its total revenue from the United States. Firm Y typically generates 60 percent of its total revenue from Canada and 40 percent of its total revenue from the United States. A weak economy in Canada will likely have a more negative effect on Firm Y because the firm relies more on its Canadian business.

Some U.S. firms, such as The Coca-Cola Company, Dow Chemical, and Exxon, generate more than half of their total revenue from foreign countries. However, they are not heavily influenced by any single foreign country's economy because their international business is scattered across many countries. The Coca-Cola Company, for example, conducts business in more than two hundred foreign countries. The demand for The Coca-Cola Company's soft drink products may decline in some

Exhibit 6.6
Comparing the Influence of Canadian Economy on Two U.S. Firms

U.S. Firm	Total Annual Revenue	Proportion of Canadian Business	Proportion of U.S. Business	Annual Revenue from Canadian Business	Annual Revenue from U.S. Business
Firm X	$100,000,000	20%	80%	$20,000,000	$80,000,000
Firm Y	$10,000,000	60%	40%	$6,000,000	$4,000,000

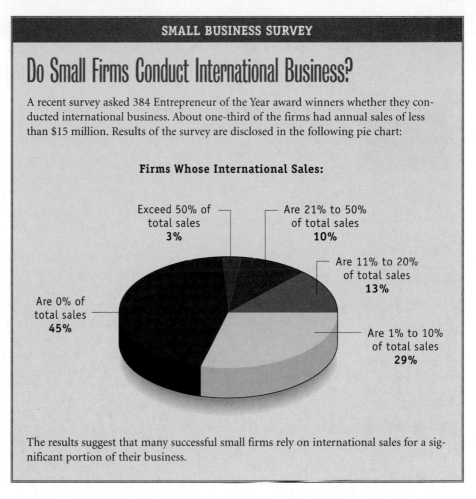

SMALL BUSINESS SURVEY

Do Small Firms Conduct International Business?

A recent survey asked 384 Entrepreneur of the Year award winners whether they conducted international business. About one-third of the firms had annual sales of less than $15 million. Results of the survey are disclosed in the following pie chart:

Firms Whose International Sales:

Exceed 50% of total sales **3%**

Are 21% to 50% of total sales **10%**

Are 11% to 20% of total sales **13%**

Are 0% of total sales **45%**

Are 1% to 10% of total sales **29%**

The results suggest that many successful small firms rely on international sales for a significant portion of their business.

countries where the weather is cooler than normal. However, this unfavorable effect can be offset by a higher demand for Coca-Cola's products in other countries where the weather is warmer than normal.

Exchange Rates

Each country has its own currency. The U.S. uses dollars ($), the United Kingdom uses British pounds (£), Canada uses Canadian dollars (C$), and Japan uses Japanese yen (¥). Exchange rates between the U.S. dollar and any currency fluctuate over time. Consequently, the number of dollars a U.S. firm needs to purchase foreign supplies may change even if the actual price of supplies charged by the foreign producer does not. When the dollar weakens, foreign currencies strengthen; thus, U.S. firms need more dollars to purchase a given amount of foreign supplies. Exchange rate fluctuations can also affect the foreign demand for a U.S. firm's product because they affect the actual price paid by the foreign customers (even if the price in dollars remains unchanged).

Political Risk

political risk the risk that the country's political actions can adversely affect a business

Political risk represents the risk that the country's political actions may adversely affect a business. Political crises have occurred in many countries throughout Eastern

CROSS-FUNCTIONAL TEAMWORK

Managing International Business Across Business Functions

When a firm plans to conduct business in a foreign country, it should request input from its managers across various departments. The production managers may assess a country according to the expenses associated with production, and therefore may focus on the following questions:

1. What is the cost of hiring the necessary labor?
2. What is the cost of developing a new facility?
3. What is the cost of purchasing an existing facility?
4. Does the country have access to the necessary materials and technology?

The answers to these questions are dependent on the specific part of the country where the firm considers producing a product.

The marketing managers may assess a country according to the potential revenue to be earned from selling a product in that country, and therefore may focus on the following questions:

1. What is the foreign demand for the firm's product?
2. What changes need to be made in the product to satisfy local consumers?

3. What types of marketing strategies would be effective in that country?
4. What is the cost of marketing the product in that country?

The financial managers may assess a country according to the costs of financing any business conducted in that country, and therefore may focus on the following questions:

1. Is it possible to obtain a local loan in that country?
2. What is the interest rate charged on local loans?
3. Should the firm use some of its retained earnings from its domestic business to support any foreign business?
4. How would the firm's earnings increase as a result of doing business in the foreign country?

Because of these cross-functional relationships, the decision to establish a business in a foreign country must consider input across departments. The production department cannot properly estimate the production costs in a specific country until the marketing department determines whether the product must be revised to satisfy the local consumers. Also, the financial managers cannot estimate the earnings from this business until they receive estimates of revenue (from the marketing department), production expenses (from the production department), and marketing expenses (from the marketing department).

Europe, Latin America, and the Middle East. U.S. firms are subject to policies enforced by the governments of the foreign countries where they do business. As an extreme form of political risk, a foreign government may take over a U.S. firm's foreign subsidiary without compensating the U.S. firm in any way. A more common form of political risk is that the foreign government imposes higher corporate tax rates on the foreign subsidiaries.

Firms must understand how government characteristics could affect their business in foreign countries. For example, some governments impose a tax on funds sent by a subsidiary to the parent firm (headquarters) in the home country. They may even restrict the funds from being sent for a certain period of time. Government tax laws on business earnings and other environmental laws vary among countries. These laws can affect the feasibility of establishing a subsidiary in a foreign country.

There are numerous examples of how political risk affected U.S. firms in the mid-1990s. A McDonald's site in China was given an eviction notice from Beijing's city government, as the twenty-year agreement to use the land was ignored. Some U.S. firms operating in Russia were surprised to learn that they had to pay a wage tax on all salaries over the minimum salary, and a large social security tax. U.S. automobile manufacturers have had agreements in various foreign countries that were not honored by those governments.

HOW EXCHANGE RATE MOVEMENTS CAN AFFECT PERFORMANCE

4 Explain how exchange rate movements can affect a firm's performance.

International trade transactions typically require the exchange of one currency for another. For example, if a U.S. firm periodically purchases supplies from a British supplier, it will need to exchange U.S. dollars for the British currency (pounds) to make the purchase. This process is shown in Exhibit 6.7. Assume that the value of the pound (£) at a given point in time is $2.00. That is, each dollar is worth one-half of a British pound. If the firm needs £1,000,000 to purchase the supplies from the British supplier, it would need $2,000,000 to obtain those pounds, as shown:

$$\text{Amount of \$ needed} = (\text{amount of £ needed}) \times (\text{Value of £})$$
$$= £1,000,000 \times \$2.00$$
$$= \$2,000,000$$

Generally, the exchange rates between each currency and the U.S. dollar fluctuate daily. When the exchange rate changes, U.S. firms involved in international trade are affected. The impact of exchange rate movements on the U.S. firm can be favorable or unfavorable, depending on the characteristics of the firm, as illustrated by the following examples.

Impact of a Weak Dollar on U.S. Importers

appreciates strengthens in value

Reconsider the previous example in which a U.S. firm needs £1,000,000 to purchase British supplies. Now assume that the value of the pound **appreciates** (or strengthens in value) against the dollar. This also means that the dollar weakens (is worth less) against the pound. For example, assume the pound is now equal to $2.02 instead of $2.00. This means that the percentage change in the value of the pound is as follows:

$$\text{Percentage change in £} = \frac{\text{New value of £} - \text{Previous value of £}}{\text{Previous value of £}}$$
$$= \frac{\$2.02 - \$2.00}{\$2.00}$$
$$= .01, \text{ or } 1\%$$

A positive percentage change in the value of a pound represents appreciation of the pound (the pound's value has increased). The reasons why the value of the British pound or any other currency may change over time are explained in the chapter appendix.

Exhibit 6.7
Example of Importing by a U.S. Firm

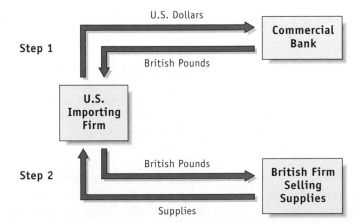

Moving Technology Across Borders

Technologies that are highly effective in one country may have to be modified substantially before they are suitable for another country. A good example of the challenges of moving technology across borders can be found in the case of AucNet, the satellite used car auctioning system. AucNet was developed in the mid-1980s in Japan, as a substitute for traditional used car auctions. It used laser disk and later satellite technology to permit dealers from around the country to view the used cars that were going to be sold. Dealers could also view the results of inspections conducted by AucNet's team of on-sight inspectors. After they had been given the opportunity to study the cars, dealers were then able to participate in on-line auctions. Participating in such auctions offered dealers two major advantages: they did not have to go to auction sites, and they did not have to take their vehicles to auction sites. As a result of its innovative approach, the company became a major force in the Japanese used car business, participating in the sale of over a million cars during its first 10 years of operation.

In 1995, AucNet entered the U.S. market, first in the Atlanta area, then expanding to California. However, since the used cars were typically much older, a simple inspection of a vehicle could not guarantee its actual condition. Also, the used car dealers in the U.S. were less specialized and therefore were interested in a broader range of cars.

To attempt to address these problems, AucNet U.S.A., Inc. took two key steps: 1) it chose to focus on the high-priced market segment of cars, and 2) it increased the scope of its inspection program. Specifically, while the Japanese inspections had been almost entirely cosmetic, for its U.S. operations it checked 120 specific items, both cosmetic and mechanical, and took each vehicle on a test drive. The final rating of each vehicle was then determined using custom designed inspection software. In addition, a digital camera was used to take three photos of each car, which could then be downloaded by potential bidders. These changes were deemed necessary to make AucNet's approach attractive to the U.S. market.

Given that the pound is now valued at $2.02, the amount of dollars needed by the U.S. firm to obtain the £1,000,000 would now be as follows:

$$\text{Amount of \$ needed} = (\text{Amount of £ needed}) \times (\text{Value of £})$$
$$= £1,000,000 \times \$2.02$$
$$= \$2,020,000$$

The amount of dollars needed is $20,000 more than the amount needed before the pound appreciated. Since the firm must now pay 1 percent more for each pound that it obtains, it pays 1 percent more when purchasing the British supplies.

The British pound and other European currencies have sometimes appreciated by 10 percent over one month. If we used a 10 percent appreciation in our example instead of 1 percent, the U.S. firm would have needed $2,200,000 to obtain the £1,000,000, which is $200,000 more than what it would have needed if the pound's value had not changed.

Our example shows how the appreciation of a foreign currency against the dollar (a weaker dollar) caused the U.S. importing firm to incur higher expenses when purchasing foreign supplies. Therefore, the weaker dollar may cause the profits of this firm to decline. This explains why a weak dollar adversely affects U.S. firms that frequently import supplies.

Impact of a Strong Dollar on U.S. Importers

depreciates weakens in value

Now consider a situation in which the value of the pound **depreciates,** or weakens in value against the dollar. This also means that the dollar strengthens against the pound. For example, assume the pound's value was $2.00, but has changed to $1.90

over the last month. This means that the percentage change in the value of the pound is as follows:

$$\text{Percentage change in £} = \frac{\text{New value of £} - \text{Previous value of £}}{\text{Previous value of £}}$$

$$= \frac{\$1.90 - \$2.00}{\$2.00}$$

$$= -.05, \text{ or } -5\%$$

The negative sign on the percentage change reflects the depreciation in value.

Recall that in our example, the U.S. firm obtains £1,000,000 to purchase British supplies. When the pound's value depreciates to $1.90, the amount of dollars needed to obtain the £1,000,000 is as follows:

$$\text{Amount of \$ needed} = (\text{Amount of £ needed}) \times (\text{Value of £})$$

$$= \text{£1,000,000} \times \$1.90$$

$$= \$1,900,000$$

The amount of dollars needed is $100,000 less than what was needed before the pound depreciated. That is, the U.S. firm can obtain the pounds for $100,000 less than before. Its payment declined by 5 percent because the pound's value declined by 5 percent.

This example shows how the depreciation of a foreign currency against the dollar (a stronger dollar) reduces the expenses of the U.S. firm that was purchasing foreign supplies. Therefore, the stronger dollar may cause the profits of this U.S. firm to increase. This explains why a strong dollar favorably affects U.S. firms that frequently import supplies.

Actual Effects of Exchange Rate Movements on U.S. Importers

To illustrate how exchange rate movements can affect firms engaged in international business, actual exchange rate movements of the British pound (£) are shown in the top of Exhibit 6.8. The amount of dollars paid by a U.S. importer that owes £1,000,000 every quarter to a British supplier is shown in the bottom of Exhibit 6.8. Notice that the pound depreciated substantially in some periods, such as 1981–84 and 1991–93. In other periods, such as 1985–87, the pound appreciated. When the pound appreciated, the amount of dollars needed to buy British imports increased. Conversely, when the pound depreciated, the amount of dollars needed to buy British imports declined. Exhibit 6.8 illustrates how the expenses of a U.S. importing firm are highly sensitive to changes in the value of the pound.

The exchange rates of currencies in less-developed countries fluctuate more than those in developed countries. For example, the Mexican peso depreciated by 45 percent during the month of December 1994. U.S. firms that do business in less-developed countries are exposed to wide swings in exchange rates.

Impact of a Weak Dollar on U.S. Exporters

Just as exchange rate movements can affect U.S. importing firms, they can also affect U.S. firms that export products to other countries. The effect of a weak dollar will be examined first, followed by the effect of a strong dollar.

Consider how a U.S. firm that exports equipment to a British firm is affected by a weak dollar. The exporting process is shown in Exhibit 6.9. If the U.S. exporter wants to receive U.S. dollars for its equipment, the British firm must first exchange its currency (pounds) into dollars at a commercial bank (Step 1 in Exhibit 6.9). Then

Exhibit 6.8
How Exchange Rate Movements
Can Affect the Price of Imports

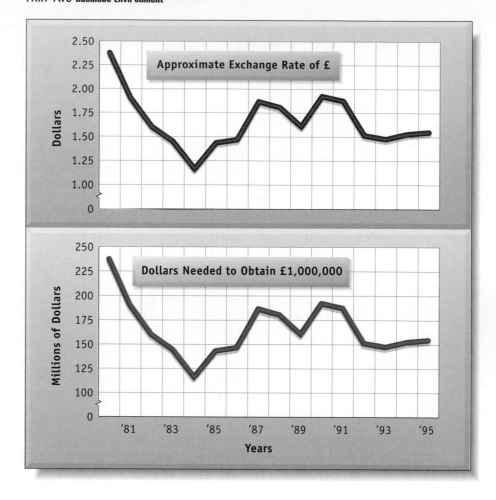

the British firm uses these dollars to purchase the equipment of the U.S. exporting firm (Step 2).

If the dollar weakens, the British firm can obtain the dollars it needs with fewer pounds. Therefore, it may be willing to purchase more equipment from the U.S. exporting firm. The U.S. firm's revenue will rise in response to a higher demand for the equipment it produces. Therefore, its profits should increase as well.

Exhibit 6.9
Example of Exporting by a
U.S. Firm

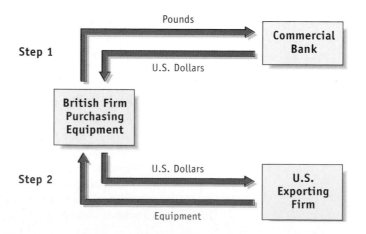

This example shows how a weak dollar can result in higher revenue and profits for U.S. firms that frequently export their products. U.S. exporting firms tend to benefit from a weak dollar because their prices are perceived as inexpensive by foreign customers who must convert their currencies into dollars. A weak dollar favorably affects U.S. firms that export heavily because foreign demand for the products they export increases substantially when the dollar is weak.

Impact of a Strong Dollar on U.S. Exporters

Now consider a situation in which the value of the pound depreciates against the dollar. As the pound's value declines, the British firm must exchange more British pounds to obtain the same amount of dollars as before. That is, it needs more pounds to purchase equipment from the U.S. firm. Consequently, it may reduce its purchases from the U.S. firm, and perhaps will search for a British producer of the equipment to avoid obtaining dollars.

This example shows how a strong dollar can result in lower revenue for U.S. firms that frequently export their products. A strong dollar adversely affects U.S. exporting firms because the prices of their exports appear expensive to foreign customers who must convert their currencies into dollars. When the dollar strengthened against some currencies in 1995, U.S. exporting firms such as Procter and Gamble, Boeing, and Eastman Kodak were adversely affected.

Hedging Against Exchange Rate Movements

hedge action taken to protect a firm against exchange rate movements

U.S. firms commonly attempt to **hedge,** or protect against exchange rate movements. They can hedge most effectively when they know how much of a specific foreign currency that they will need or will receive on a specific date in the future.

HEDGING FUTURE PAYMENTS IN FOREIGN CURRENCIES   Consider a firm that plans to purchase British supplies and will need £1,000,000 in ninety days to pay for those supplies. It can call a large commercial bank that exchanges foreign currencies and

Honda is better insulated from exchange rate movements as they are both an importer and exporter of automobiles into and out of the United States.

forward contract states an exchange of currencies that will occur at a specified exchange rate at a future point in time

forward rate the exchange rate that the bank would be willing to offer at a future point in time

spot exchange rate the exchange rate quoted for immediate transactions

request a so-called **forward contract,** which states an exchange of currencies that will occur for a specified exchange rate at a future point in time. In this case, the forward contract would specify an exchange of dollars for £1,000,000 in ninety days. In other words, the firm wants to purchase pounds ninety days forward.

The bank will quote the so-called **forward rate** or the exchange rate that the bank would be willing to offer at a future point in time. The forward rate is normally close to the **spot exchange rate,** which is the exchange rate quoted for immediate transactions. Assume that the bank quotes a ninety-day forward rate of $1.80 for the British pound. If the firm agrees to this quote, it has agreed to a forward contract. It will lock in the purchase of £1,000,000 in ninety days for $1.80 per pound, or $1,800,000 for the £1,000,000. Once the firm hedges its position, it has locked in the rate at which it will exchange currencies on that future date, regardless of the actual spot exchange rate that occurs on that date. In this way, the U.S. firm hedged against the possibility that the pound would appreciate over that period.

HEDGING FUTURE RECEIVABLES IN FOREIGN CURRENCIES   U.S. firms can also hedge when they expect to receive a foreign currency in the future. For example, consider a U.S. firm that knows it will receive £1,000,000 in ninety days. It could call a commercial bank and negotiate a forward contract in which it would provide the £1,000,000 to the bank in exchange for dollars. Assuming that the ninety-day forward rate was $1.80 (as in the previous example), the firm would receive $1,800,000 in ninety days (computed as $1.80 × £1,000,000). By using a forward contract, this firm locked in the rate at which it could exchange its pounds for dollars, regardless of the spot exchange rate that occurs on that date. In this way, the U.S. firm hedged against the possibility that the pound would depreciate over the period of concern.

LIMITATIONS OF HEDGING   A major limitation of hedging is that the hedge offsets not only unfavorable exchange rate movements but also favorable rate movements. For example, reconsider the initial example in which the firm locked in the purchase of pounds ninety days ahead at a forward rate of $1.80. If the actual spot exchange rate in ninety days was $1.70, the firm would have been better off without the hedge. However, it is obligated to fulfill its forward contract by exchanging dollars for pounds at the forward exchange rate of $1.80. This example illustrates why many U.S. firms hedge only when they expect that their future international business transactions will be adversely affected by exchange rate movements.

How Exchange Rates Affect Foreign Competition

Many U.S. firms compete with foreign firms within the U.S. market. Exhibit 6.10 shows a common situation in the United States. RCA is a U.S. firm that sells televisions in the U.S. market. It competes with many other foreign competitors that export televisions to the United States. Retail stores purchase televisions from RCA as well as other firms. Assume the stores mark up the price of each television by 20 percent. When these stores purchase Japanese televisions, they convert dollars to Japanese yen (the Japanese currency). If the value of yen depreciates against the dollar, the store needs fewer dollars to purchase the Japanese televisions. If it applies the same markup, it can reduce its price on the Japanese televisions. Therefore, increased foreign competition (due to depreciation of one or more foreign currencies) may cause RCA to lose some U.S. business.

If the foreign currency appreciates against the dollar, the foreign competitors may be unable to compete in the United States because the prices of imported prod-

Exhibit 6.10
How Exchange Rates Affect the
Degree of Foreign Competition

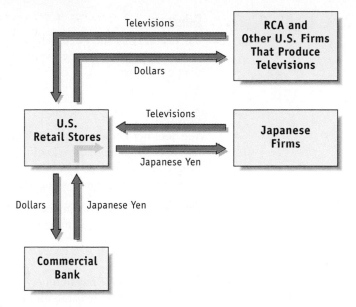

Scenario	Result
1. Japanese yen depreciates against the dollar.	U.S. retail stores can purchase Japanese televisions with fewer dollars, so the demand for Japanese televisions increases (and therefore the demand for U.S. televisions decreases).
2. Japanese yen appreciates against the dollar.	U.S. retail stores must pay more dollars to purchase Japanese televisions, so the demand for Japanese televisions decreases (and therefore the demand for U.S. televisions increases).

ucts will rise. Using our example, if the Japanese yen appreciates, the retail store would need more dollars to purchase the Japanese televisions. When applying its markup, it would need to increase its price on the Japanese televisions. Therefore, U.S. firms such as RCA may gain more U.S. business.

BUSINESS DILEMMA

Exchange Rate Effects at College Health Club

When Sue Kramer opened College Health Club (CHC), she leased the exercise equipment. However, she is considering purchasing exercise equipment from a Canadian manufacturer. The price of the equipment is C$20,000. If Sue purchases the equipment, she will have to pay the bill in ninety days. Sue recognizes that the value of the Canadian dollar changes each day. She notices that a business newspaper recently predicted that the exchange rate of the Canadian dollar will be valued at $.84 in ninety days. However, a business expert predicted that the Canadian dollar will be valued at $.88 in ninety days.

Dilemma

Sue decides that she will purchase the equipment only if her cost is less than $16,000. Estimate the price of the equipment in U.S. dollars. Should Sue purchase the Canadian equipment?

Solution

Sue does not know what the exchange rate of the Canadian dollar will be in ninety days, but she can use the two different predictions that were provided. Her purchase price can be estimated by multiplying the C$20,000 times the expected exchange rate at the time the payment is due. Her analysis is as follows:

1 If the exchange rate in ninety days is C$ = $.84:

$$\begin{aligned} \text{Expected amount of \$ needed} &= \text{C\$20,000} \times \text{Exchange rate} \\ &= \text{C\$20,000} \times \$.84 \\ &= \$16,800 \end{aligned}$$

2 If the exchange rate in ninety days is C$ = $.88:

$$\begin{aligned} \text{Expected amount of \$ needed} &= \text{C\$20,000} \times \text{Exchange rate} \\ &= \text{C\$20,000} \times \$.88 \\ &= \$17,600 \end{aligned}$$

Based on these estimates, the expected expense to CHC will be either $16,800 or $17,600, depending on which exchange rate exists in ninety days. Since the expected expense exceeds $16,000, Sue decides not to purchase the equipment. She will continue leasing equipment but will reconsider purchasing the Canadian equipment if the value of the Canadian dollar depreciates to a rate of C$ = $.80 or less. At an exchange rate of C$ = $.80, Sue will need only $16,000 to obtain C$20,000.

Additional Issues for Discussion

1 Assume that CHC becomes highly successful over time, and Sue Kramer considers establishing some health clubs in a foreign country. What characteristics would she assess in that country before deciding whether to establish health clubs there?

2 Assume that a large foreign country has no health clubs. Does this mean Sue would benefit by establishing a health club there? (Assume no political barriers exist.)

3 Do you think CHC is more exposed or less exposed to foreign competition than U.S. manufacturing firms? Why?

SUMMARY

1 The main reasons why U.S. firms engage in international business are to:

➤ attract foreign demand,
➤ capitalize on technology,
➤ use inexpensive resources, or
➤ diversify internationally.

The first two reasons reflect higher revenue, while the third reason reflects lower expenses. The fourth reason reflects less risk by reducing exposure to a single economy.

2 The primary ways in which firms conduct international business are:

➤ importing,
➤ exporting,
➤ direct foreign investment, and
➤ strategic alliances.

Many U.S. firms have used all of these strategies.

3 When firms sell their products in international markets, they assess the cultures, economic systems and conditions, exchange rate risk and political risk in those markets. A country's economic conditions affect the demand by its citizens for the firm's product. The larger the proportion of the firm's total sales generated in a

specific foreign country, the more sensitive the firm's revenue to that country's economic conditions.

4 Exchange rate movements can affect U.S. firms in various ways, depending on their characteristics. U.S. importers benefit from a strong dollar. U.S. exporters benefit from a weak dollar, but are adversely affected by a strong dollar. U.S. firms competing with foreign firms that export to the U.S. market are adversely affected by a strong dollar, because the products exported by foreign firms appear inexpensive to U.S. consumers when the dollar is strong.

KEY TERMS

appreciates
balance of trade
capitalism
communism
depreciates
direct foreign investment (DFI)
exporting
forward contract

forward rate
hedge
importing
international licensing agreement
joint venture
less-developed countries
political risk
privatization

quota
socialism
spot exchange rate
strategic alliance
tariff
trade deficit

REVIEW QUESTIONS

1 Explain why a business may want to sell its product or service in a foreign country.

2 Distinguish exporting from importing. Can a business such as McDonald's be involved in both exporting and importing?

3 Explain why many U.S. firms may increase their foreign acquisitions, due to exchange rates.

4 Explain the differences between capitalism, communism, and socialism.

5 Discuss why the U.S. market is so susceptible to foreign competition.

6 Explain the difference between a direct foreign investment and a strategic alliance undertaken by an international business.

7 Explain how tariffs or quotas impact the price of these imports?

8 Identify and explain the various types of international alliances between U.S. firms and foreign firms.

9 Identify the economic factors that must be assessed before a firm can internationalize its operation in a foreign market.

10 Identify and explain the foreign characteristics that will influence international business investment.

DISCUSSION QUESTIONS

1 Discuss the advantages and disadvantages of foreign ownership in the United States. Should some types of businesses *not* be for sale to a foreign investor?

2 Assume you are a business entrepreneur. Do you support free trade among nations, or do you believe that there should be tariffs and quotas on imported goods? How would each

position affect the economy?

3 Assume you are planning to buy a business in a foreign country. You have just heard that Americans should be better prepared when they undertake a business venture in a foreign land. The criticism is that they never prepare for risk. Comment.

4 Should Americans buy U.S.-produced goods and services, or buy

foreign goods and services? Does either practice affect the U.S. balance of trade? Comment.

5 Discuss the implications of a stronger dollar in relation to other foreign currencies for an exporter, as well as for someone who is planning to travel to a foreign country. Are there differences between the two parties?

RUNNING YOUR OWN BUSINESS

1 Explain whether your business would benefit from importing any supplies from foreign countries.

2 Will your business attempt to export any products to foreign countries? Identify which countries could be tar-

geted. Will your business compete against foreign competitors?

3 Explain how the performance of your business would be affected in any way by exchange rate movements.

INVESTING IN THE STOCK OF A BUSINESS

Using the annual report of the firm in which you would like to invest, complete the following:

1 Describe the means (if any) by which the firm engages in global business. Does it export? Does it import? Does the firm have foreign subsidiaries overseas? Joint alliances or ventures?

2 In what foreign countries does the firm do business?

Is the firm seeking to expand into new foreign markets? How does its overseas sales growth compare with its domestic sales growth?

3 Does the firm's annual report specifically mention foreign firms as a source of competition?

4 Was the firm's performance affected by exchange rate movements last year? If so, how?

CASE 1 Global Expansion by ABC Records

ABC Records is a U.S. producer of soul music, which is sold in the U.S. and exported to Europe. A year ago, the company entered into a joint venture with a distributor in London to retail its records. It is planning to import British rock into the United States, as it has just entered into a strategic alliance with this distributorship. Sales are expected to increase 20 percent a year over first-year sales of £12.5 million. ABC receives payment for its exports in British pounds. The dollar has been weakening against the British pound.

ABC Records has learned that its product line will be subject to a tariff on exported goods into Europe. The tariff is related to a common market alliance that exists

throughout Europe. The company has expressed concern because it believes that political intervention disrupts the free flow of trade as it exists in the United States.

Management is developing a strategic alliance with a French manufacturer to produce compact discs for their entire operation. The company is expected to cut production costs by 25 percent because of the French firm's increased technology. In this strategic alliance, the French manufacturer will buy all its raw materials from a company in Bonn, Germany. In addition to the distributorship in London, ABC Records plans to open new markets in six different countries throughout Western Europe by the year 2000.

Questions

1 Discuss the primary reasons why ABC Records may benefit from its international business.

2 How will ABC Records be affected if the dollar weakens further?

3 Should music imported by U.S. firms from England be subjected to a tariff?

CASE 2 Exposure to Foreign Competition

Softwood is used in the construction of residential housing. Demand for softwood is expected to grow 7 percent annually during the next few years. Canadian softwood is being imported into the United States at an alarming rate. Canadian imports currently account for about 36 percent of the U.S. softwood lumber market. This situation is of concern to many U.S. lumber producers.

Lumber producers in the United States claim that Canada is selling its lumber in the U.S. market at unfairly low prices. They believe that Canadian lumber companies are receiving heavy subsidies from the Canadian government. In Canada, most timber grows on government land and is sold to the lumber industry for a fee, known as a stumpage charge, which is set by the provinces. This practice places U.S. producers at a competitive disadvantage. In the United States, most timber is grown on privately held land and is sold at auction. Citing differences in selling practices, the U.S. lumber industry has been trying for more than a decade to curb imports of low-cost Canadian lumber.

U.S. lumber producers are petitioning Congress to seek a trade agreement with the Canadian government. This agreement would increase the cost of Canadian lumber and thus increase the cost of residential housing in the United States.

Canadian lumber producers claim that tighter environmental controls are responsible for reducing the U.S. lumber supply, thereby increasing Canada's U.S. market share from 27 percent in 1991 to the present 36 percent. A trade agreement could easily result, assuming that both sides can agree that softwood is competitively priced in the U.S. market.

Questions

1 What attracts Canadian softwood to U.S. homebuilders?

2 Is softwood competitively priced in this market?

3 Should the United States and Canada seek a trade agreement? If so, why?

4 Why is U.S. softwood priced higher than Canadian softwood?

VIDEO CASE Exposure to Global Conditions

 A pleasure sail from New Zealand to the New Hebrides Islands in 1978 came to an abrupt end for young Geoff Bourne and Barry Spanier. Their boat, a thirty-eight foot one-master that Spanier had built, was destroyed in a violent storm, and they were shipwrecked on a small island in New Zealand waters occupied only by two caretakers. It took twenty-two days to get transport off the island.

In a way, the misfortune made the fortunes of two men who, after getting out of college in California, had wandered from job to job—most connected with sailing—while taking lots of time off.

Today they own a Hawaii firm that has successfully applied new technology to an old craft, sailmaking: Spanier and Bourne Sailmakers, located in Kahului on the island of Maui and known widely as Maui Sails, has earned international recognition and growing revenues, primarily from designing windsurfing sails and equipment for a Hong Kong manufacturer of boats.

From a visit to Maui, Spanier knew there were many charter sailboats there, but no sailmakers. With $10,000 of starting capital—Bourne's savings—the friends rented a loft and went into business. They had sailmaking experience and talent, and they soon had numerous customers in Maui's charter fleet.

In 1980 a monster storm hit Maui, wrecking many boats. Maui Sails' customer base was wiped out. For some time to come, the charter skippers wouldn't be sailing or buying sails, just salvaging what they could.

Luckily, some California windsurfers, sailing in Maui's Hookipa area, brought in sails for repairs. "We had tons of high grade material for yacht sails and suggested that we could improve on the design and construction of their rigs," Spanier says. The firm became so popular with windsurfers that international sailboard brands asked for its services as a designer.

Two years later it became the exclusive research and development facility for Neil Pryde, owner of Neil Pryde Ltd., of Hong Kong, a major manufacturer of sailboards and other windsurfing equipment. Maui Sails, which had two employees, hired more—it has eleven now—and invested in tools and material.

Spanier and Bourne applied the computer to sailmaking. With the aid of a skilled programmer, Sandy Warrick, and financial backing from Pryde, who worked his company back to profitability, they developed a computerized system of designing windsurfing sails. The system cut costs and spurred sales by speeding design changes.

Questions

1 Explain how Spanier and Bourne's business may be affected by the economic conditions in Hong Kong.

Assume that Spanier and Bourne receive Hong Kong dollars as payment from the Hong Kong manufacturer, which they convert to U.S. dollars. Explain how the performance of Spanier and Bourne could be affected by a decline in the value of the Hong Kong dollar over time.

2 How could Spanier and Bourne reduce the exposure of their business to economic conditions in Hong Kong and the value of the Hong Kong dollar without giving up their business in Hong Kong?

3 Spanier and Bourne presently generate most of their revenue by selling sails to one large manufacturer of boats in Hong Kong. If that manufacturer experiences a decline in the demand for its boats, it will not purchase as many sails from Spanier and Bourne. Would Spanier and Bourne eliminate their economic exposure to the Hong Kong economy by diversifying their business among several boat manufacturers in Hong Kong?

THE Coca-Cola COMPANY ANNUAL REPORT PROJECT

The following questions apply concepts learned in this chapter to The Coca-Cola Company.

Read the graphic and the tables on pages 14–16, 31, 33, and 34 in The Coca-Cola Company annual report before answering these questions. Also read the section "Foreign Currency Management" on page 61.

1 Have The Coca-Cola Company's products achieved a global presence?

2 a. In terms of per capita consumption, what are The Coca-Cola Company's major successes?

b. Where are their major opportunies?

3 a. In the U.S., what percentage of U.S. total beverage market does The Coca-Cola Company currently supply?

b. What is The Coca-Cola Company's market share of the worldwide soft drink market?

c. What is its market share of the soft drink market in Mexico? In China? In Germany?

4 In some situations, The Coca-Cola Company may receive cash inflows from foreign countries that can be affected by exchange rate changes. How does it hedge against these fluctuations?

IN-TEXT STUDY GUIDE

Answers are in an appendix at the back of the book.

True or False

1 Economic growth is always lower in non-U.S. countries than it is in the United States.

2 When a firm focuses on one specific product in one country, the profits of the firm are normally stable over time.

3 Many U.S. firms compete with foreign firms within the U.S. market.

4 A firm's performance in a foreign country is dependent on that country's economic growth and inflation.

5 A U.S. firm's overall performance may be more stable if its product is sold in various countries, so that its business is not solely influenced by the economic conditions in a single country.

6 Competition does not exist in capitalist countries.

7 In a communist society, the government decides whether to produce more of some type of product.

8 Labor and land costs generally do not vary significantly among countries.

9 The values of most currencies are not allowed to change relative to the dollar.

10 If firms overestimate the economic growth in a particular country, they will normally overestimate the demand for their products in that country.

Multiple Choice

11 In many cases, the primary factor influencing a firm's decision to expand its business in a foreign market is the expected:
a) economic growth.
b) cost of capital.
c) labor demand.
d) economic rent.
e) bureaucracy.

12 For U.S firms with production facilities in foreign countries, production expenses will be affected by:
a) centralized government.
b) competitive forces.
c) inflation.
d) increased demand.
e) central planning bureaus.

13 Many U.S. firms have capitalized on opportunities in foreign countries by engaging in:
a) politics.
b) international business.
c) religious practices.
d) cultural diversity.
e) corrupt practices.

14 Many U.S. firms hedge only when they expect their future international business transactions to be adversely affected by:
a) government intervention.
b) increased supply.
c) increased competition.
d) political intervention.
e) exchange rate movements.

15 An exchange rate that is quoted for immediate transactions is the:
a) spot rate.
b) forward rate.
c) world bank rate.
d) prime rate.
e) international monetary fund.

16 A major limitation of hedging is that the hedge not only offsets unfavorable exchange rate movements but also offsets:
a) interest rate movements.
b) consumer price movements.
c) productivity indexes.
d) favorable rate movements.
e) inflationary movements.

17 The acquisition of a foreign business by a U.S. firm is an example of:

a) direct foreign investment.
b) exporting.
c) importing.
d) international licensing.
e) a joint venture.

18 When governments limit the amount of specific products that can be imported, they are imposing a/an:
a) tariff.
b) embargo.
c) quota.
d) cartel.
e) bribe.

19 A negative balance of trade is referred to as a:
a) trade deficit.
b) trade surplus.
c) favorable balance of payments.
d) direct investment.
e) hedge.

20 The purchase of foreign supplies by IBM is an example of:
a) direct foreign investment.
b) exporting.
c) importing.
d) international licensing.
e) a joint venture.

21 The following are possible motives for a firm engaging in international business except for:
a) domestic market.
b) attract foreign demand.
c) use inexpensive resources.
d) capitalize on technology.
e) diversify internationally.

22 The sale of film produced by Kodak in the U.S. to Chinese firms is an example of:
a) direct foreign investment.
b) exporting.
c) importing.
d) international licensing.
e) a joint venture.

23 The degree to which a firm imports goods and services is influenced by a government:
a) trade barrier.
b) trade surplus.
c) trade deficit.
d) balance of payments.
e) budget deficit.

24 The dollar weakens against the British pound if the value of the pound:
a) depreciates.
b) sells off.
c) softens.

d) appreciates.

e) declines.

25 The purchase of foreign products or services is called:

a) importing.

b) exporting.

c) hedging.

d) financial exchange.

e) economic growth.

26 An economic system that contains some features of capitalism and some features of communism is:

a) fascism.

b) bureaucratic.

c) democratic.

d) laissez-faire.

e) socialism.

27 Governments are reducing their influence in numerous countries and are allowing firms to compete in each industry through:

a) public ownership.

b) privatization.

c) central planning bureaus.

d) domestication.

e) cartel arrangements.

28 The profits of U.S. firms that do substantial business in a foreign country are highly dependent on:

a) chamber of commerce.

b) federal reserve system.

c) political risk.

d) crime rate.

e) vacation policies.

29 A tax on imported products that is imposed by governments is called a:

a) tariff.

b) quota.

c) cartel.

d) bribe.

e) custom.

30 If firms have a means of acquiring or building subsidiaries in one or more foreign countries, they are engaging in:

a) portfolio investment.

b) financial exchange.

c) arbitrage.

d) spot transactions.

e) direct foreign investment.

31 The sale of products or services to purchasers residing in other countries is called:

a) importing.

b) hedging.

c) exporting.

d) smuggling.

e) financial exchange.

32 An alliance in which a firm allows a foreign company to produce its products according to specific instructions is a(n):

a) tariff.

b) export.

c) international licensing agreement.

d) import.

e) quota.

33 According to the text, an agreement between two firms about a specific project is a:

a) sole proprietorship.

b) joint venture.

c) cartel.

d) tariff.

e) balance of payment.

34 In what kind of society does the desire for entrepreneurs to earn profits motivate them to produce products and services that satisfy customers?

a) capitalist

b) communist

c) socialist

d) domestic

e) bureaucratic

35 A contract that states an exchange of currencies that will occur for a specified amount of a particular currency at a specified future date is called a:

a) trade agreement.

b) budget deficit.

c) direct investment.

d) forward contract.

e) portfolio investment.

International Business on the World Wide Web

An amazing aspect of the World Wide Web (WWW) is its global scope. International businesses maintain a presence on the WWW and so do many countries. Links to many international sites can be found at The Internationalist (Exhibit 6.11). This site, maintained by MIT, provides detailed information by country. An executive seeking a supplier in Thailand could pull up information to schedule his trip, negotiate a contract, and learn about local customs.

Exhibit 6.11
The Internationalist Website

http://www.internationalist.com

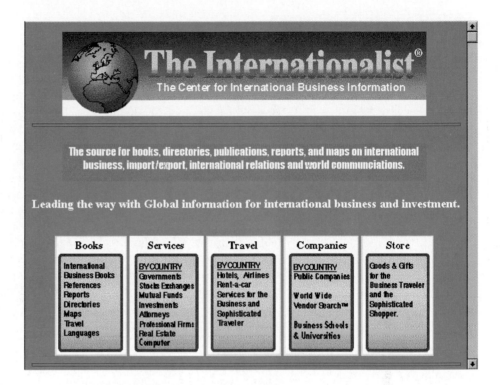

<table>
<tr><td>APPENDIX 6</td><td># The Foreign Exchange Market</td></tr>
</table>

EXCHANGE RATE QUOTATIONS

Foreign exchange markets represent a global telecommunications network among the large commercial banks that serve as financial intermediaries for foreign exchange. The major banks for foreign exchange are located in New York, Tokyo, Hong Kong, Singapore, Frankfurt, Zurich, and London. As international trade and investing has increased over time, so has the need to exchange currencies.

Exhibit 6A.1 shows the approximate foreign exchange rates of the major currencies as of July 31, 1996. These exchange rates are listed daily in every major newspaper. Directly across from the currency name (in the second column) is the spot exchange rate, for immediate delivery. The exchange rates in this column define the value of a foreign currency in U.S. dollars. The exchange rates in the third column are expressed as the number of units per dollar. According to the foreign exchange table, the British pound's value is $1.5561, which implies that .6426 pounds equal $1.00. Each exchange rate in the third column is simply the reciprocal of what is shown in the second column. The forward exchange rate is shown for a few currencies for three different points in time (30, 60, and 90 days in the future).

FACTORS THAT AFFECT EXCHANGE RATE MOVEMENTS

The value of currency adjusts to a change in demand and supply conditions in the foreign exchange market. For example, the value of the German mark with respect to the U.S. dollar changes over time in response to fluctuations in the U.S. demand for marks and German demand for dollars (supply of marks to be exchanged for dollars). In equilibrium, there is no excess or deficiency. Over time, conditions will change, causing an adjustment in the mark's value to maintain equilibrium.

Supply and demand for a currency are influenced by a variety of factors, including (1) differential inflation rates, (2) differential interest rates, and (3) government intervention.

Differential Inflation Rates

Begin with an equilibrium situation and consider what would happen to the U.S. demand for marks and the supply of German marks for sale if U.S. inflation suddenly became much higher than German inflation. The U.S. demand for German goods would increase, reflecting an increased U.S. demand for German marks (since U.S. consumers would attempt to avoid purchases of highly inflated U.S. products). In addition, the supply of marks to be sold for dollars would decline, as the German demand for highly inflated U.S. goods would decrease. Both forces would place upward pressure on the value of the mark.

Under the reverse situation, where German inflation suddenly became higher than U.S. inflation, the U.S. demand for marks would decrease (because prices of

Exhibit 6A.1
Example of Exchange
Rate Quotations

Country	Value in $	Currency per U.S. $
Argentina (Peso)	1.0012	.9988
Australia (Dollar)	.7736	1.2927
Austria (Schilling)	.09681	10.330
Belgium (Franc)	.03301	30.290
Brazil (Real)	.9766	1.0240
Britain (Pound)	1.5561	.6426
30-Day Forward	1.5556	.6428
90-Day Forward	1.5556	.6429
180-Day Forward	1.5565	.6425
Canada (Dollar)	.7274	1.3747
30-Day Forward	.7280	1.3737
90-Day Forward	.7292	1.3714
180-Day Forward	.7308	1.3684
Chile (Peso)	.002433	410.95
China (Renminbi)	.1199	8.3407
Colombia (Peso)	.0009533	1049.00
Czech. Rep. (Koruna)	. . . .	. . . .
Commercial rate	.03793	26.367
Denmark (Krone)	.1757	5.6930
Finland (Markka)	.2227	4.4906
France (Franc)	.2002	4.9960
Germany (Mark)	.6791	1.4725
30-Day Forward	.6804	1.4698
90-Day Forward	.6831	1.4639
180-Day Forward	.6876	1.4544
Greece (Drachma)	.004261	234.66
Hong Kong (Dollar)	.1293	7.7337
Hungary (Forint)	.006580	151.97
India (Rupee)	.02795	35.778
Indonesia (Rupiah)	.0004255	2350.25
Ireland (Punt)	1.6176	.6182
Israel (Shekel)	.3172	3.1530
Italy (Lira)	.0006581	1519.50
Japan (Yen)	.009361	106.83
Kuwait (Dinar)	3.3445	.2990
Malaysia (Ringgit)	.4008	2.4953
Mexico (Peso)	.1320	7.5770
Netherland (Guilder)	.6047	1.6536
New Zealand (Dollar)	.6888	1.4518
Norway (Krone)	.1570	6.3685
Pakistan (Rupee)	.02863	34.930
Peru (new Sol)	.4112	2.4318
Philippines (Peso)	.03812	26.230
Poland (Zloty)	.3705	2.6990
Portugal (Escudo)	.006591	151.72
Russia (Ruble)	.0001919	5212.00
Saudi Arabia (Riyal)	.2666	3.7505

Country	Value in $	Currency per U.S. $
Singapore (Dollar)	.7072	1.4140
Slovak Rep. (Koruna)	.03304	30.265
South Africa (Rand)	.2219	4.5065
South Korea (Won)	.001231	812.65
Spain (Peseta)	.007938	125.97
Sweden (Krona)	.1515	6.6020
Switzerland (Franc)	.8350	1.1976
Taiwan (Dollar)	.03634	27.516
Thailand (Baht)	.03958	25.267
Turkey (Lira)	.00001205	83003.00
Venezuela (Bolivar)	.002119	472.00

German goods would be too high), while the supply of marks to be exchanged for dollars would increase (as German consumers would demand more U.S. goods). These forces would place downward pressure on the value of the mark.

Differential Interest Rates

A second factor that affects exchange rates is differential interest rates. To understand its impact, consider what would happen to the U.S. demand for marks and the supply of marks for sale if U.S. interest rates suddenly became much higher than German interest rates. The demand by U.S. investors for German interest-bearing securities would decrease, as these securities would now be less attractive. In addition, the supply of marks to be sold in exchange for dollars would increase, as German investors would increase their purchases of U.S. interest-bearing securities. Both forces would place downward pressure on the mark's value.

Government Intervention

A country's government can intervene to affect a currency's value. Direct intervention occurs when a country's central bank (such as the Federal Reserve Bank for the United States or the Bank of England for the United Kingdom) sells some of its currency reserves for a different currency. For example, if the Federal Reserve Bank desired to weaken the dollar, it could sell some of its dollar reserves in exchange for foreign currencies. In essence, it has increased the U.S. demand for foreign currencies, which could cause those currencies to appreciate against the dollar. If the Federal Reserve Bank desired to strengthen the dollar, it could sell some of its foreign currency reserves in exchange for dollars. This action reflects an increase in the supply of foreign currencies to be exchanged for dollars. As an indirect method of intervention, the government could influence those economic factors (such as inflation or interest rates) that affect a currency's value.

A firm is exposed to economic conditions (Chapter 4), industry conditions (Chapter 5), and global conditions (Chapter 6). The economic conditions that affect a firm's performance are economic growth, inflation, and interest rates. Economic growth influences the demand for products and services produced by firms. Inflation influences the production expenses of materials, machinery, or employees. Interest rates influence the demand for products that are typically purchased with borrowed funds. They also influence the cost of financing. In general, a firm's performance is improved as a result of strong economic growth, low inflation, and low interest rates.

The industry conditions that affect a firm's performance are the demand for a specific type of product (industry demand), the industry competition, the labor environment, and the regulatory environment. A firm's performance is typically improved when industry demand is high, industry competitors are weak, the supply of available labor is high, and when regulations do not impose excessive regulations.

The global conditions that affect a firm's performance are economic conditions in foreign countries and exchange rates. A U.S. firm's performance may be improved when the foreign countries where it sells some of its products experience a high rate of economic growth. A U.S. firm may also benefit from a weak dollar if it exports products, or from a strong dollar if it imports products.

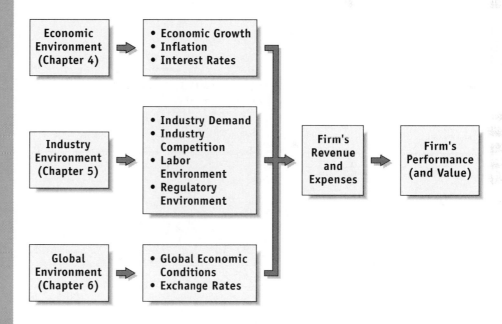

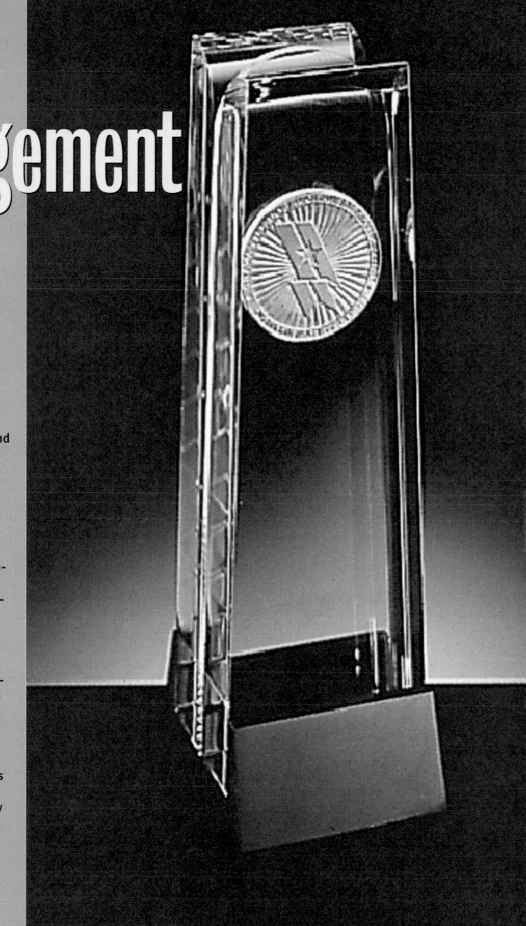

Management represents the use of human resources and other resources in a manner that best achieves the firm's objectives. Four key components of management are (1) understanding the characteristics necessary for managers to be effective, (2) assignments of job responsibilities, (3) management of the process by which the products are produced, and (4) monitoring and improving the quality of products produced. Chapter 7 provides a background on the characteristics necessary for managers to be effective, while Chapter 8 explains how job responsibilities are assigned. Chapter 9 describes how the resources used in the production process can be allocated efficiently, while Chapter 10 explains how the quality of products produced can be monitored and improved.

199

CHAPTER 7

Fundamentals of Effective Management

Management represents the utilization of human resources (employees) and other resources (such as machinery) in a manner that best achieves the firm's plans and objectives. According to a recent survey by Shareholder Surveys, shareholders ranked good management and long-term vision as the two most important characteristics of a firm. Effective management can improve the firm's performance, and therefore increase the firm's value for shareholders.

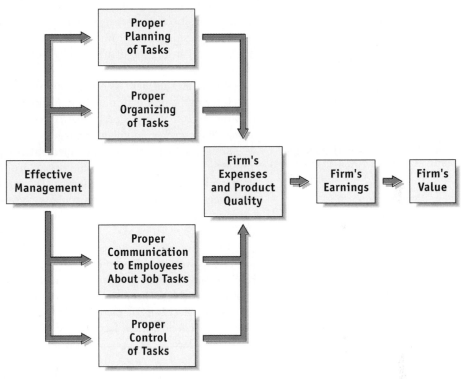

Consider the case of Intel Corporation, which produces computer chips, boards, and software for computer firms. What types of planning should Intel do over the next one to five years? How can Intel ensure that its various business tasks are being conducted properly? What types of management skills are needed to ensure Intel's continued success? This chapter discusses the fundamentals of management, which can be used to answer these questions.

The **Learning Goals** of this chapter are to:

1 Identify the levels of management.

2 Identify the key functions of managers.

3 Describe the skills that managers need.

4 Describe methods in which managers can use their time effectively.

LEVELS OF MANAGEMENT

1 | **Identify the levels of management.**

top (high-level) management
includes positions such as president, chief executive officer, chief financial officer, and vice-president that make decisions regarding the firm's long-run objectives

middle management often responsible for the short-term decisions

supervisory (first-line) management usually highly involved with the employees who engage in the day-to-day production process

Employees who are responsible for managing other employees or other resources serve as managers, even if their official title is different. The functions of managers vary with their respective levels within the firm. **Top (high-level) management** includes positions such as president, chief executive officer (who commonly also serves as president), chief financial officer, and vice-president. They each make decisions regarding the firm's long-run objectives (such as three to five years ahead).

Middle management is often responsible for the short-term decisions, as they are closer to the production process. Middle managers resolve problems and devise new methods to improve performance. Middle management includes positions such as regional manager and plant manager.

Supervisory (first-line) management is usually highly involved with the employees who engage in the day-to-day production process. Supervisors deal with problems such as worker absenteeism and customer complaints. Supervisory management includes positions such as account manager and office manager. The types of functions that each level of management conducts are summarized in Exhibit 7.1.

The relationships among the top, middle, and supervisory managers can be more fully understood by considering a simple example. Exhibit 7.2 shows the responsibilities of all managers in light of new plans by a firm to expand production and increase sales. The middle and top managers must make production, marketing, and finance decisions that would achieve the new plans. The supervisory managers provide specific instructions to the new employees who are hired to achieve a higher production level.

The construction supervisor shown here focuses on employee input as part of the organization's emphasis on employee involvement and job satisfaction.

Exhibit 7.1
Comparison of Different Levels of Management

Top Management Title	Types of Decisions
President	1) Should we create new products?
	2) Should we expand?
	3) How can we expand? Through acquisitions?
Chief Financial Officer	1) Should more funds be borrowed?
	2) Should we invest available funds in proposed projects?
Vice-President of Marketing	1) Should an existing product be revised?
	2) Should our pricing policies be changed?
	3) Should our advertising strategies be changed?
Middle Management Regional Sales Manager	1) How can we boost sales in a particular city?
	2) How can complaints by one of the largest customers be resolved?
	3) Should an additional salesperson be hired?
Plant Manager	1) Should the structure of the assembly line be revised?
	2) Should new equipment be installed throughout the plant?
Supervisory Management Account Manager	1) How can workers who process payments from various accounts be motivated?
	2) How can conflicts between two workers be resolved?
Supervisor	1) How can the quality of work by assembly-line workers be assessed?
	2) How can assembly-line tasks be assigned across workers?
	3) How can customer complaints be handled?

FUNCTIONS OF MANAGERS

2 | **Identify the key functions of managers.**

Most managerial functions can be classified into one of the following categories:

➤ Planning
➤ Organizing
➤ Leading
➤ Controlling

Planning

planning represents the preparation of the firm for future business conditions

The **planning** function represents the preparation of the firm for future business conditions. Firms conduct various types of planning, as explained next.

strategic plan intended to identify the firm's main business focus over a long-term period, perhaps three to five years

STRATEGIC PLANNING A firm's **strategic plan** is intended to identify the firm's main business focus over a long-term period, perhaps three to five years. The strate-

Exhibit 7.2
Comparison of Responsibilities
Among Managers

Top Management

1. Set new plan to expand production and increase sales.
2. Communicate those plans to all managers.

Middle and Top Managers

1. Determine how many new employees to hire.
2. Determine how to charge lower prices to increase sales.
3. Determine how to increase advertising to increase sales.
4. Determine how to obtain funds to finance the expansion.

Supervisory Managers

1. Provide job assignments to the new employees who are hired.
2. Set time schedules for new employees who are hired.

mission statement describes the firm's primary goal

gic plan is based on the firm's **mission statement,** which describes the firm's primary goal. For example, here is the mission statement of Bristol-Myers Squibb:

> ▌▌ *The mission of Bristol-Myers Squibb is to extend and enhance human life by providing the highest quality health and personal care products.* ▌▌

Most mission statements are general, like that of Bristol-Myers. The mission of General Motors is to be the world leader in transportation products, while the mission of Amoco Corporation is to provide quality petroleum and chemical products to customers and high returns to stockholders. Each mission statement tends to stress excellence in some specified industry. The strategic plan typically consists of goals and strategies that can be used to satisfy the firm's mission. For example, some of the main goals and strategies listed in a recent annual report of Bristol-Myers Squibb are as follows:

Goals

> ▌▌ *Leadership in each product category and in each geographic market in which we compete. We aim to achieve number one or number two position with increasing market shares.* ▌▌

❚❚ *Superior customer satisfaction by providing the highest quality products and services to our customers. We will strive to be rated number one or two with continuous improvement as rated by our customers.* ❚❚

❚❚ *Superior steady shareholder returns, as measured by a number one or two competitive position in economic performance within our industry.* ❚❚

❚❚ *An organization which is committed to winning through teamwork, empowerment, customer focus, and open communications.* ❚❚

Strategies

❚❚ *Our mission and goals will be achieved by adhering to the following core strategies:*
• *Achieve unit growth fueled internally by new products, geographic expansion, and marketing innovation, and externally through acquisition, joint venture and licensing agreements.*
• *Dedicate ourselves to being recognized as the best in research and development across our businesses . . .*
• *Achieve continuous improvement in our cost structure . . .*
• *Attract, develop, motivate, and retain people of the highest caliber. The company's reporting, reward and recognition systems will be built around attainment of the goals identified above.* ❚❚

tactical planning smaller scale plans (over one or two years) that are consistent with the firm's strategic (long-term) plan

TACTICAL PLANNING   High-level and middle managers also engage in **tactical planning,** or smaller scale plans (over one or two years) that are consistent with the firm's strategic (long-term) plan. Tactical planning normally focuses on a short-term period, such as the next year or so. To develop their tactical plan, managers of AT&T and other firms assess the economic conditions, the general demand for various products, the level of competition among firms producing those products, and changes in technology. They use their vision to capitalize on opportunities in which they have some advantages over other firms in that industry. If a firm's strategic plan is to increase its market share by 20 percent, its tactical plans may represent plans for increasing sales in specific regions that have less competition. As time passes, additional tactical planning will be conducted in accordance with the strategic plan.

operational planning establishes the methods used for the near future (such as the next year) to achieve the tactical plans

OPERATIONAL PLANNING   Another form of planning, called **operational planning,** establishes the methods used for the near future (such as the next year) to achieve the tactical plans. Using our previous example of a firm whose tactical plan is to increase sales, the operational plan may specify the means by which the firm can increase sales. That is, the operational plan may specify an increase in the amount of funds allocated to advertising and the hiring of additional salespeople.

An important part of the planning process at Springfield Remanufacturing Corporation, a former Baldrige Award winner, are scoreboards. Boards like the one shown in this picture keep employees informed about how they are meeting production goals.

The goals from operational planning are somewhat dependent on the firm's long-term goals. For example, top managers of a firm may establish a goal of 12 percent annual growth in sales over the next several years. The salespeople of the firm may be asked to strive for a 1 percent increase in total sales per month during the upcoming year. Their month-to-month goals are structured from the long-term goals established by top management.

policies guidelines for how tasks should be completed

When firms engage in operational planning, they must abide by their **policies,** or guidelines for how tasks should be completed. For example, a policy on the hiring of employees may require that a specific process be followed. Policies enforced by firms ensure that all employees conduct specific tasks in a similar manner. They are intended to prevent employees from conducting tasks in a manner that is inefficient, dangerous, or illegal.

procedures steps necessary to implement a policy

Most policies contain **procedures,** or steps necessary to implement a policy. For example, a policy for hiring may specify that an ad is to be placed in the local newspaper for so many days and posted in a visible spot at the firm. It may also specify a maximum number of days that an applicant has to accept or reject a job offer. These procedures attempt to prevent unfair treatment to people that may apply for a position. Without procedures, managers could make decisions that conflict with the company's goals.

contingency planning alternative plans developed for various possible business conditions

CONTINGENCY PLANNING   Some plans of firms may not be finalized until specific business conditions are known. For this reason, firms use **contingency planning,** in which alternative plans are developed for various possible business conditions. That is, the plan to be implemented is contingent on the business conditions that occur. For example, a firm that produces sports equipment may plan to boost its production of rollerblades in response to recent demand. However, it may develop an alternative plan for using its resources to produce other equipment instead of rollerblades if demand declines. It may also develop a plan for increasing its production if the demand for its rollerblades is much higher than expected.

Some contingency planning is conducted to prepare for possible crises that may occur. For example, airlines may establish contingency plans in the event that various problems occur, as illustrated in Exhibit 7.3.

Exhibit 7.3
Illustration of
Contingency Planning

Situation	Contingency Plan
Overbooked reservations	To reduce the number of customers who need that flight, offer customers who are willing to be bumped (wait for next flight) a free round-trip ticket to the destination of their choice in the future.
Minor airplane repair needed	Have airline engineers available at each major airport in the event that a minor repair is needed.
Major airplane repair needed	If the airplane is not suitable for flying, attempt to reroute the passengers who were supposed to be on that plane by reserving seats for them on other flights.

The relationships among planning functions are shown in Exhibit 7.4. Notice how the tactical plan is dependent on the strategic plan. Also, the operational plan is based on the tactical plan. The contingency plan offers alternatives to consider instead of the operational plan in specific situations (such as a higher or lower demand for the product than anticipated).

Exhibit 7.4
How Planning Functions are
Related

Example

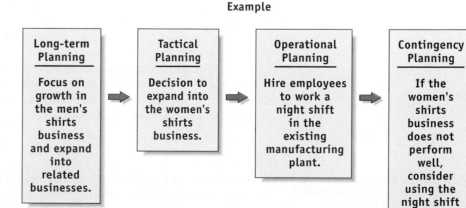

CROSS-FUNCTIONAL TEAMWORK

Interaction of Functions to Achieve the Strategic Plan

The development of a strategic plan requires interaction among the firm's managers who are responsible for different business functions. Recall that the strategic plan of Bristol-Myers Squibb that was mentioned earlier includes goals of increased market share, customer satisfaction, and continuous improvement. Its strategies to achieve those goals include the creation of new products, continuous improvement in cost structure (high production efficiency), and retaining good employees.

The management function of Bristol-Myers Squibb can help achieve the firm's goals by assessing the needs of consumers in order to create new products. It can also attempt to assess the customer's satisfaction level of their existing products, and use marketing strategies to increase the market share of these products. The financing function of Bristol-Myers Squibb can help achieve the firm's goals by determining the level of borrowing that will be sufficient to support the firm's operations.

Since the business functions are related, a strategic plan can be implemented only when the interaction among business functions is recognized. A strategic plan that focuses on increased sales will likely require more production and financing. Exhibit 7.5 discloses some common ways in which the goals of a strategic plan can be achieved by this function.

Exhibit 7.5
How Various Business Functions Are Used to Achieve the Strategic Plan

Function	Typical Goals or Strategies That Can Be Achieved by This Function
Management	High production efficiency
	High production quality
	Customer satisfaction
	Employee satisfaction
Marketing	Innovation (new products)
	Increase market share of existing products
	Customer satisfaction
Finance	Reduce financing costs
	Efficient use of funds

To fully understand how these plans fit together, assume that your firm is created to produce men's shirts. Assume your strategic plan specifies goals of expanding into related products. In this case, your tactical plan may focus on producing one other product along with men's shirts, such as women's shirts. The operational plan would specify the changes in the firm's operations that are necessary to produce and sell women's shirts. Specifically, the plan would determine how much more material must be purchased each month, how the women's shirts will be priced, and where the women's shirts will be sold. A contingency plan could be created in the event that excessive competition develops in the market for women's shirts. If this occurs, the contingency plan may be to expand into different products, such as men's pants.

Organizing

organizing the organization of employees and other resources in a manner that is consistent with the firm's goals

The **organizing** function represents the organization of employees and other resources in a manner that is consistent with the firm's goals. Once a firm's goals are established (from the planning function), resources are obtained and organized to achieve those goals. For example, employees of Chrysler Corporation are organized among assembly lines to produce cars or trucks in a manner consistent with Chrysler's goals.

The organizing function occurs continuously throughout the life of the firm. This function is especially important for firms that frequently restructure their operations. Organizational changes such as the creation of a new position or the promotion of an employee are made frequently. These changes may even cause revisions in job assignments of those employees whose job positions have not changed.

To illustrate the importance of the organizing function, consider a construction company that builds homes. The general contractor assigns tasks to the employees. From the laying of the foundation to painting, most tasks must be completed in a particular order. Since all tasks cannot be completed simultaneously, the contractor has workers working on different homes. In this way, employees can apply their respective specialties (such as painting, electrical, and so on) to whatever homes are at the proper stage of construction. In the next chapter we will look at organizational structure in more detail.

Leading

leading the process of influencing the habits of others to achieve a common goal

The **leading** function is the process of influencing the habits of others to achieve a common goal. It may include the communication of job assignments to employees and possibly the methods to complete those assignments. It may also include serving as a role model for employees. The leading should be conducted in a manner that is consistent with the firm's strategic plan.

The leading function involves not only instructions on how to complete a task but also incentives to complete it correctly and quickly. Some forms of leading may help motivate employees. One method is to delegate authority by assigning employees more responsibility. Increased responsibility can encourage employees to take more pride in their jobs and raise their self-esteem. If employees are brought closer to the production process and allowed to express their concerns, problems can be resolved more easily. Managers who allow much employee feedback may prevent conflicts between management and employees, or even conflicts among employees.

initiative the willingness to take action

For managers to be effective leaders, they need **initiative,** which is the willingness to take action. Managers who have all other skills but lack initiative may not be very effective. Some managers who recognize the need to enact changes are unwilling to take action because making changes takes more effort than leaving the situation as is, and change may upset some employees. For example, consider a manager who recognizes that the firm's expenses could be reduced, without any adverse effect on the firm, by eliminating a particular department. Yet, this manager may refrain from suggesting any action because it might upset some employees. Managers are more likely to initiate change if they are directly rewarded for suggesting any changes that enhance the firm's value.

autocratic leadership style that retains full authority for decision making

LEADERSHIP STYLES While all managers have their own leadership styles, each style can be classified as autocratic, free rein, or participative. Managers who use an **autocratic** leadership style retain full authority for decision making; employees have little or no input. For example, if managers believe that one of their manufacturing plants will continue to incur losses, they may decide to close the plant without asking for input from the plant's workers. Autocratic managers may believe that employees cannot offer input that would contribute to a given decision. Employees are instructed to carry out tasks ordered by autocratic leaders, and are therefore discouraged from being creative. In general, employees who desire responsibility are likely to become dissatisfied with such a management style.

Herb Kelleher's personality and passion are critical elements of his leadership of Southwest Airlines.

free-rein leadership style that delegates much authority to employees

participative leadership style that allows the leaders to accept some employee input, but the leaders usually use their authority to make decisions

Managers who use a **free-rein** (also called "laissez-faire") management style delegate much authority to employees. This style is the opposite extreme of the autocratic style. Free-rein managers communicate goals to employees but allow employees to choose how to complete the objectives. For example, managers may inform workers in a manufacturing plant that the plant's performance must be improved, and then allow the workers to implement an improvement strategy. Employees working under a free-rein management style are expected to manage and motivate themselves daily.

The **participative** (also called democratic) leadership style allows the leaders to accept some employee input, but the leaders usually use their authority to make decisions. This style requires frequent communication between managers and employees. Participative management can allow employees to express their opinions, but it does not pressure employees to make major decisions. For example, managers of a General Motors plant may consider the ideas of assembly-line workers on how to improve the plant's performance, but the managers will make the final decisions.

A comparison of leadership styles is provided in Exhibit 7.6. The optimal leadership style varies with the situation and with employees' experience and personalities. The free-rein style may be appropriate if employees are highly independent, creative, and motivated. An autocratic style may be most effective for managing employees with low skill-levels or high turnover rates. Participative management is effective when employees can offer a different perspective because of closer attention to daily tasks.

Exhibit 7.6
How Leadership Style Affects
Employee Influence on
Management Decisions

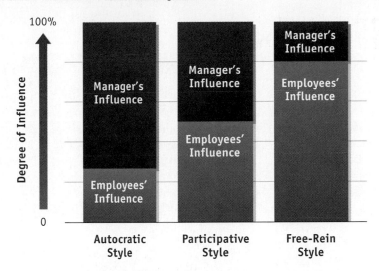

Within a given firm, all three leadership styles may be used. For example, the top management of General Motors may use autocratic leadership to determine the types of automobiles (large versus small cars, luxury versus economy cars, and so on) to design in the future. These plans are made without much employee input because top management can rely on recent surveys of consumer preferences along with their own vision of what types of cars will be in demand in the future.

Once top management identifies the types of automobiles to produce, a participative leadership style may be used to design each type of car. That is, top management may decide general design guidelines on a particular type of car to be produced (such as specifying a small economy car), and employees may be asked for their suggestions on developing this type of car. These employees have experience on specific assembly-line operations and can offer useful input based on various production or quality problems they experienced with other cars. The top managers will make the final decisions after receiving the engineers' proposed designs, which are based on input from numerous employees. This example reflects a participative style because managers will use their authority to decide on the particular type of product to be produced, but will solicit input from many employees.

After the design of a specific car is completed, managers allow a free-rein style for some parts of the production process. For example, a group of employees may be assigned to a set of assembly-line tasks. They may be allowed to assign the specific tasks among themselves. They may also be allowed to rotate their specific jobs to avoid boredom. This example reflects the free-rein style because the employees are allowed to choose how to achieve the firm's objectives.

Controlling

controlling the monitoring and evaluation of tasks

The **controlling** function represents the monitoring and evaluation of tasks. To evaluate tasks, managers should measure performance in comparison with the standards and expectations they set. That is, the controlling function assesses whether the plans set within the planning function are achieved. Standards can be applied to production volume and cost, sales volume, profits, and several other variables used to measure a firm's performance. The strategic plan of Bristol-Myers Squibb (disclosed earlier) states that its reward systems will be based on standards set by the goals identified within that plan. An example of how the controlling function can be used to assess a firm's operations is shown in Exhibit 7.7.

Exhibit 7.7
Example of the Controlling Function

	Actual Level Last Week	Standards (Expected Level)	Assessment
Sales Volume	300 units	280 units	OK
Production Volume	350 units	350 units	OK
Labor Expenses	$10,000	$9,000	Too high
Administrative Expenses	$14,500	$15,000	OK
Equipment Repair	$3,000	$1,000	Too high

Some standards such as profits are general and apply to all departments of a firm. Thus, no single department is likely to be entirely accountable if the firm's profits are not sufficient. However, other standards focus on a particular operation of the firm. For example, production volume, production cost per unit, and inventory level standards can be used to monitor production. A specified volume of sales can be used as a standard to monitor the effectiveness of marketing strategies. The main reason for setting standards is to detect and correct deficiencies. When deficiencies are detected, managers must take corrective action. For example, if labor and equipment repair expenses are too high, the firm would attempt to identify the reason for these deficiencies so that it could prevent them in the future. If a firm finds that its sales volume is below standards, its managers would determine whether to revise the existing marketing strategies or penalize those employees who are responsible for the deficiency. Deficiencies that are detected early may be more easily corrected.

In some cases, the standards rather than the strategies need to be corrected. For example, a particular advertising strategy to boost automobile sales may fail when interest rates are high, since consumers are unwilling to borrow money to purchase automobiles at those interest rates. The failure to reach a specified sales level may be due to the high interest rates rather than a poor advertising strategy.

Integration of Management Functions

management the utilization of human resources (employees) and other resources (such as machinery) in a manner that best achieves the firm's plans and objectives

To illustrate how the four different functions of **management** are used, consider a firm that makes children's toys and decides to restructure its operations. Because of low sales, the top managers create a new strategic plan to discontinue production of plastic toys and to begin producing computer games. This planning function will require the use of the other management functions, as shown in Exhibit 7.8. The organizing function is needed to reorganize the firm's production process so that it can produce computer games. The leading function is needed to provide employees with instructions on how to produce the computer games. The controlling function is needed to determine whether the production process established to produce computer games is efficient, and whether the sales of computer games are as high as forecasted. The controlling function may also provide feedback as to whether employees satisfied the firm's expectations.

In a small business, the owner may frequently perform all the management functions. For example, an owner of a small business may revise the strategic plan (planning function), reorganize the firm's production facility (organizing function),

Exhibit 7.8
Integration of Management
Functions

 Planning

> Top Managers:
> Change of strategic plan to replace
> plastic toy production with
> computer game production.

Communicate the plan
to middle management and ask
middle management to
implement the plan.

 Control

> Top Management:
> Assess the expenses and sales from
> producing computer games every
> month. Determine whether
> computer games business
> should be expanded.

 Organizing

> Middle Managers:
> Reorganize the plastic toy
> production plant so that it can now
> be used to produce computer
> games. Retrain the plant's
> employees for this production,
> and hire four new employees to
> help with the technical
> production aspects.

Communicate the
reorganization to supervisors
and ask them to implement
the new production
process.

 Control

> Middle Management:
> Determine whether the production
> is efficient (based on monitoring
> the plant's output and expenses
> each month).

 Leading

> Supervisors:
> Explain each employee's tasks
> required to produce computer
> games, and explain how to
> perform the tasks.

Communicate
the tasks.

> Employees:
> Perform the tasks assigned;
> may have some input on job
> assignments.

 Control

> Supervisors:
> Monitor employees to ensure that
> they are completing their new
> assignments properly.

assign new tasks to the employees (leading function), and then assess whether all these revisions lead to acceptable results (controlling function).

Leadership Styles for Global Business

When U.S. firms establish businesses in foreign countries (called "foreign subsidiaries"), they must determine the type of leadership style to use in those countries. These firms do not automatically apply whatever style they use in the United States, because the conditions in the foreign countries are different. In some countries that have just recently encouraged private ownership of businesses (such as Hungary, Argentina, and China), the people in those countries are not accustomed to making business decisions that would maximize the value of the business. Many people only had experience in managing government-owned businesses. Consequently, the management decisions were sometimes focused on satisfying government goals that conflicted with maximizing the value of the business. Furthermore, the businesses had little or no competition, so managers could make decisions without concern about losing market share. Given those conditions, some U.S. firms have used a more autocratic leadership style for their foreign subsidiaries. That is, instructions come from the U.S. headquarters, and the managers of the foreign subsidiaries are responsible for carrying out those instructions. When these managers have problems, they contact U.S. headquarters to receive advice.

While U.S. firms have recently allowed free-rein and participative styles in the United States, they may be reluctant to give too much power to managers of some foreign subsidiaries. As the managers of the foreign subsidiaries gain experience working for the firm and in a competitive environment, they may be given more power to make decisions.

When a U.S. firm has foreign subsidiaries in several different countries, its choice of a leadership style may vary with the characteristics of the foreign country. For example, it may allow a participative style in some industrialized countries where managers are experienced in making business decisions that are focused on maximiz-

These workers exercising at a Hitachi shipyard in Japan are used to a much different management style than workers in the U.S.

ing the firm's value. Yet, the same firm may impose an autocratic style in any country where most business managers were not accustomed to making business decisions in this manner. No one particular leadership style is always appropriate for all countries. The firm must consider the country's characteristics before deciding which leadership style to use. Furthermore, the proper leadership style for any particular country may change over time in response to changes in the country's conditions.

MANAGERIAL SKILLS

3 **Describe the skills that managers need.**

To perform well, managers rely on four types of skills:

➤ Conceptual skills
➤ Interpersonal skills
➤ Technical skills
➤ Decision-making skills

Conceptual Skills

conceptual skills the ability to understand the relationships between the various tasks of a firm

Managers with **conceptual skills** have the ability to understand the relationships between the various tasks of a firm. They see how all the pieces fit together. For example, top managers of Motorola understand how the production process is related to the marketing and finance functions. They may not be as concerned with the precise method of any specific task, but have a general understanding of the firm's operations. This enables them to anticipate the potential problems that could arise for the firm if a particular production plant experiences shortages. Managers need conceptual skills to make adjustments when problems like this occur. Managers with good conceptual skills have back-up strategies when problems in the production process occur. This allows the firm to continue using its resources effectively.

Conceptual skills are commonly used by the top-level and middle-level managers who are not directly involved in the production assembly process. These skills are necessary to optimally utilize employees and other resources in a manner that can achieve the firm's goals. Managers with good conceptual skills tend to be creative and are willing to consider various methods of achieving goals.

Consider the conceptual skills of Louis Gerstner, chief executive officer (CEO) of IBM. When he became CEO in 1993, Gerstner recognized that IBM had excessive production costs. To reduce these costs, he reorganized the firm's operations. This was a primary reason why IBM's stock prices rose by more than 90 percent within two years after Gerstner became CEO.

Interpersonal Skills

interpersonal skills the skills necessary to communicate with customers and employees

Virtually all managers perform tasks that require good **interpersonal skills,** which are the skills necessary to communicate with customers and employees, as discussed next.

COMMUNICATION WITH CUSTOMERS   Many managers must communicate with customers to ensure satisfaction. They listen to customer complaints themselves and attempt to respond in an acceptable manner. They may also bring other complaints to the attention of top management. Managers lacking good interpersonal skills might ignore customer complaints. Consequently, problems would go unnoticed until a sufficient number of dissatisfied customers stopped buying products. By that time, it could be too late for the firm to regain customers' trust.

One of the most important interpersonal skills is the ability to ask good questions. Without this, the real story behind customer or employee dissatisfaction may not be uncovered.

COMMUNICATION WITH EMPLOYEES   Managers need good interpersonal skills when communicating with employees. They must be able to clearly communicate assignments to employees and must communicate with employees who have made mistakes on the job so that they can be corrected. In addition, they must listen to complaints from employees and attempt to resolve their problems.

Middle- and top-level managers who use good interpersonal skills in communicating with lower management will be more informed about problems within the firm. Interpersonal skills are often used by top and middle managers when their decisions are influenced by information of other managers. For example, financial managers who develop next year's budget rely on projections of sales volume and prices provided by the marketing department. They also rely on production cost projections provided by the production department. All these managers must communicate with each other, since their projections are interrelated.

Technical Skills

Managers need technical skills to understand the types of tasks that they manage. Managers who are closer to the actual production process use their technical skills more frequently than high-level managers. For example, first-line managers of an assembly line of a computer manufacturer must be aware of how computer components are assembled. A technical understanding is important for all managers who evaluate new product ideas or are involved in solving problems.

Decision-Making Skills

Managers need decision-making skills so that they can use existing information to determine how the firm's resources should be allocated. The types of decisions made by managers vary with the position. Some typical decisions regarding the utilization of the firm's resources are as follows:

➤ Should more employees be hired?
➤ Should more machinery be purchased?
➤ Should a new facility be built?
➤ Should the assembly-line operation be revised?
➤ Should more supplies be ordered?
➤ Should salaries be adjusted?

These decisions affect either the revenue or the operating expenses of the firm, and therefore affect the firm's earnings. Managers who make proper decisions can improve the firm's earnings and thereby improve the firm's value.

STEPS FOR DECISION MAKING   The process of making a decision involves several specific stages. First, any possible decisions that are consistent with the firm's strategic plan are identified. Then, information relevant to each possible decision is compiled. Using this information, the costs and benefits of each possible decision are estimated. From these estimates, the best decision can be determined by one or more managers and can be implemented. As time passes, this decision should be evaluated to determine if any changes are necessary. The stages of the decision-making process are summarized in Exhibit 7.9.

Exhibit 7.9
Stages Involved in Making a Decision

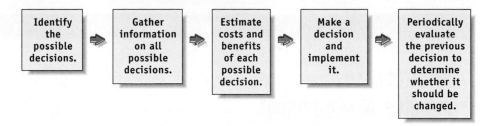

As an example, consider the task of accommodating increased production at Winn-Dixie supermarket. Managers first think of alternative means of achieving this goal, such as hiring more labor or allowing more overtime for existing labor. The relevant information to be compiled would allow the costs and benefits of each alternative to be estimated. This includes the cost of hiring more labor and the overtime wage that would be paid to existing labor. Once the information is compiled, a cost-benefit analysis is conducted and the best alternative is selected. As time passes, the cost of each alternative may change and the managers may reconsider their decisions.

Summary of Management Skills

The various management skills that have been described are summarized in Exhibit 7.10. All of these skills are necessary for managers to be successful.

HOW MANAGERS MANAGE TIME

4

Describe methods in which managers can use their time effectively.

Managers have a limited amount of time to manage their responsibilities. They use **time management**, which represents the manner by which managers allocate their time when managing tasks. While there is no perfect formula for managers to use their time efficiently, the following guidelines should be followed:

Exhibit 7.10
Summary of Key Managerial Skills

Skill	How the Skill Is Needed by a Firm
Conceptual	Used to understand how the production level must be large enough to satisfy demand, and how demand is influenced by the firm's marketing decisions.
Interpersonal	Used to inform employees about the goals of the firm and about specific policies that they must follow; also used to hear complaints from employees or customers, and to resolve any conflicts among people.
Technical	Used to understand how components must be assembled to produce a product; also used to understand how machines and equipment should be used.
Decision-Making	Used to determine whether the firm should expand, change its pricing policy, hire more employees, or obtain more financing; proper decision-making requires an assessment of the costs and benefits of various possible decisions that could be implemented.

SPOTLIGHT ON TECHNOLOGY

Software to Improve Management

Effective management is particularly difficult in a small business where a single manager is responsible for many tasks. Recently, computer software packages have been developed to help managers in other areas. This new category of software, referred to as "MBA-ware" by *PC Magazine,* supports a wide range of activities, including the following:

➤ **Personnel Hiring:** Software for screening job applicants, based upon psychological principles, can be used to assess attitudes and potential fit with the company. Software of this type has long been used at a number of well-known companies, such as Mrs. Field's Cookies.

➤ **Personnel Evaluation:** Reviewing and evaluating personnel has long been a sensitive task, dreaded by many managers. Software is available that helps managers in constructing and writing reviews, as well as recording employee progress toward goals. Such software can aid managers in getting through the review process, and can be extremely valuable in documenting poor performance leading to an employee termination. Such documentation can be extremely valuable if the terminated employee sues his or her former employer.

➤ **General Management:** A wide range of software products are available to assist managers in day-to-day management activities. Among these, calendar and scheduling software can be used for maintaining appointments and for time management. Personnel software can form the basis of a personnel system: keeping track of assorted information such as vacation usage, medical benefits, pension contributions, and so forth. In addition, some versions of personnel software provide managers with templates for creating complete personnel manuals. Contact management software can help sales personnel keep track of customer calls. Financial software is available to aid managers in making reasonable projections of future business. A wide range of software is also available for supporting specific activities, such as creating presentations and business planning.

➤ **Negotiating:** A number of software packages have been developed that employ psychological models to help managers come up with negotiating strategies for various situations. The software design is based on the principle that varying negotiating styles should be employed when dealing with different types of individuals.

➤ **Decision Making:** A growing number of software packages are designed to help managers make decisions more rationally. Using tested decision-making techniques, they force managers to identify and prioritize alternatives in such a way that they can be ranked in an internally consistent fashion.

➤ **Creativity:** Software also exists that is designed to stimulate managerial creativity. Such packages employ techniques drawn from brainstorming research, and may also employ question-and-answer sessions designed to inspire managers with new ideas.

While it is unlikely that such software will ever substitute for managerial experience, more and more managers will undoubtedly use such tools to supplement their own management techniques.

---

time management the manner by which managers allocate their time when managing tasks

➤ Set proper priorities.
➤ Schedule long time intervals for large tasks.
➤ Minimize interruptions.
➤ Set short-term goals.
➤ Delegate some tasks to employees.

Each of these guidelines is discussed in turn.

Set Proper Priorities

One of the main reasons for time management problems is that managers lose sight of their role. Consider a regional sales manager who has two responsibilities: (a) resolving any problems with salespeople or with existing sales orders (such as production delays and defective products), and (b) entertaining new clients. Assume that the proper allocation of time is 90 percent to resolving problems and 10 percent to entertaining new clients. Yet, a sales manager may allocate much more time to entertaining because it is more enjoyable. Consequently, problems with sales orders may accumulate. This is a classic example of how a manager's time may be improperly allocated. A more effective manager would limit the time toward entertainment, recognizing that more time should be devoted toward resolving problems with sales orders. Time management is a matter of priorities. Those managers who set priorities according to what is best for the firm, rather than what they enjoy the most, are more successful.

Schedule Long Time Intervals for Large Tasks

Managers may be able to efficiently complete large tasks by scheduling large intervals (blocks) of time to focus on those tasks. Within each block, managers can focus all of their attention on the large task. In general, more work on a large project can be accomplished within one three-hour interval than in three separate one-hour intervals that are spread throughout a day or a week. When using short time intervals, managers waste time refreshing their memories on the issue of concern and the potential solutions. They would be more efficient if they could focus on the issue for a longer interval.

The best strategy for an issue that requires less than one day of work may be to focus completely on that issue until the work is done. Short appointments that must be made during a given day and are unrelated to the large tasks should be consolidated so that they do not continually break up the time allocated to the large tasks.

Minimize Interruptions

Virtually all managers are interrupted during the normal working day. Some of the interruptions may require immediate attention, but others can be put off until later. Managers should stay focused on the task at hand before allowing interference by unscheduled interruptions (except for emergencies). Managers may have assistants available who can screen calls and take messages. However, even managers without assistants may allow phone answering machines to take messages, rather than answer each call while in the middle of a task.

Some managers have a natural tendency to create their own interruptions. For example, they may stop in offices of other employees to socialize. While socializing during work hours may help reduce stress or boredom, managers should attempt to complete some amount of work before taking a social break. In this way, the break is a reward for accomplishing some work, not simply a means of putting off work.

Set Short-Term Goals

A common problem for managers is meeting deadlines, especially on large tasks. One reason for this problem is that managers procrastinate (put off their assignment) because the task seems overwhelming. A second reason is that many managers may find alternative tasks to work on rather than those tasks with deadlines far into the future. As the work that needs to be done is pushed toward the deadline, completing the work on time becomes more difficult.

Managers should set short-term goals so that they can chip away at large tasks. For example, consider a manager who is assigned the task of purchasing a new computer system for the firm. The manager should break down the assignment into smaller tasks, such as (A) obtaining all the relevant information from other employees on the features that the computer system should have, (B) calling firms that sell computer systems to specify the features needed, so that the firm can quote a price, and (C) visiting firms where a similar computer system is in place to determine how

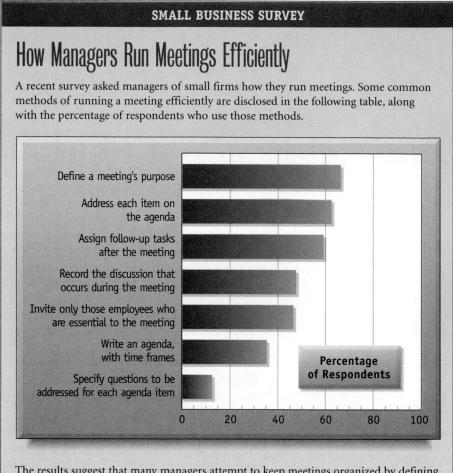

SMALL BUSINESS SURVEY

How Managers Run Meetings Efficiently

A recent survey asked managers of small firms how they run meetings. Some common methods of running a meeting efficiently are disclosed in the following table, along with the percentage of respondents who use those methods.

The results suggest that many managers attempt to keep meetings organized by defining the meeting's purpose and providing an agenda. However, most managers do not specify questions to be addressed for each agenda item.

well it works. Task C cannot be done until Task B is completed, and Task B cannot be done until Task A is completed.

If the assignment must be done in ten weeks, the manager may set a goal that Task A be completed over the first three weeks, Task B be completed over the fourth and fifth weeks, and Task C be completed over the sixth and seventh weeks. This schedule allows a few extra weeks before the deadline in case any unexpected problems cause a task to take more time than what was planned.

Delegate Some Tasks to Employees

Managers only have so much time to complete the tasks they are assigned. If they can delegate some authority to their employees, they will have more time to be creative. By delegating, managers may even increase the job satisfaction of employees who prefer extra responsibility. However, managers should delegate only those tasks that employees can handle.

·COLLEGE·
HEALTH CLUB

Planning at College Health Club

Sue Kramer, president of College Health Club (CHC), is attempting to develop a long-term plan for her business. Her health club has been moderately successful so far, but Sue wants her business to grow over time. She decides to establish the following plans:

1 A strategic plan that would be used to identify the future direction of the business over a period of three to five years.
2 A tactical plan that would comprise smaller-scale plans over the next year or so that are consistent with her strategic plan.
3 An operational plan that would include methods used to achieve the tactical plans.

Dilemma

Sue believes that her concept of a health club that focuses on college students could be applied to other college campuses, but no other college campuses are nearby. Offer suggestions on how Sue could develop a strategic plan to attract college students to health clubs.

Solution

Sue offered convenience to college students by establishing the health club across the street from the campus, and set the membership price at a level that the students could afford. She plans to further capitalize on this strategy, as explained in her strategic plan.

1 *Strategic Plan*   Focus on providing health club services to college students around the state by establishing health clubs near various college campuses. Provide convenient services at a reasonable price.
2 *Tactical Plan*   Assess various college campuses throughout the state. Also determine whether competitive health clubs have already attracted those students. Estimate the costs of establishing a health club next to each campus.
3 *Operational Plan*   Determine which college campus has the most potential for establishing a new health club. Survey the students on that campus to determine whether there would be a demand for health club services. Get quotes on the rent for various places near the campus. Forecast the annual expenses and revenue if a health club were established. If the idea seems feasible, develop an official business plan that would be presented to a commercial bank to obtain financing for this new business.

If a new health club were created, Sue would monitor the performance there and determine whether to consider expanding the service to other campuses. Her ultimate goal would be a chain of many health clubs around the state. While Sue has a long-term vision, she cannot achieve her long-term plans immediately. She plans to pursue one new health club at a time to ensure that she can adequately manage the business as it expands. She would need to hire employees to help manage any new health clubs. Her strategic plan set the foundation for developing her tactical and operational plans.

Additional Issues for Discussion

1 What situations would discourage Sue Kramer from pursuing her strategic plan?

2 Explain why Sue Kramer needs good interpersonal skills to be successful when running her health club.

3 As Sue hires employees (mostly students who would work part-time) for the existing health club over time, which leadership style should Sue use?

SUMMARY

1 The levels of management are:

➤ top (high-level) management, which concentrates on the firm's long-run objectives;

➤ middle management, which is responsible for intermediate and short-term decisions;

➤ supervisory management, which is highly involved with employees who engage in the day-to-day production process.

2 The key functions of management are:

➤ planning for the future (objectives),

➤ organizing resources to achieve objectives,

➤ leading employees by providing them with instructions on how they should complete their tasks,

➤ controlling, which allows for monitoring and evaluating employee tasks.

3 The most important managerial skills needed are:

➤ conceptual skills, used to understand relationships between various tasks;

➤ interpersonal skills, used to communicate with other employees and with customers;

➤ technical skills, used to perform specific day-to-day tasks, such as accounting skills to develop financial statements or electrical skills to understand how the wiring of a product is arranged;

➤ decision-making skills, used to assess alternative choices on the allocation of the firm's resources.

4 Some of the key guidelines for effective time management are:

➤ set proper priorities, in order to focus on the most important job responsibilities;

➤ schedule long time intervals for large tasks, in order to focus on large tasks until the work is done;

➤ minimize interruptions, in order to complete assignments;

➤ set short-term goals, in order to chip away at long-term projects;

➤ delegate tasks that employees can complete on their own.

KEY TERMS

autocratic	management	procedures
conceptual skills	middle management	strategic plan
contingency planning	mission statement	supervisory (first-line) management
controlling	operational planning	tactical planning
free-rein	organizing	time management
initiative	participative	top (high-level) management
interpersonal skills	planning	
leading	policies	

REVIEW QUESTIONS

1 Explain how you would utilize the guidelines for time management for an important project due today.

2 Describe the different leadership styles that you could develop and what style would be most appropriate if you wanted to consult with employees before making a decision.

3 Define the concept of management and explain what resources are available in a manager's budget to make decisions.

4 When U.S. firms establish businesses in foreign countries (called "foreign subsidiaries"), management must determine the appropriate leadership style. Discuss the appropriate style for each of the following: an underdeveloped Third World country and an advanced industrialized country.

5 Distinguish management from leadership. Do you think a person could be effective in one area and ineffective in the other?

6 Explain the stages of decision making for a manager who has just decided to enter a new market with an existing product line.

7 Describe the various functions a manager will perform on the job.

8 Identify and give examples of the functions of managers and how they vary at each level of management within the firm.

9 Discuss the different types of skills that a manager should possess. Explain what skills are necessary for a supervisor within a machine shop.

10 Discuss how a manager would implement the various types of planning functions within a firm. With which type of planning function would a president of a firm be most likely involved?

DISCUSSION QUESTIONS

1 Assume you are thinking of becoming a manager. What are the most important skills you should have to become an effective manager?

2 Discuss how global competition is changing our thinking about managing firms and subsidiaries in foreign countries.

3 In your opinion, what is the most important management function that drives all the other functions? Explain.

4 Have you witnessed illustrations of effective and ineffective management? Cite some examples of both.

5 Explain the different leadership styles you would use if you were the manager of a project you were doing with other students.

RUNNING YOUR OWN BUSINESS

1 Describe the strategic plan of your business. Within this plan, state the business opportunities that exist and the general direction of your business to capitalize on those opportunities.

2 Explain in detail how your business will operate to achieve your strategic plan.

INVESTING IN THE STOCK OF A BUSINESS

Using the annual report of the firm in which you would like to invest, complete the following:

1 What is the firm's mission and strategic plan?

2 How does the firm intend to achieve its strategic plan? Is it restructuring its operations to achieve its objectives?

CASE 1 Applying Management Skills

Maggie Wiltz manages a high-fashion specialty store in Atlanta, Georgia. Her daily activities start one hour before her store normally opens for business. She starts her day by opening the morning mail. Maggie must read numerous memos before the day starts. These memos are typically important in their relationship to the coming day's business activities.

Half an hour before the store opens, Maggie has a meeting with her employees. Important issues must be discussed, most notably the fact that sales were off in the first quarter by 10 percent. She also wants to discuss with her employees her concern over returned merchandise.

Maggie's employees are relatively new and inexperienced. She elects to use a participative leadership style. She believes she should select the appropriate leadership style to fit the situation. Once Maggie starts the meeting, she wants the employees to participate and provide solutions to the topics discussed. Yet the employees cannot state why they believe sales are declining. The employees do, however, participate in discussions focused on the return of merchandise; they believe a quality issue is involved.

Once the store opens, Maggie encounters frequent interruptions from her employees. Another item on her agenda for the day is a midday luncheon with the Rotary Club, where she is to be the guest speaker. Later in the day, at the close of business, Maggie is to meet with her regional sales manager to discuss the topic of excessive return of merchandise. She intends to provide him with the solutions that resulted from the meeting with her employees. She does not look forward to this meeting.

Questions

1 Define time management. What recommendations could you make for Maggie's improvement in this area?

2 Discuss the management functions that Maggie utilizes on her job.

3 Should Maggie have developed a plan of action before her meeting with her employees?

4 Discuss the management skills that Maggie is using in this case.

CASE 2 Developing a Plan for the Official All-Star Cafe

Robert Earl, who created Planet Hollywood restaurants, is developing a strategy that is focused on his plans to spread more "chains" around Planet Earth. The first "link" in his planet chain is the sports-themed Official All-Star Cafe, which opened this past year in New York City's Times Square. Housed inside this restaurant are memorabilia of well-known sports figures such as Andre Agassi.

Mr. Earl hopes that his Official All-Star Cafe will help him capitalize even more on a boom in such restaurants that is sweeping major cities in the United States as well as becoming increasingly more pervasive on the international level.

Many experts in this industry say the trend is far from reaching its plateau. "We're not seeing the end of the theme-restaurant phenomenon, we're seeing the beginning," states E. Zagat, co-publisher of the Zagat dining guide. "But there's room for growth only where the themes are big enough. If your theme gets too narrow, you might fall flat on your face."

At least for the time being, many theme restaurants have a formula that is drawing in large numbers of patrons. The guests get a much bigger experience for relatively the same price as offered at a regular restaurant. According to the review in Zagat's guide, an average dinner, with drink and tip, costs about $24 at Planet Hollywood. Mr. Earl expects prices at the sports cafe to be similar.

There is no need to promote high-priced food. With this concept, many restaurants can offer good value with very amusing surroundings. Rather than rely on food alone, most theme restaurants offer clothing and other merchandise carrying the restaurant's logo. This often generates huge revenue, and converts the customers into walking billboards for the restaurants. Mr. Earl doesn't consider himself to be in the restaurant business, but actually more in the trademark business.

Mr. Earl estimates the All-Star Cafe will derive about 30 percent of its revenue from selling a wide range of sports clothing and other souvenirs. The nonfood portion might even eventually reach 50 percent.

The decision has been made to go after the sports-hobby enthusiast as well as the individual who is out to have a good time while seeking an excellent meal that offers good value.

Questions

1 Discuss the management function which stands out in the creative process that describes how Mr. Earl has used the concept of the Official All-Star Cafe.

2 Discuss the management skills that were utilized in the creation of the Official All-Star Cafe.

3 Develop a mission statement Mr. Earl could have used

when he created the Official All-Star Cafe.

4 Discuss the decision made by Mr. Earl to diversify into multiple product lines. Is this profitable?

VIDEO CASE How Effective Management Can Be the Key to Success

Donald J. Dalton has made a handicap an asset. He runs a company that matches disabled people with computer products that help them overcome their disabilities. Micro Overflow Corporation, of Naperville, Illinois, is a success—a fact explainable at least in part by the fact that Dalton is a quadriplegic.

Many times, he has left home before sunrise, driven hours to evaluate a client's needs, driven more hours to speak at a dinner where he publicized his company, and gotten back home around midnight. The next day, more of the same.

Micro Overflow keeps costs down. It had no choice at the start. A new enterprise in an unproven industry, it couldn't get financing. That meant it couldn't hire people to take some of the burden off Dalton and the staff. For the first eighteen months, there were no salaries. All profits were plowed back into the company.

The staff worked out of Dalton's one-car garage. A twelve- by twenty-foot space held four work stations, two phone lines, a fax machine, a five-computer local area network, a bulletin board, and—typically—a half dozen "assistive technology" systems being assembled, tested, and readied for delivery to clients.

Dalton's company today has eight employees and three thousand square feet of office space. It served more than 320 clients last year, up from 23 its first year and 63 the second. Annual sales are at the $600,000 level.

A mission statement helps the company keep focused. Through "the implementation of modern technologies," it says, "Micro Overflow strives to remove the 'dis' from disability."

Questions

1 A key to the success of Micro Overflow is the effective time management of Donald Dalton, the owner. Explain how Dalton uses his time efficiently. Explain how technology helps Donald Dalton to use his time efficiently.

2 According to the video, Micro Overflow benefits from an employee team approach. Explain how the team approach can enhance the firm's performance.

3 Assume that a small team of employees made all the key decisions about one part of Micro Overflow's business, and that this part of the business was highly successful. Also assume that these employees recognize how much influence they had in the recent success of Micro Overflow. Is there any concern that Donald Dalton (the owner of Micro Overflow) would have about this team?

THE Coca-Cola COMPANY ANNUAL REPORT PROJECT

The following questions apply concepts learned in this chapter to The Coca-Cola Company. Read pages 6–8 and page 29 in The Coca-Cola Company annual report before answering these questions.

1 The Coca-Cola Company has built its credibility by consistently hitting its long-term targets (goals). Why do you think this builds credibility among its stockholders?

2 One of the most critical elements of effective management is providing a corporate vision. What does The Coca-Cola Company want its managers to see?

3 a. A second critical element of good management is the ability to learn and develop. How does The Coca-Cola Company encourage the learning process?

b. How does The Coca-Cola Company distinguish learning from training?

4 It is important for a manager to recognize the accomplishments of others. How does The Coca-Cola Company Chairman, Roberto Goizueta do this?

Answers are in an appendix at the back of the book.

True or False

1 Strategic planning establishes the methods used for the near future (such as the next year) to achieve desired objectives.

2 The controlling function represents the organization of employees and other resources in a manner that is consistent with the firm's goals.

3 The leading function involves not only instructions on how to complete a task but also incentives to complete it correctly and quickly.

4 Top management is usually highly involved with employees that are engaged in the day-to-day production process.

5 Contingency planning refers to guidelines on departmentalizing tasks.

6 In a small business, the owner may frequently perform all the management functions.

7 A firm must consider the foreign country's characteristics before deciding which leadership style is most appropriate.

8 A mission statement typically consists of a firm's goals.

9 Conceptual skills are only needed by the assembly-line employees who are directly involved in the production assembly process.

10 The free-rein leadership style is more appropriate than the autocratic style if employees are highly independent, creative, and motivated.

Multiple Choice

11 The function of management used to provide feedback as to whether employees satisfied the firm's expectations is:
a) planning.
b) controlling.
c) organizing.
d) leading.
e) time management.

12 The skills managers use to understand the relationships between the various tasks of the firm are:
a) interpersonal.
b) technical.
c) decision-making.
d) conceptual.
e) problem-solving.

13 The following are guidelines that should be followed when using time management except for:
a) setting proper priorities.
b) centralizing responsibility.
c) scheduling long intervals of time for large tasks.
d) minimizing interruptions.
e) delegating some tasks to employees.

14 Since they are closer to the production process, middle managers are often responsible for the:
a) strategic plans.
b) setting objectives.
c) long-term decisions.
d) visionary process.
e) short-term decisions.

15 The goals from operational planning are somewhat dependent on the firm's:
a) interpersonal skills.
b) technical skills.
c) strategic plans.
d) leadership styles.
e) organizational structure.

16 The following are typical goals that can be achieved by the management function except for:
a) high production efficiency.
b) high production quality.
c) limited competition.
d) customer satisfaction.
e) employee satisfaction.

17 So that they can use existing information to determine how the firm's resources should be allocated, managers need:
a) standing plans.
b) autocratic management.
c) single-use plans.
d) decision-making skills.
e) to prioritize schedules.

18 The style of leadership that is the opposite extreme of the autocratic style is:
a) free-rein.
b) authoritative.
c) manipulation style.
d) boss-centered.
e) commanding style.

19 In the airline industry, having situations involving overbooked reservations would be an example of the need for:

a) interpersonal planning.
b) leadership.
c) autocratic management.
d) authoritative management.
e) contingency planning.

20 A manager's leadership style should be conducted in a manner that is consistent with the firm's:
a) competition.
b) strategic plan.
c) customers.
d) industry demands.
e) labor union.

21 For managers to understand the types of tasks they supervise, they must possess:
a) contingency plans.
b) interpersonal skills.
c) top-management skills.
d) technical skills.
e) tactical plans.

22 Which of the following is the first step involved in making a decision?
a) gathering information.
b) estimating costs and benefits of each possible decision.
c) identifying the possible decisions.
d) making a decision and implementing it.
e) evaluating the decision to determine whether any changes are necessary.

23 When employees have little or no input in decision making, managers use a(n):
a) free-rein style.
b) interpersonal communication style.
c) autocratic leadership style.
d) participative style.
e) employee-centered style.

24 The type of leadership style that is effective when employees can offer a different perspective to the manager is:
a) autocratic.
b) command-oriented.
c) contingency.
d) authoritative.
e) participative.

25 The managers of foreign subsidiaries are responsible for carrying out instructions provided to them from:
a) the corporate headquarters.
b) time management.
c) contingency planning.
d) standing plans.
e) single-use plans.

26 The position of chief financial officer is considered to be a:
a) supervisory position.
b) top-management position.
c) first-line management position.
d) bottom-line position.
e) middle management position.

27 To prevent employees from conducting tasks in a manner that is inefficient, dangerous, or illegal, firms enforce:
a) kickbacks.
b) reciprocity.
c) policies.
d) time management.
e) prioritizing tasks.

28 A strategic plan that focuses on increased sales will likely require more:
a) production and financing.
b) policies and rules.
c) prioritizing tasks.
d) authoritarian management.
e) autocratic management.

29 Managers who lack initiative may not be very effective even if they possess the necessary:
a) financial backing.
b) reciprocity.
c) support.
d) skills.
e) patronage.

30 The role of a manager is to establish standards of production, which would include the following except for:
a) profits.
b) affirmative action.
c) sales volume.
d) production cost.
e) production volume.

31 The skills that managers need to communicate with customers and employees are:
a) organizing skills.
b) control skills.
c) motivating skills.
d) conceptual skills.
e) interpersonal skills.

32 The firm's primary goal is described by the strategic plan based on the firm's:
a) tactical plan.
b) mission statement.
c) operating plan.
d) bottom-up plan.
e) contingency plan.

33 High-level and middle managers engage in smaller-scale plans that are consistent with the firm's strategic plan. These smaller-scale plans are known as:

a) tactical plans.

b) mission statements.

c) leadership plans.

d) bottom-up plans.

e) contingency plans.

34 A series of steps necessary to be completed when implementing a policy is a:

a) contingency.

b) job.

c) position.

d) rule.

e) procedure.

35 The function of management that represents the monitoring and evaluation of tasks is:

a) planning.

b) organizing.

c) controlling.

d) leading.

e) motivating.

Management Training on the World Wide Web

To say that a comic strip would inspire training materials for effective management may seem a little far-fetched. However, that is exactly what Scott Adams' Dilbert character has become. The Dilbert Comic strip is tacked to offfice walls around the country and *Training Magazine* has called him "possibly the nation's leading commentator on life in the modern workplace." The Dilbert character is now a part of a series of business training videos that are being used by the likes of IBM, GTE, and others. An additional source for Dilbert's pointed insights is the Dilbert Zone located at http://www.unitedmedia.com/comics/dilbert/

Exhibit 7.11
The Dilbert Zone

(Reprinted by permission of United Feature Syndicate, Inc.)

http://www.unitedmedia.com/comics/dilbert/

Organizational Structure

Each firm should have a strategic plan that identifies the future direction of its business. The responsibilities of its managers should be organized to achieve the strategic plan.

Each firm establishes an organizational structure, or the structure within the firm that identifies responsibilities for each job position and the relationships among those positions. An organizational structure also indicates how all the job responsibilities fit together. The organizational structure affects the efficiency with which a firm produces its product, and therefore affects a firm's value.

Consider the case of Heinz, which manufactures hundreds of different products. Should a different manager be responsible for overseeing the operations of each product? How much responsibility should Heinz assign to those employees who produce Heinz products? What factors should Heinz consider when determining how much authority to assign to its employees? This chapter provides a background on organizational structure, which can be used to address these questions.

The **Learning Goals** of this chapter are to:

1 Explain how an organizational structure may be used by a firm to achieve its strategic plan.

2 Identify methods that can be used to departmentalize tasks.

HOW A FIRM'S ORGANIZATIONAL STRUCTURE ACHIEVES ITS STRATEGIC PLAN

1

Explain how an organizational structure may be used by a firm to achieve its strategic plan.

organizational structures the structure within the firm that identifies responsibilities for each job position and the relationship among those positions

organization chart a diagram that shows the interaction among employee responsibilities

chain of command identifies the job position to which each type of employee must report

No one specific **organizational structure** is optimal for all firms. The means by which responsibilities are organized for a large multinational manufacturing firm such as DuPont may not necessarily be appropriate for a small firm such as Starbucks.

A firm's organizational structure can be illustrated with an **organization chart,** which is a diagram that shows the interaction among employee responsibilities. Exhibit 8.1 provides an example of an organization chart.

Chain of Command

The organizational structure indicates the **chain of command,** which identifies the job positions to which all types of employees must report. The chain of command also indicates who is responsible for various activities. Since employees often encounter problems that require communication with other divisions, it helps to know who is responsible for each type of task.

Heinz needs an organizational structure that can manage the production of all its products that are produced for sale in numerous countries.

Exhibit 8.1
Example of an Organization Chart

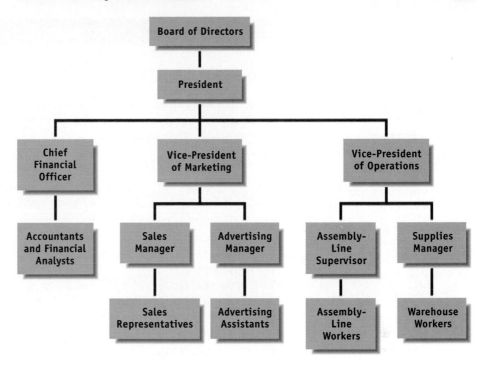

The president (who also typically holds the position of chief executive officer) has the ultimate responsibility for the success of a firm. The president normally attempts to coordinate all divisions and provide direction for the firm's business. For most firms, many managerial duties are delegated to other managers. Vice-presidents normally oversee specific divisions or broad functions of the firm and report to the president.

Authority of the Board of Directors

board of directors a set of executives that is responsible for monitoring the activities of the firm's president and other high-level managers

Each firm has a **board of directors,** or a set of executives that is responsible for monitoring the activities of the firm's president and other high-level managers. Directors are selected by shareholders; they serve as representatives for the shareholders, as confirmed by a recent quote from Sears' annual report:

❚❚ *The board of directors regularly reviews the corporation's structure to determine whether it supports optimal performance and thus serves the best interests of shareholders by delivering shareholder value.* ❚❚

inside board members board members who are also managers of the same firm

outside board members board members who are high-level managers of other firms

Directors have the authority to approve or disapprove key business proposals made by a firm's managers, such as acquisitions or layoffs. For example, IBM's decision to acquire Lotus and Boeing's decision to lay off workers required board approval. Those board members who are also managers of the same firm (such as the chief executive officer) are referred to as **inside board members.** Board members who are high-level managers of other firms are referred to as **outside board members.** In general, the board focuses only on key decisions and is not normally involved in the day-to-day activities of the firm. Board members attend a board meeting that is generally scheduled every few months or are called when their input is needed regarding a key business decision.

SMALL BUSINESS SURVEY

Who Are the Board Members of Small Firms?

A recent survey asked the chief executive officers (CEOs) of small firms (with less than $50 million in annual sales) about the background of their outside board members. The results of the survey follow.

Background	Percentage of Firms Whose Board Members Have That Background
Executives of other firms	69%
Major investors in the firm	36%
Retired business executives	30%
Attorneys	29%
Accountants	22%
Bankers	18%
Business consultants	13%
Customers	2%
Others	3%

The results suggest that these firms rely heavily on either executives or major investors to serve as their outside board members. The attorneys, accountants, and business consultants that are hired as outside board members typically also perform other duties (such as legal or banking duties) for the firm.

The largest one thousand U.S. firms have about twelve directors on their board on average. The average annual compensation to directors for serving on the boards of the largest industrial firms in the United States is about $68,000. Some firms, such as General Electric and PepsiCo, provide the directors with their stock as partial compensation. This type of compensation may motivate the directors to serve the interests of the firm's shareholders, because the board members will benefit if the firm's stock price rises. Some firms, such as Travelers Group, pay their board members entirely with stock so that they can ensure that the board members will focus on decisions that may boost the stock's price for shareholders.

Directors not only oversee the key decisions of managers but may also initiate changes in a firm. For example, the board may decide that the firm's chief executive officer needs to be replaced or that the firm's businesses should be restructured. The boards of numerous well-known firms such as American Express, W. R. Grace, Honeywell, IBM, and KMart have recently initiated major changes. In many cases, the board becomes more involved after a period of poor performance by the firm. Board members of numerous firms have become more active in recent years as a result of pressure from shareholders.

A board of directors may be more willing to take action if most of its members are outside members (and therefore are not employees of the firm). The outside board members may suggest policies that will benefit shareholders, even if the policies are not supported by the firm's top managers. For example, they may suggest that the salaries of some high-level managers be reduced. Such a policy is less likely to be suggested by those inside board members who are also employed by the firm as high-level managers.

Monitoring by Institutional Investors

The high-level managers of a firm are monitored not only by the board of directors, but also by institutional investors (such as life insurance companies and pension plans) that hold a large amount of the firm's shares. The institutional investors do not have direct control over the firm, but may publicly criticize any major decisions of high-level managers that are not intended to increase the value of the firm's stock. They may also inform the firm's board members of their views. Board members may listen to those institutional investors that are major shareholders of the firm. Large shareholders can influence the composition of the board because shareholders are allowed to vote for board members.

Span of Control

Top management determines the firm's **span of control,** or the number of employees managed by each manager. When an organizational structure is designed to have each manager supervise just a few employees, it has a narrow span of control. Conversely, when it is designed to have each manager supervise numerous employees, it has a wide span of control. For a firm with numerous employees who perform similar tasks, a wide span of control is used, since these employees can be more easily managed by one or a few managers. However, for a firm with highly diverse tasks, more managers with various skills may be needed to manage the different tasks, resulting in a narrow span of control.

Exhibit 8.2 illustrates how the span of control can vary among firms. The organizational structure on the left reflects a narrow span of control. Each employee oversees only one other employee. The nature of the business may require highly specialized skills in each position, so that employees may focus more on their own tasks and do not have to monitor a large set of employees. The organizational structure on the right reflects a wide span of control. The president directly oversees all other employees. Such a wide span of control is more typical of firms in which many employees have similar positions that can be easily monitored by a single person.

Organizational Height

The organizational structure can also be described by its height. A tall organizational structure implies that there are many layers from the bottom of the structure to the top of the structure. Conversely, a short (or flat) organizational structure implies that there is not much distance from the bottom of the structure to the top, because there are not many layers of employees between the bottom and top. Many firms that are able to use a wide span of control tend to have a flat organizational structure, as they do not require as many layers. Conversely, firms that need to use a narrow span of control tend to have a tall organizational structure with many layers. Notice that in Exhibit 8.2, the organizational structure with the narrow span of control is tall, while the organizational structure with the wide span of control is flat.

Centralization

Some firms make an effort to maintain most authority among the high-level managers, which is referred to as **centralization.** For these firms, middle and supervisory

The gentleman pictured above may not be a household name, but major U.S. corporations make a point to meet him. As CEO of CalPERS (the California Public Employees' Retirement System), James E. Burton oversees the management of $100 billion investment dollars.

span of control the number of employees managed by each manager

centralization an effort to maintain most authority among the high-level managers

Exhibit 8.2
Distinguishing between a Narrow and a Wide Span of Control

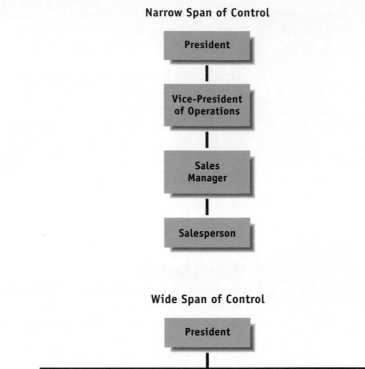

Narrow Span of Control

President

Vice-President of Operations

Sales Manager

Salesperson

Wide Span of Control

President

| Sales-person 1 | Sales-person 2 | Sales-person 3 | Sales-person 4 | Sales-person 5 | Sales-person 6 |

managers are more responsible for day-to-day tasks and for reporting to the top managers, but are not allowed to make many decisions.

Decentralization

decentralized authority is spread among several divisions or managers

autonomy divisions can make their own decisions and act independently

In recent years, many firms have **decentralized,** meaning that authority is spread among several divisions or managers. An extreme form of decentralization is **autonomy,** in which divisions can make their own decisions and act independently. The trend by firms to decentralize is due to its potential advantages. The delegation of authority can improve the morale of the employees, who may have more enthusiasm if the firm assigns them more responsibilities. In addition, these managers become more experienced in decision making. Therefore, they will be more qualified for high-level management positions in the future. Many technology firms have been innovative as a result of being decentralized, as more managers have become more creative.

Decentralization can be useful in accelerating the decision-making process. Decisions are made more quickly if they are not stalled while waiting for approval from top managers. Many firms, including IBM, have decentralized to accelerate their decision making.

Johnson and Johnson is a prime example of a firm that has benefited from decentralization. It has 168 operating divisions scattered among 53 countries, and most of the decision making is done by the managers at those divisions. This has enabled each of Johnson and Johnson's units to make quick decisions in response to local market conditions.

How Decentralized Is Your Company?

Decentralization is one of the key design dimensions in an organization. It is closely related to several behavioral dimensions of an organization, such as leadership style, degree of participative decision making, teamwork, and the nature of power and politics within the organization.

The following questionnaire allows you to get an idea about how decentralized your organization is. (If you do not have a job, have a friend who does work complete the questionnaire to see how decentralized his or her organization is.) Which level in your organization has the authority to make each of the following eleven decisions? Answer the questionnaire by circling one of the following:

0 = The board of directors makes the decision.
1 = The CEO makes the decision.
2 = The division/functional manager makes the decision.
3 = A sub-department head makes the decision.
4 = The first-level supervisor makes the decision.
5 = Operators on the shop floor make the decision.

Decision Concerning:		Circle Appropriate Level				
a. The number of workers required.	0	1	2	3	4	5
b. Whether to employ a worker.	0	1	2	3	4	5
c. Internal labor disputes.	0	1	2	3	4	5
d. Overtime worked at shop level.	0	1	2	3	4	5
e. Delivery dates and order priority.	0	1	2	3	4	5
f. Production planning.	0	1	2	3	4	5
g. Dismissal of a worker.	0	1	2	3	4	5
h. Methods of personnel selection.	0	1	2	3	4	5
i. Method of work to be used.	0	1	2	3	4	5
j. Machinery or equipment to be used.	0	1	2	3	4	5
k. Allocation of work among workers.	0	1	2	3	4	5

Add up all your circled numbers. Total = _____ . The higher your number (for example, 45 or more), the more decentralized your organization. The lower your number (for example, 25 or less), the more centralized your organization.

ADVANTAGES   The decentralized organizational structure can improve the firm's performance for the following reasons. First, it reduces operating expenses because salaries of some employees who are no longer needed are eliminated. Second, it accelerates the decision-making process, as lower-level employees are assigned more power. Third, it motivates some employees by assigning them more responsibilities. Fourth, it allows those employees who are closely involved in the production of a particular product to offer their input.

DISADVANTAGES   A decentralized organizational structure could force some managers who do not have sufficient experience to make major decisions. Also, if middle and supervisory managers are assigned an excessive amount of responsibilities, they may be unable to complete all of their tasks.

PROPER DEGREE OF DECENTRALIZATION   The proper degree of decentralization for any firm is dependent on the skills of managers who could be assigned more responsibilities. Decentralization can be beneficial when the managers who are given more power are capable of handling their additional responsibilities. For example, assume that historically, top managers determined annual raises for all assembly-line workers, but decided to delegate this responsibility to supervisors who monitor those workers. The supervisors are closer to the assembly line and are possibly in a better position to assess worker performance. Therefore, this type of decentralization may be appropriate. The top managers may still have final approval of the raises that supervisors propose for their workers.

As a second example, assume that top managers allow supervisors of assembly lines to decide the price to bid for a specific business that is presently for sale. Assembly-line supervisors are not normally trained for this type of task and should not be assigned such a task. The proper price to bid for a business requires a strong financial background and should not be delegated to managers without the proper skills.

The two examples demonstrate that high-level managers should retain authority for those tasks that require the specialized skills of high-level managers, but should delegate authority when the tasks can be handled by other managers. Routine decisions should be made by the employees who are closely involved with the tasks of concern. This may improve decision making, since other managers are closer to the routine tasks and may have greater insight than top managers on these matters.

Some degree of centralization is necessary when determining how funds should be allocated to support various divisions of a firm. If managers of each division were given the authority to make this decision, they might request more funds to expand even if there was no reason for the divisions to expand. Centralized management of funds can prevent division managers from making decisions that conflict with the goal of maximizing the firm's value.

EFFECT OF DOWNSIZING ON DECENTRALIZATION   As firms expanded during the 1980s, additional management layers were created resulting in taller organization charts. However, in the 1990s, many firms attempted to cut expenses by eliminating job positions. This so-called **downsizing** has resulted in flatter organization charts with fewer layers of managers. Notice from Exhibit 8.3 how Continental Airlines, IBM, General Motors, and Sears have downsized in recent years.

downsizing an attempt by a firm to cut expenses by eliminating job positions

Exhibit 8.3
Downsizing by Four Different Firms

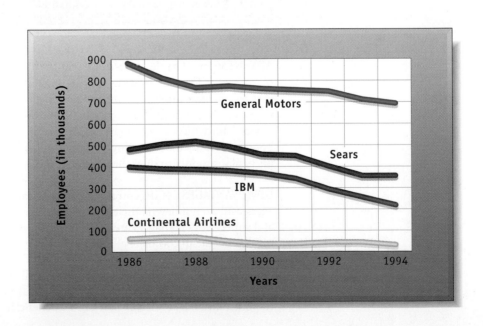

Exhibit 8.4
Effect of Downsizing on Span of Control

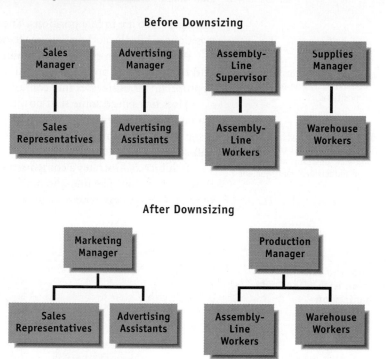

As some management positions were eliminated, many of those responsibilities were delegated to employees who previously reported to the managers whose positions were eliminated. For example, Amoco eliminated a middle layer of its organizational structure. When managers in the middle of the organization chart are removed, other employees must be assigned more power to make more decisions. That is, downsizing has resulted in a greater degree of decentralization.

Downsizing has also affected each manager's span of control. The decentralization caused by eliminating many middle managers resulted in more diverse responsibilities to the remaining managers. Consequently, the organizational structure of many firms was revised to reflect a wider span of control, as illustrated in Exhibit 8.4.

Downsizing not only has removed some management layers and created a wider span of control, but also has combined various job responsibilities within the organizational structure. While job assignments have traditionally focused on production tasks, more attention is now given to customer satisfaction. Many firms recognize that they rely on the same customers for additional business in the future, and have revised their strategic plan to focus more on achieving repeat business from their customers. In many cases, customers would prefer to deal with a single employee rather than several different employees. Consequently, employees are not as specialized because they must have diverse skills to accommodate the customers.

Line Versus Staff Positions

The job positions in an organizational structure can be classified as line positions or staff positions. **Line positions** are established to make decisions that achieve specific business goals. Conversely, **staff positions** are established to support the efforts of line positions, rather than to achieve specific goals of the firm. For example, managers at Black and Decker who are involved in the production of power tools are in line positions. Employees in staff positions at Black and Decker offer support to the

line positions established to make decisions that achieve specific business goals

staff positions established to support the efforts of line positions

managers who are in line positions. The staff positions provide assistance to the line positions, while the authority to make decisions is still assigned to line positions.

An organization chart that contains only line positions and no staff positions is referred to as a **line organization.** This type of organizational structure may be appropriate for businesses that cannot afford to hire staff for support.

Most firms need some staff positions to provide support to the line positions. An organizational structure that includes line positions and staff positions and assigns authority from higher-level management to employees is referred to as a **line-and-staff organization.**

Exhibit 8.5 illustrates a comparison between a line organization and a line-and-staff organization. The line-and-staff organization in this exhibit contains a director of computer systems, who oversees the computer system, and a director of legal ser-

line organization an organization chart that contains only line positions and no staff positions

line-and-staff organization an organizational structure that includes line positions and staff positions and assigns authority from higher-level management to employees

Exhibit 8.5
Comparison of a Line Organization with a Line-and-Staff Organization

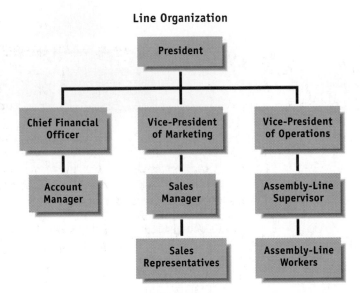

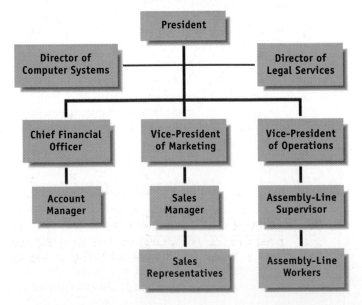

vices, who is involved with hiring and training employees. These two positions are staff positions because they can assist the finance, marketing, and production departments, but do not have the authority to make decisions that achieve specific business goals.

Creating a Structure that Allows More Employee Input

Firms commonly rely on the input of employees from various divisions for special situations. For this reason, they may need to temporarily adjust their formal organizational structure so that some extra responsibilities may be assigned. The following are two common methods for revising the organizational structure to obtain employee input:

➤ Matrix organization
➤ Intrapreneurship.

Each of these methods is discussed in turn.

matrix organization the interaction among various parts of the firm to focus on specific projects

MATRIX ORGANIZATION　Firms are often confronted with special circumstances that require input from their employees. A **matrix organization** represents the interaction among various parts of the firm to focus on specific projects. Because the projects may take up only a portion of the normal workweek, participants can continue to perform their normal tasks and are still accountable to the same boss for those tasks. For example, a firm that plans to install a new computer system may need input from each division on the specific functions of the system that are necessary. This example is illustrated in Exhibit 8.6. The team of employees periodically works on any assigned project until the project is completed. Some employees may be assigned to two or more projects during the specific period. Exhibit 8.6 shows that one representative was chosen from the finance, marketing, and production divisions; each representative can offer insight from the perspective of his or her respective division. The horizontal thin line in Exhibit 8.6 shows the interaction among the representatives from different divisions. A computer systems employee is the manager of this

Louisville Slugger bat makers bring a significant amount of individual skill to their jobs. The production process benefits from input by employees directly involved in the production.

Exhibit 8.6
A Matrix Organization for a Special Project to Design a New Computer System

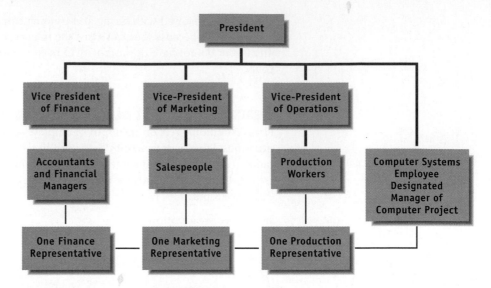

project; this person would report the recommendations of the matrix organization to the president or to some other top manager.

An advantage of the matrix approach is that it involves employees who can offer insight from different perspectives. Each participant who has been assigned to a specific group (or team) has particular skills that are used to contribute to the project. This teamwork involves all participants in decision making, which may provide more employee satisfaction than typical day-to-day assignments. Firms such as Intel, IBM and Boeing have commonly used teams of employees to complete specific projects.

One possible disadvantage of a matrix organization is that no employee may feel responsible because responsibilities are assigned to teams of several employees. Therefore, a firm that uses teams to complete various tasks may designate one job position with the responsibility of organizing the team and ensuring that the team assignment is completed before the deadline. The person designated as project manager (or team leader) of a specific project does not necessarily have authority over the other participants for any other tasks.

Another disadvantage of the matrix organization is that any time used to participate in projects reduces the time allocated for normal tasks. In some cases, ultimate responsibility is not clear, causing confusion. Digital Equipment Corporation eliminated its matrix structure for this reason.

INTRAPRENEURSHIP   Some firms not only require input from employees on specific issues but also encourage employees to offer ideas for revising operations that would enhance the firm's value. These firms may even create a special subsidiary within their organizational structure in which particular employees are given the responsibilities of innovation. In this way, the costs and benefits of innovation can be estimated separately from the rest of the business operations.

Particular employees of a firm can be assigned to create ideas, as if they were entrepreneurs who were running their own firms. This process is referred to as **intrapreneurship,** as employees are encouraged to think like entrepreneurs within the firm. However, they differ from entrepreneurs in that they are employees rather than owners of the firm. Some employees may even be assigned responsibilities to develop new products or ideas for improving existing products. Intrapreneurship can pull employees away from normal, day-to-day production tasks. However, it can also allow firms to be more innovative because employees are encouraged to search for

intrapreneurship assignment of particular employees of a firm to create ideas, as if they were entrepreneurs who were running their own firms

CHAPTER EIGHT Organizational Structure

How Information Systems Enhance Organizational Structures

Information technology has allowed greater flexibility in the organizational structure of firms. An excellent example is the U.S. property and casualty (P&C) insurance industry. The traditional structure for P&C companies consists of a central headquarters, which performs high-level management activities, and a national network of local agents, who are owned either by the company or by many independent agents. Within the P&C industry it is the network of agents who provide the critical link between customers and the P&C headquarters.

One exception to this typical P&C structure is United Services Automobile Association (USAA), which services all customers directly from its San Antonio, Texas, headquarters.

USAA's highly centralized structure might lead one to conclude that its customer service suffers in comparison with other P&C companies, whose local agents get to know customers and establish personal relationships. The opposite is true, however. Historically, USAA ranks at the top of P&C companies for service and commitment to customers.

Computers are present in every aspect of USAA's P&C business. Incoming correspondence is immediately scanned to optical disks and indexed into a document processing system that was the most advanced in the world when it was constructed. All information relating to a given USAA member is indexed by member number so that customer service representatives can instantly access the information when a customer calls. A USAA customer service representative can access specific information on a particular customer's policy or claim, along with copies of relevant correspondence, in less time than it takes the local agent to walk across the room to the file cabinet. USAA has also made extensive use of computers to eliminate the need for space to maintain hard copies of all documents. Becoming the industry leader in information technology has enabled USAA to prosper.

---

new ideas. Many firms, including Apple Computer and 3M Company, have used intrapreneurship to encourage new ideas.

Intrapreneurship is likely to be more successful if employees are rewarded with some type of bonus for innovations that are ultimately applied by the firm. The firm should also attempt to ensure that any ideas that employees develop are seriously considered. If managers shoot down ideas for the wrong reasons (jealousy, for instance), employees may consider leaving the firm and implement their ideas (by starting their own business).

Informal Organizational Structure

All firms have both a formal organizational structure and an informal organizational structure. An **informal organizational structure** represents an informal communications network among a firm's employees. The network (sometimes called a "grapevine") is developed as a result of employee interaction that occurs over time. Some employees interact because they work on a similar task. Interaction among employees in unrelated divisions often occurs in a common lunch area, at social events, or even as a result of a decision that requires input from two different divisions.

informal organizational structure
an informal communications network among a firm's employees

ADVANTAGES   The informal organizational structure can benefit a firm in the following ways. Employees that need help in performing a task may benefit from others. If employees had to use the formal structure to seek help, they would require assistance from the person to whom they report. This may be inconvenient when that particular person is not available, and can slow the production process. An informal structure may also allow employees to substitute for one another, which can ensure that a task will still be completed on time. An informal structure can reduce the amount of manager involvement.

Self-directed work team members at the Bristol Myers Squibbs ConvaTec plant in Deeside, Wales, set their own schedules and allocate resources. Most workers enjoy having this control and involvement.

Another advantage of an informal structure is that friendships result from it. Friendships with other employees is a common reason for employee satisfaction with their jobs. It could be the major factor that discourages them from looking for a new job. This is especially true of lower-level jobs that pay low wages. Because friendship can strongly influence employee satisfaction, firms commonly encourage social interaction by organizing social functions.

Informal communication can occur among employees on different levels. This allows for information to travel informally from the top down or from the bottom up throughout the organization.

DISADVANTAGES Along with the advantages just described, an informal structure also has some disadvantages. Perhaps the main disadvantage is that employees obtain unfavorable information about the firm through the informal structure. Whether the information is true or is a gross exaggeration, it can have a major impact on employee morale. Unfavorable information that would have an adverse impact tends to travel faster and further throughout an informal structure. Second, some employees may have some influence over others in an informal structure. If any poor employees have an influence over others, the firm would be adversely affected.

METHODS OF DEPARTMENTALIZING TASKS

departmentalize assign tasks and responsibilities to different departments

When developing or revising an organizational structure, high-level management must first identify all the different tasks and responsibilities that the firm performs. The next step is to **departmentalize** those tasks and responsibilities, which means to assign tasks and responsibilities to different departments. The manner by which to departmentalize tasks and responsibilities is dependent on the characteristics of the business. Four of the more popular methods of departmentalizing are as follows:

➤ By function
➤ By product
➤ By location
➤ By customer

Exhibit 8.7
Departmentalizing by Function

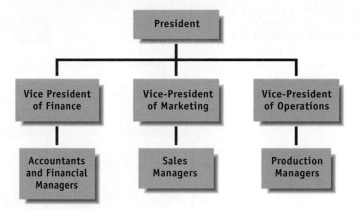

Departmentalize by Function

Many small firms departmentalize by function, meaning that tasks and responsibilities are allocated according to employee functions. The organization chart shown in Exhibit 8.7 is departmentalized by function. The finance, marketing, and production divisions are separated. This system works well when the firm is engaged in the production of just one or a few products.

Departmentalize by Product

For larger firms with many products, departmentalizing by product is common. The allocation of tasks and responsibilities is separated according to the type of product produced. The organization chart shown in Exhibit 8.8 is departmentalized by product (soft drink, food, and restaurant). This type of organizational structure is used by General Motors, which has created divisions for Buick, Cadillac, Oldsmobile, and Chevrolet.

Many large firms departmentalize by both product and function, as shown in Exhibit 8.9. The specific divisions are separated by product and each product division is departmentalized by function. Thus, each product division may have its own marketing, finance, and production divisions. It may appear that this system is inefficient because of the need for several divisions. Yet, if the firm is large enough, a single division would need to hire as many employees as are needed for several divisions. Separation by product allows employees to become more familiar with a single product rather than having to keep track of several different products.

When a firm is departmentalized by product, the expenses involved in the production of each product can be more easily estimated. Therefore, the firm can be viewed as a set of separate business divisions (separated by product) and each divi-

Exhibit 8.8
Departmentalizing by Product

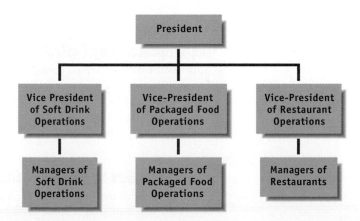

Exhibit 8.9
Departmentalizing by Product
and Function

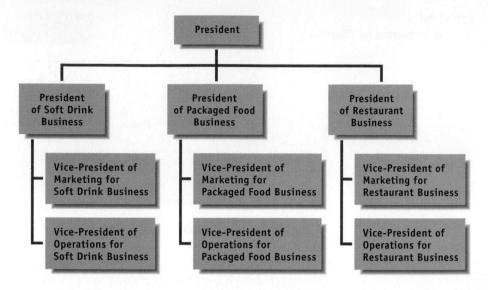

sion's profits can be determined over time. This allows the firm to determine the contribution of each business division to its total profits, which is useful when the firm is deciding which divisions should be expanded.

For a small or medium-sized firm with just a few products, departmentalizing by product would cause an inefficient use of employees, resulting in excessive expenses. A single financial manager should be capable of handling all financial responsibilities, and a single marketing manager should be capable of handling all marketing responsibilities. Thus, there is no reason to departmentalize by product.

Departmentalize by Location

Another method of separating tasks and responsibilities is to departmentalize by location. Regional offices could be established to cover specific geographical regions. This system may be appealing if corporate customers in particular locations frequently purchase a variety of the firm's products. Such customers would be able to contract the same regional office to place all of their orders. Large accounting firms departmentalize by location in order to be close to their customers.

When a firm is departmentalized by location, its expenses involved in each location can be more easily estimated. Therefore, the firm can be viewed as a set of divisions separated by location, with each location generating its own profits. This allows the firm to identify the locations that have been performing well, which may help determine which locations should attempt to expand their business.

Departmentalize by Customer

Some firms have separated divisions according to the type of customer. For example, some airlines have a separate reservations division to focus exclusively on group trips. Computer firms such as IBM have designated some salespeople to focus exclusively on selling computers to school systems. They also have some divisions that focus on retail stores, while others focus on large corporate customers.

Departmentalize by Various Characteristics

Some large firms use more than one method to departmentalize tasks. For example, they may departmentalize some tasks by location and others by product. Other firms

CROSS-FUNCTIONAL TEAMWORK

Interaction Among Departments

While the organizational structure formally indicates to whom each employee reports, it still allows interaction among different departments. For example, a firm may departmentalize by function, so that one executive is responsible for the management of operations, a second executive is responsible for the marketing function, and a third executive is responsible for the financing function.

While each function appears independent of the others on the organization chart, executives in charge of their respective functions must interact with the other departments. Exhibit 8.10 shows how the marketing, production, and finance departments rely on each other for information before making decisions. The marketing department needs to be aware of any changes in the production of a product and the volume of the product that will be available before it finalizes its marketing strategies. The production department needs customer satisfaction information as it considers redesigning products. It also needs to receive forecasts of expected sales from the marketing department, which affects the decision of how much to produce. The marketing and production departments provide the finance department with their forecasts of funds needed to cover their expenses. The finance department uses this information along with other information to determine whether it needs to obtain additional financing for the firm.

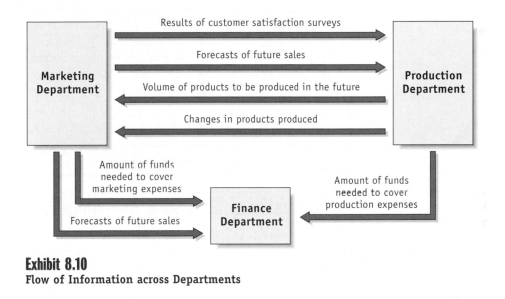

Exhibit 8.10
Flow of Information across Departments

departmentalize by location and product. Their offices are geographically distributed so that salespeople are easily accessible to local customers. In addition, their operating units are separated by product so that each unit can specialize in the production of a specific product.

GLOBAL BUSINESS

Organizational Structure of a Multinational Corporation

The organizational structure of a multinational corporation is complex because responsibilities must be assigned not only to U.S. operations but also to all foreign operations. To illustrate, consider General Motors, which has facilities in Europe, Canada, Asia, Latin America, Africa, and the Middle East. It has departmentalized by location, so either a president or a vice-president is in charge of each foreign region. Specifically, it has a president assigned to GM of

Mexico, a president assigned to GM of Brazil, a vice-president of Asian and Pacific operations, a president assigned to GM of Canada Limited, and a vice-president assigned to Latin American, African, and Middle East operations. In Europe, it has a vice-president assigned to sales and marketing and a second vice-president assigned to Europe's manufacturing plants. That is, the European operations are also departmentalized by function.

Even when firms departmentalize their U.S. operations by product or by function, they commonly departmentalize their foreign operations by location. Since some foreign operations are distant from the firm's headquarters, departmentalizing operations in any foreign country by product or function would be difficult. If the foreign operations were departmentalized by product, an executive at the U.S. headquarters would have to oversee each product produced in the foreign country. If the operations were departmentalized by function, an executive at the U.S. headquarters would have to oversee each function conducted at the foreign facility. Executives at the U.S. headquarters are not normally capable of monitoring the foreign operations because they are not there on a daily or even a weekly basis. Consequently, it is more appropriate to assign an executive at the foreign facility with the responsibility of overseeing a wide variety of products and functions at that facility.

In recent years, some multinational corporations have begun to develop a board of directors that has international business experience. In this way, the board is more capable of monitoring the firm's foreign operations. Furthermore, some multinational corporations are more willing to promote managers within the firm who have substantial experience in international business. Thus, they sometimes assign employees to their foreign facilities so that they can gain that experience.

BUSINESS DILEMMA

Organizational Structure Of College Health Club

When Sue Kramer created College Health Club (CHC), the organizational structure consisted of only herself and one part-time employee. However, she is planning to establish a second health club near a college campus about sixty miles away from the club she presently owns.

Sue recognizes that an organizational structure could be created by departmentalizing by (1) function, (2) product (service), or (3) location. Sue must decide whether to departmentalize by function, by product (service), or by location. These characteristics are summarized next.

Function
1 Marketing: To attract more members.
2 Production: To produce the services for its members.

Product (Service) Offered
1 Ensure that weight machines are working properly.
2 Provide aerobics classes.

Location
1 First health club located next to a local college.
2 Second health club to be located next to a college sixty miles away.

Dilemma

Another way of describing Sue's dilemma is as follows. Should Sue departmentalize responsibilities according to function so that one person conducts the marketing and another manages the production? Or should Sue departmentalize responsibilities by service so that one person focuses on tasks related to the weight machines while another focuses on tasks related to aerobics classes? Or should Sue departmentalize responsibilities by location so that one person manages all functions and services of the health club at the local college campus, while another person manages all functions and services of the health club at the campus sixty miles away?

Solution

Given that the two health clubs are sixty miles apart, Sue may prefer to departmentalize by location. She could focus on the duties at the new health club and allow one or more employees to manage the existing health club. There is no reason to departmentalize by service because it would force one person to manage the weight machines at both clubs (which are sixty miles apart) and another to manage aerobics classes at both clubs. It would be more efficient if the two tasks were performed at each health club by one person. This method avoids travel time between the two clubs. Even if Sue allows someone to perform the key functions at one of the health clubs, she would still have the authority as president to oversee or change any major decisions at that club.

Additional Issues for Discussion

1 As the memberships at CHC increase, Sue Kramer will hire some college students on a part-time basis. Would most of these positions be line positions or staff positions? Why?

2 Sue Kramer considered hiring a college student for an intrapreneurship position for the summer months only. How could this student be beneficial to CHC?

3 If Sue Kramer hires employees at CHC, what types of jobs would possibly be needed? To whom would these employees report?

SUMMARY

1 The organizational structure of a firm identifies responsibilities for each job position within a firm and the relationships among those positions. The structure enables employees to recognize which job positions are responsible for the work performed by other positions.

Most firms use a line-and-staff organizational structure. However, they may also use a matrix organization to obtain employee input on various projects. They may also encourage intrapreneurship in which some employees are assigned to create new products or ideas.

2 The main methods of departmentalizing are by:

➤ Function, in which tasks are separated according to employee functions;

➤ Product, in which tasks are separated according to the product produced;

➤ Location, in which tasks are concentrated in a particular division to serve a specific area; and

➤ Customer, in which tasks are separated according to the type of customer that purchases the firm's products.

KEY TERMS

autonomy
board of directors
centralization
chain of command
decentralized
departmentalize
downsizing

informal organizational structure
inside board members
intrapreneurship
line organization
line positions
line-and-staff organization
matrix organization

organization chart
organizational structure
outside board members
span of control
staff positions

REVIEW QUESTIONS

1 Explain why no one specific organizational structure is optimal for all firms.

2 Define organizational structure and how it can affect the value of the firm.

3 In operating a global business, explain why the organizational structure of a multinational corporation is so complex.

4 Describe the different spans of control you would use for a firm with numerous employees who perform similar tasks and for a firm with highly diverse tasks.

5 Assume you are creating a new organizational structure for your firm that allows more employee input. Identify and explain the two common methods you could implement.

6 Explain the difference between line positions and staff positions within an organization and cite examples of each.

7 Explain the advantages and disadvantages of an informal organizational structure.

8 Define inside board members and outside board members. What type of compensation may motivate these directors to serve the interests of the firm's shareholders?

9 Explain how cross-functional teamwork interacts among departments.

10 Define and explain the advantages and disadvantages of decentralization of management.

DISCUSSION QUESTIONS

1 Assume you are high-level management and you are revising the organizational structure of your firm. Identify and explain the main methods for departmentalizing the tasks and responsibilities to the different departments.

2 Assume you have just been named the project manager for a firm. You must bring together line-and-staff personnel in formulating a temporary organizational structure for this project. What type of organizational structure would you recommend and why?

3 In your opinion, describe how departmentalization would become the building block for organizational structure.

4 As a manager, why must you distinguish delegation from accountability for your employees?

5 Express your opinion of the informal organization. Is it the same as the "grapevine"? Should a manager ever use the "grapevine" with employees?

RUNNING YOUR OWN BUSINESS

1 Describe the organizational structure of your business.

2 Provide an organization chart and describe the responsibilities of any employees that you plan to hire.

3 How might this structure change as the business grows?

INVESTING IN THE STOCK OF A BUSINESS

Using the annual report of the firm in which you would like to invest, complete the following:

1 Describe the organizational structure of the firm.

2 Does it appear that there are many high-level managers in the firm?

3 Has the firm downsized in recent years by removing middle managers from its organizational structure?

CASE 1 Creating An Organizational Structure

Janet Shugarts is president of a barbecue sauce manufacturer in Austin, Texas. A manager in production has come up with a new barbecue recipe that he claims will be the best on the market because it's hot and spicy and has a flavor that the competition cannot match.

Janet has just received new marketing research information. The research indicates that the taste and preference of most Europeans is for a hot and spicy barbecue sauce. The marketing manager is excited about this new product and believes it can be exported into Western Europe.

Janet has just come out of a meeting with her four managers. They have decided to create a sales office in Paris, France. The plan is to create a project team to establish a production facility within a year in this country. The marketing manager will head up this project team and has requested that this subsidiary be decentralized, to provide him with an opportunity to make timely decisions in this local market.

Because of this expansion, Janet is planning to increase her work force by 20 percent based on an already existing work force of 120 employees. She has recently hired a human resource manager to take charge of the recruiting and selection function. The "grapevine" is circulating a rumor around the plant. The rumor hints that employees may attempt to bring in a union. The human resource manager is alarmed because of his position on the organization chart. His position is listed as a support position, and thus he can only advise and make recommendations to a line manager concerning issues relating to recruiting and selection.

Questions

1 Has Janet created an organizational structure? If so, how?

2 Why would the marketing manager request decentralization of authority in Paris, France?

3 Does this organization reflect a line-and-staff organizational structure? If so, explain.

CASE 2 Restructuring at Apple Computer

With its cash flow problems and loss of market share, will Apple Computer be able to survive this latest knockdown? Gilbert Amelio, the new CEO of Apple, believes these troubles are fixable and that this is an organizational problem of arranging resources to achieve goals. Some people believe, however, that Apple's problems will continue. Apple has been unable to market enough innovative and snazzy machines to justify higher prices and maintain a significant chunk of the personal computer (PC) market. Its global PC share dropped to 7.8 percent, down from 8.3 percent a year earlier.

Apple must develop a new strategy in which it should consider merging with a strong partner. Amelio's rescue plan includes the development of new products and eliminating the "dogs" within its product line. This would require intrapreneurship to create new products or ideas.

The issue of downsizing is prevalent because of Apple's streamlining of the Macintosh product line, and Apple's EWorld, its on-line service, may be axed. This may follow massive across-the-board layoffs.

Apple needs to restructure its organization. It will create new departments such as research and development and new job descriptions to meet the high technological demands of the computer industry. The R&D department will be a support function and advise the marketing department with regard to new products.

Questions

1 Explain how Apple's problems relate to its organization.

2 Define intrapreneurship and indicate what it means for Apple.

3 Should the research and development department be a line or staff function at Apple? Explain.

VIDEO CASE Reorganizing to Achieve Business Success

The healthy growth and profits it had enjoyed for sixty-three years were rudely interrupted in 1986 at Bradbury and Stamm Construction Company (BSC), one of New Mexico's largest private contractors.

A disastrous energy market in neighboring Texas, traditional source of most capital for New Mexican development, and passage of the Tax Reform Act of 1986, which removed significant investment incentives, sent New Mexico's building industry into a tailspin. Hundreds of companies declared bankruptcy.

Under Jim King, a fourteen-year employee who became BSC's third president that year, the Albuquerque firm acted to ensure that it wouldn't have to follow suit.

Next, responsibility was spread across a wider spectrum of the company. The tall organization chart was eliminated, and four self-sufficient teams were created to handle large projects and smaller projects. Each team had its own manager.

Three women were promoted to team technician slots and eventually became project managers—first of their gender in so high a position among New Mexican contractors.

Today BSC, which has 198 employees—30 more than three years ago, but half the number it had before 1986—is doing well. Annual sales are at the $65 million to $70 million level.

"We're a whole lot leaner, smarter, and more customer-oriented than just a few years ago," says Jim King. "We've learned to respond positively to obstacles, and we've thrown away the panic button."

Questions

1 Bradbury and Stamm Construction (BSC) originally used a tall organizational structure, with several layers of management. Describe how it changed its organizational structure. How do you think BSC may benefit from the change in the organizational structure?

2 What is a potential disadvantage of the new organizational structure used by BSC, as compared with its original organizational structure?

3 Should BSC also allow its production workers to make decisions normally made by its executives, such as where to expand, how much to pay when acquiring another company, and how much money to borrow?

THE Coca-Cola COMPANY ANNUAL REPORT PROJECT

The following questions apply concepts in this chapter to The Coca-Cola Company. Read the first two paragraphs of page 3 and the organization chart on page 72 in The Coca-Cola Company annual report before answering these questions.

1 Explain how The Coca-Cola Company changed its management structure in 1996.

2 Review The Coca-Cola Company's organizational structure on page 72. Why do you think The Coca-Cola Company has an organizational structure that is divided (decentralized) in geographic divisions?

3 **a.** How many of the individuals on the board of directors are company employees? (See page 73)

b. Why do you think few Company employees are on the board?

c. There are at least two famous individuals on the board; can you name them? (See page 73)

d. The Coca-Cola Company employed 32,000 people in 1996. Based on the Company's net operating revenues, how much revenue did each employee generate?

IN-TEXT STUDY GUIDE

Answers are in an appendix at the back of the book.

True or False

1 When a firm is departmentalized by location, its expenses involved in each location can be more easily estimated.

2 The organization chart indicates the reports to and interaction among employee responsibilities.

3 The organization chart ensures that each employee is directly accountable to a member who sits on the board of directors.

4 Most firms departmentalize their foreign operations by function.

5 Authority is always maintained at the highest level of management.

6 An organizational structure indicates how all the job responsibilities fit together.

7 An informal organizational structure (also called the "grapevine") represents a formal communications network among employees of a firm.

8 Job positions in an organizational structure can be classified as line or staff positions.

9 Departmentalization by function works well when the firm is engaged in the production of many different products.

10 An organizational structure that is designed to have each manager supervise just a few employees has a narrow span of control.

Multiple Choice

11 When the managers of a financing function rely on the marketing managers to make decisions, this is an example of:
a) contingency planning.
b) autocratic leadership.
c) departmentalization.
d) board of directors.
e) cross-functional teamwork.

12 An example of a firm that would departmentalize by type of customer is a(n):
a) airline industry.
b) candy store.
c) large accounting firm.
d) food distributor.
e) newspaper.

13 An organizational structure that includes line positions and staff positions and assigns authority from higher-level management to employees is referred to as a:
a) line organization.
b) staff organization.
c) customer organization.
d) line-and-staff organization.
e) product organization.

14 Many staff positions serve the line function in a(n):
a) command role.
b) assistance role.
c) direct authority role.
d) responsibility center.
e) line organization.

15 Some management layers have been removed and a wider span of control has been created through:

a) unity of command.
b) downsizing.
c) division of work.
d) specialization.
e) contingency planning.

16 An organization that represents the interaction between various parts of the firm to come together on specific projects is a:
a) matrix organization.
b) functional organization.
c) product organization.
d) geographic organization.
e) customer orientation.

17 It is common for larger firms with many products to departmentalize by:
a) function.
b) customer.
c) manufacturing process.
d) geographic area.
e) product.

18 A tall organizational structure reflects:
a) many layers.
b) one owner.
c) one manager.
d) numerous stockholders.
e) numerous board members.

19 The responsibilities of a firm's managers should be organized to achieve the:
a) grapevine.
b) formal contingency.
c) strategic plan.
d) chain of command.
e) bureaucratic organization.

20 The process that identifies responsibilities for each job position and the relationships among those positions is the:
a) organizational structure.
b) planning function.
c) leadership application.
d) job description.
e) control cycle.

21 Jobs that are established to make decisions that achieve specific business goals are:
a) staff positions.
b) line positions.
c) line-and-staff functions.
d) temporary jobs.
e) job placement.

22 An organizational structure that includes only line positions and no staff positions is referred to as a:
a) product organization.

b) line organization.
c) single position organization.
d) supportive organization
e) single linear organization.

23 In recent years many firms have decided to spread authority among several divisions or managers; this is called:
a) centralization.
b) decentralization.
c) chain of command.
d) intrapreneurship.
e) authority.

24 The ultimate responsibility for the success of a firm lies with the:
a) president.
b) employee.
c) customer.
d) competition.
e) labor union.

25 The board of directors serve as representatives of the:
a) employees.
b) customers.
c) shareholders.
d) competition.
e) labor unions.

26 According to the text, large accounting firms departmentalize by:
a) decentralizing.
b) centralization.
c) location.
d) customer.
e) specialization.

27 Downsizing results in:
a) autocratic management.
b) centralization.
c) decentralization.
d) a matrix organization.
e) intrapreneurship.

28 Board members who are managers of the same firm (such as the chief executive officer) are referred to as:
a) chain of command.
b) organization chart.
c) outside board members.
d) centralized authority.
e) inside board members.

29 A set of executives that is responsible for monitoring the activities of the firm's president and other high-level managers is called a(n):

a) board of directors.
b) chain of command.
c) span of control.
d) unity of command.
e) organization chart.

30 An extreme form of decentralization in which divisions can make their own decisions and act independently is called:
a) centralization.
b) autonomy.
c) span of control.
d) span of management.
e) departmentalization.

31 Span of control is determined by:
a) consultants.
b) staff.
c) top management.
d) employees.
e) customers.

32 Assigning tasks and responsibilities to different departments means to:
a) specialize.
b) decentralize.
c) downsize.
d) departmentalize.
e) autonomize.

33 A diagram that shows the formal structure of the firm is a(n):
a) organization chart.
b) chain of command.
c) corporate charter.
d) strategic plan.
e) organization.

34 Board members who are high-level managers of other firms are called:
a) board leaders.
b) inside board members.
c) outside board members.
d) institutional investors.
e) creditors.

35 A process whereby particular employees of a firm can be assigned to create ideas, as if they were entrepreneurs, is referred to as:
a) staff organization.
b) intrapreneurship.
c) co-ownership.
d) leadership.
e) line organization.

Managing by Telecommuting

Many of today's organizational structures are based upon the notion of a "place of business." What happens to such structures if the place of business disappears? One major long-term impact of the Internet will be to increase our ability to work out of our homes. But working at home using a computer to communicate, often referred to as telecommuting, brings with it many challenges. How do home-based workers prevent distractions from interfering with their work? How can a manager monitor a home-based employee's productivity? Many sites on the WWW address these problems. A good place to start is *HomeWorker* magazine's home page (Exhibit 8.11), which features articles on many of these subjects as well as links to other telecommuting sites.

Exhibit 8.11
Home Worker Magazine Web Site

http://www.homeworker.com/

INCOME OPPORTUNITIES'
HOME WORKER™

**CONNECTING
PEOPLE
WORKING
FROM HOME**

Associate Publisher **Bruce Helmis** welcomes you to **HomeWorker**!

JANUARY/FEBRUARY

Give 'Em Something To Talk (Or Write) About

Fighting the Solitaire of a Home Office

The Homeworking Phenomenon: Looking Beyond The Hype

CHAPTER 9

Production
Management

Firms are created to produce one or more products or services. Production management (also called operations management) represents the management of a process in which resources (such as employees and machinery) are used to produce products and services. The process by which a firm's products (or services) are produced can affect the firm's value.

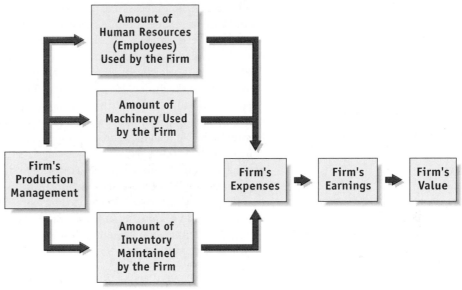

Consider the case of McDonnell Douglas, which produces airplanes for airlines and governments. How can McDonnell Douglas determine the combination of employees and machines to produce each airplane? Should it focus its production at one plant or utilize several different production sites? Where is the optimal site for producing its product? How should its facilities be designed to make the most efficient use of space? This chapter provides a background on production management, which can be used to address these questions.

The **Learning Goals** of this chapter are to:

1   Identify the key resources used for production.

2   Identify the factors that affect the plant site decision.

3   Describe how various factors affect the design and layout decision.

4   Describe the key tasks that are involved in production control.

RESOURCES USED FOR THE PRODUCTION PROCESS

1 **Identify the key resources used for production.**

production process (conversion process) a series of tasks in which resources are used to produce a product or service

production management (operations management) the management of a process in which resources (such as employees and machinery) are used to produce products and services

Whether a firm produces products or services, it needs a **production process** (also called **conversion process**), or a series of tasks in which resources are used to produce a product or service. A process identifies the mixture of resources allocated for production, the assignment of tasks, and the sequence of tasks.

Many possible production processes can achieve the production of a specific product. Thus, effective **production management** can develop an efficient (relatively low-cost) and high-quality production process for producing specific products and services. Specifically, production management can achieve efficiency by determining the proper amount of materials to use, the proper mix of resources to use, the proper assignments of the tasks, and the proper sequence of the tasks. The success of some firms, such as Motorola and Kraft Foods, is partially attributed to their production management. The success of service-oriented firms such as Southwest Airlines is attributed to their low cost production air transportation for customers. The profits and value of each firm are influenced by its production management.

The main resources that firms use for the production process are human resources (employees), materials, and other resources (such as buildings, machinery, and equipment).

Human Resources

Firms must identify the type of employees needed for production. Skilled labor is necessary for some forms of production, while unskilled labor can be used for other forms. Some forms of production are labor-intensive in that they require more labor than materials. The operating expenses involved in hiring human resources are dependent both on the number of employees and on their skill levels. Because of the

Many different materials go into producing a finished product. These Levi's jeans have finished the "stone-washing" process.

employee skill level required, a computer development firm incurs much larger salary expenses than a grocery store.

Materials

The materials used in the production process are normally transformed by the firm's human resources into a final product. Tire manufacturers rely on rubber, automobile manufacturers rely on steel, and book publishers rely on paper. Service firms such as travel agencies and investment advisors do not rely as much on materials because they do not engage in manufacturing.

Other Resources

A building is needed for most forms of production. Manufacturers use factories and offices. Service firms use offices. The site may be owned or rented by the firm. Since the purchase of a building can be expensive, some firms simply rent the buildings they use. Renting also allows the firm to move at the end of the rent period without having to sell the building. Machinery and equipment are also needed for many manufacturing firms.

Combining the Resources for Production

work station an area in which one or more employees are assigned a specific task

assembly line consists of a sequence of work stations, in which each work station is designed to cover specific phases of the production process

Managers attempt to utilize the resources just described in a manner that achieves production at a low cost. They combine the various resources with the use of work stations and assembly lines. A **work station** is an area in which one or more employees are assigned a specific task. A work station may require not only employees but also machinery and equipment.

An **assembly line** consists of a sequence of work stations, in which each work station is designed to cover specific phases of the production process. The production of a single product may require several work stations, with each station using employees, machinery, and materials. Since the cost of all these resources along with the building can be substantial, efficient management of the production process can reduce expenses, which can convert into higher profits.

A typical example of the production process is shown in Exhibit 9.1. Employees use buildings, machinery, and equipment to convert materials into a product or service. For example, printing firms train employees to use their machines for typesetting, printing, and binding, which produces books. Travel agencies train employees to use their offices and computers for hotel and airline reservations.

Exhibit 9.1
Resources Used in Production

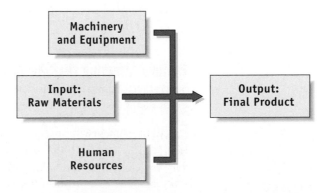

Exhibit 9.2
Illustration of Coca-Cola's Efforts
to Reduce Operating Expenses

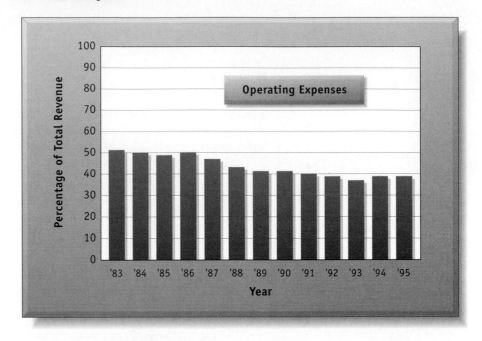

Many different combinations of employees can be allocated among various tasks. At one extreme, one employee may cover all tasks of the production process. However, most production processes are more efficient if different employees are assigned different tasks. In this way, employees can utilize their unique types of expertise.

Firms frequently attempt to improve their production process so that they can reduce their operating expenses. Exhibit 9.2 shows how The Coca-Cola Company has reduced its operating expenses (in proportion to its total revenue) since 1983.

SELECTING A SITE

2 | **Identify the factors that affect the plant site decision.**

A critical decision in production management is the selection of a site (location) for the factory or office. Location can significantly affect the cost of production and therefore the firm's ability to compete against other firms. This is especially true for industrial firms such as Bethlehem Steel and Chrysler Corporation, which require a large investment in plant and equipment. Site selection can also affect revenue because it may influence the demand for the product produced if the product is to be sold at the site.

Factors Affecting the Site Decision
Several factors must be considered when determining the optimal site. The most relevant factors are identified here.

COST OF WORKPLACE SPACE   The cost of purchasing workplace space (such as buildings or offices) can vary significantly among locations. This was one major reason why companies located in northern cities relocated to the South during the last ten years. The cost of workplace space is likely to be high near the center of any busi-

This GM facility in Mexico produces bumpers. Cost of space, cost of labor, tax incentives, access to transportation, and supply of labor would all play a major role in selecting a site for this type of product.

ness district, where the land cost is high. W. R. Grace and IBM recently moved some of their facilities to locations where land prices are lower.

The cost of leasing workplace space can also vary substantially among locations. Exhibit 9.3 shows annual office rental rates per square foot in various major cities. Notice that the office rental rates are generally higher in the northeastern states than in other areas. The rental rate is typically higher in those cities where the cost of land is high.

COST OF LABOR   The cost of hiring employees varies significantly among locations. Salaries within a city tend to be higher than outside the city for a given occupation. Salaries are also generally higher in the North than the South for a given occupation. This is another reason why many companies have relocated to the South.

TAX INCENTIVES   Some local governments may be willing to offer tax credits to attract companies into their area. This incentive is provided to increase the employment level and improve the economic conditions of an area.

SOURCE OF DEMAND   If the firm plans to sell its product in a specific location, it may establish its site there. The transporting and servicing costs of the product could be minimized by producing at a site near the source of demand.

ACCESS TO TRANSPORTATION   When companies sell products to areas across the nation, they may choose a site near their main source of transportation. They also need to be accessible so that materials can be delivered to them. Some factories and offices are established near interstate highways, rivers, and airports for this reason.

SUPPLY OF LABOR   Firms that plan to hire specialized workers must be able to attract the labor needed. They may choose a location where a large supply of workers with that particular specialization exists. For instance, high-tech companies tend to locate near universities where there is an abundance of educated labor.

Exhibit 9.3
Comparison of Office Rental Rates (Per Square Foot Per Year) among Cities

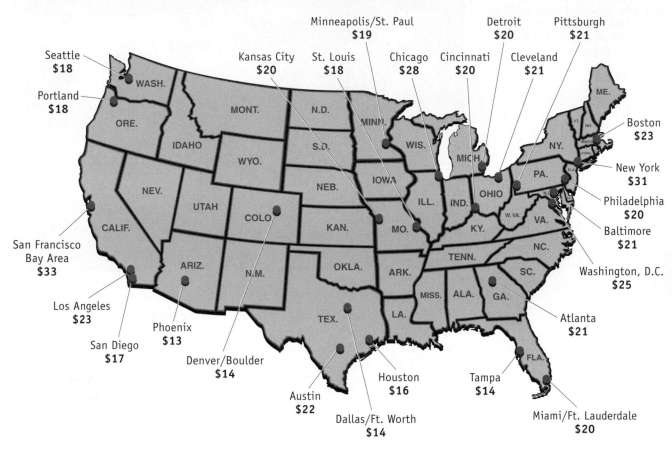

Evaluating Possible Sites

When a firm considers various sites, it must compare the desirability of each site. First, it may assign a weight to represent the importance of each of the various factors that will influence its decision. Labor-intensive firms would likely place a high weight on the cost of human resources; other firms would not be as concerned about this factor.

Once the firm has determined which factors should have the most influence on its decision, it attempts to rate these factors for each possible site. An easy method to compare alternative sites is to develop a site evaluation matrix, as shown in Exhibit 9.4. Each row represents a list of possible sites. The columns represent various factors that need to be evaluated. These factors may be rated from 1 (outstanding) to 5 (poor). The overall rating assigned to any potential site could be determined by averaging the ratings for that site. However, if some factors are more important than others, they deserve to have a relatively higher influence on the overall ratings.

The site evaluation matrix in Exhibit 9.4 is simplified in that it focuses on only two factors for each city. The land cost is presumed to be a more important factor and has an 80 percent weight. The supply of labor is allocated the remaining 20 percent weight. The weighted rating shown in Exhibit 9.4 is equal to the rating times the weight of the rating. The weighted rating for each factor is combined to determine the total rating for each city. For example, the Austin, Texas, site received a land cost rating of 3, which converts to a weighted rating of 2.4 (computed as 3 × .8). It also

Exhibit 9.4
Example of a Site Evaluation Matrix

Possible Sites	Land Cost		Supply of Labor		Total Rating
	Rating	Weighted Rating (80 % Weight)	Rating	Weighted Rating (20% Weight)	
Austin, TX	3	2.4	1	.2	2.6
Chicago, IL	4	3.2	2	.4	3.6
Los Angeles, CA	5	4.0	3	.6	4.6
Omaha, NE	1	.8	3	.6	1.4

received a supply of labor rating of 1, which converts to a rating of .2 (computed as 1 × .2). Its total rating is 2.6 (computed as 2.4 + .2).

Once the firm determines a rating for each factor, it can derive the total rating for each site considered. Based on the ratings that were assumed for each of the four sites in Exhibit 9.4, the Omaha site had the best rating and thus would be selected as the site.

If another firm assessed the same four sites in Exhibit 9.4, it might come to a different conclusion, for two reasons. First, it may use different factors in its matrix. Second, it may rate the factors differently. For example, one city may have an abundance of people who have computer development skills, but may not have many people with skills to manage a bank.

Once a particular area (such as a city or county) has been chosen, the precise location must be decided. Some of the factors already mentioned will influence this decision. In addition, factors such as traffic, crime rate, and worker access to public transportation may influence this decision.

GLOBAL BUSINESS

Selecting a Foreign Production Site

The selection of a foreign production site by a U.S. firm is critical because location affects the firm's operating expenses and therefore its earnings. Consider the case of Warner-Lambert, a U.S. firm that produces pharmaceutical and consumer products, including Listerine, Halls cough drops, Clorets mints, Certs mints, and Trident gum. Warner-Lambert has operations in more than one hundred countries. Its extensive development of foreign operations was motivated by global demand for its products. Warner-Lambert's marketing goal is "every product, everywhere." It is attempting to sell its products in virtually every country. Consequently, it established production sites that were convenient to the foreign markets where it planned to expand. It also considered the land and labor costs in the foreign countries when determining where to establish production facilities. In addition, it considered the locations of its other sites, since each site could accommodate consumer demand within that region. Warner-Lambert has substantial production facilities in Europe, the Middle East, Africa, Latin America, and the Far East, and recently expanded its operations in Australia, New Zealand, and various parts of Europe.

The selection of a production site by any multinational corporation is crucial because costs vary substantially among countries. Annual office rental rates per square foot are about $15 in Mexico City, $58 in Paris, and $125 in Tokyo. The cost of human resources is generally much lower in less-developed countries. Yet, the supply of labor in those countries may be inadequate. Furthermore, consumer demand for products in those countries may be low, which forces the foreign facility to transport the products to other countries with much higher demand. Multinational corporations must assess the trade-offs involved. If the products are lightweight (involving low transportation expenses), multinational corporations might be willing to use facilities in less-developed countries but transport the products to areas where demand is higher.

SELECTING THE DESIGN AND LAYOUT

3 **Describe how various factors affect the design and layout decision.**

design represents the size and structure of the plant or office

layout represents the arrangement of the machinery and equipment within the factory or office

Once a site for a manufacturing plant or office is chosen, the design and layout must be determined. The **design** represents the size and structure of the plant or office. The **layout** represents the arrangement of the machinery and equipment within the factory or office.

The design and layout decisions directly affect operating expenses because they determine the costs of rent, machinery, and equipment. They may even affect the firm's interest expenses because they influence the amount of money that firms borrow to purchase property or machinery.

A recent study by the management consulting firm Ernst and Young found that firms can improve their profits by using innovative ideas for their plant design and layout. Firms may assign employee teams the responsibility of identifying methods to make their plant design and layout more efficient. Employees may be highly motivated to offer cost-cutting solutions when they realize that the alternative solution would involve layoffs.

Factors Affecting Design and Layout

Design and layout decisions are influenced by the following characteristics.

SITE CHARACTERISTICS Design and layout decisions are dependent on some characteristics of the site selected. For example, if the site is in an area with high land costs, a high-rise building may be designed so that less land will be needed. The layout of the plant will then be affected by the design.

PRODUCTION PROCESS Design and layout are also dependent on the production process to be used. If an assembly-line operation is to be used, all tasks included in this operation should be in the same general area. A **product layout** positions the tasks in the sequence that they are assigned. For example, one person may specialize in creating components, while the next person assembles components, and the next person packages the product. The product layout is commonly used for assembly-line production.

product layout positions the tasks in the sequence that they are assigned

Alternatively, some products (such as airplanes, ships, or homes) are completely produced in one fixed position, which requires a **fixed-position layout.** The employees go to the position of the product, rather than having the product come to them.

fixed-position layout employees go to the position of the product, rather than waiting for the product to come to them

The design and layout should allow the sequence of tasks to take place efficiently. For example, the production process is commonly completed near the outside of the plant so that the finished products can be easily loaded onto trucks.

flexible manufacturing a production process that can be easily adjusted to accommodate future revisions

Many firms now use **flexible manufacturing,** a production process that can be easily adjusted to accommodate future revisions. This enables the firm to restructure its layout due to changes in the types of products demanded. Merck and Company commonly uses flexible manufacturing, which allows it to produce more than one product within an assembly line. Many auto plants use flexible manufacturing so they can produce whatever cars or trucks are in demand. The production process must be flexible to accommodate customer demand.

A flexible layout normally requires that employees have flexible skills. While employees may have some specialization, they must have other skills when the layout of the plant is rearranged to focus on the production of other products.

This Fisher Price plant in Matamoros, Mexico is an example of a product layout plant. The product moves through a variety of stations on its way to becoming a portable crib.

PRODUCT LINE   Most firms produce more than one product or service at their site. Firms with a narrow product line focus on the production of one or a few products, which allows them to specialize. Other firms with a broad product line offer a wide-range of products. Firms with such a broad product line must have a design and layout that can be revised as the product line is revised.

As market preferences change, demand for products changes. The layout must be revised to accompany these changes. For example, the recent popularity of minivans has caused many automobile manufacturers to allocate more of their layout for the production of minivans. The allocation of more space for one product normally takes space away from others, unless the initial design and layout allowed extra space for expansion.

DESIRED PRODUCTION CAPACITY   When planning both design and layout, the firm's desired production capacity (maximum production level possible) must be considered. Most firms attempt to plan for growth by allowing flexibility to increase the production capacity over time. The design of the building may allow for additional levels to be added on. The proper layout can open up more space to be used for more production. For example, Ford recently revised its assembly-line operations to produce 25 percent more cars.

If firms do not plan for growth, they will be forced to search for a new site once demand for their product exceeds their production capacity. When firms maintain their existing site and develop a second site to expand, they will need to duplicate their machinery and job positions assigned at the original site. Consequently, production efficiency will tend to decrease. To avoid this problem, they may relocate to a site with a larger capacity. Reassessing all potential plant sites and developing a new design and layout can be costly. Firms could avoid these costs by ensuring that the layout at their initial site allows for growth.

While it is desirable to have a layout that allows for growth, it is also expensive. A firm must invest additional funds to obtain additional land or floor space. This investment ties up funds that may be better used by the firm for other purposes. Furthermore, if growth does not occur, the firm would not have an efficient layout because some of the space will continue to be unused.

Reducing the Layout Space

Recently, many firms have reduced their investment in property and buildings to reduce their expenses. Many large firms such as IBM, General Motors, and Exxon have more than one hundred thousand employees. They incur massive expenses in the property or buildings that they own or rent. The potential for reducing costs is great if these firms can more efficiently use their work space and sell whatever property or buildings they do not need. Alternatively, they can reduce expenses by canceling their rent agreements on buildings they were renting.

Hewlett-Packard has reduced its investment in plant and equipment relative to its other assets, as shown in Exhibit 9.5. This frees up funds that can be used for

Exhibit 9.5
How Hewlett-Packard Increased Its Production Efficiency by Reducing Its Investment in Plant and Equipment

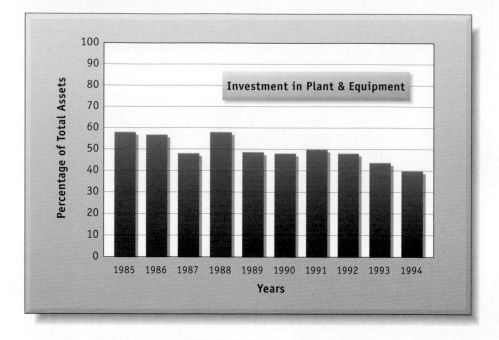

hotelling (just-in-time office) firm provides an office with a desk, a computer, and a telephone for any employee who normally works at home but needs to use work space at the firm

PRODUCTION CONTROL

4 **Describe the key tasks that are involved in production control.**

production control involves purchasing materials, inventory control, routing, scheduling, quality control

other purposes. AT&T, Eastman Kodak, and Mobil Oil expect to save more than $100 million by reducing their work space.

Downsizing is responsible for the need to reduce work space at many firms. When firms reduced (downsized) their work force, they no longer needed as many offices. In addition, firms attempted to reduce work space because of the large expense associated with owning large amounts of property and building space.

As firms reduce their work space, they may need to adjust their layout to accommodate their employees. One solution is to allow more employees to work at home. Given the improvement in telecommunications (computer networks and fax machines), some employees may be able to do most of their work at home. AT&T is experimenting with this strategy for some employees. When the employees who work at home need to come in to work, they use work spaces that are not permanently assigned to anyone. For example, a firm may have an office available with a desk, a computer, and a telephone for any employee who normally works at home but needs to use work space at the firm. This concept is referred to as **hotelling** (or **just-in-time office**). Such shared office space may be a little less convenient for employees, but can help reduce operating expenses. Salespeople who travel frequently commonly use a home office rather than a company office.

Once the plant and design have been selected, the firm can engage in **production control,** which involves the following:

➤ Purchasing materials
➤ Inventory control
➤ Routing
➤ Scheduling
➤ Quality control

Purchasing Materials

Managers perform the following tasks when purchasing supplies. First, they must select a supplier. Second, they attempt to obtain volume discounts. Third, they determine whether to delegate some production tasks to suppliers. These tasks are discussed next.

SELECTING A SUPPLIER OF MATERIALS   In selecting among various suppliers, firms consider characteristics such as price, speed, quality, servicing, and credit availability. A typical approach to evaluating suppliers is to first obtain prices from each supplier. Next, a sample is obtained from each supplier and inspected for quality. Two or three suppliers may be selected according to these criteria. Then, these suppliers are asked to provide further information on their speed of delivery and their service warranties in case any delivery problems occur. The firm may then try out a single supplier and evaluate its reliability over time.

Alternatively, a firm may initially use a few suppliers and later select the supplier that has provided the best service. Some firms may avoid depending on a single supplier, since any problems originating from that supplier could have a major impact on the firm. For example, the Chevrolet Caprice (produced by General Motors) was delayed in 1994 because the supplier of ashtrays did not deliver them to General Motors on time. Orders at Apple Computer were delayed when it could not obtain a sufficient supply of memory chips and monitors.

OBTAINING VOLUME DISCOUNTS   Firms that purchase a large volume of materials from suppliers may obtain a discounted price on supplies. This practice has enabled firms such as AT&T, Allied Signal, Chrysler, and Wal-Mart to reduce their production expenses in recent years.

outsourcing act of purchasing parts from a supplier rather than producing the parts

DELEGATING PRODUCTION TO SUPPLIERS   Manufacturers commonly use **outsourcing,** which is the act of purchasing parts from suppliers rather than producing the

The Stewart & Stevenson Company won a large contract for supplying trucks to the U.S. armed forces through the innovative use of materials. The company designed this truck to fit armed forces product requirements; however all of the parts that went into the truck were parts that were already in use in other vehicles. The company was able to get the winning bid by saving on the design and manufacture of new parts.

Exhibit 9.6
Effects of Deintegration

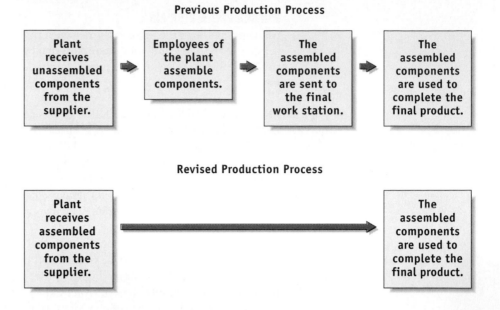

Previous Production Process

| Plant receives unassembled components from the supplier. | → | Employees of the plant assemble components. | → | The assembled components are sent to the final work station. | → | The assembled components are used to complete the final product. |

Revised Production Process

| Plant receives assembled components from the supplier. | ⟶ | The assembled components are used to complete the final product. |

parts. Outsourcing can reduce a firm's expenses if suppliers can produce the parts at a lower cost than manufacturers. Some manufacturers have even begun delegating some parts of the production process to suppliers. Consider a unionized manufacturing firm that is located in a big city where wages are generally high. Assume that historically, this firm ordered several components from a supplier and assembled the components at its own plant. If the supplier is nonunionized, it may be better to have the supplier partially assemble the components before sending them to the manufacturer. Some of the assembly task is thereby shifted to the supplier. Partial assembly by the supplier may cost less than paying high-wage employees at the manufacturing plant.

deintegration strategy of delegating some production tasks to suppliers

This strategy of delegating some production tasks to suppliers is referred to as **deintegration** and is illustrated in Exhibit 9.6. The production process within the plant is no longer as integrated, because part of the production is completed by the supplier before the supplies or components are delivered to the manufacturing plant. Automobile manufacturers have deintegrated their production processes by delegating some production tasks to suppliers or other firms. For example, General Motors has delegated the production of its radiator caps, vacuum pumps, and many other parts to suppliers. Chrysler purchases assembled parts of automobiles from Tenneco, a supplier. Ford Motor Company purchases automobile seats that are fully assembled from Lear Seating. This act of deintegration has saved unionized manufacturers hundreds of dollars per automobile, because the supplier's cost of labor is lower than that of the manufacturer.

The concept of deintegration is not restricted to automobile manufacturing. Firms such as General Mills and Snapple have also delegated some production to other firms.

Inventory Control

inventory control the process of managing inventory at a level that minimizes costs

Inventory control is the process of managing inventory at a level that minimizes costs. It requires the management of materials inventories, work-in-process inventories, and finished goods inventories, as explained next.

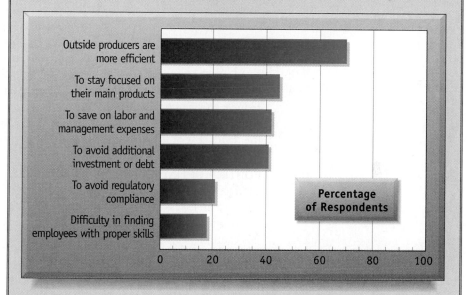

SMALL BUSINESS SURVEY

Why Do Firms Outsource Rather Than Produce Some Products Themselves?

A recent survey of the chief executive officers (CEOs) of four hundred high-growth businesses asked what caused them to outsource rather than produce some products (including supplies) themselves. The results are summarized in the following chart.

It appears from the survey that many firms recognize that they can benefit from specializing in what they do best, and relying on other firms for supplies or parts needed for their production process.

carrying costs costs of maintaining (carrying) inventories

order costs costs involved in placing orders

just-in-time (JIT) system that attempts to reduce materials inventories to a bare minimum by frequently ordering small amounts of materials

materials requirements planning (MRP) a process for ensuring that materials are available when needed

CONTROL OF MATERIALS INVENTORIES When firms carry excessive inventories of materials, they may need to borrow more funds to finance these inventories. This increases their so-called **carrying costs,** or their costs of maintaining (carrying) inventories. While they can attempt to reduce their carrying costs by frequently ordering small amounts of materials, this strategy increases the costs involved in placing orders (called **order costs**). Any adjustment in the materials purchasing strategy will normally reduce carrying costs at the expense of increasing order costs, or vice versa.

A popular method for reducing carrying costs is the **just-in-time (JIT)** system originated by Japanese companies. This system attempts to reduce materials inventories to a bare minimum by frequently ordering small amounts of materials. It can reduce the costs of maintaining inventories. However, there is a cost of managerial time required for frequent ordering and a cost of frequent deliveries. In addition, the just-in-time system could result in a shortage if applied improperly. U.S. firms such as Applied Magnetics Corporation and Black and Decker Corporation have improved their productivity by effectively using just-in-time management.

Materials requirements planning (MRP) is a process for ensuring that the materials are available when needed. Normally requiring the use of a computer, MRP helps managers determine the amount of specific materials that should be purchased at any given time. The first step of MRP is to work backward from the finished product toward the beginning and determine how long in advance materials are needed before products are completely produced. As the firm forecasts the demand for its product in the future, it can determine the time at which the materials need to arrive to achieve a production level that will accommodate the forecasted demand.

CONTROL OF WORK-IN-PROCESS INVENTORIES   Firms must also manage their **work-in-process inventories,** which represent inventories of partially completed products. They attempt to avoid shortages of all three types of inventories. The direct consequence of a shortage in raw materials inventory or work-in-process inventory is an interruption in production, while the direct consequence of a shortage in completed goods is foregone sales. A shortage of completed products inventory is commonly caused by a shortage of raw materials inventory or work-in-process inventory.

> **work-in-process inventories** represent inventories of partially completed products

Bristol-Myers Squibb Company has attempted to reduce the time from when raw materials are purchased until the completion and sale of the final product. This reduces the length of time during which funds must be borrowed to finance purchases, because the firm receives cash from the sale of the product sooner. Therefore, the firm's cost of financing is reduced.

CONTROL OF FINISHED GOODS INVENTORIES   As demand for a firm's product changes over time, managers need to monitor the anticipated supply-demand differential. If an excess supply of a product is anticipated, firms could avoid excessive inventories by redirecting their resources toward the production of other products. For example, Ford Motor Company redirects resources away from the production of cars that are not selling as well as expected. Alternatively, firms that experience an excess supply of products could continue their normal production schedule and implement marketing strategies (such as advertising) that would increase demand.

If excess demand is anticipated, firms become concerned about possible shortages and must develop a strategy to boost production volume. They may schedule overtime for workers or may hire new workers to achieve higher levels of production.

When the forecasted demand is underestimated, the firm may not produce a sufficient volume to accommodate all customers. Compaq Computer experienced shortages of its laptop computers in 1994 because it underestimated demand. In 1995, Apple Computer experienced a shortage because it underestimated the demand for its computers. It had more than $1 billion in computer orders that it could not accommodate immediately. For this reason, some firms maintain more inventories than their expected volume of sales.

Many firms, such as Land's End and Cemex, have improved their efficiency by using computer networks. Changes in inventory level are updated as soon as a customer order is received. IBM has consistently reduced its inventory in an effort to reduce its costs, as shown in Exhibit 9.7. Its inventory as a percentage of its total assets was cut by more than half over the period 1985–1995.

Routing

> **routing** the sequence (or route) of tasks necessary to complete the production of a product

Routing represents the sequence (or route) of tasks necessary to complete the production of a product. Raw materials are commonly sent to various work stations so that they can be used as specified in the production process. A specific part of the production process is completed at each work station. For example, the production of a bicycle may require (1) using materials to produce a bike frame at one work sta-

Exhibit 9.7
Illustration of IBM's Efforts to Minimize Inventory

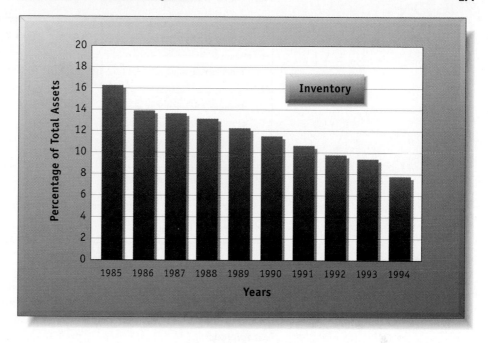

tion, (2) assembling wheels at a second work station, and (3) packaging the frames and wheels that have been assembled at a third work station.

The routing process is periodically evaluated to determine whether it can be improved to allow a faster or less expensive production process. General Motors, Chrysler, and United Parcel Service have recently streamlined their routing process to improve production efficiency.

Scheduling

scheduling the act of setting time periods for each task in the production process

production schedule a plan for the timing and volume of production tasks

Scheduling is the act of setting time periods for each task in the production process. A **production schedule** is a plan for the timing and volume of production tasks. For example, the production schedule for a bicycle may set a time of two hours for each frame to be assembled and one hour for each wheel to be assembled. Scheduling is useful because it sets the expected amount of production that should be achieved at each work station over a given day or week. Therefore, each employee recognizes what is expected. Furthermore, the scheduling allows managers to forecast how much will be produced by the end of the day, week, or month.

SCHEDULING FOR SPECIAL PROJECTS   Scheduling is especially important for special long-term projects that must be completed by a specific deadline. If many related tasks must be completed in a specific sequence, scheduling can indicate when each task should be completed. In this way, managers can detect whether the project is likely to be completed on time. If any tasks are not completed on time, managers must search for ways to make up the time on other tasks.

Gantt chart illustrates the expected timing for each task within the production process

One method of scheduling tasks of a special project is to use a **Gantt chart** (named after its creator, Henry Gantt), which illustrates the expected timing for each task within the production process. To show how a Gantt chart can be applied, consider an example in which a chemical firm must produce five hundred gallon containers of Chemical Z for a manufacturer. The production process involves creating large amounts of Chemicals X and Y, which are then mixed in a tank to pro-

Exhibit 9.8
Example of a Gantt Chart

Production Tasks	Week 1	Week 2	Week 3	Week 4	Week 5
1. Produce Chemical X.	■				
2. Produce Chemical Y.					
3. Mix Chemicals X and Y in a tank to produce Chemical Z.			■		
4. Pour Chemical Z into 500 one-gallon containers.				■	
5. Package the one-gallon containers into cases.					□

duce Chemical Z. Next, Chemical Z must be poured in gallon containers and then packaged in cases to be delivered. Notice that while the first two tasks can be completed at the same time, each remaining task cannot begin until the previous task is completed.

The bar for each task on the Gantt chart can be marked when that task is completed, as shown in Exhibit 9.8. According to the exhibit, the first four tasks have been completed, so the focus is now on the fifth task.

Another method of scheduling tasks of a special project is the **program evaluation and review technique (PERT),** which schedules tasks in a manner that will minimize delays in the production process. The PERT involves the following steps:

program evaluation and review technique (PERT) schedules tasks in a manner that will minimize delays in the production process

1 The various tasks involved in the production process are identified.
2 The tasks are arranged in the order in which they must take place; this sequence may be represented on a chart with arrows illustrating the path or sequence of the production process.
3 The time needed for each activity is estimated.

An example of PERT as applied to a firm's production of Chemical Z is shown in Exhibit 9.9. The production of Chemical X (Task 1) and Chemical Y (Task 2) can

Exhibit 9.9
Determining the Critical Path Based on a Sequence of Production Tasks

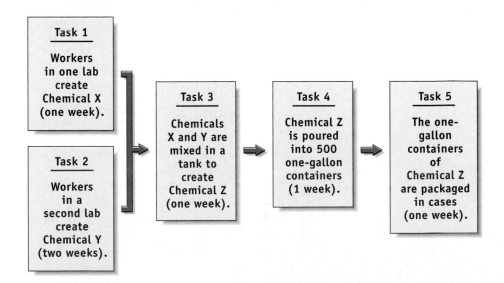

Agile Manufacturing

Many experts believe we are about to enter a new era in manufacturing: the era of mass customization. What distinguishes mass customization from today's mass production is that factory products will no longer consist of multiple copies of the same item. Instead, product specifications will be fed through information pipelines, and factory equipment will reconfigure itself to produce the exact product desired. Further, experts predict that these customized products will cost about the same as today's mass-produced equivalent.

The techniques needed to create such factories of the future are collectively grouped under the heading of agile manufacturing and will depend heavily on information technology. Optical scanning systems combined with telecommunications will be used to get product specifications into the plant. Computer-aided design and computer-aided manufacturing (CAD/CAM) represent the next step. Product specifications, scanned in or drawn by operators, will be translated into instructions for industrial robots and computer-controlled machinery. These pieces of equipment have great flexibility. Rather than accommodating only a single set of repetitive motions, suitable only for doing the same task over and over again, the equipment will be able to do many different activities. This variety of activities will allow a variety of products to be produced.

The U.S. economy is already experiencing some of the benefits of agile manufacturing. A valve maker in Georgia uses CAD/CAM technology to produce customized valves for customers in under three days. In the textile business, agile factories in the United States are able to quickly produce small lots of specialized fabrics to order.

In the near future, agile factories may be the norm in U.S. manufacturing. Experts warn, however, that the appearance of such factories will not necessarily translate into new manufacturing jobs. The key to achieving agility is automation, so the labor required to run such plants will be limited. Substantial growth however, is expected in the high-tech jobs associated with designing, building, and maintaining the equipment used in these factories.

---

critical path the path that takes the longest time to complete

be conducted simultaneously. The mixing of chemicals X and Y (Task 3) cannot begin until Tasks 1 and 2 are completed.

Each sequence of tasks is referred to as a path. For example, the sequence of Tasks 1, 3, 4, and 5 represents one path. A second path is the sequence of Tasks 2, 3, 4, and 5. The accumulated time for this path is four weeks. The **critical path** is the path that takes the longest time to complete. In our example, the critical path is the sequence of Tasks 2, 3, 4, and 5; that path takes five weeks. It is important to determine the time necessary to complete the steps within the critical path, since the production process will take that long.

The five-week period has no slack time (extra time) for the workers involved in the critical path. Once the critical path is determined, the slack time on any other paths can be estimated. Since the other path in Exhibit 9.9 has a completion time of four weeks, it has slack time of one week over a five-week period. Knowing the time involved in the critical path allows one to reduce inefficiencies that can be caused by slack time on other paths. Some of the workers assigned to Task 1 may be assigned to help with the second task of the critical path sequence. This may reduce the time necessary to complete the critical path.

Reviewing the tasks that are part of the critical path can be used to avoid delays or increase production speed. Tasks estimated to take a long time are closely monitored, since any delays in these tasks are more likely to cause a severe delay in the entire production process. Furthermore, firms attempt to determine whether these tasks can be performed more quickly so that the critical path is completed in less time.

Managers who oversee special projects recognize that the time necessary for each task may be uncertain. For this reason, they may create an alternative "worst-case" estimate of the time period for each task to be completed. The accumulation of worst-case times of all tasks along the critical path creates a worst-case time for the project to be completed. In our previous example, the expected time of the project

Quality control is a critical element when manufacturing any product. Here IBM technicians are putting new laptop computers through a variety of tests before shipping the finished product to consumers.

was five weeks, but the worst-case time may be seven weeks. That is, the project should be completed in five weeks, but it could take as long as seven weeks if some unfavorable conditions occur (employees call in sick, equipment breaks, and so on). Managers who oversee such a project may guarantee to the customer that the product will be ready within seven weeks. They may be less willing to guarantee five weeks because of conditions that could delay the production schedule.

Possible problems such as a shortage of materials, the absence of a worker, or a machine breakdown could disrupt the production schedule. Proper planning can limit the adverse effects of such disruptions or even reduce the likelihood of the disruptions. For example, an excess of materials could be maintained to avoid shortages. Alternative job assignments could be developed in case a worker is absent. Preventive maintenance of the machinery could prevent a possible breakdown.

Quality Control

quality control a process of determining whether the quality of a product meets the desired quality level

Quality control is a process of determining whether the quality of a product meets the desired quality level, and identifying improvements (if any) that need to be made in the production process. Quality can be measured by assessing the various characteristics (such as how long the product lasts) that enhance customer satisfaction. The actual quality of a product can be compared with the desired quality level to determine whether the quality needs to be improved. Given the importance of quality, the following chapter is devoted to this topic.

BUSINESS DILEMMA

Production At College Health Club

Sue Kramer, president of College Health Club (CHC), is reviewing the production of CHC's health club services.

SITE   The health club was established at a site next to the college campus where it attracts most of its customers. Thus, its site was established near its source of demand, since most of the demand comes from the college campus.

DESIGN AND LAYOUT   The design of the health club allows for some expansion so that it could attract more members without being overcrowded. The layout of the club is intended to separate members who use the exercise equipment from those taking aerobics classes.

PRODUCTION EFFICIENCY   Most of the expenses at CHC (such as rent) are fixed. Therefore, the average cost of serving each customer would decline substantially if CHC could increase its memberships.

Business Dilemma

Sue Kramer begins to consider whether to relocate the site of her health club. She wants to determine whether a site closer to the business district of the city would be more appropriate than next to a college campus outside the city. Using the typical factors that can affect a site decision (which were identified in this chapter), determine which factors favor a site closer to the business district and which factors favor the present site. Should Sue relocate CHC near the business district or leave CHC near the college campus?

Solution

Factors such as cost of human resources and supply of labor are not relevant in this case because Sue's club does not rely on many employees. If Sue moves the site closer to the business district, the club will attract more customers from that area. One advantage of locating near the business district is that professionals can pay higher membership fees. However, Sue's main decision to establish the club next to the college campus was because its source of demand was the students. If she moves the site away from the college, she will lose many of the customers who are students at the college.

Recall that Sue's initial plan was to focus on the college students, because she thought no other club was focusing on that target market. Since the source of demand was the key factor involved in the site decision, and the students at the college represent the target market, Sue decides to keep the site next to the college campus.

Additional Issues for Discussion

1 The cost of land is much higher near the middle of the city than it is outside the city, where CHC is located. How does this affect CHC's expenses?

2 The design of the health club allows for some expansion. What is a disadvantage of having extra room to allow for expansion?

3 CHC has been open for about six months. How might Sue Kramer forecast membership (demand) over the next six months?

1 The key resources used for production are human resources, materials, and other resources (such as the plant, machinery, and equipment).

2 The plant site decision is influenced by:

➤ cost of workplace space,
➤ cost of labor,
➤ tax incentives,
➤ source of demand for the product produced,
➤ access to transportation, and
➤ supply of labor.

A site evaluation matrix can be used to assign a rating to each relevant factor and derive a total rating for each possible site.

3 The design and layout of a plant are influenced by the:

➤ site characteristics,
➤ production process,
➤ product line, and
➤ desired production capacity.

4 Production control involves:

➤ purchasing materials, which requires selecting a supplier, negotiating volume discounts, and possibly delegating production to suppliers;
➤ inventory control, which involves managing various inventories at levels that minimize costs;
➤ routing, which determines the sequence of tasks necessary to complete production;
➤ scheduling, which sets time periods for the tasks required within the production process; and
➤ quality control, which can be used to identify improvements (if any) that need to be made in the production process.

assembly line
carrying costs
conversion process
critical path
deintegration
design
fixed-position layout
flexible manufacturing
Gantt chart
hotelling
inventory control

just-in-time (JIT)
just-in-time office
layout
materials requirements
    planning (MRP)
operations management
order costs
outsourcing
product layout
production control
production management

production process
production schedule
program evaluation and review
    technique (PERT)
quality control
routing
scheduling
work station
work-in-process inventories

1 In managing a plant, production control is extremely important. Name the five tasks involved.

2 If you were a plant manager, what primary resources would you use for production?

3 You are moving your plant from the West Coast to the East Coast. What key location decisions should be considered?

4 Compare just-in-time (JIT) inventory with materials requirements planning (MRP).

5 Define PERT. Explain what steps are involved with PERT. Why is it necessary to identify the critical path when working on a project?

6 What characteristics influence design and layout decisions?

7 Define and explain quality control.

8 Why is a production schedule so important for a manager?

9 Explain the use of work stations and assembly lines.

10 Define deintegration. How would the use of this method of delegating be beneficial to a manufacturer?

DISCUSSION QUESTIONS

1 How would production management apply to the Chicago Bulls basketball team?

2 Assume you are a project manager for a large construction company. You have been given an assignment to develop a schedule for the construction of a skyscraper. Discuss how you would implement a schedule.

3 Assume you are a production manager for an automotive plant. What resources would you consider using to make it an efficient plant? Discuss.

4 Assume your company has given you an assignment to relocate the plant to a new region. What factors would you consider in making the decision?

5 What type of layout is appropriate for the following: (a) aircraft manufacturer, such as Boeing, (b) automotive plant, such as General Motors, (c) new housing construction?

RUNNING YOUR OWN BUSINESS

1 Describe the production process of your business. That is, describe the tasks that are required to produce your product or service. Describe the number of employees and other resources (such as machinery) that are needed for production.

2 Describe the facilities needed for production. Would it require that you rent space in a shopping mall? Describe in general terms the design and layout of the facilities.

3 Estimate the rent expense during the first year for the facilities needed to run your business. Also estimate (if possible) the annual utility expense (such as electricity) for your business facilities.

INVESTING IN THE STOCK OF A BUSINESS

Using the annual report of the firm in which you would like to invest, complete the following:

1 Describe (in general terms) the firm's production process. What products are produced? Where are the production facilities located? Are the facilities concentrated in one location or scattered?

2 Have the firm's operations been restructured in recent years to improve efficiency? If so, how?

3 Does your firm need to consider labor supply issues when selecting a site?

CASE 1 Selecting the Best Plant Site

Richard Capozzi, an entrepreneur in the high-fashion Italian shoes industry, is planning to relocate his manufacturing operation to the western part of the United States. He is presently considering two different locations. One possible location is outside Los Angeles, and the other is in Oklahoma City.

In analyzing the plant site decision, he is considering several factors. In Los Angeles the cost of land is high. However, local government officials are willing to make tax concessions. This plant location is accessible to transportation; a railroad is adjacent to the plant and an eight-way interstate is in close proximity. Capozzi has identified the West Coast region as his target market for this type of shoe. An artist by trade, he has developed a unique design that should create mass-market appeal in this geographic area.

The Oklahoma City location has several advantages. Land cost is lower than in Los Angeles. Also, a large sup-

ply of trained labor is available in this region.

Another key consideration Capozzi must deal with is raw material availability. The raw material is imported from Italy and is received at the port of entry in Los Angeles. Transportation costs would be lower for the Los Angeles plant, a fact which weighs heavily in Mr. Capozzi's decision.

Questions

1 What will influence the plant site decision for Mr. Capozzi, and which alternative appears to be optimal?

2 How can each relative factor be rated or evaluated to determine the optimal plant location?

3 How should the decision regarding plant layout and design be determined?

4 What resources will Mr. Capozzi need to implement the production plan?

CASE 2 Improving the Production Process

Wabash National, a manufacturer of truck trailers (located in Lafayette, Indiana), has demonstrated that it is possible to build a globally competitive company from scratch in a stodgy industry. Wabash gained its edge by making customized trailers and innovative products for fast-growing companies such as Federal Express. It retains its edge by pushing employees to work hard and by coming up with new ways to raise productivity.

Wabash continually attempts to build employee commitment. Since it is a nonunion plant, it implements a team approach as its management style. Employee participation programs are designed to identify problems and resolve them through empowerment. A commitment to quality is generated by communicating with employees through a successful orientation and training program. Management acts and sleeps the Wabash way: Communicate with employees, but don't steal much time from production. This is achieved through a production control program.

An effective inventory control system at Wabash was achieved through a team effort to resolve an excess inventory of axles. Hundreds of axles were piled up outside the plant, making retrieval difficult and increasing carrying costs. The team devised a way to flag order changes early so that the purchasing department could alert vendors to alter deliveries.

By implementing such production control programs, Wabash increased its productivity, as measured by sales per employee, by 18 percent. This success is expected to continue because of the close working relationship that management has developed with employees.

Questions

1 What is production control?

2 What are the elements present within the production control system at Wabash?

3 How did Wabash deal with its excessive inventory problem?

4 What is the most valued resource at Wabash?

VIDEO CASE How Production Can Be a Key to Success

In buying the ninety-year-old Burt Company of Portland, Maine, in 1985, John Kendall knew he was taking a big gamble.

The manufacturing business, owned for three generations by a family named Burt, had only one product, a poker chip. Hand-built of compression-molded clay, the chip was a Burt invention, and the company had enjoyed a worldwide monopoly.

Now an identical chip was being made in low-wage Mexico and sold to casinos by a full-service supplier of gaming accessories (tables, dice, and so on). The Burt Company, which couldn't compete on price, was losing $30,000 a month. Unless Kendall could turn the firm (which he renamed CHIPCO) around, the odds favored its demise.

Kendall went to Las Vegas, Atlantic City, and Europe to see the company's distributors and casino executives. If they could have everything they wanted in a new chip, what would that be?

From what he learned, he listed requirements, including: prices no higher than existing chip prices; clay or ceramic material, not slippery like plastic; ten-gram weight; washable; unbreakable; customized designs; prompt deliveries; suitable for automated handling; and security against counterfeiting.

Ceramic chip blanks were injection-molded in large quantities, keeping cost low and production capacity high. An injection-moldable resin kept chip weight at ten grams. A new decoration-coloration process permitted customization of chips without retooling expense or long delivery delays. A system was developed to implant invisible bar codes on chips, making them counterfeit-proof and permitting automated handling.

CHIPCO's first delivery of its Pro-Tech™ chips was to a casino in Puerto Rico in November, 1988. Deliveries of the old chips had been good for years; after all, the chips were virtually indestructible. These were, too, but decorations made them "designer" chips, and many a patron took one home as a souvenir. The casino reordered in a month and again six months later.

A new casino profit center had been born. If a casino ordered "designer" chips instead of plain, at 65 cents a pop, and the customer bought chips for $1 or $5, everytime a customer took a chip as a souvenir, the difference went to the casino's bottom line.

Kendall's sales rose, and his bottom line improved, too, but his first profitable year didn't come until 1991, after six years of losses. Sales then were $1.2 million; last year they were $2.8 million.

Questions

1 Explain how John Kendall (owner of CHIPCO) established the requirements for the casino chip that he wanted to produce. One of John Kendall's production requirements was that the price of the chips produced should be no higher than the price charged for existing chips. Why is this considered a production requirement when it focuses on the price charged for the chips?

2 The new production process of the casino chips included a new coloration process (of coloring the chip) that allowed chips to be customized without lengthy production (retooling) delays. Explain why this process may be more efficient than a process that customizes casino chips by the weight or shape of the chip.

3 John Kendall presently focuses much of his business in Atlantic City, Las Vegas, Puerto Rico, and Europe. Do you think he could reduce his production cost over the next several years by moving his production site from Portland, Maine, to a production site in either Atlantic City or Las Vegas? Given the trend in the casino industry, why might his business be spread beyond the locations just mentioned?

THE *Coca-Cola* COMPANY ANNUAL REPORT PROJECT

The following questions apply concepts learned in this chapter to The Coca-Cola Company. Read the section "Bottling Partners" on page 40 in The Coca-Cola Company annual report before answering these questions.

1 What major production task has The Coca-Cola Company delegated to other organizations?

2 Why do you think The Coca-Cola Company might choose to produce its concentrates and syrups in foreign countries when possible?

3 How might a trucking strike in a particular geographic area affect The Coca-Cola Company's production?

IN-TEXT STUDY GUIDE

Answers are in an appendix at the back of the book.

True or False

1 Downsizing created the need to reduce work space at many firms.

2 The critical path is the path that takes the shortest time to complete on a PERT diagram.

3 Hotelling represents the sequence of tasks necessary to complete the production of a product.

4 A work station represents an area in which one or more employees are assigned a specific task.

5 Inventories of partially completed products are called work-in-process.

6 Most firms delegate all of the production tasks to suppliers.

7 Design and layout decisions do not affect operating expenses.

8 General Motors, Chrysler, and United Parcel Service have recently streamlined their routing process to improve production efficiency.

9 A fixed-position layout is commonly used for assembly-line production.

10 Quality control can be measured by assessing the various characteristics that enhance customer satisfaction.

Multiple Choice

11 A firm can limit the adverse effects of disruptions in the production schedule with proper:
a) accounting methods.
b) quality control.
c) financing.
d) competition.
e) planning.

12 Firms are forced to search for new sites once demand for their product exceeds their:
a) quality control.
b) production capacity.
c) inspection requirements.
d) routing schedules.
e) purchase plans.

13 A critical decision in production management is the selection of a:
a) contingency plan.
b) competitor.

c) customer mix.

d) consultant.

e) site.

14 Production management influences each firm's:

a) industry demand.

b) competition.

c) profits and values.

d) union.

e) benefits policy.

15 A system that attempts to reduce material inventories to a bare minimum by frequently ordering small amounts of materials from suppliers is called:

a) routing.

b) just-in-time.

c) scheduling.

d) quality control.

e) deintegration.

16 The process by which a firm's products (or services) are produced can affect the firm's:

a) value.

b) competition.

c) hotelling.

d) tax incentives.

e) materials.

17 Design and layout decisions are influenced by the following characteristics except for:

a) production process.

b) desired production capacity.

c) product line.

d) purchasing applications.

e) site.

18 The act of setting time periods for each task in the production process is called:

a) routing.

b) scheduling.

c) inventory control.

d) dispatching.

e) quality control.

19 To avoid delays or increase production speed, the tasks that are part of the _____ are reviewed.

a) purchasing applications

b) Gantt path

c) critical path

d) raw material inventory

e) hotelling.

20 A production process that can be easily adjusted to accommodate a revision in the production process is:

a) work-in-process.

b) flexible manufacturing.

c) routing.

d) scheduling.

e) quality control.

21 The process of managing raw materials at a level that minimizes costs is called:

a) scheduling.

b) routing.

c) dispatching.

d) production planning.

e) inventory control.

22 A sequence of work stations in which each work station is designed to cover specific phases of the production process is called a/an:

a) assembly line.

b) hotelling.

c) deintegration.

d) product location.

e) Gantt chart.

23 A process that ensures that the materials are available when needed is called:

a) deintegration.

b) work-in-process.

c) raw materials.

d) materials requirements planning.

e) quality control.

24 A strategy of delegating some production tasks to suppliers is referred to as:

a) routing.

b) dispatching.

c) deintegration.

d) quality assurance.

e) hotelling.

25 The management of a process in which resources (such as employees and machinery) are used to produce products and services is called:

a) production management.

b) office management.

c) quality control.

d) deintegration.

e) employee turnover.

26 A process of determining whether the quality of a product meets the desired quality level, and identifying improvements (if any) that need to be made in the production process is called:

a) materials requirements planning.

b) deintegration.

c) hotelling.

d) work-in-process.

e) quality control.

27 A concept adopted by a firm that creates an office available with a desk, a computer, and a telephone for any employee who normally works at home but needs to use work space at the firm is referred to as:
a) flexible manufacturing.
b) deintegration.
c) production control.
d) hotelling.
e) quality control.

28 A method of scheduling tasks which illustrates the expected timing for each task within the production process is a:
a) Venn diagram.
b) Gantt chart.
c) MRP system.
d) just-in-time system.
e) production plan.

29 A production process where employees go to the position of the product, rather than waiting for the product to come to them is a(n):
a) assembly line.
b) batch process.
c) fixed-position layout.
d) unit production process.
e) mass production process.

30 The elements of a production control system include the following except for:
a) layout and design.
b) inventory control.
c) routing.
d) scheduling.
e) quality control.

31 A _____ represents a series of tasks in which resources are used to produce a product or service.
a) layout chart.
b) Venn diagram.
c) organization chart.
d) production process.
e) chain of command.

32 When firms store excessive inventories of materials, this increases their cost of operation in the form of:
a) purchasing costs.
b) production costs.
c) carrying costs.
d) quality control.
e) human resources.

33 The factors that affect a site decision include the following except for:
a) cost of workplace space.
b) tax incentives.
c) source of demand.
d) access to transportation.
e) quality assurance.

34 Once a site for the manufacturing plant is chosen, the next step to be determined is:
a) design and layout.
b) production control.
c) hotelling.
d) deintegration.
e) inventory control.

35 The sequence of tasks necessary to complete the production of a product is:
a) dispatching.
b) quality control.
c) purchasing.
d) routing.
e) deintegration.

Surfing the Net

Exhibit 9.10
Manufacturers Information Net
Home Page

http://www.mfginfo.com/

Manufacturing Information on the World Wide Web

One of the by-products of the information age is that production has become less labor intensive and more technology intensive. As a result, manufacturers are increasingly well represented on the WWW. A good place to start looking for information on manufacturing is the Manufacturers Information Net home page (Exhibit 9.10).

mfginfo

- Software
- Computers
- Manufacturers
- Job Shops
- Suppliers
- Services

- Machine Tools
- Cutting Tools
- Hydraulic Products
- CAM
- CAD
- DNC
- Used Machinery
- Machinery Builders
- New Machinery Dealers

- ON LINE MANUFACTURING DISCUSSION GROUPS

Best Viewed With Netscape 1.2

CHAPTER 10

Improving Production Quality and Efficiency

In recent years, firms have given more attention to the quality of the products or services they produce. The act of monitoring and improving the quality of products and services produced is commonly referred to as total quality management (TQM). Firms have also given more attention to production efficiency, which refers to the ability to produce products at a low cost. A firm's earnings and therefore its value can be influenced by TQM and production efficiency.

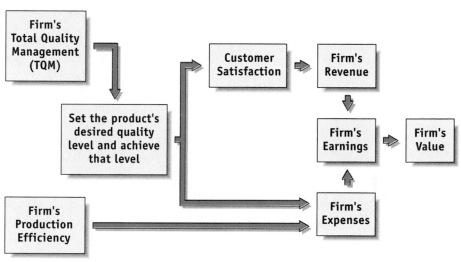

Consider the case of Motorola, which produces cellular telephones, two-way radios, and various other electronic devices. The superior quality of its products made Motorola the winner of the first Malcolm Baldrige National Quality Award. How can Motorola measure the quality of its products? How can it ensure that its production process achieves specific quality standards? How can it improve its production efficiency? This chapter provides a background on TQM and production efficiency, which can be used to address these questions.

The Learning Goals of this chapter are to:

1. Show how total quality management (TQM) can be applied to monitor and enhance the quality of the products and services produced.

2. Identify the key methods used to improve production efficiency.

IMPROVING PRODUCTION QUALITY WITH TQM

Show how total quality management (TQM) can be applied to monitor and enhance the quality of the products and services produced.

1

total quality management (TQM)
the act of monitoring and improving the quality of products and services produced

The **total quality management (TQM)** concept was developed by W. Edwards Deming and was used extensively by some Japanese firms before being used in the United States. According to W. Edwards Deming, some of the key guidelines for improving quality are (1) provide managers and other employees with the education and training for them to excel in their jobs, (2) encourage employees to take responsibility and to provide leadership, and (3) encourage all employees to search for ways to improve the production process. These guidelines are consistent with giving employees the skills and the freedom to be creative, rather than to impose more restrictions that force employees to focus only on producing a large number of units just to meet some production quota. Deming discouraged the focus on production quotas, so that employees could allocate more of their time toward leadership and the improvement of the production process.

During the 1980s and 1990s, TQM was used to some degree by most U.S. firms. It typically uses teams of employees to assess quality and offer suggestions for improvement.

TQM also stresses the need for firms to measure quality from the customer's perspective. In the past, firms assessed quality solely from their own perspective. For instance, a high-technology computer may satisfy a firm, but it will only satisfy a customer if it is easy to use. Firms are now more aware that their assessment of quality must focus on customer opinions rather than their own. Firms are now paying more attention to quality because it can determine whether customers will purchase the product again. Customers are more likely to purchase the product again from the same producer if they are satisfied with the quality, whether the product is a car, a pair of shoes, or a cordless phone.

W. Edwards Deming developed the TQM concept. When U.S. firms didn't listen, Deming took his efforts to Japan. Deming is seen as a hero of the Japanese industrial resurgence.

The chip clean room at Motorola. These Motorola employees are working in a clean room. One speck of dust or dirt can destroy both the product and the equipment in this room. Motorola knows that workers need extensive training to be effective in this environment.

Firms now realize that it is easier to retain existing customers than it is to attract new customers who are unfamiliar with their products or services. Historically, firms that focused on quality and customer satisfaction had an advantage over their competitors. Today, most firms recognize the importance of customer satisfaction. Yet, some firms are much better at ensuring customer satisfaction than others.

While firms can improve their quality in numerous ways, consider the efforts of Corning Telecommunications Products, which won the Malcolm Baldrige National Quality Award in 1995. First, it developed a technologically advanced product (fiber that transmits phone calls). Second, Corning's purchases of supplies focused less on price and more on quality characteristics (such as durability). The quality of its products are partially dependent on the quality of its supplies. Third, it substantially reduced the number of customer complaints about its products in recent years. Fourth, it created an interactive computer system so that employees can monitor customer feedback. This helped employees realize what customers liked or disliked about Corning's products and servicing.

Other firms such as Motorola and Saturn, which are noted for their focus on TQM, use their own strategies for improving quality. While the strategies vary among firms, they all tend to focus on a goal of increasing customer satisfaction. Consider these quotes from recent annual reports:

❚❚ *We instituted Amoco Progress to unite the best practices of quality management throughout the corporation.* ❚❚

—Amoco

❚❚ *The Commitment to Excellence philosophy is Anheuser-Busch's effort to incorporate the key total quality management principles of customer satisfaction, employee involvement, and continuous process improvement into its culture.* ❚❚

—Anheuser-Busch

❚❚ McDonnell Douglas is working toward one overriding objective in commercial aircraft: to become the low-cost producer of the highest quality aircraft available to airlines. ❚❚

—McDonnell Douglas

❚❚ It's impossible to separate performance for our shareholders from performance for our customers. Our commitment encompasses both. We are committed to rewarding shareholders with above-average returns while constantly exceeding the expectations of our customers. ❚❚

—Westinghouse

The use of total quality management normally involves the following functions:

➤ Specify the desired quality level.
➤ Achieve the desired quality level.
➤ Control the quality level.

Specify the Desired Quality Level

The quality of a product or service typically measures the likelihood that it will perform properly over its expected life. The quality of a computer may be defined by how well it works and how long it lasts. It may also be measured by how easy it is to use. Alternatively, it may be defined by the degree of repairs necessary: the more repairs, the lower the quality. Quality may also be defined by how quickly the manufacturer repaired a computer that experienced problems. Each of the characteristics just described can affect customer satisfaction, and therefore should be considered as indicators of quality.

Firms must decide on the amount of resources they will use to enhance a product's quality. At one extreme, they can set a high quality level, which will result in high expenses and a high price. At the other extreme, they can set a low quality level to maintain low expenses, and charge a lower price. A low quality level does not mean that the product was produced incorrectly. It normally means that the production process was simplified to reduce expenses, so that the firm can charge a low price. Low-quality products are appealing to customers who can only afford to pay low prices and who are unwilling to pay higher prices for high-quality products.

When firms set the quality level, they assess the demand for products within different market segments (such as a high-quality segment and a low-quality segment). They also assess the quality levels of products produced by competitors. They attempt to set the quality and price of their products at levels that will satisfy some segment of the market. The Chevrolet Cavalier fits customers who focus more on price and less on quality, while the Cadillac fits customers who focus more on quality.

When setting quality, the focus should be on quality characteristics that customers desire. For example, consider an economy car that could be improved by installing a larger (faster) engine or a higher-quality interior. Assume, however, that a customer survey determines that these improvements would not substantially increase customer satisfaction. Instead, customers are most concerned with possible production defects. In this case, the car manufacturer may decide to focus on ensuring proper production (so that there are fewer defects) rather than upgrading specific parts of the car. With this approach, the firm's desired quality level is focused on increasing customer satisfaction.

Given that the future demand by customers for the firm's product may be influenced by the level of customer satisfaction, the firm sets a desired quality level that may result in a higher future demand for its product. Conversely, if the firm had set quality goals that were not relevant to customers, its efforts might not have had any favorable effect on future demand.

Achieve the Desired Quality Level

Once the desired quality level is set, employees involved in any stage of the production process can offer suggestions on how the product or service should be produced to achieve that quality level. Employee teams can be organized to provide their suggestions. Having people from different parts of the production process on the same team may enable any potential conflict across the production process to be detected. Higher-quality products will normally require higher-quality materials or more hours of labor to produce the final product. The production process that is developed will specify the types of materials needed to achieve the desired quality level, and the amount of time taken by human resources on each part of the process.

Training may be necessary to achieve the level of quality that the firm desires. Motorola now spends heavily on training and development to maintain quality control. In 1995, it experienced only 30 defects per 1 million components produced. This compares favorably with the 7,000 defects per 1 million components that Motorola experienced eight years earlier.

Control the Quality Level

Quality control is used to determine the production process to ensure that it meets specified quality standards. Once the desired quality level has been defined, firms can assess whether that quality level was achieved. To ensure that the quality is maintained, firms conduct a periodic valuation of the characteristics used to measure product quality. Recently, Microsoft detected some defects in its computer software, General Motors detected defects in fuel tanks of specific types of cars, and Philip Morris detected defects in some of its cigarettes. By detecting defects, these firms were able to correct the production process and maintain customer satisfaction.

Boeing (manufacturer of aircraft) incurred expenses of more than $1 billion in 1993 for implementing a system to remove production defects and raise its quality level. However, Boeing's production process was improved substantially as a result of its ability to identify defects. By 1995, its defects declined by about 40 percent. If firms properly resolve deficiencies detected by quality control, they may be able to increase revenue and cover the expenses associated with quality control.

CONTROL BY COMPUTERS   Quality control may be conducted by computers. The firm's computers may monitor each component of a product produced to determine whether specifications are satisfied. Computer-controlled machinery has electronic sensors that can screen out defective parts. Firms such as Eastman Kodak use computers and software to enhance quality control.

CONTROL BY EMPLOYEES   Employees are also used to assess quality. One person may be assigned to assess components at each stage of the assembly line. Alternatively, a team of employees may be responsible for assessing the quality of products at different stages of the production process. Many firms use a **quality control circle,** which is a group of employees who assess the quality of a product and offer sugges-

quality control circle a group of employees who assess the quality of a product and offer suggestions for improvement

Laser beams are used to align wheels at Ford's Kentucky truck plant. This use of technology improves the speed and accuracy of the production process.

tions for improvement. Quality control circles usually allow for more interaction among workers and managers, and provide workers with a sense of responsibility. Most automobile manufacturers (including Chrysler and Ford) and computer manufacturers (including IBM) have successfully used quality control circles.

Specific employees of Saturn Corporation (a subsidiary of General Motors) conduct a weekly review of their production process. They search for defects and quickly communicate this information to the employees who are involved with that part of the production process.

sampling some of the products produced are randomly selected and tested to determine whether they satisfy the quality standards

CONTROL BY SAMPLING   Only by testing each unit produced for any possible flaw could quality control ensure that all products satisfied the desired quality level. This is virtually impossible. Firms tend to assess quality control by **sampling,** in which some of the products produced are randomly selected and tested to determine whether they satisfy the quality standards. Firms may check one unit per one hundred units produced and concentrate specifically on possible flaws that have been detected in previous checks.

CONTROL BY MONITORING COMPLAINTS   Quality should be assessed not only when the product is produced but also after the product is sold. Some products may not show quality deficiencies until after customers use them. One method of assessing the quality of products that have been sold is to monitor the proportion of products returned, or to monitor customer complaints. In 1995, Continental Airlines doubled its customer complaint staff so that it could more quickly identify and

---

SELF-SCORING EXERCISE

Are You Highly Satisfied As a Customer?

Think of an organization or business with whom you have frequent contact and inter-action. How satisfied are you with the products or services provided to you by this organization or business? Would the organization or business be competitive in the Customer Satisfaction category for a Malcolm Baldrige National Quality Award?

Complete the following eight questions to rate the quality of the organization's or business's customer satisfaction. Use a scale of 1 (definitely not), 2 (probably not), 3 (unsure), 4 (probably yes), and 5 (definitely yes).

____ 1. Do you believe the organization knows what you expect as a customer?

____ 2. Has the organization improved the quality of its customer relationships over a period of time?

____ 3. Do you receive the same standard of service from different people in this organization?

____ 4. Do you believe that each and every employee is committed to serving your needs and satisfying you as a customer?

____ 5. Whenever you have had even the smallest complaint about the organization, has that complaint been resolved satisfactorily?

____ 6. Have you ever completed any sort of customer satisfaction survey, card, or feedback form for the organization?

____ 7. Have you heard that people were more satisfied with the organization's prod-ucts and services in the past than today?

____ 8. Compared with similar organizations, do you consider this organization to be superior in serving customers?

____ Total points

Scoring

35–40: This organization provides world-class customer service and deserves quality recognition in this area.

28–34: This organization provides high-quality service to its customers.

20–27: This organization is mediocre in its service to customers.

8–19: This organization needs to improve its service to customers.

---

resolve quality deficiencies. However, this method does not necessarily indicate the degree of customer satisfaction. It detects only those situations in which customers were extremely dissatisfied.

AT&T has a Consumer Communications Services unit that attempts to ensure customer satisfaction. Chrysler has recently attempted to obtain more feedback from its dealers on customer complaints about its production.

CONTROL BY SURVEYS   More customer feedback can be obtained by conducting surveys. Firms can allow customers to offer opinions on product quality control by sending them a survey months after the sale. For example, Toys Я Us and Saturn survey their customers to determine the level of customer satisfaction. The survey can also ask for feedback on the quality of specific parts or functions of the product.

CORRECTING DEFICIENCIES   The quality control process not only detects quality deficiencies but also is used to correct them. If quality is deficient, it is likely caused by one of the following factors. First, the materials provided by suppliers could be inadequate. Second, the quality of work by employees could be inadequate. Third, the machinery and equipment used to produce a product could be malfunctioning.

If the cause of the quality deficiency is materials, the firm either may require the existing supplier to improve the quality or may obtain materials from a different supplier in the future. If the cause is the work of employees, the firm may need to retrain or reprimand those employees. If the cause of quality deficiency is the machinery, the firm may need to use replacements or make repairs.

When a firm detects production deficiencies, it not only must correct the production process but also may need to correct customer complaints. If the deficiencies were not detected before the product was sold, customers may experience problems with the products. The firm should attempt to respond quickly to customers who purchased the products or services with such quality deficiencies. In this way, it can reduce customer dissatisfaction. For example, when Chevy recently recalled its S-10 pickup trucks to fix a gas pipe, it contacted most of the customers by phone and offered them loaners until the trucks were fixed.

Total quality management is commonly used to correct a firm's perceived deficiencies and therefore improve customer satisfaction. Consider the case of Fairview-AFX, a developer of training facilities, which attempted to assess its customer service record in the early 1990s. Fairview's salespeople called their biggest customers to obtain feedback on their service. About 75 percent of the customers were not satisfied with Fairview's service because of delays in completing work. Recognizing that it might lose much business to competitors, Fairview established a Customer Care program, which obligated employees to complete their work on schedule. Second, it began to contact customers after performing work to ensure that the work was done properly. Third, it set up a communications system between its offices in different cities to monitor inventory so that it could properly estimate delivery times. This resulted in fewer delays in the work it performed and helped to accelerate the production process. Consequently, Fairview was able to substantially improve customer satisfaction.

Global Quality Standards

Firms that conduct international business may attempt to satisfy a set of global quality standards. These standards have been established by the International Standards Organization (ISO) which has representatives from numerous countries. Firms are not required to meet these standards. However, by voluntarily meeting these standards, they can become certified, which may boost their credibility when selling products to foreign customers. The process of being certified commonly costs at least $20,000 and takes at least one year. The standards focus on the design, manufacturing process, installation, and service of a product. Independent auditors review the firm's operations and decide whether to certify the firm. Foreign customers may be more comfortable if the firm has met the international standards. A publication called *ISO 9000* specifies the standards for production quality.

Recently, another set of standards have been established (called *ISO 14000)* for environmental effects of the production process. Some firms are concerned about qualifying for the quality standards because they may have to disclose confidential information about their production process that could possibly be leaked to competitors.

Firms may also have to meet other standards to sell their products in specific foreign countries. For example, the Japanese government assesses any products that are sold in Japan to ensure that they are safe. Japan's safety standards have discouraged firms based in the United States and other countries from attempting to sell

This Coca-Cola Company plant in the Philippines was one of the first to earn ISO 9000 certification.

products in Japan. The standards established by Japan may serve as a barrier that protects local firms in Japan from foreign competitors.

In addition to meeting standards on global quality, firms must adapt their products to satisfy unique characteristics of countries. U.S. firms that produce automobiles for the United Kingdom must place the steering wheel on the right side. U.S. firms that produce tires to be sold in less-developed countries may use more rubber to withstand rougher road surfaces.

METHODS TO IMPROVE PRODUCTION EFFICIENCY

2 | **Identify the key methods used to improve production efficiency.**

production efficiency the ability to produce products at a low cost

Firms strive to increase their **production efficiency,** which reflects a lower cost for a given amount of output and a given level of quality. Managers continually search for ways to manage human and other resources in a manner that improves production efficiency. Some firms are motivated to reduce their expenses because they are losing market share to their competitors or because their earnings are inadequate. If such a trend continues, these firms will not survive. Even firms that have recently performed well must recognize the need to continually improve, since other competitors may become more efficient.

When Louis Gerstner became chief executive officer of IBM in 1993, he set a goal that IBM's management use resources efficiently when producing computers and related products. IBM's restructuring led to an increase in production efficiency, which had several favorable effects. First, the reduction in expenses allowed IBM to lower its prices and therefore become more competitive. Sales of IBM computers increased as demand for its product increased in response to lower prices. IBM's profits increased as a result of its higher sales and more efficient production process (lower operating expenses). Finally, IBM's stock price increased as a result of its higher profits. IBM's stock doubled by 1995. The key to IBM's improvement was more efficient management of its production process.

benchmarking a method of evaluating performance by comparison to some specified (benchmark) level, typically a level achieved by another company

Many firms that set production efficiency goals use **benchmarking,** which is a method of evaluating performance by comparison to some specified (benchmark)

level. For example, a firm may set a goal of producing baseball caps at a cost of $3 per cap, which is the average cost incurred by the most successful producer of baseball caps.

The top managers of some firms set production efficiency targets (or goals) that cannot be achieved under the present conditions. These targets are referred to as **stretch targets** because they are stretched beyond the ordinary. Stretch targets may be established in response to a decline in the firm's market share or performance. For example, 3M Company created a stretch target that 30 percent of its sales be derived from sales of products it created in the last four years. This target was intended to encourage more development of new products so that 3M did not rely on its innovations from several years ago. Boeing also created stretch targets to improve upon its relatively slow process for producing airplanes. It set stretch targets on its time schedule for producing various pieces of the airplane. It also set stretch targets to substantially lower its production expenses so that it could lower its prices. If expenses could be reduced substantially, Boeing could reduce prices and therefore convince airlines to purchase new airplanes rather than repair old ones.

Firms can improve production efficiency through the following methods:

➤ Technology
➤ Economies of scale
➤ Restructuring

Each of these methods is discussed in turn.

Technology

Firms may improve their production efficiency with new technology. New machinery conducts tasks more quickly because of increased technology. Computer systems used by numerous manufacturing firms have improved as a result of technology, and have increased the speed at which various tasks can be completed.

Many production processes have become **automated,** whereby tasks are completed by machines without the use of employees. Since expenses incurred from machinery can be less than those incurred from human resources, automation is one form of technology that may improve production efficiency. Guidelines for effective automation are summarized in Exhibit 10.1.

---

stretch targets production efficiency targets (or goals) that cannot be achieved under the present conditions

automated tasks are completed by machines without the use of employees

---

Exhibit 10.1
Guidelines for Effective Automation

To effectively capitalize on the potential benefits from automation, the following guidelines should be considered:

1. Planning—Automation does not normally just involve speeding up work, but may require the elimination of some production steps. Planning is necessary to decide the type of automation that would be most appropriate (computers versus other machinery).
2. Use Automation Where the Benefits are Greatest—It may not be efficient to evenly allocate automation among all parts of the production process. Some workers will not be able to use a computer for their type of work.
3. Training—To make sure that the automation implemented is effectively utilized, any workers that use new computers or machinery should be trained.
4. Evaluate Costs and Benefits over Time—By assessing the costs and benefits of automation, a firm can decide whether to implement additional automation or revise its existing automation.

The latest technology and higher accountability are a critical part of any control effort as seen in this advertisement for Wood-Mizer.

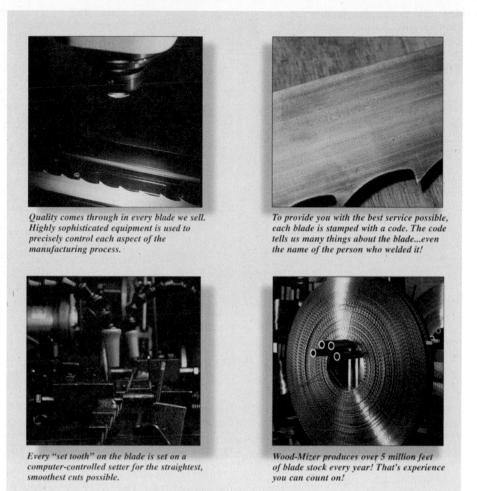

Quality comes through in every blade we sell. Highly sophisticated equipment is used to precisely control each aspect of the manufacturing process.

To provide you with the best service possible, each blade is stamped with a code. The code tells us many things about the blade...even the name of the person who welded it!

Every "set tooth" on the blade is set on a computer-controlled setter for the straightest, smoothest cuts possible.

Wood-Mizer produces over 5 million feet of blade stock every year! That's experience you can count on!

Many firms such as Albertsons (a grocery chain) and Home Depot improved production efficiency with the use of computer technology. For example, computers can keep track of the daily or weekly volume of each type of product that is purchased at the cash register of a retail store. Therefore, the firm does not need an employee to monitor the inventory of these products. The computer may even be programmed to automatically reorder some products once the inventory is reduced to a specified level. Some hospitals use pharmacy robots that stock and retrieve drugs. This technology increases production without additional labor expenses.

Many firms improve technology through ventures with other firms, whereby the firms pool their specific types of expertise or knowledge. Nucor and U.S. Steel created an alliance to develop a new method for converting iron ore into steel. Apple, IBM, and Motorola created an alliance to improve technology for computer hardware. Motorola created an alliance with United Parcel Service (UPS), in which UPS helped Motorola reduce its time on product deliveries by 75 percent. All of these examples reflect the advancement of technology in ways that can reduce operating expenses, and therefore increase the firm's value.

Economies of Scale

economies of scale as the quantity produced increases, the cost per unit decreases

Firms may also be able to reduce costs by achieving **economies of scale**, which reflects a lower average cost incurred from producing a larger volume. To recognize

This IBM production facility faces tremendous challenges in mass producing computer boards. One minor flaw will make these expensive parts worthless.

fixed costs represent operating expenses that do not change in response to the number of products produced

variable costs operating expenses that vary directly with the number of products produced

how economies of scale can occur, consider that two types of costs are involved in the production of a product: fixed costs and variable costs. **Fixed costs** represent operating expenses that do not change in response to the number of products produced. For example, the cost of renting a specific factory is not affected by the number of products produced there.

Variable costs are operating expenses that vary directly with the number of products produced. As output increases, the variable costs increase, while the fixed costs remain constant. The average cost per unit typically declines as output increases for firms that incur large fixed costs.

Automobile manufacturers incur a large fixed cost because they have to pay for their large facilities (including all the machinery) even if they do not produce many cars. Therefore, they need to produce a large number of cars to reduce the average cost per car produced.

Consider the production of a paperback book that requires some materials (ink and paper) and some manual labor. Assume that a book printing company incurs a fixed cost (rent plus machinery) of $40,000 per month. These expenses exist regardless of the number of books printed. Assume that the variable cost of producing each book is $2 per book. The total cost of producing books each month is equal to the fixed cost plus the variable cost. The total cost is estimated for various production levels in Exhibit 10.2. The key measure of production efficiency is the average cost per unit, which is measured as the total cost divided by the number of units produced. Notice how the average cost declines when the production volume increases. This relationship exists because the fixed cost is not affected by the production volume. Therefore, the fixed costs can be spread over a larger production volume. No extra fixed cost is incurred when producing additional products.

Assume that each of the books produced can be sold for $10. Exhibit 10.3 shows the total revenue and total costs for various quantities of books produced. The total revenue is equal to the quantity produced times the price of $10 per book. The profits represent the difference between the total revenue and the total cost. Notice that the firm experiences losses at small quantities. This is because the fixed costs are incurred even though the production volume is low. At the quantity level of 5,000 books, the total revenue is equal to the total cost. The quantity of units sold at which

Exhibit 10.2
Relationship between Production Volume and Costs

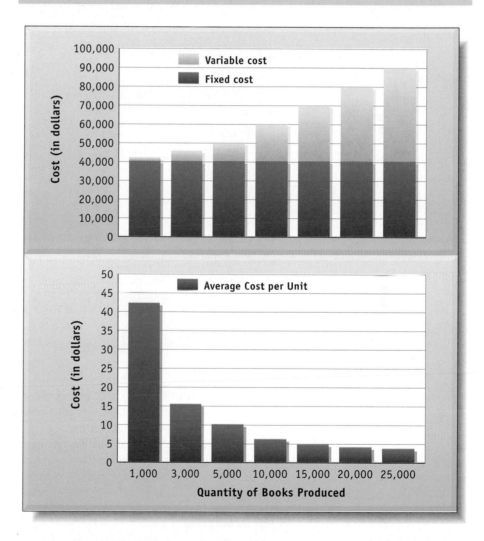

Quantity of Books Produced	Fixed Cost	Variable Cost ($2 Per Unit)	Total Cost	Average Cost Per Unit
1,000	$40,000	$2,000	$42,000	$42.00
3,000	$40,000	$6,000	$46,000	$15.33
5,000	$40,000	$10,000	$50,000	$10.00
10,000	$40,000	$20,000	$60,000	$6.00
15,000	$40,000	$30,000	$70,000	$4.67
20,000	$40,000	$40,000	$80,000	$4.00
25,000	$40,000	$50,000	$90,000	$3.60

break-even point the quantity of units sold at which total revenue equals total cost

total revenue equals total cost is referred to as the **break-even point.** At any quantity beyond 5,000 books, the firm experiences profits. The profits are larger for larger quantities produced. This results from the lower average cost incurred from the production of more books.

Some firms strive to achieve a large market share so that they can achieve economies of scale. For example, Compaq Computer typically sets a goal to obtain a

Exhibit 10.3
Relationship between Volume
and Profitability

Quantity of Books Produced	Total Revenue (= Quantity × Price)	Total Cost	Profits
1,000	$10,000	$42,000	−$32,000
3,000	$30,000	$46,000	−$16,000
5,000	$50,000	$50,000	$0
10,000	$100,000	$60,000	$40,000
15,000	$150,000	$70,000	$80,000
20,000	$200,000	$80,000	$120,000
25,000	$250,000	$90,000	$160,000

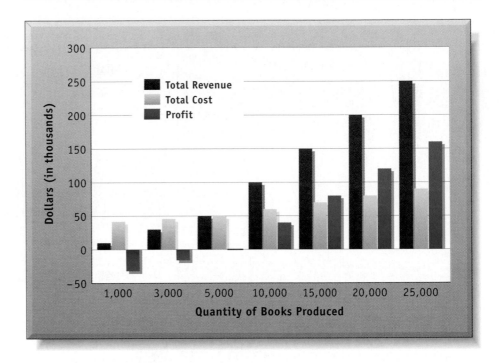

substantial market share for each of its products. This results in a large production
volume so that Compaq can achieve economies of scale. One of the largest expenses
in the production of computers is the research and development to improve computers. That expense is incurred whether Compaq sells only twenty computers or fifty
thousand computers. Therefore, the average cost per unit is reduced when Compaq
produces a large amount of a specific computer.

Restructuring

restructuring the revision of the production process in an attempt to improve
efficiency

Restructuring represents the revision of the production process in an attempt to
improve efficiency. When restructuring reduces the expense of producing products
or services, it can improve the firm's profits and therefore increase the firm's value.
For example, when Amoco restructured its operations over the 1992–95 period, it
reduced its expenses by $1.2 billion. This resulted in an extra $1.2 billion in earnings
(before taxes). Mobil Corporation restructured its operations in 1995, which was
expected to reduce expenses by more than $1 billion per year. The stock price of

Using Information Technology to Improve Product Quality

Information technology is increasingly being employed to enhance and monitor product quality. A particularly good example can be found in the elevator industry. The quality of elevators is critical; few people can remember their last trip on an elevator, but everybody can remember the last time they were stuck in one. Otis Elevator, in particular, has been a leader in using information technology to improve product quality. A major problem in preventing elevator failures is that small discrepancies that characteristically lead up to a failure (such as the elevator not being precisely aligned with the floor when it comes to a stop) are often ignored. Thus, the first indication of a problem to an elevator service company may be the emergency call telling them someone is trapped.

To identify such small problems before they become emergencies, Otis developed a Remote Elevator Monitoring (REM) system. The REM system used a small computer to monitor elevator performance. In addition, some installations employed telecommunications linkages, allowing the elevator itself to call Otis headquarters in the event of any unexpected problems. As a result, the REM system made it possible for service personnel to be sent to a building before small problems escalated to an emergency.

By promoting these capabilities, Otis was able to charge a premium for its elevators, based upon their perceived quality. Incorporating information technology into products to enhance quality can also lead to other economic benefits to the firm. In many industries, ongoing maintenance and servicing of products is, in itself, a huge market. Consequently, the manufacturer can use its expertise in the technology as a competitive advantage in competing for the service business, as Otis did with its elevators.

Mobil increased by more than 4 percent on May 1, 1995, when Mobil announced its plans to restructure. This example shows how the value of the firm rose in direct response to a restructuring plan that would reduce expenses.

reengineering the redesign of a firm's organizational structure and operations

Many firms periodically assess all aspects of their business to determine whether they should restructure in any way. Many use **reengineering,** which is the redesign of a firm's organizational structure and operations. The reengineering may result in some minor revisions, such as the procedures used to take phone messages or to send packages at the firm. Alternatively, the revisions may be much larger, such as a new facility or a new assembly-line operation for production.

Reengineering requires that the company forget the old way of doing things and attempt to build the best system from scratch. Reengineering has been used by Delta Airlines, Digital Equipment Corporation, Hallmark, Westinghouse Electric, and many other firms. It requires the efforts of many different types of managers within the firm who are willing to think about the optimal method for production, without being forced to focus on the method that is presently being used. Reengineering is normally conducted by obtaining input from the employees who understand how the production process works. These employees are likely to recognize any inefficient parts of the process that should be eliminated or revised.

A popular method for obtaining employee feedback is to organize employees into cross-functional teams, in which one employee who is responsible for each specific function of the production process is assigned to the team. For example, a manufacturing firm may have a team that consists of one employee who orders supplies, one who works on the assembly line, one who is responsible for selling the finished product, and one who assesses the quality of the product. Allied Signal has organized more than ten thousand teams to determine how to improve its production efficiency.

Employees who are asked for input on restructuring do not have to completely understand every function of the production process, because they can rely on others on their team for specific details. The team of employees can attempt to create a production process that is most efficient. The expenses and other characteristics of this proposed process can be estimated and compared with those of the existing process. When using the team concept, no single employee has excessive influence on the proposed methods for restructuring. Thus, any proposals by the team reflect the support of several employees and are not intended to benefit just one particular employee.

Some employees may attempt to focus on changes that will give them more job security or power. This can reduce the potential benefits of reengineering, because the proposed restructuring of the production process may be intended to enhance each employee's position rather than the firm's efficiency. Firms may attempt to prevent such a problem by rewarding those employees who develop cost-cutting ideas that the firm actually uses.

The following statements from recent annual reports confirm how some firms are attempting to restructure their operations:

> **We believe our restructuring programs will reduce operating costs by approximately $170 million.**
>
> —Westinghouse

> **We have totally reengineered operations. . . . We now possess a conscious culture with an expense structure that enables us to compete with an increasingly efficient and competitive marketplace.**
>
> —Fleet Financial

> **Through the reengineering process, we are promoting significant changes throughout this 75-year-old company. We are discarding decades-old processes and starting with a clean sheet of paper.**
>
> —Zenith

downsizing the act of reducing the number of employees

DOWNSIZING When firms restructure, they also typically engage in **downsizing,** or the act of reducing the number of employees. Firms identify various job positions that could be eliminated without affecting the volume or the quality of products produced. Some downsizing occurs as a result of technology because automated production processes replace human resources (as explained earlier). However, numerous firms downsize even if they have no plans to further automate their production process.

In recent years, Mobil Corporation cut 4,700 jobs, American Airlines cut 6,000 jobs, and Procter and Gamble cut 13,000 jobs. Boeing, Chrysler, IBM, Eastman Kodak, TRW, and numerous other firms have also cut thousands of jobs. A reduction in employees results in a reduction of salaries paid by the firm. Firms frequently used downsizing during the recession of the early 1990s. Many firms were experiencing financial problems and restructured their operations to reduce expenses. Job positions were eliminated, resulting in a reassignment of tasks to the remaining employees. Firms noticed that they were able to achieve similar production volume with fewer employees. Even after the recession ended, firms continued to downsize because competition was so intense in many industries. Exhibit 10.5 shows that more than 400,000 jobs were cut each year from 1991 to 1995. Firms that had an ineffi-

Interaction of Functions Involved in Total Quality Management

Total quality management requires an ongoing product assessment, beginning from the time product materials are ordered and continuing until the customer has purchased and used the product. Consequently, TQM requires an interaction of business functions. The key management functions involved in TQM are ordering the proper types and amounts of supplies, achieving efficient (low-cost) production of the product, and ensuring that the product satisfies the firm's production standards.

The key marketing functions involved in TQM are achiev-

ing efficient use of marketing strategies, ensuring customer satisfaction, and obtaining feedback from customers on how to improve the product. When marketing managers receive a similar criticism about a product from many customers, they should contact the production managers, who may redesign the product. This interaction between management and marketing functions is shown in Exhibit 10.4.

The financing function is indirectly affected, as changes in expenses or revenue resulting from TQM may alter the amount of new financing that the firm needs.

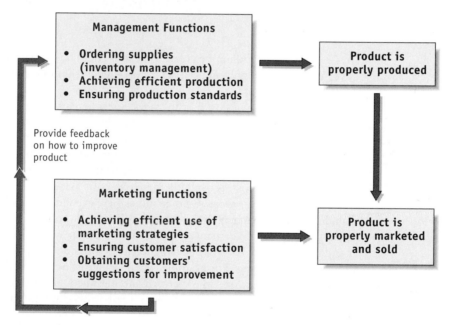

Exhibit 10.4
Interaction between Management and Marketing Functions When Implementing Total Quality Management

cient production process were forced to become more efficient to compete with those firms that had already downsized.

To illustrate the potential savings from downsizing, consider that a firm's cost of employees (labor cost) may be as much as its cost of the materials used to produce the final product. Many large firms, such as IBM and General Motors, spend more than $1 billion in salaries and other compensation each year. If a firm could find a way to cut one hundred employees, and if the average compensation of these employees was $30,000, the savings would be $3 million (computed as $30,000 \times 100 employees). For those large firms that eliminated thousands of jobs, the cost sav-

Exhibit 10.5
Downsizing by U.S. Firms
Over Time

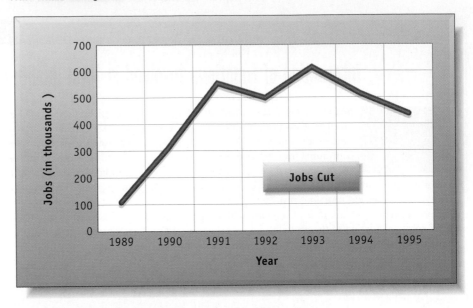

corporate anorexia firms become so
obsessed with eliminating their inefficient
components that they downsize too much

ings exceeded $100 million per year. If the jobs could be cut without any other
adverse effects, $100 million per year in cost savings should result in an additional
$100 million in profit.

Downsizing also has its disadvantages. Some firms become so obsessed with
eliminating their inefficient components that they downsize too much. This is
referred to as **corporate anorexia.** Downsizing can have the following adverse effects.
First, there may be costs associated with the elimination of job positions, such as
efforts to find other job positions within the firm or outside the firm for the employees whose jobs were cut. Second, there may be costs associated with training some
remaining employees whose responsibilities were expanded. Third, the morale of the
remaining employees may decline if they believe their position may be cut, which
could reduce their performance. Fourth, downsizing may result in lower quality, as
the remaining employees may be assigned more work and might not detect defects in
the production process. For example, when Delta Airlines reduced its workforce by
10,000 employees, its "on-time" performance declined. Firms must consider such
possible adverse effects before they can accurately estimate the cost savings that
would result from downsizing.

BUSINESS DILEMMA

· COLLEGE ·
HEALTH CLUB

Total Quality Management at College Health Club (CHC)

Sue Kramer, president of College Health Club, frequently hears of numerous business success stories that were attributed to the use of total quality management
(TQM). However, most of the TQM examples were manufacturing firms that had
elaborate production processes. CHC simply produces a health club service. Yet, Sue
believes that the TQM principles could be applied to the production and sale of
health club services.

Dilemma

Sue's goal is to apply TQM within her health club business. Offer some suggestions on how Sue could attempt to improve the performance of CHC by applying TQM.

Solution

Recall that the key functions involved in TQM are (1) defining a desired quality level, (2) developing a production process that achieves that level, and (3) controlling the quality level with continuous monitoring and assessment.

No simple formula can measure the quality of a health club service. Sue decides that the best way to measure the quality of the services she provides is to determine whether customers are satisfied with the services. Sue identifies various criteria that may affect customer satisfaction. She asks the customers to rate each of the following criteria, from a 1 ("not satisfied") to a 5 ("very satisfied"):

1 Does CHC have all the desired weight machines and equipment?
2 Does CHC have enough weight machines and equipment so that customers do not have to wait their turn?
3 Is CHC's location convenient?
4 Are CHC's business hours (from 8:00 A.M. to 10:00 P.M. seven days a week) acceptable?
5 Are CHC's aerobics classes effective?
6 Does CHC offer enough aerobics classes?

This survey will help determine the quality level of the health club services as perceived by the customers. Sue can then determine whether the quality level is acceptable to her. If the average score of any criterion is less than 4.0, Sue plans to focus on that item to improve quality and therefore boost customer satisfaction. She will obtain more detailed feedback on any criterion with an unacceptable score, to determine how customer satisfaction can be improved.

To control the quality level over time, Sue plans to place index cards with this survey and a comments box near the exit of CHC. Thus, anytime customers have concerns about the quality of CHC's services, they can fill out these cards. A high level of customer satisfaction will improve CHC's revenue and could also improve production efficiency due to economies of scale.

Sue recognizes that she not only should search for new members but also should make an effort to keep existing members.

Additional Issues for Discussion

1 How can the quality of a health club be measured?
2 Since so many factors affect quality, how can Sue Kramer decide which factors to focus on for her health club?
3 Explain how the concept of quality control applies to CHC.

SUMMARY

1 Total quality management normally involves:

➤ specifying the desired quality level, in which the firm develops a quality standard that can be measured and monitored over time;

➤ achieving the desired quality level, in which the firm establishes a production process that satisfies the quality standard it established;

➤ controlling the quality level in which the firm monitors the quality level over time and considers adjustments to achieve continuous improvement.

2 The key methods used to improve production efficiency are:

➤ technology, which increases the speed of the production process,

➤ economies of scale, which reduces the average cost per unit as a result of a higher production volume, and

➤ restructuring, which represents a revision of the production process to reduce production expenses.

KEY TERMS

automated
benchmarking
break-even point
corporate anorexia
downsizing

economies of scale
fixed costs
variable costs
production efficiency
quality control circle

reengineering
restructuring
sampling
stretch targets
total quality management (TQM)

REVIEW QUESTIONS

1 Identify some key business functions of management, marketing, and finance that must be performed when implementing a TQM program.

2 Identify the methods for improving production efficiency for a firm.

3 Describe corporate anorexia. When can downsizing create adverse effects for a firm?

4 Identify and explain a TQM application for a manufacturing firm that would emphasize efficiency.

5 Discuss how employees can be used to assess the quality level for products produced in a firm.

6 Define downsizing and identify some factors that may force a firm to downsize.

7 Define stretch targets for a production manager and discuss why they are established.

8 Identify and explain the use of quality control circles and cite examples where they have enjoyed success.

9 Identify and explain why production managers would be interested in the break-even point. Why would one be interested in achieving economies of scale?

10 Discuss the global quality standards which a firm can attempt to achieve in international business.

DISCUSSION QUESTIONS

1 Discuss the concept of a quality control circle at a local plant in your hometown.

2 Apply the TQM process to a problem at your college or university. How was this problem resolved? Did it meet your satisfaction?

3 Identify a firm in your local area that achieves the highest level of quality and sets a primary objective of customer satisfaction.

4 Assume you are a plant manager and that your primary objective is to increase production efficiency. Discuss the methods that you could consider to achieve this goal.

5 You have just been assigned to a team in your class and given a research assignment. You are asked to implement a TQM process. Discuss how continuous improvement will take place during this project.

RUNNING YOUR OWN BUSINESS

1 Describe how your business can ensure: (a) customer satisfaction, (b) the quality of the product or service you plan to produce, and (c) that customers are treated properly by any employees that you hire.

2 Describe how technology will enable you to improve

the quality of the product or service you plan to produce. Describe how your production or customer service may possibly improve over time as a result of technology.

3 Discuss how economies of scale relate to your business.

INVESTING IN THE STOCK OF A BUSINESS

Using the annual report of the firm in which you would like to invest, complete the following:

1 Does the firm appear to pay attention to customer satisfaction? Explain.

2 Has the firm improved the quality of its products or

services in recent years? If so, how?

3 See if you can find information on your firm as it relates to reengineering. Check your annual report and a business magazine or newspaper.

4 Does your firm benefit from economies of scale? Try to identify the fixed and variable costs.

CASE 1 Using TQM to Assess Employee Quality

Every year, employees put in writing what they think, not just of one another's performance, but of their supervisors' performance as well. Their evaluations help determine how much those supervisors get paid.

Laitram Corporation, a manufacturing firm based in Harahan, Louisiana, has addressed the evaluation issue by implementing a total quality management (TQM) concept using peer surveys. The challenge lies in finding a way to determine pay for employees.

The company operates under what it calls the Laitram Continuous Improvement Program. The essence of the program, like that of TQM, is enhancing cooperative effort among the people who work together in the company.

The late W. Edwards Deming, for decades the leading figure in the American quality movement, spoke of such "merit rating" with scorn: "It nourishes short-term performance, annihilates long-term planning, builds fear, demolishes teamwork, nourishes rivalry and politics."

Despite Deming's concerns, numerous quality-oriented firms have reached the conclusion that there is no satisfactory alternative to the individual performance review as a tool for evaluating and rewarding employees.

A new twist at Laitram has been the development of a

multi-rater program. It entails the review of supervisors' performances by their employees. Although this type of program is still unusual in U.S. industry, such programs are gaining acceptance.

Each employee is required to make an end-of-the-year confidential report on his or her supervisor's performance. Laitram also conducts peer surveys, which ask employees about firsthand experiences with other employees. When surveys are used to gather more accurate information about activities within the company, employees tend to accept the surveys, because employees who typically have never received recognition for doing great work are finally recognized.

Questions

1 What is total quality management (TQM)? How can it solve the problems of determining employee pay increases?

2 Discuss the impact of merit reviews according to W. Edwards Deming's principles.

3 Discuss how supervisors' job performance is evaluated at Laitram Corporation. What are the potential benefits and costs of this method?

CASE 2 Applying TQM to Education

Heather Peart, an electronics student in Brooklyn's George Westinghouse Vocational and Technical High

School, is involved in an experiment. With help from companies such as Ricoh, IBM, and Xerox, Peart and her

Westinghouse classmates are participating in an educational experiment: learning—and using—total quality management (TQM), the popular business technique.

In the school's electronics classes, the students use TQM principles to complete repairs well ahead of deadlines, with minimal mistakes. Westinghouse also uses TQM to improve attendance and parental involvement. The venture seems to be paying off: Since the schoolwide program began in 1990, Westinghouse's dropout rate has fallen from 12.9 percent to 2.1 percent.

The federal government has become involved by endorsing TQM applications in public schools throughout the country. For the first time in 1996, the government will award the Baldrige Quality Award for education. The award will recognize constant improvement and better results, from higher test scores to lower dropout rates. Judges will evaluate teaching methods by measuring how students are learning and determining the benefits derived. The objective has become the measurement of learning, not simply teaching.

Educators are trying to adapt quality principles of TQM by using the same techniques and vocabulary as is used in today's industry, including terms such as "customer satisfaction" and "brainstorming." Schools all over the country are using TQM concepts.

Whether TQM is used in the classroom or students are applying these principles in the workshop, this technique has had success in enhancing a quality orientation by providing instant feedback to students charged with marking their progress.

Questions

1 What is TQM, and what are its objectives at Westinghouse Vocational?

2 Will TQM principles and practices enhance education in American public schools? Explain.

3 How can TQM create success for students who are enrolled in workshops in the business environment?

4 Why do you think the dropout rate at Westinghouse High School decreased? What does this mean for businesses?

VIDEO CASE How the Focus on Quality Can Lead to Success

Robotron Corporation, a Southfield, Michigan, manufacturer, used to think the equipment it produced for the auto industry was above average in quality, says CEO Leonard Brzozowski. That, he adds, "was largely because none of our customers ever complained about it."

However, when Robotron sold machines to Sanyo Manufacturing Company, it relized that it had quality problems.

The Japanese firm was unhappy with the equipment. Brzozowski went to its plant and "learned that they had a completely different expectation of quality than our usual American customers." Inspection was more demanding. Tolerances allowed were much smaller.

"For the first time," Brzozowski says, "we realized that the philosophy, engineering, management, and shop practices of our company did not qualify us for global competition." He and other managers "resolved to launch a revolution" at Robotron.

A group of employees were immediately driven to a Sanyo plant in Michigan. "Their opportunity to actually see the customer's disappointment, hear his complaints, and compare our equipment with that manufactured by Sanyo," Brzozowski says, accomplished more than scores of meetings or managers' speeches could have. The ride home was filled with discussions about things to do to improve quality.

Soon Robotron had established new inspection procedures, bought more accurate inspection tools, changed internal control procedures, and developed yardsticks against which to measure progress.

It began sending out teams to check on customer satisfaction within six months after equipment deliveries. A hot line that any customer could call was set up, and customers were given home numbers of Brzozowski and his staff.

At the time of the Sanyo incident, the company had virtually no foreign revenue. Today at least 20 percent of its sales are exports, many of them the result of marketing pacts with foreign firms.

Also, the company has developed bonding products for manufacturers outside the auto industry. In three years sales of such products have risen from zero to $1.3 million, almost 10 percent of total sales.

Questions

1 Describe the ways in which Robotron improved the monitoring of its production process.

2 Why did Robotron need to survey customers who purchased its products. Isn't it enough to monitor the production process to make sure that the products are produced properly?

3 Some employees may argue that customer satisfaction surveys are not necessary for products that last a long time, because the firm may not rely on repeat purchases from its customers. Offer your opinion.

THE 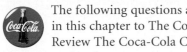 COMPANY ANNUAL REPORT PROJECT

The following questions apply concepts learned in this chapter to The Coca-Cola Company. Review The Coca-Cola Company annual report when answering these questions.

1 How does The Coca-Cola Company know if it is manufacturing a "good" product?

2 How can The Coca-Cola Company ensure that it is manufacturing the "best possible" product at all times and at all locations?

3 Do you think The Coca-Cola Company benefits from economies of scale? Explain.

4 How can The Coca-Cola Company benefit from the process of benchmarking?

IN-TEXT STUDY GUIDE

Answers are in an appendix at the back of the book.

True or False
1 Economies of scale reflect a lower average cost incurred from producing a larger volume.

2 Many firms improve technology through ventures with other firms, whereby the firms pool their specific types of expertise or knowledge.

3 Firms tend to assess quality control by inspecting the finished product, in which some of the products produced are randomly selected and tested to determine whether they satisfy the quality standards.

4 Firms now realize that providing the quality level that satisfies customers may make it easier to retain existing customers rather than attract new customers who are unfamiliar with their products or services.

5 When firms periodically assess all aspects of their business to determine whether they should restructure in any way, this is referred to as a quality control circle.

6 Restructuring represents the revision of the production process in an attempt to improve efficiency.

7 Firms strive to increase their production efficiency, which reflects the amount of revenue that is generated by a given amount of output.

8 Some downsizing occurs as a result of technology because automated production processes replace employees.

9 Total quality management focuses only on quality assessment that begins from the time product materials are ordered until the product has been produced.

10 The break-even point refers to the quantity of units sold at which the total revenue is equal to the fixed costs of production.

Multiple Choice
11 Methods for improving production efficiency would include the following except for:
a) pricing policies.
b) restructuring.
c) economies of scale.
d) technology.

12 The process used to detect and correct quality deficiencies is:
a) downsizing.
b) break-even analysis.
c) quality control.
d) research and development.
e) financial management.

13 The _____ of a product or service typically measures the likelihood that it will perform properly over its expected life.
a) downsizing
b) quality
c) cost
d) reengineering
e) restructuring

14 The use of total quality management normally involves the following functions except for:
a) downsizing.
b) specifying the desired quality level.
c) controlling the quality level.
d) achieving the desired quality level.

15 A set of standards established for environmental effects of the production process is called:
a) quality circles.
b) production schedules.
c) random samples.
d) production restructuring.
e) *ISO 14000.*

16 Since the expenses incurred from machinery can be less than those incurred from human resources, _____ is one form of technology that may improve production efficiency.
a) downtime
b) downsizing
c) absenteeism

d) automation

e) grapevine

17 A popular method for obtaining employee feedback is by using:

a) cross-functional teams.

b) marketing research.

c) research and development.

d) automation.

e) economies of scale.

18 No single employee has excessive influence on proposed methods of restructuring when using the:

a) competitive forces.

b) ISO 1000.

c) grapevine.

d) production routing form.

e) team concept.

19 When firms become so obsessed with eliminating their inefficient components that they downsize too much, this creates:

a) quality circles.

b) cross-functional teams.

c) corporate anorexia.

d) reengineering applications.

e) production efficiency.

20 Some firms strive to achieve a large market share so that they can achieve:

a) cost overruns.

b) economies of scale.

c) production inefficiencies.

d) quality control inspection.

e) stretch targets.

21 _____ is normally conducted by obtaining input from the employees who understand how the production process works.

a) Downsizing

b) Sampling

c) Dividend policy

d) Reengineering

e) Automation

22 Production efficiency goals that cannot be achieved under the present conditions are referred to as:

a) quality circles.

b) management strategies.

c) production controls.

d) corporate anorexia.

e) stretch targets.

23 TQM stresses the need for firms to measure quality from the perspective of the:

a) competition.

b) customer.

c) government.

d) environment.

e) industry.

24 The production process that ensures meeting specified quality standards is known as:

a) sampling circles.

b) economies of scale.

c) quality control.

d) stretch targets.

e) corporate anorexia.

25 _____ is commonly used to correct a firm's perceived deficiencies and therefore improve customer satisfaction.

a) TQM

b) Automation

c) Corporate anorexia

d) Downsizing

e) Sampling

26 Firms can obtain feedback from customers by conducting:

a) production control.

b) inventory control.

c) JIT inventories.

d) surveys.

e) routing procedures.

27 The term used to describe a firm's restructuring process and the reduction in the number of employees is:

a) organizational structure.

b) total quality management.

c) quality control circles.

d) span of control.

e) downsizing.

28 The procedure of randomly selecting and testing products to determine whether they satisfy quality standards is called:

a) sampling.

b) restructuring.

c) reengineering.

d) downsizing.

e) corporate anorexia.

29 Managers continually search for ways to manage human and other resources in a manner that improves:

a) sampling.

b) production efficiency.

c) corporate anorexia.

d) revenue downsizing.

e) cost overruns.

30 The operating expenses that vary directly with the number of products produced are:

a) direct costs.

b) fixed expenses.

c) variable costs.

d) semifixed costs.

e) fixed costs.

31 The total quality management concept was originally developed in Japan by:

a) Frederick Taylor.

b) A. H. Maslow.

c) Malcolm Baldrige.

d) W. Edwards Deming.

e) Frederick Hertzberg.

32 To make sure that automation is effectively utilized, any workers that use new computers or machinery should be:

a) unionized.

b) trained.

c) downsized.

d) forced to work individually.

e) supervisors only.

33 The two types of costs involved in the production of a product are:

a) revenue and semivariable.

b) budgetary and overhead.

c) fixed and variable.

d) expense and financial.

e) responsibility and direct.

34 The quantity of units sold at which total revenue equals total cost is referred to as the:

a) responsibility center.

b) profit center.

c) revenue budget.

d) cost center.

e) break-even point.

35 _____ represents operating expenses that do not change in response to the number of products produced.

a) Fixed costs

b) Revenue centers

c) Break-even points

d) Responsibility centers

e) Budgetary centers

Quality Information on the World Wide Web

The WWW offers much information relating to quality control and total quality management (TQM). The American Society of Quality Control web site (Exhibit 10.6) maintains links to much of this information. This site provides an up-to-date bibliography of quality-related publications, a calendar of quality workshops, and a quality chat/forum for on-line discussion of quality implementation issues. In addition, it supplies information on applying for the prestigious Malcolm Baldrige National Quality Award.

Exhibit 10.6
American Society of
Quality Control Web Site

http://www.asqc.org/

If you are using a text browser, follow this link.

SUMMARY OF PART III

The chapters in Part III describe some of the key components of effective management. These components are (1) recognition of the skills necessary to be effective managers (Chapter 7), (2) proper assignments of job responsibilities (Chapter 8), (3) efficient allocation of resources for production (Chapter 9), and (4) proper monitoring and improvement of product quality (Chapter 10).

The key skills needed for managers to be effective are conceptual skills (to understand relationships among tasks of a firm), interpersonal skills, technical skills, and decision-making skills.

In addition to skills, effective management requires that job responsibilities are properly assigned within the organizational structure. Ideally, the organizational structure allows some control over each job assignment so that all types of tasks can be monitored. Yet, an organizational structure may also attempt to ensure employee input on various tasks by assigning extra responsibilities to employees. Job tasks and responsibilities can be departmentalized by function, product, location, or type of customer. The method of departmentalizing job tasks and responsibilities is dependent on the characteristics of the business.

Effective management also requires an efficient production process, which involves the selection of a plant site, and the design and layout of the production facilities. The plant site decision is influenced by land cost, access to transportation, and other factors that affect the cost of production. Design and layout decisions are influenced by the characteristics of the plant site, production process, product line, and desired production capacity.

Effective management also requires an effort to continuously improve the quality of each product that is produced. Quality management forces employees to specify the desired quality level, to consider how the production process can be revised to achieve that quality level, and to continuously monitor the quality level by using various quality control methods.

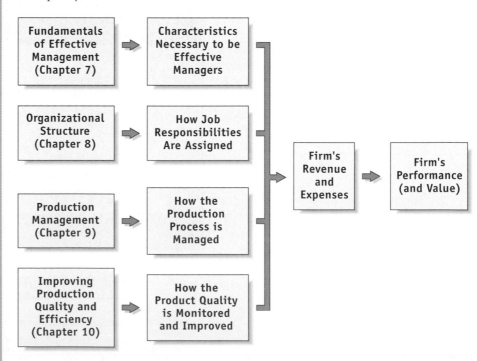

Managing Employees

CHAPTER 11
Motivating Employees
CHAPTER 12
Hiring, Training, and Evaluating Employees

While Part III focused on organizational structure and production, Part IV focuses on human resources (employees), another critical component of management. Part IV contains two chapters that explain how managers can improve the performance of their employees. Chapter 11 describes the methods that can be used to motivate employees. Motivation may be necessary for many employees to perform well. To the extent that managers can effectively motivate employees, they can increase the performance of employees and therefore increase the performance of the firm. Chapter 12 explains proper methods used to hire, train, and evaluate the performance of employees. If managers can use these methods effectively, they should be able to improve the firm's performance.

CHAPTER 11

Motivating Employees

A firm has a strategic plan that identifies opportunities and the future direction of the firm's business. When the firm develops strategies to achieve the strategic plan, it relies on its managers to utilize employees and other resources to make the strategies work. The performance of a firm is highly dependent on the performance of its employees. By motivating employees to properly perform the tasks they are assigned, firms can maximize the firm's value.

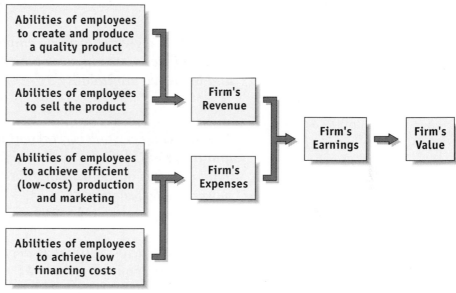

Consider the case of Wal-Mart Stores, which has a chain of retail stores that sell a wide variety of merchandise. Employees are needed to receive merchandise shipped to them and to periodically stock the shelves. Some employees serve as cashiers, while others are responsible for managing the stores. How can Wal-Mart motivate these employees to perform well at work? Would Wal-Mart employees be more motivated if they were more satisfied with their jobs? How can Wal-Mart ensure a high level of job satisfaction among its employees? This chapter provides a background on motivating employees, which can be used to address these questions.

The **Learning Goals** of this chapter are to:

1 Describe the theories on motivation.

2 Explain how firms can enhance job satisfaction and therefore enhance motivation.

THEORIES ON MOTIVATION

1 **Describe the theories on motivation.**

job satisfaction degree to which employees are satisfied with their jobs

The motivation of employees is influenced by **job satisfaction,** or the degree to which employees are satisfied with their jobs. Firms recognize the need to satisfy their employees, as illustrated by the following statements from recent annual reports:

> *You will see a greater focus on employee satisfaction . . . which will lead us to higher quality, better growth, and improved profitability.*
>
> —Kodak

> *The new Quaker State is representative of a new spirit and the promise of a better future for every Quaker State employee. It is the realization that they have it in their power to effect change.*
>
> —Quaker State

> *Bethlehem's success ultimately depends on the skill, dedication and support of our employees.*
>
> —Bethlehem Steel

Since employees who are satisfied with their jobs are more motivated, managers can motivate employees by ensuring job satisfaction. Some of the more popular theories on motivation are summarized here, followed by some general guidelines that can be used to motivate workers.

Hawthorne Studies

Workers in a Western Electric Plant near Chicago in the late 1920s were studied to identify how a variety of conditions affected their level of production. When the lighting was increased, the production level increased. Yet, the production level also increased when the lighting was reduced. These workers were then subjected to various break periods; again, the production level increased for both shorter breaks and longer breaks. One interpretation of these results is that workers become more motivated when they feel as though they are allowed to participate. Supervisors may be able to motivate workers by giving them more attention and by allowing them to participate. The Hawthorne studies, which ignited further research on motivation, are summarized in Exhibit 11.1 and suggest that human relations can affect a firm's performance.

hierarchy of needs needs are ranked in five general categories. Once a given category of needs is achieved, people become motivated to reach the next category

Maslow's Hierarchy of Needs

In 1943, the **hierarchy of needs** theory was developed by Abraham Maslow, a psychologist. This theory suggests that people rank their needs into five general cate-

Exhibit 11.1
Summary of Hawthorne Studies

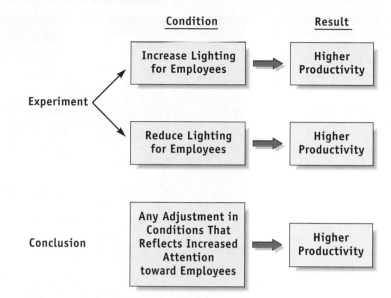

physiological needs the more basic requirements for survival

safety needs job security and safe working conditions

social needs need to be part of a group

esteem needs respect, prestige, and recognition

self-actualization the need to fully reach one's potential

gories. Once they achieve a given category of needs, they become motivated to reach the next category. The categories are identified in Exhibit 11.2, with the most crucial needs on the bottom. **Physiological needs** are for the more basic requirements for survival, such as food and shelter. Most jobs can help achieve these needs.

Once these needs are fulfilled, **safety needs** (such as job security and safe working conditions) become the most immediate goal. Some jobs satisfy these needs. People also strive to achieve **social needs,** or the need to be part of a group. Some firms attempt to help employees achieve their social needs, either by grouping workers in teams or by organizing social events after work hours. People may also become motivated to achieve **esteem needs,** such as respect, prestige, and recognition. Some workers may achieve these needs by being promoted within their firms or by receiving special recognition for their work. The final category of needs is **self-actualization,** which represents the need to fully reach one's potential. For example, people may achieve

Exhibit 11.2
Maslow's Hierarchy of Needs

Sun Microsystems' company picnic fills a social need as well as
encouraging employees to work
together while having fun.

self-actualization needs by starting a specific business that fits their main interests and
by being successful in running this business.

    The hierarchy of needs theory can be useful for motivating employees because it
suggests that employees may be in different classes of the hierarchy. Therefore, their
most immediate needs may differ. If managers recognize employee needs, they will
be better able to offer rewards that motivate employees.

Herzberg's Job Satisfaction Study

In the late 1950s, a study by Frederick Herzberg surveyed two hundred accountants
and engineers about job satisfaction. Herzberg attempted to identify the factors that
made them feel dissatisfied with their jobs at a given point in time. He also attempted
to identify the factors that made them feel satisfied with their jobs. His study found
the following:

Common Factors Identified by Dissatisfied Workers	Common Factors Identified by Satisfied Workers
Work conditions	Achievement
Supervision	Responsibility
Salary	Recognition
Job security	Advancement
Status	Growth

hygiene factors work-related factors
perceived to be inadequate

    Employees become dissatisfied when work-related factors in the left column
(called **hygiene factors**) are perceived as inadequate. They are commonly satisfied

motivational factors work-related
factors that please employees

when the work-related factors in the right column that please employees (called **motivational factors**) are offered.

The results suggest that factors such as work conditions and salary must be adequate to prevent workers from being dissatisfied. Yet, better-than-adequate work conditions and salary will not necessarily lead to a high degree of satisfaction. Instead, a high degree of worker satisfaction is most easily achieved by offering additional benefits, such as responsibility. If managers can increase worker satisfaction by assigning workers more responsibility, they may motivate workers to be more productive. A summary of Herzberg's job satisfaction study is illustrated in Exhibit 11.3.

Notice how the results of Herzberg's study correspond with the results of Maslow's hierarchy. Herzberg's hygiene factors generally correspond with Maslow's basic needs (such as job security). This suggests that if hygiene factors are adequate, they fulfill some of the more basic worker needs. Fulfillment of these needs can prevent dissatisfaction, as employees become motivated to achieve a higher class of needs. Herzberg's motivational factors (such as recognition) generally correspond with Maslow's more ambitious hierarchy needs.

Several U.S. firms, such as Ford Motor Company, TRW, and Polaroid Corporation, are implementing workshops to stress teamwork and company loyalty. These workshops build self-esteem by focusing on employees' worth to the company. In this way, the workshops may enable employees to achieve a higher class of needs, thereby increasing job satisfaction.

McGregor's Theory X and Theory Y

Another major contribution to motivation was provided by Douglas McGregor, who developed Theory X and Theory Y. Each of these theories represents supervisors' possible perception of workers. The views of Theories X and Y are summarized as follows on the next page.

This Jim's Restaurant employee has been provided the tools to perform safely and effectively. This steel mesh glove protects the employee and the company from unnecessary physical or financial harm.

Exhibit 11.3
Summary of Herzberg's Job
Satisfaction Study

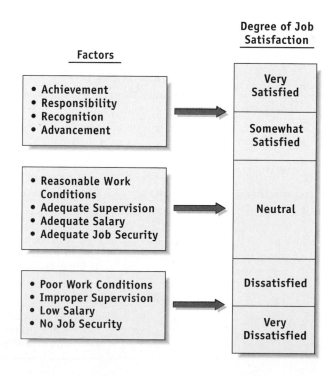

Theory X	Theory Y
Employees dislike work and job responsibilities and will avoid work if possible.	Employees are willing to work and prefer more responsibility.

The way supervisors view employees can influence the manner in which they treat them. Supervisors who believe in Theory X will likely use tight control over workers, with little or no delegation of authority. In addition, employees would be closely monitored to ensure that they perform their tasks. Conversely, supervisors who believe in Theory Y would delegate more authority, since workers are perceived as responsible. These supervisors would also allow more opportunities for employees to use their creativity. This management approach would fulfill employee needs to be responsible and to achieve respect and recognition. Consequently, these employees would likely be more motivated because their level of job satisfaction should be higher.

A summary of Theories X and Y is illustrated in Exhibit 11.4. Most employees would prefer that their supervisors follow Theory Y rather than Theory X. Yet, some supervisors may be unable to use Theory Y for specific situations. In these cases, they are forced to retain more authority over employees rather than delegate tasks.

Theory Z

In the 1980s, a new theory on job satisfaction was developed. This theory, called Theory Z, was partially based on the Japanese style of allowing all employees to participate in decision making. Participation can increase job satisfaction because it gives employees responsibility. Job descriptions tend to be less specialized so that employees will develop varied skills and have a more flexible career path. To increase job satisfaction, many U.S. firms have begun to allow employees more responsibility.

Expectancy Theory

expectancy theory employee's efforts are influenced by the expected outcome (reward) for those efforts

Expectancy theory suggests that an employee's efforts are influenced by the expected outcome (reward) for those efforts. Therefore, an employee's level of motivation is dependent on the compensation or recognition to be received. Employees will be

Exhibit 11.4
Summary of McGregor's Theories X and Y

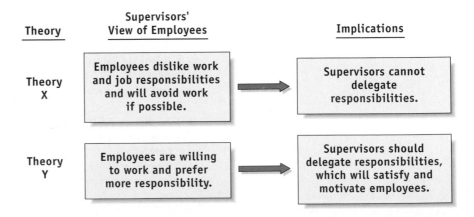

more motivated to achieve goals if they are achievable and offer some reward. This theory is somewhat related to the other theories, but offers additional insight into how managers should motivate their employees.

As an example, consider a firm that offers the salesperson who achieves the highest volume of annual sales a one-week vacation in Paris. This type of reward will motivate employees only if two requirements are fulfilled. First, the reward must be desirable to employees. Second, employees must believe they have a chance to earn the reward. If the firm employs one thousand salespeople, and only one reward is offered, employees may not be motivated because their perceived chance of being the top salesperson may be too low. Motivation may be absent even in smaller groups if all employees expect that a particular salesperson will generate the highest sales volume.

Motivational rewards are more difficult to offer for jobs in which output cannot be measured. For example, employees that repair the firm's machinery or service customer complaints do not contribute to the firm in a manner that can be easily measured or compared with other employees. However, performance may still be measured by customer satisfaction surveys or by various other performance indicators.

Equity Theory

equity theory compensation should be equitable, or in proportion to each employee's contribution

The **equity theory** of motivation suggests that compensation should be equitable, or in proportion to each employee's contribution. As an example, consider a firm with three employees, where Employee 1 contributes 50 percent of the total output, Employee 2 contributes 30 percent, and Employee 3 contributes 20 percent. Assume that the firm plans to allocate $100,000 in bonuses based on the relative contributions of each employee. Using the equity theory, the $100,000 would be allocated as shown in Exhibit 11.5.

If employees believe that they are undercompensated, they may request greater compensation. If their compensation is not increased, employees may reduce their contribution. Equity theory emphasizes how employees can become dissatisfied with their jobs if they believe that they are not equitably compensated.

Supervisors may prevent job dissatisfaction by attempting to provide equitable compensation. However, their perception of an employee's contribution may differ from that of the employee. Supervisors commonly find that their employees tend to overestimate their contribution. That is, if each employee of a particular firm were

Exhibit 11.5
Example of Equity Theory

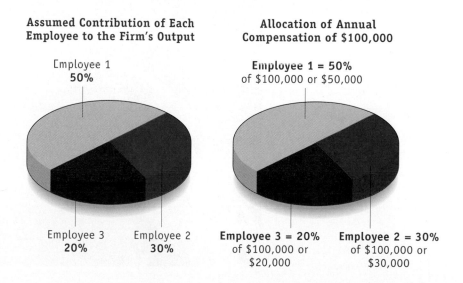

Assumed Contribution of Each Employee to the Firm's Output

Employee 1
50%

Employee 3
20%

Employee 2
30%

Allocation of Annual Compensation of $100,000

Employee 1 = 50%
of $100,000 or $50,000

Employee 3 = 20%
of $100,000 or $20,000

Employee 2 = 30%
of $100,000 or $30,000

Exhibit 11.6
Summary of Reinforcement
Theory

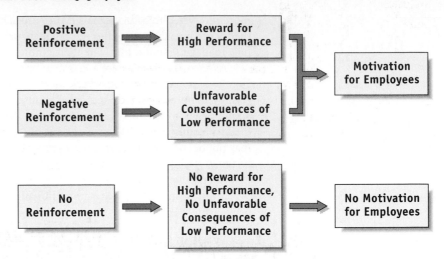

asked the percentage of his or her contribution to the firm's total output, the sum of these percentages would likely be greater than 100 percent. Thus, some employees will be dissatisfied with their compensation regardless of how the compensation is distributed. If a firm could define how to measure employee contributions, and compensate according to those contributions, its employees would be more satisfied and motivated.

Reinforcement Theory

reinforcement theory reinforcement can control behavior

positive reinforcement motivates employees by providing rewards for high performance

Reinforcement theory, summarized in Exhibit 11.6, suggests that reinforcement can control behavior. **Positive reinforcement** motivates employees by providing rewards for high performance. The various forms of positive reinforcement range from an oral compliment to a promotion or large bonus. Employees may differ in how they react to various forms of positive reinforcement. The more they appreciate the form of reinforcement, the more they will be motivated to continue high performance.

Recently retired baseball manager Tommy Lasorda (Los Angeles Dodgers) was well known for giving umpires like Eric Gress negative reinforcement on occasion.

negative reinforcement motivates employees by encouraging them to behave in a manner that avoids unfavorable consequences

Negative reinforcement motivates employees by encouraging them to behave in a manner that avoids unfavorable consequences. For example, employees may be motivated to complete their assignments today to avoid admitting the delay in a group meeting, or to avoid negative evaluations by their supervisors.

The various forms of negative reinforcement range from a reprimand to job termination. Some supervisors may prefer to consistently offer positive reinforcement for high performance rather than penalize for poor performance. However, offering positive reinforcement for all tasks that are adequately completed may be difficult. Furthermore, if an employee who has performed poorly is not given negative reinforcement, others may think that employee was given preferential treatment, which could cause a decline in the general performance of the other employees.

Motivational Guidelines Offered by Theories

If supervisors can increase employees' job satisfaction, they may motivate employees to be more productive. All of the theories on motivation are briefly summarized in Exhibit 11.7. Based on these theories, some general conclusions can be offered on motivating employees and providing job satisfaction:

1 Employees commonly compare their perceived compensation and contribution with others. To prevent job dissatisfaction, supervisors should attempt to ensure that employees are appropriately compensated for their contributions.

2 Even if employees are offered high compensation, they will not necessarily be very satisfied. They have other needs as well, such as social needs, responsibility, and self-esteem. Jobs that can fulfill these needs may provide more satisfaction, and therefore may also provide motivation.

3 Employees may be motivated if they believe that it is possible to achieve a level that will result in a desirable reward.

Exhibit 11.7
Comparison of Motivation Theories

Theory	Implications
Theory developed from Hawthorne studies	Workers can be motivated by attention.
Maslow's hierarchy of needs	Needs of workers vary, and managers can motivate workers to achieve these needs.
Herzberg's job satisfaction study	Compensation, reasonable working conditions, and other factors do not ensure job satisfaction but only prevent job dissatisfaction. Thus, other factors (such as responsibility) may be necessary to motivate workers.
McGregor's Theory X and Theory Y	Based on Theory X, workers will avoid work if possible, and cannot accept responsibility. Based on Theory Y, workers are willing to work and prefer more responsibility. If Theory Y exists, managers can motivate workers by delegating responsibility.
Expectancy theory	Workers are motivated if potential rewards for high performance are desirable and achievable.
Equity theory	Workers are motivated if they are being compensated in accordance with their perceived contribution to the firm.
Reinforcement theory	Good behavior should be positively reinforced and poor behavior should be negatively reinforced to motivate workers in the future.

HOW FIRMS CAN ENHANCE JOB SATISFACTION AND MOTIVATION

2 Explain how firms can enhance job satisfaction and therefore enhance motivation.

Many of the theories on motivation suggest that firms can motivate employees to perform well by ensuring job satisfaction. In general, the key characteristics that affect job satisfaction are money, security, work schedule, and involvement at work. Thus, the more common job enrichment programs used to enhance job satisfaction for employees are as follows:

➤ Adequate compensation program
➤ Job security
➤ Flexible work schedule
➤ Employee involvement programs

To the extent that firms can offer these job enrichment programs to employees, they may be able to motivate employees. Each program is discussed in turn.

Adequate Compensation Program

Firms can attempt to satisfy employees by offering adequate compensation for the work involved. However, adequate compensation will not necessarily motivate employees to make their best effort. Therefore, firms may attempt to ensure that those employees with the highest performance each year are granted the highest percentage raises.

merit system allocates raises according to performance (merit)

A **merit system** allocates raises according to performance (merit). For example, a firm may decide to give its employees an average raise of 5 percent, but the poorly performing employees may receive 0 percent while the highest performing employees receive 10 percent. This system provides positive reinforcement for employees who have performed well and negative reinforcement for those who have performed poorly. The merit system is normally more effective than the alternative **across-the-board system,** in which all employees are allocated a similar raise. The across-the-board system offers no motivation because the raise is unrelated to employee performance.

across-the-board system all employees are allocated a similar raise

Firms may attempt to align raises not only with employee performance but with other rewards as well. **Incentive plans** provide employees with various forms of compensation if they meet specific performance goals. For example, a firm may offer a weekly or monthly bonus based on the number of components an employee produced, or the dollar value of all products an employee sold to customers.

incentive plans provide employees with various forms of compensation if they meet specific performance goals

EXAMPLES OF COMPENSATION PROGRAMS   The compensation of Saturn Corporation is composed of base pay and "reward" pay that is tied to specific performance goals. The base pay is set lower than the norm for each job within the industry. However, the additional reward pay (tied to specific goals) can allow the total compensation to exceed the norm. Employees are more motivated to perform well because they benefit directly from high performance.

About one-fourth of the employees of Enterprise Rent-A-Car Company are compensated according to the firm's profits. Steelworkers at Nucor can earn annual bonuses that exceed their annual base salary. Many salespeople earn bonuses based on their own sales volume.

Kodak uses an incentive plan that allows each executive to earn a bonus based on his or her performance. The performance targets are set by the outside board members who are not employees of Kodak. The bonuses are based on performance measures such as revenue and earnings. Procter and Gamble Company provides bonuses to executives based on some nonfinancial measures, such as integrity and leadership.

The bonuses of CEOs at Salomon Brothers, General Electric, TRW, and many other firms are tied to the firm's performance. Performance measures may include revenue, earnings, production efficiency, and customer satisfaction.

Firms recognize how tying compensation to performance may increase job satisfaction and motivate employees. The following policies stated in recent annual reports confirm this:

> *A company lives or dies by results, and at Campbell, executive pay is linked directly to performance . . . and 100 percent of all incentive bonuses are tied to company performance.*
> —Campbell's Soup Company

> *We also recognize that compensation must reward performance and instill accountability.*
> —Digital Equipment Corporation

> *We are working hard to change the culture of the company by emphasizing and rewarding results, not activity.*
> —IBM

In addition to linking compensation with performance, some firms also grant stock to their employees as partial compensation for their work. The value of this type of compensation is dependent on the firm's stock price. To the extent that employees can enhance the firm's stock price with hard work, they can enhance their own compensation.

This form of compensation was initially used only for CEOs. In recent years, other top managers of firms have been granted stock as well, to keep them focused on enhancing the value of stock. Some firms have applied this concept to all or most of their employees. For example, all employees of Avis are given some shares of Avis stock. This may motivate them to perform well because their performance may enhance the value of the stock they own. One limitation of this approach is that some employees who own a small amount of stock may not believe that their work habits will have much influence on profits (and therefore on the stock price) of the firm. Thus, they will not be motivated if they do not expect that their stock's price will increase as a result of their efforts.

DEVELOPING A PROPER COMPENSATION PLAN   Most compensation plans that tie pay to performance are intended to motivate employees to achieve high performance. A compensation plan can motivate employees if it contains the following characteristics:

1 *Align Compensation Plan with Business Goals* Compensation formulas for employees should be set only after the goals of the business are established. This ensures that employees are rewarded in line with their ability to satisfy business goals.

2 *Align Compensation with Specific Employee Goals* A compensation plan will motivate employees more if it clearly specifies individual employee goals. Goals for an individual assembly-line employee should focus on specific job responsibilities

Mary Kay employees reap the benefits of salary rewards and status when they reach specific sales targets. This employee can eventually work her way up to a Cadillac. A successful outcome benefits both employee and company.

that the employee can control. Conversely, individual goals that specify high performance for the entire production plant are not under the control of a single employee, and therefore the employee will not be as motivated to perform well.

As an example, employees of a Monsanto chemical plant are compensated according to the performance of a group to which they belong within the firm. This compensation scheme has worked because the groups are small enough to allow employees to believe they have some control over the performance measurement. The employees were initially compensated according to the performance of the entire plant. Employees were not satisfied with this system because they did not believe they could influence the performance of the entire plant.

3 *Establish Achievable Goals for Employees* The compensation plan will work better if the goals specified for each employee are achievable. By offering numerous achievable bonuses, managers can increase each employee's perception of the chance to earn a reward. Firms with limited budgets for offering bonuses could offer rewards that are less extravagant but still desirable.

Rewards that are desirable and achievable will motivate employees only if they are aware of the bonuses. If the firm decides at the end of the year to offer rewards, it is too late to motivate employees for that year. Levels of motivation will be higher if employees know about the potential for bonuses at the beginning of the year.

4 *Allow Employee Input on Compensation Plan* The compensation plan should be developed only after receiving input from employees on how they should be rewarded. While some employee requests may be unreasonable, allowing employee input can improve job satisfaction.

Job Security

Employees who have job security may be more motivated to perform well. They are less likely to be distracted at work because of a concern about finding a more secure job.

While firms recognize how job security can motivate their employees, they may not be able to guarantee job security. A weakened U.S. economy lowers the demand for the goods and services provided by U.S. firms, so that these firms cannot afford

Spreading Motivation Across Business Functions

When a firm uses compensation or other incentives to motivate employees, it must attempt to implement this program across all of its business functions. Since business functions interact, motivating employees who perform one type of function will have limited effects if employees performing other functions are not motivated.

Consider an example in which a firm's production employees are given new incentives to perform well, while marketing employees are not given any new incentives. The quality of the product achieved by the production department is somewhat dependent on the feedback it receives from marketing employees who conduct customer satisfaction surveys. Also, the pro-

duction department's ability to produce an adequate supply of a product is dependent on the sales forecasts provided by the marketing department. If the sales forecast is too low, the production department may produce an insufficient volume, resulting in shortages.

Production tasks can also affect marketing tasks because effective marketing strategies will result in higher sales only if a sufficient volume of products is produced. Employees assigned to a specific function rely on employees assigned to other functions. Thus, employees who are assigned to a given function and are motivated can achieve high performance only if the other employees they rely on are motivated.

to retain all of their employees. Even when the economy is strong, some firms are pressured to lay off employees to reduce expenses.

Firms can provide more job security by training employees to handle various tasks so that they can be assigned other duties if their typical assignments are no longer needed. Yet, the firm may not have any job openings to which employees can be reassigned. Further, the job openings may be so different that reassignments are not possible. Workers on an assembly line would not normally be qualified to perform accounting or financial analysis jobs for an automobile manufacturer.

JOB SECURITY IN JAPAN Employees of Japanese firms tend to have much more job security and are commonly given lifetime job guarantees. Because employment is secure, employees may be less resistant to changes within a firm. For example, Japanese firms have automated their production to a greater degree than U.S. firms. Employees who are replaced by robots are less resistant to change because they recognize that they will be trained for other jobs within the firm. Also, Japanese firms are more willing to provide the training because employees are less likely to switch to a competitive firm after receiving the training. Lifetime job guarantees encourage employees to remain at the same firm. Furthermore, employees who are given lifetime job guarantees take a greater interest in serving the firm because their future employment is dependent on the firm's survival. U.S. employees may not have the same attitude toward their firm because they may view it as a temporary place of employment until they switch to another firm.

Flexible Work Schedule

One method of increasing job satisfaction is to implement programs that allow for a more flexible work schedule (called **flextime programs**). Some firms have experimented with a **compressed work week,** which compresses the work load into fewer days per week. The most common example is to change a five-day, eight-hour-per-day work week into four days at ten hours per day. The main purpose of this schedule is to allow employees to have three-day weekends. When employees are on a schedule that they prefer, they are more motivated to perform well.

flextime programs programs that allow for a more flexible work schedule

compressed work week compresses the work load into fewer days per week

Using Computers to Motivate Employees

In the 1950s and 1960s, using a computer on the job meant sitting at a keyboard, performing mind-numbing data entry tasks. In today's business world, the situation is often radically different. Rather than making jobs more boring, computers are often used to expand the scope of a job and motivate employees. As a result, potential users are often eager to start using such systems.

As an example, consider the application of computers to mortgage loans. For most of this century, mortgage loans for housing were simple financial instruments, offered primarily by savings and loan (S&L) institutions. However, the number and types of financial institutions able to offer mortgages increased dramatically in the 1980s. These changes to the mortgage industry meant that many banks' branches were unable to offer mortgage products as part of their customer service. Both the branches and the bank headquarters considered the situation undesirable; not only did it mean a potential revenue stream was being lost, but it also precluded the bank from becoming a one-stop financial center for its customers.

To alleviate the problem, the Bank of Boston's advanced technology group developed a program called the Mortgage Originator. It applied rules for mortgage origination derived from managers at the bank's headquarters. It also maintained a full database of existing mortgage products, contained rules for qualifying customers in accordance with reselling guidelines, and even allowed its users to determine if customers could qualify for larger mortgages. Using the system, branch officers could create complex mortgages for customers. They were motivated to use the system by virtue of its ability to increase the scope of their jobs.

---

job sharing two or more persons may share a particular work schedule

Another form of a flexible work schedule is **job sharing,** where two or more persons may share a particular work schedule. For example, a firm that needs a forty-hour work week for deliveries may hire two people to share that position. This allows employees to work part-time to fulfill other obligations such as school or family.

Employee Involvement Programs

Based on theories summarized earlier, employees would be more motivated if they play a bigger role in the firm, either by being more involved in decisions or by being assigned more responsibility. Various methods are used by firms to allow more employee involvement and responsibility.

job enlargement program to expand (enlarge) the jobs assigned to employees

JOB ENLARGEMENT   One method of increasing employee responsibility is to use **job enlargement,** which is a program to expand (enlarge) the jobs assigned to employees. Job enlargement has been implemented at numerous firms such as Motorola and Xerox Corporation, which experienced downsizing in the 1990s. The program was implemented not only to motivate employees but also to reduce operating expenses.

job rotation allows a set of employees to periodically rotate their job assignments

JOB ROTATION   **Job rotation** allows a set of employees to periodically rotate their job assignments. For example, an assembly-line operation may involve five different types of assignments. Each worker may focus on one assignment per week and switch assignments at the beginning of the next week. In this way, a workers does five different assignments over each five-week period.

Job rotation not only may reduce boredom but also can prepare employees for other jobs if their primary job position is eliminated. In this way, employees can remain employed by the firm. For example, if the demand for a specific type of car declines, the manufacturer of that car may attempt to reassign the employees who worked on that car to work on other cars or trucks.

SELF-SCORING EXERCISE

Are You an Empowered Employee?*

Read each of the following statements carefully. Then, to the right, indicate which answer best expresses your level of agreement (5 = strongly agree, 4 = agree, 3 = sometimes agree/sometimes disagree, 2 = disagree, 1 = strongly disagree, and 0 = undecided/do not know). Mark only one answer for each item, and remember to respond to all items. Remember that *work group* means all persons who report to the same manager as you do, regardless of their job titles.

_____ 1. I feel free to tell my manager what I think.	5	4	3	2	1	0
_____ 2. My manager is willing to listen to my concerns.	5	4	3	2	1	0
_____ 3. My manager asks for my ideas about things affecting our work.	5	4	3	2	1	0
_____ 4. My manager treats me with respect and dignity.	5	4	3	2	1	0
_____ 5. My manager keeps me informed about things I need to know.	5	4	3	2	1	0
_____ 6. My manager lets me do my job without interfering.	5	4	3	2	1	0
_____ 7. My manager's boss gives us the support we need.	5	4	3	2	1	0
_____ 8. Upper management (directors and above) pays attention to ideas and suggestions from people at my level.	5	4	3	2	1	0

Scoring

To determine if you are an empowered employee, add your scores.

32–40: You are empowered! Managers listen when you speak, respect your ideas, and allow you to do your work.

24–31: You have *some* power! Your ideas are considered sometimes and you have some freedom of action.

16–23: You must exercise caution. You cannot speak or act too boldly and your managers appear to exercise close supervision.

 8–15: Your wings are clipped! You work in a powerless, restrictive work environment.

*If you are not employed, discuss these questions with a friend who is employed. Is your friend an empowered employee?

EMPOWERMENT AND PARTICIPATIVE MANAGEMENT   In recent years, supervisors of many firms have delegated more authority to their employees. This strategy is referred to as **empowerment,** as it allows employees power to make more decisions. The concept of empowerment is more specific than job enlargement because it focuses on increased authority, whereas job enlargement may not necessarily result in more authority. Empowerment may motivate those employees who are more satisfied when they have more authority. Also, they may be in a better position to make decisions on the tasks they perform than supervisors who are not directly involved in those tasks.

The strategy of empowerment is related to the concept of **participative management,** in which employees are allowed to participate in various decisions. For example, Chrysler has a program in which individual workers are asked for suggestions on cost cutting or improving quality. Managers are asked to review these suggestions and respond to the workers within a few days.

empowerment allows employees power to make more decisions

participative management employees are allowed to participate in various decisions to be made by their supervisors or others

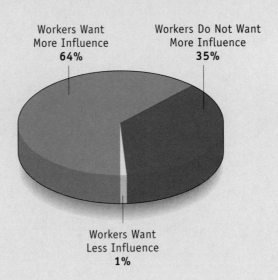

SMALL BUSINESS SURVEY

Do Employees Want More Influence in Business Decisions?

Employees may desire to be involved in business decision making because it increases their degree of influence on the firm's performance. In recent years, the restructuring of firms has resulted in substantially more responsibilities for many employees. A survey of 4,500 workers of various firms was conducted to determine whether workers still wanted to have more influence in business decisions. The results are disclosed in the following chart:

Workers Want
More Influence
64%

Workers Do Not Want
More Influence
35%

Workers Want
Less Influence
1%

The results suggest that even with the recent efforts of firms to give their employees more power and responsibility, employees would generally prefer more responsibility.

---

management by objectives (MBO) allows employees to participate in setting their goals and determining the manner by which they achieve their tasks

Technically, empowerment assigns decision-making responsibilities to employees, while participative management simply allows the employees input in decisions. In reality, both terms are used to reflect more responsibilities for employees, whether they have complete or partial influence on decisions. The higher level of involvement by employees is supported by Theory Z, which was discussed earlier.

A popular form of participative management is **management by objectives (MBO),** which often allows employees to set their goals and determine the manner by which they achieve their tasks. Their participation can be beneficial because they are closer to the production process. In addition, they may use their own creativity to achieve the goals, if their tasks can be completed in various ways.

MBO is commonly applied to salespeople by assigning a monthly sales *quota* (or goal) that is based on historical sales. Yet, the actual sales volume may be dependent on the state of the economy. Care must be taken to assign a goal that is achievable.

For production employees, a production volume goal is specified. Some employees may reduce their quality of work to reach the goal. Thus, objectives must be stated to ensure adequate quality as well as quantity.

teamwork a group of employees with varied job positions are given the responsibility to achieve a specific goal

TEAMWORK   Another form of employee involvement is **teamwork,** in which a group of employees with varied job positions are given the responsibility to achieve a specific goal. Goodyear Tire and Rubber Company uses more than two thousand

These Motorola engineers are working on the design of a sophisticated DSP GPS System. To solve difficult technological design problems, the input of many Motorola highly trained people is needed.

project teams to achieve its goals. A classic example of teamwork is Chrysler's strategy to create new ideas. Chrysler has encouraged workers on its assembly line to offer ideas on production and quality control. More than one thousand assembly-line workers from its Belvidere plant teamed up with Chrysler's engineers to design the Chrysler Neon. They also helped design the training program to produce the Neon. The level of job satisfaction at the Belvidere plant increased substantially after involving assembly-line workers in decisions.

Chrysler has continued to design cars with input from assembly-line workers. Executives establish general guidelines on a type of automobile that would satisfy consumers. The workers are then assembled in teams to work out the design details.

When Jaguar (a subsidiary of Ford Motor Company) desired to improve its customer service, its executives initially attempted to instruct employees to provide better service. However, motivating employees was difficult because they were not satisfied with their jobs. The executives decided to create worker involvement groups to develop a plan for improved customer service. The employees were more willing to deal with the problem once they were allowed to search for the best solution.

open-book management educates employees on their contribution to the firm and enables them to periodically assess their own performance levels

OPEN-BOOK MANAGEMENT Another form of employee involvement is **open-book management,** which educates employees on their contribution to the firm and enables them to periodically assess their own performance levels. Open-book management educates employees on how they affect the key performance measures that are relevant for the firm's owners. In this way, it encourages employees to make decisions and conduct tasks as if they were the firm's owners.

The three distinct characteristics of open-book management are:

1 The firm educates all employees on the key performance measurements that affect the firm's profits and value, and ensures that these performance measurements are widely available to employees over time (like an "open book" on the firm's performance). For example, various revenue, expense, and production figures may be displayed daily or weekly in the work area.

2 As employees are given the power to make decisions, they are trained to understand how the results of their decisions will affect the firm's overall performance.

Thus, salespeople recognize how their efforts affect the firm's total revenue, while engineers recognize how their efforts reduce the cost of producing a product. Many job positions are not tied directly to revenue or total expenses. Therefore, it is helpful to break performance into pieces that employees can relate to, such as number of customer complaints, proportion of product defects, and percentage of tasks completed on time. Each of these pieces influences the total demand for the firm's product (and therefore the firm's revenue), as well as the expenses incurred.

3 The compensation of employees is typically aligned with their contribution to the firm's overall performance. They may earn some stock, so that they are not only employees but also shareholders. This reinforces their focus on making decisions that will enhance the firm's value and therefore its stock price. In addition, firms may provide annual pay raises only to employees who helped improve the firm's performance. While educating employees on how their work affects the firm's value is useful, a firm may still need to compensate employees for their performance in order to motivate them. Firms may set specific annual performance targets for employees and then continually update employees on performance levels throughout the year.

Comparison of Methods Used to Enhance Job Satisfaction

The methods that can enhance job satisfaction and therefore motivate employees are compared in Exhibit 11.8. Each type of program offers a different method of enhancing an employee's job satisfaction. When firms develop a set of programs that satisfy employees, they will be more effective in motivating employees to achieve high performance. Therefore, programs can improve a firm's profits and value.

While firms have increased their use of these programs, most have not been able to offer job security. In the 1990s, many firms attempted to become more efficient by downsizing, which eliminated numerous job positions. In 1995 alone, more than four hundred thousand jobs were cut by U.S. firms. Although workers are more satisfied with the additional responsibilities assigned to them in recent years, they still have little job security.

Exhibit 11.8
Methods Used to Enhance Job Satisfaction

Program	Description
1. Adequate compensation program	Align raises with performance. Align bonuses with performance. Provide stock as partial compensation.
2. Job security	Encourage employees to have a long-term commitment to the firm.
3. Flexible work schedule	Allow employees flexibility on the timing of their work schedule.
4. Employee involvement programs	Implement job enlargement. Implement job rotation. Implement empowerment and participative management. Implement teamwork. Implement open-book management.

Motivating Employees Across Countries

The techniques used to motivate employees in the United States may not necessarily be successful for motivating employees in other countries. For example, consider a U.S. firm that has just established a production plant in Eastern Europe. European employees' views on conditions necessary for job satisfaction may differ from those of U.S. production workers. In general, U.S. firms have successfully motivated production workers in the United States by giving them more responsibilities. However, the assignment of additional responsibilities may not motivate production workers in Eastern Europe, especially if those workers have less experience and education. These workers could even be overwhelmed by the extra responsibilities. They might be less capable of striving for efficiency, since their past work experience was in an environment that did not stress efficiency.

In some situations, a U.S. firm may be more capable of motivating foreign workers than U.S. workers. For example, General Motors established a plant in what was then East Germany to produce automobiles. When it trained the workers at this plant, it explained the need for production efficiency to ensure the plant's survival. It asked the workers to provide suggestions on how the plant could increase its production efficiency. These workers offered ten times the number of suggestions that were offered by workers of other General Motors plants in Europe. An entire automobile can be assembled in twenty hours at the East German plant, which is faster than the production time at any other General Motors plant. The efficiency of the workers at the East German plant may be attributed to the background of the workers. While these workers did not have many years of experience on automobile assembly lines, they also had not learned any bad habits that were more prevalent when production assembly systems were less efficient. Thus, these workers were more capable of learning an efficient production system.

Overall, the firm's ability to motivate workers in a specific country may depend on characteristics that are not under the firm's control. Workers who would lose their jobs if the firm performs poorly may be more motivated, regardless of the firm's motivation strategies. Workers based in countries with fewer opportunities may be more motivated, since they may appreciate their existing jobs more than workers in other countries. Given these differences, a firm may consider using varying motivation strategies for workers in different countries. In general, a firm should attempt to determine what conditions would increase the job satisfaction of workers in a particular country, and provide those conditions for workers who perform well.

BUSINESS DILEMMA

COLLEGE HEALTH CLUB

Motivation at College Health Club

Sue Kramer, president of College Health Club (CHC), is searching for a way to motivate Lisa Lane, who was hired mainly as an aerobics instructor but also performs other minor tasks. Lisa works part-time and will graduate from college in one year. Sue makes all the decisions, even those related to the scheduling and format of aerobics classes. If CHC's business increases, Sue wants to hire Lisa full-time to help with various tasks and decisions. Lisa's main focus right now is completing her degree.

While Lisa is an adequate aerobics instructor, she has much potential for running a business and will likely become bored if used only as an instructor.

Dilemma

Sue wants to enhance Lisa's job satisfaction so that Lisa will be willing to continue her part-time job until Sue can afford to hire her full-time. However, Sue is not presently in a position to increase Lisa's hourly wage. Sue needs to develop alternative ways in which she can satisfy Lisa and encourage her to remain employed at CHC. Offer your own recommendations to Sue on the ways in which she may encourage Lisa to remain employed at CHC.

Solution

While Sue could enhance Lisa's job satisfaction in various possible ways, she decides on the following:

1 Allow Lisa some flexibility on what hours she would serve as instructor for aerobics classes (although the classes would have to be offered at times desired by CHC members).

2 Allow Lisa to offer input on various decisions, such as ways to increase membership and the types of exercise classes to be offered. If Lisa is more involved in decision making, she might be more willing to take a full-time position at CHC rather than at some other firm once she obtains her degree.

This strategy not only allows Lisa more power but also may improve decision making, because Lisa is more involved with the classes and may have ideas about what would satisfy the customers (members).

Sue also considers promising Lisa a future full-time job to discourage her from seeking another job in the future. This would provide Lisa with job security. Sue cannot afford to hire Lisa full-time unless CHC's membership grows. So she promises Lisa a full-time job in one year if membership grows to four hundred.

Overall, Sue is attempting to enhance Lisa's job satisfaction with flextime, empowerment, and job security.

Additional Issues for Discussion

1 Do you think Sue Kramer's esteem and self-actualization needs are fulfilled in her present position at CHC?

2 Do you think Lisa Lane's esteem and self-actualization needs are fulfilled in her present position at CHC?

3 Explain how expectancy theory may be used to explain how Sue is motivated to perform well at CHC.

SUMMARY

1 The main theories on motivation are as follows:

➤ The Hawthorne studies suggest that employees are more motivated when they receive more attention.

➤ Maslow's hierarchy of needs theory suggests that employees are satisfied by different needs, depending on their position within the hierarchy. Firms can satisfy employees at the low end of the hierarchy with job security or safe working conditions. Once basic needs are fulfilled, employees have other needs that must be met. Firms can attempt to satisfy these employees by allowing social interaction or more responsibilities.

➤ Herzberg's job satisfaction study suggests that the factors that prevent job dissatisfaction are different from those that enhance job satisfaction. An adequate salary and working conditions prevent job dissatisfaction, while responsibility and recognition enhance job satisfaction.

➤ McGregor's Theories X and Y suggest that when supervisors believe employees dislike work and responsibilities (Theory X), they do not delegate responsibilities and employees are not motivated; when supervisors believe that employees prefer responsibilities, they delegate more responsibilities, which motivates employees.

➤ Theory Z suggests that employees are more satisfied when they are involved in decision making, and therefore may be more motivated.

➤ Expectancy theory suggests that employees are more motivated if compensation is aligned with goals that are achievable and offer some reward.

➤ Equity theory suggests that employees are more motivated if their compensation is aligned with their relative contribution to the firm's total output.

➤ Reinforcement theory suggests that employees are more motivated to perform well if they are rewarded for high performance (positive reinforcement) and penalized for poor performance (negative reinforcement).

2 Firms can enhance job satisfaction and therefore motivate employees by providing:

➤ an adequate compensation program, which aligns compensation with performance,
➤ job security,
➤ a flexible work schedule, and
➤ employee involvement programs.

KEY TERMS

across-the-board system	incentive plans	open-book management
compressed work week	job enlargement	participative management
empowerment	job rotation	physiological needs
equity theory	job satisfaction	positive reinforcement
esteem needs	job sharing	reinforcement theory
expectancy theory	management by objectives (MBO)	safety needs
flextime programs	merit system	self-actualization
hierarchy of needs	motivational factors	social needs
hygiene factors	negative reinforcement	teamwork

REVIEW QUESTIONS

1 Distinguish Theory X from Theory Y perceptions of management.

2 Describe Herzberg's job satisfaction study on worker motivation.

3 Identify the categories of Maslow's hierarchy of needs theory.

4 Discuss how managers utilize strategic planning to motivate their employees and to maximize the value of the firm.

5 Identify and explain methods that will enhance job satisfaction and motivate employees.

6 Describe how empowerment is related to participative management.

7 Discuss the equity theory of motivation.

8 Identify and explain how a manager could utilize reinforcement theories of motivation.

9 Describe how expectancy theory can motivate behavior.

10 Discuss the methods used to motivate employees in the United States. Should the same methods be used to motivate employees in other countries?

DISCUSSION QUESTIONS

1 Assume that you are a manager who recognizes that your employees are motivated by money. How could you stimulate their performance at work?

2 Would motivational techniques be more important for the Atlanta Braves than for an organization such as General Motors?

3 Assume that you are a manager of a video store. Which theory of motivation would best motivate employee behavior?

4 Would you consider using negative reinforcement to improve the performance of lazy employees?

5 Do you think the various theories of motivation support one another?

RUNNING YOUR OWN BUSINESS

1 How can you empower your employees (if at all) so that they have an incentive to perform well?

2 Describe how you might encourage your employees to use teamwork.

3 Describe how each of the theories discussed in this chapter would apply to your employees or yourself.

INVESTING IN THE STOCK OF A BUSINESS

Using the annual report of the firm in which you would like to invest, complete the following:

1 Does the firm appear to recognize that its employees are the key to its success?

2 Does the firm empower its workers? Does it encourage teamwork? Provide details.

CASE 1 Using Motivation to Enhance Performance

Tom Fry is a plant manager for Ligonier Steel Corporation, located in Ligonier, Pennsylvania. The plant is small, with 250 employees. Its productivity growth rate has stagnated for the past year and a half.

Tom is concerned and decides to meet with employees in various departments. During the meeting, employees disclose that they do not have a chance to interact with one another while on the job. Because they do not receive any recognition for their suggestions, their input of ideas for improvement has stopped.

After a week elapses, Tom calls a meeting to announce a new program. He plans to offer rewards for high performance so that employees will be motivated to surpass their quotas. Bonuses will be offered to employees who exceed their quotas. Tom believes this program will work because of his perception that "money motivates employees."

A few months later, Tom notices that productivity has increased, and employees are enjoying the bonuses they have earned. Tom decides to provide an additional means of motivation. He wants employees to continue to interact with one another to solve work problems and share information. Supervisors now recognize individual accomplishments. They congratulate employees when suggestions are made and identify an employee of the month in the company newsletter to recognize outstanding performance. Tom strongly supports this feature of the program.

The goal is for employees to grow and develop to their fullest potential. Individuals may be retrained or go back to college to permit job growth within the plant. Employees' ideas and contributions are now perceived as a way to enhance their individual career paths. The results have been overwhelming. Tom Fry, supervisors, and employees have all enjoyed the benefits that have made Ligonier Steel a satisfying place to work, for everyone.

Questions

1 Describe the motivation theory that applies to this case.

2 What needs can employees at Ligonier Steel satisfy in performing their jobs?

3 Describe how bonuses motivated the employees at Ligonier Steel.

4 Describe other rewards besides bonuses that can motivate behavior at work.

CASE 2 Motivating Young Employees

Joyce Cline, a manager of a Houston country club, has 125 employees working under her direction. Many of these employees are young and working their way through college. She assumes that many of these younger employees are unmotivated, easily distracted, and arrogant. Joyce has stereotyped these workers as "slackers."

Because of her negative employee perceptions, Joyce has developed a manipulative style of management. She has coerced these employees and threatened them to motivate their behavior at work.

Because of these inherent problems, Janice Ickes, the human resource director, is consulted, and she meets with Joyce. Janice's perception of younger employees is different. She believes that younger employees are misunderstood, and that job instability and the breakdown of traditional employer-employee relationships are responsible for motivation problems. Janice believes that employees are willing to work and prefer more responsibility.

Employees should be encouraged to exercise creativity in performing their jobs. Consequently, these employees are likely to be more motivated because they should be more satisfied with their jobs.

Joyce admits that maybe there could be a better way to manage younger people. She assures Janice that she will consider her advice and develop a new attitude in managing younger people.

Questions

1 Describe Joyce's initial approach to the motivation of employees at work.

2 Describe Janice's approach to the motivation of employees at work.

3 To what does Janice attribute the motivational problems of these younger employees?

4 Will Janice's approach motivate all employees?

VIDEO CASE Motivating Employees as a Means of Survival

A few years ago, Nevada Communication Services (referred to as "The Continuum" on the video) was one sick health-care enterprise. Its revenues for the year were down to $315,000, less than half what they had been two years earlier, and they were continuing to shrink.

Diane Ross, Nevada Communication's president and founder, met the challenge of less demand by offering a greater supply of services.

Four steps have been crucial in what has proved to be a successful expansion of services, she says. First, she and the staff—currently twenty—committed themselves to a vision of what the company would become and wrote a business plan. The writing process "provided us with a road map giving a clearer picture of where we were, where we were going, and what we had to do to accomplish our goals. It also served as a great reality check."

Second, the staff has been turned into a team. Classes have been held to explain each of the company's services and the needs of those served. Staff members have been trained in areas outside their job descriptions, so they can fill in if there is a shortage of help. Monthly pot-luck dinners are held at which the staff—a diverse group from diverse fields—comes together "to share, celebrate, and sometimes grieve," Ross says.

Third, everyone shares responsibility for the enterprise's future. "All of us market. Each staff member is responsible for areas for improvement, from spotting a faulty piece of equipment and taking immediate action to addressing a customer complaint."

And fourth is what Ross calls "our biggest challenge." She explains: "We have encouraged staff to open their minds to seeing different perspectives and to take a chance on doing something in a different way. Take a risk. Make a mistake."

Questions

1 Explain how Nevada Communication Services may have increased its employee satisfaction level and motivation with its new policies.

2 Would the new policies enacted by Nevada Communication Services be effective for any firm? Can you think of any reason why some employees may not necessarily be satisfied?

3 The policies enacted by Nevada Communication Services were successful in motivating its employees. Yet, these policies may have some possible adverse effects, even if they do motivate employees. State some possible adverse effects that could result from these policies.

THE Coca-Cola COMPANY ANNUAL REPORT PROJECT

The following questions apply concepts learned in this chapter to The Coca-Cola Company. Read page 29 in The Coca-Cola Company annual report before answering these questions.

1 Given that The Coca-Cola Company attempts to improve the abilities of all its employees to find opportunities that others cannot, do you think that a Theory X management style would be appropriate at The Coca-Cola Company?

2 Would rigid salary scales be appropriate for The Coca-Cola Company?

3 How might methods of motivating employees differ across countries within The Coca-Cola Company? Do you think you would be motivated to work at The Coca-Cola Company?

IN-TEXT STUDY GUIDE

Answers are in an appendix at the back of the book.

True or False

1 Most compensation plans that tie pay to performance are intended to motivate employees to achieve high performance.

2 The performance of a firm is highly dependent on the performance of its employees.

3 A merit system allocates raises for all employees according to sales of the firm.

4 The compensation plan of a firm should be completely developed by its employees, without managers' input.

5 Open-book management encourages employees to make decisions and conduct tasks as if they were the firm's owners.

6 According to Frederick Herzberg, better-than-adequate work conditions and salary always lead to a high degree of job satisfaction.

7 A supervisor who believes in Theory Y will use tight control over workers and would discourage creativity.

8 Equity theory suggests that an employee's efforts are influenced by the expected outcome of those efforts.

9 Employees of Japanese firms tend to have much more job security than U.S. employees.

10 The hierarchy of needs theory, developed by Abraham Maslow, states that all employees need to be paid adequately, and that they will be very satisfied with their jobs if they are paid adequately.

Multiple Choice

11 The compensation of employees is typically aligned with their contribution to the firm's:
a) hierarchy of needs.
b) industry demand.
c) overall performance.
d) reinforcement theory.
e) hygiene theory.

12 By _____ employees to properly perform the tasks they are assigned, management can maximize the firm's value.
a) motivating
b) threatening
c) coercing
d) manipulating
e) harassing

13 A form of employee involvement that educates employees on their contribution to the firm and enables them to periodically assess their own performance levels is:
a) Theory X management.
b) open-book management.
c) Theory Y management.
d) Theory Z management.
e) Theory J management.

14 In addition to linking compensation with performance, some firms grant employees _____ for good performance.
a) negative reinforcement
b) suspensions
c) demotions
d) time-share
e) common stock

15 A form of employee involvement in which a group of employees with varied job positions are given the responsibility to achieve a specific goal is:
a) teamwork.
b) Theory X management.
c) job rotation.
d) demotivation.
e) manipulation.

16 A method of increasing job satisfaction is to implement:
a) Theory X management.
b) negative reinforcement.
c) punishment.
d) flextime programs.
e) avoidance techniques.

17 The degree to which employees are satisfied with their jobs is:
a) job satisfaction.
b) motivation.
c) behavior modeling.
d) exploitiveness.
e) coerciveness.

18 When firms delegate more authority to their employees, this strategy is referred to as:
a) Theory X management.
b) empowerment.
c) hygiene theory.
d) coerciveness.
e) manipulation.

19 A form of participative management that allows employees to participate in setting their goals and determining the manner by which they achieve their tasks is:
a) equity theory of motivation.
b) expectancy theory of motivation.
c) management by objectives.
d) Theory X management.
e) Theory Y management.

20 A program to expand the jobs assigned to employees is called:
a) hygiene theory.
b) downsizing.
c) positive reinforcement.
d) equity theory of motivation.
e) job enlargement.

21 Social interaction and acceptance by others are examples of:
a) physiological needs.
b) esteem needs.
c) safety needs.
d) social needs.
e) self-actualization needs.

22 The reinforcement theory that motivates employees by encouraging them to behave in a manner that avoids unfavorable consequences is _____ reinforcement.
a) positive
b) punishment
c) avoidance

d) negative
e) extinction

23 Needs that are satisfied with food, clothing, and shelter are called _____ needs.
a) safety
b) social
c) affiliation
d) self-esteem
e) physiological

24 In the late 1950s, a study by Frederick Herzberg surveyed two hundred accountants and engineers about:
a) job satisfaction.
b) downsizing.
c) reinforcement theory.
d) Theory X management.
e) expectancy theory.

25 _____ states that workers will be motivated if they are compensated in accordance with their perceived contributions to the firm.
a) Expectancy theory
b) Equity theory
c) Need theory
d) Theory Y
e) Reinforcement theory

26 An employee involvement program that periodically moves individuals from one job assignment to another is:
a) job enlargement.
b) job enrichment.
c) job rotation.
d) job sharing.
e) flextime.

27 The following are methods used to enhance job satisfaction except:
a) employee involvement programs.
b) Theory X management.
c) job security.
d) adequate compensation programs.
e) flexible work schedules.

28 According to Herzberg, employees are commonly satisfied when offered:
a) downsizing.
b) negative reinforcement.
c) motivational factors.
d) less responsibility.
e) Theory X management.

29 Theory Z suggests that employees are more satisfied when they are involved in:
a) coercive tactics.
b) manipulation.
c) punishment.

d) extinction.

e) decision making.

30 In an across-the-board system, all employees receive similar:

a) raises.

b) job assignments.

c) offices.

d) work schedules.

e) performance appraisals.

31 _____ can reduce boredom and prepare employees for other jobs if their primary job is eliminated.

a) Job evaluation

b) Job rotation

c) Reengineering

d) Performance appraisal

e) Reinforcement

32 If managers recognize employee needs, they are better able to offer rewards that would _____ employees.

a) exploit

b) coerce

c) motivate

d) manipulate

e) threaten

33 One implication of the Hawthorne studies is that workers can be motivated by receiving:

a) attention.

b) money.

c) stock.

d) bonuses.

e) profit sharing.

34 Plans offered to employees that provide various forms of compensation if they meet specific performance goals are:

a) projects.

b) programs.

c) affirmative action plans.

d) reinforcement theories.

e) incentive plans.

35 Two or more persons sharing a particular work schedule is called:

a) job enlargement.

b) job enrichment.

c) job sharing.

d) flextime.

e) job rotation.

Surfing the Net

Exhibit 11.9
Foundation for Enterprise
Development Web Site

http://www.fed.org/fed

Employee Ownership Information on the World Wide Web

Firms can motivate employees by offering them stock as partial ownership in the firm, known as equity compensation. The Foundation for Enterprise Development web site (Exhibit 11.9) maintains links to sources of information on equity compensation and other business-related topics.

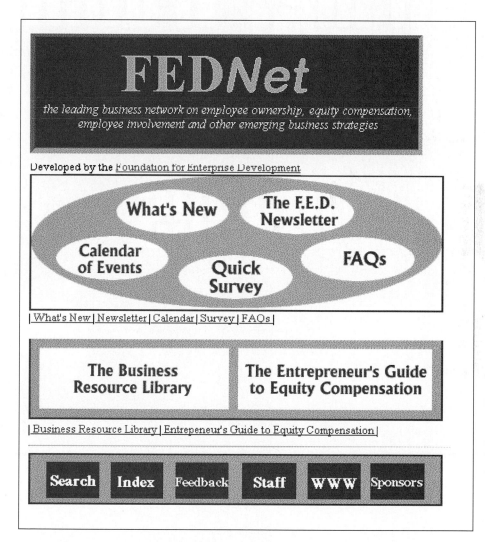

FED*Net*

the leading business network on employee ownership, equity compensation, employee involvement and other emerging business strategies

Developed by the Foundation for Enterprise Development

What's New

The F.E.D. Newsletter

Calendar of Events

Quick Survey

FAQs

| What's New | Newsletter | Calendar | Survey | FAQs |

The Business Resource Library

The Entrepreneur's Guide to Equity Compensation

| Business Resource Library | Entrepeneur's Guide to Equity Compensation |

Search   Index   Feedback   Staff   WWW   Sponsors

CHAPTER 12

Hiring, Training, and Evaluating Employees

A key to a firm's performance is its human resources (employees). Therefore, a firm's performance is dependent on how human resources are managed. The management of human resources involves recruiting employees, developing their skills, and evaluating their performance.

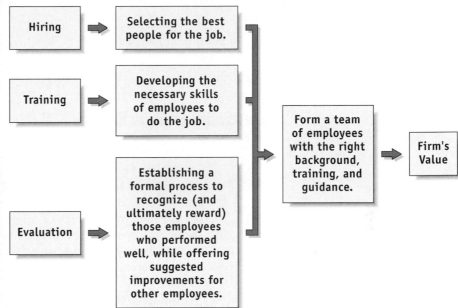

Hiring	→	Selecting the best people for the job.
Training	→	Developing the necessary skills of employees to do the job.
Evaluation	→	Establishing a formal process to recognize (and ultimately reward) those employees who performed well, while offering suggested improvements for other employees.

→ Form a team of employees with the right background, training, and guidance. → Firm's Value

Consider the case of Southwest Airlines, which has seen great success in recent years and has rapidly expanded its routes throughout most of the United States. What information should Southwest use to determine how many pilots and other types of employees to hire? What type of training can Southwest provide to new pilots beyond that which was received when the pilots pursued their pilot's license? How can Southwest evaluate the performance of its pilots and other employees? This chapter focuses on managing the hiring, training, and evaluating of employees, which can be used to address these questions.

The **Learning Goals** of this chapter are to:

1 Explain human resource planning by firms.

2 Differentiate among the types of compensation that firms offer to employees.

3 Describe the skills of employees that firms develop.

4 Explain how the performance of employees can be evaluated.

HUMAN RESOURCE PLANNING

1 **Explain human resource planning by firms.**

human resource planning the act of planning to satisfy a firm's needs for employees

Human resource planning is the act of planning to satisfy a firm's needs for employees. It is composed of three tasks:

➤ Forecasting employee needs
➤ Job analysis
➤ Recruiting

Forecasting Employee Needs

If employee needs can be anticipated in advance, the firm has more time to satisfy those needs. Some needs for human resources occur as workers retire or take a job with another firm. Retirement can be forecasted with some degree of accuracy. However, forecasting when an employee will take a job with another firm is difficult.

Additional needs for employees result from expansion. These needs may be determined by assessing growth trends in a firm. For example, if the firm is expected to increase production by 10 percent (in response to increased sales), it may prepare for the creation of new positions to achieve the projected production level. Positions that handle accounting and marketing related tasks may not be affected by the increased production level.

If the firm foresees a temporary need for higher production, it may avoid hiring new workers, since it would soon have to lay them off. Layoffs not only affect the laid-off workers but also scare those workers who are still employed. In addition, firms that become notorious for layoffs will be less capable of recruiting people for new positions.

Since firms avoid hiring during a temporary increase in production, they must achieve their objective in some other way. A common method is to offer overtime to existing workers. An alternative method is to hire temporarily for part-time or seasonal work.

Once new positions are created, they must be filled. This normally involves a job analysis and recruiting, which are discussed in turn.

Job Analysis

job analysis the analysis used to determine the tasks and the necessary credentials for a particular position

job specification states the credentials necessary to qualify for the job position

job description states the tasks and responsibilities of the job position

Before a firm hires a new employee to fill an existing job position, it must decide the tasks and responsibilities that would be performed by that position, and the credentials (education, experience, and so on) needed to qualify for that position. The analysis used to determine the tasks and the necessary credentials for a particular position is referred to as **job analysis.** This analysis should include input from the position's supervisor as well as from other employees whose tasks are related. The job analysis allows the supervisor of the job position to develop a job specification and job description. A **job specification** states the credentials necessary to qualify for the job position. A **job description** states the tasks and responsibilities of the job position. An example of a job description is provided in Exhibit 12.1. People who consider applying for the job position use the job specification to determine whether they could qualify for the position, and use the job description to determine what is involved in the position.

Exhibit 12.1
Example of a Job Description

Title: Sales Representative
Department: Sales
Location: Southern Division, Atlanta, Georgia

Position Summary
The sales representative meets with prospective customers to sell the firm's products, and to ensure that existing customers are satisfied with the products they have purchased.

Relationships
➤ Reports to the regional sales manager for the Southern Division
➤ Works with five other sales representatives, although each representative has responsibility for his or her own region within the Southern Division.

Main Job Responsibilities
1. Serve existing customers; call on main customers at least once a month to obtain feedback on the performance of products previously sold to them; take any new orders of products.
2. Visit other prospective customers and explain the advantages of each product.
3. Check on those customers who are late in paying their bills; provide feedback to the billing department.
4. Meet with the production managers at least once a month to inform them about any product defects cited by customers.
5. Assess the needs of prospective customers; determine whether other related products could be produced to satisfy customers; provide feedback to production managers.
6. Will need to train new sales representatives in the future if growth continues.
7. Overnight travel is necessary for about eight days per month.
8. Sales reports must be completed once a month.

Recruiting

Various forms of recruiting are used to ensure an adequate supply of qualified candidates. Some firms have a **human resource manager** (sometimes called the "personnel manager") who helps each specific department recruit candidates for its open positions. To identify potential candidates for the position, the human resource manager may check files of recent applicants who applied before the position was even open. These files are usually created as people submit their applications to the firm over time. In addition, the manager may place an ad in local newspapers. This increases the pool of applicants, as some people are unwilling to submit an application unless they are informed of an open position at the firm.

Most well-known companies tend to receive a large supply of qualified applications for each position. Many firms retain applications for only a few months so that the number of applications does not become excessive.

INTERNAL VERSUS EXTERNAL RECRUITING Recruiting can occur internally or externally. **Internal recruiting** seeks to fill open positions with persons already employed by the firm. Numerous firms post job openings so that existing employees can be informed. Some employees within the firm may desire the open positions more than their existing positions.

Internal recruiting can be beneficial because existing employees have already been proven. Their personalities are known, and their potential capabilities and limitations can be thoroughly assessed. Internal recruiting also allows a way for existing workers to receive a **promotion** (an assignment of a higher-level job with more responsibility and compensation) or to switch to more desirable tasks. This is impor-

human resource manager helps each specific department recruit candidates for its open positions

internal recruiting an effort to fill open positions with persons already employed by the firm

promotion an assignment of a higher-level job with more responsibility and compensation

tant to employees because the potential for advancement motivates them to perform well. Such potential also reduces job turnover, and therefore reduces the costs of hiring and training new employees. About two-thirds of the employees that Walt Disney hired for management positions were recruited internally.

Firms can do more internal recruiting if their employees are assigned responsibilities and tasks that train them for advanced positions. This strategy conflicts with job specialization because it exposes employees to more varied tasks. Yet, this is necessary to prepare them for other jobs and to reduce the possibility of boredom. Even when firms are able to fill a position internally, the previous position that the employee held becomes open, and the firm must recruit for that position.

external recruiting an effort to fill positions with applicants outside the firm

External recruiting is an effort to fill positions with applicants outside the firm. Some firms may recruit more qualified candidates when using external recruiting, especially for some specialized job positions. While external recruiting allows the evaluation of applicants' potential capabilities and limitations, human resource managers do not have as much information as they do for internal applicants. The applicant's resume shows a list of previously performed functions, along with a description of responsibilities. Yet, it does not indicate how the applicant responds to orders or interacts with other employees. This type of information is more critical for some jobs than others.

SCREENING APPLICANTS The recruiting process used to screen job applicants involves several steps. The first step is to assess each application to screen out unqualified applicants. While the information provided on an application is limited, it usually serves as an adequate initial screening method to determine whether the applicant has the minimum background, education, and experience necessary to qualify for the position.

The second step for screening applicants is the interview process. Some firms conduct initial interviews of college students at placement centers on college campuses. Other firms conduct initial interviews at their location. The human resource manager may be able to assess the personalities of remaining applicants from a per-

When recruiting employees, a company such as Microsoft is more concerned with intellectual contributions than specific personalities.

Exhibit 12.2
Example of Questionnaire to Obtain Employee Opinions about a Job Applicant

Applicant's Name _____

Position to be filled _____

	Strongly Agree	Agree	Unsure	Disagree	Strongly Disagree
The applicant possesses the necessary skills to perform the tasks required.					
The applicant would work well with others.					
The applicant would be eager to learn new skills.					
The applicant has good communication skills.					
The applicant would accept responsibility.					
Do you detect any deficiencies in the applicant (if so, describe them)?					
Do you recommend that we hire the applicant? Why, or why not?					

Signature of employee who is assessing applicant: _____

sonal interview, as well as obtain additional information that was not included on the application. Specifically, an interview can indicate an applicant's promptness, communication skills, and attitude. Furthermore, an interview allows the firm to obtain more detailed information about the applicant's past experience.

If the first two screening steps can substantially reduce the number of candidates, the human resource manager can allocate more time during the interview process to assess each remaining applicant. Even if these steps for screening have effectively reduced the number of candidates, the first interview with each remaining candidate will not necessarily lead to a selection. A second and even third interview may be necessary. These interviews may involve other employees of the firm that have some interaction with the position of concern. The input of these employees can often influence the hiring decision. A typical questionnaire to obtain employee opinions about an applicant is shown in Exhibit 12.2.

A third step for screening applicants is to contact the applicant's references. However, this screening method has limited benefits because applicants normally list only those references that are likely to provide strong recommendations. A recent survey by the Society for Human Resource Management found that more than 50 percent of the human resource managers are sometimes provided inadequate information about a job applicant's personality traits. More than 40 percent of these managers stated that they sometimes receive inadequate information about the applicant's skills and work habits.

Another possible step that firms use to screen applicants is an **employment test,** which is a written test of each candidate's abilities. Some tests are designed to assess intuition or willingness to work with others. Other tests are designed for specific skills, such as computer skills.

employment test a written test of each candidate's abilities

Some firms also request a physical examination for the candidates they plan to hire. This serves as a final screen. The examination can determine whether the candidate is physically able to conduct the tasks that would be assigned. In addition, the examination may detect any medical problems. If the firm still decides to hire the candidate, it can at least document any medical problems that existed before the candidate was employed by the firm. This can protect a firm from being blamed for causing a person's medical problems because of unsafe work conditions.

Along with physical examinations, some firms ask candidates to take drug tests. Firms are adversely affected when their employees take drugs, for two reasons. First, the firm may incur costs of health care and counseling for these employees. Second, the performance of these employees will likely be low, and may even reduce the performance of other co-workers.

MAKE THE HIRING DECISION   By the time the steps for screening applicants are completed, the application list should have been reduced to a small number of qualified candidates. The Boston Beer Company (producer of Samuel Adams Beer) has three full-time recruiters who screen carefully before hiring. It took them two years to recently hire a person for a sales position. Such careful screening enables them to recruit people who remain employees at Boston Beer Company for a long time. Careful recruiting can result in low turnover.

Once the screening is completed, the top candidate can be selected from this list and offered the job; the remaining qualified applicants can be considered if the top candidate does not accept the job offer. A summary of the steps used to screen job applicants is provided in Exhibit 12.3. Notice that each step reduces the list of applicants who would possibly qualify for the position.

Exhibit 12.3
Steps for Screening Job Applicants

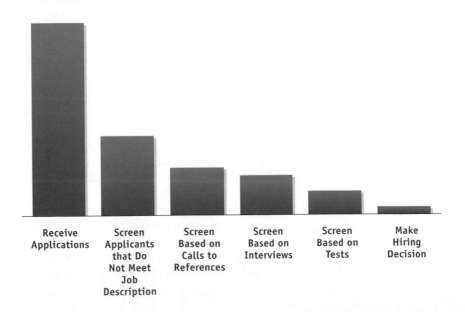

| Receive Applications | Screen Applicants that Do Not Meet Job Description | Screen Based on Calls to References | Screen Based on Interviews | Screen Based on Tests | Make Hiring Decision |

Exhibit 12.4
Summary of Tasks Involved in
Human Resource Planning

The final selection of a candidate may include a few alternates in case the ideal candidate declines the job offer. Once a person is hired, he or she becomes acquainted with health and benefits plans, and additional details of the job. A summary of the various phases necessary to fill a position is provided in Exhibit 12.4.

PROVIDING EQUAL OPPORTUNITY   When recruiting candidates for a job position, managers should not discriminate based on factors that are unrelated to potential job performance. Federal laws prohibit such discrimination. The following are some of the more relevant laws imposed to prevent discrimination or improper treatment:

➤ The Equal Pay Act of 1963 states that men and women performing similar work must receive the same pay.
➤ The Civil Rights Act of 1964 prohibits discrimination based on race, gender, religion, or national origin.
➤ The Age Discrimination in Employment Act of 1967, amended in 1978, prohibits employers from discriminating against people who are at least forty years old.
➤ The Americans with Disabilities Act (ADA) of 1990 prohibits discrimination against people who are disabled.
➤ The Civil Rights Act of 1991 enables females, minorities, and disabled people who believe that they have been subject to discrimination to sue firms. This act protects against discrimination in the hiring process or the employee evaluation process. It also protects against sexual harassment in the workplace.

COMPENSATION PACKAGES THAT FIRMS OFFER

2 Differentiate among the types of compensation that firms offer to employees.

Firms attempt to reward their employees by providing adequate compensation. The level of compensation is usually determined by comparing what employees at other firms with similar job characteristics earn. Information on compensation levels can be obtained by conducting a salary survey, or from various publications that report salary levels for different jobs. The wide differences in compensation among job positions are attributed to differences in the supply of people who have a particular skill and the demand for people with that skill. For example, demand for employees who have extensive experience in business financing decisions is high, but the supply of people with such experience is limited. Therefore, firms offer a high level of compensation to attract these people. Conversely, the supply of people who can qualify as a clerk is large, so firms can offer relatively low compensation to hire clerks.

compensation package represents the total monetary compensation and benefits offered to employees

A **compensation package** represents the total monetary compensation and benefits offered to employees. Some employees consider their salary to be their compensation. Yet, the benefits that some firms offer may be valued more than the salary. The typical elements of a compensation package are salary, commissions, bonuses, profit sharing, benefits, and perquisites.

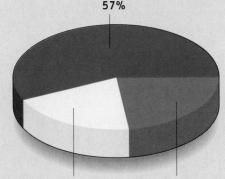

SMALL BUSINESS SURVEY

Do Firms Reward Employees for Customer Satisfaction?

A recent survey of 164 chief executive officers (CEOs) asked whether their nonsales employees (not directly involved with the sale of products) are rewarded for their roles in satisfying customers. The results of the survey are summarized in the following chart:

Firms that reward nonsales
employees for satisfying
customers
57%

Firms considering the strategy
of rewarding employees for
satisfying customers
23%

Firms that are not rewarding employees
for satisfying customers and are not
considering such a strategy
20%

The results suggest that most firms now recognize the importance of customer satisfaction, and are attempting to motivate employees to ensure customer satisfaction.

Salary

salary (or **wages**) represents the dollars paid for a job over a specific period

Salary (or **wages**) represents the dollars paid for a job over a specific period. The salary can be expressed per hour, per pay period, or per year, and is fixed over a particular time period.

Commissions

commissions represent compensation for meeting specific sales objectives

Commissions normally represent compensation for meeting specific sales objectives. For example, salespeople at many firms receive a base salary, plus a percentage of their total sales volume as monetary compensation. Salespeople at IBM have been given commissions based on their sales volume, but recently the commissions have been aligned with the earnings resulting from their sales. This is a direct method of motivating them to increase sales. For jobs in which employee performance cannot be as easily measured, commissions are not used.

Bonuses

bonus an extra one-time payment at the end of a period in which performance was measured

A **bonus** is an extra one-time payment at the end of a period in which performance was measured. It is usually offered less frequently than commissions (such as once a year). A bonus may be offered for efforts to increase revenue, reduce expenses, or improve customer satisfaction. In most cases, the bonus is not set by a formula; thus, supervisors have some flexibility in determining the bonus for each employee. The total amount of bonus funds that are available for employees may be dependent on the firm's profits for the year of concern.

Profit Sharing

profit sharing a portion of the firm's profits that is provided to employees

Some firms, such as Continental Airlines and General Motors, offer employees **profit sharing,** or a portion of the firm's profits paid to employees. Boeing, Chase Manhattan, and many other firms provide stock to some of their employees. This motivates employees to perform in a manner that improves profitability.

Employee Benefits

employee benefits additional privileges beyond compensation payments such as a paid vacation; health, life, or dental insurance; and pension programs

Employees may also receive **employee benefits,** which represent additional privileges beyond compensation payments such as a paid vacation; health, life, or dental insurance; and pension programs. These employee benefits are not taxed. Many firms provide substantial employee benefits to their employees. The cost of providing health insurance has soared in recent years. Many firms, such as Johnson and Johnson and Tenneco, have responded by offering preventive health-care programs. Some firms now give employees incentives to stay healthy, by reducing the insurance premiums charged to employees who receive favorable scores on cholesterol levels, blood pressure, fitness, and body fat. KMart Corporation recently linked its employee retirement benefits to its earnings as an employee incentive.

Perquisites

perquisites additional privileges beyond compensation payments and employee benefits

Some firms offer **perquisites** (or "perks") to high-level employees, which are additional privileges beyond compensation payments and employee benefits. Common perquisites include free parking, a company car, club memberships, telephone credit cards, and an expense account.

Comparison Across Jobs

The forms of compensation allocated to employees vary with their jobs, as shown in Exhibit 12.5. Employees who are directly involved in the production process (such as

Exhibit 12.5
How Forms of Compensation Can Vary across Job Descriptions

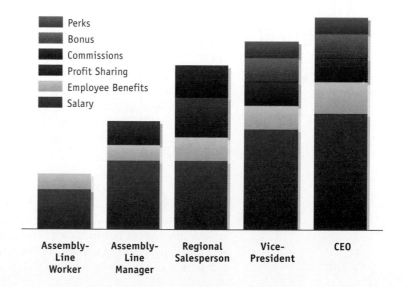

Perks
Bonus
Commissions
Profit Sharing
Employee Benefits
Salary

Assembly-Line Worker | Assembly-Line Manager | Regional Salesperson | Vice-President | CEO

assembly-line workers) tend to receive most of their compensation in the form of salary. Low-level managers may also receive most of their compensation as salary, but may receive a small bonus and profit sharing.

Employees involved in sales commonly receive a large proportion of their compensation in the form of commissions. High-level managers, such as vice-presidents and chief executive officers (CEOs), normally have a high salary and the potential for a large bonus. Their employee benefits are also relatively large, and they normally are awarded various perks as well.

Compensating Employees Across Countries

 The manner by which a firm compensates its employees may vary across countries. Salary may be perceived as less important in a country where personal income tax rates are high. If a large portion of the salary is taxed, employees may prefer other forms of compensation. The health benefits that a firm offers may be less important in countries that provide free medical services.

Some U.S. firms, such as Gillette and PepsiCo, offer their employees opportunities to purchase their stock at below-market prices. Most employees in the United States perceive this form of employee compensation as desirable. However, employees in other countries perceive it as less desirable. The rules for individuals who purchase stock vary among countries. For example, individuals in Brazil, China, and India are restricted from purchasing or owning stock under some circumstances. The taxes imposed on the profits earned by individuals on their stocks also vary across countries, which makes stock ownership more desirable for employees based in particular countries. Furthermore, individuals in some countries are more comfortable investing in bank deposits rather than in stocks.

Since employees based in different countries may have varying views about compensation, a firm with employees in several countries should consider tailoring its compensation plans to fit the characteristics of each country. The firm may provide higher salaries in one country and more health benefits in another. Before establishing a compensation plan in a given country, the firm should assess the specific tax laws of that country and survey individuals to determine the types of compensation that are most desirable. When a firm designs a compensation plan to fit the country's characteristics, it can improve employee job satisfaction.

DEVELOPING SKILLS OF EMPLOYEES

3 Describe the skills of employees that firms develop.

Firms that hire employees provide training to develop various employee skills. Motorola has created its own university which allows each of its employees to receive at least one week of training per year. A recent study by the management consulting firm Ernst and Young found that those firms that invest in training programs are more profitable. Some of the more common types of training provided to employees are discussed next.

Technical Skills

Employees must be trained to perform the various tasks they perform daily. As technology improves at factories owned by firms such as General Motors, Westinghouse, and McDonnell Douglas, employees receive more training. These firms spend mil-

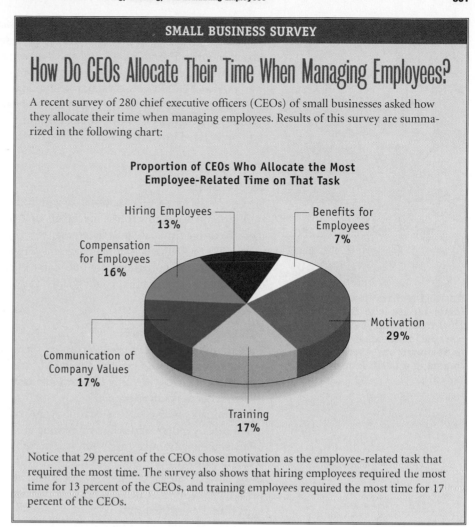

SMALL BUSINESS SURVEY

How Do CEOs Allocate Their Time When Managing Employees?

A recent survey of 280 chief executive officers (CEOs) of small businesses asked how they allocate their time when managing employees. Results of this survey are summarized in the following chart:

Proportion of CEOs Who Allocate the Most Employee-Related Time on That Task

- Hiring Employees 13%
- Benefits for Employees 7%
- Compensation for Employees 16%
- Motivation 29%
- Communication of Company Values 17%
- Training 17%

Notice that 29 percent of the CEOs chose motivation as the employee-related task that required the most time. The survey also shows that hiring employees required the most time for 13 percent of the CEOs, and training employees required the most time for 17 percent of the CEOs.

lions of dollars every year on training. As computer technology improves, employees of travel agencies, mail order clothing firms, retail stores, and large corporations must receive more training on using computers. In addition, employees who are assigned to new jobs will require extra training. Firms must recognize that expenses may be incurred each year to continually develop each employee's skills.

Decision-Making Skills

Firms can benefit from providing their employees with some guidelines to consider when making decisions and creating ideas. For example, Xerox trains all of its employees to follow a six-step process when creating ideas and making decisions. Kodak employees who recently created new products are asked to share their knowledge with other employees who are attempting to develop new products. Motorola trains its employees to apply new technology to develop new products.

Customer Service Skills

Employees who frequently deal with customers need to have customer service skills. Many employees in tourism industries such as airlines and hotels are trained to satisfy customers. The hotel chain Marriott International provides an eight-hour training session on serving customers, with refresher sessions provided after the first and second months. The training is intended not only to ensure customer satisfaction but also to provide employees with an orientation that makes them more comfortable (and increases employee satisfaction). Since Marriott began implementing its training sessions, it has reduced its employee turnover. Walt Disney provides extensive training to its newly hired employees. Customer service skills are also necessary for employees hired by firms to sell products or deal with customer complaints.

Safety Skills

Firms educate employees about safety within the work environment. This includes training employees how to use machinery and equipment in factories owned by large manufacturing firms, such as Caterpillar and Goodyear Tire. The United Parcel Service (UPS) implements training programs for its employees on handling hazardous materials. Training programs not only comfort employees but also reduce healthcare and legal expenses that could be incurred as a result of work-related injuries.

Marriott realizes how critical customer service is to their success. They train employees in many ways including seminars on how to deal with unreasonable customers in a positive manner.

Human Relations Skills

Some training seminars may be necessary for supervisors who lack skills in managing other employees. In general, this type of training helps supervisors to recognize that their employees not only deserve to be treated properly but also will perform better if they are treated properly.

Seminars on diversity are commonly provided by firms to help employees of different races, genders, and religions become more sensitive to other views. Denny's offers employee training on diversity to prevent racial discrimination. Diversity training may allow for an environment in which people work together more effectively, thereby improving the firm's performance. It also may prevent friction between employees, which can possibly prevent discrimination or harassment lawsuits filed against the firm.

Training seminars are also designed to improve relationships among employees across various divisions, so that employees can work within teams. For example, Motorola and Xerox provide seminars for employees on teamwork. Anheuser-Busch organizes regular meetings between employees and executives.

EVALUATION OF EMPLOYEE PERFORMANCE

4 **Explain how the performance of employees can be evaluated.**

Employees often perceive performance evaluation as a method for allocating raises. Yet, if supervisors properly conduct the evaluation, it can also provide feedback and direction to employees. An evaluation should indicate an employee's strengths and weaknesses, and may influence an employee's chances of being promoted within the firm in the future.

Segmenting the Evaluation into Different Criteria

The overall performance of most employees is normally based on multiple criteria. Therefore, evaluations can be conducted more properly by segmenting the evaluation into the criteria that are relevant for each particular job position. For example,

---

SPOTLIGHT ON TECHNOLOGY

Using Computers to Manage and Train Employees

Traditionally, computers have been employed to perform relatively low-level tasks. That situation is changing, however. In many companies, computers are being used to manage and train employees. One of the most advanced work management systems ever developed was created by Mrs. Field's Cookies. In the mid-1980s, it installed computer terminals in hundreds of its retail stores, located primarily in malls and downtown areas across the country. Terminals connected directly with the company's main computer performed a number of activities that would normally have been the responsibility of store managers, including the following:

➤ *Production Scheduling:* Based on historical data, the system instructed workers on when to bake cookies, as well as how many and what type.

➤ *Promotion and Sales Advice:* The system regularly suggested various promotional and sales techniques that could be used to increase traffic.

➤ *Recruiting and Training:* The system included applications which interviewed potential job candidates, and provided various on-line training activities for employees.

Using this system, Mrs. Field's Cookies achieved a productivity level that was unusually high in the industry. In large part, this productivity was a direct result of being able to eliminate an entire layer of management through the use of computers.

While computers may be able to efficiently perform routine decision-making tasks, they are often unable to perform all the tasks that the managers they replace would normally perform. For example, computers may be unable to recognize the potential effects of new competition or how to deal with specific employee problems. Nevertheless, they can improve the firm's performance if their limitations are recognized.

---

consider employees who have excellent technical skills for their jobs, but are not dependable. Since they rate high on one criterion and low on another, their overall performance may be evaluated as about average. However, an average rating for overall performance does not specifically pinpoint the favorable or unfavorable work habits of these employees.

The segmenting of performance evaluation into different criteria can help supervisors pinpoint specific strengths and weaknesses. Evaluating each criterion separately provides more specific information to employees about how they may improve. In our example, the employees who receive a low rating on dependability can focus on improving that behavior. Furthermore, these employees can see from their evaluation that their supervisors recognized their strong technical skills. Without a detailed evaluation, employees may not recognize what tasks they do well (in the opinion of supervisors) and specific weaknesses that need to be improved.

OBJECTIVE VERSUS SUBJECTIVE CRITERIA   Some performance criteria are objective, such as parts produced per week, number of days absent, percentage of deadlines missed, and the proportion of defective parts caused by employee errors. Examples of direct measures of performance are provided for specific job positions in Exhibit 12.6 to illustrate how the examples vary by type of job. Other characteristics not shown in Exhibit 12.6 that are commonly assessed for some job positions include organization, communication, and decision-making skills.

Some criteria are less objective but still important. For example, the quality of work cannot always be measured by part defects, because many jobs are not focused on producing a single product. Therefore, quality of work may be subjectively assessed by a supervisor. Also, the willingness of an employee to help other employees is an important criterion that is subjective.

Exhibit 12.6
Examples of Direct
Measures of Performance

Job Position	Direct Measures of Performance
Salesperson	Dollar volume of sales over a specific period
	Number of new customers
	Number of delinquent accounts collected
	Net sales per month in territory
Manager	Number of employee grievances
	Cost reductions
	Absenteeism
	Unit safety record
	Timeliness in completing appraisals
	Employee satisfaction with supervisor
	Division production
	Diversity of new hires
Administrative assistant	Number of letters prepared
	Word processing speed
	Number of errors in filing
	Number of jobs returned for reprocessing
	Number of calls screened

Using a Performance Evaluation Form

Supervisors are typically required to complete a performance evaluation form at the end of each year. An example of such a form is shown in Exhibit 12.7. When supervisors measure the performance of employees, they normally classify the employee in one of several categories such as the following: (1) outstanding, (2) above average, (3) average, (4) below average, and (5) poor. The set of criteria can be more specific for particular jobs within the firm. For example, assembly-line workers may be rated by the total components produced and production quality. A company salesperson may be evaluated by the number of computers sold and the quality of service provided to customers. It is important that employees are informed of the criteria by which they will be rated. Otherwise, they may allocate too much time toward tasks that supervisors view as not important.

Assigning Weights to the Criteria

The evaluation of all relevant criteria can be combined to determine an overall performance level of each employee. Some firms use weighting systems to determine the overall performance of employees, in which the criteria used to evaluate the employee are weighted and rated. For example, bank tellers may be rated according to their speed in handling customer transactions, their quality (accuracy) in handling money transactions, and their ability to satisfy customers. The speed may be monitored by supervisors over time, while accuracy is measured by balancing the accounts at the end of each day, and customer satisfaction is measured from customer feedback over time.

The different criteria must also be weighted separately, since some of the employee's assignments may be perceived as more important than others. Using our example, assume that the weights are determined as follows:

Exhibit 12.7
Example of Performance Appraisal Form

Employee Name _____ Date _____
Position _____

Behavior Ratings: Check the one characteristic that best applies.
Quality of Work (refers to accuracy and margin of error):
    _____ **1.** Makes errors frequently and repeatedly
    _____ **2.** Often makes errors
    _____ **3.** Is accurate; makes occasional errors
    _____ **4.** Is accurate; rarely makes errors
    _____ **5.** Is exacting and precise

Quality of Work (refers to amount of production or results):
    _____ **1.** Usually does not complete work load as assigned
    _____ **2.** Often accomplishes part of a task
    _____ **3.** Handles work load as assigned
    _____ **4.** Turns out more work than requested
    _____ **5.** Handles an unusually large volume of work

Timeliness (refers to completion of task, within time allowed):
    _____ **1.** Does not complete duties on time
    _____ **2.** Is often late in completing tasks
    _____ **3.** Completes tasks on time
    _____ **4.** Usually completes tasks in advance of deadlines
    _____ **5.** Always completes all tasks in advance of time frames

Attendance and Punctuality (refers to adhering to work schedule assigned):
    _____ **1.** Is usually tardy or absent
    _____ **2.** Is often tardy or absent
    _____ **3.** Normally is not tardy or absent
    _____ **4.** Makes a point of being on the job and on time
    _____ **5.** Is extremely conscientious about attendance

Responsibility (refers to completing assignments and projects):
    _____ **1.** Usually does not assume responsibility for completing assignments
    _____ **2.** Is at times reluctant to accept delegated responsibility
    _____ **3.** Accepts and discharges delegated duties willingly
    _____ **4.** Accepts additional responsibility
    _____ **5.** Is a self-starter who seeks out more effective ways to achieve results or seeks additional responsibilities

Cooperation with Others (refers to working and communicating with supervisors and co-workers):
    _____ **1.** Has difficulty working with others and often complains when given assignments
    _____ **2.** Sometimes has difficulty working with others and often complains when given assignments
    _____ **3.** Usually is agreeable and obliging; generally helps out when requested
    _____ **4.** Works well with others; welcomes assignments, and is quick to offer assistance
    _____ **5.** Is an outstanding team worker; always assists others and continually encourages cooperation by setting an excellent example

Performance Summary (include strong areas and areas for future emphasis in improving performance or developing additional job skills):

Employee Comments or Concerns:

Signatures:
Human Resource Manager _____ **Date** _____
Employee _____ **Date** _____
Supervisor _____ **Date** _____

Speed in handling customer transactions	30%
Accuracy in handling customer transactions	50%
Satisfying customers	20%
	100%

The sum of the weights of all criteria should be 100 percent. The weighting system should be communicated to employees when they begin a job position so that they understand what characteristics are most important within the evaluation.

To demonstrate how an overall performance measure is derived, assume that in our example the supervisor rated the bank teller as shown in Exhibit 12.8. The overall rating is the weighted average of 4.5; this rating is in between "above average" and "outstanding." Other bank tellers could also be periodically rated in this manner. At the end of each year, the ratings may be used to determine the raise for each teller. The ratings may also be reviewed along with other characteristics (such as experience) when the employees are considered for a promotion.

This system of developing an overall rating is more appropriate when a few key criteria can be used to assess an employee throughout a period. However, when employees have numerous job assignments, accounting for all types of assignments within the performance evaluation is more difficult. Yet, some of the assignments may be combined into a single characteristic, such as "customer service" or "ability to get jobs done on time."

Some supervisors may believe that a weighted system is too structured and does not account for some relevant characteristics, such as ability to get along with other employees. However, characteristics like these could be included within the weighting system.

Steps for Proper Performance Evaluation

Firms can follow specific steps to demonstrate fairness to employees and also satisfy legal guidelines in recognizing employee rights.

1 Supervisors should communicate job responsibilities to employees when they are hired. Supervisors should also communicate any changes in employee job responsibilities over time. This communication can be done orally, but should be backed up with a letter to the employee. The letters are not as personal as oral communication, but provide documentation in case a disagreement arises in the future about assignments and responsibilities. The letters may not only provide support to defend

Exhibit 12.8
Developing an Overall Rating

Characteristic	Rating	Weight	Weighted Rating
Speed in handling customer transactions	4 (above average)	30%	4 × 30% = 1.2
Accuracy in handling customer transactions	5 (outstanding)	50%	5 × 50% = 2.5
Satisfying customers	4 (above average)	20%	4 × 20% = .80
			Overall rating = 4.5

against employee lawsuits, but also force supervisors to pinpoint the specific tasks for employees in a particular job position.

2 When supervisors notice that employees have deficiencies, they should inform them of those deficiencies. This communication may occur in the form of a standard periodic review. Supervisors may prefer to inform employees of deficiencies immediately, rather than wait for the review period. Employees should be given a chance to respond to the criticism. Supervisors may also allow a short period of time for employees to correct the deficiencies.

Supervisors should also communicate with employees who were evaluated favorably so that those employees recognize that their efforts are appreciated.

3 Supervisors should use consistency among employees when conducting performance evaluations. That is, two employees who have a similar deficiency should be treated equally in the evaluation process. Many supervisors would prefer communicating deficiencies only to those employees who are more willing to accept criticism. Yet, it is only fair to treat the deficiencies similarly among employees.

Action Due to Performance Evaluations

Some performance evaluations require supervisors to take action. Employees that receive a very favorable evaluation may deserve some type of recognition or even a promotion. If supervisors do not acknowledge such favorable performance, employees may either lose their enthusiasm and reduce their effort, or search for a new job at a firm that will reward them for high performance. Supervisors should acknowledge high performance so that such performance continues in the future.

Employees that receive an unfavorable evaluation must also be given attention. Supervisors must determine the reasons for poor performance. Some reasons (such as a family illness) may have a temporary adverse impact on performance and can be corrected. Other reasons, such as a bad attitude, may not be temporary.

When supervisors give employees an unfavorable evaluation, they must decide whether to take any additional actions. If the employees were unaware of their own deficiencies, the unfavorable evaluation can pinpoint the deficiencies that employees must correct. In this case, the supervisor may simply need to monitor the employees closely and ensure that the deficiencies are corrected.

However, if the employees were already aware of their deficiencies before the evaluation period, they may be unable or unwilling or correct them. This situation is more serious, and the supervisor may need to take action. The action should be consistent with the firm's guidelines, and may include reassigning the employees to new jobs, suspending them temporarily, or firing them. A supervisor's action taken on a poorly performing worker can affect the attitudes of other employees. If no penalty is imposed on an employee for poor performance, other employees may rebel by reducing their productivity as well.

Firms must follow certain procedures to fire an employee. These procedures are intended to prevent firms from firing employees without reason. Specifically, supervisors should identify deficiencies in employees' evaluations and give them a chance to respond.

Dealing with Lawsuits by Fired Employees

It is not uncommon for employees to sue the firm after being fired. Some lawsuits argue that the fired employee did not receive due process. Others argue that the firing is attributed to discrimination based on race, gender, age, religion, or national origin. Complaints of discrimination are first filed with the Equal Employment

Opportunity Commission (EEOC), which is responsible for enforcing the discrimination laws. About 20 percent of complaints filed with the EEOC are judged as having a reasonable cause for the fired employee to take action, while 80 percent of the complaints are judged to have no reasonable cause. However, even when the EEOC believes the complaint is not valid, the fired employee can still sue the firm.

The surge of employee lawsuits in recent years is partially attributed to the following factors. First, as of 1991, plaintiffs were allowed the right to trial by jury. The common perception is that juries are more sympathetic toward plaintiffs than judges are. Also, juries are perceived as more unpredictable, which concerns firms that are sued by employees. A second reason for the surge in lawsuits is the increase in potential damages that can be awarded to plaintiffs. As a result of the Civil Rights Act of 1991, plaintiffs can be awarded not only for compensatory damages (such as back pay) but also for punitive damages (to penalize the firm) and legal expenses. Therefore, plaintiffs and their attorneys can now receive much larger amounts of money.

Much media attention has been given to employee lawsuits. Firms recognize that such lawsuits can be very costly. However, firms should not ignore an employee's deficiencies just because of fear that the employee will sue. Such a situation will reduce the motivation of other employees if they recognize that one employee is receiving special treatment. The court system has generally sided with firms in cases in which supervisors followed proper procedures in firing employees.

In recent years, many employees who were dismissed have charged that the dismissal was based on discrimination because of race, religion, gender, or age. Many firms with numerous employees have been sued for this reason, even when their supervisors have followed all proper procedures. While the laws that prohibit discrimination have good intentions, the court system has not effectively separated the frivolous cases from the valid ones. Consequently, legal expenses for many firms have risen substantially.

Dow Chemical makes sure that evaluations are consistent and fair by allowing lower-level employees to evaluate their managers.

CROSS-FUNCTIONAL TEAMWORK

How Job Responsibilities Across Business Functions Can Complicate Performance Evaluations

Firms have increasingly encouraged employees to perform a variety of business functions to achieve higher levels of job satisfaction and efficiency. While this form of job enlargement has been successful, it can complicate the evaluation of an employee's performance. Consider an employee of a sporting goods store whose only responsibility was stringing tennis rackets. The performance of this employee was judged by the number of tennis rackets strung and the quality of the stringing (as measured by customer feedback).

The employee's responsibilities were then enlarged to include visiting country clubs and selling tennis rackets to them. While the employee's initial job was focused on assembly of tennis rackets, the enlarged responsibilities involved marketing the tennis rackets. Furthermore, other employees would also be involved in the stringing of rackets and the sales calls to country clubs.

The performance evaluation of the employee has become more complicated for two reasons. First, more than one task now needs to be assessed. Second, other employees are also involved in completing these tasks, which makes it difficult to measure one employee's individual contribution. That is, a firm can easily assess the performance of a team of employees, but cannot easily assess the performance of each employee within the team.

Some firms have attempted to settle lawsuits before trial to reduce their legal expenses and negative publicity. However, settling a lawsuit that has no merit may result in other frivolous lawsuits by employees.

Despite the surge of employee lawsuits, firms must still attempt to ensure that their employees are doing the jobs that they are paid to do. While firms cannot necessarily avoid employee lawsuits, they can attempt to establish training and performance evaluation guidelines that will reduce the chances of employee lawsuits.

Employee Evaluation of Supervisors

upward appraisals used to measure the managerial abilities of supervisors

Some firms allow employees to evaluate their supervisors, which can be used to measure the managerial abilities of supervisors. These so-called **upward appraisals** have been used by many firms, including AT&T and Dow Chemical. An upward evaluation is more effective if it is anonymous. Otherwise, workers may automatically offer a very favorable evaluation so that their supervisor might return the favor, or to avoid retaliation. Evaluations of the supervisor may identify deficiencies so that the supervisor can more effectively manage employees in the future. The evaluation form for supervisors should allow each criterion to be evaluated separately so that they can recognize which characteristics need to be improved.

BUSINESS DILEMMA

·COLLEGE·
HEALTH CLUB

Performance Evaluation at College Health Club

Sue Kramer, president of College Health Club (CHC), is planning to establish a second health club about sixty miles away, next to a college campus. If she decides to establish the second club, she will need someone to manage it daily. This manager will need to purchase weight machines, offer aerobics classes, and attract memberships. A second health club could boost Sue's earnings substantially over time. However, if the club is not managed properly, it could incur losses and could even put Sue out of business.

Sue believes this second club will be successful if it is able to attract local college students as members and ensure that they are sufficiently satisfied to continue their membership. The club's success would also be based on its ability to maintain expenses at a low level. Before hiring a manager, Sue decides to consider the key work characteristics of the manager that would make this second health club successful. These characteristics would serve as the criteria that Sue can use to periodically evaluate the performance of this manager.

Dilemma

Sue's specific goal is to develop a list of three key characteristics that would help determine the manager's performance. Offer your input on the key characteristics that Sue should assess to determine the manager's performance.

Solution

Sue recognizes that the key characteristics are those that would make the second club successful. Since memberships are critical to generate revenue, Sue decides that the manager's ability to sell new memberships is the most relevant characteristic to use in evaluating the manager. The number of new memberships per period would be used to measure this characteristic.

Second, Sue decides that the manager's ability to achieve customer (member) satisfaction is relevant because that would determine future membership renewals. Sue could conduct a survey of existing members to assess customer satisfaction.

Third, she decides that the manager's ability to purchase and repair the equipment at a low cost is relevant. Sue could monitor the expense of the club per period to assess this characteristic. While other criteria may also be considered, these characteristics are most important for ensuring that the second club's revenue would be high and its costs low.

Additional Issues for Discussion

1 Should Sue ask any job applicants to take drug tests?

2 What type of criteria can Sue use to measure the performance of an aerobics instructor that she hired?

3 Why is it important for Sue Kramer to write a detailed job description for managing the new health club (assuming that she decides to open a new health club)?

4 What steps should Sue take if the new manager is not working out?

SUMMARY

1 The main functions involved in human resource planning are

➤ anticipating human resource needs,
➤ job analysis, and
➤ recruiting.

2 Compensation packages offered by firms can include salary, commissions, bonuses, profit sharing, employee benefits, and perquisites.

3 After firms hire employees, they commonly provide training to enhance technical skills, decision-making skills, customer service skills, safety skills, and human relations skills.

4 The performance of employees can be evaluated by segmenting the evaluation into different criteria, assigning an evaluation rating to each criterion, and weighting each criterion. The overall performance rating is the weighted average of all criteria that were assigned a rating.

Once supervisors evaluate employees, they should discuss the evaluations with them and identify any specific strengths, as well as any specific weaknesses that need to be improved.

KEY TERMS

bonus
boycott (chap. appendix)
commissions
compensation package
craft unions (chap. appendix)
employee benefits
employment test
external recruiting
human resource manager
human resource planning
industrial unions (chap. appendix)
injunction (chap. appendix)

internal recruiting
international unions (chap. appendix)
job analysis
job description
job specification
labor union (chap. appendix)
Landrum-Griffin Act (chap. appendix)
local unions (chap. appendix)
lockout (chap. appendix)
national unions (chap. appendix)
Norris-LaGuardia Act (chap. appendix)
perquisites

picketing (chap. appendix)
profit sharing
promotion
right-to-work (chap. appendix)
salary
strike (chap. appendix)
Taft-Hartley Act (chap. appendix)
upward appraisals
wages
Wagner Act (chap. appendix)
yellow-dog contract (chap. appendix)

REVIEW QUESTIONS

1 How can management reduce the employee need for union representation? (see the chapter appendix.)

2 Discuss the types of skills that an employee could receive from a firm's training program.

3 Describe the tasks involved in developing a human resource plan.

4 How can segmenting the evaluation into different criteria help the supervisor pinpoint specific strengths and weaknesses of an employee's job performance?

5 Distinguish internal from external recruiting that is undertaken by a firm.

6 Discuss the steps involved in the recruiting process to screen job applicants.

7 Discuss the validity of employees evaluating their supervisors' job performance.

8 Discuss the implications for a firm to be an equal opportunity employer.

9 Discuss the various types of compensation packages that could be offered to employees in performing their jobs.

10 Distinguish a job description from a job specification for an employee position.

DISCUSSION QUESTIONS

1 Assume you are a human resource manager and have been assigned to develop a compensation policy with supplemental pay benefits for your employees. Discuss. What do you think the most desired benefit is today for employees?

2 Discuss the popularity of nonunion plants. (See the chapter appendix.)

3 Assume you are a manager and have an employee with three years' work experience who refuses to be retrained. This employee further refuses to discuss his performance appraisal with you. What is your next step?

4 Discuss the legal implications that impact human resource management practices.

5 Assume you have just opened a Jeep Cherokee dealership. Which of your employees would be paid salaries, hourly wages, commissions, and bonuses?

RUNNING YOUR OWN BUSINESS

1 Develop a job description for the employees that you would need to hire for your business. Include the required education and skills within the job description.

2 Describe the training (if any) that you would have to provide to any employees you hire for your business.

3 Describe how you would compensate your employees. Would you offer bonuses as an incentive? If so, describe how you would determine the bonus.

4 Describe the criteria you would use to evaluate the performance of your employees.

INVESTING IN THE STOCK OF A BUSINESS

Using the annual report of the firm in which you would like to invest, complete the following:

1 Does the firm periodically provide special training to its employees? If so, provide details.

2 Does the firm offer bonuses to its employees as an

incentive? If so, are the bonuses tied to employee performance? Provide details.

3 Does the firm offer any other programs that are designed to achieve employee satisfaction, such as a flexible work schedule? If so, provide details.

CASE 1 Filling Job Positions

George DeCaro, a human resource manager of Bobcat International, has just received a directive from the president of the company. The directive reads: "We have just completed our strategy for the year. The thrust of this strategy is to increase our market share by 22 percent over the next three years." It continues: "We must be ready for this challenge by increasing production, and the human resource department must staff the organization with thirty-seven new jobs."

George's task is to forecast job requirements each year for the next three years. George recognizes that both internal and external recruiting will have to be undertaken. The firm's philosophy is to promote from within whenever possible. This procedure promotes high morale and contributes to the overall success of the organization. Some jobs will have to be filled externally. He ponders the

sources for recruiting potential job candidates for semiskilled plant jobs that pay an hourly rate.

George works well with the firm's president and wants to request a meeting to demonstrate how the human resource department will perform a vital role in helping the firm meet its objectives.

Questions

1 What is the human resource plan? Discuss its major tasks.

2 What is job analysis? How should it be used in this case?

3 Discuss George's sources for recruiting potential employees for the plant jobs.

4 What should be on George's agenda for the meeting with the company's president?

CASE 2 Training on the Job

Norton Manufacturing Company, in Fostoria, Ohio, is a crankshaft producer that supplies the auto industry. Norton began in 1950 as a two-man shop. As the company expanded, it successfully made the transition to manufacturing crankshafts, which became its market niche. The growth of this company has been phenomenal; over the past five years corporate sales have increased tenfold. The

technology of the crankshaft industry has changed dramatically during this time period. Therefore, the need for technical skills training is critical.

In the past year, Norton assessed the technical skills of its machine operators. One assessment covered math, and Norton found that some of its operators had mastered the subject only to a seventh-grade level. The understanding of math applications is an important criterion for the firm's success. To address this need, Norton responded by giving employees twenty hours of classroom training using the job instruction technique of employee training. This met with significant success. The quantitative skills of Norton's employees improved dramatically.

More recently, Norton contracted with a local vocational school to have an instructor based at the plant, offering perhaps two hours of instruction every week to each of the three shifts.

Classroom training will consist of "machine-shop math," basic blueprint reading, statistical process control, and other concepts. Employees benefit immediately from such training because they can apply it to the job. The training program at Norton is an integral part of the company's turnaround.

Questions

1 Does training pay for itself at Norton?
2 What led to the development of a training program at Norton?
3 What skills are being enhanced at this company?
4 Assume that Norton's management considered increasing the training. Is it possible that excessive training could reduce the firm's performance? How?

VIDEO CASE Managing Employees in a Volatile Business

Rhino Foods of Burlington, Vermont, had comfortably been making various dessert products for years when, in 1991, Ben and Jerry's Homemade, a large producer of ice cream and ice cream novelties, put Rhino dough in a new product it was introducing, chocolate-chip cookie dough ice cream.

Ben and Jerry's released the flavor to retailers in April and by June was selling it in large quantities. Ted Castle (president of Rhino Foods), who had been supplying thirty-two thousand pounds of cookie-dough pellets a week, was asked to quadruple that amount in three weeks. If he didn't answer yes within forty-eight hours, he was told, Ben and Jerry's would get a secondary supplier. As he drove to Burlington from Ben and Jerry's headquarters in Waterbury, Vermont, forty minutes away, Castle stewed over the need to expand production in a rush that could lead to accidents, errors, even loss of the Ben and Jerry's account altogether. Also, he had limited funds.

But the opportunity was too good to miss. He bought new equipment and had a wall moved for more space, and negotiated extended-payment terms from suppliers. Procedures for making the dough pellets had to be redesigned, and Castle, a believer in employee empowerment, relied for ideas on the employees who were doing the work.

Ben and Jerry's was providing 80 percent of Rhino's business. But occasionally it cut orders, leaving some skilled production workers with little to do. Castle hated layoffs for their effect on remaining employees' morale, on unemployment compensation insurance rates, and on the quality of job-seekers when Rhino was ready to rehire. Also, it was costly to train new workers.

Brainstorming among employees produced a creative solution: exchanges with other companies that also had up-and-down staffing needs. Two firms have taken six Rhino employees temporarily, and Rhino, which has a staff of sixty, is planning to repay the favor.

To avoid overdependence on Ben and Jerry's, new products were created and marketers hired. Sales accounts were maintained by building relationships: Customers receive regular phone calls to be sure things are going well.

Today Ben and Jerry's represents only 50 percent of Rhino sales. Castle is very glad he didn't miss that big opportunity.

Questions

1 Explain how the reliance of Rhino on Ben and Jerry's complicated Rhino's management of its employees.
2 The executives of Rhino Foods met with its other employees to discuss potential solutions for the abrupt shifts in the number of employees needed. Is it wise for the executives to ask other employees for their input on potential solutions to this problem?
3 Explain how a major marketing effort used by Rhino Foods can possibly reduce the problem of frequent hiring and layoffs. Also explain how a strategy by Rhino to diversify its food products (rather than produce only cookie dough) can possibly reduce the problem of frequent hiring and layoffs.

THE Coca-Cola COMPANY ANNUAL REPORT PROJECT

The following questions apply concepts learned in this chapter to The Coca-Cola Company. Read page 29 in The Coca-Cola Company annual report before answering these questions.

1 a. Why has The Coca-Cola company focused on improving business assessment skills of employees?
    b. Can "business assessment" skills be taught?

2 a. Explain how long-term incentive awards are used by The Coca-Cola Company.
    b. What is used to measure the performance of employees?

3 What challenges do you think are unique to multinational firms such as The Coca-Cola Company, with respect to hiring, training and evaluating employees?

IN-TEXT STUDY GUIDE

Answers are in an appendix at the back of the book.

True or False

1 Job analysis represents the forecasting of a firm's employee needs.

2 Layoffs not only affect laid-off workers but also can scare the workers who are still-employed.

3 Employee benefits such as health insurance and dental insurance are taxed.

4 Personal tax rates vary across countries.

5 The overall performance evaluation of most employees is based on multiple criteria.

6 One task of human resource planning is recruiting.

7 Employees who frequently deal with customers need no training in customer service skills.

8 Employees perceive performance evaluation as a method for allocating wage increases.

9 When forecasting employee needs, employee retirements can be forecasted with some degree of accuracy.

10 A job specification states the credentials necessary to qualify for the position.

Multiple Choice

11 The set of weighted or rated criteria that firms use to assess employee contributions is called a:
a) job analysis.
b) job specification.
c) performance evaluation.
d) job description.
e) recruiting process.

12 The instrument that specifies credentials necessary to qualify for the job position is a:
a) job specification.
b) job description.
c) job analysis.

d) job evaluation.
e) performance evaluation.

13 The act of planning to satisfy a firm's needs for employees is:
a) recruiting.
b) selecting.
c) compensation planning.
d) organizing.
e) human resource planning.

14 At the time employees are hired, supervisors should communicate the:
a) application form.
b) job responsibilities.
c) type of interview.
d) employment test.
e) reference checks.

15 The individual responsible for performance evaluation is generally the employee's:
a) labor union.
b) board of directors.
c) customers.
d) supervisor.
e) business agent.

16 An upward performance appraisal for a supervisor is more effective if it is:
a) anonymous.
b) arbitrary.
c) criticized.
d) subjective.
e) verbal.

17 A primary function of the _____ is to help specific departments recruit candidates.
a) chief executive officer
b) chief financial officer
c) board members

d) human resource manager

e) plant manager

18 The tasks and responsibilities of job positions are disclosed in a(n):

a) job specification.

b) job sequence.

c) job description.

d) yellow-dog contract.

e) employment test.

19 Firms can increase the degree of internal recruiting if their employees are assigned responsibilities and tasks that train them for:

a) downsizing.

b) advanced positions.

c) demotion.

d) reinforcement.

e) receiving perquisites.

20 A firm's human resource manager can obtain detailed information about the applicant's past work experience through a(n):

a) employment test.

b) physical exam.

c) interview.

d) orientation program.

e) job analysis.

21 A final screening process that some firms request of candidates they plan to hire is a(n):

a) job specification.

b) physical examination.

c) application form.

d) resume.

e) orientation.

22 The process used to determine the tasks and the necessary credentials for a particular position is referred to as:

a) job analysis.

b) job screening.

c) human resource planning.

d) human resource forecasting.

e) recruiting.

23 To ensure an adequate supply of qualified candidates, firms use various forms of:

a) job descriptions.

b) job specifications.

c) recruiting.

d) reference checks.

e) human resource planning.

24 Numerous firms post job openings on their job sites, which is referred to as:

a) external recruiting.

b) on-the-job training.

c) job instruction training.

d) vestibule training.

e) internal recruiting.

25 By establishing training and performance guidelines, firms can attempt to reduce:

a) lawsuits.

b) human resource plans.

c) job analysis.

d) job descriptions.

e) job specifications.

26 An effort to fill positions with applicants outside the firm is called:

a) promotion.

b) internal recruiting.

c) external recruiting.

d) transfer.

e) on-the-job training.

27 An extra one-time payment at the end of a period in which performance was measured is a:

a) salary.

b) wage.

c) stock option.

d) piece rate.

e) bonus.

28 Additional privileges beyond compensation payments and employee benefits are:

a) salaries.

b) wages.

c) commissions.

d) perquisites.

e) bonuses.

29 Employees involved in sales commonly receive a large proportion of their compensation in the form of:

a) pensions.

b) commissions.

c) stock.

d) bonuses.

e) profit sharing.

30 When a business creates a new position, it involves job analysis and:

a) reengineering.

b) recruiting.

c) wage compensation.

d) position description.

e) downsizing.

31 Employees who are directly involved in the production process (such as assembly-line workers) tend to receive most of their compensation in the form of a:

a) bonus.
b) commission.
c) salary.
d) stock.
e) perquisites.

32 The following are objective criteria in performance evaluation except for:

a) parts produced per week.
b) number of days absent.
c) percentage of deadlines missed.
d) defective parts produced by employee errors.
e) willingness of an employee to help other employees.

33 If firms wish to avoid hiring during a temporary increase in production, they can offer _____ to existing workers.

a) overtime
b) vacations

c) training programs
d) affirmative action
e) orientation programs

34 Firms allowing employees to be promoted from within is an example of:

a) external recruiting.
b) downsizing.
c) testing.
d) profit sharing.
e) internal recruiting.

35 A step in the recruiting process that involves screening applicants is the:

a) training procedure.
b) orientation procedure.
c) upward appraisal.
d) interview.
e) probation period.

Surfing the Net

Information on Human Resource Management

Vast quantities of human-resource-related information are available on the Internet. A good place to start looking for such information is the Society for Human Resource Management, whose home page (Exhibit 12.9) maintains links to articles and many different information sources. This site, as well as many others, maintains a current list of employment opportunities. If you need information on a particular human resource issue, use the search function to find relevant information.

Exhibit 12.9
The Society for Human Resource Management

http://www.shrm.org

Welcome to SHRM® Online

The **Society for Human Resource Management's** home on the World Wide Web.

[Join SHRM | News Update | Inside SHRM | HR Info Center |
| Reading Rack | Goods & Services | SHRM FAQ | HR Links | Job Listings]

Labor Unions

labor union established to represent the views, needs, and concerns of labor

A **labor union** is established to represent the views, needs, and concerns of labor. A union can attempt to recognize the needs of its workers, and then negotiate with the firm's management to satisfy those needs. The needs may include job security, safer working conditions, and higher salaries. The union may be able to negotiate for the workers better than they can themselves, because the workers do not have the time nor the expertise for negotiating with management. Furthermore, management would not have the time to deal with each worker's needs separately. The union serves as the representative for all workers.

BACKGROUND ON UNIONS

craft unions organized according to a specific craft (or trade), such as plumbing

industrial unions organized for a specific industry

local unions composed of members in a specified local area

national unions composed of members throughout the country

international unions include members that work in other countries

Unions can be classified as either craft or industrial. **Craft unions** are organized according to a specific craft (or trade), such as plumbing. **Industrial unions** are organized for a specific industry. The Textile Workers Union has about 140,000 members, while the United Steelworkers Union has about 700,000 members. Unions can also be classified as either local or national. **Local unions** are composed of members in a specified local area. **National unions** are composed of members throughout the country. Some local unions are part of a national union. **International unions** include members that work in other countries.

History of Union Activities

The popularity of unions has been affected by various laws, summarized next.

Norris-LaGuardia Act allowed unions to publicize a labor dispute

yellow-dog contract a contract requiring employees to refrain from joining a union as a condition of employment

THE NORRIS-LAGUARDIA ACT   Before 1932, the courts commonly accommodated employer requests to issue injunctions against unions. In 1932, the **Norris-LaGuardia Act** was passed by Congress. It allowed unions to publicize a labor dispute. It also prohibited employers from forcing workers to sign a **yellow-dog contract**, which was a contract requiring employees to refrain from joining a union as a condition of employment.

Wagner Act prohibited firms from interfering with workers' efforts to organize or join unions

THE WAGNER ACT   Even with the Norris-LaGuardia Act, firms were able to discourage employees from joining or organizing unions. The **Wagner Act** prohibited firms from interfering with workers' efforts to organize or join unions. Employers could not discriminate against employees who participated in union activities. In addition, the act required employers to negotiate with the union representing employees.

Taft-Hartley Act an amendment to the Wagner Act, prohibited unions from pressuring employees to join

right-to-work allows states to prohibit union shops

THE TAFT-HARTLEY ACT   While the Wagner Act reduced employer discrimination against union participants, it was unable to reduce strikes. The **Taft-Hartley Act**, an amendment to the Wagner Act, prohibited unions from pressuring employees to join. An exception is the union shop, where new employees are required to join the union. The **right-to-work** section of this act allows states to prohibit union shops (several states have used this power).

THE LANDRUM-GRIFFIN ACT   In 1959, Congress passed the **Landrum-Griffin Act** (originally called the Labor-Management Reporting and Disclosure Act of 1959). This act required labor unions to specify in their bylaws the membership eligibility requirements, dues, and collective bargaining procedures.

Trends in Union Popularity

Union membership declined slightly in the early 1930s, as firms discouraged workers from participating in labor activities. After the Wagner Act was passed in 1935, union membership increased rapidly. By 1945, about one-fourth of all workers were union members. However, union membership consistently declined during the 1980s and 1990s. By 1995, less than 13 percent of all workers were union members. One of the reasons for the decline was the inability of some unionized firms to compete with nonunion firms whose expenses were lower.

NEGOTIATIONS BETWEEN UNIONS AND MANAGEMENT

Contracts between unions and management commonly last for two to three years. An attempt is made to agree to a new contract before the existing contract expires. The union obtains feedback from its members on what working provisions need to be improved. Unions will also obtain data on existing wages and employee benefits provided for jobs similar to those of members. Management assesses existing conditions and determines the types of provisions it may be willing to make.

Before the actual negotiations begin, unions may offer a proposed revision of the existing contract. This proposal often includes very high demands, which management will surely refuse. Management may also offer a proposed revision of the existing contract that the union will surely refuse. Normally, the original gap between the two sides is very large. This establishes the foundation for negotiations.

When unions and management meet to negotiate a new contract, the more critical issues to be discussed are as follows:

➤ Salaries
➤ Job security
➤ Management rights
➤ Grievance procedures

Salaries

A general concern of unions is to improve or at least maintain the worker's standard of living. Unions are credited for negotiating high wages for their workers. Unionized grocery store owners commonly receive at least double the salaries of nonunionized employees in the same job positions. Airline pilot captains of unionized airlines, such as American and Delta, earn more than $100,000 per year, while pilot captains of nonunionized airlines commonly earn less than $50,000 per year.

Unions attempt to negotiate for salary increases that will at least match expected increases in the cost of living. They also monitor salaries of workers at other firms to determine the salary increases that they will request. For example, the United Auto Workers (UAW) announced on September 4, 1996 that Ford would be the target company in 1996 negotiations. The UAW contract with Ford will be used as the basis for negotiating with Chrysler or GM.

SELF-SCORING EXERCISE

The Frazzle Factor

Read each of the following statements, and rate yourself on a scale of 0 to 3, giving the answer that best describes how you generally feel (3 points for *always*, 2 points for *often*, 1 point for *sometimes*, and 0 points for *never*). Answer as honestly as you can, and do not spend too much time on any one statement.

Am I Angry?
_____ 1. I feel that people around me make too many irritating mistakes.
_____ 2. I feel annoyed because I do good work or perform well in school, but no one appreciates it.
_____ 3. When people make me angry, I tell them off.
_____ 4. When I am angry, I say things I know will hurt people.
_____ 5. I lose my temper easily.
_____ 6. I feel like striking out at someone who angers me.
_____ 7. When a co-worker or fellow student makes a mistake, I tell him or her about it.
_____ 8. I cannot stand being criticized in public.

Am I Overstressed?
_____ 1. I have to make important snap judgements and decisions.
_____ 2. I am not consulted about what happens on my job or in my classes.
_____ 3. I feel I am underpaid.
_____ 4. I feel that no matter how hard I work, the system will mess it up.
_____ 5. I do not get along with some of my co-workers or fellow students.
_____ 6. I do not trust my superiors at work or my professors at school.
_____ 7. The paperwork burden on my job or at school is getting to me.
_____ 8. I feel people outside the job or the University do not respect what I do.

Scoring

To find your level of anger and potential for aggressive behavior, add your scores from both quiz parts.

40–48: The red flag is waving, and you had better pay attention. You are in the danger zone. You need guidance from a counselor or mental health professional, and you should be getting it now.
30–39: The yellow flag is up. Your stress and anger levels are too high, and you are feeling increasingly hostile. You are still in control, but it would not take much to trigger a violent flare of temper.
10–29: Relax, you are in the broad normal range. Like most people, you get angry occasionally, but usually with some justification. Sometimes you take overt action, but you are not likely to be unreasonably or excessively aggressive.
0–9: Congratulations! You are in great shape. Your stress and anger are well under control, giving you a laid-back personality not prone to violence.

If the firm has experienced high profits in recent years, a union may use this as reason to negotiate for large wage increases. Conversely, firms that recently experienced losses will argue that they cannot afford to make pay increases. Pilots at Continental Airlines did not receive a salary increase over several years, which caused poor relations between the pilots and management at Continental.

Job Security

Job security is a key issue from the perspective of workers. They want to be assured of a job until retirement. Management may not be willing to guarantee job security, but may at least specify the conditions in which workers would be laid off. Workers with less seniority are more likely to be laid off.

While unions are unable to force management to guarantee lifetime jobs, they are somewhat successful at obtaining supplemental unemployment benefits for workers. Firms that offer these benefits contribute an amount for each hour worked into a fund. The fund is used to compensate workers who are laid off. This compensation is a supplement to the normal unemployment compensation workers receive.

Unions may also attempt to prevent management from replacing workers with machines. Management may agree to such demands if the unions reduce some of their other demands. Unions would emphasize this issue in industries such as automobile manufacturing, where some tasks are highly repetitive, and therefore workers are more likely to be replaced by machines.

For some workers, job security may be more important than higher wages. Therefore, firms that are willing to provide job security may not have to provide large increases in wages. A recent agreement between American Airlines and its workers provides more job security in exchange for no increase in wages.

Management Rights

Management expects to have various rights as to how it manages its workers. For example, the union-management contract may state a specified number of work hours. Management may also retain the rights to make their own hiring, promotional, and transferring decisions, without influence by unions.

Grievance Procedures

A grievance is a complaint made by an employee or the union. Contracts between a union and management specify procedures for resolving a grievance. The first step normally calls for a meeting between the employee, his or her supervisor, and a union representative. If this meeting does not resolve the grievance, the union normally meets with high-level managers.

CONFLICTS BETWEEN UNIONS AND MANAGEMENT

picketing walking around near the employer's building with signs complaining of poor working conditions

boycott refusing to purchase products and services

strike discontinuation of employee services

Unions use various methods to bargain for better working conditions or higher compensation. Employees may attempt to pressure management by **picketing,** or walking around near the employer's building with signs complaining of poor working conditions. Employees can also **boycott** the products and services offered by refusing to purchase them.

A more dramatic method of bargaining is a **strike,** which is discontinuation of employee services. The impact of a strike on a firm is dependent on the firm's ability to carry on operations during the strike. For example, if all machinists of a manufacturing firm strike, the firm's production will be severely reduced unless its other workers can substitute. Most firms carry an inventory of finished products that may be used to accommodate orders during the strike. However, even a large inventory will not be sufficient if the strike lasts long enough.

The publicity of a strike can reduce a firm's perceived credibility. Even though a strike is only temporary, it can create permanent damage. Some firms have long-term arrangements with other companies to provide a specified volume of supplies periodically. If these companies fear that their orders will not be satisfied because of a strike, they will search for a firm that is less likely to strike.

Exhibit 12.A1
Example of How a Strike Can Affect A Firm's Value

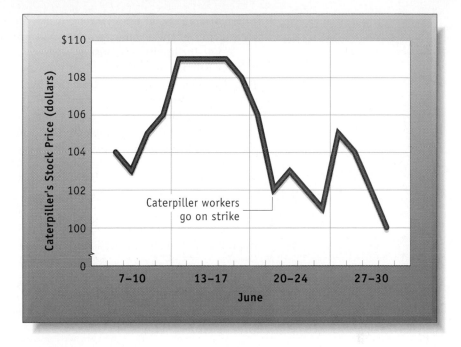

To illustrate how the dissatisfaction of employees can affect a firm's value, consider the case of Caterpillar. About fourteen thousand of Caterpillar's workers went on strike on June 21, 1994. Exhibit 12A.1 shows the stock price of Caterpillar around the time of the strike. Notice how the stock price declined by more than $4.00 per share in response to the strike. The strike lasted more than seventeen months. Caterpillar replaced many of the strikers with temporary workers and experienced record earnings over the strike period. By the end of the strike, about one-third of the strikers returned to work without any compromise by Caterpillar.

Management may respond to union pressure by obtaining an **injunction,** which is a court order to prevent the union from a particular activity such as picketing.

injunction a court order to prevent the union from a particular activity such as picketing

Caterpillar struggled through a lengthy work stoppage. However, the company held its ground and eventually ended up with a favorable agreement. Since the company and union reached agreement, the value of the firm has increased.

lockout prevents employees from working until an agreement between management and labor is reached

Alternatively, it could use a **lockout,** which prevents employees from working until an agreement between management and labor is reached.

Another common response by management is to show how large benefits to workers will possibly result in the firm's failure, which would effectively terminate all jobs. The management of Northwest Airlines and US Air used this approach in the mid-1990s to prevent excessive demands by the union. US Air also offered its pilots partial ownership of the firm in place of salary increases.

The amount of bargaining power of a union is partially dependent on whether the firm can easily replace employees who go on strike. For example, an airline cannot easily replace pilots in a short period of time because of the extensive training it must provide. Other workers with specialized mechanical skills also have some bargaining power. When thirty-three thousand machinists of Boeing (a producer of aircraft) went on strike in 1995, they forced Boeing to provide a larger salary increase as an incentive to end the strike. However, a strike by workers at Bridgestone/Firestone (a producer of tires) was not as successful, as the firm hired replacement workers.

Management's Criticism of Unions

Unions are criticized by management for several reasons, some of which are discussed here.

HIGHER PRICES OR LOWER PROFITS   If unions achieve high wages for employees, firms may pass the increase on to consumers in the form of higher prices. If firms do not pass the increase on, their profits may be reduced and the shareholders of the firm will be adversely affected. In essence, the disadvantages to the consumers or shareholders offset the benefits to employees.

A related criticism is that high wages resulting from the union can reduce the firm's ability to compete internationally. This was a major criticism during the 1980s, as many foreign competitors increased their market share in the United States.

ADVERSE IMPACT ON ECONOMIC CONDITIONS   A decision to strike by some unions can severely damage a given industry. Unions have the power to close large manufacturing plants, an airline's operations, or even garbage collection. Some shutdowns can have a severe impact on the local area.

PRODUCTION INEFFICIENCY   Some unions have negotiated for a minimum number of workers to perform a specific task. In some cases, the number of workers has exceeded the number actually needed. A related criticism is that workers are sometimes perceived to be protected from being fired if they are in a union. Management may be unwilling to fire an unproductive person if it believes the union will file a grievance. If it retains unproductive workers, its efficiency is reduced, and its cost of production increases.

How Firms Reduce the Employee's Desire for a Union

The management of some firms has consistently maintained good relations with labor. Consequently, labor has not attempted to organize a union. The following are some of the more common methods for management to maintain good relations:

1 Management should promote employees from within so that employees are satisfied with their career paths.

2 Management should attempt to avoid layoffs so that employees do not feel

AFL-CIO strikers wait it out at a Texas power plant. While union membership has decreased in recent years, they remain an important factor in many industries. The recent trend of corporate downsizing has many experts predicting a return of union strength.

threatened whenever business slows down. This may be achieved by reassigning job positions to some employees who are no longer needed in their original positions.

3 Management should allow employees responsibility and input into some decisions. Recent labor contracts between labor and management at General Motors require labor-management committees to be created at each plant to develop methods for improving efficiency. This is a classic example of considering input from employees.

4 Management should maintain reasonable working conditions to demonstrate fairness to employees.

5 Management should offer reasonable and competitive wages so that employees feel properly rewarded and are not continually quitting to take other jobs.

The points just listed represent the key working provisions for which unions negotiate. If the firm adequately maintains these provisions, workers may not need to organize a union.

The performance of a firm is highly dependent on the performance of its employees. Firms commonly attempt to improve employee performance by increasing job satisfaction. The following methods can be used to improve job satisfaction. First, firms can provide compensation that is linked with employee performance. This strategy rewards employees directly for their efforts. Second, firms may provide job security to their employees, which may reduce work-related stress. Third, firms may allow their employees to have a flexible work schedule, which allows employees to have more input on their daily or weekly work schedule. Fourth, firms may implement more employee involvement programs to give employees more input on most business decisions.

Firms can improve their performance by using proper methods of hiring, training, and evaluating their employees. Proper hiring methods ensure that employees have the right background for the types of jobs that may be assigned. Proper training enables employees to apply their skills to perform specific tasks. Proper evaluation methods ensure that employees are rewarded when they perform well, and that they are informed of any deficiencies so that they can correct them in the future.

Marketing can be broadly

defined as the actions of firms to plan and execute the design, pricing, distribution, and promotion of products. A firm's marketing mix represents the combination of product, pricing, distribution, and promotion strategies used to sell products. Examples of marketing decisions include the product decision by Kodak to design a miniature video camera, the pricing decision by Ford to price its new Mustang, the distribution decision by Nike on how to distribute its running shoes across various outlets around the world, and the promotion decision by United Airlines to use television advertising when promoting its airline services.

To recognize how all four strategies are used by a single firm, consider a computer firm that identifies a software package that consumers need. The firm could develop the software (product strategy), set a price for the software (pricing strategy), decide to sell the software through specific computer stores (distribution strategy), and decide to advertise the software in magazines (promotion strategy). Chapter 13 focuses on product and pricing strategies, Chapter 14 focuses on distribution strategies, and Chapter 15 focuses on promotion strategies.

CHAPTER 13

Product and Pricing Strategies

Product strategies dictate the means by which firms generate revenue, while pricing strategies influence the demand for the products produced. A firm's product and pricing strategies affect its value as follows:

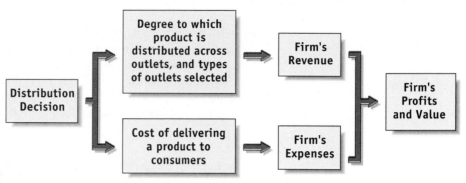

Consider the case of First Team Sports, which produces rollerblades and street hockey equipment. What factors would First Team Sports consider when deciding whether to produce other types of sports equipment? In what ways can First Team Sports differentiate its rollerblades and street hockey equipment from those of its competitors? What factors should First Team Sports consider when pricing its rollerblades? This chapter provides a background on product and pricing strategies, which can be used to address these questions.

The **Learning Goals** of this chapter are to:

1 Identify the main factors that affect a product's target market.

2 Identify the steps involved in creating a new product.

3 Explain the common methods used to differentiate a product.

4 Identify the main phases of a product life cycle.

5 Identify the factors that influence the pricing decision.

BACKGROUND ON PRODUCTS

product physical goods as well as services that can satisfy consumer needs

The term **product** can be broadly defined to include physical goods as well as services that can satisfy consumer needs. Firms must continually improve existing products and develop new products to satisfy customers over time. In this way, they generate high sales growth, which normally increases their value. Exhibit 13.1 compares Motorola's sales growth and stock price with that of Boeing. Notice how Motorola has achieved consistently strong sales growth, and its value (as measured by its stock

Exhibit 13.1
**How Sales Growth Can
Affect the Firm's Value**

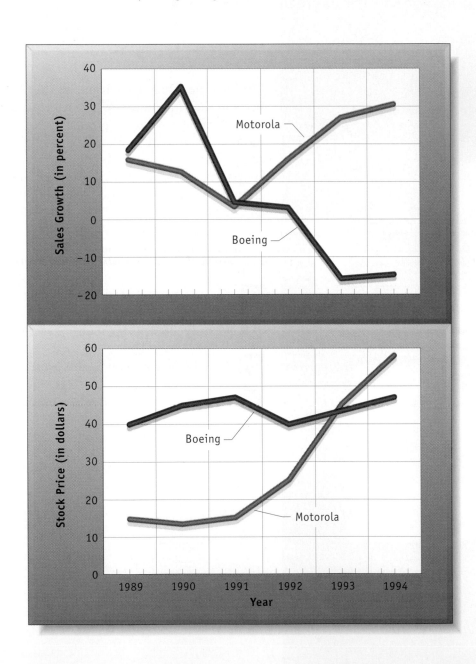

price) has risen as well. Conversely, Boeing has experienced lower sales growth in recent years, which has prevented its value from rising as much.

Most products can be classified as (1) convenience products, (2) shopping products, and (3) specialty products. **Convenience products** are widely available to consumers, are purchased frequently, and are easily accessible. Milk, newspapers, soda, and chewing gum are typical examples of convenience products.

Shopping products differ from convenience products in that they are not purchased frequently. When consumers are ready to purchase shopping goods, they first shop around and compare quality and prices of competing products. Furniture and appliances are examples of shopping products.

Specialty products are considered by specific consumers to be special, which means that these consumers would make a special effort to purchase them. A Rolex watch and a Jaguar automobile are examples of specialty products. When evaluating specialty products, consumers base their purchasing decision primarily on personal preference, not on comparative pricing.

convenience products widely available to consumers, are purchased frequently, and are easily accessible

shopping products are not purchased frequently

specialty products considered by specific consumers to be special, which means that these consumers would make a special effort to purchase them

Product Line

A **product line** represents a set of related products or services offered by a single firm. For example, Coke, Diet Coke, Caffeine-Free Diet Coke, and Sprite are all part of a single product line at The Coca-Cola Company. Pepsi, Diet Pepsi, Mountain Dew, and All-Sport are all part of a single product line at PepsiCo.

A product line tends to expand over time as a firm recognizes other consumer needs. The Coca-Cola Company recognizes that consumers differ with respect to their desire for a specific taste, caffeine versus no caffeine, and diet versus regular. They have expanded their product line of soft drinks to satisfy various needs. Compaq Computer has added new portable computers to its product line over time, while Taco Bell has added various low-fat food items to its menus.

product line a set of related products or services offered by a single firm

This Coca-Cola Company customer service representative is prepared to field questions about the many beverages in Coca-Cola's product line.

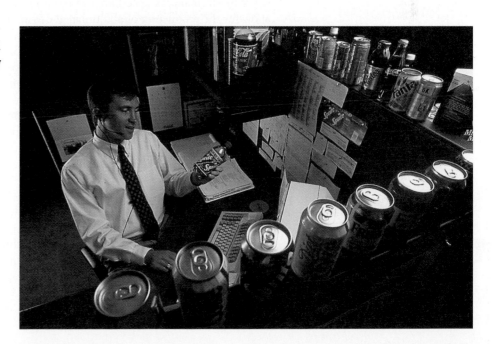

Exhibit 13.2
Product Mix of PepsiCo

Note: PepsiCo's product mix breakdown was measured by the proportion of sales generated by each product line.

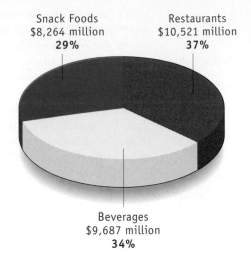

Snack Foods
$8,264 million
29%

Restaurants
$10,521 million
37%

Beverages
$9,687 million
34%

Product Mix

product mix the assortment of products offered by a firm

The assortment of products offered by a firm is referred to as the **product mix.** Most firms tend to expand their product mix over time as they identify other consumer needs or preferences. Quaker State originally focused on motor oil but has added windshield washer fluid, brake fluid, and many other automobile products to its product mix. Before firms add more products to their product mix, they should determine whether a demand for new products exists and whether they are capable of efficiently producing those products. A firm may even decide to discontinue one of the products in its product mix.

DIVERSIFYING THE PRODUCT MIX   To avoid being completely dependent on one market, firms tend to diversify their product mix when their primary product is subject to wide swings in demand. In this way, they are not as reliant on a single product whose performance is uncertain. Firms with flexible production facilities that can allow for the production of additional goods are more capable of diversifying their product mix.

A common diversification strategy is for a firm to diversify products within its existing production capabilities. For example, hospital supply companies offer a wide variety of supplies that can be sold to each hospital. Walt Disney, which had focused on producing films for children, now offers films for adults. Clothing manufacturers such as Donna Karan offer several types of clothes that can be sold to each retail outlet. A product mix that contains several related products can allow for more efficient use of salespeople. PepsiCo's product mix, summarized in Exhibit 13.2, focuses on beverages, snack foods, and restaurants.

IDENTIFYING A TARGET MARKET

1

Identify the main factors that affect a product's target market.

target market a group of individuals or organizations with similar traits who may purchase a particular product

The consumers who purchase a particular product may have specific traits in common, which cause their needs to be similar. Firms attempt to identify these traits so that they can target their marketing toward people with those traits. Marketing efforts are usually targeted toward a particular **target market,** which is a group of individuals or organizations with similar traits who may purchase a particular product.

consumer markets exist for various consumer products and services (such as cameras, clothes, and household items)

industrial markets exist for industrial products that are purchased by firms (such as plastic and steel)

Target markets can be broadly classified as consumer markets or industrial markets. **Consumer markets** exist for various consumer products and services (such as cameras, clothes, and household items), while **industrial markets** exist for industrial products that are purchased by firms (such as plastic and steel). Classifying products into consumer versus industrial markets provides only a broad description of the types of customers who purchase those products. Efforts are made by firms to more narrowly describe their target markets.

Common traits used to describe a target market are the consumer's gender, age, and income bracket. For example, the target market for dirt bikes may be males under thirty years of age, while the target market for three-month cruises may be for wealthy males or females over fifty years of age. Eddie Bauer produces a line of casual clothes for a target market of customers between thirty and fifty years of age, while Carters produces clothes for babies.

Factors That Affect the Size of a Target Market

As time passes, the demand for products changes. Firms attempt to be in a position to benefit from a possible increase in demand for particular products. For example, some hotels in Los Angeles and New York have anticipated an increase in Japanese guests and have offered new conveniences to capture that portion of the market. Common conveniences offered are Japanese translators, rooms with bamboo screens, and a Japanese-language newspaper for these guests.

As consumer preferences change, the size of a particular target market can change. Firms monitor consumer preferences over time to anticipate how the size of their target market may be affected. The following are key factors that affect consumer preferences and therefore affect the size of the target market:

➤ Demographics
➤ Geography
➤ Economic factors
➤ Social values

demographics characteristics about the human population or specific segments of the population

DEMOGRAPHICS The total demand for particular products or services is dependent on the **demographics,** or characteristics about the human population or specific segments of the population. As demographic conditions change, so does the demand. For example, demographic statistics show an increase in women who work outside the home. Firms have adjusted their product lines to capitalize on these changes. Clothing stores have created more lines of business clothing for women. Food manufacturers have created easy-to-fix frozen foods to accommodate the busy schedules of wage-earning women. The tendency for people to have less free time and more income has resulted in increased demand for more convenient services, such as quick oil change and tire replacement services.

One of the most relevant demographic characteristics is age, because target markets are sometimes defined by age levels. Demographic statistics show that the population has grown older. Consequently, sports cars are not as popular. Customers are more interested in cars that are dependable and safe. Automobile manufacturers have adjusted to the demographics by supplying fewer sports cars.

While the population has generally grown older, the number of children in the United States has recently increased. During the period 1989–95, there were at least 4 million births annually, a birth rate that the United States had not experienced since 1964 (the last year of the baby boom). Many of these recently born children have two

Exhibit 13.3
Changes in Consumer Characteristics

	1974	1994
U.S. population	214 million	260 million
Percentage of population that is at least sixty-five years of age	10%	13%
Children under eighteen who live in poverty	15%	23%
Households with income over $100,000	2 million	5.6 million
Black households with income over $100,000	29,000	214,000
Percentage of high school graduates who enter college the following fall	47%	63%

parents who work outside the home and spend large sums of money on their children. Firms such as OshKosh B' Gosh and The Gap have capitalized on this trend by producing high-quality (and high-priced) children's clothing.

To illustrate how characteristics of the population can change over time, consider the changes over the twenty-year period 1974–94, as shown in Exhibit 13.3. In general, the population has grown larger, while both the number of people living in poverty and the number of households earning more than $100,000 annually have increased. These statistics imply a reduction in the proportion of people in the middle class. Such information is relevant to firms because it suggests that the size of specific target markets may be changing over time.

GEOGRAPHY   The total demand for a product is also influenced by geography. Snow tires are targeted in northern states, while surfboards are targeted along the east and west coasts of the United States. Tastes are also influenced by geography. The demand for spicy foods is higher in the southwestern states than in other states.

ECONOMIC FACTORS   As economic conditions change, so do consumer preferences. During a recessionary period, the demand for most types of goods is reduced. Specialty and shopping products are especially sensitive to these conditions. During a recession firms may promote necessities rather than specialty products. In addition, their pricing may be more competitive during such a period. When the economy becomes stronger, firms have more flexibility to raise prices, and may also promote specialty products more than necessities.

Interest rates can also have a major impact on consumer demand. When interest rates are low, consumers are more willing to purchase goods with borrowed money. The demand for products such as automobiles, boats, or homes is especially sensitive to interest rate movements because these products are often purchased with borrowed funds.

SOCIAL VALUES   As the social values of consumers change, so do their preferences. For example, the demand for cigarettes and whiskey has declined in response to consumer awareness about the health dangers of using these products. If a firm producing either of these products anticipates the change in preferences, it can begin to shift its marketing mix. Alternatively, it could modify its product to capitalize on the trend. For example, it could reduce the alcohol content of the whiskey or the tar and nicotine content of the cigarettes. It may also revise its promotion strategy to inform the public of these changes.

In response to a trend towards $160 basketball shoes for kids, Hakeem Olajuwon and Spalding teamed together to offer a high quality but reasonably priced basketball shoe. The shoe retails for $45.

GLOBAL BUSINESS

Targeting Foreign Countries

 When firms sell their product mix in foreign countries, they must recognize that consumer characteristics vary across countries. Consider the case of CPC International, a U.S. firm that produces numerous food products including Skippy peanut butter, Mazola corn oil, and Hellmann's mayonnaise. CPC's global marketing strategy is to penetrate any foreign markets where there would be sufficient demand. Yet, CPC recognizes that some of its products will be more successful than others in particular foreign markets. Thus, it considers the characteristics of the foreign country before it decides which products to market in that country. In a recent annual report, CPC states: "We are emphatically global in our strategy of building a few core businesses worldwide; in our ability to spot worldwide trends. . . . At the same time we are decisively local in our detailed understanding of cultures, consumer trends, and competitive environments in 59 countries; in our ability to adapt our products to local eating habits and our marketing programs to cultural nuances and developing trends."

To illustrate how each product of CPC is targeted to those specific countries, consider the following brief summary of just a few of CPC's products:

1 CPC sells mayonnaise in Argentina, Brazil, and Chile, and has recently introduced it in Mexico and Venezuela. It has experienced high sales of the mayonnaise in the Czech and Slovak Republics, and has recently marketed mayonnaise in Poland.

2 CPC has been very successful in its sales of cornstarch in Latin America, where demand for cornstarch, used to prepare cakes and cereals, is strong. CPC also sells cornstarch in Asia, where it is used as a cooking aid.

3 CPC sells ready-to-eat desserts and dessert mixes in Europe, including Yabon cakes in France and Ambrosia rice puddings in the United Kingdom. It also sells dessert mixes in Latin America under the Kremel, Maizena, and Maravilla brands.

4 CPC sells pasta in Europe under the Napolina and Knorr brands, and in Asia under the Royal and Best Foods brands.

In general, the product mix marketed by CPC in any given country is dependent on the characteristics of the people in that country. CPC periodically changes the product mix that is marketed to a particular country in response to changes in that country's characteristics.

CREATING NEW PRODUCTS

2 Identify the steps involved in creating a new product.

In a given year, firms may offer more than twenty thousand new products. The vast majority of these products will be discontinued within six months. This information suggests how difficult it is to create new products that are successful. Yet, the profits from a single successful product may offset losses resulting from several failed products.

The creation of a new product does not have to represent a famous invention. Most new products are simply improvements of existing products. Consequently, existing products become **obsolete,** or less useful than in the past, for two reasons. They may no longer be in fashion, which is called **fashion obsolescence.** For example, the demand for bell-bottom pants declined once they were no longer in style. Alternatively, products may become inferior to new products that are technologically more advanced, which is called **technological obsolescence.** For example, when

obsolete less useful than in the past

fashion obsolescence no longer in fashion

technological obsolescence inferior to new products

Hewlett-Packard creates faster printers, the old models are subject to technological obsolescence.

Use of Marketing Research to Create New Products

When firms develop products, they assess the market to monitor the marketing strategies of their competitors. However, monitoring competitors may cause the firm to be a follower rather than a leader. Many firms would prefer to make product decisions that are more innovative than those of their competitors. To obtain more insight on what consumers want, firms use **marketing research**, which is the accumulation and analysis of data in order to make a particular marketing decision.

marketing research accumulation and analysis of data in order to make a particular marketing decision

Marketing research is useful for making product decisions. Computer firms build computers and automobile manufacturers design their new cars to accommodate their perception of what consumers want. Perceptions by firms of consumer preferences are more accurate when backed by marketing research.

A marketing survey may identify the preference by many consumers for a specific product that is not available. It may also identify deficiencies of the firm's existing products, which can be used to correct these deficiencies. The design and quality of a product may be revised to accommodate consumer preferences.

New and revised products may be tested with marketing research. The products can be given to prospective customers, who are asked to assess various features of the products. This type of research allows firms to make further revisions that will satisfy customers.

To have confidence in the implications drawn from marketing research, sample groups of consumers that can represent the target market are studied. Many marketing research studies lead to a marketing decision that will cost millions of dollars. If the marketing research leads to incorrect conclusions, the decision could result in a large loss to the firm.

One limitation of using marketing research to identify consumer preferences is that tastes change rapidly. Some products, such as clothing, may have been popular when the marketing research was conducted but are out of style by the time they are designed and distributed to the market.

Use of Research and Development to Create Products

Firms invest funds in research and development (R&D) to design new products or to improve the products they already produce. Manufacturing firms tend to invest more money in research and development than service firms, because technology can improve manufactured products more easily than services.

Firms that spend money on research and development expect the benefits to exceed the expenses. Procter and Gamble's research and development resulted in its two-in-one shampoo and conditioner technology. It attributes the success of its Pantene Pro-V to its product technology. This product is now the leading shampoo in various countries. Procter and Gamble has improved the technology of Tide detergent more than seventy times. Technological development can allow one firm an advantage over its competitors.

To illustrate the importance of research and development to some firms, the level of annual investment in research and development by ten firms is shown in Exhibit 13.4. Each of these firms typically spend more than $1 billion on research and development per year.

Some firms have created alliances to conduct research and development. They share the costs and their technology in attempting to develop products. An alliance

What Are the Keys to Creating Successful Products?

A recent survey asked 550 manufacturers of products to rate the sources of new product ideas. Each possible source listed in the following charts was rated 1 to 5, with 5 meaning that the source was frequently used by a firm for creating new product ideas. The average score across the 550 manufacturers is disclosed for each possible source of new product ideas.

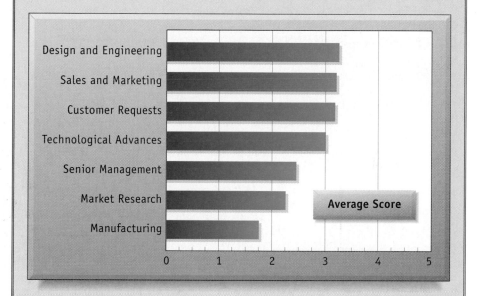

The results suggest that new product ideas most frequently come from the engineering and marketing functions, and are less frequently initiated by the senior management or from the manufacturing process.

not only combines expertise from two or more firms, but also may reduce the costs to each individual firm.

To expand their product line, many firms have recently increased their investment in research and development. For example, Abbott Laboratories has consistently increased its investment in research and development, as shown in Exhibit 13.5. Since Abbott Laboratories produces various health-care drugs, its future performance is heavily dependent on its ability to create new drugs.

USING PATENTS TO PROTECT RESEARCH AND DEVELOPMENT One potential limitation of research and development is that it may lead to the production of products that are later copied by other firms. That is, the firms that create the ideas are not always able to protect competitors from copying the idea. Consequently, the potential to recover all the expenses incurred from research and development may be dependent on whether the ideas can be protected from competitors. Firms apply for **patents,** which allow exclusive rights to the production and sale of a specific product. The use of patents can allow firms such as IBM, Kodak, and 3M to benefit from their inventions because it prevents competitors from copying the idea. The 3M Company,

patents allow exclusive rights to the production and sale of a specific product

Exhibit 13.4
Firms That Invest Heavily in Research and Development (R&D)

Firm	Products Produced	Total Spending on R&D in 1994 (in millions)
1. General Motors	Automobiles	$7,036
2. Ford Motor Company	Automobiles	5,214
3. IBM	Computer technology	3,382
4. AT&T	Communications systems	3,110
5. Hewlett-Packard	Computer technology	2,027
6. Motorola	Communications systems	1,860
7. Boeing	Airplanes	1,704
8. Digital Equipment	Computer technology	1,301
9. Chrysler	Automobiles	1,300
10. Johnson and Johnson	Health-care products	1,278

which created the Post-it notes, commonly has at least four hundred patents per year. Patents have even been created for specific sunglasses and microwave popcorn.

Steps Necessary to Create a New Product

The following steps are typically necessary to create a new product:

➤ Develop product idea.
➤ Assess the feasibility of a product idea.
➤ Design and test the product.

Exhibit 13.5
Illustration of Increased Focus on Research and Development at Abbott Laboratories

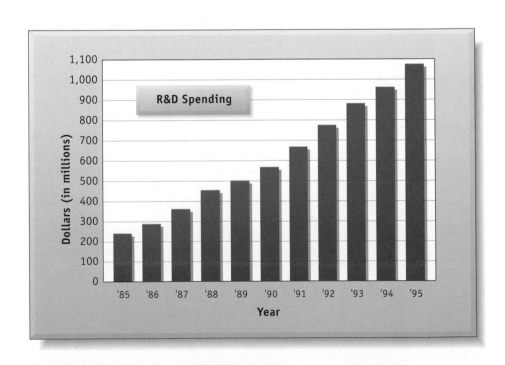

➤ Distribute and promote the product.
➤ Post-audit the product.

DEVELOP PRODUCT IDEA   The first step in creating a new product is to develop an idea. A common method of developing new ideas for products is to identify consumer needs or preferences that are not being satisfied by existing products. The ultimate goal is to develop a product that is superior to existing products in satisfying the consumer.

Many firms have recently emphasized satisfying the customer. The commitment of some firms to customer satisfaction is confirmed by the following statements in recent annual reports:

❚❚ *Kodak's future is in total customer satisfaction.* ❚❚

—Eastman Kodak

❚❚ *I [Louis Gerstner, CEO] want everyone in IBM to be obsessed with satisfying our customers.* ❚❚

—IBM

❚❚ *We aim to redouble our efforts . . . toward one simple goal: meeting the needs of our customers.* ❚❚

—Apple Computer

Identifying consumer preferences may involve monitoring human behavior. For example, an airline may monitor flights to determine the most disturbing inconveniences, such as cramped seating. This leads to ideas for an improved product, such as wider seats. To satisfy consumer preferences, rental car companies at airports now allow their key customers to go straight from the airplane to their cars (rather than stand in line at the counter).

An alternative to monitoring behavior is surveying people about their behavior. Surveys may be conducted by employees or consulting firms. Again, the goal is to identify consumer preferences that have not been fulfilled. Recognition of an increased consumer concern about health led to many ideas for new products and revisions of existing products. For example, food manufacturers responded by creating cereals and frozen dinners that are more nutritious.

Each consumer preference that deserves attention is the result of a limitation or deficiency of an existing product. The firm must determine how these deficiencies can be corrected by the creation of a new product or improvement in an existing product. In the mid-1990s, IBM decided that it needed to improve the processing speed of its computers. IBM incurred substantial expenses as a result of this decision to improve its products. However, the demand for these improved products increased, resulting in higher revenue.

ASSESS THE FEASIBILITY OF A PRODUCT IDEA   Any idea for a new or improved product should be assessed by estimating the costs and benefits. The idea should be undertaken only if the benefits outweigh the costs. For example, if an airline widens its seats to satisfy customers, the most obvious cost is the work involved in performing this task. Yet, other costs are involved as well. The widening of seats may cause

CROSS-FUNCTIONAL TEAMWORK

Interaction Among Product Decisions and Other Business Decisions

 **When marketing managers create a new product,** they must design it in a manner that will attract customers. They must also decide the price at which the product should be sold. These marketing decisions require communication between the marketing managers and the managers that oversee production. Marketing managers explain to the production managers how they would like products to be designed. The production managers may offer revisions that can improve the design of the product. They also provide estimates on the costs of production. Yet, the cost per unit is typically dependent on the volume of products to be produced; therefore, the cost per unit can be estimated only after marketing managers suggest the volume that will need to be produced to satisfy the demand. Since the pricing decisions are partially influenced by the cost of producing products, the prices cannot be determined by the marketing managers until receiving cost estimates from the production managers.

Once the marketing managers have received the necessary input from the production managers and have developed plans for the design and pricing of a product, a financial analysis by financial managers is necessary to ensure that the proposal is feasible. The financial analysis involves estimating the revenue to be generated by the firm as a result of creating this product. It also involves estimating production expenses. Using these estimates, the financial managers can determine whether the new product will provide an adequate return to the firm to make the firm's investment in the development of this product worthwhile. The marketing managers should attempt to develop the product only if the financial analysis suggests that it will provide an adequate return to the firm. If the marketing managers decide to develop this product, they would inform the production managers, who may need to hire additional production employees. In addition, the financial managers must be informed because they may need to obtain funds to finance production.

While marketing managers may be responsible for the creation of new products, they rely on input from the production and financial managers when deciding whether each product is worthwhile, and when deciding the design and price of the new product.

the airline to reduce its seating capacity. The cost of this reduction is forgone revenue (less revenue because fewer seats are available). In addition, the widening of seats may prevent the use of the airplane for a period. Any forgone revenue during that period also represents a cost of improving the product. The benefits of the wider seats are greater satisfaction to consumers, which may result in a greater demand for the airline's service, resulting in more revenue.

DESIGN AND TEST THE PRODUCT   If the firm believes the new (or revised) product is feasible, it must determine the design and other characteristics of the product. The new product may be tested before being fully implemented. For example, the airline may first revise its seating structure in a few planes to determine consumer reaction. If the actual costs exceed the benefits, the proposed changes will not be made on other airplanes. However, if the change has a favorable impact, it may be performed on the entire fleet.

DISTRIBUTE AND PROMOTE THE PRODUCT   When firms introduce new products or improve existing products, they typically attempt to inform consumers. New or improved products are introduced to consumers with various marketing techniques. As an example, an airline that widens its seats may advertise this feature in the media. Additional expenses required to promote the revised design should be accounted for when determining whether it is worthwhile to create a new design.

POST-AUDIT THE PRODUCT   After the new product has been introduced into the market, the actual costs and benefits should be measured and compared with the

Exhibit 13.6
Steps Involved in Creating
or Revising a Product

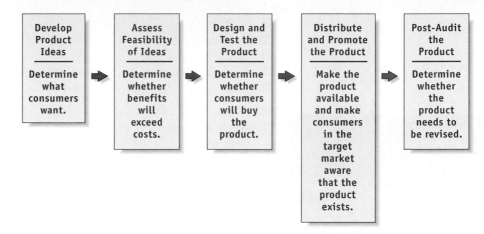

Develop Product Ideas	Assess Feasibility of Ideas	Design and Test the Product	Distribute and Promote the Product	Post-Audit the Product
Determine what consumers want.	Determine whether benefits will exceed costs.	Determine whether consumers will buy the product.	Make the product available and make consumers in the target market aware that the product exists.	Determine whether the product needs to be revised.

costs and benefits that were forecasted earlier. This comparison determines whether the cost-benefit analysis was reasonably accurate. If costs were severely underestimated or benefits were severely overestimated, the firm may need to adjust its method of analysis for evaluating other new products in the future. In addition, the post-audit of costs and benefits can be used for future development of the same product. For example, if the actual costs of improving the airplanes outweigh the benefits, the airline may revert to its original product design when new airplanes are needed.

SUMMARY OF STEPS USED TO CREATE OR REVISE A PRODUCT   A summary of the steps involved in creating or revising a product is shown in Exhibit 13.6. Notice that the whole process is initiated by attempting to satisfy consumer preferences.

PRODUCT DIFFERENTIATION

3 **Explain the common methods used to differentiate a product.**

product differentiation effort of a firm to distinguish its product from competitive products in a manner that makes it more desirable

Product differentiation is the effort of a firm to distinguish its product from competitive products in a manner that makes it more desirable. Some products are differentiated from competitive products by their quality. For example, Starbucks has become a popular coffee shop around the country because of its special coffee, even though its prices are high. Kay-Bee Toys used a marketing strategy of specializing in a small selection of high-quality toys, rather than competing with Wal-Mart and Toys "Я" Us for the entire line of toys.

All firms look for some type of competitive advantage so that their product is distinguished from the rest. The following are some of the more common methods used to differentiate the product:

➤ Unique design
➤ Unique packaging
➤ Unique branding

Unique Design

Some products are differentiated by their design. Consider a homebuilder who is presently building homes and will sell them once they are completed. The builder can attempt to build homes to satisfy buyers by assessing the following questions:

1 Would consumers in this neighborhood prefer one- or two-story homes?
2 Is a basement desirable?
3 Is a fireplace desirable?
4 What is a popular size for homes in this neighborhood?
5 What type of architecture is popular in this neighborhood?

Once the builder considers these and other issues, the homes will be built with specifications that would attract buyers.

Various characteristics could make one product better than others, including a product's safety, reliability, and ease of use. Firms such as AT&T, Kodak, and Mercedes have a reputation for their reliability, which helps create a demand for their products. Producers attempt to improve reliability by using high-quality materials, providing service, and offering warranties. However, attempts to improve reliability usually result in higher costs.

Unique Packaging

A packaging strategy can determine the success or failure of a product, especially for products whose quality levels are quite similar. In an attempt to differentiate themselves from the competition, some firms have repackaged various grocery products in unbreakable or easily disposable containers.

Many packaging strategies are focused on convenience. Motor oil is now packaged in containers with convenient twist-off caps, and many canned foods have pull-tabs. Tide detergent is packaged in both powder and liquid so that consumers can choose their preferred form.

Packaging can also provide advertising. For example, many food products such as microwave dinners are packaged to explain the preparation instructions on the outside. These instructions also demonstrate how simple the preparation is. Packaging also informs consumers about the nutrition of foods or the effectiveness of health-care products. The advertising on the package may be the key factor that encourages consumers to purchase one product instead of others.

Unique Branding

Branding is a method of identifying products and differentiating them from competitors. Brands are typically represented by a name and a symbol. A **trademark** is a brand whose form of identification is legally protected from use by other firms. Some trademarks have become so common that they represent the product itself. For example, "Coke" is often used to refer to any cola drink, and "Kleenex" is frequently used to refer to any facial tissue. Some symbols are more recognizable than the brand name. Easily recognized symbols are displayed by Levi's jeans, Nike, Pepsi, and Mercedes.

FAMILY VERSUS INDIVIDUAL BRANDING   Companies that produce goods assign either a family or an individual brand to their products. **Family branding** is the branding of all or most products produced by a company. The Coca-Cola Company sells Coca-Cola, Diet Coke, Cherry Coke, and other soft drinks. Ford, RCA, IBM, and Quaker State use family branding to distinguish their products from the competition.

Companies that use **individual branding** assign a unique brand name to different products or groups of products. For example, Procter and Gamble produces Tide, Bold, and Era. General Mills produces numerous brands of cereal. Many clothing manufacturers may use different brand names. One product line may be mar-

Product packaging is particularly important for consumer products. These Olympic cereal boxes were probably more expensive to produce than the cereal inside.

branding a method of identifying products and differentiating them from competitors

trademark a brand whose form of identification is legally protected from use by other firms

family branding branding of all or most products produced by a company

individual branding assign a unique brand name to different products or groups of products

keted to prestigious clothing shops. A second line may be marketed to retail stores. To preserve the prestige, the top quality brand may not be sold in retail stores.

PRODUCER VERSUS STORE BRANDS Most products can be classified either as a producer brand, a store brand, or a generic brand. **Producer brands** represent the manufacturer of products. Examples of producer brands are Black and Decker, Frito-Lay, and Fisher Price. These brands are usually well known because they are sold to retail stores nationwide. **Store brands** represent the retail store where the product is being sold. For example, Sears and J.C. Penney offer some products with their own label. Even if store brands were produced by firms other than the retailer, the names of the producers are not identified. Store brand products do not have as much prestige as popular producer brands; however, they often have a lower price.

Some products are not branded by the producer or the store. These products have a so-called **generic brand.** The label on generic products simply describes the product. Generic brands have become increasingly popular over the last decade because their prices are relatively low. They are most popular for products that are likely to be similar among brands, such as napkins and paper plates. Customers are comfortable purchasing generic brands of these products because there is not much risk in buying a cheaper product.

BENEFITS OF BRANDING Branding continually exposes the company's name to the public. If the company is respected, new products may be trusted because they carry the company brand name. If they carried a different name, new products introduced by a firm would not likely sell as well.

Many firms with a brand name use their name to enter new markets. The Coca-Cola Company uses its name to promote new soft drinks that it creates. Nabisco can more easily penetrate the market for various specialty foods because of its reputation for quality food products. These firms not only are able to offer new products but also may enter new geographic markets (such as foreign countries) because of their brand name.

The brand of a product is especially useful for differentiating a product when there are only a few major competitors. For example, many consumers select among only two or three brands of some products, such as toothpaste or computers.

The importance of branding is emphasized in a recent annual report of Procter and Gamble:

> ❚❚ *Consumers have to trust that a brand will meet all their needs all the time. That requires superior product technology. And it also requires sufficient breadth of product choices. We should never give consumers a . . . reason to switch away from one of our brands.* ❚❚

Having an established brand name is often crucial to store space allocation. For example, Coca-Cola and Pepsi often receive the majority of a store's soft drink shelf space. The same is true for some cereals, detergents, and even dog food. Retail stores normally allocate more space for products with popular brand names.

Recently firms have entered into agreements called **co-branding,** in which two noncompeting products are combined at a discounted price. For example, Blockbuster Entertainment Group has begun to issue Visa cards. Blockbuster Video customers can get discounts on video rentals by using their Visa card.

---

producer brands represent the manufacturer of products

store brands represent the retail store where the product is being sold

generic brand products not branded by the producer or the store

Intel successfully branded the Intel inside image for what was previously a no-name part of the computer.

co-branding two noncompeting products are combined at a discounted price

Exhibit 13.7
Methods Used to
Differentiate Products

Method	Achieve Superiority by:
Unique design	Higher level of product safety, reliability, or ease of use.
Unique packaging	Packaging to get consumers' attention or to improve convenience.
Unique branding	Using the firm's image to gain credibility, or using a unique brand name to imply prestige.

Summary of Methods to Differentiate Products

A summary of methods used to achieve product differentiation is provided in Exhibit 13.7. Firms can attempt to combine various methods to differentiate their products. For example, Kodak could create a product that is technologically superior to others. Yet, it can also differentiate its product by packaging it in a special manner and by using the Kodak family brand name.

PRODUCT LIFE CYCLE

4 **Identify the main phases of a product life cycle.**

product life cycle the typical set of phases that products experience over their life

Most products experience specific phases over their lifetime. The **product life cycle** is the typical set of phases that products experience over their life. The marketing decisions made about a particular product may be dependent on the prevailing phase of the cycle. The typical product life cycle has four specific phases:

➤ Introduction
➤ Growth
➤ Maturity
➤ Decline

Introduction

introduction phase the initial period in which consumers are informed about the product

The **introduction phase** is the initial period in which consumers are informed about the product. The promotion of a product is intended to introduce the product and make consumers aware of it. In some cases, the product is first tested in particular areas to determine consumer reaction. Recently, the concept of direct satellite television was tested in various locations. The initial cost of producing and advertising a product may exceed the revenue received during this phase. The price of the product may initially be set high if no other competitive products are in the market yet. This strategy is referred to as **price skimming.**

price skimming the price of the product may initially be set high if no other competitive products are in the market yet

Growth

growth phase the period in which sales of the product increase rapidly

The **growth phase** represents the period in which sales of the product increase rapidly. The marketing of a product is typically intended to reinforce the product's features. Cable television networks are in the growth phase. Other firms that are aware of the product's success may attempt to create a similar or superior product. The price of the product may be lowered once competitive products enter the market.

Exhibit 13.8
Product Life Cycle Phases

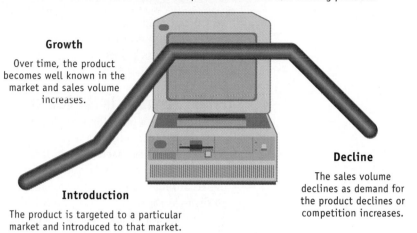

Maturity
Sales volume hits a peak at the end of the growth phase. Then sales begin to level off as a result of competition from new and existing products.

Growth
Over time, the product becomes well known in the market and sales volume increases.

Decline
The sales volume declines as demand for the product declines or competition increases.

Introduction
The product is targeted to a particular market and introduced to that market.

Maturity

maturity phase the period in which competitive products have entered the market, and sales of the product level off because of competition

The **maturity phase** is the period in which competitive products have entered the market, and sales of the product level off because of competition. At this point, most marketing strategies are used to ensure that customers are still aware that the product exists. Alternatively, some marketing strategies may offer special discounts to maintain market share. The firm may also revise the design of the existing product (product differentiation) to maintain market share. Standard cable television service is an example of a product at the maturity phase.

Decline

decline phase the period in which sales of the product decline, either because of reduced consumer demand for that type of product or because competitors are gaining market share

The **decline phase** represents the period in which sales of the product decline, either because of reduced consumer demand for that type of product or because competitors are gaining market share. If firms do not prepare for a decline phase on some products, they may experience an abrupt decline in business. Some firms begin to prepare two or more years before the anticipated decline phase by planning revisions in their existing products or services.

The product life cycle is illustrated in Exhibit 13.8. The length of a cycle tends to vary among types of products. It also varies among the firms that sell a particular type of product, because some firms lengthen the cycle by continually differentiating their product to maintain their market share.

PRICING STRATEGIES

5 **Identify the factors that influence the pricing decision.**

Whether a firm produces industrial steel, textbooks, or haircuts, it needs to determine prices for its product. Managers typically attempt to set a price that will maximize the firm's value. The price charged for a product affects the firm's revenue and therefore its earnings. Recall that the revenue from selling a product is equal to its price times the quantity sold. While a lower price reduces the revenue received per unit, it typically results in a higher quantity of units sold. A higher price increases the revenue received per unit, but results in a lower quantity of units sold. Thus, an obvious trade-off is involved when determining price for a product.

Firms set the prices of their products by considering the following:

➤ Cost of production
➤ Supply of inventory
➤ Competitors' prices

Pricing According to the Cost of Production

Some firms set a price for a product by estimating the per-unit cost of producing a product and then adding a markup. This method for pricing products is commonly referred to as **cost-based pricing.** If this method is used, the firm must also account for all production costs that are attributable to the production of that product. Pricing according to cost attempts to ensure that production costs are covered. Virtually all firms consider production costs when setting a price. The difference in price between a Cadillac and a Saturn is partially attributed to the difference in production costs. However, other factors may also influence the pricing decision.

ECONOMIES OF SCALE   The per-unit cost of production may be dependent on production volume. For products subject to economies of scale, the average per-unit cost of production decreases as production volume increases. This is especially true for products or services that have high fixed costs (costs that remain unchanged regardless of the quantity produced), such as automobiles. A pricing strategy must account for economies of scale. If a high price is charged, not only does sales volume decrease, but also the average cost of producing a small amount increases. For those products or services that are subject to economies of scale, the price should be sufficiently low to achieve a high sales volume (and therefore lower production costs).

Pricing According to the Supply of Inventory

Some pricing decisions are directly related to the supply of inventory. For example, computer firms such as IBM or Compaq typically reduce prices on existing personal computers to make room for new models that will soon be marketed. Automobile dealerships frequently use this strategy as well. Most manufacturers and retailers tend to reduce prices if they need to reduce their inventory.

Pricing According to Competitors' Prices

Firms commonly consider the prices of competitors when determining the prices of their products. They can use various pricing strategies to compete against other products, as explained next.

PENETRATION PRICING   If a firm wants to be sure that it can sell its product, it may set a lower price than those of competitive products to penetrate the market. This pricing strategy is called **penetration pricing** and has been used in various ways by numerous firms, including airlines, automobile manufacturers, and food companies.

The success of penetration pricing depends on the responsiveness of consumers to a reduced price. The demand for a product that is **price-elastic** is highly responsive to price changes. Some grocery products such as napkins and paper plates are price-elastic, as price may be the most important criterion that consumers use when

Pricing Information-Based Products

As information technology is increasingly incorporated into products, manufacturers are having to rethink their traditional pricing strategies. Traditionally, most product costs have come from labor and raw materials. This means that the variable cost of each unit produced (the costs directly associated with a given unit) was a critical factor in the pricing decision. The information technology components of products have a markedly different cost structure, however. While it may cost tens or hundreds of millions of dollars to design and test a single chip, once chips are in production, the variable cost of producing additional chips is very small (such as a few dollars or even pennies). The same is true for producing software. As a result, while incorporating information technology into a product may dramatically improve product

quality, it can have little impact on the variable cost of that product. Therefore, variable cost is less useful in deciding on price.

How should manufacturers recoup the investment they made in incorporating information technology into their products? One way is to raise product prices to reflect the higher value of the redesigned products to consumers. However, other opportunities are available to gain revenue from the technology. Licensing the product to other manufacturers, as Adobe did with its PostScript printer language, is one way of deriving revenue. Another is to market the specialized test equipment needed to service the new technology. Some companies even use technology as a source of ongoing revenue from prior customers, periodically offering upgrades to the on-board information systems in their products.

Whether or not a product contains information technology, it is ultimately the market that determines if the "price is right." As such technologies become increasingly important to product performance, however, companies will have to be more creative in their product and pricing strategies.

deciding which brand to purchase. Philip Morris lowered its price for Marlboro cigarettes by about 30 percent in the mid-1990s and was able to increase its market share from about 20 percent to 31 percent. Taco Bell increased its Mexican-style fast-food market share to 76 percent after reducing its prices.

When Southwest Airlines entered the airline industry, its average fare was substantially lower than the average fare charged by other airlines for the same routes. Southwest not only pulled customers away from other competitors, but also created some new customer demand for airline services because of its low prices.

However, penetration pricing is not always successful. Allstate Insurance increased its market share by lowering its insurance prices (premiums), but its profits declined because it lowered its prices too much.

price-inelastic the demand for a product is not very responsive to price changes

The demand for a product that is **price-inelastic** is not very responsive to price changes. Firms should not use penetration pricing if their products are price-inelastic, because most consumers would not switch to competitive products to take advantage of lower prices. For some products, such as deli products and high-quality automobiles, personalized service and perceived quality may be more important than price. The demand for many services is not responsive to price reductions, because consumers may prefer one firm over others. For example, consumers may be unwilling to switch dentists, hair stylists, or stockbrokers because a competitor reduced its price.

defensive pricing the act of reducing product prices to defend (retain) market share

DEFENSIVE PRICING Some pricing decisions are defensive rather than offensive. If a firm recognizes that the price of a competitive product has been reduced, it may use **defensive pricing**, which is the act of reducing product prices to defend (retain) market share. For example, airlines commonly reduce their airfares in response to a competitor who lowered its airfares. This response tends to allow all airlines to retain their market share, but their revenue will decrease (because of the lower price).

Exhibit 13.9
Estimation of Costs and Revenue at Various Quantities Produced

Quantity (Q)	Fixed Cost	Variable Cost (Q × $.60)	Total Cost	Total Revenue (Q × $1.80)	Profits
1,000	$4,000	$600	$4,600	$1,800	−$2,800
3,000	4,000	1,800	5,800	5,400	−400
4,000	4,000	2,400	6,400	7,200	800
7,000	4,000	4,200	11,200	12,600	1,400
10,000	4,000	6,000	16,000	18,000	2,000
15,000	4,000	9,000	13,000	27,000	14,000
20,000	4,000	12,000	16,000	36,000	20,000
25,000	4,000	15,000	19,000	45,000	26,000
30,000	4,000	18,000	22,000	54,000	32,000

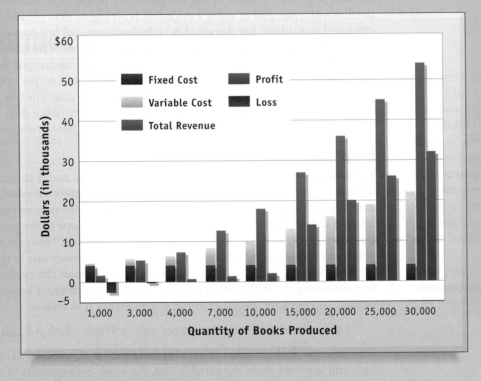

ADDITIONAL PRICING DECISIONS

In addition to setting the price of a product, firms must decide whether to offer special discounts, periodic sales prices, and credit terms for specific customers. Each of these decisions is discussed separately.

Discounting

Since some consumers are willing to pay more for a product than others, a firm may attempt to charge different prices to different customers. For example, restaurants and hotels often offer discounts for senior citizens. Magazines offer student discounts on subscriptions. Airlines tend to charge customers on business at least twice the fares of customers who are paying for the flight themselves. Discounting can enable the firm to attract consumers that are more price conscious, while charging higher prices to other consumers that are less price conscious.

Sales Prices

Many firms use sales prices as a means of discounting for those consumers who may make purchases only if the price is reduced. For example, retail stores tend to place some of their products on sale in any given week. This strategy not only attracts customers who may have been unwilling to purchase those products at the full price, but also encourages them to buy other products while they are at the store.

Many products, such as televisions and shoes, have normally been priced high by stores to allow for a major reduction in the prices when they are on sale. Since most consumers recognize that these products may soon be priced at a 20 to 40 percent discount, they tend to purchase these products only when they are on sale.

Credit Terms

Regardless of the price charged for a product, firms must determine whether they should allow the product to be purchased on credit. Supplier firms commonly allow manufacturing firms to purchase supplies on credit. They would obviously prefer cash sales, since a cash payment avoids the possibility of bad debt and also provides an immediate source of funds. However, they may still offer credit to attract some manufacturing firms that do not have cash available.

Firms can encourage their customers to pay off their credit by offering a discount. For example, the terms "2/10 net 30" imply that a 2 percent discount can be taken if the bill is paid within ten days, and the bill must be paid in full within thirty days.

A change in credit terms can affect the firm's sales. Thus, firms may revise credit terms as a marketing tool. If a firm desired to increase demand, it may offer an

The GM Card rebates 5% of purchases back to the consumer in the form of a discount against the purchase price of a new car.

extended period to pay off the credit, such as 2/10 net 60. A disadvantage of this strategy is that many credit balances will be paid off at a slower rate. In addition, the level of bad debt tends to be higher for firms that offer such loose credit terms.

Many retail stores offer credit to customers through MasterCard and Visa credit cards. Retailers pay a percentage of their credit sales (usually around 4 percent) to the bank that sponsors the card. The advantage of these cards is that the credit balance is paid by the card sponsor, who in turn is responsible for collecting on customer credit. Retail stores such as J.C. Penney and Sears offer their own credit cards.

BUSINESS DILEMMA

· COLLEGE ·
HEALTH CLUB

Product Differentiation at College Health Club

Some of the key concepts in this chapter are integrated in the following discussion of College Health Club's (CHC) marketing decisions. Sue Kramer recently reviewed the firm's product and pricing policies, and created the following assessment.

CHC's primary product is health-club services. The target market has been working men and women between the ages of nineteen and thirty who are or were enrolled in the nearby college.

Since the facilities are not being fully utilized during the mornings and early afternoons, CHC's needs to reevaluate its target market. Additional markets should be targeted to more efficiently utilize the facilities. Homemakers should be targeted, since they could utilize the facilities during these off-peak periods. Yet, because they may have children at home, the product (services) that CHC offers may have to be expanded to attract this new market.

The price of an annual membership is $250. This price is lower than most competitors. CHC's sales volume is adequate, but the facilities are rarely crowded. CHC could accommodate a larger group of customers, especially during the morning and early afternoon hours.

Dilemma

Sue considers methods to make CHC more desirable than the competition. CHC's initial success was attributed to its price and convenience for the students at the local college. However, Sue wants to differentiate the services for members to ensure continued interest by students. She also wants to retain the members even after they graduate from college.

Sue follows the steps discussed in this chapter for considering improvements in the service her club offers to members. First, she surveys existing members to determine whether they have specific preferences that she could provide to keep them as long-term customers. The following are the main suggestions of members:

1 Install a small bar in CHC.
2 Install televisions throughout CHC so that customers could watch specific programs while exercising. Some of the televisions would have a video cassette recorder along with several cassettes on aerobics and exercising.
3 Establish a refreshments area (or at least vending machines) for customers who want to take a break. This would encourage more social interaction between customers and differentiate CHC from competitors. As friendships develop, customers

will be less likely to switch to an unfamiliar competitor health club.

4 Install a child care section in CHC so that customers could place their children there whenever they came to the club.

Sue wants to assess the costs and benefits of each of these ideas so that she can decide which ideas (if any) to implement. Offer your opinion on which of these ideas (if any) Sue should implement.

Solution

Sue decides that the bar is not worth considering, because she wants CHC's focus to be on health and does not want to have the responsibility of managing a bar and applying for the necessary ownership licenses. The bar would use up valuable space in the health club, and some college student members are minors. Sue also believes that CHC members would not quit their membership for lack of a bar, since other popular casual bars are nearby.

Sue now focuses on the feasibility of the televisions and the refreshments area. She could purchase three televisions for about $1,500, which could be installed in three separate areas of CHC for members. Since a CHC membership is presently $250, the televisions are considered a feasible purchase if they would bring in six new (or renewal) memberships. That is, six new or renewal memberships would cover the $1,500 expense of three new televisions. Sue believes that the televisions are worth purchasing.

Sue also decides to install some vending machines. This would take up less room than a refreshment stand, and Sue would not need to hire employees to provide refreshments. The vending area would allow for social interaction among members.

Sue also decides to add a child care section that would be available during off-peak periods (mornings). In the afternoon when the club is more crowded, this section would be cleared for more exercise space. While Sue recognizes that she might have to buy an insurance policy to cover the potential liability from child care, she believes that the child care section would result in a substantial increase in members.

Each of Sue's decisions was made based on comparing the estimated costs of improving the health club services with the potential extra revenue that would result from increased memberships.

Additional Issues for Discussion

1 How could Sue more closely evaluate the feasibility of targeting homemakers for off-peak periods?

2 When Sue created CHC, she focused on the target market of students at the college nearby. Her promotions and advertising were focused on the college students. If she now decides to target homemakers as well, how might she revise her promotion and advertising?

3 Would prestige pricing be an effective strategy for CHC, based on its target market?

CHAPTER 14

Distribution Strategies

A distribution channel represents the path of a product from the producer to the customer. The channel often includes marketing intermediaries, or firms that participate in moving the product toward the customer.

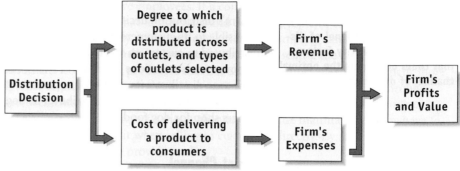

A firm's distribution decisions can affect its value by influencing the amount of customers that the product reaches (and therefore influencing revenue). Distribution decisions can also affect the costs of delivering a product from the point of production to the consumer.

Consider the case of Wilson Company, which produces a variety of tennis rackets. Should Wilson distribute its tennis rackets directly to consumers, or should it distribute them to retail stores? Should it sell its rackets exclusively to sporting goods stores or to any retail merchandise stores? Should it use a wholesaler or its own employees to distribute the rackets to retail stores? This chapter provides a background on strategies used to distribute products to customers, which can be used to address these questions.

The **Learning Goals** of this chapter are to:

1 Explain advantages and disadvantages of a direct channel of distribution, and identify factors that could determine the optimal channel of distribution.

2 Differentiate between types of market coverage.

3 Explain how the distribution process can be accelerated.

4 Explain how retailers can serve manufacturers.

5 Explain how wholesalers can serve manufacturers and retailers.

6 Explain the strategy and potential benefits of vertical channel integration.

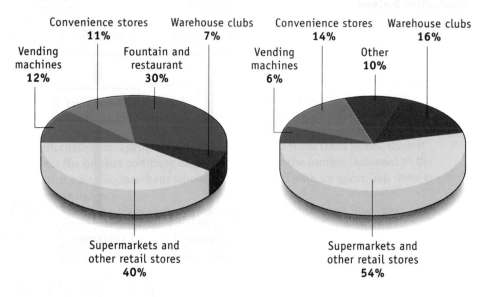

Exhibit 14.4
Intensive Distribution of Products by PepsiCo

PepsiCo's Soft Drink Distribution Channels

Convenience stores 11%
Warehouse clubs 7%
Vending machines 12%
Fountain and restaurant 30%
Supermarkets and other retail stores 40%

PepsiCo's Snack Chip Distribution Channels

Convenience stores 14%
Warehouse clubs 16%
Vending machines 6%
Other 10%
Supermarkets and other retail stores 54%

Intensive Distribution

intensive distribution distribute the product across most or all possible outlets

To achieve a high degree of market coverage for all types of consumers, **intensive distribution** is used to distribute the product across most or all possible outlets. Firms that use intensive distribution ensure that consumers will have easy access to the product. Intensive distribution is used for products such as chewing gum and cigarettes, which do not take up much space in outlets and do not require any expertise for employees of outlets to sell the products.

Intensive distribution is also used by PepsiCo to distribute its soft drinks and snacks. Exhibit 14.4 show how PepsiCo's products are sold through those retail outlets that focus on food and drinks. PepsiCo distributes its soft drinks and snack foods to virtually every supermarket, convenience store, and warehouse club in the United States and in some foreign countries.

Selective Distribution

selective distribution distribute the product among selected outlets

Selective distribution is used to distribute the product among selected outlets. That is, some outlets are intentionally avoided. For example, some specialized computer equipment will be sold only at outlets that emphasize computer sales, since some expertise may be necessary. Some college textbooks will be sold only at college bookstores and not at retail bookstores. Liz Claiborne distributes its clothing only to upscale clothing stores.

Exclusive Distribution

exclusive distribution the use of only one or a few outlets

Exclusive distribution involves the use of only one or a few outlets. This is an extreme form of selective distribution. For example, some luxury items may be distributed exclusively to a few outlets that cater to very wealthy consumers. By limiting the distribution, the firm can create or maintain the prestige of the product. Some Nike brands are sold exclusively to Foot Locker's retail stores.

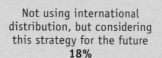

Are Catalogs Using International Distribution?

A recent survey of small firms specializing in catalog sales asked these firms whether they were attempting to distribute their catalogs (and therefore their products) internationally. The results of the survey are provided in the following chart:

Not using international distribution, but considering this strategy for the future
18%

Not using international distribution, and is not planning to use this strategy in the future
18%

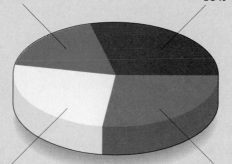

Not using international distribution, but receiving international orders anyway
26%

Using international distribution
27%

The results suggest that 71 percent of all catalog firms surveyed are either distributing their products internationally or considering such a strategy. Many catalog firms appear to recognize the potential to expand their business internationally without necessarily establishing subsidiaries in foreign countries.

Some products require specialized service that may have exclusive distribution. A firm producing high-quality jewelry may prefer to distribute exclusively to one particular jewelry store in an area where the employees receive extensive training.

Selecting the Optimal Type of Market Coverage

A comparison of the alternative degrees of market coverage achieved by distribution systems is provided in Exhibit 14.5. The optimal degree of coverage is dependent on the characteristics of the product.

Marketing research can determine the optimal type of coverage by identifying where consumers desire to purchase products or services. For example, a marketing survey could determine whether a firm should distribute its videocassettes for sale through video stores only, or through grocery stores as well. If the survey leads to a decision to distribute through grocery stores, the firm can then use additional marketing research to compare the level of sales at its various outlets. This research will help determine whether the firm should continue distributing videocassettes through grocery stores. Marketing research shows that Foot Locker retail stores attract

Exhibit 14.5
Alternative Degrees of Market Coverage

	Advantage	Disadvantage
Intensive Distribution	Gives consumers easy access.	Many outlets will not accept some products if consumers are unlikely to purchase those products there.
Selective Distribution	The distribution is focused on those outlets where there will be demand for the products, and/or where employees have expertise to sell the products.	Since the distribution is selective, the products will not be as accessible as they would be if intensive distribution were used.
Exclusive Distribution	Since the distribution is focused on a few outlets, the products are perceived as prestigious. Also the producer can ensure that the outlets where the products are distributed are able to service the product properly.	The product's access to customers is limited.

teenagers who are willing to spend $80 or more for athletic shoes. Nike distributes its shoes to Foot Locker because it views these teenagers as its target market.

SELECTING THE TRANSPORTATION USED TO DISTRIBUTE PRODUCTS

Any distribution of products from producers to wholesalers or from wholesalers to retailers requires transportation. The cost of transporting some products can exceed the cost of producing them. An inefficient form of transportation can result in higher costs and lower profits for the firm. For each form of transportation, firms should estimate timing, cost, and availability. This assessment allows the firm to choose an optimal method of transportation. The most common forms of transportation used to distribute products are described next.

Truck

Trucks are commonly used for transport because they can reach any destination on land. They can usually transport quickly and can make several stops. For example, The Coca-Cola Company uses trucks to distribute its soft drinks to retailers in a city.

Rail

Railroads are useful for heavy products, especially when the sender and receiver are located close to railroad stations. For example, railroads are commonly used to send coal to electric plants. However, if a firm is not adjacent to the station, it must reload the product on to a truck. Because the road system allows much more accessibility than railroad tracks, railroads are not useful for short distances. For long distances, however, they can be the cheapest form of transportation.

Air

Transportation by airline can be quick and relatively inexpensive for light items such as computer chips and jewelry. For a large amount of heavy products such as steel or

The Port of Houston is one of the largest in the United States. Water carriers remain a dominant form of transportation for bulk products such as grains, coal, chemicals, and petroleum products.

wood, truck or rail is a better alternative. Even when air is used, trucks are still needed for door-to-door service (to and from the airport).

Water

For some coastal or port locations, transportation by water deserves to be considered. Shipping is necessary for the international trade of some goods such as automobiles. Water transportation is often used for transporting bulk products.

Pipeline

For products such as oil and gas, pipelines can be an effective method of transportation. However, the use of pipelines is limited to only a few types of products.

Additional Transportation Decisions

The selection of the proper form of transportation (such as truck, rail, and so on) is only the first step in developing a proper system for transporting products. To illustrate how complex the transporting of products can be, consider the case of PepsiCo, which may receive orders of its snack foods and soft drinks from one hundred stores in a single city every week. It must determine an efficient way to load the products and then create a route to distribute those products among stores. It must decide the best route and the number of trucks needed to cover the one hundred stores. It must also decide whether to distribute snack foods and soft drinks simultaneously, or allow some trucks to distribute snack foods and others to distribute soft drinks.

Frito-Lay, a subsidiary of PepsiCo, uses nine hundred trucks to deliver snack foods to grocery, convenience, and drugstores. While its distribution network has been effective, Frito-Lay continues to consider ways to reduce its cost of distribution.

In reality, no perfect formulas are available to determine the ideal distribution system. Most firms attempt to estimate all the expenses associated with each possible way of delivering products that are ordered. Firms compare the total estimated expenses of each method and select the one that is most efficient.

HOW TO ACCELERATE THE DISTRIBUTION PROCESS

3 Explain how the distribution process can be accelerated.

The structure of a firm's distribution system affects its performance. A lengthy distribution process has an adverse effect. First, products will take longer to reach customers, which may allow competitors to provide products to the market sooner. This may cause retail stores or customers to order their products from other firms.

A slow distribution process will also result in a long time period from when the firm invests funds to produce the product until it receives revenue from the sale of the product. In most cases, firms will not receive payment until after customers receive the products. Consequently, firms are forced to invest their funds in the production process for a longer period of time.

To illustrate the importance of speed in the distribution process, consider that the actual time taken to distribute a typical cereal box from the producer to the retailer (the grocery store) is about one hundred days. Now consider a cereal firm that receives $100 million per year in revenue from the sale of cereal, and could reduce its distribution time from one hundred days to sixty days on average. In a typical year, this firm would receive its $100 million of revenue forty days earlier than before, meaning it would have forty extra days to reinvest those funds in other projects. Thus, a reduction in distribution time can enhance the firm's value.

Streamline the Channels of Distribution

Many firms are attempting to streamline the channels of distribution so that the final product reaches customers more quickly. For example, by eliminating some of its six regional warehouses, National Semiconductor reduced its typical delivery time by 47 percent and its cost of distribution by 2.5 percent. It now sends its microchips directly to customers around the world from its distribution center. This restructuring has removed one level of the distribution process, as shown in Exhibit 14.6.

Restructuring a distribution process commonly results in the elimination of warehouses. When products are light (such as microchips) and can be easily deliv-

Exhibit 14.6

Example of a Restructured Distribution Process

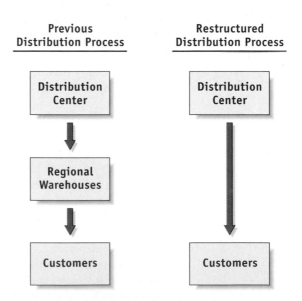

Exhibit 14.7
Relationship between
Production and Distribution

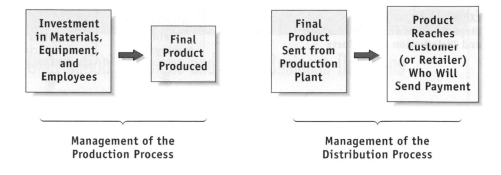

The distribution process can also be accelerated by improving its interaction with the production process. Notice from Exhibit 14.7 how the production process interacts with the distribution process. As an example, if automobiles are produced but not distributed quickly, the production process may be halted until there is room to store the newly produced automobiles. Alternatively, if an insufficient quantity of automobiles is produced, the manufacturer will not be able to distribute the amount of automobiles that dealers desire, no matter how efficient its distribution process is.

ered by mail to customers, warehouses may not be needed. However, heavy products (such as beverages) cannot be easily delivered by mail, thus warehouses are necessary.

Integrate the Production and Distribution Processes

The distribution process can also be accelerated by improving its interaction with the production process. Notice from Exhibit 14.7 how the production process interacts with the distribution process. As an example, if automobiles are produced but not distributed quickly, the production process may be halted until there is room to store the newly produced automobiles. Alternatively, if an insufficient quantity of automobiles is produced, the manufacturer will not be able to distribute the amount of automobiles that dealers desire, no matter how efficient its distribution process is.

Saturn ensures that its production and distribution processes interact. Its factories must always have the supplies and parts needed to produce a large volume of automobiles. Then, the automobiles must be distributed to numerous dealerships around the country. Local or economic conditions can cause the amount of new automobiles that dealerships periodically need to change abruptly. Thus, Saturn's production and distribution process must be able to respond quickly to abrupt changes in the demand by dealerships. Since Saturn allows interaction between its production process and distribution process, it can adjust to satisfy demand.

Compaq Computer has also used interaction between production and distribution to accelerate its process of distributing computers to more than thirty thousand wholesalers and retail stores. It has reduced the time from which a final product is produced until it leaves the production plant from four weeks to two weeks. Computer technology is now used to indicate which products should be loaded on to specific trucks for delivery purposes.

Exhibit 14.8 provides another perspective on the tasks involved from the time supplies and materials used to produce a product are ordered until the product is delivered to retailers. This exhibit shows how the distribution of products relies on production. If any step within the production process breaks down and lengthens the production period, products will not be distributed on a timely basis.

Assuming that the production process is properly conducted, the firm still needs an efficient distribution system to ensure that products are consistently available for customers. One of the keys to an efficient distribution system is to ensure that any intermediaries used to transfer products from producers to consumers maintain an adequate inventory. The producer must maintain sufficient inventory in anticipation of orders from wholesalers, retailers, or customers. If it does not, it will experience shortages. This task is especially challenging when the firm produces a wide variety of products and sells them to several different intermediaries or customers.

These questions help Sue arrive at a conclusion. Members would like to purchase exercise clothing at the club because it is a convenient place for them to shop. However, Sue does not want to use up valuable space in the club to create a retail shop that would primarily serve customers. The membership is too small to set up a shop.

Sue decides on a compromise solution. She decides to display six different styles of exercise clothing produced by the manufacturer with a poster explaining that members can purchase any of the styles. She would maintain an inventory of the clothing in the back room. Her strategy is to serve as a retailer of only these six styles without using up much space in her health club.

Additional Issues for Discussion

1 If Sue agrees to sell exercise clothing produced by the manufacturer, would the distribution system be a direct channel, a one-level channel, or a two-level channel?

2 Sue had considered producing her own line of CHC exercise clothing and selling it at her health club. Would this type of distribution system be a direct channel, a one-level channel, or a two-level channel?

3 Assume that Sue decides to produce her own line of CHC clothing to sell at her health club. Does this situation reflect intensive distribution, selective distribution, or exclusive distribution?

SUMMARY

1 The advantages of a direct channel of distribution are:

➤ the full difference between the producer's cost and the price paid by the consumer goes to the producer;
➤ the producer can easily obtain firsthand feedback on the product, allowing for quick service on customer complaints and for the opportunity to quickly correct any deficiencies.

The disadvantages of a direct channel of distribution are:

➤ the producer must employ more salespeople;
➤ the producer may have to provide credit to customers and incur the risk of bad debt (some intermediaries might be willing to incur this risk);
➤ the producer must provide all product promotions (some intermediaries might be willing to promote the products for producers).

The optimal channel of distribution is dependent on ease of transportation; the greater the ease, the more likely that intermediaries could be used. It is also dependent on the degree of standardization; the more standardized the product, the more likely that intermediaries could be used.

2 The three types of market coverage are:

➤ intensive distribution, which is used to distribute the product across most or all outlets;
➤ selective distribution, which is used to intentionally avoid some outlets;
➤ exclusive distribution, which uses only one or a few outlets.

3 A quick distribution process not only satisfies customers but also reduces the amount of funds that must be used to support this process. Firms may accelerate their distribution process by reducing the channels of

distribution. Alternatively, they may improve the interaction between the distribution and production processes. The distribution process relies on the production process to have products ready when needed.

4 Retailers serve as intermediaries for manufacturers by distributing products directly to customers. Each retailer is distinguished by its characteristics, such as number of outlets (independent versus chain), quality of service (self-service versus full-service), variety of products offered (specialty versus variety), and whether it is a store or a nonstore retailer.

5 Wholesalers serve manufacturers by:

➤ maintaining the products purchased at their own warehouse, which allows manufacturers to maintain smaller inventories;
➤ using their sales expertise to sell products to retailers;

➤ delivering the products to retailers;
➤ assuming credit risk in the event that the retailer does not pay its bills;
➤ providing information to manufacturers about competitive products being sold in retail stores.

Wholesalers serve retailers by:

➤ maintaining sufficient inventory so that retailers can order small amounts frequently;

➤ sometimes promoting the products they sold to the retailers;
➤ setting up product displays for retailers;
➤ offering products on credit to retailers;
➤ informing retailers about policies implemented by other retailers regarding the pricing of products, allocation of space, and so on.

6 Vertical channel integration is the managing of more than one level of the distribution system by a single firm. For example, a manufacturer of a product may create an intermediary such as a retail store to distribute the product. Alternatively, an intermediary may decide to produce the product instead of ordering it from manufacturers. In either example, a single firm serves as a manufacturer and an intermediary, and would no longer rely on another firm to manufacture or distribute its product.

KEY TERMS

agents
chain
direct channel
exclusive distribution
full-service retail store
independent retail store

intensive distribution
market coverage
marketing intermediaries
merchants
one-level channel
selective distribution

self-service retail store
specialty retail store
two-level channel
variety retail store
vertical channel integration

REVIEW QUESTIONS

1 What type of distribution system would a manufacturer use for the following products: (a) Calvin Klein jeans, (b) hometown newspapers, (c) Kenmore automatic washers?
2 What mode of transportation should be considered by an orchid grower in Hawaii who sends orchids to retail stores in other states? Why?
3 A manufacturer who sells staple products to mini-mart service stations would utilize wholesalers and retailers to reach the final customer. Why?

4 Explain why Liz Claiborne distributes its clothing at upscale clothing stores as opposed to discount chain stores.
5 In the United States, the distribution network is well organized. However, in foreign countries, especially Third World countries, distribution networks are not well organized. Why has this happened?
6 How can marketing research determine the optimal type of distribution coverage for the firm?

7 Identify and explain the relationship between production and distribution in reaching the ultimate consumer.
8 Discuss the advantages and disadvantages of direct channel distribution.
9 Discuss the factors that would determine an optimal channel of distribution.
10 Compare and contrast one-level and two-level channels of distribution.

DISCUSSION QUESTIONS

1 Discuss the likely events resulting from the elimination of intermediaries for the following products: (a) Rolling Rock beer, (b) Levi's jeans, (c) Grand Cherokee.

2 The president of a soft drink firm states, "No matter how productive we are, we cannot get anything accomplished unless you intermediaries get this product on the retailers' shelves." Comment.
3 Only recently have community colleges started to realize that they, like manufacturers, must give thought to their distribution systems. What dis-

tribution decisions might community colleges have to make?

4 Describe an appropriate channel of distribution for (a) a loaf of bread sold in a local grocery store, (b) a Buick Regal, (c) a door-to-door salesperson.

5 Select the appropriate distribution (intensive, selective, or exclusive) for the following products: (a) Ethan Allen furniture, (b) Marlboro cigarettes, (c) Starter jackets, (d) Reebok shoes, (e) *USA Today*.

RUNNING YOUR OWN BUSINESS

1 Describe how your business will distribute the product to the customers.

2 Describe whether the cost of distributing your product will be affected substantially if there is a large increase in the price of gasoline or in the postal rates.

INVESTING IN THE STOCK OF A BUSINESS

Using the annual report of the firm in which you would like to invest, complete the following:

1 How does the firm distribute its products to consumers? Does it rely on wholesalers? Does it rely on retail stores?

2 Has the firm revised its distribution methods in recent years? If so, provide details.

CASE 1 Distribution of Comic Books

As a boy, Stephen Geppi enjoyed reading comic books. Little did he realize then that ten-cent comic books would eventually turn into a multimillion-dollar industry.

When Geppi saw his nephew reading a comic book, he realized that the ten-cent comics he read as a boy were now considered collector's items worth hundreds of dollars.

Geppi started to search for comics at garage sales, flea markets, swap shops, and through the mail. He discovered he could make more money from the comics than from his full-time job. He decided to quit his job and open his own business. He went from owning Geppi's Comics World, his first retail store, to Diamond Comic Distributors, which is the largest distributor of U.S. comics in the world.

Switching from a retail outfit to a distributor in 1982 was an accident; the distributor that Geppi was buying from was almost bankrupt. Geppi stepped in to ensure his own future supply of comics. Diamond has continued to be successful through acquiring other comic book distributors and has expanded to a global distribution network.

Today Geppi has a 45 percent market share in a $500 million industry.

Geppi tries to do more than compete on delivery, time, and price. He offers a variety of services to the retailer, such as catalogs and advertising for retailers. His goal is to develop technology, from the vendor to the retailer, in the form of bar coding and point-of-sale systems to improve automation and inventory control. He plans to develop a competitive edge to lock in retailers to the vast array of services offered by his firm.

Questions

1 How has Diamond Comic Distributors developed a competitive advantage over other distributors?

2 What channels of distribution are in place for Diamond Comic Distributors?

3 Discuss how Diamond will develop goals for inventory control in the future.

4 What type of market coverage is extended by Diamond Comic Distributors?

CASE 2 Distribution Decisions by Transtar

Transtar Industries is a wholesaler in business to sell transmission parts for trucks. It recently installed a computerized order system. The system allows a customer (such as a truck repair shop) to order inventory parts from anywhere in the United States. Transtar can ship it directly to the customer.

Monte Ahuja, president of Transtar, developed an objective that his company would sell more than transmission parts. His plan was to sell technical expertise to provide his customers who own repair shops with information pertaining to truck transmission availability. Previously, the average transmission shop dealt with seven or so transmissions, but with recent technological changes and the increased number of imports entering the United States, shops must now handle as many as ninety different transmissions. Ahuja has placed his company in a position to be more competitive in the industry by putting more emphasis on information rather than price. He offers numerous product catalogs and handbooks that provide extensive, detailed descriptions and diagrams of every transmission, as well as specific parts needed to complete the repairs. Technical support is given by way of an 800 phone line that provides mechanics with a description of the product features offered by Transtar and data pertaining to Transtar transmission availability.

With the staggering selection of transmissions, shops cannot begin to keep all the essential parts. To help alleviate this problem, Transtar has organized a national computer network linking its twelve regional offices around the country. This will provide information on the status of in-stock inventory, orders expected to come in, and delivery schedules expected to go out. With this information, salespeople can access data on the availability of a product anywhere in the United States and have it shipped to them directly. Shipment within twenty-four hours can be guaranteed because of an automated warehouse system and a computerized UPS delivery program. Transtar presently carries more than $11 million in inventory, a figure the president claims is ten times more than any inventory a competitor carries.

Questions

1 Is Transtar a wholesaler or a retailer?
2 What is the new market coverage that Transtar is now providing to its customers?
3 Is Transtar considered an intermediary? How many levels are within Transtar's channels of distribution?
4 Does Transtar have a quick distribution process? If so, how?

VIDEO CASE Using Distribution to Achieve Success

Task Lighting Corporation of Kearney, Nebraska began with a lighting product designed by Kenneth Anderson and a partner. But the product, called Luché, couldn't be patented and soon was copied by competitors.

Anderson then came up with another lighting product that could be protected from competitors by a patent. Lumére was a four-inch module with two low-voltage bulbs and male and female plugs on opposite ends. The modules could be connected to make a low-voltage fixture of virtually any length.

Product defects were a problem almost immediately. Also, some customers didn't follow installation instructions. Large numbers of modules were returned, occasionally accompanied by angry letters or phone calls. Problems multiplied. Task couldn't afford an in-house sales force.

Today product defects are a tiny fraction of what they were. Task solved the problem with a number of modifi-

cations and by training distributors with the proper installation procedures so they could pass this information on to their customers. The use of distributors resulted in a large increase in sales.

Questions

1 Explain why the distribution strategy of using intermediaries was necessary to improve customer satisfaction for the lighting product sold by Task Lighting. That is, why did this strategy satisfy customers more than if the product was sent directly by Task Lighting without using any intermediaries?
2 In addition to customer satisfaction, explain another way that the use of intermediaries was beneficial to Task.
3 Assume that Task Lighting could revise the lighting product such that it needs no special training or instructions. Also assume that Task could use some other forms of marketing the product (at a low cost) to inform customers about the product. Under these conditions, why would Task possibly discontinue its use of intermediaries?

THE Coca-Cola COMPANY ANNUAL REPORT PROJECT

The following questions apply concepts learned in this chapter to The Coca-Cola Company. Read pages 29, 32 and 40 in The Coca-Cola Company annual report before answering these questions.

1 In 1995, how many new plants were opened by The Coca-Cola Company and its subsidiaries?

2 Does The Coca-Cola Company utilize intensive distribution, selective distribution, or exclusive distribution?

3 In what non-traditional locations has The Coca-Cola Company expanded its distribution?

IN-TEXT STUDY GUIDE

Answers are in an appendix at the back of the book.

True or False

1 A lengthy distribution process adversely affects a firm's performance.

2 If a producer of a product deals directly with a customer, marketing intermediaries are involved.

3 Manufacturers can vertically integrate their operations by establishing retail stores.

4 Distribution decisions do not affect the cost of delivering a product.

5 Intensive distribution is used for products such as automobiles and appliances.

6 Wholesalers commonly offer manufacturers sales expertise.

7 Products that are standardized are more likely to involve intermediaries.

8 Specialized products are offered at most retail stores.

9 The retailer's decision to purchase particular products may be primarily due to the wholesaler's persuasion.

10 Manufacturers always control the prices charged to consumers when they sell their products to marketing intermediaries.

Multiple Choice

11 A firm's distribution process can be accelerated by improving its interaction with its:
a) social responsibilities.
b) human resource process.
c) financing process.
d) production process.
e) accounting process.

12 Wholesalers use their sales expertise when selling products to:
a) retailers.
b) producers.
c) employees.
d) managers.
e) advertisers.

13 Wholesalers often receive feedback from:
a) competition.
b) adversaries.
c) environmentalists.
d) unions.
e) retailers.

14 An example of a direct channel is:
a) mail-order clothing firm.
b) wholesaler to retailer to consumer.
c) industrial distributor to user.
d) retailer to consumer.
e) manufacturer sells to franchise who sells to individual consumer.

15 Restructuring a distribution process commonly results in the elimination of:
a) production.
b) warehouses.
c) manufacturer.
d) product lines.
e) product mixes.

16 The optimal channel of distribution is dependent on:
a) the recent performance of the firm.
b) the amount of funds borrowed.
c) product characteristics.
d) advertising.
e) promotion.

17 Retail stores that generally offer help in the purchase of products and provide servicing for the products they sell are:
a) full-service.
b) self-service.
c) limited service.
d) full-credit.
e) one-stop shopping.

18 Marketing intermediaries that match buyers and sellers of products without becoming the owner are called:
a) full-service.
b) agents.
c) marketers.
d) merchant-wholesalers.
e) retailers.

19 The degree of product distribution among outlets is called the:
a) one-level channel.
b) zero-level channel.
c) two-level channel.
d) quick distribution process.
e) market coverage.

20 To distribute a product among designated outlets, you would use:
a) intensive distribution.
b) exclusive distribution.
c) selective distribution.
d) mass distribution.
e) single-outlet distribution.

21 An advantage of an intensive distribution is that it gives consumers easy access to:
a) wholesalers.
b) products.
c) packaging.
d) marketing.
e) promotion.

22 When manufacturers sell directly to customers, they have full control over the:
a) retailers.
b) wholesalers.
c) prices charged.
d) demand-pull strategy.
e) cost-push strategy.

23 If a product can be easily transported, it is more likely to involve:
a) zero-level marketing.
b) direct marketing.
c) direct selling.
d) intermediaries.
e) cash-and-carry producers.

24 Stores that tend to focus on only one or a few types of products are:
a) specialty retailers.
b) variety department stores.
c) retail outlets.
d) discount stores.
e) cash-and-carry retailers.

25 When the wholesaler purchases the products from the manufacturer and sells them to retailers on credit, it normally assumes the:
a) package design.
b) credit risk.
c) promotional expenses of the manufacturer.
d) manufacturer's guarantee.
e) producer's risk.

26 When firms can avoid a(n) _____ _____, they may be able to earn a higher profit per unit on their products.
a) supply schedule.
b) demand schedule.
c) marketing intermediary.
d) price equilibrium.
e) inventory control.

27 The manner by which a firm's products are made accessible to its customers is determined by its:
a) advertising strategies.
b) product decisions.
c) pricing strategies.
d) distribution decisions.
e) package designs.

28 The first step in developing a system for distributing products is the selection of the proper form of:
a) advertising messages.
b) financing.
c) promotion.
d) design and layout of production.
e) transportation.

29 By purchasing products from the manufacturer and selling them to the retailers, wholesalers serve as:
a) producers.
b) intermediaries.
c) end users.
d) cash-and-carry producers.
e) chain stores.

30 A situation in which two or more levels of distribution are managed by a single firm is called:
a) vertical channel integration.
b) horizontal channel integration.
c) multilevel marketing.
d) wheel of retailing.
e) conglomeration.

31 With a direct channel of distribution, the full difference between the manufacturer's cost and the price paid by the consumer goes to the:
a) manufacturer.
b) wholesaler.
c) retailer.

d) intermediary.
e) merchant.

32 For a manufacturer to expose its product to as many consumers as possible, its market coverage should be:
a) selective distribution.
b) intensive distribution.
c) exclusive distribution.
d) zero-level distribution.
e) multilevel distribution.

33 A distribution channel represents the path of a product from producer to:
a) retailer.
b) wholesaler.
c) consumer.
d) manufacturer.
e) industrial distributor.

34 According to the text, an extreme form of selective distribution is:
a) zero-based marketing.
b) exclusive distribution.
c) multilevel marketing.
d) physical distribution.
e) wholesale intermediaries.

35 A retail store that has only one outlet is a(n):
a) independent.
b) chain.
c) franchise.
d) vertical integration.
e) horizontal integration.

Distribution Information on the World Wide Web

A major challenge facing marketing managers on the World Wide Web (WWW) is distribution. Although some products can be sold successfully by mail, consumers won't buy many products without seeing them. The problem is that a "web surfer" can be calling from anywhere in the world. Thus, companies operating on the WWW need to be able to direct customers to appropriate retailers and service locations.

The MapQuest web site (Exhibit 14.10) is a one-stop shopping map resource for most of the world. They supply on-line maps which can be "zoomed in" to extremely

Exhibit 14.10
MapQuest Interactive
Atlas Web Site

http://www.mapquest.com

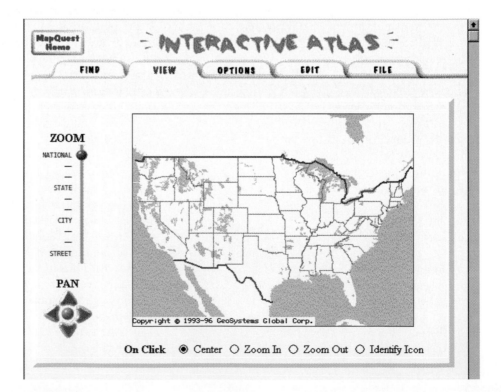

Exhibit 14.11
Zoomed-in Map Picturing Boca Raton, Florida.

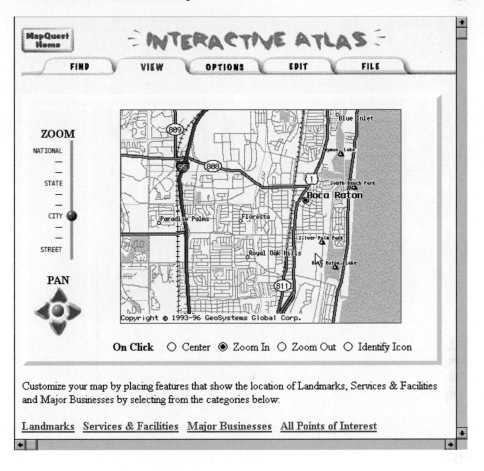

high levels of detail. Businesses can place their distribution sites on these maps and then allow consumers to identify the best sites on their own. For example, a few clicks on the U.S. map can bring the user to a local map of Boca Raton, Florida (Exhibit 14.11), the birthplace of the IBM PC. The maps are also useful for business travelers, employees considering relocation, and those trying to pinpoint distribution or travel routes throughout the world.

CHAPTER 15

Promotion Strategies

Firms regularly attempt to inform customers about the favorable features of their products. They engage in promotion, which is the act of informing or reminding consumers about a specific product or brand. Firms can use promotion to increase their value:

Consider the case of Nike, which produces shoes and apparel. How can Nike benefit from promotion? What promotion strategies and types of advertising should Nike implement? This chapter provides a background on promotion strategies, which can be used to address these questions.

The **Learning Goals** of this chapter are to:

1 Explain how promotion can benefit firms.

2 Describe the various forms of media used for advertising products.

3 Describe the steps involved in personal selling.

4 Describe the sales promotion methods that are used.

5 Describe how firms can use public relations to promote products.

6 Explain how firms select the optimal mix of promotions to use.

2

'96 Mill Enhancements

The future of band sawmilling is here today!

Longer, fully supported swing arms adjust for different log lengths. Larger diagonal bed bracing improves bed rigidity and strength.

New, heavy-duty carriage design lengthens track bearing life.

Longer, fully supported swing arms and hydraulic roller toeboards (on hydraulic mills only) are just two of the enhancements we have made for 1996. These improvements and additions, combined with our TRU•SHARP blades and remanufacturing service, a low-cost finance program, and excellent customer service, enable us to provide you with the best portable bandsaw mill available today.

Your satisfaction and profitability are our goals!

New electric brake package now standard on all Super, Super hydraulic and hydraulic mill trailers.

Call 1-800-553-0182 to receive a 28-page All-Products Catalog or to speak with a Sales Representative.

All Wood-Mizer sawmills are covered by our 15-day money back guarantee. You're satisfied or your money back!

Rugged hydraulic roller toeboards compensate for log taper and allow fast log positioning (on hydraulic mills only).

"Mushroom head" bed rail support bolts enhance shock-loading capability of bed and lengthen mill life when cutting maximum capacity logs.

SAVE up to $702! (See back page.)

The Proof's in the Performance!

Because of their specialized nature, industrial products such as the Wood-Mizer super hydraulic saw are promoted by direct mail.

to previous Ford customers. Talbots (a clothing firm) sends ads to a mailing list of its previous customers. Another approach is for firms to call a magazine that is read by their targeted consumers and attempt to purchase the magazine's subscriber list. This approach is quite common. Many mailing lists can be separated by state or even zip code. Burger King has developed a mailing list of 5 million children who are members of the Burger King Kids Club. American Airlines has a database of 28 million names which it can use to send direct mail. Recent increases in the price of paper and postage have caused advertising by direct mail to become more expensive.

telemarketing the use of telephone for promoting and selling products

TELEMARKETING **Telemarketing** uses the telephone for promoting and selling products. Many local newspaper firms heavily use telemarketing to attract new subscribers. Phone companies and cable companies also use telemarketing to sell their services.

COMPUTER ON-LINE SERVICES Numerous firms have begun to advertise on computer on-line services including the Internet. For example, General Motors and

Exhibit 15.7
Forms of Advertising

Forms of Advertising	Typical Area Targeted
Newspaper	Local
Magazine	National
Radio	Local
Television	National or local
Direct mail	National or local
Telemarketing	Local
Computer on-line services	National
Outdoor	Local
Transportation	Local
Specialty	National or local

AT&T advertise on the on-line Pathfinder Service. Coors advertises its beer on Prodigy. Some of the advertising simply provides a toll-free phone number that consumers can call to obtain more information. Other advertising provides more detailed information about the firm's products. Some firms even provide financial reports to advertise their recent performance.

OUTDOOR ADS   Outdoor ads are shown on billboards and signs. This type of ad is normally enlarged, since consumers are not likely to stop and look at it closely. Vacation-related products and services use outdoor advertising. For example, Disney World ads and Holiday Inn Hotel ads are displayed on billboards along many highways.

TRANSPORTATION ADS   Advertisements are often displayed on forms of transportation, such as on buses and on the roofs of taxi cabs. They are distinguished here from the outdoor ads just described because they are moving rather than stable. The ads generally attempt to provide a strong visual effect that can be recognized by consumers while the vehicle is moving. Marlboro and other cigarette brands are commonly advertised in this way.

SPECIALTY ADS   Other forms of nonmedia advertising are also possible, such as T-shirts, hats, and bumper stickers. T-shirts advertise a wide variety of products, from shoes such as Adidas or Nike to soft drinks such as Coca-Cola and Pepsi.

Summary of Forms of Advertising
Exhibit 15.7 summarizes the forms of advertising. It also designates each form according to whether it reaches the national market (nationwide advertising) or the local market.

PERSONAL SELLING

3 Describe the steps involved in personal selling.

personal selling a personal sales presentation used to influence one or more consumers

Personal selling is a personal sales presentation used to influence one or more consumers. It requires a personal effort to influence a consumer's demand for a product. Salespeople conduct personal selling on a retail basis, on an industrial basis, and on an individual basis. The sales effort on a retail basis is usually less challenging because the consumers usually have already entered the store with plans to purchase.

In addition, many salespeople in retail stores do not earn a commission. Consequently, they are not as motivated to make a sale.

Selling on an industrial basis involves selling supplies or products to companies. Salespeople in this capacity are normally paid a salary plus commission. The volume of industrial sales achieved by a salesperson is highly influenced by that person's promotional efforts.

Selling on an individual basis involves selling directly to individual consumers. Some insurance salespeople and financial planners fit this description. Their task is especially challenging if they do not represent a well-known firm, since they must prove their credibility.

Salespeople that sell on an industrial and individual basis generally perform the following steps:

- Identify the target market
- Contact potential customers
- Makes sales presentation
- Answer questions
- Close the sale
- Follow up

Identify the Target Market

An efficient salesperson will first determine the type of consumers interested in the product. This reduces time wasted on consumers that will not purchase the product, regardless of the sales effort. If previous sales have been made, the previous customers may be the most obvious starting point.

Industrial salespeople can identify their target market by using library references and the yellow pages of a phone book. If they sell safety equipment, they would call almost any manufacturer in their area. If they sell printing presses, their market would be much more limited.

Individual salespeople have more difficulty in identifying their market because they are unable to obtain information on each household. Thus, they may send a brochure to the "resident" at each address, asking the households to call them if interested. The target market initially represents all households, but is then reduced to those consumers that call back. Specific subdivisions of households that fit the income profile of typical consumers may be targeted.

Contact Potential Customers

Once potential customers are identified, they should be contacted by phone, mail, or in person, and provided with a brief summary of what the firm can offer them. Interested customers will make an appointment to meet with salespeople. Ideally, appointments should be made to allow the salesperson efficient use of time. For example, an industrial salesperson working the state of Florida should not make appointments in Jacksonville (northeast Florida), Miami (southeast), and Pensacola (northwest) within the same week. Half the week would be devoted to travel alone. The most logical approach is to fill the appointment schedule within a specific area. Individual salespeople should also attempt to schedule appointments on a specific day when they are near the same area.

Make Sales Presentation

A sales presentation can range from demonstrating how a printing press is used to explaining the benefits of an insurance policy. Industrial salespeople usually bring

Exhib
Summ
Perso

rebat
facture

coup(
zines,
of a pr

samp
ples to
brand

Sales people are increasingly sophisticated in their preparation for customer sales calls. Here Merck sales specialist Shannon Fiddiman checks a computer detail on a client prior to making a sales call.

equipment with them. They also provide free samples of some products to companies. The sales presentation generally involves the use of each product, the price, and the advantages over competitive products. The presentation should focus on how a particular product satisfies customer needs.

Answer Questions

Questions by potential customers normally occur during the course of the sales presentation. Salespeople should anticipate common questions and prepare responses to these questions.

Close the Sale

Most salespeople would prefer to make (or "close") a sale right after the sales presentation, while the product's advantages are in the minds of potential customers. For this reason, they may offer some incentive to purchase immediately, such as a discounted price.

Follow Up

A key to long-term selling success is the attention given to purchasers even after the sale is made. This effort increases the credibility of salespeople and encourages existing customers to call those people when they need additional products.

IN-TEXT STUDY GUIDE

Answers are in an appendix at the back of the book.

True or False

1 The production managers must be aware of the anticipated demand so that they can produce a sufficient volume of products.

2 The promotion mix is the combination of promotion methods that a firm uses to increase the acceptance of its products.

3 Once potential customers are identified, they should be contacted by phone or mail, and provided with a brief summary of what the firm can offer them.

4 A premium is a gift or prize provided to consumers who purchase a specific product.

5 Forms of advertising include newspapers, magazines, radio, and television.

6 The most common sales promotion methods are rebates, coupons, sampling, displays, and premiums.

7 The promotion budget for a specific product is primarily influenced by the sales presentation and closing attempts by a salesperson.

8 Before implementing a promotion strategy, firms attempt to determine whether its benefits will exceed their cost.

9 Public relations is generally more expensive than other promotion methods.

10 A key to successful selling is the follow-up service to customers provided by salespeople.

Multiple Choice

11 If a firm's target market is made up of a wide variety of customers throughout a specific region, it would likely use _____ to promote its product.
a) personal selling
b) advertising
c) door-to-door sales
d) one-on-one communication
e) target marketing

12 The promotional mix for a firm includes the following except for:
a) target marketing.
b) personal selling.
c) advertising.
d) sales promotion.
e) public relations.

13 A common goal of many sales representatives is to become a(n):

a) financial manager.
b) production manager.
c) purchasing agent.
d) accountant.
e) sales manager.

14 Advertisements that are created by many firms and televised separately rather than within a show are called:
a) commercials.
b) specialty ads.
c) infomercials.
d) sales promotions.
e) personal selling.

15 The use of the telephone for promoting and selling products is known as:
a) advertising.
b) telemarketing.
c) sales promotion.
d) promotional mix.
e) public relations.

16 If marketing managers anticipate a larger demand for a product in response to new promotion strategies, they must inform their:
a) labor union.
b) legal division.
c) clerical department.
d) production department.
e) telemarketing department.

17 A common method for promoting products and services, although it is generally more expensive than other methods, is:
a) advertising.
b) public relations.
c) telemarketing.
d) ultra-marketing.
e) publicity.

18 The main steps involved in personal selling include the following except for:
a) identify the target market.
b) follow up.
c) contact potential customers.
d) make sales presentation.
e) advertising.

19 The following are sales promotion methods, except for:
a) newspaper ads.
b) rebates.

SALE

4 Desc
meth

sales
that are

c) coupons.
d) sampling.
e) premiums.

20 The act of informing or reminding consumers about a specific product or brand is referred to as:
a) personal selling.
b) production.
c) finance.
d) promotion.
e) research and development.

21 When firms direct their promotion directly at the target market, they provide information to the consumers who would most likely purchase the products. This is a:
a) push strategy.
b) purchase decision.
c) promotional mix decision.
d) sales discount.
e) pull strategy.

22 The element of the promotional mix which requires a personal effort to influence a consumer's demand for a product is:
a) sales promotion.
b) publicity.
c) personal selling.
d) public relations.
e) marketing.

23 When firms promote products, they highlight the advantages over all other products. They emphasize the product's:
a) publicity.
b) features.
c) sales promotion.
d) labeling.
e) life cycle.

24 Even if a firm's product is properly produced, priced, and distributed, it still needs to be:
a) manufactured.
b) inspected.
c) graded.
d) promoted.
e) market tested.

25 A visual method that retail stores use in promoting particular products is a:
a) display.
b) rebate.
c) coupon.
d) premium.
e) market.

26 Forms of advertising would include the following except for:
a) direct mail.
b) outdoor ads.
c) personal selling.
d) computer on-line services.
e) transportation.

27 Public relations can be used to enhance the image of a product or firm. What strategy could a firm use to communicate to the general public?
a) TV advertising
b) sales promotion
c) direct mail
d) personal selling
e) press conferences

28 Ads that promote the firm, rather than a specific product, are classified as:
a) coupons.
b) displays.
c) premiums.
d) institutional advertising.
e) nonmedia advertising.

29 A salesperson who has just completed an effective sales presentation should attempt to:
a) analyze the market.
b) win at all costs.
c) close the sale.
d) exploit the customer.
e) maximize sales returns and allowances.

30 When producers promote their products to wholesalers or retailers, their promotion effort is called a:
a) push strategy.
b) premium price strategy.
c) sales promotion.
d) market segmentation.
e) pull strategy.

31 Sampling can sometimes provide samples through:
a) newspapers.
b) direct mail.
c) magazines.
d) radio.
e) television.

32 A nonpersonal sales presentation about a specific brand is:
a) institutional advertising.
b) personal selling.
c) brand advertising.
d) comparative advertising.
e) reminder advertising.

33 Firms that hire _____ to promote products must consider the perceptions of the consumers in each country.
a) accountants
b) economists
c) suppliers
d) clients
e) celebrities

34 The promotion budget varies substantially across firms and may even vary for each firm's product line over time. Its characteristics are influenced by the following except for:

a) size of human resource department.
b) competition.
c) phase of the product life cycle.
d) economic conditions.

35 The type of advertising that is used for grocery products such as cereal, peanut butter, and dog food is:
a) institutional advertising.
b) reminder advertising.
c) the push strategy.
d) industry advertising.
e) public relations advertising.

Promotions on the World Wide Web

One common use of the World Wide Web (WWW) is to provide companies with a forum for informing consumers about their products. One popular promotional site was established by General Motors in 1995 (Exhibit 15.13). The GM site not only offers extensive information on all of its products but also provides dazzling special effects, including video snippets, audio tracks, and virtual reality tours through GM cars.

Exhibit 15.13
General Motors Web Site

http://www.gm.com

GM productline takeaspin spotlight crossroads

"Finding out what the customer wants is easy. Doing something about it, that's the hard part."

Listen to Liz Wetzel, a member of the GM Design Team.

General Motors

Travel to the other GM divisional sites on the world wide web.

Experience the Shockwave enhanced version of our website.

Welcome to the General Motors Homepage! This site is designed to give you the fullest, most interesting, and up-to-date web experience possible today. Enjoy.

Product Line provides a high level overview of the cars, trucks, vans, and sport utility vehicles offered by the various GM divisions. It includes a picture of each vehicle, a list of available models, and a brief description of key features.

Take a Spin uses Quicktime VR technology to explore featured vehicles inside and out. Sit in the driver's seat for a 360 degree interior view, or rotate the vehicle for a 360 degree exterior view.

The key marketing strategies described in Chapter 13 through 15 can be summarized as follows. First, a firm uses market research to define a consumer need. Once a product is developed to satisfy this need, a pricing decision is made. The pricing policy affects the demand for the product and therefore affects the firm's revenue. Then, a method of distributing the product to consumers must be determined. The use of intermediaries tends to make the product more accessible to customers, but also results in higher prices. Finally, a promotion strategy must be designed to make consumers aware of the product, or to convince them that this product is superior to others.

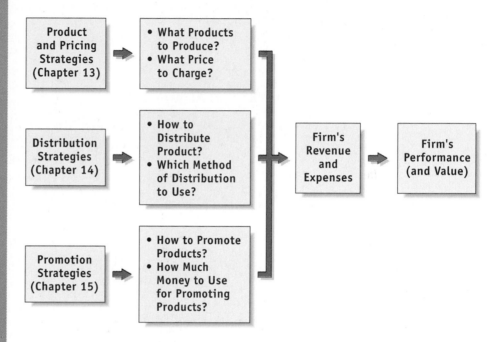

The marketing strategies just described are continually used even after a product follows the typical life cycle. For example, marketing research may be conducted to determine whether an existing product should be revised or targeted toward a different market. The pricing policy could change if the target market is revised or if the production costs change. The decision regarding the channel of distribution should be periodically reviewed to determine whether some alternative channel is more feasible. The promotional strategy may be revised in response to changes in the target market, pricing, phase of the life cycle, or the channel of distribution.

Financial management

represents the analysis of financial data, as well as determining how to obtain funds and use funds. Chapter 16 explains how a financial analysis of a firm can be conducted to determine how it is performing, and why. This type of analysis is used to detect a firm's deficiencies, so that they can be corrected.

Finance is the means by which firms obtain funds (financing), and invest funds in business projects. Firms may obtain funds to build a new factory, purchase new machinery, purchase more supplies, or even purchase an existing business owned by another company. Chapter 17 describes the common methods that firms use for financing, and also identifies the types of financial institutions that provide financing. It also explains the factors that influence the ideal type of financing. Chapter 18 describes the tasks that are necessary for determining whether to invest in a particular business project. In addition, it explains why firms sometimes use their funds to acquire other firms. The chapters on financing and business investment are closely related since financing supports the firm's investment in new business projects.

CHAPTER 16

Accounting and Financial Analysis

Accounting is the summary and analysis of a firm's financial condition. Financial statements are created to disclose detailed information about a firm's recent performance and its financial condition. Accounting information is used by managers of all types of businesses to make decisions. To the extent that the financial analysis resulting from accounting can detect deficiencies in the firms' operations, it can allow managers to revise those operations, and can therefore enhance the firm's value.

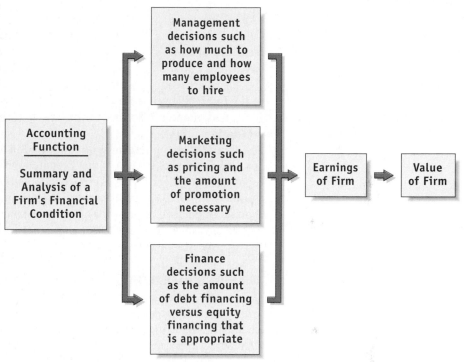

To illustrate how accounting and financial analysis can enhance the firm's value, consider the case of Delta Airlines, which experienced negative earnings from 1991 to 1996. How can a financial analysis be used to identify the cause of Delta's financial problems? What financial characteristics should Delta assess when conducting a financial analysis? Why would the financial analysis of Delta include an analysis of the entire airline industry? This chapter provides a background on accounting and financial analysis, which can be used to address these questions.

The **Learning Goals** of this chapter are to:

1 Explain how firms use accounting.

2 Explain how to interpret financial statements.

3 Explain how to evaluate a firm's financial condition.

HOW FIRMS USE ACCOUNTING

1 **Explain how firms use accounting.**

accounting the summary and analysis of a firm's financial condition

bookkeeping the recording of a firm's financial transactions

financial accounting accounting performed for reporting purposes

Firms use **accounting** to report their financial condition, support decisions, and control business operations.

Reporting

One accounting task is to report accurate financial data. **Bookkeeping** represents the recording of a firm's financial transactions. For example, the recording of daily or weekly revenue and expenses is part of the bookkeeping process.

Firms are required to periodically report their revenue, expenses, and earnings to the Internal Revenue Service (IRS) so that their taxes can be determined. The type of accounting performed for reporting purposes is referred to as **financial accounting.**

Financial accounting must be conducted in accordance with generally accepted accounting principles (GAAP) that explain how financial information should be reported. The Financial Accounting Standards Board (FASB), Securities Exchange Commission (SEC), and IRS establish the accounting guidelines. The use of a common set of guidelines allows for more consistency in reporting practices among firms. Consequently, a comparison of financial statements between two or more different firms may be more meaningful.

REPORTING TO SHAREHOLDERS Publicly owned firms are required to periodically report their financial condition for existing or potential shareholders. Shareholders assess financial statements to evaluate the performance of firms in which they invested. If the analysis determines that the firm has performed poorly, existing shareholders may attempt to replace the board of directors or may sell their stock. Some shareholders do not take the time to analyze the firms in which they invest. Instead, they consider the advice of financial advisors who analyze firms for them.

REPORTING TO CREDITORS Firms also report their financial condition to existing and prospective creditors. The creditors assess the financial statements of firms to determine the probability that the firms will default on loans. Creditors that plan to provide short-term loans assess financial statements to determine the level of the firm's liquidity (ability to sell existing assets). Conversely, creditors that plan to provide long-term loans may assess the financial statements to determine whether the firm is capable of generating sufficient income in future years to make interest and principal payments on the loan far in the future.

CERTIFYING ACCURACY Private accountants provide accounting services for the firms with which they are employed. While they usually have an accounting degree, they do not have to be certified.

public accountants provide accounting services for a variety of firms for a fee

certified public accountants accountants that meet specific educational requirements and pass a national examination

Public accountants provide accounting services for a variety of firms for a fee. A license is required to practice public accounting. Accountants that meet specific educational requirements and pass a national examination are referred to as **certified public accountants** (CPAs).

A common job for a public accountant is auditing to ensure that the firm's financial statements are accurate. All publicly owned firms must have their financial

The CPA. Never Underestimate The Value.™

Accountants must meet specific licensing requirements in order to be recognized as a CPA (certified public accountant).

statements audited by an independent accounting firm. When public accountants audit a firm, they examine the firm's financial statements for accuracy. A public accountant's stamp of approval does not imply anything about a firm's performance, but only that the information contained within the financial statements is accurate.

Decision Support

Firms use financial information developed by accountants to support decisions. For example, a firm's financial managers may use historical revenue and cost information for budgeting decisions. The marketing managers use sales information to evaluate the impact of a particular promotional strategy. The production managers use seasonal sales information to determine the necessary production level in the future. The type of accounting performed to provide information to help managers make decisions is referred to as **managerial accounting.** Financial accounting also reports information, but to shareholders and the IRS (outside the firm). To provide a complete set of information, the information generated by managerial accounting can be included with other information (such as industry characteristics).

managerial accounting the type of accounting performed to provide information to help managers of the firm make decisions

Control

By reviewing financial information, managers monitor the performance of individuals, divisions, and products. As with the decision-support role, managers use managerial accounting to maintain control. Accounting information on sales is used to monitor the performance of various products and the salespeople who sell them. Information on operating expenses is used to monitor production efficiency.

Managers evaluate their firm's financial statements to monitor the firm's operations and to identify the firm's strengths and weaknesses. The firm's financial statements can be generated and analyzed as frequently as necessary to identify problems and quickly resolve them before they become serious.

Another accounting task used for control is **auditing,** which is an assessment of the records that were used to prepare the firm's financial statements. **Internal auditors** specialize in evaluating various divisions within a firm to ensure that they are operating efficiently.

auditing an assessment of the records that were used to prepare the firm's financial statements

internal auditors specialize in evaluating various divisions of a business to ensure that they are operating efficiently

INTERPRETING FINANCIAL STATEMENTS

2 | **Explain how to interpret financial statements.**

income statement indicates the revenue, costs, and earnings of firms over a period of time

balance sheet reports the book value of all assets, liabilities, and owner's equity of firms at a given point in time

The purpose of financial statements is to inform interested parties about the operations and financial condition of firms. The most important financial statements are the **income statement** and the balance sheet. The income statement indicates the revenue, costs, and earnings of firms over a period of time (such as a quarter or year), while the **balance sheet** reports the book value of all assets, liabilities, and owner's equity of firms at a given point in time.

It is possible for a firm to show high earnings on its income statement while being financially weak according to its balance sheet. It is also possible for a firm to show low earnings or even losses on its income statement while being financially strong according to its balance sheet. Because the two statements reveal different financial characteristics, both financial statements must be analyzed along with other information to perform a complete evaluation.

Understanding the information reported on income statements and balance sheets is a necessary ingredient in financial analysis. These financial statements are explained briefly next.

Exhibit 16.1
Example of Income Statement: Taylor Inc.

Net Sales		$20,000,000
Cost of Goods Sold		16,000,000
Gross Profit		$4,000,000
Selling Expense	$1,500,000	
General & Administrative Expenses	1,000,000	
Total Operating Expenses		2,500,000
Earnings Before Interest and Taxes (EBIT)		1,500,000
Interest Expense		500,000
Earnings Before Taxes		$1,000,000
Income Taxes (at 30%)		300,000
Net Income		$700,000

net sales the total sales adjusted for any discounts

cost of goods sold the cost of materials used to produce the goods that were sold

gross profit is equal to net sales minus the cost of goods sold

operating expenses composed of selling expense and general and administrative expenses

earnings before interest and taxes (EBIT) the earnings before interest and taxes minus interest expenses

earnings after taxes the earnings before taxes minus taxes

Income Statement

The annual income statement for Taylor Inc., a manufacturing firm, is presented in Exhibit 16.1. The income statement items shown in Exhibit 16.1 are explained next. These items are disclosed in the income statements of most manufacturing firms. **Net sales** reflect the total sales adjusted for any discounts. The **cost of goods sold** represents the cost of materials used to produce the goods that were sold. For example, the cost of steel used to produce automobiles is counted as part of the cost of goods sold for Ford Motor Company. The **gross profit** is equal to net sales minus the cost of goods sold. That is, gross profit measures the degree to which the revenue from selling products exceeded the cost of materials used to produce them.

Operating expenses are composed of selling expenses and general and administrative expenses. For example, the cost of labor and utilities and advertising expenses at Ford Motor Company are counted as part of operating expenses. The gross profit minus a firm's operating expenses equals **earnings before interest and taxes (EBIT).** The earnings before interest and taxes minus interest expenses equals earnings before taxes. Finally, earnings before taxes minus taxes equals net income (sometimes referred to as **earnings after taxes**).

Firms commonly measure each income statement item as a percentage of total sales, as illustrated in Exhibit 16.2 for Taylor Inc. The exhibit shows how each dollar of sales is used to cover various expenses that were incurred to generate the sales.

Exhibit 16.2
How Funds Received from Sales Were Used by Taylor Inc.

Net Sales		100.0%
Cost of Goods Sold		80.0
		20.0%
Selling Expense	7.5%	
General & Administrative Expenses	5.0%	
Total Operating Expenses		12.5%
Earnings Before Interest and Taxes (EBIT)		7.5%
Interest Expense		2.5%
Earnings Before Taxes		5.0%
Income Taxes (at 30%)		1.5%
Net Income		3.5%

Notice that 80 cents of every dollar of sales is used to cover the cost of the goods sold, while 12.5 cents of every dollar of sales is needed to cover operating expenses; 2.5 cents of every dollar of sales is needed to cover interest expenses, and 1.5 cents of every dollar of sales is also needed to pay taxes. That leaves 3.5 cents of every dollar of sales as net income. This breakdown for a firm can be compared with other firms in the industry. Based on this information, the firm may notice that it is using too much of its revenue to cover the cost of goods sold (relative to other firms in the industry). Therefore, it may search for ways to reduce the cost of producing its goods.

Balance Sheet

asset anything owned by a firm

liability anything owed by a firm

basic accounting equation Assets = Liabilities + Owner's Equity

Anything owned by a firm is an **asset.** Anything owed by a firm is a **liability.** Firms normally support a portion of their assets with funds of the owners, called "owner's equity" (also called "stockholder's equity"). The remaining portion is supported with borrowed funds, which creates a liability. This relationship is described by the following **basic accounting equation:**

$$\text{Assets} = \text{Liabilities} + \text{Owner's Equity}$$

For example, consider a person who purchases a car repair shop for $200,000. Assume that the person used $40,000 of savings for the purchase and borrowed the remaining $160,000 from a local bank. The accounting statement for this business would show assets of $200,000, liabilities of $160,000, and owner's equity of $40,000. As the business acquires equipment and machinery, its total asset value increases. The funds used to purchase more assets are obtained either by additional borrowing or by additional support from the owner. Any increase in assets will therefore be matched by an equal increase in liabilities and owner's equity.

current assets assets that will be converted into cash within one year

The balance sheet for Taylor Inc. as of the end of the year, is illustrated in Exhibit 16.3. The assets listed on a balance sheet are separated into current assets and fixed assets. **Current assets** are assets that will be converted into cash within one year. They include cash, marketable securities, accounts receivable, and inventories. Cash typically represents checking account balances. Marketable securities are short-term securities that can be easily sold and converted to cash quickly if additional funds are needed. Marketable securities will earn interest for the firm until they are sold or redeemed at maturity. Accounts receivable reflect sales that have been made for which payment has not yet been received. Inventories are composed of raw materials, partially completed products, and finished products that have not yet been sold.

fixed assets assets that will be used by a firm for more than one year

depreciation a reduction in the value of the assets to reflect deterioration in assets over time

Fixed assets are assets that will be used by a firm for more than one year. They include the firm's plant and equipment. In Exhibit 16.3, depreciation is subtracted from plant and equipment to arrive at net fixed assets. **Depreciation** represents a reduction in the value of the assets to reflect deterioration in assets over time. Specific accounting rules are used to measure the depreciation of fixed assets.

accounts payable money owed by the firm for the purchase of materials

notes payable short-term loans to the firm made by creditors such as banks

Liabilities and owner's equity are also shown in Exhibit 16.3. Current (short-term) liabilities include accounts payable and notes payable. **Accounts payable** represent money owed by the firm for the purchase of materials. **Notes payable** represent short-term loans to the firm made by creditors such as banks. Long-term liabilities (debt) are liabilities that will not be repaid within one year. These liabilities commonly include long-term loans provided by banks and the issuance of bonds.

owner's equity includes the par (or stated) value of all common stock issued, additional paid-in capital, and retained earnings

Owner's equity includes the par (or stated) value of all common stock issued, additional paid-in capital, and retained earnings. Additional paid-in capital represents the dollar amount received from issuing common stock that exceeds par value. Retained earnings represent the accumulation of the firm's earnings that are reinvested in the firm's assets rather than distributed as dividends to shareholders.

Exhibit 16.3
Example of Balance Sheet: Taylor Inc.

Assets	
Current Assets	
Cash	$200,000
Marketable Securities	300,000
Accounts Receivable	500,000
Inventory	1,000,000
Total Current Assets	$2,000,000
Fixed Assets	
Plant and Equipment	$10,000,000
Less Accumulated Depreciation	2,000,000
Net Fixed Assets	$8,000,000
Total Assets	$10,000,000
Liabilities & Owner's Equity	
Current Liabilities	
Accounts Payable	$600,000
Notes Payable	400,000
Total Current Liabilities	$1,000,000
Long-Term Debt	$5,000,000
Owner's Equity	
Common Stock	
($5 par value, 200,000 shares)	$1,000,000
Additional Paid-In Capital	$2,000,000
Retained Earnings	$1,000,000
Total Owner's Equity	$4,000,000
Total Liabilities and Owner's Equity	$10,000,000

A firm can use its balance sheet to determine the percentage of its investment in each type of asset. An example is provided in Exhibit 16.4. Notice that 80 percent of the firm's assets are allocated to net fixed assets. Most manufacturing firms allocate a large portion of their funds to net fixed assets, since these are the assets used in the production process.

The liabilities and owner's equity can also be broken down to determine where the firm is obtaining most of its financial support. Notice that 50 percent of the firm's funds were obtained by issuing long-term debt, and another 30 percent of the funds were obtained from issuing stock. Retained earnings made up 10 percent of the firm's funds.

RATIO ANALYSIS

3 | **Explain how to evaluate a firm's financial condition.**

ratio analysis an evaluation of the relationship between financial statement variables

Now that the key components of the income statement and balance sheet have been reviewed, the discussion will focus on evaluating these financial statements. An evaluation of the relationship between financial statement variables is called **ratio analysis.** Firms can assess their financial characteristics by comparing their financial ratios with those of other firms in the same industry. In this way, they can deter-

Exhibit 16.4
Breakdown of Balance Sheet

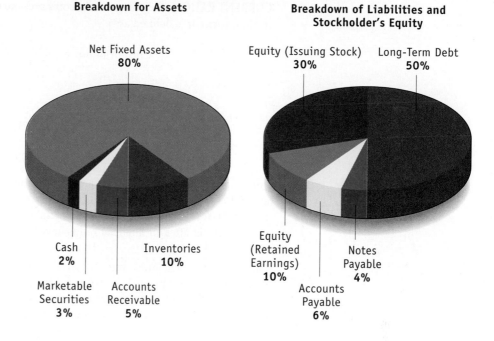

Breakdown for Assets

Net Fixed Assets
80%

Cash
2%

Marketable
Securities
3%

Accounts
Receivable
5%

Inventories
10%

**Breakdown of Liabilities and
Stockholder's Equity**

Equity (Issuing Stock)
30%

Long-Term Debt
50%

Equity
(Retained
Earnings)
10%

Accounts
Payable
6%

Notes
Payable
4%

mine how their financial condition differs from other firms that conduct the same type of business.

Firms can also assess the ratios over time to determine whether financial characteristics are improving or deteriorating. The industry average serves as a benchmark for what would be considered normal for the firm. Differences from the norm can be favorable or unfavorable, depending upon the size and direction of the difference.

Financial ratios are commonly classified according to the characteristics they measure, such as:

➤ measures of liquidity,
➤ measures of efficiency,
➤ measures of financial leverage,
➤ measures of profitability.

The ratios that are used to assess each of these characteristics are defined and discussed next. Each ratio is computed for Taylor Inc. based on the financial statements for Taylor that were disclosed earlier.

Measures of Liquidity

liquidity the firm's ability to meet short-term obligations

The **liquidity** represents the firm's ability to meet short-term obligations. Since short-term assets are commonly used to pay short-term obligations (which are current liabilities), most liquidity measures compare current assets with current liabilities. The greater the level of current assets available relative to current liabilities, the greater the firm's liquidity.

A high degree of liquidity can enhance the firm's safety, but an excessive degree of liquidity can reduce the firm's return. For example, an excessive amount of cash is a waste and can reduce a firm's returns. Firms that have excessive cash, marketable securities, accounts receivable, and inventories could have invested more funds in assets such as machinery or buildings (fixed assets) that are used for production. Firms attempt to maintain sufficient liquidity to be safe, but not excessive liquidity. Two common liquidity measures are identified next.

CURRENT RATIO   The current ratio compares current assets with current liabilities in ratio form. It is defined as:

$$\text{Current Ratio} = \frac{\text{Current Assets}}{\text{Current Liabilities}}$$

For Taylor:

$$\text{Current Ratio} = \frac{\$2,000,000}{\$1,000,000}$$

$$= 2.00$$

For most manufacturing firms, the current ratio is between 1.0 and 1.5. For Taylor, current assets are twice the amount of its current liabilities. A more detailed comparison of Taylor's liquidity and other financial ratios to the industry is conducted later in this chapter after all financial ratios have been discussed.

QUICK RATIO   The quick ratio requires a slight adjustment in the current ratio. Inventory may not be easily converted into cash and therefore may be excluded when assessing liquidity. To get a more conservative indication of a firm's liquidity, the quick ratio does not include inventory in the numerator:

$$\text{Quick Ratio} = \frac{\text{Cash} + \text{Marketable Securities} + \text{Accounts Receivable}}{\text{Current Liabilities}}$$

For Taylor:

$$\text{Quick Ratio} = \frac{\$1,000,000}{\$1,000,000}$$

$$= 1.00$$

Since the quick ratio does not include inventory in the numerator, it is smaller than the current ratio for any firm that has some inventory. The greater the firm's quick ratio, the greater its liquidity.

Measures of Efficiency

Efficiency ratios measure how efficiently a firm manages its assets. Two of the more popular efficiency ratios are described next.

INVENTORY TURNOVER   Firms prefer to generate a high level of sales with a low investment in inventory because fewer funds are tied up. However, very low levels of inventory can also be unfavorable because they can result in shortages, which can reduce sales. To assess the relationship between a firm's inventory level and sales, the inventory turnover ratio can be used:

$$\text{Inventory Turnover} = \frac{\text{Cost of Goods Sold}}{\text{Inventory}}$$

For Taylor:

$$\text{Inventory Turnover} = \frac{\$16,000,000}{\$1,000,000}$$

$$= 16.00$$

Wal-Mart uses a sophisticated computer network to track sales of items and ensure that inventories move quickly. This leads to a high asset turnover ratio compared to others in the industry.

This ratio suggests that Taylor turns its inventory over sixteen times during the year. The cost of goods sold is used instead of sales in the numerator to exclude the markup that is reflected in sales.

The average inventory over the period of concern should be used in the denominator when it is available, since inventory can change substantially during that period. When it is not available, the year-end inventory is used.

ASSET TURNOVER   Firms prefer to support a high level of sales with a relatively small amount of assets so that they efficiently utilize the assets they invest in. Firms that maintain excess assets are not investing their funds wisely. To measure the efficiency with which firms use their assets, the asset turnover ratio can be calculated. It is defined and computed for Taylor as follows:

$$\text{Asset Turnover} = \frac{\text{Net Sales}}{\text{Total Assets}}$$

$$= \frac{\$20,000,000}{\$10,000,000}$$

$$= \$2.00$$

Taylor's sales during the year were two times the level of its total assets. Like all other financial ratios, the asset turnover should be evaluated over time and in comparison with the industry norm.

Measures of Financial Leverage

Financial leverage represents the degree to which firms use borrowed funds to finance the firm's assets. Firms that borrow a large proportion of their funds have a high degree of financial leverage. This can favorably affect the firm's owners when the firm performs well, because the earnings generated by the firm can be spread among a relatively small group of owners. However, when the firm experiences poor performance, a high degree of financial leverage is dangerous. Firms with a high degree of financial leverage incur higher fixed financial costs (interest expenses) that must be paid regardless of their levels of sales. These firms are more likely to experience debt repayment problems and therefore are perceived as having more risk. Conversely, firms that obtain a larger proportion of funds from equity financing incur smaller debt payments and therefore have less risk.

While a high proportion of equity financing reduces risk, it may also force earnings to be widely distributed among shareholders. Firms that rely heavily on equity typically have a large number of shareholders that share the firm's earnings. This may dilute the earnings that shall be distributed to each shareholder as dividends.

DEBT-TO-EQUITY RATIO   A measure of the amount of long-term financing provided by debt relative to equity is called the debt-to-equity ratio. This ratio is defined and computed for Taylor as follows:

$$\text{Debt-to-Equity Ratio} = \frac{\text{Long-Term Debt}}{\text{Owner's Equity}}$$

$$= \frac{\$5,000,000}{\$4,000,000}$$

$$= 1.25$$

For Taylor, long-term debt is 1.25 times the amount of owner's equity.

times interest earned ratio measures the ability of the firm to cover its interest payments

TIMES INTEREST EARNED   The **times interest earned ratio** measures the ability of the firm to cover its interest payments. If a firm has a low level of earnings before interest and taxes (EBIT) relative to the size of its interest expense, a small decrease in EBIT in the future could force a firm to default on the loan. Conversely, a high level of EBIT relative to the annual interest expense suggests that even if next year's EBIT declines substantially, the firm will still be able to cover the interest expense. The times interest earned ratio is defined and computed for Taylor as follows:

$$\text{Times Interest Earned} = \frac{\text{Earnings Before Interest and Taxes (EBIT)}}{\text{Annual Interest Expense}}$$

$$= \frac{\$1,500,000}{\$500,000}$$

$$= 3.0$$

A times interest earned ratio of 3.0 suggests that the earnings before interest and taxes of Taylor was three times Taylor's interest expense.

Measures of Profitability

Profitability indicates the performance of a firm's operations during a given period. The dollar amount of profit generated by the firm can be measured relative to the firm's level of sales, assets, or equity. The ratios that measure these relationships are discussed next.

net profit margin a measure of net income as a percentage of sales

NET PROFIT MARGIN   The **net profit margin** is a measure of net income as a percentage of sales. This ratio measures the proportion of every dollar of sales that ultimately becomes net income. The net profit margin is computed for Taylor as follows:

$$\text{Net Profit Margin} = \frac{\text{Net Income}}{\text{Net Sales}}$$

$$= \frac{\$700{,}000}{\$20{,}000{,}000}$$

$$= 3.50\%$$

Even with a low profit margin, firms with a high volume of sales can generate a reasonable return for their shareholders. However, firms with a low volume of sales may need a higher profit margin to generate a reasonable return for their shareholders.

return on assets (ROA) measures the net income of the firm as a percentage of the total amount of assets utilized by the firm

RETURN ON ASSETS A firm's **return on assets (ROA)** measures the return to the firm as a percentage of the total amount of assets utilized by the firm. It is defined and computed for Taylor as follows:

$$\text{Return on Assets} = \frac{\text{Net Income}}{\text{Total Assets}}$$

$$= \frac{\$700{,}000}{\$10{,}000{,}000}$$

$$= 7.00\%$$

The ROA provides a broad measure of a firm's performance. The higher the ROA, the more efficiently the firm utilized its assets to generate net income.

return on equity (ROE) measures the return to the common stockholders (net income) as a percentage of their investment in the firm

RETURN ON EQUITY The **return on equity (ROE)** measures the return to the common stockholders as a percentage of their investment in the firm. This ratio is closely

The internal control problem McGuire's management faces should be obvious: discouraging would-be bill-snatchers. This is not a small problem, since approximately $100,000 is literally "hanging around" the restaurant. Furthermore, at the end of the day, there is not enough cash in the cash register to cover the amount of sales. This was observed by a bar manager when reviewing the accounting data; cash receipts did not match up with the sales register receipts.

Because the bar has recently hired security to monitor its employees, it has now created a liquidity problem. Management is considering video cameras to run contin-

uously. However, this would require a large investment on the part of the owners.

Questions

1 If you were management at McGuire's, what type of internal controls would you implement pertaining to the dollar bills?

2 How would financial statements be assessed to prevent the cash shortage in the cash register?

3 What type of ratio analysis can management use to monitor their liquidity?

VIDEO CASE Responding to Problems Detected by Financial Analysis

Gary Brown was running a successful company when suddenly, the bank phoned and said the firm's $350,000 line of credit was being frozen and its loans were about to be called in.

Though Brown knew GBA Systems, of Greensboro, North Carolina, was flourishing, it was instantly $100,000 short and teetering on the brink of bankruptcy. The bank was concerned about the firm's excessive financial leverage, based on its high debt ratios.

Brown put together a game plan for correcting the high debt ratios. Expenses were cut drastically. Ten of the fifty-six employees were laid off, and three were put on part-time; two branch offices were closed; eight company cars were sold, leaving three; Brown took a 35 percent pay cut, and there were smaller cuts down the line.

Follow-up with customers was intensified, resulting not only in increased customer satisfaction but also in better collections. The firm used creative ways to improve cash flow. A Christmas-season offer to give 5 percent of billings to charity on outstanding balances that were paid by December 15 brought accounts receivable nearly to

zero. Underprivileged Greensboro residents had a happier holiday, and so did GBA, which saved interest costs by operating with its own cash instead of borrowed funds.

Today, housed in a new, $2 million mansion that makes a statement about the company's strength and stability, GBA Systems has a financial statement that also looks good. It is in its bankers' good graces, too. Sales last year—to one thousand clients, now served by forty-eight employees—topped $5 million.

Questions

1 Why is there such a focus on a firm's financial leverage by creditors (such as banks) and by the firm itself?

2 One solution by Gary Brown (owner of GBA Systems) was to reduce GBA's accounts receivable. How can this help resolve the problem of excessive debt?

3 Gary Brown could have reduced GBA's debt by allowing someone to invest equity in the firm, thereby becoming a partner. The funds invested by the partner could be used to pay off some of the debt, which would reduce the firm's financial leverage. Why might Gary Brown prefer not to use this solution?

THE CocaCola COMPANY ANNUAL REPORT PROJECT

The following questions apply concepts learned in this chapter to The Coca-Cola Company. Read pages 48–49 in The Coca-Cola Company annual report before answering these questions.

1 Discuss the trend in the net income over time generated by The Coca-Cola Company.

2 Discuss the trend in the size of per-share dividend payments paid by The Coca-Cola Company to share-

holders since 1985. (See the selected financial data on pages 48–49).

3 On pages 50 and 51 notice that accounts receivable have increased from $1,470 million in 1994 to $1,695 million in 1995. Discuss possible explanations for this increase.

4 Using this annual report or the business section of a major newspaper, find the stock symbol for The Coca-Cola Company. On August 21, 1996 The Coca-Cola Company traded at 50 7/8 per share, the dividend was $.50, and the price/earnings ratio was 39. How do those numbers compare to where The Coca Cola Company is today? What does this information say about The Coca-Cola Company's return to shareholders?

IN-TEXT STUDY GUIDE

Answers are in an appendix at the back of the book.

True or False

1 A U.S. firm that has subsidiaries (including offices and factories) in foreign countries typically generates earnings in the foreign currencies of the countries where those subsidiaries are located.

2 Accounting is the summary and analysis of a firm's financial condition.

3 The return on equity (ROE) measures the return to the creditors who lent funds to the firm.

4 Certified public accountants provide accounting services for the firms with which they are employed, but do not require a college degree in accounting.

5 The times interest earned ratio measures the ability of the firm to cover its interest payments.

6 Bookkeeping represents the recording of a firm's financial transactions.

7 Ratio analysis reports the book value of all assets, liabilities, and owner's equity of firms at a given point in time.

8 The two primary financial statements for a firm are the balance sheet and the bookkeeping statement.

9 Efficiency ratios measure how efficiently a firm manages its assets.

10 Financial leverage represents the degree to which firms use borrowed funds to finance the firm's assets.

Multiple Choice

11 The financial statement that summarizes revenue, costs, and earnings of firms over a period of time (such as a quarter or year) is the:
a) balance sheet.
b) income statement.
c) cash budget.
d) retained earnings statement.
e) sources and uses of funds statement.

12 Any firm with foreign subsidiaries must consolidate the financial data from all subsidiaries when preparing its:
a) mission statement.
b) foreign exchange.
c) balance of payment.

d) financial statements.
e) domestic policy.

13 In order for managers to make all types of business decisions, they must utilize:
a) accounting information.
b) informal communication.
c) grapevine techniques.
d) nepotism.
e) family relationships.

14 Firms use financial information developed by accountants to:
a) support financial data.
b) analyze job descriptions.
c) support decisions.
d) prepare job specifications.
e) analyze working conditions.

15 Individuals who provide accounting services to a variety of firms for a fee are:
a) industrial accountants.
b) internal auditors.
c) payroll clerks.
d) controllers.
e) public accountants.

16 Firms prefer to support a high level of sales with a relatively small amount of assets, so that they efficiently utilize the assets they invest in. This can be measured by:
a) liquidity analysis.
b) activity ratios.
c) asset turnover.
d) return on equity.
e) leverage ratios.

17 Publicly owned firms are required to periodically report their financial condition for existing or potential:
a) suppliers.
b) customers.
c) employees.
d) shareholders.
e) unions.

18 All of the following are characteristics commonly used to classify financial ratios except for:
a) revenue.
b) liquidity.

c) efficiency.
d) leverage.
e) profitability.

19 The type of accounting performed for reporting purposes is referred to as:
a) ratio analysis.
b) financial accounting.
c) managerial accounting.
d) cost accounting.
e) payroll accounting.

20 The statement that reports the book value of all assets, liabilities, and owner's equity of firms at a given point in time is the:
a) income statement.
b) cash budget.
c) profit and loss statement.
d) revenue statement.
e) balance sheet.

21 The consolidation process allows changes in exchange rates to have an impact on the firm's:
a) balance of payment.
b) reported earnings.
c) competition.
d) industry demand.
e) balance of trade.

22 The type of accounting performed to provide information to help managers of the firm make decisions is referred to as:
a) certified public accounting.
b) external auditing.
c) public accounting.
d) government accounting.
e) managerial accounting.

23 A ratio that measures net income as a percentage of sales is the:
a) net profit margin.
b) leverage ratio.
c) liquidity ratio.
d) activity ratio.
e) asset turnover.

24 The guidelines that explain how financial information should be reported should be in accordance with:
a) Financial Accounting Standards Board (FASB).
b) American Association of Accountants.
c) American Bookkeepers Association.
d) generally accepted accounting principles (GAAP).
e) Securities Exchange Commission (SEC).

25 Long-term financing undertaken by the firm can be assessed through:
a) liquidity ratios.

b) current ratios.
c) acid test ratios.
d) activity ratios.
e) debt-to-equity ratio.

26 The individuals who assess the financial statements of firms to determine the probability that the firms will default on loans are:
a) shareholders.
b) owners.
c) creditors.
d) preferred stockholders.
e) common stockholders.

27 A firm's operating expenses are subtracted from gross profit to determine its:
a) net sales.
b) cost of goods sold.
c) profit or loss.
d) balance sheet.
e) earnings before interest and taxes (EBIT).

28 Assets that will be converted into cash within one year are:
a) fixed assets.
b) current assets.
c) plant and equipment.
d) owner's equity.
e) liabilities.

29 The firm's assets are financed with its:
a) cost of goods sold.
b) earnings before interest and taxes.
c) liabilities and owner's equity.
d) plant and equipment.
e) net sales.

30 The major limitations of ratio analysis include the following except:
a) comparing some firms with an industry average may be difficult because the firm operates in more than one industry.
b) the industry used as a benchmark may include firms that are involved in a variety of different businesses.
c) accounting practices vary among firms.
d) all industries have similar characteristics.
e) firms may have large seasonal swings in sales.

31 The cost of materials used to produce the goods that were sold is known as:
a) net sales.
b) cost of goods sold.
c) sales return and allowances.
d) gross profit.
e) net income.

32 A ratio that measures the firm's dollar amount of profit relative to the return on sales, assets, or equity is a(n):
a) current ratio.
b) liquidity ratio.
c) profitability ratio.
d) activity ratio.
e) leverage ratio.

33 The par (or stated) value of common stock issued, additional paid-in capital, and retained earnings is called:
a) sales revenue.
b) cost of goods sold.
c) gross profit.
d) net income.
e) owner's equity.

34 An evaluation of the relationship between financial statement variables is called:
a) ratio analysis.
b) asset turnover.
c) cost of goods sold.
d) operating expenses.
e) gross profit.

35 A reduction in the value of the assets to reflect deterioration in assets over time is:
a) cost of goods sold.
b) gross profit.
c) sales revenue.
d) depreciation.
e) owner's equity.

Accounting Information on the Internet

Accounting and financial information is constantly changing in today's dynamic business environment. One way for a manager to keep on top of the changes is to rely on on-line sources. Oregon State University maintains a web site (Exhibit 16.8) that points to key sources of accounting and financial information. One of the best uses of this site is to file an on-line resume for accounting and financial employment opportunities. It also serves as an up-to-date resource for information on financial markets.

Exhibit 16.8
Oregon State University's
Accounting and Finance Web Site

http://www.bus.orst.edu

Accounting and Finance On-Line Resources

These sites, listed in alphabetical order, provide a broad range of information on accounting and finance topics, ranging from research to jobs:

- AccWeb - lists jobs and resumes for accountants
- Financial Economics Network
- FINWeb - Financial Economics
- Global Financial Network
- International Accounting Network. This information is available through three locations. Fastest service from North America will generally be through RAW at Rutgers. Two other two sites, at ANet at Southern Cross University in New South Wales, Australia, and Summa at the University of Exeter in the United Kingdom, are valuable when RAW is busy.
- Resources for Economists on the Internet
- RiskWeb - Information on risk management and insurance, including working papers, and a searchable database (including abstracts) of articles in important journals.

these links

- Accounting and Finance Organizations
- Financial Institutions
- Financial Markets
- Financial Planning
- Accounting and Finance Journals, Articles and Reports
- US Government Accounting and Finance Resources
- Accounting and Finance Departments
- Accounting and Finance Courses on-line
- Accounting and Consulting Firms
- Accounting Software Providers
- Internal Audit On-line Resources
- Tax On-line Resources
- Other Accounting and Finance Lists
- Other Business Resources

CHAPTER 17

Financing

Firms obtain capital (long-term funds) in the form of debt or equity. Debt financing is the act of borrowing funds. Equity financing is the act of receiving investment from owners (by issuing stock or retaining earnings). The manner in which a firm decides to finance its business can affect its financing costs. By making the proper financing decisions, a firm can minimize the cost of financing its operations, which can enhance its value.

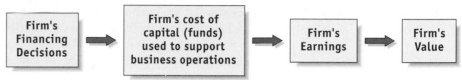

Consider the case of Lone Star Steakhouse and Saloon, which has experienced an annual sales growth rate of about 200 percent. As Lone Star establishes new restaurants around the United States, it needs substantial funds to finance its expansion. How can Lone Star finance its expansion? What types of financial institutions would provide financing to Lone Star? What factors would influence Lone Star's decision to borrow money versus issue new stock? This chapter provides a background on financing, which can be used to address these questions.

The **Learning Goals** of this chapter are to:

1   Identify the common methods of debt financing for firms.

2   Identify the common methods of equity financing for firms.

3   Explain how firms issue securities to obtain funds.

4   Describe how firms determine their composition of financing.

METHODS OF DEBT FINANCING

1   **Identify the common methods of debt financing for firms.**

Firms borrow funds to invest in assets such as buildings, machinery, and equipment. Those firms that invest in more assets typically need to borrow more funds. Service firms spend more money on employees and less on machinery and factories. Thus, they may not need to borrow as much funds, because they do not have to purchase machinery for production purposes. Conversely, industrial firms tend to have large investments in assets such as buildings and machinery, and therefore need to borrow more **capital**. The common methods of **debt financing** are described next.

capital long-term funds

debt financing the act of borrowing funds

Borrowing from Financial Institutions

Firms obtain loans from financial institutions. When firms apply for loans, they must organize a detailed financial plan that specifies the projections of future revenue and expenses. The plan should demonstrate how the firm will generate sufficient revenue over time to repay the loan.

Many loans are for three years or longer. Lenders assess the creditworthiness of firms according to several factors, including the: (1) firm's planned use of borrowed funds, (2) financial condition of the firm's business, (3) outlook of the industry or environment surrounding the firm's business, and (4) available collateral of the business that can be used to back the loan. Because the lender must assess the financial condition of any business to which it lends, it requires financial statements. The lender will assess the financial statements to determine whether the firm will be able to make its loan repayments on schedule.

If the lender determines that the firm is creditworthy, it will attempt to establish terms of the loan that are acceptable to the firm. The terms of the loan specify the amount to be borrowed, maturity, collateral, and the rate of interest on the loan.

PLEDGING COLLATERAL   Firms that need to borrow may be asked to pledge a portion of their assets as collateral to back the loan. A common form of collateral is the asset with which the borrowed funds would be used. Lenders are more comfortable providing loans when the loans are backed by collateral. As an example, a firm that borrows funds to purchase a machine may offer that machine as collateral. If lenders expect that they could sell an asset for 70 percent of its existing value, they may finance 70 percent of the purchase and require the asset to be used as collateral. If the firm defaults on the loan, the lender could sell the asset for an amount that covers the loan.

Firms may also pledge their accounts receivable (payments owed to the firm for previous sales of products) as collateral. If these firms default on loans, lenders would take control of their accounts receivable. To ensure that the accounts receivable collateral sufficiently covers the loan balance, lenders could provide a loan amount that is just a fraction of the collateral they require. Thus, even if some customers never pay off their accounts receivable, the collateral may still cover the full amount of the loan.

SETTING THE LOAN RATE   Banks can determine the average rate of interest that they pay on their deposits (which represents their cost of funds) and add on a pre-

Heavy equipment, such as this EBY back-hoe, often serves as its own collateral.

mium when setting the loan rate. Since the deposit rates change over time in response to general interest rate movements, loan rates change as well.

The premium is dependent on the credit risk of the loan or the probability of default. If the firm appears to be in good financial condition, and the collateral covers the loan amount, the premium may be about 4 percentage points. For example, if the lender's cost of funds is 6 percent, the loan rate may be 10 percent. However, if the borrowing firm is perceived to have more credit risk, the premium may be more than 4 percentage points. The rate of interest typically charged on loans to the most creditworthy firms that borrow is called the **prime rate.**

prime rate the rate of interest typically charged on loans to the most creditworthy firms that borrow

FIXED-RATE VERSUS FLOATING-RATE LOANS When firms need funds, they must choose between a fixed-rate loan and a floating-rate loan. Most commercial loans charge floating interest rates that move in tandem with market interest rates. Consider a firm that can obtain a five-year floating-rate loan with an interest rate that is adjusted by the bank once a year according to changes in the prime rate. Assume the initial loan rate of interest is 8 percent (based on the prevailing prime rate), but the loan rate will be adjusted once a year. Alternatively, the firm can obtain a fixed-rate loan of 10 percent. Which loan is preferable? The answer depends on future interest rate movements, which are uncertain. Firms that expect interest rates to rise consistently over the five-year period prefer to use a fixed-rate loan so that they can avoid the upward adjustments on a floating-rate loan. Firms that expect interest rates to decline or remain stable over the five-year period prefer to use a floating-rate loan.

Exhibit 17.1 shows the trend of interest rates that would occur under three different scenarios. If the firm has a fixed-rate loan, the interest rate charged on its loan is i_1, regardless of how market interest rates move over time. If the firm has a floating-rate loan, the interest rate charged on its loan would be i_2 if market interest rates increased over time, or i_3 if market interest rates decreased over time. Firms that obtain floating-rate loans are adversely affected by rising interest rates, because the interest rate on their loans will increase.

The interest rate charged on a new loan is based on the general level of interest rates at that time. The top part of Exhibit 17.2 shows how the prime rate has

Exhibit 17.1
Interest Rate Charged on Loans under Three Different Scenarios

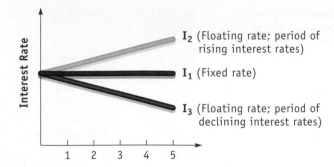

changed over time. The lower part of the exhibit shows the interest expense that a firm would have incurred if it was charged the prime rate on a $1 million loan at that time.

Exhibit 17.2
Effect of Interest Rates on Interest Expenses Incurred by Firms

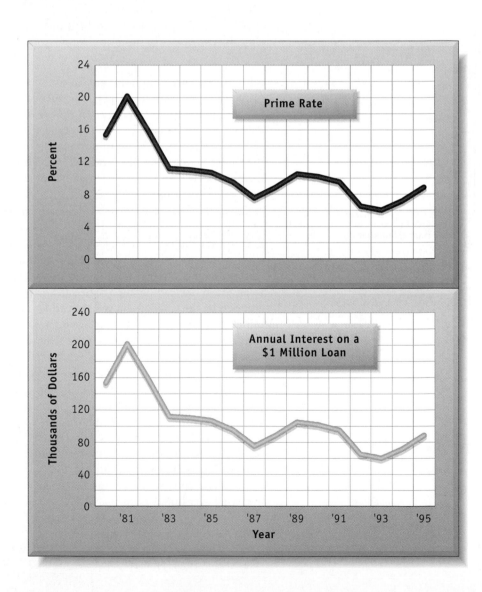

Example of a corporate bond certificate.

Issuing Bonds

bonds long-term debt securities (IOUs) purchased by investors

Large firms may obtain funds by issuing **bonds,** which are long-term debt securities (IOUs) purchased by investors. Some large firms prefer to issue bonds rather than obtain loans from financial institutions because the interest rate may be lower. Bondholders are creditors, not owners of the firm that issued the bonds.

par value the amount that the bondholders receive at maturity

Small firms that are not well known are unable to issue bonds. Even if they could issue their own bonds, the typical amount of funds borrowed through the issuance of bonds would exceed the amount of funds that they would need.

The **par value** of a bond is the amount that the bondholders receive at maturity. Most bonds have a maturity of between ten and thirty years. The coupon (interest) payments paid per year are determined by applying the so-called coupon rate to the par value. If the coupon rate is 10 percent, the coupon payments paid per year will be $100 for every $1,000 of par value. The coupon payments are normally paid semi-annually and are fixed over the life of the bond.

The coupon rate of bonds is influenced by the general level of interest rates at the time the bonds are issued. Firms typically prefer to issue bonds at a time when interest rates are relatively low. Therefore, they can lock in a relatively low coupon rate over the life of the bond. However, forecasting interest rates is difficult, so firms cannot easily time the bond issue when interest rates have hit their bottom. Also, firms that need funds immediately cannot wait until interest rates are at a more desirable level.

indenture a legal document that explains the firm's obligations to bondholders

secured bonds bonds backed by collateral

unsecured bonds bonds that are not backed by collateral

call feature provides the right for the issuing firm to repurchase the bonds before maturity

When a firm plans to issue bonds, it creates an **indenture,** which is a legal document that explains its obligations to bondholders. For example, it states the collateral (if any) that is backing the bonds. **Secured bonds** are bonds backed by collateral, while **unsecured bonds** are bonds that are not backed by collateral. The indenture also states whether the bonds have a **call feature,** which provides the right for the issuing firm to repurchase the bonds before maturity. To recognize the benefits of a call feature, consider a firm that issued bonds when interest rates were very high. If interest rates decline a few years later, the firm could issue new bonds at the lower interest rate and use the proceeds to repay the old bonds. Thus, the call feature gives firms the flexibility to replace old bonds with new bonds that have a lower interest rate. Firms that have a call feature typically need to pay a higher rate of interest.

DEFAULT RISK OF BONDS   The interest rate paid on bonds issued by firms is influenced not only by prevailing interest rates but also by the firm's risk level. Firms that have more risk of default must provide higher interest to bondholders in order to compensate for the risk involved. Rating agencies such as Moody's Investor Service and Standard and Poor's Corporation rate the bonds according to their quality (safety). Investors can use the ratings to assess the risk of the firm issuing the bonds.

A summary of the different ratings that can be assigned is shown in Exhibit 17.3. While each rating agency uses its own method for rating bonds, most bonds

Exhibit 17.3
Summary of Risk Ratings
Assigned by Rating Agencies

	RATING ASSIGNED BY:	
	Moody's	Standard & Poor's
Highest quality	Aaa	AAA
High quality	Aa	AA
High-medium quality	A	A
Medium quality	Baa	BBB
Medium-low quality	Ba	BB
Low quality (speculative)	B	B
Poor quality	Caa	CCC
Very poor quality	Ca	CC
Lowest quality (in default)	C	DDD,D

will be rated within a similar risk level by the agencies. Investors may prefer to rely on the rating agencies rather than develop their own evaluation of the firms that issue bonds. At a given point in time, firms with higher ratings will be able to issue bonds with lower interest rates.

If the financial condition of a firm weakens, the rating on the bonds that it issued can be reduced by a rating agency. For example, in 1995 Moody's Investor Service lowered its ratings of bonds that were issued by KMart Corporation because of KMart's weakened financial condition. This was the fourth downward revision of KMart's debt by Moody's in the last three years. As a firm's bond ratings decline, it is less able to issue new bonds because investors are concerned about the lower rating (higher risk). Rating agencies assign ratings after evaluating the financial condition of each firm. They closely assess the amount of debt that a firm has, and the firm's ability to cover interest payments on its existing debt. Firms are periodically reevaluated, since their ability to repay debt can change in response to economic or industry conditions, or even conditions unique to the firm.

protective covenants restrictions imposed on specific financial policies of the firm

Bondholders may attempt to limit the risk of default by enforcing so-called **protective covenants,** which are restrictions imposed on specific financial policies of the firm. These covenants are enforced to ensure that managers do not make decisions that could increase the firm's risk, and therefore increase the probability of default. For example, some protective covenants may restrict the firm from borrowing beyond some specified debt limit until the existing bonds are paid off.

Issuing Commercial Paper

commercial paper a short-term debt security normally issued by firms in good financial condition

Many firms also issue **commercial paper,** which is a short-term debt security normally issued by firms in good financial condition. Its normal maturity is between three and six months. Thus, the issuance of commercial paper is an alternative to obtaining loans directly from financial institutions. The minimum denomination of commercial paper is usually $100,000. The typical denominations are in multiples of $1 million. Various financial institutions commonly purchase commercial paper. The interest rate on commercial paper is influenced by the general market interest rates at the time of issuance.

Impact of the Debt Financing Level on Interest Expenses

To illustrate how the level of debt financing (whether by borrowing from financial institutions or by issuing IOUs) affects interest expenses, consider a firm that borrows $1 million for a five-year period at an interest rate of 9 percent. This firm will pay $90,000 in interest in each of the next five years (computed as $1,000,000 \times 9\%$). Thus, the firm will need sufficient revenue to cover not only its operating expenses (such as salaries) but also its interest expenses. If the firm had borrowed $2 million, it would have to pay $180,000 in annual interest (computed as $2,000,000 \times 9\%$). When firms borrow money excessively, they have large annual interest payments that are difficult to cover. For this reason, they have a higher probability of defaulting on the loans than they would if they had borrowed less funds.

Common Creditors that Provide Debt Financing

commercial banks obtain deposits from individuals and primarily use the funds to provide business loans

savings institutions obtain deposits from individuals and primarily use the deposited funds to provide mortgage loans

Various types of creditors can provide debt financing to firms. **Commercial banks** obtain deposits from individuals and primarily use the funds to provide business loans. **Savings institutions** (called "thrift institutions") also obtain deposits from individuals and primarily use some of the deposited funds to provide business loans.

finance companies typically obtain funds by issuing debt securities (IOUs) and lend most of their funds to firms

pension funds receive employee and firm contributions toward pensions and invest the proceeds for the employees until the funds are needed

insurance companies receive insurance premiums from selling insurance to customers, and invest the proceeds until the funds are needed to pay insurance claims

mutual funds investment companies that receive funds from individual investors, which they pool and invest in securities

bond mutual funds investment companies that invest the funds received from investors in bonds

While savings institutions focus most of their loans on individuals who need mortgage loans, they have increased their amount of business loans in recent years.

Finance companies typically obtain funds by issuing debt securities (IOUs) and lend most of their funds to firms. In general, finance companies tend to focus on loans to less established firms that have a higher risk of loan default. However, the finance companies charge a higher rate of interest on these loans to compensate for the higher degree of risk.

Pension funds receive employee and firm contributions toward pensions and invest the proceeds for the employees until the funds are needed. They commonly use their funds to invest in bonds that are issued by firms.

Insurance companies receive insurance premiums from selling insurance to customers, and invest the proceeds until the funds are needed to pay insurance claims. They commonly use their funds to invest in bonds that are issued by firms.

Mutual funds are investment companies that receive funds from individual investors, which they pool and invest in securities. Mutual funds can be classified by the type of investments that they make. Some mutual funds (called **bond mutual funds**) invest the funds received from investors in bonds that are issued by firms.

METHODS OF EQUITY FINANCING

2   **Identify the common methods of equity financing for firms**

equity financing the act of receiving investment from owners (by issuing stock or retaining earnings)

The common methods of **equity financing** are retaining earnings and issuing stock, as explained next.

Retaining Earnings

Firms can obtain equity financing by retaining earnings rather than by distributing the earnings to their owners. Managers of firms retain earnings to provide financial support for the firm's expansion. For example, if a firm needs $10 million for expansion and has just received $6 million in earnings (after paying taxes), it may retain the $6 million as equity financing and borrow the remaining $4 million.

Many small firms tend to retain most of their earnings to support expansion. Larger corporations tend to pay out a portion of their earnings as dividends, and retain only part of what was earned. Large firms can more easily obtain debt financing, so they can afford to pay out a portion of their earnings as dividends.

Issuing Stock

common stock a security that represents partial ownership of a particular firm

Common stock is a security that represents partial ownership of a particular firm. Only the owners of common stock are permitted to vote on certain key matters concerning the firm, such as election of the board of directors, approval to issue new shares of common stock, and approval of merger proposals. Firms can issue common stock to obtain funds. When new shares of stock are issued, the number of shareholders who own the firm increases.

preferred stock a security that represents partial ownership of a particular firm and offers specific priorities over common stock

Preferred stock is a security that represents partial ownership of a particular firm and offers specific priorities over common stock. If a firm does not pay dividends over a period, it must pay preferred stockholders all dividends that were omitted before paying common stockholders any dividends. Also, if the firm goes bankrupt, the preferred stockholders have priority claim to the firm's assets over common stockholders. However, if a firm goes bankrupt, there may not be any assets left for preferred stockholders, since creditors (such as lenders or bondholders) have first claim. Preferred stockholders normally do not have voting rights. Firms issue common stock more frequently than preferred stock.

ISSUING STOCK TO VENTURE CAPITAL FIRMS   Firms can issue stock privately to a **venture capital firm**, which is composed of individuals who invest in small businesses. These individuals act as investors in firms rather than as creditors. They expect a share of the businesses in which they invest. Their investments typically support projects that have potential for high returns but also have high risk.

venture capital firm composed of individuals who invest in small businesses

Entrepreneurs who need equity financing can attend venture capital forums in which they are allowed a short time (fifteen minutes or so) to convince the venture capital firms to provide them with equity financing. If an entrepreneur's presentation is convincing, venture capital firms may arrange for a longer meeting with the entrepreneur to learn more about the business that needs financing.

Venture capital firms recognize that some of the businesses they invest in may generate little or no return. However, the providers of venture capital hope that the successful businesses will more than make up for any unsuccessful businesses in which they invested. Venture capital firms commonly assess businesses that would require an equity investment somewhere between $200,000 and $2,000,000. Small projects are not popular because their potential return is not worth the time involved in assessing their feasibility.

GOING PUBLIC   If a small privately held business desires to obtain additional funds, it may consider an **initial public offering (IPO)** of stock (also called "going public"), which is the first issue of stock to the public. Consider the case of the Great American Backrub store, which was created in New York City in 1992. While it generated about $600,000 in annual revenue as of 1995, it wanted to open fifteen more stores within a year. To support the expansion, it engaged in an IPO to raise $6.25 million. Even though it had a short history, it was able to raise funds because it had hired good managers with substantial experience. In 1995, many specialty beer companies such as Boston Beer Company (producer of Samuel Adams beer), Redhook Ale

initial public offering (IPO) the first issue of stock to the public

Boston Beer Company's IPO was unique in that they offered individual investors the opportunity to purchase 33 shares of the initial offering. Many IPOs are limited to institutional buyers only.

SPOTLIGHT ON TECHNOLOGY

Using the Internet for Stock Offerings

Just as the Internet has impacted many other business areas, it seems destined to change how businesses acquire financing. In 1995, for example, Spring Street Brewing, a New York microbrewery that makes Wit beer, conducted a public offering on the World Wide Web (WWW). The $5 million offering, which was qualified by the Securities and Exchange Commission (SEC) and was lawful in twenty states, took advantage of new federal regulations that reduced the reg-

istration requirements for small offerings. To comply with remaining securities laws, circulars for potential investors were made available as files for direct transfer over the Internet.

One reason cited by Spring Street Brewing for its Internet offering was to make it easier for customers to invest directly in the company. The company had already slanted the offering toward those customers by making minimum stock purchase relatively low ($227.50) and by giving owners of the stock special privileges, such as invitations to special events and product discounts. They believed that the demographics of Internet users, who tend to be young, well-educated, and affluent consumers, closely matched those of the key consumers of specialty beers such as Wit. For this reason, the Internet seemed the logical way to communicate with these individuals.

Brewery, and Pete's Brewing (producer of Pete's Wicked Ale) engaged in IPOs to financially support their planned growth.

Insurance companies and pension funds commonly purchase large amounts of stocks issued by firms. In addition, **stock mutual funds** (investment companies that invest pooled funds received from individual investors in stocks) purchase large amounts of stocks issued by firms. An IPO would allow for additional funds without boosting the existing debt level and without relying on retained earnings. Firms can obtain a large amount of funds by going public without increasing future interest payments to creditors. For example, Revlon obtained more than $100 million from an IPO in 1995 and used some of the funds to reduce its existing debt.

Along with its advantages, IPOs have some disadvantages. First, firms that go public are responsible for informing shareholders of their financial condition. There are expenses associated with developing periodic financial reports that must be filed with the Securities and Exchange Commission (SEC) by all firms that issue stock to the public. Furthermore, the financial information filed by these firms is accessible to investors. Some firms may prefer not to disclose information that would indicate the success (and perhaps the wealth) of the owners.

A second disadvantage is that when small businesses attempt to obtain funding from the public, they may have difficulty in convincing the public about the feasibility of their business opportunities. This limits the amount of funding that can be obtained from an initial public offering. It also forces the firm to sell part of the ownership at a relatively low cost. If a firm goes public and cannot obtain funding at a reasonable price, its original owners would feel as though they gave away part of the firm for nothing.

A third disadvantage of an IPO is that the ownership structure is diluted. That is, the proportion of the firm owned by the original owners is reduced once shares are sold to the public. This may result in less control of the firm by the original owners, which means that other investors have more influence on the firm's board of directors and therefore on major decisions by the firm. Also, the profits earned by the firm that are distributed among owners as dividends must be allocated among more owners.

A fourth disadvantage of an IPO is that investment banks charge high fees for advising and placing the stock with investors. The firm also incurs legal fees,

stock mutual funds investment companies that invest funds received from individual investors in stocks

accounting fees, and printing fees. The fees may be about 10 percent of the total amount of funds received from the IPO. Thus, an IPO of $20 million may result in fees of $2 million.

IPOs are generally more popular when most stock prices are high, as firms may receive a higher price for their newly issued stock under these conditions. For example, stock prices in 1995 were very high, and there were more than five hundred IPOs in that year, which resulted in funding of more than $42 billion for the firms that issued the new stock.

LISTING THE STOCK   Once a firm has issued stock to the public, it lists its stock on a stock exchange. This allows the investors to sell the stock they purchased from the firm to other investors over time. The stock exchange serves as a **secondary market**, or a market where existing securities can be traded among investors. Thus, investors have the flexibility to sell stocks that they no longer wish to hold.

The most popular stock exchanges in the United States are the New York Stock Exchange (NYSE), the American Stock Exchange (AMEX) and the over-the-counter (OTC) market. Each exchange has a set of listing requirements that firms must satisfy to have their stocks listed on that exchange.

> **secondary market** a market where existing securities can be traded among investors

Comparison of Equity Financing with Debt Financing

A comparison of equity financing with debt financing is illustrated in Exhibit 17.4. Notice from the exhibit that the forms of debt financing (loans and bonds) require the firm to make interest and principal payments. Conversely, the forms of equity financing (retained earnings and stock) do not require any payments. The financing with stock may result in dividend payments, but these payments can be omitted if the firm cannot afford them. Also, there are no principal payments to the stockholders, as the stock has no maturity.

Firms use a variety of financing methods to obtain funds. General Motors frequently obtained funds by borrowing from banks, issuing bonds, and issuing new stock. Zenith Electronics recently obtained $24 million from the issuance of stock,

Exhibit 17.4
Summary of Firm's Debt and Equity Financing Methods

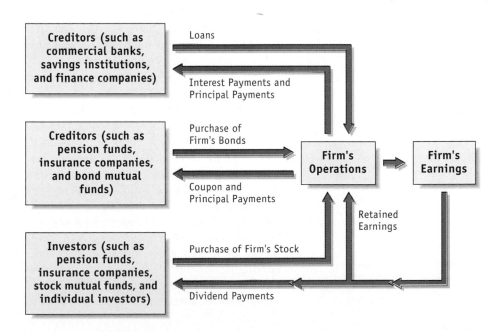

$55 million from the issuance of bonds, and also negotiated a $90 million credit agreement among financial institutions.

HOW FIRMS ISSUE SECURITIES

3 Explain how firms issue securities to obtain funds.

public offering the selling of securities to the public

A **public offering** of securities (such as bonds or stocks) represents the selling of securities to the public. A firm that plans a public offering of securities can receive help from investment banks, which originate, underwrite, and distribute the securities.

Origination

Investment banks advise the firms on the amount of stocks or bonds they can issue. The issuance of an excessive amount of securities can cause a decline in market prices, because the supply of securities issued may exceed the demand. Also, the issuance of bonds requires the determination of a maturity date, a coupon rate, and collateral.

Underwriting

underwritten the investment bank guarantees a price to the issuing firm, no matter what price the securities are sold for

best-efforts basis the investment bank does not guarantee a price to the issuing firm

underwriting syndicate a group of investment banks that share the obligations of underwriting the securities

When securities offerings are **underwritten,** the investment bank guarantees a price to the issuing firm, no matter what price the securities are sold for. In this way, the investment bank bears the risk that the securities might only be sold at low prices. Alternatively, the investment bank may attempt to sell the securities on a **best-efforts basis,** in which it does not guarantee a price to the issuing firm.

For large issues of securities, the investment bank may create an **underwriting syndicate,** which is a group of investment banks that share the obligations of underwriting the securities. That is, each investment bank in the syndicate is allocated a portion of the securities and is responsible for selling that portion.

Distribution

prospectus a document that discloses relevant financial information about the securities and financial information about the firm

private placement the selling of securities to one or a few investors

flotation costs costs paid to investment banks for their advising, their efforts to sell the securities, printing expenses, and registration fees

The issuing firm must register the issue with the Securities and Exchange Commission (SEC). It provides the SEC with a **prospectus,** which is a document that discloses relevant financial information about the securities (such as the amount) and financial information about the firm.

Once the SEC approves the registration, the prospectus is distributed to investors who may purchase the securities. Some of the more likely investors are pension funds and insurance companies that have large amounts of funds to invest. Some issues are completely sold within hours. When issues do not sell as well, investment banks may lower the price of the securities to increase demand.

Some firms may prefer to use a **private placement,** which represents the selling of securities to one or a few investors. An investment bank may still be used for advisory purposes and for identifying a financial institution (such as an insurance company) that may purchase the entire issue. Firms consider private placements because the actual selling costs are lower for private placements because there is only one or a few investors. However, a disadvantage of a private placement is that many investors cannot afford to purchase an entire issue. Consequently, privately placing the securities may be difficult.

Firms that issue securities incur **flotation costs,** which are costs paid to investment banks for advising, selling the securities, printing expenses, and registration fees.

OTHER METHODS OF OBTAINING FUNDS

In addition to debt financing and equity financing, firms may obtain funds in other ways, as discussed next.

Financing from Suppliers

When a firm obtains supplies, it may be granted a specific period to pay its bill. The supplier is essentially financing the firm's investment over that period. If the firm is able to generate adequate revenue over that time to pay the bill, it will not need any more financing. However, even if it needs more financing, the supplier's willingness to wait for payment saves the firm some financing costs.

Exhibit 17.5 shows the benefits of supplier financing. The top diagram shows that the firm receives supplies on March 1, but does not have to pay its bill until August 1. By August 1, the firm will have sold the product that required the use of the supplies. Thus, it can use a portion of the revenue received from selling the product to pay the supplier.

The lower diagram shows that with no supplier financing, the firm must obtain funds from another source. For example, it may borrow funds from a commercial bank on March 1 to pay the supplier at that time. When it receives its payment for the product on August 1, it can use a portion of the revenue received to pay off the debt. In this case, the firm had to borrow funds for five months and incurs interest expenses over that period. The difference between these two scenarios is that the firm incurs only the expense of the supplies when supplier financing is provided, but incurs the expense of supplies plus interest expenses if supplier financing is not provided.

Leasing

leasing renting the assets for a specified period of time

Some firms prefer to finance the use of assets by **leasing,** or renting the assets for a specified period of time. These firms rent the assets and have full control over them

Exhibit 17.5
How Firms Can Benefit from Supplier Financing

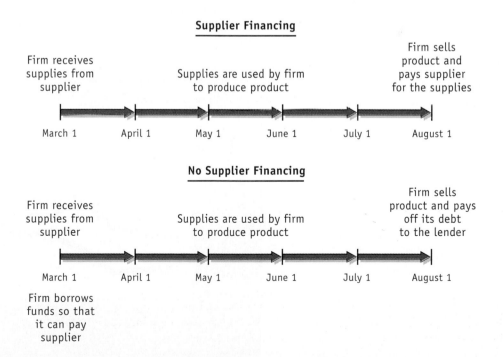

Supplier Financing

| Firm receives supplies from supplier | Supplies are used by firm to produce product | Firm sells product and pays supplier for the supplies |

| March 1 | April 1 | May 1 | June 1 | July 1 | August 1 |

No Supplier Financing

| Firm receives supplies from supplier | Supplies are used by firm to produce product | Firm sells product and pays off its debt to the lender |

| March 1 | April 1 | May 1 | June 1 | July 1 | August 1 |

Firm borrows funds so that it can pay supplier

over a particular period. They return the assets at the time specified in the lease contract. Many firms that lease assets cannot afford to purchase them. By leasing, they make periodic lease payments, but do not need a large initial outlay.

Some firms prefer to lease rather than purchase when they expect that they may not need the assets for a long period of time. For example, consider a new firm that does not know how much factory space it will need until it can assess the demand for its product. This firm may initially lease factory space so that it can switch factories without having to sell its existing factory if it needs more space.

DECIDING THE CAPITAL STRUCTURE

4 **Describe how firms determine their composition of financing.**

capital structure the composition of debt versus equity financing

All firms must decide on a **capital structure,** or the composition of debt versus equity financing. No particular capital structure is perfect for all firms. However, some characteristics should be considered when determining the appropriate capital structure. The use of debt (such as bank loans or bonds) as a source of funds is desirable because the interest payments made by the firm on its debt are tax deductible. Firms can claim their interest payments during the year as an expense, thereby reducing their reported earnings and their taxes. When firms use equity as a source of funds, they do not benefit in this way.

While debt offers a tax-deductibility advantage, too much debt can increase the firm's risk of default on its debt. A higher level of debt results in a higher level of interest payments each year, which can make it difficult for a firm to cover all its debt payments. When creditors are concerned about the firm's ability to make future interest payments, they are less willing to provide additional credit. A firm's ability to increase its debt level is also constrained by the amount of collateral available.

Firms tend to retain some earnings as an easy and continual form of equity financing. When they need additional funds to support their operations, they typically use debt financing if they have the flexibility to do so. However, when they approach their debt capacity, they may have to retain more earnings or issue stock to obtain additional capital.

The capital structure levels of two different computer firms are shown in Exhibit 17.6. Honeywell has typically maintained its debt (as a percentage of total capital)

Exhibit 17.6
Capital Structure Levels across Firms

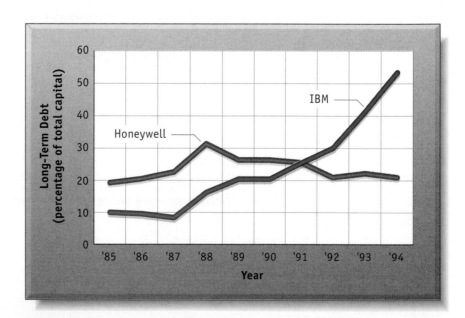

between 20 percent and 30 percent. However, IBM has recently used a much higher proportion of debt. Each firm's capital structure changes over time as it obtains new financing to support its growth.

Revising the Capital Structure

Many firms revise their capital structure in response to changes in economic conditions, such as economic growth and interest rates. If economic growth declines and their earnings decline, they may reduce debt because it is more difficult to cover interest payments. When interest rates decline, they may increase debt because the interest payments would be relatively low.

To reduce the strain of meeting high interest payments, Avon, McGraw-Hill, Northwest Airlines, American Airlines, and Westinghouse recently reduced their debt levels by hundreds of millions of dollars. As an extreme example, Avon reduced its total debt from $1.1 billion in 1988 to $178 million in 1994. This represents a debt reduction of $922 million, which reflects an 84 percent decline in the amount of debt held. Westinghouse recently issued stock and used part of the proceeds to reduce its debt level by $1.7 billion. Black and Decker reduced its financial leverage (proportion of debt relative to equity used) in the 1990s, as shown in Exhibit 17.7. Notice how its annual interest payments declined over time in response to its reduction in financial leverage.

Exhibit 17.7
Effect of Black and Decker's Decision to Reduce Its Financial Leverage

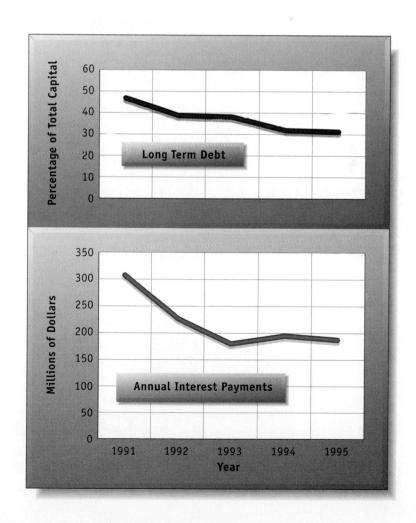

Conversely, other firms, such as IBM and Coca-Cola, have increased debt because they expected that they could easily cover future interest payments that result from the additional debt. For example, The Coca-Cola Company began increasing its debt level to support projects that it believes will generate returns well above the cost of the debt. Campbell's Soup recently increased its long-term debt by $100 million. Kraft recently decided to buy back $6 billion of its stock over a three-year period, which will increase its reliance on debt financing.

How the Capital Structure Affects the Return on Equity

A firm's earnings performance (as measured by its return on equity) can be significantly influenced by the capital structure decision. Consider a firm that had earnings of $1 million last year and has $10 million in assets. The firm's return on equity (measured as earnings divided by owner's equity) depends on the amount of the firm's assets that were financed with equity versus debt. Exhibit 17.8 shows how the firm's return on equity is dependent on its financial leverage. If the firm used all equity to finance its $10 million in assets, its return on equity (ROE) would be:

$$\text{ROE} = \frac{\$1,000,000}{\$10,000,000}$$
$$= 10\%.$$

At the other extreme, if the firm used only 20% equity ($2 million) to finance its assets, its ROE would have been:

$$\text{ROE} = \frac{\$1,000,000}{\$2,000,000}$$
$$= 50\%.$$

While using little equity (mostly debt) can achieve a higher return on equity, it exposes a firm to the risk of being unable to cover its interest payments. To illustrate

Exhibit 17.8
How a Firm's Return on Equity Is Dependent on Financial Leverage

Note: Assume the firm had a net income of $1 million last year and has $10 million in assets.

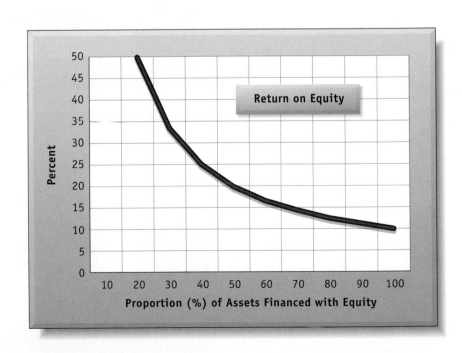

SMALL BUSINESS SURVEY

Financing Choices of Small Firms

A recent survey by Arthur Andersen determined how small firms are financing their businesses, with the results as shown:

	Proportion of Firms that Recently Used This Type of Financing
Commercial bank loans	36%
Credit cards	27
Retained earnings	24
Private loans	18
Personal bank loans	17
Supplier credit	14
Leasing	10
Other	13

Results of this survey show how small firms use a wide variety of methods to obtain funds. The use of commercial bank loans, credit cards, and private loans reflect debt financing, while the use of retained earnings reflects equity financing.

the risk, Exhibit 17.9 shows how the annual interest expense incurred by a firm (with $10 million in assets) is dependent on the firm's degree of financial leverage. This exhibit assumes a 10 percent interest rate. For example, if the firm uses all equity, it

Exhibit 17.9
How a Firm's Interest Expense Is Dependent on Financial Leverage

Note: Assume the firm has $10 million in assets; also assume a 10 percent interest rate on debt.

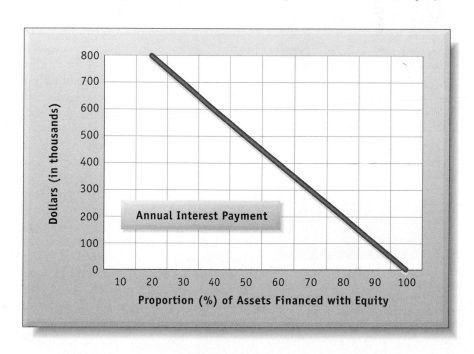

does not incur any interest expenses. At the other extreme, if it uses only 20 percent ($2 million) of equity financing and relies on 80 percent ($8 million) of debt financing, it will incur an interest expense of $800,000 per year.

The relationship shown in Exhibit 17.9 is simply intended to illustrate how a high degree of financial leverage can force high interest expenses. In reality, the impact of high financial leverage may be even more pronounced than that shown in Exhibit 17.9, because lenders may charge a high interest rate to firms that wish to borrow an excessive amount. An extra premium on the interest rate would compensate those lenders for the risk that the firm may be unable to repay its debt.

Firms weigh the potential higher return on equity that results from using mostly debt financing against its risk resulting from high interest payments. Many firms compromise by balancing their amount of equity and debt financing. For example, a firm could finance its $10 million in assets by using $5 million of equity and the remaining $5 million of debt. Assuming an interest rate of 10 percent on debt, the interest expense would be $500,000 (computed as 10% × $5,000,000), as shown in Exhibit 17.9.

GLOBAL BUSINESS

Global Financing

The management of foreign receipts is critical to Euro-Disney. Given Euro-Disney's large amount of sales, effective balancing of foreign transactions can have a significant impact on profitability.

When U.S. firms establish businesses in foreign countries (called "foreign subsidiaries"), they must obtain sufficient funds to support them. Consider the case of Euro-Disney, a French subsidiary of Walt Disney Company. About 49 percent of Euro-Disney's stock was owned by Walt Disney Company, and the remainder was owned by the public. In 1994, Euro-Disney was experiencing financial problems because its theme park was not attracting a sufficient number of customers. It needed to obtain more financial support. However, it was concerned about increasing its debt, since it was already having problems covering its interest payments on debt. It worked out a financial strategy in which it would sell $750 million of stock to Walt Disney Company. It would also issue new stock to the public to obtain additional funds. Furthermore, the banks that had provided loans to Euro-Disney agreed to forgive interest payments that were owed by Euro-Disney over an eighteen-month period. Many of the European banks who were holding Euro-Disney's debt also purchased some of Euro-Disney's stock.

Euro-Disney's financing strategy focused on obtaining French francs, since that is the currency it uses to pay most of its expenses. Also, its revenue is in French francs. When it needs to make payments on its debt or dividend payments to its shareholders, it can use the francs received from its theme park's business. Thus, when paying creditors or shareholders, Euro-Disney does not have to convert the francs into any other currency. This is important because it enables Euro-Disney to avoid potential adverse effects of exchange rate movements.

Consider the potential effects on Euro-Disney if it obtained U.S. dollars to resolve its financial problems. As it generated French francs from its theme park business, it would have had to convert some of those francs to dollars to make interest or dividend payments. If the value of the French franc declined over time, Euro-Disney would need a larger amount of francs to obtain the amount of dollars necessary to make the payments. This would place a greater financial strain on Euro-Disney. This example illustrates that financing foreign projects is complex because it not only involves a decision of debt versus equity financing but also involves selecting the currency to use for financing.

DIVIDEND POLICY

dividend policy decision regarding how much of the firm's quarterly earnings should be retained (reinvested in the firm), versus distributed as dividends to owners

The board of directors of each firm decides how much of the firm's quarterly earnings should be retained (reinvested in the firm), versus distributed as dividends to owners. This decision, referred to as **dividend policy,** is important because it influences the amount of additional financing that firms must obtain. For example, consider a firm that earned $30 million after payment of taxes. Assume that it will need $40 million for various expenses in the near future. If it retains all of the earnings, it will need an additional $10 million. At the other extreme, if it pays out the entire $30 million as dividends, it will need to obtain an additional $40 million.

The dividends paid out per share is shown for three different firms in Exhibit 17.10. Notice that the dividend payout can vary substantially among firms. Polaroid has maintained a stable dividend, while J. P. Morgan has steadily increased its dividend over time. Chrysler's dividend has been unstable.

Some firms target their dividend payment as a percentage of future earnings. For example, General Mills set a dividend target of 50 percent of earnings, while Goodyear Tire set a dividend target of between 20 and 25 percent of earnings.

Factors that Affect a Firm's Dividend Policy

There is no optimal dividend policy to be used by all firms. However, a firm's unique characteristics may influence its dividend policy. Two characteristics that can influence the dividend policy are shareholder expectations and the firm's financing needs.

SHAREHOLDER EXPECTATIONS A firm's shareholders may expect to receive dividends if they have historically been receiving them. If the firm discontinues or reduces the dividend payment, shareholders could become dissatisfied. Thus, many firms make an effort to either maintain or increase dividends from year to year. Monsanto has increased its annual dividends every year for more than twenty straight years. ConAgra has increased its dividends by 14 percent or more every year

Exhibit 17.10
Dividend Payouts (Dividends Divided by Earnings) across Firms

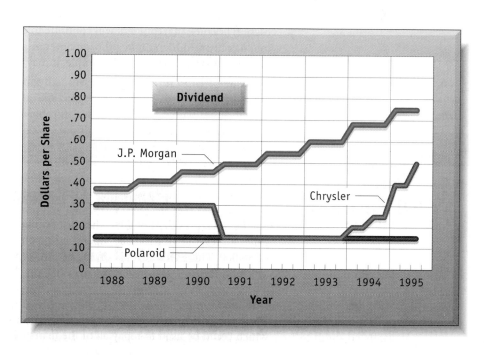

15 A group of investment banks that share the obligations of underwriting the securities is a(n):
a) bond indenture.
b) corporate charter.
c) savings and loan institution.
d) mutual savings bank.
e) underwriting syndicate.

16 Long-term debt securities purchased by investors are called:
a) corporate bonds.
b) common stock.
c) preferred stock.
d) accounts payable.
e) notes payable.

17 Bondholders may attempt to limit the risk of default by enforcing restrictions imposed on specific financial policies of the firm known as:
a) retained earnings.
b) preferred underwriting.
c) protective covenants.
d) corporate charters.
e) promissory notes.

18 A firm that has no need for additional funds may distribute most of its earnings as:
a) interest.
b) dividends.
c) notes payable.
d) assets.
e) net profit.

19 Those firms that invest in more assets typically need to:
a) borrow more funds.
b) buy their accounts payable.
c) sell their notes payable.
d) increase dividends.
e) buy treasury stock.

20 Expenses paid to investment banks are flotation costs, which include the following except for:
a) selling costs.
b) printing expenses.
c) registration fees.
d) advising costs.
e) coupon payments.

21 Some firms prefer to finance the use of assets by renting the assets for a specified period of time. This is referred to as:
a) capital structure.
b) leasing.
c) retained earnings.
d) sales revenue.
e) notes payable.

22 When firms borrow funds, they must choose between a fixed-rate loan and a(n):
a) accounts receivable.
b) inventory loan.
c) floating-rate loan.
d) note receivable.
e) revenue loan.

23 A firm weighs the potential higher return on equity that results from using mostly debt financing against its risk resulting from:
a) low inventory turnover.
b) high accounts receivable turnover.
c) high retained earnings turnover.
d) sale of treasury stock.
e) high interest payments.

24 When a business borrows money, the following terms are specified except for:
a) dividend payments.
b) rate of interest.
c) collateral.
d) amount to be borrowed.
e) maturity.

25 Lenders assess the creditworthiness of firms by the following factors except for:
a) planned use of borrowed funds.
b) financial condition of the firm.
c) industry outlook.
d) available collateral.
e) other industries that the firm has avoided.

26 The board of directors of each firm must decide how much of its quarterly earnings should be reinvested in the firm. The reinvested earnings are referred to as:
a) common stock.
b) retained earnings.
c) dividends.
d) preferred stock.
e) working capital.

27 When U.S. firms establish businesses in foreign countries (called "foreign subsidiaries"), they must obtain:
a) a balance of payments.
b) a trade deficit.
c) a budget deficit.
d) sufficient funds.
e) balanced budgets.

28 The corporation must register the security issue with the:
a) Federal Trade Commission.
b) Securities and Exchange Commission.
c) Internal Revenue Service.

d) Department of Commerce.

e) Bureau of Labor.

29 When firms apply for loans, they must organize and project their future revenue and expenses in a detailed:

a) marketing mix.

b) production plan.

c) accounting plan.

d) financial plan.

e) production schedule.

30 Firms that conduct international business must consider the potential effects of:

a) exchange rate movements.

b) domestic turnovers.

c) international dividends.

d) international indentures.

e) international proxies.

31 Shareholder expectations and the firm's financing needs are two characteristics that can influence the firm's:

a) exchange rates.

b) governmental relationships.

c) dividend policy.

d) foreign exchange.

e) counter trade.

32 When financial managers estimate future cash flows to decide whether to finance with debt or equity, they rely on input from:

a) the U.S. Treasury.

b) executives of competitor firms.

c) governmental officials.

d) marketing managers.

e) the Central Planning Bureau.

33 The interest rate paid on bonds issued by firms is influenced not only by prevailing interest rates but also by the firm's:

a) retained earnings.

b) risk level.

c) dividend policy.

d) earnings per share.

e) return on equity.

34 When Euro-Disney was experiencing financial problems, the primary reason was its theme park was not attracting a sufficient number of:

a) customers.

b) current liabilities.

c) notes payable.

d) corporate bonds.

e) long-term liabilities.

35 Firms obtain capital (funds) in the form of:

a) assets and liabilities.

b) revenues and expenses.

c) equity and assets.

d) working capital and cost of goods sold.

e) debt and equity.

Figure 17.11
Venture Connect Web Site

Financing Information on the Internet

The Internet is increasingly being used to facilitate small business financing. Dozens of venture capital companies, particularly those servicing the high-tech and health-care industries, have established Internet sites. Through those sites, they can be contacted directly by entrepreneurs who are seeking capital to start up or expand small companies. Other Internet sites have been established to match potential investors with companies needing those funds. These companies, such as Venture Connect (Exhibit 17.11), play an important role in the financing of small businesses.

The site where ideas and capital come together

This site provides a place where businesses in need of capital can connect with funding and where investors may find ventures in which to invest. Those with services to offer to both start-ups and existing companies can place a listing in Business Services. Those with business for sale, business opportunities or unique products are welcome also.

Why not advertise on the World Wide Web where you can reach a global market 24 hours a day 7 days a week!

CHAPTER 18

Business Investment

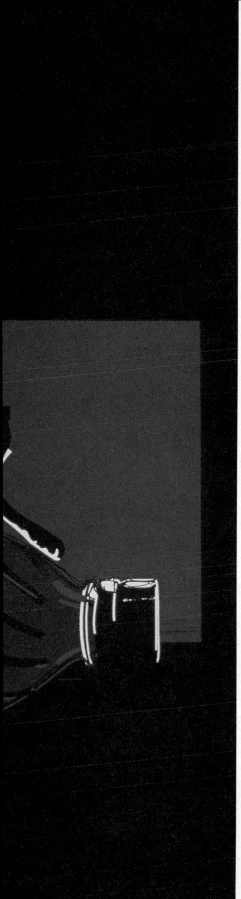

While the previous chapter focuses on how firms obtain funds (financing), this chapter focuses on how firms utilize funds (business investment). A firm has a wide variety of ways in which it can utilize its funds. It makes long-term investment decisions about whether to expand its existing business, develop new businesses, or purchase other companies. It also makes short-term investment decisions regarding its amount of investment in cash, accounts receivable, and inventory. Proper investment decisions will affect its earnings and therefore its value.

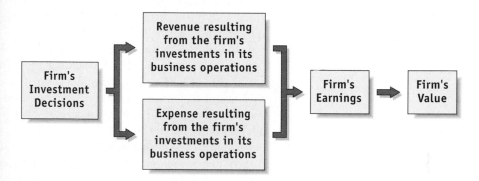

To illustrate how business investing can affect the value of a business, consider the case of PepsiCo, which invests more than $2 billion a year in its snack food, beverage, and restaurant businesses. How can PepsiCo determine how much funds to invest in long-term projects? How can Pepsi determine the investment necessary to launch a new product such as JOSTA (chapter opening photo) in a foreign market? How can it determine whether it should invest most of its funds in new snack food businesses, beverage businesses, or restaurant businesses? This chapter provides a background that can be used to answer these questions.

The **Learning Goals** of this chapter are to:

1 Describe the tasks necessary to make business investment decisions.

2 Explain how capital budgeting can be used by a firm to determine whether it should invest in a project.

3 Describe the factors that motivate investment in other firms (acquisitions).

4 Explain how firms make decisions for investing in short-term assets.

INVESTMENT DECISIONS

Describe the tasks necessary to make business investment decisions.

1

capital budgeting comparison of the costs and benefits of a proposed project to determine whether it is feasible

Firms continually evaluate potential projects in which they invest, such as the development of a new building or the purchase of a machine. To decide whether any proposed project should be implemented, firms conduct **capital budgeting,** which is a comparison of the costs and benefits of a proposed project to determine whether it is feasible. The costs of a project include the initial outlay (payment) for the project, along with the periodic costs of maintaining the project. The benefits of a project are the revenue it generates.

For example, when PepsiCo establishes a new restaurant, the initial outlay includes the construction of the building, the furniture needed, silverware, glassware, and cooking facilities. It also includes costs of food as well as labor. The benefits of this project are the revenue that will be generated by the restaurant over time. In most cases, the precise amount of costs and benefits of a project is not known in advance and can only be estimated.

Exhibit 18.1 shows how firms such as Ford Motor Company and Southwest Airlines have increased their investment in assets over time. Ford's investment is focused on production facilities to produce more automobiles, while Southwest Airlines has invested in more airplanes. Any large investment in assets considered by a firm requires a capital budgeting analysis.

Many decisions that result from capital budgeting are irreversible. That is, if the project does not generate the benefits expected, it is too late to reverse the decision. For example, if a restaurant is unsuccessful, its selling price would likely be much lower than the cost of establishing it.

To illustrate how an inaccurate budgeting analysis can affect the firm, consider the case of Converse, which invested in a company called Apex One in May 1995.

Textron made a multimillion dollar capital investment when they built this helicopter plant. Their annual report provides a clear criteria to measure the success of the investment.

Exhibit 18.1
How Investment in Assets Has
Grown for Two Firms

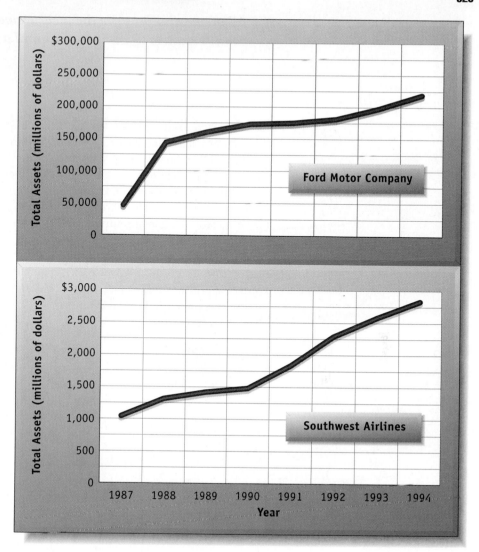

The expenses involved in this project's operations were underestimated, while the revenue from this project was overestimated. Converse terminated the project just three months after it made the initial outlay and incurred a $41.6 million loss on this project. To illustrate how firms focus on each project's return versus its cost, consider the following statements from recent annual reports:

> **❚❚** *Our goal is to achieve a return on invested capital over the course of each business cycle that exceeds the company's cost of capital.* **❚❚**
>
> —Boise Cascade

> **❚❚** *With a return on capital roughly three times our cost of capital, this strategy [of borrowing more funds to expand] makes even more sense now than before.* **❚❚**
>
> —The Coca-Cola Company

> **❚❚** *All of our divisions use the measurement of return on invested capital relative to the cost of capital as their standard.* **❚❚**

—Textron

How Interest Rates Affect Investment Decisions

Interest rates determine the cost of borrowed funds. A change in interest rates can affect the cost of borrowing as well as the project's feasibility. Firms require a return on projects that exceeds their cost of funds. If they use borrowed funds to finance a project and pay 20 percent on those funds, they would require a return of at least 20 percent on that project. If interest rates decrease, the cost of financing decreases, and the firm's required rate of return decreases. Thus, a project once perceived by the firm as unfeasible may be feasible once the firm's required rate of return is lowered.

Firms use a lower discount rate to derive the present value of cash flows when interest rates are reduced, because their required rate of return is reduced. This boosts the present value of future cash flows and increases the likelihood that the project's net present value will be positive.

Capital Budget

capital budget targeted amount of funds to be used for purchasing assets such as buildings, machinery, and equipment that are needed for long-term projects

Firms plan a **capital budget,** or a targeted amount of funds to be used for purchasing assets such as buildings, machinery, and equipment that are needed for long-term projects. The size of the capital budget is influenced by the amount and size of feasible business projects.

Exhibit 18.2 uses PepsiCo as an example to show how a firm's capital budget can be allocated across its various businesses. PepsiCo distributes its capital budget across snack foods, beverages, and restaurants. It has recently allocated more of its budget to restaurants because of the potential opportunities in that business.

Notice from Exhibit 18.2 how a capital budget can also be segmented by geographic markets. PepsiCo has recently allocated about 65 percent of its capital budget for projects in the United States and 35 percent for projects in foreign countries.

Exhibit 18.2
Example of How Capital Expenditures Can Be Allocated across Businesses and Markets: PepsiCo

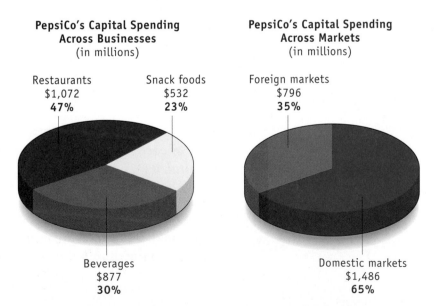

PepsiCo's Capital Spending Across Businesses
(in millions)

Restaurants
$1,072
47%

Snack foods
$532
23%

Beverages
$877
30%

PepsiCo's Capital Spending Across Markets
(in millions)

Foreign markets
$796
35%

Domestic markets
$1,486
65%

Many firms such as ConAgra, AT&T, Exxon, and Ford Motor Company spend hundreds of millions of dollars on capital expenditures every year. To recognize how firms allocate their funds toward capital expenditures, consider the following statements from recent annual reports:

> ▌▌ *Approximately 43 percent of the company's capital expenditures was directed toward additional capacity for new and existing products, while about 12 percent was committed to environmental protection. . . . The remaining capital was utilized to maintain the company's existing asset base.* ▌▌
>
> —Dow

> ▌▌ *Worldwide capital expenditures [of $7.1 billion] were devoted primarily to product development in continued support of the Corporation's programs to improve vehicle quality, performance, and styling.* ▌▌
>
> —General Motors

> ▌▌ *Capital expenditures were . . . up $50 million from the prior year, due to a high level of cost saving projects [and] industry restructuring programs.* ▌▌
>
> —Campbell's Soup

Hotel chains such as Marriott generally budget a certain percentage of income toward capital improvement projects. This is necessary in order to maintain the quality of the hotel and to ensure up-to-date amenities.

Classification of Capital Expenditures

The types of potential capital expenditures considered by a firm can be broadly classified into the following three categories.

EXPANSION OF CURRENT BUSINESS If the demand for a firm's products increases, a firm invests in additional assets (such as machinery or equipment) to produce a large enough volume of products that will accommodate the increased demand. For example, Amoco increased its capital budget by 31 percent in 1995 because it anticipated an increase in demand for its products. Numerous computer firms also increased their capital budget at that time to capitalize on expectations of an increased demand for computer products. PepsiCo recently invested $500 million in Poland to expand its business there.

DEVELOPMENT OF NEW BUSINESS When firms expand the line of products that they produce and sell, they need new facilities for production. They may also need to hire employees to produce and sell the new products. Chrysler recently invested $35 million to engage in business related to automobile manufacturing and to improve its exporting capabilities.

INVESTMENT IN ASSETS THAT WILL REDUCE EXPENSES Machines and equipment wear out or become technologically obsolete over time. Firms replace old machines and equipment to capitalize on new technology, which may allow for lower expenses over time. For example, a new computer may be able to generate a firm's financial reports more economically than an older computer. The benefits of lower expenses may outweigh the initial outlay needed to purchase the new computer.

Firms also purchase machines that can perform the work of employees. For example, machines rather than employees could be used on an assembly line to package a product. The benefits of these machines are the cost savings that result from employing fewer workers. To determine whether the machines are feasible for this purpose, the cost savings must be compared with the price of the machines.

Capital Budgeting Tasks

The process of capital budgeting is composed of five tasks:

- ➤ Proposing new projects
- ➤ Estimating cash flows of projects
- ➤ Determining whether projects are feasible
- ➤ Implementing feasible projects
- ➤ Monitoring projects that were implemented

PROPOSING NEW PROJECTS   New projects are continually proposed within the firm as various departments or divisions offer input on new projects to consider.

ESTIMATING CASH FLOWS OF PROJECTS   Each potential project affects the cash flows of the firm. Estimating the cash flows that will result from the project is a critical part of the capital budgeting process. Revenue received from the project represents cash inflows, while payments to cover the project's expenses represent cash outflows. The decision whether to make a capital expenditure is based on the size of the periodic cash flows (defined as cash inflows minus cash outflows per period) that are expected to occur as a result of the project.

DETERMINING WHETHER PROJECTS ARE FEASIBLE   Once potential projects are proposed and their cash flows estimated, the projects must be evaluated to determine whether they are feasible. Specific techniques are available to assess the feasibility of projects. One popular method is the net present value (NPV) technique. This technique compares the expected periodic cash flows resulting from the project with the initial outlay needed to finance the project. This is discussed in more detail later in this chapter. If the present value of the project's expected cash flows is above or equal to the initial outlay, the project is feasible. Conversely, if the present value of the project's expected cash flows is below the initial outlay, the project is not feasible.

In some cases, the evaluation involves deciding between two projects designed for the same purpose. Such projects are referred to as **mutually exclusive** when only one of the projects can be accepted. For example, a firm may be considering two machines that perform the same task. The two alternative machines are mutually exclusive, since the purchase of one machine precludes the purchase of the other.

When the decision of whether to adopt one project has no bearing on the adoption of other projects, the project is said to be **independent.** For example, the purchase of a truck to enhance delivery capabilities and the purchase of a large computer system to handle payroll processing are independent projects. That is, the acceptance (or rejection) of one project does not influence the acceptance (or rejection) of the other project.

The authority to evaluate the feasibility of projects may be dependent on the types of projects evaluated. Larger capital expenditures normally are reviewed by high-level managers. Smaller capital expenditures may be made by other managers.

mutually exclusive only one of the projects can be accepted

independent the decision of whether to adopt one project has no bearing on the adoption of other projects

IMPLEMENTING FEASIBLE PROJECTS   Once the firm has determined which projects are feasible, it must focus on implementing those projects. All feasible projects should be given a priority status so that those projects that fulfill immediate needs can be implemented first. As part of the implementation process, the firm must obtain the necessary funds to finance the projects.

MONITORING PROJECTS THAT WERE IMPLEMENTED   Even after a project has been implemented, it should be monitored over time. The project's actual costs and benefits should be compared with those that were estimated before the project was implemented. The monitoring process may detect errors in the previous estimation of the project's cash flows. If any errors are detected, the employees that were responsible for project evaluation should be informed of the problem so that future projects can be evaluated more accurately.

A second purpose of monitoring is to detect and correct inefficiencies in the current operation of the project. Furthermore, monitoring can help determine if and when a project should be abandoned (liquidated) by the firm.

Summary of Capital Budgeting Tasks

The five tasks necessary to conduct capital budgeting are summarized in Exhibit 18.3. The most challenging task is the estimation of cash flows, because it is difficult to accurately measure the revenue and expenses that will result from a particular project.

Exhibit 18.3
Summary of Capital Budgeting Tasks

Task	Description
Proposing new projects	Propose new projects that reflect expenditures necessary to support expansion of existing businesses, development of new businesses, or the replacement of old assets.
Estimating cash flows of projects	Cash flows in each period can be estimated as the cash inflows (such as revenue) resulting from the project minus cash outflows (expenses) resulting from the project.
Determining whether projects are feasible	A project is feasible if the present value of its future cash flows exceeds the initial outlay needed to purchase the project.
Implementing feasible projects	Feasible projects should be implemented, with priority given to those projects that fulfill immediate needs.
Monitoring projects that were implemented	Projects that have been implemented need to be monitored to determine whether their cash flows were estimated properly. Monitoring may also detect inefficiencies in the project and can help determine when a project should be abandoned.

CAPITAL BUDGETING ANALYSIS

2

Explain how capital budgeting can be used by a firm to determine whether it should invest in a project.

A firm performs a capital budgeting analysis of each project by comparing the project's initial outlay with the project's expected benefits. The benefits represent the cash flows generated by the project. Before providing an example of a firm's capital budgeting analysis, the procedure for estimating the present value of future cash flows is provided.

Background on Present Value

Because money has a time value, a payment received by a firm at a future point in time has less value than the exact payment received today. For this reason, future payments are commonly discounted to determine their present value. For example, if a payment of $50,000 is received in one year, it can be discounted to determine its present value. Assume that the firm could achieve a return of 10 percent over the next year on funds available today. It could use this interest rate to discount the $50,000 payment to be received in one year.

$$\begin{aligned}\text{Present value } (PV) \\ \text{of \$50,000 payment} \\ \text{to be received in} \\ \text{one year}\end{aligned} \quad = \quad \frac{\$50,000}{(1+.10)}$$

$$= \quad \$45,455$$

This means that the $50,000 payment to be received in one year has a present value of $45,455. If the firm received $45,455 today (instead of $50,000 in one year) and invested the funds at 10 percent, the funds would accumulate to $50,000 at the end of the year.

Capital budgeting analysis compares future cash flows resulting from the project with the initial outlay needed to purchase the project. The initial outlay is made immediately (if the project is implemented), but the cash flows resulting from the project may be received over several years. Since the timing of the cash flows differs from that of the initial outlay, the cash flows must be converted to a present value so that they can be compared with the initial outlay.

The present value of a project's future cash flows is determined by discounting the cash flows at the rate of return that the firm could have earned on the funds if it had used them for an alternative project with similar risk. That is, the discount rate reflects the return that the firm would require to make the investment. The firm must earn at least that return, or it would simply invest the funds in the alternative project.

For example, assume a firm can invest in a project today that would generate a lump-sum cash flow (CF) of $10,000 from the investment in one year. If the firm has a required return (r) on this investment of 12 percent, the present value (PV) of the cash flow is as follows:

$$PV = \frac{CF \text{ at end of Year 1}}{(1 + r)}$$

$$= \frac{\$10,000}{(1 + .12)^1}$$

$$= \$8,929$$

This suggests that if the cash amount of $8,929 were available today and could be invested at 12 percent, it would be worth $10,000 in one year. If the initial outlay is more than $8,929, the firm should not make the investment, because the initial outlay would exceed the present value of the cash flow generated by the investment.

Now adjust the example to determine the present value of the $10,000 cash flow if it was received at the end of the second year instead of the first year. The present value of this project based on a required return of 12 percent is as follows:

$$PV = \frac{CF \text{ at end of Year 2}}{(1 + r)^2}$$

$$= \frac{\$10,000}{(1 + .12)^2}$$

$$= \$7,972$$

The exponent of the denominator was adjusted to discount the amount based on a period of two years instead of one year. Notice that the present value of cash flows in Year 2 is less than the present value of cash flows in Year 1. The further out the time at which a given amount is received, the lower the present value.

The present value of a cash amount in any year could be estimated by adjusting the exponent to reflect the number of years in the future. As one final example, the present value of a $10,000 cash flow received three years from now is estimated next (assuming the required return is 12 percent).

$$PV = \frac{CF \text{ at end of Year 3}}{(1 + r)^3}$$

$$= \frac{\$10,000}{(1 + .12)^3}$$

$$= \$7,118$$

Now consider a project that generates a cash flow of $10,000 for the firm in Years 1, 2, and 3. Each cash flow can be discounted separately to derive its present value; then, the discounted cash flows are added to determine the present value of the investment. The present value of these cash flows are estimated next.

$$PV = \frac{CF \text{ at end of Year 1}}{(1 + r)^1} + \frac{CF \text{ at end of Year 2}}{(1 + r)^2} + \frac{CF \text{ at end of Year 3}}{(1 + r)^3}$$

$$= \frac{\$10,000}{(1 + .12)^1} + \frac{\$10,000}{(1 + .12)^2} + \frac{\$10,000}{(1 + .12)^3}$$

$$= \$8,929 + \$7,972 + \$7,118$$

$$= \$24,019$$

This example is illustrated in Exhibit 18.4. It shows how the present value of cash flows is determined by discounting the cash flows in each year at the investor's

Exhibit 18.4

Example of Discounting Cash Flows

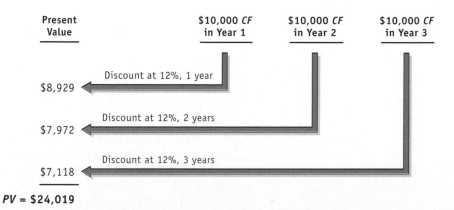

required rate of return. Then, those discounted cash flows are added together to determine the present value of the cash flows. If the initial outlay necessary to purchase this project is less than $24,019, the project is feasible and should be implemented. However, if the initial outlay necessary to purchase the project is more than $24,019, the project is not feasible and should not be implemented.

ESTIMATING THE NET PRESENT VALUE   To reinforce the use of capital budgeting analysis, consider a firm that decides to purchase a used delivery truck for $15,000 that will be used to make extra deliveries and will last only two years. By having this truck, the firm estimates that it will generate an extra $8,000 in cash flow at the end of next year and an extra $12,000 at the end of the following year. Assume the firm requires a return of 15 percent on this project. The present value of these cash flows is estimated as follows:

$$PV = \frac{\$8,000}{(1 + .15)^1} + \frac{\$12,000}{(1 + .15)^2}$$

$$= \$6,957 + \$9,074$$

$$= \$16,031$$

net present value equal to the present value of cash flows minus the initial outlay

The **net present value** of a project is equal to the present value (PV) of cash flows minus the initial outlay (I). In our example, the net present value (NPV) is as follows:

$$NPV = PV - I$$
$$= \$16,033 - \$15,000$$
$$= \$1,031$$

When the net present value is positive, the present value exceeds the initial outlay and the project is feasible. When the net present value is negative, the present value of cash flows is less than the initial outlay and the project is not feasible. Projects are undertaken only when they are expected to generate benefits (present value of cash flows) that exceed the cost (initial outlay).

Now let's progress to larger-scale decisions by firms. Assume that a firm considers opening up a new store, which would require an initial outlay of $2,000,000. The firm has estimated its revenue and expenses as shown in the first three columns of Exhibit 18.5 over a four-year period. To simplify the example, assume that all transactions of the firm are done on a cash basis (no accounts payable or receivable). At the end of four years, the firm expects to sell the store for $1,000,000 (after paying taxes on the proceeds of the sale). The amount of money that a firm can receive from selling a project is referred to as the **salvage value.** Assume that the firm requires a 20 percent rate of return on this project. Assume a tax rate of 30 percent charged on earnings generated by the project.

salvage value amount of money that a firm can receive from selling a project

The steps for the firm to determine whether this project is feasible are as follows. First, the earnings should be derived by subtracting expenses from revenue, as shown in column 4 of Exhibit 18.5. Second, the tax on the earnings is estimated as 30 percent of each year's earnings, as shown in column 5.

The third step is to subtract the taxes from profits to derive the cash flows shown in column 6. The fourth step is to discount the cash flows received by the firm (including the salvage value) using the firm's required rate of return (20 percent) as the discount rate. The discounted cash flows for each year (shown in column 7) are then added at the bottom of column 7 to determine the present value (PV) of future cash flows.

Exhibit 18.5
Capital Budgeting Example

(1) End of Year	(2) Revenue	(3) Expenses	(4) Earnings	(5) Tax (30%)	(6) After-Tax Cash Flow	(7) Discounted Value of Cash Flow
1	$4,000,000	$4,000,000	0	0	0	0
2	5,000,000	4,000,000	$1,000,000	$300,000	$700,000	$486,111
3	6,000,000	5,000,000	1,000,000	300,000	700,000	405,093
4	7,000,000	5,000,000	2,000,000	600,000	1,400,000	675,154
Salvage Value					1,200,000	482,253
					PV =	$2,048,611
					I =	$2,000,000
					NPV =	$ 48,611

Steps
1. Subtract expenses (in column 3) from revenue (in column 2) to derive earnings (shown in column 4) each year.
2. Apply the 30 percent tax rate on earnings to determine the tax on earnings each year (as shown in column 5).
3. Subtract the taxes from earnings to determine the after-tax cash flow each year (as shown in column 6).
4. Discount the after-tax cash flow each year, as shown in column 7.

The process of discounting the project's cash flows to derive its present value is illustrated in Exhibit 18.6. In this example, the cash flows had to first be determined before they could be discounted. Notice that because of the time value of money, the $700,000 cash flow in Year 3 has a much lower present value than the $700,000 cash flow in Year 2.

The present value is equal to $2,048,611 in our example. To derive the project's net present value (*NPV*), the project's initial outlay (*I*) of $2,000,000 is subtracted from the present value. In our example, the *NPV* = $48,611. This means that the present value of future cash flows resulting from the project is expected to exceed the project's initial outlay (*I*) by $48,611. Since the *NPV* is positive, the proposed project should be undertaken. When the present value of the project's cash flows exceeds the

Exhibit 18.6
Deriving a Project's Net Present Value

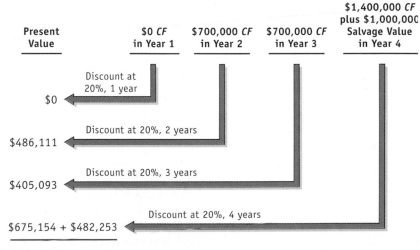

PV = $2,048,611

Texas Instruments' Assessment of Proposed Capital Expenditures

Deciding between potential investments requires considerable analysis. The decision can be even more difficult in large companies, where different departments may be competing for a limited pool of money. For example, how does a firm compare the need for a new computer in the accounting department with the need for a new piece of production equipment in a manufacturing division?

Texas Instruments (TI), the diversified technology firm headquartered in Dallas, faced precisely such a problem during the mid-1980s. Spurred by double-digit growth in many of its defense divisions, managers found themselves overwhelmed by preparing the capital expenditure proposals the company required for all asset purchases of over $1,000. Not only was the volume of such proposals staggering, but the variety of methods required to analyze the investment potential of each type tended to outstrip the knowledge levels of those responsible for preparing the proposals (who were often engineers by training).

To address the problem, one department within TI's

Defense Systems Engineering Group developed a computer program specifically to prepare such proposals. The system, called the Capital Expert, took approximately a year to develop. It was constructed using advanced expert systems technology and incorporated hundreds of rules relating to asset analysis. These rules, in turn, were developed through extensive interviews with experts in preparing capital proposals.

The system operated by asking the user a series of questions. The Capital Expert then performed a cash flow analysis, using TI production projections and depreciation schedules built into the system. Upon completion of the analysis, it printed out a TI-approved capital proposal form, completely filled in, as well as miscellaneous exhibits, including charts.

Users of the system, particularly those not intimately familiar with the capital proposal process, found that the system increased their productivity. Preparing such proposals manually often took from two to three days. By using the system, users could often prepare such proposals in an hour.

Ultimately, the Capital Expert was a victim of its own success. The two key people responsible for the actual development and maintenance of the system were both promoted out of their department, so there was no one to keep it updated. Finally, in the late 1980s, the U.S. defense business experienced drastic cutbacks. Fewer contracts meant less need to train new people to prepare proposals. As a result of these factors, the system was quietly retired by 1990, but not before it delivered an estimated savings of $1 million to TI.

initial outlay (cost) of the project, the return of the project is expected to exceed the cost of capital used to support the project.

Global Investing

U.S. firms frequently consider investing funds in foreign projects. During 1996, The Coca-Cola Company invested about $1.5 billion to expand its worldwide business. The Coca-Cola Company typically invests the bulk of its capital budget overseas, because international markets offer more opportunities for the company.

When U.S. firms such as Coca-Cola consider the purchase of a foreign company, they conduct a capital budgeting analysis to determine whether this type of project is feasible. The capital budgeting analysis required to assess a foreign project is more complex than a domestic project, because of the need to assess specific characteristics of the foreign country. First, the initial outlay required to purchase the foreign firm will depend on the exchange rate at that time. If Coca-Cola purchased a small Mexican firm for P1,000,000 in September of 1994 when the peso was worth $.30, the initial outlay would have been $300,000 (computed as $.30 × P1,000,000). However, if the acquisition was made in September 1995 when the peso was worth $.16, the ini-

Since virtually every corner of the world offers opportunity for The Coca-Cola Company, it must consider many issues when making business investment decisions.

tial outlay would have been $160,000 (computed as P1,000,000 × $.16). The lower the value of the foreign currency needed, the lower the initial outlay needed by the U.S. firm to acquire the foreign company. Firms prefer to invest in foreign companies (or any other foreign projects) under these conditions.

Firms that consider foreign projects must also determine the required rate of return for the foreign project to be feasible. Many foreign projects are considered to be more risky than domestic projects, which forces U.S. firms to require higher rates of return on foreign projects than on domestic projects. Foreign projects in less-developed countries are especially risky, because the probability is high that these projects could be terminated by the governments of those countries. When a U.S. firm requires a higher return, it uses a higher discount rate to derive the present value of the project's future cash flows. This point is especially important in light of recent trends by U.S. firms to invest in large projects based in less-developed countries. General Motors typically invests more than $100 million per year in less developed countries. The large amount of investment by General Motors in less-developed countries suggests that the projects in those countries are expected to generate very high returns, which makes these projects worthwhile even if they are riskier than projects in the United States.

Many other factors also deserve to be considered for foreign projects. The prior discussion is intended to illustrate how a capital budgeting analysis must consider the specific characteristics of the country where the project is to be implemented.

MERGERS

Describe the factors that motivate investment in other firms (acquisitions).

3

A firm may invest in another company by purchasing all the stock of that company. This results in a **merger,** in which two firms are merged (or combined) to become a single firm owned by the same owners (shareholders). Mergers may be feasible if they can increase the firm's value either by increasing the return to the firm's owners or by reducing the firm's risk without a reduction in return.

CROSS-FUNCTIONAL TEAMWORK

Cross-Functional Relationships Involved in Business Investment Decisions

 When financial managers make capital budgeting decisions, they rely on information from the production and marketing departments, as shown in Exhibit 18.7. The expected cash inflows resulting from a project are dependent on the expected sales to be generated by the project, which are normally forecasted by the marketing department. The expected cash outflows resulting from a proj- ect are dependent on the expected expenses incurred from the project. Those expenses that are attributed to marketing (such as promotion expenses) can be forecasted by the marketing department. Those expenses that are attributed to production (such as labor expenses) can be forecasted by the production department. The financial manager's ability to estimate a project's net present value is dependent on the input provided by marketing and production managers.

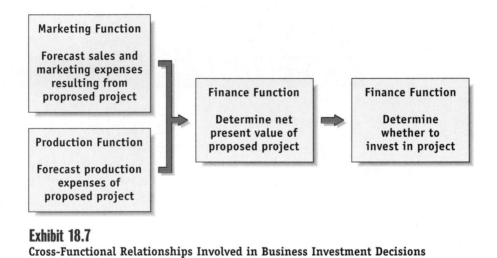

Exhibit 18.7
Cross-Functional Relationships Involved in Business Investment Decisions

---

merger two firms are merged (or combined) to become a single firm owned by the same owners (shareholders)

horizontal merger combination of businesses that engage in the same types of business

vertical merger combination of a firm with a potential supplier or customer

conglomerate merger combination of two firms in unrelated businesses

Mergers can be classified as one of three general types. A **horizontal merger** is the combination of businesses that engage in the same types of business. For example, the recent merger between Chemical Banking Corporation and Chase Manhattan Corporation represents a horizontal merger, as it combines two of the largest commercial banks. A **vertical merger** is the combination of a firm with a potential supplier or customer. For example, General Motors recently purchased a battery manufacturer that could produce the batteries for many of its automobiles. A **conglomerate merger** is the combination of two firms in unrelated businesses. For example, the merger between ITT Corporation and Caesar's World (casinos) is a conglomerate merger. The term *conglomerate* is sometimes used to describe a firm that is engaged in a variety of unrelated businesses.

Corporate Motives for Mergers

Mergers are normally initiated as a result of one or more of the following motives.

IMMEDIATE GROWTH   A firm that plans for growth may prefer to achieve its objective immediately through a merger. Consider a firm whose production capacity cannot fully satisfy demand for its product. The firm would need two years to build additional production facilities. To achieve an immediate increase in production, the firm may search for a company that owns the appropriate facilities. By acquiring either part or all of such a company, the firm could achieve immediate growth in its production capacity, which allows for growth in its sales. When Walt Disney purchased Capital Cities/ABC, it created more growth potential than if it simply attempted to expand its existing businesses.

ECONOMIES OF SCALE Growth may also be desirable to reduce the production cost per unit. Products that exhibit economies of scale can be produced at a much lower cost per unit if a large amount is produced. A merger may allow for the combination of two production facilities, which achieves a lower production cost per unit.

For example, assume that Firm A and Firm B produce a similar product. Also assume that each firm uses an assembly-line operation for about eight hours per day and sells its product to its own set of customers. Firm A sells five hundred units per month, while Firm B sells four hundred units per month. The variable cost per unit is $10 for each firm. Each firm pays $6,000 per month to rent its own factory. This rent is a fixed cost because it is not affected by the amount of the product produced. If Firm A acquired Firm B, it would be able to serve both sets of customers, which would result in a higher production level. The factory could be used for sixteen hours a day to run a second shift for the assembly line.

Based on the initial assumptions, the average cost per unit for each firm is shown in Exhibit 18.8. Notice that when Firm A acquires Firm B, the average cost per unit is lower than it was for either individual firm. This occurs because only one factory is needed when the firms are merged. Thus, the average cost per unit declined when Firm A made more efficient use of the factory.

There may be additional ways for the combination of firms to reduce costs, beyond the savings resulting from renting only one factory. For example, assume each firm has its own accountant. Each firm pays a salary for this position, which reflects a fixed cost. However Firm A's accountant may be able to cover all the accounting duties for the combined firm, which means that it need not incur the cost of Firm B's accountant. Therefore, it can further reduce costs by removing any job positions in Firm B that can be handled by Firm A's existing employees.

Horizontal mergers are more likely to achieve economies of scale than vertical or conglomerate mergers, because they involve firms that produce similar products. Firms with similar operations can allow for the elimination of similar positions once the firms are combined. The merger between Chemical Banking Corporation and Chase Manhattan was expected to result in millions of dollars saved each year, because the

Exhibit 18.8
Illustration of How an Acquisition Can Generate Economies of Scale

Firm	Total Output Produced	Variable Cost per Unit	Variable Cost	Fixed Cost (Rent)	Total Cost	Average Cost per Unit
A	500 units	$10	$5,000	$6,000	$11,000	($11,000/500) = $22.00
B	400 units	$10	$4,000	$6,000	$10,000	($10,000/400) = $25.00
A & B Combined	900 units	$10	$9,000	$6,000	$15,000	($15,000/900) = $16.67

combined operations of the two firms would result in lower salary expenses. The merger between Lockheed and Marietta Corporation, the largest merger of defense contractors in U.S. history, was expected to result in major cost savings.

MANAGERIAL EXPERTISE The performance of a firm is highly dependent on the managers who make the decisions for a firm. Since the firm's value is influenced by its performance, its value is influenced by its managers. To illustrate this point, consider a firm called "Weakfirm" that has had weak performance recently because of its managers. This firm's value should be low if its performance has been weak and is not expected to improve.

However, assume that another firm in the same industry, called "Strongfirm," has more competent managers. If the managers of Strongfirm were managing the operations of Weakfirm, the performance of Weakfirm might have been much higher. Given this information, Strongfirm may consider purchasing Weakfirm. The price for Weakfirm should be relatively low because of its recent performance. Yet, once Strongfirm purchases Weakfirm, it could improve Weakfirm's performance. The owners (shareholders) of Strongfirm will benefit because their firm would be able to acquire another firm at a relatively low price and turn it into something more valuable. In other words, the additional earnings generated by Strongfirm following the acquisition may exceed the cost of the acquisition.

The example just described occurs frequently. Some firms that have had relatively weak performance (compared with other firms in the industry) become targets. Consequently, weak firms are always in danger of being acquired. Kohlberg Kravis Roberts acquired RJR Nabisco because it believed it could improve the firm's performance by using its own managerial expertise.

Some mergers can be beneficial when each firm relies on the other firm for specific managerial expertise. For example, consider Disney's recent acquisition of the ABC television network. Disney produced movies which were sold to television networks. When television networks began to produce their own movies, Disney could have been prevented from selling its movies to various networks. By acquiring the ABC network, Disney can rely on the network to show some of its movies, while the ABC network can be assured that it will be supplied with various popular Disney movies. Disney has expertise as the producer of the product (movies), and ABC has expertise as the distributor of that product. Both firms may benefit as a result of the acquisition.

TAX BENEFITS Firms that incur negative earnings (losses) are sometimes attractive candidates for mergers because of potential tax advantages. The previous losses incurred by the company prior to the merger can be carried forward to offset positive earnings of the acquiring firm. While the losses of the acquired firm have occurred prior to the acquisition, they reduce the taxable earnings of the newly merged corporation. To illustrate the potential tax benefits, consider an acquisition in which the acquiring firm applied a $1 million loss of the acquired firm to partially offset its earnings. If the acquiring firm was subject to a 30 percent tax rate, it could reduce its taxes by $300,000 (computed as 30 percent times the $1,000,000 in earnings that is no longer subject to tax because of applying the $1,000,000 loss).

LEVERAGED BUYOUTS

leveraged buyout a purchase of a company (or the subsidiary of the company) by a group of investors with borrowed funds

A **leveraged buyout**, or LBO, represents a purchase of a company (or the subsidiary of the company) by a group of investors with borrowed funds. In many cases, the investors are the previous managers of the business. For example, consider a diversified firm that plans to sell off its financial services division to obtain cash. The management of this division may attempt to borrow the necessary funds to purchase the division themselves and become the owners. The newly owned business would be supported with mostly borrowed funds.

A well-known LBO was the acquisition of RJR Nabisco by Kohlberg Kravis Roberts (KKR) for about $25 billion. About 94 percent of the funds used to purchase RJR Nabisco were borrowed funds.

Any business with characteristics that can adequately operate with a large amount of borrowed funds is a potential candidate for an LBO. Such characteristics include established product lines, stable cash flow, and no need for additional fixed assets. These characteristics increase the probability that a sufficient amount of cash flows will consistently be forthcoming to cover periodic interest payments on the debt. Growth is not normally a primary goal, since the firm does not have excess cash to expand and may have already borrowed up to its capacity.

While the LBO can place a strain on cash, it does offer an advantage. The ownership of the business is restricted to a small group of people. All earnings can be allocated to this group, which allows the potential for high returns to the owners (although most earnings will likely be reinvested in the business in the early years). However, since businesses that experience LBOs have a debt-intensive capital structure (high degree of financial leverage), they are risky.

DIVESTITURES

divestiture the sale of an existing business by the firm

A **divestiture** represents the sale of an existing business by the firm. There are several motives for enacting divestures. First, firms may divest (sell) businesses that are not part of their core operations, so that they can focus on what they do best. For example, Eastman Kodak, Kmart, W.R. Grace, and Ford Motor Company recently sold various businesses that were not closely related to their core businesses.

A second motive for divestitures is to obtain funds. Divestitures generate funds for the firm, because one of the firm's businesses is sold in exchange for cash. For example, Westinghouse made divestitures to focus on its core businesses, and also to obtain funds so that it could pay off some of its existing debt. ITT Corporation sold a commercial finance business for about $900 million so that it could use the funds to expand in the entertainment business.

A third motive for divesting is that the "break-up" value of a firm is sometimes believed to be worth more than the firm as a whole. In other words, the sum of a firm's individual asset liquidation values exceeds the market value of the firm's combined assets. This encourages firms to sell off what would be worth more when liquidated than retained.

SHORT-TERM INVESTMENT DECISIONS

4   **Explain how firms make decisions for investing in short-term assets.**

working capital management the management of a firm's short-term assets and liabilities

Working capital management represents the management of a firm's short-term assets and liabilities. A firm's short-term assets include cash, short-term securities, accounts receivable, and inventory. Its short-term liabilities include accounts payable and short-term loans. Working capital management is typically focused on the proper amount of investment in a firm's cash, in short-term securities, accounts receivable, and inventory. All of these strategies can be classified as a firm's investment strategies. Working capital management can be segmented into liquidity management, accounts receivable management, and inventory management.

Liquidity Management

liquid access to funds to pay bills when they come due

liquidity management means by which short-term assets and liabilities are managed to ensure adequate liquidity

Treasury bills short-term debt securities issued by the U.S. Treasury

Firms that are **liquid** have adequate access to funds to pay bills when they come due. **Liquidity management** represents the means by which short-term assets and liabilities are managed to ensure adequate liquidity. To remain liquid, firms may maintain cash and short-term securities. For example, they may invest in **Treasury bills,** which are short-term debt securities issued by the U.S. Treasury. Treasury bills have maturities of thirteen weeks, twenty-six weeks, and one year. Treasury bills offer a relatively low return. They provide a firm with easy access to funds because they can easily be sold to other investors. When firms need funds to pay bills, they sell the Treasury bills and use the proceeds to pay the bills. DuPont holds about $1 billion in cash and short-term securities, which makes up about 2.5 percent of DuPont's total assets. Coca-Cola holds about $1 billion in cash and short-term securities, which makes up about 8 percent of its total assets.

Firms normally attempt to limit their holdings of cash and short-term securities so that they can use their funds for other purposes that generate higher returns. For example, UAL Corporation (owner of United Airlines) has substantially reduced its holdings of these short-term assets over time, as shown in Exhibit 18.9. Its current ratio (measured as its short-term assets divided by its short-term liabilities) peaked in 1987, but has declined consistently since 1990.

Firms can be liquid without holding cash and short-term securities, if they have easy access to borrowed funds. Most firms have a **line of credit** with one or more banks, which is an agreement that allows access to borrowed funds upon demand over some specified period (usually for one year). If a firm experiences a temporary shortage of funds, it can use its line of credit to obtain a short-term loan immediately. The interest charged by the banks on the loan is normally tied to some specified market-determined interest rate. Thus, the interest rate will be consistent with existing market rates at the time of the loan. Firms with a line of credit do not need to go through the loan application process. They can normally reapply for a new line of credit each year.

line of credit an agreement that allows access to borrowed funds upon demand over some specified period

The Coca-Cola Company typically maintains a line of credit of at least $2 billion. Given its $1 billion in cash and short-term securities, plus access to $2 billion, it is very liquid because it is unlikely to need $3 billion at a given time to pay its bills.

Exhibit 18.9
Liquidity Management by UAL Corporation (owner of United Airlines)

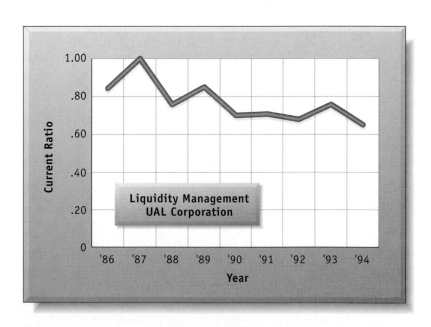

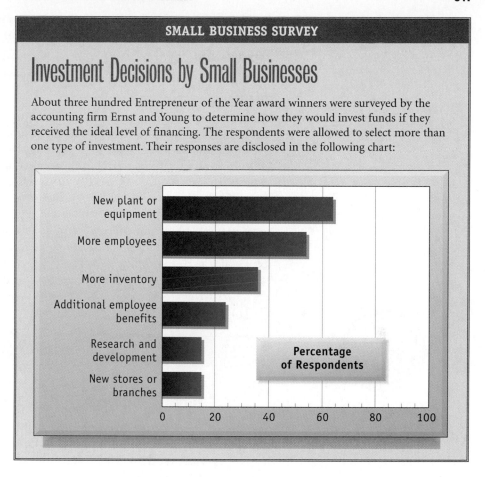

SMALL BUSINESS SURVEY

When firms build up an excessive amount of cash, they search for ways to use the excess. For example, Chrysler and Dow Chemical recently used excess cash to repurchase some of their existing stock. Time Warner and Westinghouse used excess cash to pay off some of their existing debt.

Accounts Receivable Management

Firms have accounts receivable when they grant credit to customers. By granting credit, they may generate more sales than if they required an immediate cash payment. However, allowing credit has two potential disadvantages. The first is that the credit balance may last a long time before it is paid by customers. Consequently, the firm does not have use of cash until several months after the sale was made. This may force the firm to borrow funds until the cash is received, and the firm will have to pay interest on those funds.

The second potential disadvantage of extending credit to customers is that the customers may default on the credit provided. In this case, the firm never receives payment for the products it sold to customers.

Accounts receivable management sets the limits on credit available to customers, and the length of the period in which payment is due. The goal is to be flexible enough so that sales increase as a result of credit granted, but strict enough to avoid customers who would pay their bills late (beyond the period specified) or not at all.

accounts receivable management sets the limits on credit available to customers, and the length of the period in which payment is due

Given the possibilities of late payments or no payments (default) on the credit, firms need to closely assess the creditworthiness of any customers who wish to pay their bills with credit.

Inventory Management

When firms maintain large amounts of inventory, they can avoid stockouts (shortages). However, they invest a large amount of funds by holding so much inventory, and they could have used those funds for other purposes. Consider the case of Wal-Mart, which continuously attempts to order enough of each product to satisfy customers. Yet, it does not want to order an excessive amount of any product, so that it can use its funds more efficiently.

inventory management determines the amount of inventory that is held

Inventory management determines the amount of inventory that is held. Managers attempt to hold just enough inventory to avoid stockouts, without tying up funds in excess inventories. This task is complicated because it requires forecasts of future sales levels, which can be erratic. If sales are more than expected, stockouts could occur unless excess inventory was held.

BUSINESS DILEMMA

·COLLEGE·
HEALTH CLUB

Capital Budgeting at College Health Club

Sue Kramer, president of College Health Club (CHC), notices that the Silver Health Club in a nearby town is for sale for $100,000. It is close to another college campus but has not made much of an effort to attract that college's students. This club's largest expense is the rent. Sue believes that she could improve the performance of the Silver Health Club if she purchased it, but its price seems high.

Sue decides to conduct a capital budgeting analysis of Silver Health Club. She estimates her cash inflows each year and subtracts the estimated cash outflows to derive annual cash flows. Her cash outflows include the hiring of a manager to oversee the club's business, since Sue would still focus most of her time at CHC. She estimates that her cash flows would be $5,000 in each of the first two years and $20,000 over each of the following three years. All cash flows are expected to occur at the end of each year. Sue also estimates that she would be able to sell this health club in five years for $120,000 (after taxes). She decides that she would need to generate a rate of return of at least 20 percent from this health club to make it worth purchasing.

Dilemma

Sue's goal is to determine whether to purchase the health club. Conduct a capital budgeting analysis to determine the net present value of Silver Health Club. Based on your analysis, should Sue purchase the Silver Health Club?

Solution

Sue's capital budgeting analysis of the target firm is disclosed in Exhibit 18.10. The cash flows shown in column 2 of Exhibit 18.10 are discounted at a rate of 20 percent

Exhibit 18.10
Capital Budgeting Analysis of a
Firm that CHC May Acquire

End of Year	Estimated Cash Flow	Discounted Cash Flow (at 20%)
1	$5,000	$4,167
2	$5,000	$3,472
3	$20,000	$11,574
4	$20,000	$9,645
5	$20,000	$8,038
	+$120,000	$48,225
	(Salvage Value)	

Present Value	=	$85,121
− Initial Outlay	=	$100,000
= Net Present Value	=	−$14,879

(which represents Sue's required rate of return) to derive their present value in column 3. Notice that the salvage value of $120,000 (the expected sales price of the firm) is also included in the estimated cash flows for Year 5. The discounted annual cash flows are summed at the bottom of Column 3 to derive the present value of future cash flows.

The present value of the Silver Health Club's future cash flows is estimated to be $85,121, which is less than the initial outlay (purchase price) of $100,000. Therefore, the net present value from acquiring the Silver Health Club is negative, causing Sue to reject this project. The present value of future cash flows does not cover the amount she would have to pay for the Silver Health Club. Sue decides to monitor the status of the Silver Health Club over time. If its price were lowered, she would reassess whether to acquire it by conducting a new capital budgeting analysis.

Additional Issues for Discussion

1 If Sue were willing to require a lower rate of return on the Silver Health Club, how would this affect the present value of Silver Health Club's future cash flows?

2 When Sue estimates the value of Silver Health Club, what is the key information used to estimate its value? Could this information be wrong?

3 A key motive for Sue to consider purchasing Silver Health Club is her belief that she could improve its performance by managing it better. Would economies of scale be a motive for Sue to consider expansion by purchasing another health club?

SUMMARY

1 Capital budgeting analysis is normally applied to determine whether projects that have been proposed are feasible. If the present value of the project's expected cash flows exceeds the project's initial outlay, the project has a positive net present value and should be implemented. If the present value of the project's expected cash flows is less than the project's initial outlay, the project has a negative net present value and should not be implemented.

2 The process of capital budgeting is composed of five tasks:

➤ proposing new projects that deserve to be assessed;

➤ estimating cash flows of projects, which represent the cash inflows (derived from revenue) minus cash outflows (derived from expenses) per period;

➤ determining which projects are

feasible, which can be accomplished by comparing the present value of the project's cash flows with the project's initial outlay;

➤ implementing feasible projects based on a priority status;

➤ monitoring projects that were implemented, so that any errors from estimating project cash flows are recognized and may be avoided when assessing projects in the future.

3 Firms consider investing funds to acquire other companies as a result of one or more of the following motives:

➤ A firm can achieve immediate growth by acquiring another firm, whereas growth without a merger will be slower.

➤ Mergers can create a higher volume of sales for a firm, which allows it to spread its fixed cost across more units, thereby reducing costs (economies of scale).

➤ Mergers can allow firms to combine resources and contribute those resources in which they have the most managerial expertise.

➤ Mergers can allow the acquiring firm to reduce its taxable earnings when it acquires a company that recently incurred a loss.

4 Firms invest in short-term assets such as cash, accounts receivable, and inventory. They invest in a sufficient amount of cash and short-term securities to maintain adequate liquidity. However, excessive investment in cash and short-term securities represents an inefficient use of funds. Firms desire to invest in sufficient accounts receivable so that they can increase revenue over time. However, they must impose adequate credit standards so that they can avoid excessive defaults on credit they provided.

Firms desire to invest in a sufficient amount of inventory so that they can avoid stockouts. However, excessive investment in inventory represents an inefficient use of funds.

KEY TERMS

accounts receivable management	inventory management	net present value
capital budget	leveraged buyout	salvage value
capital budgeting	line of credit	tender offer (chapter appendix)
conglomerate merger	liquid	Treasury bills
divestiture	liquidity management	vertical merger
horizontal merger	merger	white knight (chapter appendix)
independent	mutually exclusive	working capital management

REVIEW QUESTIONS

1 Identify short-term investment decisions undertaken by a firm.

2 How do interest rates affect the capital budgeting analysis?

3 Identify the classifications of capital expenditures.

4 Discuss the major tasks involved in the capital budgeting process.

5 Discuss the investment decisions that financial managers must consider in achieving the firm's objectives.

6 Discuss the process of capital budgeting analysis when a firm assesses a foreign project.

7 Discuss why a firm's management would consider a divestiture.

8 Explain how cross-functional teamwork is involved in business investment decisions.

9 Discuss the pros and cons of carrying a small versus a large inventory for a retailer.

10 Identify and explain the different types of mergers that can take place between firms.

DISCUSSION QUESTIONS

1 Assume your firm is considering several projects. Should you invest in these projects? Why?

2 Explain why a horizontal merger could reduce competition in the automobile industry.

3 Assume you are a financial manager. How would you work with production and marketing managers in making capital budgeting decisions to introduce a new product? What must the product generate to make it economically feasible?

4 Jason Boone has just opened a go-cart track. He has timed the opening of the go-cart track with the annual county fair. Because his business has grown rapidly, cash flow remains a problem. Analyze Jason's financial problems. Could this be a good business?

5 Why might a horizontal merger achieve economies of scale?

RUNNING YOUR OWN BUSINESS

1 Describe any big purchases (such as a computer or a machine) that you may need to make for your business someday. What factors would be a part of a cost/benefit analysis of this purchase?

2 Describe how much inventory you would have to maintain to avoid shortages.

3 Would your business generate accounts receivable? If so, how would you manage this asset?

INVESTING IN THE STOCK OF A BUSINESS

1 What is the firm's capital budget for this year? Is this budget higher or lower than last year's?

2 What types of new projects has the firm invested in recently?

3 Has the firm divested any of its operations? If so, did it divest to focus more on its core business?

4 Has the firm been involved in any recent merger activity? If so, what is their justification for this action?

CASE 1 Benefits of an Acquisition

When Packard Bell Electronics acquired Zenith Data Systems Corporation, it had access to Zenith's cash. This should improve Packard Bell's current cash problems and allow it to become the biggest seller of personal computers in the United States. Packard Bell's revenue would grow from about $4 billion to about $5.5 billion. While sales continue to increase, profitability is still a concern because the retail market is very competitive for personal computers.

The merger combination should help both Packard Bell and Zenith Data. Zenith Data has suffered stagnant growth the past few quarters because it had virtually no presence in the booming retail market. Packard Bell, on the other hand, has grown tremendously at retail, but lacks much of a hold in the corporate office market. By combining operations, Packard Bell would gain instant access to the big corporate and government accounts of Zenith Data, while Zenith Data can benefit from Packard Bell's growth in the retail market.

The acquisition was a result of Packard Bell's need for cash because of the difficulty it had maintaining profitability in the cutthroat PC retail market it dominates.

Questions

1 What type of merger is this?

2 What immediate problem is addressed with this acquisition by Packard Bell?

3 Could both companies benefit from this merger?

CASE 2 Ford's Merger Decision

Ford Motor Company announced a major decision to merge the company's European business with its North American one. Since each continent has separate management structures, products, factories and even ways of doing things, this amounts to a merger of two companies that makes most real takeovers seem small.

The investment in assets over time has produced sig-

nificant results to make Ford a world leader in the production of automobiles. Jac Nasser, a new vice-president at Ford, along with the other three vice-presidents, was responsible for developing a new financial strategy called Ford 2000. Many of these new products must go through a capital budget process. Ford has announced a major expansion program, involving expanding their current business and improving their market share throughout Europe. It is developing new product lines to be more competitive with European producers. Globalization will produce savings of around $3 billion a year, resulting from lower product-engineering and development costs.

Development of new products is essential at Ford, especially if they compete successfully in Europe. A major task is to undertake a capital budgeting analysis to fully appreciate whether a new product line will generate positive net present values associated with a project.

Questions

1 What are the planned capital expenditures by Ford Motor Company?

2 Did a horizontal merger take place at Ford?

3 Should a product always have positive net present values for it to be considered?

4 If U.S. interest rates rise, how might this affect the feasibility of projects assessed by Ford?

VIDEO CASE How Business Investment Decisions Determine Success

A philosophy that guides Andrew Bernhardt in running Qualitad, a Rutland, Vermont, manufacturer of plastic packaging, is: Don't count on another company to perform a vital function for you; do it yourself.

To produce and assemble its own plastic containers, Qualitad bought three forming machines. It bought the most sophisticated equipment for extruding plastic.

If Qualitad invests funds into new machinery or producing a new product, it must conduct a capital budgeting analysis. Its future performance is highly dependent on the decisions that result from its capital budgeting analyses.

Bernhardt sees a lot of opportunity for his company in microwave products. When a key customer asked for containers from which individual portions of frozen food could be eaten after microwaving, Qualitad developed microwave platters. It has since developed bowls, casseroles, and jumbo platters, all dishwasher-safe but

priced as disposable. (They also are recyclable.) And it is doing research on other items.

Qualitad now ships to Europe and expects to expand in that market. It also expects expansion at home.

Questions

1 When Qualitad assessed whether to purchase machines and equipment for producing plastic containers, what factors do you think were considered? That is, what are the potential benefits of this type of business investment and what are the costs?

2 Qualitad is presently considering the development of various microwave products. How can Qualitad estimate the potential benefits and the cost of each of these products?

3 When Qualitad considers the development of a new microwave product, why might its estimated costs be wrong? Why might its estimated revenue from this product be wrong?

THE *Coca-Cola* COMPANY ANNUAL REPORT PROJECT

The following questions apply concepts learned in this chapter to The Coca-Cola Company. Read page 21 and page 41 up to the section "Bottling Operations," and pages 49–50 in the annual report of The Coca-Cola Company before answering these questions.

1 What does The Coca-Cola Company do with the cash flow it receives (see page 21)?

2 **a.** What is The Coca-Cola Company's criterion for investing in a project?

b. What types of investment does The Coca-Cola Company currently undertake in emerging markets? In developed markets?

3 Describe the trend in capital expenditures of The Coca-Cola Company over the last 10 years. (See "Capital Expenditures" under "Balance Sheet Data" on page 49.)

Answers are in an appendix at the back of the book.

True or False

1 When the decision of whether to adopt one project has no bearing on the adoption of other projects, the project is said to be independent.

2 The capital budgeting analysis required to assess a foreign project is more complex than a domestic project because of the need to assess specific characteristics of the foreign country.

3 Capital budgeting involves the comparison of assets and revenue.

4 One of the most popular methods available to assess the feasibility of projects is the net present value (NPV) technique.

5 A payment received by a firm at a future point in time has more value than the exact payment received today.

6 The amount of money that a firm can receive from selling a project is referred to as the net present value.

7 When interest rates rise and firms use a higher discount rate, this also increases the present value of future cash flows and increases the likelihood that a project's net present value will be positive.

8 To decide whether any proposed project should be implemented, firms conduct capital budgeting.

9 Estimating the cash inflows and outflows that would result from the project is a critical part of the capital budgeting process.

10 A project is never feasible if the present value of its future cash flows exceeds the initial outlay needed to purchase the project.

Multiple Choice

11 A targeted amount of funds to be used for purchasing assets such as buildings, machinery, and equipment needed for long-term projects is a(n):
a) revenue budget.
b) capital budget.
c) accounting plan.
d) marketing plan.
e) production schedule.

12 The present value (*PV*) of cash flows minus the initial outlay (*I*) equals the:
a) net present value.
b) capital budget.
c) profit objective.

d) production quota.
e) market forecast.

13 When U.S. firms consider the purchase of a foreign company, they conduct a _____ to determine whether this type of project is feasible.
a) Gantt chart
b) production plan
c) sales forecast
d) capital budgeting analysis
e) PERT diagram

14 Since the firm's value is influenced by its performance, its value is influenced by its:
a) supplier's fraud.
b) government.
c) price fixing.
d) investment fraud.
e) managers.

15 The size of the capital budget is influenced by the amount and size of:
a) industry supply.
b) industry prices.
c) feasible business projects.
d) competitive forces.
e) market forecasts.

16 The merger between ITT Corporation (telecommunications) and Caesar's World (casinos) is a:
a) horizontal merger.
b) conglomerate merger.
c) vertical merger.
d) bond indenture.
e) divestiture.

17 A firm's short-term assets include the following except for:
a) cash.
b) accounts receivable.
c) bonds.
d) short-term securities.
e) inventory.

18 Firms that have adequate access to funds so that they can pay their bills are considered to be:
a) leveraged.
b) trading on the equity.
c) nonprofitable.
d) bankrupt.
e) liquid.

19 When firms maintain large amounts of inventory, they can avoid:

a) stockouts.
b) trade credit.
c) leveraging.
d) liquidity.
e) debt financing.

20 To be flexible enough so that sales increase as a result of credit granted, but strict enough to avoid customers who would pay their bills late or not at all, is a goal of:
a) leverage management.
b) accounts receivable management.
c) accounts payable management.
d) trade credit management.
e) inventory control.

21 Products that exhibit _____ can be produced at a much lower cost per unit if a large amount is produced.
a) economies of scale
b) production bottlenecks
c) substandard production schedules
d) machine breakdowns
e) antiquated equipment

22 The types of potential capital expenditures considered by a firm can be classified by: development of new business; investment in assets that will reduce expenses; and:
a) sales revenue.
b) sales discount.
c) sales return and allowances.
d) purchase discounts.
e) expansion of current business.

23 The process of capital budgeting for a firm is composed of the following except for:
a) determining whether projects are feasible.
b) monitoring projects that were implemented.
c) estimating cash flows of projects.
d) inventory control.
e) proposing new projects.

24 A firm's project is feasible when its present value exceeds the:
a) future outlay.
b) future value.
c) initial outlay.
d) future present value.
e) discounted cash value.

25 When a U.S. firm requires a higher return, it uses a higher discount rate to derive the present value of the project's:
a) initial cash flows.
b) future cash flows.

c) discounted cash value.
d) net present value.
e) immediate cash on hand.

26 Economies of scale are more likely to be achieved by:
a) vertical mergers.
b) horizontal mergers.
c) conglomerate mergers.
d) divestitures.
e) accounts receivable management.

27 Firms that incur negative earnings are sometimes attractive candidates for mergers because of potential:
a) tax advantages.
b) cash advantages.
c) profit exploitation.
d) retained earnings.
e) divestitures.

28 A purchase of a company (or the subsidiary of the company) by a group of investors with borrowed funds is a(n):
a) common stock purchase.
b) purchase from retained earnings.
c) equity purchase.
d) preferred stock purchase.
e) leveraged buyout.

29 The three general types of mergers are horizontal, conglomerate, and:
a) cooperative.
b) vertical.
c) divestiture.
d) bureaucratic.
e) parallel.

30 Short-term securities that offer a relatively low return, but provide a firm with easy access to funds because they can easily be sold to other investors are:
a) Treasury notes.
b) Treasury bonds.
c) Treasury bills.
d) corporate bonds.
e) common stock.

31 Attempting to hold just enough inventory to avoid stockouts, without tying up funds in excess inventories, is complicated because it requires:
a) forecasts of future sales levels.
b) accounts receivable management.
c) accounts payable management.
d) notes payable.
e) notes receivable.

32 The sale of an existing business is known as a(n):
a) preferred stock.
b) common stock.

c) divestiture.
d) accounts receivable management.
e) inventory control.

33 The result of a firm investing in another company by purchasing all the stock of that company is a(n):
a) divestiture.
b) leveraged buyout.
c) economies of scale.
d) line of credit.
e) merger.

34 The management of a firm's short-term assets and liabilities is:

a) accounts receivable management.
b) working capital management.
c) sales management.
d) plant and equipment management.
e) fixed asset management.

35 An agreement that allows a firm access to borrowed funds upon demand over some specified period of time is a:
a) bond indenture.
b) stock flotation.
c) note receivable.
d) line of credit.
e) note payable.

Surfing the Net

Investment Information on the Internet

An important source of financial and investment information on companies is documents filed with the Securities and Exchange Commission (SEC). New York University's Edgar web site (Exhibit 18.11) provides a convenient location for accessing such information.

Exhibit 18.11
NYU's Edgar Web Site

http://edgar.stern.nyu.edu/edgar.html

NYU EDGAR

Welcome to the EDGAR Development Project at the NYU Stern School of Business Information Systems Department. If you use this site please read this important disclaimer.

Get Corporate SEC Filings

Mutual Fund Database Prototype - now with Expanded Fund Families

NEW **Search and View Corporate Profiles**

Alternatives: **Edgar Site at SEC** and **Other NYU Edgar Server**

Frequently Asked Questions

The RR Donnelley Library of SEC Materials

Software and Data and **Advanced Software Course**

Reciprocal Links and **Other Interesting Links**

Introduction and **What is EDGAR?**

This project was sponsored in 1994 and 1995 by the National Science Foundation and implemented in conjunction with the Internet Multicasting Service.

The Merger Process

MERGER ANALYSIS

When a firm plans to engage in a merger, it must conduct the following tasks:

➤ Identify potential merger prospects.
➤ Evaluate potential merger prospects.
➤ Make the merger decision.

Identify Potential Merger Prospects

Firms attempt to identify potential merger prospects that may help them achieve their strategic plan. If the firm plans for growth in its current line of products, it would consider purchasing (or "acquiring") companies in the same business. If it needs to restructure its production process, it may attempt to acquire a supplier. If it desires a more diversified product line, it may attempt to acquire companies in unrelated businesses. The firm's long-run objectives influence the selection of merger prospects that are worthy of evaluation.

The size of firms is also a relevant criterion, since some firms may be too small to achieve the desired objectives, while others may be too large to acquire. The location is another possible criterion, since a firm's product demand and production costs are dependent on its location.

Evaluate Potential Merger Prospects

Once merger prospects have been identified, they must be analyzed thoroughly, using publicly available financial statements. The financial analysis of these prospects may detect problems that would eliminate some prospects from further consideration. Yet, prospects with deficiencies that could be corrected should still be considered. Along with the firm's financial condition, additional characteristics of each prospect must be assessed, including its reputation and labor-management relations. From this assessment, potential problems that may not be disclosed on financial statements can be detected.

An evaluation of the prospect's specific characteristics is necessary, such as its facilities, its dependency on suppliers, and pending lawsuits. Unfortunately, the firm planning the acquisition may not be able to complete a full evaluation of such specific characteristics unless the prospect provides the information. The firm planning the acquisition may contact the prospect to request more detailed information. The prospect may comply if it is willing to consider the possibility of a merger.

Make the Merger Decision

Once the firm has identified a specific prospect it wishes to acquire, it can assess the feasibility of acquiring that prospect by using capital budgeting analysis. Thus the acquisition prospect can be evaluated just like any other project. The cost of this project is the outlay necessary to purchase the firm. The benefits are the extra cash flows that will be generated over time as a result of the acquisition. If the present value of those future cash flows to be received by the acquiring firm exceeds the initial outlay, the acquisition is feasible.

MERGER PROCEDURES

If an attempt is made to acquire a prospect, that prospect becomes the "target." It is set apart from all the other prospects that were considered. To enact the acquisition, firms will normally hire an investment bank (such as First Boston, Morgan Stanley, or Salomon Brothers) for guidance. Some firms that continuously acquire or sell businesses may employ their own investment banking department to handle many of the necessary tasks. Most tasks can be classified into one of the following:

➤ Financing the merger
➤ Tender offer
➤ Integrating the businesses
➤ Postmerger evaluation

Financing the Merger

A merger normally requires a substantial amount of long-term funds, as one firm may purchase the existing stock of another firm. One common method for a firm to finance a merger is by issuing more of its own stock to the public. As new stock is sold to the public, the proceeds are used to purchase the target's stock. Alternatively, the acquiring firm may trade its new stock to the shareholders of the target firm in exchange for their stock. Instead of issuing new stock, the acquiring firm may also borrow the necessary funds to purchase the target's stock from its shareholders.

Tender Offer

The acquiring firm first contacts the management of the target firm to negotiate a merger. The acquiring firm normally pays a premium on the target firm's stock to make the deal worthwhile to the target firm's stockholders. Consider IBM's acquisition of Lotus Development Corporation in 1995. Exhibit 18A.1 shows how the stock price of Lotus jumped on June 5 in response to IBM's offer to acquire the firm.

tender offer a direct bid by the acquiring firm for the shares of the target firm

When two firms cannot come to terms, the acquiring firm may attempt a **tender offer.** This is a direct bid by the acquiring firm for the shares of the target firm. It does not require prior approval of the target firm's management. Thus, a tender offer could accomplish a merger even if the management of the target firm disapproves.

The acquiring firm must decide the price at which it is willing to purchase the target firm's shares and then officially extend this tender offer to the shareholders. The tender offer normally represents a premium of 20 percent or more above the prevailing market price, which may be necessary to encourage the shareholders of the target firm to sell their shares. The acquiring firm can achieve control of the target firm only if enough of the target firm's shareholders are willing to sell.

Integrating the Businesses

If a merger is achieved, various departments within the two companies may need to be restructured. The key to successfully integrating the management of two compa-

Exhibit 18A.1
Stock Price Response to Merger
Announcement on June 5, 1995

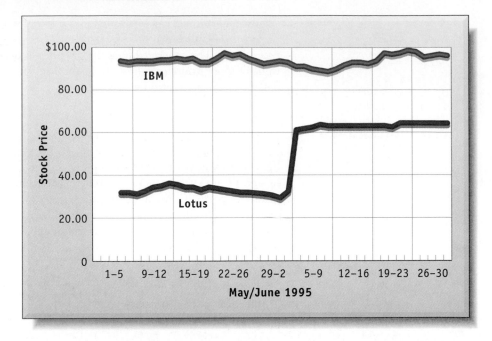

nies is to clearly communicate the strategic plan of the firm. In addition, the organizational structure should be communicated to clarify the roles of each department and position. This includes identifying to whom each position will report, and who is accountable for various tasks. If the roles are not clearly defined up front, the newly integrated management will not function properly.

Tensions are especially high in the beginning stages of a newly formed merger, since the employees of the acquired firm are not fully aware of the acquiring firm's plans. Once the merger has occurred, the personnel involved in the initial evaluation of the target firm should guide the integration of the two firms. For example, if the primary reason for a horizontal merger was to reduce the duplication of some managerial functions (to increase production efficiency), management of the newly formed firm should make sure that these reasons for initiating the merger are realized.

A newly formed merger typically requires a period in which the production, financing, inventory management, capital structure, and dividend policies must be reevaluated. Policies are commonly revised to conform to the newly formed firm's characteristics. For example, to deal with the larger volume of sales, inventory of the combined firm may need to be larger than for either original business (although perhaps not as large as the sum of both businesses).

While identifying ways by which a merger could be beneficial is often easy, it may not be as easy to achieve those benefits without creating any new problems. As a final point, the process of creating the merger can also be much more expensive than originally anticipated, and can often place a financial strain on the acquiring company (especially when the target fights the takeover effort). Therefore, firms that are considering acquisitions should attempt to anticipate all types of expenses that may be incurred as a result of the acquisitions.

Postmerger Evaluation

After the merger, the firm should periodically assess the merger's costs and benefits. Were the benefits as high as expected? Were there unanticipated costs involved in the merger? Was the analysis of the target firm too optimistic? Once the merger takes place, it cannot be easily reversed. Thus, any errors detected from the analysis that led to the merger cannot be washed away. However, lessons can be learned from any errors so that future merger prospects will be more accurately evaluated.

DEFENSE AGAINST TAKEOVER ATTEMPTS

In some cases, managers of a target firm may not approve of the attempt by the acquiring firm. They may believe that the price offered for their firm is below what it is worth, or that their firm has higher potential if it is not acquired. They may view the potential acquiring firm as a shark approaching for the kill (takeover). Under such conditions where the takeover attempt is hostile, management of the target firm can choose from a variety of "shark repellents" to defend itself.

A common defensive tactic against a takeover attempt is an attempt to convince shareholders to retain their shares. Another tactic to avoid a merger is a private placement of stock. By selling shares directly (privately) to specific institutions, the target firm can reduce the acquiring firm's chances of obtaining enough shares to gain controlling interest. The more shares outstanding, the larger the amount of shares that must be purchased by the acquiring firm to gain controlling interest.

A third defensive tactic is for the target firm to find a more suitable company (called a **white knight**) that would be willing to acquire a firm and rescue it from the hostile takeover efforts of some other firm. The white knight rescues the target firm by acquiring the target firm itself. While the target firm would no longer retain its independence, it may prefer being acquired by the white knight firm.

white knight a more suitable company that would be willing to acquire a firm and rescue it from the hostile takeover efforts of some other firm

The performance of the firm can be assessed by conducting a financial analysis, as discussed in Chapter 16. A financial analysis is also used to identify the reasons for poor performance, such as excessive (or deficient) investment in its long-term or short-term assets, or an excessive amount of debt used to finance its investment.

The key financial management decisions made by a firm can be classified as either financing (explained in Chapter 17) or investing funds in business projects (Chapter 18). Firms use either debt financing or equity financing to obtain funds. The common methods of debt financing are obtaining bank loans, issuing bonds, and issuing commercial paper. The common methods of equity financing are retaining earnings or issuing stock. The ideal type of financing is dependent on the firm's characteristics. If the firm does not have a large amount of debt, it may consider debt financing to capitalize on the tax advantage of using debt. However, if the firm already has a large amount of debt financing, it may use equity financing instead.

When firms consider using funds to invest in business projects, they must determine whether the return on the investment is sufficient to make the investment feasible. Capital budgeting analysis is used to determine whether the project is feasible. This analysis determines whether the present value of cash flows exceeds the initial outlay of the project.

In addition to business projects, firms also invest in short-term assets such as accounts receivable and inventory. An investment in accounts receivable is necessary to attract some customers who prefer to purchase products on credit. An investment in inventory is necessary to avoid stockouts. Yet, excessive investment in accounts receivable or in inventory is an inefficient use of funds, because the funds could have been used for other purposes.

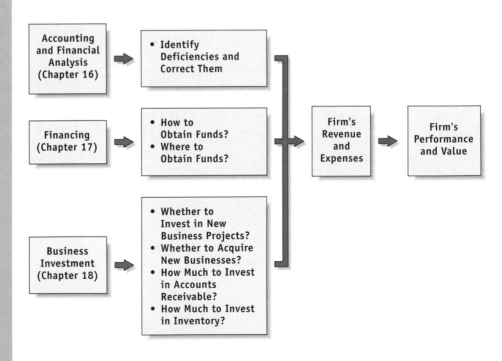

Part VII further explores topics that were introduced in previous chapters and provides a synthesis of the text. Chapter 19 explains how firms use computer information systems to facilitate their operations. Chapter 20 describes the types of risk to which firms are exposed and the methods of managing that exposure. Chapter 21 provides a synthesis of all the key business functions that have been emphasized throughout the text. These functions can be properly conducted only by recognizing how they interact with one another.

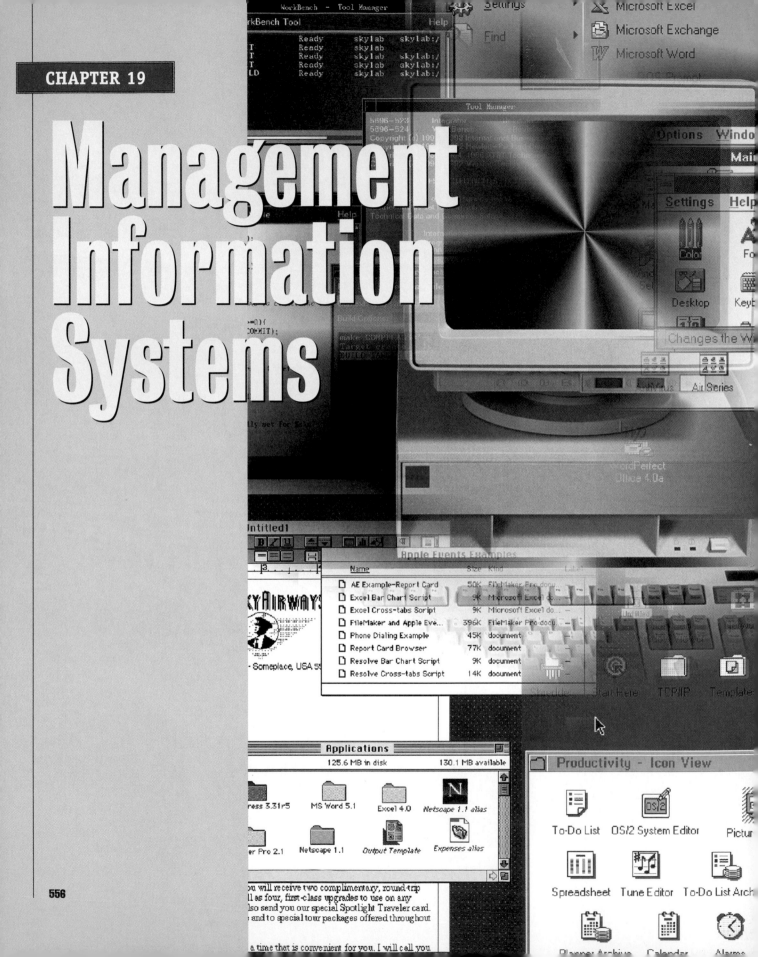

CHAPTER 19

Management Information Systems

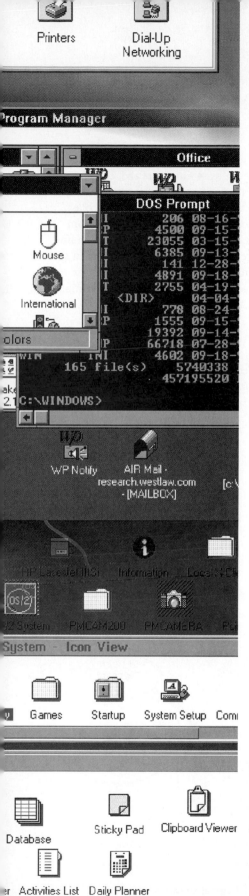

Management information systems (MIS) is the business function that oversees the adoption, use, and management of information technologies, which include both computers and telecommunications. Over the past fifty years, these technologies have shown that they can impact the value of the firm in many ways. Decision support systems and end user applications, which enhance managerial decision making, have opened the door to both improved revenue and reduced costs. Traditional data processing systems have streamlined existing business processes, making firms more efficient. Internal information systems, which permit many users to access the same information simultaneously, have improved efficiency and have led to the development of business opportunities that were previously impossible. Interorganizational systems, which allow information to be shared across organizational boundaries, have improved the efficiency of transactions and have promoted better relationships between suppliers and customers. They have also led to the development of entirely new distribution channels. These contributions represent only a partial listing of the ways in which information technologies can potentially increase the value of the firm.

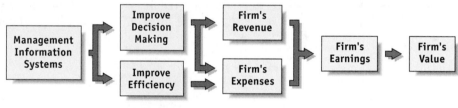

Consider the case of United Parcel Service (UPS), which delivers packages to numerous residences and firms around the world. How can UPS use management information systems to keep track of these packages? How can it use management information systems to deliver packages more quickly? This chapter discusses concepts about management information systems that can be used to address these questions.

The **Learning Goals** of this chapter are to:

1 Describe the key components of a computer and explain their purpose.

2 Discuss the different ways in which computers and related technologies contribute to today's businesses.

3 Describe some of the key challenges of managing today's information technologies.

4 Identify emerging technologies and their implications.

WHAT IS A COMPUTER?

1

Describe the key components of a computer and explain their purpose.

electronic computer a device capable of processing and storing vast quantities of information

mainframes large computers used primarily to service entire organizations

hardware the physical components of a computer

system architecture the basic logical organization of computers

An **electronic computer** is a device capable of processing and storing vast quantities of information. Such computers, which did not even exist fifty years ago, come in many forms. The early tube-based computers of the 1950s could fill a small warehouse, generating heat equivalent to several hundred hair dryers running full blast. Today's computers more closely resemble the microcomputer of Exhibit 19.1, comfortably fitting on a desktop and drawing less power than a light bulb. Today's **mainframes,** large computers used primarily to service entire organizations, have been so miniaturized that their key circuitry often fits into a casing the size of a pizza box. These physical changes in computers have been accompanied by even more dramatic changes in performance, as illustrated in Exhibit 19.2.

Computer Hardware

The physical components of a computer are collectively called **hardware.** Although computer hardware is constantly changing, the basic logical organization of computers, often referred to as **system architecture,** has been relatively stable since the mid-1950s. Specifically, nearly all computers are built around four key components:

Exhibit 19.1
A Typical Microcomputer

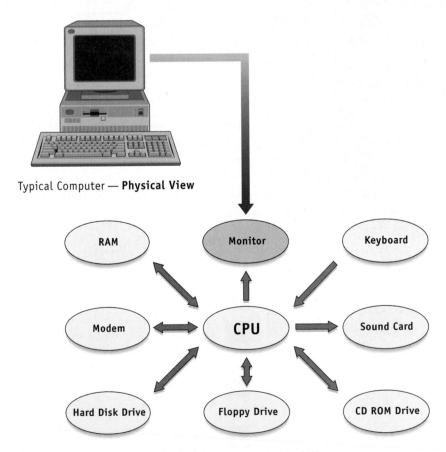

Typical Computer — **Physical View**

Typical Computer — **Logical View**

Exhibit 19.2
How Much Have Computers
Improved?

The physical changes in computer hardware over the past forty years have been accompanied by even more dramatic changes in actual performance.

For many key computer components, price-performance ratios have been improving by a factor of ten every five years.

To put such improvements into perspective, had automobiles experienced the rate of price-performance improvement, the luxury car that cost $10,000 in the mid-1960s would now sell for under a nickel (including a liberal allowance for inflation).

megahertz [MHz] millions of cycles per second

random access memory (RAM) space in which to temporarily store information

megabytes millions of characters

winchester drives sealed magnetic disks

Advanced Micro Devices produces CPV's which compete with Intel's Pentium series.

1 *Central Processing Unit (CPU):* The heart of the computer, the CPU (or processor), performs all calculations and moves information between the computer's other components. More than any other single component, CPUs (such as Intel's Pentium chip) determine the basic behavior and capabilities of a particular computer. Generally, the faster the processor (as measured in millions of cycles per second, or **megahertz [MHz]**), the faster the computer.

2 *Primary Storage:* For a computer to function, its processor must have scratch space in which to temporarily store information. On today's computers, such storage typically takes the form of **random access memory (RAM)** chips. The amount of RAM installed on a particular system is measured in millions of characters (or **megabytes**). Many applications will not run unless a certain amount of RAM is installed, and most applications run faster when more RAM is installed.

3 *Secondary Storage:* Because RAM is expensive and temporary, computers also have secondary storage available. Today, most secondary storage is in the form of sealed magnetic disks, commonly referred to as **Winchester drives** or **hard disks.**

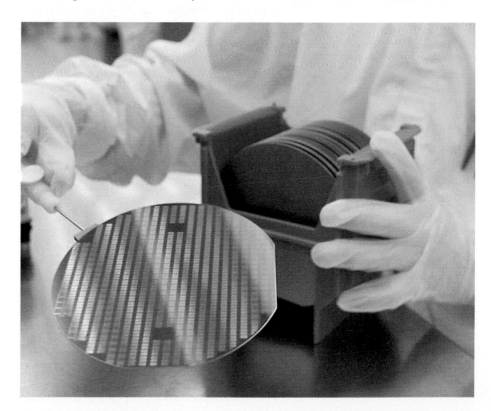

hard disks sealed magnetic disks

floppy disks removable secondary storage

magnetic tapes removable secondary storage

compact disks (CD-ROMS) optical techniques

gigabytes billions of characters

There are also many forms of removable secondary storage, which can be carried from machine to machine. Common forms of secondary storage include **floppy disks** and **magnetic tapes** which store information magnetically and **compact disks,** often referred to as **CD-ROMs** which use optical techniques. As was the case for RAM, quantities of secondary storage are usually measured in megabytes. Recently, however, increases in hard disk capacities have made units of **gigabytes** (billions of characters) increasingly common.

4 *Peripherals:* The devices attached to the CPU which are not primary or secondary storage are peripherals. Thousands of different types of general purpose and special purpose peripherals exist. Among those most often found on today's desktop computers are a keyboard, a mouse, a monitor, a printer, a modem, and a sound card. On business machines, peripherals often include scanners and network connectors.

Computer Software

computer program collection of step-by-step instructions to the processor

word processor program is intended to create documents

spreadsheet program is intended to perform financial analysis

database program is intended to generate reports from a firm's client list

software programs that determine the specific tasks a computer will perform at any given time

application programs and data associated with performing a specific task

software packages applications purchased off the shelf

Unlike most pieces of complex machinery, which are designed to accomplish a specific task, computers have no predefined purpose, making them general purpose machines. The CPU can do many things; what it lacks is specific direction. To provide that direction, a collection of step-by-step instructions to the processor, referred to as a **computer program,** is loaded into primary storage (RAM), then run by the CPU. By changing the program that is loaded into RAM, the user can dramatically change how the computer behaves. One program is intended to create documents (a **word processor**), while another program is intended to perform financial analysis (a **spreadsheet)**, and yet another program is intended to generate reports from a firm's client list (a **database**).

Just as the actual machinery of the computer is referred to as hardware, the programs that determine the specific tasks a computer will perform at any given time are called **software.** The programs and data associated with performing a specific task, such as word processing, are collectively referred to as an **application.** Applications can be developed from scratch by computer programmers. They can also be purchased off the shelf, in which case they are called **software packages.** Such packages are typically sold on removable secondary storage media, such as floppy disks or CD-ROMs.

WHAT ARE COMPUTERS USED FOR?

2

Discuss the different ways in which computers and related technologies contribute to today's businesses.

The potential uses for computers are limited only by the imagination of programmers and users. In today's businesses, however, five general types of use have become particularly common:

➤ Computational models
➤ Data processing systems
➤ Internal information systems
➤ End user productivity tools
➤ Interorganizational systems

Each of these is considered in turn.

Computational Models

Ever since their invention, computers have held a tremendous advantage over humans in their ability to perform computations. Today's desktop computers, for

Computer models are critical when organizing sophisticated operations such as American Airlines' flight schedule. Equipment must be routed to maximize revenue while minimizing costs. The possible configurations of equipment and routes are almost limitless.

example, can perform several million multiplications in a second. A human performing the same number of computations would take roughly twelve years, assuming the individual was willing to work fifty-five hour weeks without vacations and could multiply two fourteen-digit numbers together in an average time of about a minute. Simply stated, where problems require many computations, the use of computers is necessary.

The computational ability of computers has proven indispensable for creating models which help firms better understand and control business situations. Such computer models are fundamentally different from physical models in that they describe a problem in purely numeric terms. For example, if General Motors wanted to predict the wind resistance of a new model of automobile, the physical model would require creating a scale model of the car, placing it in a wind tunnel, measuring the forces at different wind velocities, then scaling the results up to the car's actual size. The computer model of the same problem would use airflow equations and three-dimensional vector images to simulate the wind blowing over the car body. The computer model offers many advantages: there is no need to construct complex equipment (such as the wind tunnel), the same computer can be used to model many different situations, and the computer can often be used to model situations that are impossible to simulate physically (such as the movement of future interest rates).

statistical analysis applies statistical principles to understanding relationships between data elements and predicting future behaviors

optimization models used to represent situations that have many possible combinations of inputs and outputs

"what-if" analysis generating different potential business scenarios to answer questions

Computer models may take many forms. **Statistical analysis** of data, common in finance and operations management, applies statistical principles to understanding relationships between data and certain outcomes. Such analysis often entails billions of computations. **Optimization models,** such as linear programming, are used to represent situations that have many possible combinations of inputs and outputs. Such models are frequently used to help businesses choose their mix of products or design their distribution systems. **"What if" analysis** involves generating different potential business scenarios to answer questions such as, "What if our sales were 10 percent higher?" or "What if interest rates rose by two points?" Managers typically use "what-if" analysis to determine the sensitivity of a business situation to changes in many factors, such as inflation, growth, market share, and costs. Computers are necessary for such analysis, as hundreds of scenarios are often considered.

decision support systems (DSS)
computer models that are used to
improve managerial decision making

Computer models that are used to improve managerial decision making are called **decision support systems (DSS).** DSS applications can come in two forms. The first is as a complete application designed to help managers make specific decisions. For example, plant location software can help managers decide where to place a new facility. DSS applications are also available in tool form, such as the spreadsheet software that managers use to make financial projections. Rather than focusing on a specific problem, such tools are designed to help managers create their own models in a given situation.

Data Processing Systems

As early as the late 1950s, it became clear that computer power could be used for purposes other than fast arithmetic. As more sophisticated forms of secondary storage were developed, such as magnetic tape and hard disks, computers began to replace traditional paper-based record-keeping systems. Among the advantages of these computer-based systems are the following:

➤ *Accuracy:* Paper-based systems are subject to arithmetic and transcription errors. Computer-based systems can be designed to greatly reduce these problems.
➤ *Speed:* Using computer-based systems, the time required to sort, look up, and format information is a fraction of that required in paper-based systems. Further, the speed of routine tasks, such as closing a company's books at year end, is similarly improved.
➤ *Space:* The physical space required for record keeping can often be significantly reduced by using a computer-based system. For example, a manager at the United Services Automobile Association (USAA) predicted that the on-line correspondence system they were implementing would ultimately save seventeen acres of storage compared with the company's existing paper-based system.
➤ *Flexibility:* Storing information on computers makes it possible to rapidly create new summaries of information that would have taken days or months to prepare manually. Today's information systems often provide report-writing tools. These tools permit managers to create their own customized output without the need for programmers.

One area in which data processing systems did not generally produce the initially expected benefits was in labor costs. Some savings were often realized from eliminating the clerical personnel at the heart of the manual system. Such savings, however, were nearly always more than offset by the need to add higher-priced computer programmers and operators. Thus, while early efforts to automate often led to huge increases in capacity and accuracy, they rarely led to reductions in actual labor costs.

Internal Information Systems

In the late 1960s, information systems began to appear in business. These information systems differed from data processing systems in a number of ways (see Exhibit 19.3). Most important, information systems were designed to allow many users to interact with the same pool of data at the same time, an impossibility on data processing systems which performed only one job at a time.

The move to internal information systems had far-reaching implications for organizations. Such information systems made it possible for many people to simultaneously interact with the same central data source. Airline reservation clerks around the world could all examine the same seat on a particular flight, booking it for a passenger if necessary. Plant managers could examine sales figures and market-

Exhibit 19.3
Data Processing Systems Versus Information Systems

Characteristic	Data Processing Systems	Information Systems
Number of users	One user at a time.	Many users could simultaneously use the system, through a process called *time sharing*. In addition many people could access the same shared pool of data.
Operation	*Batch Processing:* Performed a single job at a time, referred to as a *batch*. Users submitted complete batch jobs to the machine, then came back later when the job was complete.	*Interactive Processing:* System could perform many jobs at once, and users could interact with the system using their terminal while a job was being performed. Users interacting with the system were said to be *on-line*.
System users	Limited to data processing personnel. Managers had access to printed output only.	Both managers and data processing personnel.
Task domain	Automating existing administrative processes.	Automating existing processes *and* creating new processes that take advantage of the capabilities of the technology and have no equivalent form in manual systems.

Federal Express information systems track every step that a package takes. Customers can check the status of a package 24 hours a day by phone or through their web site at http://www.fedex.com/.

interorganizational systems (IOS)
employ computers and telecommunications technology to move information across the boundaries of the firm

ing forecasts, while marketing managers could simultaneously check inventory levels and production schedules. A delivery company could track the status of a customer's package anywhere in the world, no matter where the customer was calling from. Such applications went far beyond automating firms' existing procedures. They allowed companies to develop entirely new ways of conducting business.

End User Productivity Tools

From the 1950s to the 1970s, the high cost of computer systems put them out of the reach of most individuals and small businesses. By the early 1980s, however, computers such as the Apple II and the IBM personal computer (PC) had been introduced, making it possible to acquire significant computing capacity for a few thousand dollars. Initially, a lack of high-quality software hampered the adoption of such systems. Soon, however, commercial programmers made an important realization: They could make far more money by selling low-priced software to millions of PC owners than they could by marketing software to a few thousand mainframes. As a result, during the 1980s and 1990s, a huge variety of high-quality software for PCs was introduced. Today, PC software exists in virtually every category imaginable, with tens of thousands of software titles currently being sold. Some of the categories that are most important to managers are summarized in Exhibit 19.4.

Interorganizational Systems

Interorganizational systems (IOS) employ computers and telecommunications technology to move information across the boundaries of the firm. Such IOS represent the logical extension of a company's internal information systems to its customers, to its suppliers, and to other interested parties.

IOS come in many forms. Systems such as automatic teller machines (ATMs) and airline reservation systems that allow the user to interact directly with a com-

Exhibit 19.4
Examples of Common Software Categories

Category	Description	Examples	Typical Price Range for PCs
Desktop publishing	Tools ranging from those suitable for creating and editing basic documents (word processing software) to more advanced layout and desktop publishing tools that create files that can be sent directly to commercial typesetters and printers.	*Word Processors:* WordPerfect Microsoft Word	$100–$400
		Desktop Publishing: PageMaker Quark	$400–$800
Graphic design	Tools for drawing pictures, creating charts, and manipulating images, such as photographs brought in with a scanner.	Harvard Graphics Corel Draw Hijaak Adobe Photoshop	$100–$600
Financial analysis tools	A category dominated by spreadsheet applications, which allow data and formulas to be laid out on a large grid, similar to the large sheets of ruled paper that businesses once used to make financial projections.	Lotus 1-2-3 Microsoft Excel	$100–$400
Accounting software	A broad range of software products, ranging from simple accounting packages which can perform basic accounting for individuals and small businesses to more advanced modular accounting packages, serving the needs of medium and large businesses.	*Basic Accounting:* QuickBooks Pro Peachtree	$50–$300
		Advanced Accounting: Solomon	$2,000–$100,000+
Personal productivity and management	A wide variety of tools, such as calendar tools, contact managers, daily diaries, and organizers. These tools help individuals organize their time and information more effectively. More sophisticated versions of the tools also exist for organization-level productivity management, such as project management software.	*Personal Tools:* Calendar Creator Plus Day-Timer Organizer Act!	$50–$100
		Project & Workgroup Microsoft Project	$200–$400
Information resource software	Software that delivers information and advice to businesses. Such software includes reference software, such as encyclopedias on CD-ROM, professional advisory software, such as tax preparation software and legal software, and on-line databases, such as phone directories and census databases. Many on-line sources of information are also available.	*Encyclopedia* Microsoft's Encarta	$50–$100
		Professional Advisory Turbo Tax (Tax) AskDan (Legal)	$50–$200
		Databases: SelectPhone	$50–$200

remote job entry systems systems that allow the user to interact directly with a company's internal systems

electronic data interchange (EDI) allows the computers of two or more companies to communicate directly with each other

pany's internal systems are referred to as **remote job entry systems.** They not only make doing business easier for the customer but also save the company clerical costs.

Another form of IOS, **electronic data interchange (EDI),** allows the computers of two or more companies to communicate directly with each other, without human intervention. EDI systems can produce significant savings in ordering costs, while improving order processing time and accuracy. Even managers skeptical of the benefits of EDI may find they have no choice but to install them, because a growing num-

Exhibit 19.4
Examples of Common Software Categories (continued)

Category	Description	Examples	Typical Price Range for PCs
Workgroup software	Applications that facilitate communications and information sharing between individuals in a network environment.	Lotus Notes	$1,500–$50,000
Database management systems (DBMS)	Tools to facilitate the storing, organizing, and retrieving of information. As well as existing on its own, these DBMS are often used to create other applications, such as accounting systems, commercial databases, and information managers.	Microsoft Access Paradox	$100–$400
Programming tools	Tools to allow the creation of programs. Range from programming languages, suited primarily to computer professionals, to visual development environments that emphasize prebuilt components and can be used effectively by managers.	*Programming Languages* Visual C++ COBOL *Visual Environments* Visual Basic Delphi PowerBuilder	$300–$500 $200–$1,500
Utilities	Tools that permit individuals to more effectively use, protect, and maintain the hardware and software resources on their computers.	Norton Utilities RAM Doubler Stacker	$50–$100

ber of companies, such as Wal-Mart, refuse to do business with vendors who will not hook up electronically.

A third type of IOS is the commercial information service, which provides a packaged assortment of information services to customers, referred to as subscribers. These services, the better known of which include CompuServe, Prodigy, and America Online, bundle together many different IOS applications, such as Sabre (airline reservation), technical support forums for hardware and software vendors, and electronic shopping malls. They also provide numerous additional services, such as electronic mail, news, and games, to attract subscribers. Most recently, they have provided subscribers with direct connections to the Internet, the global network connecting academic, government, and business institutions (see the Spotlight on Technology feature later in this chapter). Users subscribe to these services by paying a small monthly fee, usually starting around $10 per month. They may pay extra for using special services, such as research databases that contain detailed information on public and private companies.

MANAGING TODAY'S INFORMATION TECHNOLOGIES

3 **Describe some of the key challenges of managing today's information technologies.**

The growing importance of information technology to today's businesses means that every manager, not just MIS managers, must become familiar with issues relating to the management of information technology. The following five areas are particularly important:

➤ Managing the firm's information system architecture
➤ Acquiring software
➤ Managing the development of information systems
➤ Managing the implementation of information systems
➤ Managing the security of information systems

Managing the Firm's Information System Architecture

The concept of a system architecture of an individual computer can be generalized to the organization as a whole. With today's technologies, many different system architectures are possible. That choice of architecture can, in turn, play a critical role in determining the capabilities of the firm. For example, it can determine the ability of employees to share information and work together, impact how quickly a company can respond to customer requests, and even alter the ways in which a company can offer its goods and services. Several common architectures are considered next.

stand-alone systems consists of one or more computers

STAND-ALONE SYSTEM   The **stand-alone system** architecture, illustrated in Exhibit 19.5, consists of one or more computers, usually PCs or other desktop computers, which function independently. Each system has its own software and its own data, and typically services the needs of a single user. The stand-alone architecture, sometimes referred to as a "sneaker network" because users must carry disks between machines to transfer data, is most common in small businesses. Its primary advantages are low cost and technological simplicity. Its main weakness is the difficulty of moving information between users. For this reason, stand-alone architectures are generally impractical for firms that extensively use shared information.

mainframe (multiuser) system uses a single central computer

MAINFRAME (MULTIUSER) SYSTEM   The **mainframe (multiuser) system** architecture, illustrated in Exhibit 19.6, uses a single central computer, usually referred to as a mainframe, that performs data processing for all users in the organization. Users typically interact with the mainframe through **terminals**, devices that combine the

terminals devices that combine the functions of a monitor and a keyboard

functions of a monitor and a keyboard. Under the mainframe architecture, all data

Exhibit 19.5
Stand-Alone System Architecture

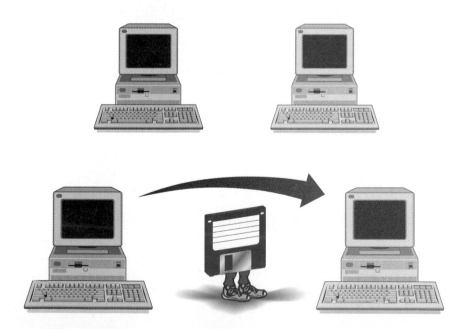

Exhibit 19.6
Mainframe (Multiuser)
System Architecture

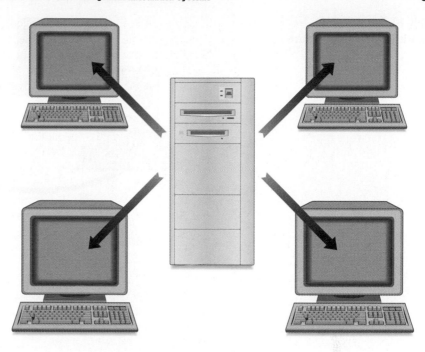

storage and computer hardware are centralized, usually under the control of an MIS department within the organization. While other computers may be present in the organization, such as those used by engineering groups for scientific purposes, such systems are usually kept entirely separate from the company's business systems.

The primary advantage of the multiuser system, which was most popular from the late 1960s to the early 1980s, is that all programs and data are centrally located. The ability to share data led to the development of applications such as on-line reservation systems. It also made possible sophisticated production management systems capable of sharing data across the entire scope of a business, from raw materials to sales of finished products. The main drawback of the multiuser system is that it tends to prevent users from taking advantage of the sophisticated applications and tools that are now available for PCs but not mainframe computers.

NETWORK SYSTEM In the past ten years, new system architectures have emerged which provide the benefits of both stand-alone and multiuser architectures. A **network system** architecture connects individual computers together in ways that allow them to share information.

The typical network architecture, illustrated in Exhibit 19.7, consists of one or more machines, known as **file servers,** that store and provide access to centralized data. Connected to these file servers are many individual computers, referred to as **work stations.** Work stations can run their own software, but can also access the software and data on the file server, duplicating the benefits of the multiuser system.

Networks are classified according to how the individual work stations are connected. When all are directly connected by network cabling to the file server, as is often the case in a building or headquarters complex, the architecture is called a **local area network (LAN).** When telecommunications technologies are employed to connect pieces of the network, the architecture is called a **wide area network (WAN).** Such telecommunications technologies can be as simple as the use of conventional phone lines and **modems,** devices that permit the digital signals inside computers to be transmitted over lines designed primarily for voice communication. They can also

network system connects individual microcomputers together in ways that allow them to share information

file servers one or more machines that store and provide access to centralized data

work stations access the software and data on the file server

local area network (LAN) individual work stations are directly connected by network cabling to the file server

wide area network (WAN) when telecommunications technologies are employed to connect pieces of the network

modems devices that permit the digital signals inside computers to be transmitted over lines designed primarily for voice communication

Exhibit 19.7
Network System Architecture

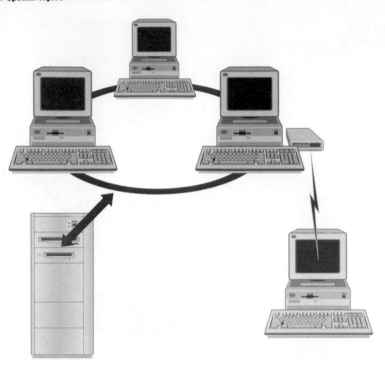

be far more exotic, including the use of leased phone lines, satellites, microwave linkages, and cellular connections.

To construct a network, both hardware and software must be acquired. Network hardware costs include running network cables throughout an office complex, purchasing network adapters for each work station, and purchasing hubs necessary to connect clusters of work stations. In addition, networks require their own specialized software. At a minimum, that software will include a **network operating system,** such as Novell's Netware or Microsoft's Windows NT, which handles the communications between machines. Recently, many companies have also installed **workgroup software,** such as Lotus Notes, which provides a broad array of user-friendly features, such as electronic mail, document management systems, and work-sharing systems. Together, the hardware and software costs can easily amount to several thousand dollars per work station.

In many respects, network architectures marry the benefits of the stand- alone and mainframe architectures. The connectivity aspect of a network provides easy access to and sharing of information. Since users access the network with PC-based work stations, the full range of PC software can be run. The main drawbacks of networks over previous architectures are the added costs. In addition, the task of administering and maintaining a network is far more complex than that of keeping stand-alone PCs up and running. Thus, the cost of hiring specially trained network engineers and administrators must be considered when establishing a network.

network operating system handles the communications between machines

workgroup software provides a broad array of user-friendly features, such as electronic mail, document management systems, and work-sharing systems

Acquiring Software

Without the proper software, computers are little more than noisy paperweights. The acquisition of software is therefore a critical issue for managers seeking to use information technology effectively. The issue can be further broken down into two **parts:**

how to acquire packaged software and how to acquire customized software, which is written specifically to meet the needs of the organization.

PACKAGED SOFTWARE Much, if not all, of the software used in any organization will be packaged software. Such software can be purchased off the shelf and used with no actual programming. The decision regarding which software to purchase should not be made lightly. Issues that a manger should consider include the following:

1 *Compatibility:* Few firms today have the luxury of establishing their information systems from scratch. How the new software will match existing hardware and software must be addressed. Questions the manager should ask include:

    a. Will the company's existing hardware handle the new software?
    b. Can the new software convert the information created by the old software?
    c. Can the new software exchange information with other applications that the firm uses?

2 *Upgradeability:* Because computer hardware advances so quickly, businesses should anticipate the need to upgrade their software regularly, usually every two to three years. The package's upgrade policy and history is therefore important over the long run. Questions the manager should ask include:

    a. How often are upgrades introduced?
    b. What do upgrades typically cost?

3 *Support:* It is not unusual for the cost of a software package to be far less than the cost of learning to use it. These costs include required training, productivity declines during the period when the application is being learned, and the use of technical support. Such costs must be factored into the software acquisition decision. Questions the manager should ask include:

    a. How hard will it be to learn the new software?
    b. What training resources are available?
    c. What are the vendor's technical support policies?

In addition, managers should consider the long-term implications of every software decision. Compatibility issues and the need to retrain users mean that all software acquisition decisions ultimately interrelate. Thus, a company should plan a full reevaluation of its entire software policy every four to five years. At such times, software decisions with long-term implications, such as changing PC and network operating systems, should be made and a plan for future acquisitions established.

CUSTOMIZED SOFTWARE Although packaged software provides an inexpensive solution for many of the firm's needs, on occasion a firm needs software to accomplish a task that is not directly supported by any existing package. Such situations frequently present three alternatives:

➤ *Modify the company's business processes to fit an existing software package.* Although many managers may balk at having to change the way they do business to accommodate the needs of a $100 software tool, sometimes such an approach can make sense. Packaged software, such as accounting applications and project management tools, are usually designed around sound business practices. As a result, adopting a software package can sometimes provide the means for improving administrative processes in the firm.

➤ *Customize an existing application.* Particularly in the accounting area, custom development often starts with a basic package that is modified to meet the firm's specific needs. The amount of programming that must be done is much less than writing an entire system from scratch. Yet modifications to the basic package may make it difficult and expensive to upgrade when new versions of the basic package are introduced. If the required modifications are extensive, the alternative may be as expensive as programming the entire application from scratch.

➤ *Build an entirely new application.* Particularly for complex, specialized applications, creating an application from scratch is often necessary. The chief advantage of such an approach is it allows the application to be designed specifically to meet the needs of the organization. Weighed against this benefit are the high costs of custom development. Custom development also carries two significant risks: the risk of major cost overruns and the risk that the application will not be completed. These risks increase with the size of the application, the complexity of the application, and the firm's lack of experience with the technologies involved.

Even after choosing one of the three alternatives, the manager still faces a classic make-or-buy decision. Should the firm employ a staff of programmers to build and maintain the application? Should it employ third parties, such as consultants or accounting firms, to develop its systems? If so, will it work side-by-side with the firm in developing the system, or will it demand a **turnkey system,** ready for use upon delivery from the vendor? Such decisions can have a major impact on the long-term success of the application. In today's rapidly changing technology environment, applications must be updated every two to five years or they become obsolete. In choosing a development strategy, the organization must map out a path that ensures such ongoing maintenance is carried out.

turnkey system ready for use upon delivery from the vendor

Managing the Development of Information Systems

Whenever a company wants to create an information systems for its own purposes, it must address the problem of how to manage the development of that system. Large software development projects have much in common with other large development projects, such as building a skyscraper or a ship. They can involve many people, can require large amounts of coordination, can take a long time to complete, and can come with hefty price tags; $10 million systems development projects are not uncommon. There are also differences, however. Consider the problem of gauging the progress of software development. Someone who is building a submarine and wants to see how things are going can walk through the dry dock where it's being built and inspect it. With software development projects, walking through the work area will always yield roughly the same view: a group of people sitting in front of work stations typing, talking, or thinking. Simply assessing whether a software development project is on track can represent a significant undertaking, whether it is being done internally or under contract with a third-party developer.

systems development life cycle (SDLC) involves decomposing a system into its functional components

PROJECT MANAGEMENT TECHNIQUES   The traditional approach to managing systems development, sometimes referred to as the **systems development life cycle (SDLC),** involves decomposing a system into its functional components. For example, an accounting application would be broken down into modules and submodules, each representing a distinct function in the overall accounting process. Project management techniques, such as PERT charts or critical path analysis, are then employed to organize and monitor the development of the system as a whole. Using such techniques, managers are able to assess how the development is proceeding compared with the original development plan.

Unfortunately, the accuracy of project management techniques is not guaranteed. A major source of inaccuracies is the discovery of errors in the code, commonly referred to as **bugs.** For example, a module or submodule may appear to be complete on paper. When that module is connected to other modules, however, previously undiscovered problems may indicate a need for substantial additional work.

bugs errors in the code

INCREMENTAL DEVELOPMENT TECHNIQUES In recent years, incremental development techniques, which distribute testing more uniformly throughout the development cycle, have gained in popularity. Such techniques usually involve the rapid creation of a working system with limited functionality, known as a **prototype.** Once the initial prototype has been created, additional features are added, with testing being performed at each stage of development. This ongoing testing reduces the number of bugs uncovered at the end of the development process. As the application approaches full functionality, it is often made available to a carefully selected subset of sophisticated users, a process known as **alpha testing.** These users run the software, reporting problems to the developers and making suggestions for additional functionality. Once a fully functional version of the application has been created, a wider group of users is given the software, in a process called **beta testing.** These users, who more closely resemble "average" users in their level of experience, generally focus their attention on detecting bugs. The size and scope of alpha and beta testing programs varies widely, but can be huge. Prior to its introduction of Windows 95, for example, Microsoft had literally hundreds of thousands of beta test sites, most of whom had paid for the privilege of being testers in order to acquire the software before its general release.

prototype creation of a working system with limited functionality

alpha testing as the application approaches full functionality, it is often made available to a carefully selected subset of sophisticated users

beta testing once a fully functional version of the application has been created, a wider group of users is given the software

Managing the Implementation of Information Systems

Managers often assume that the actual development of a system or acquisition of appropriate software represents the major obstacle to creating a successful information system. Experience teaches us otherwise, however. Managing system implementation, the process of transferring a system to its intended users, often proves far more difficult than technical development. For some categories of software, it is unsuccessful implementation, rather than technical or economic issues, that leads to most systems being abandoned.

The heart of the implementation challenge is overcoming user resistance to a new system or technology. Users uncomfortable with a new system may resort to **passive resistance.** They might overstate the difficulties associated with learning the technology, in effect claiming that they are not using it because they cannot figure out how it works. Users may also indirectly express their displeasure by overstating the impact of any bugs they discover or by dwelling on situations in which the system creates unnecessary work. Users have also been known to engage in **active resistance.** They may, for example, intentionally type in bad data or repeatedly crash the system to make it unusable. Such behaviors can be curtailed with constant management supervision. But as soon as management's attention wanders, resisting users simply return to their old practices. Faced with such active resistance, managers often conclude that the benefits of a system are simply not worth the effort required to keep it in use.

Managers can employ a number of techniques to increase the odds of a successful implementation. Among the most important of these are the following:

passive resistance users uncomfortable with a new system overstate difficulties associated with learning the technology

active resistance users type in bad data or repeatedly crash the system to make it unusable

➤ *Ensure that the system has top management support.* In study after study, top management support has been reported as a factor that contributed to successful implementation. Absent such support, users are less hesitant in resisting the system.

➤ *Ensure that a need for the system has been established and communicated to users.* Users must be aware that a bona fide need for the system exists. The more visible the need, the better. For example, a system that keeps inferior products from getting to the customer has obvious appeal.

➤ *Allow potential users to participate in the system design and development process.* Such participation can lead to an increased sense of involvement for users, giving them a sense of system ownership. That sense of ownership, in turn, can cause users to see themselves as partners in trying to ensure a system's success.

➤ *Design systems that are intrinsically motivating for users.* Where a system (a) provides its users with a greater sense of control over their jobs, (b) makes its users' jobs more interesting, and (c) improves the quality of its users' job performance in visible ways, potential users are unlikely to resist the system. They may even gravitate toward using it.

Managing the Security of Information Systems

The widespread use of information technology in organizations has significant security implications for management. Information technology increases firms' vulnerability to both espionage and sabotage.

espionage process of illegally gathering information

ESPIONAGE   A serious security threat aggravated by information technology is **espionage**, the process of illegally gathering information. Prior to the widespread adoption of information systems, the physical nature of paper records (such as customer lists) made them both hard to steal and hard to analyze. The situation changes when such information is stored on computers, however. Sensitive data, such as a company's entire customer list and sales history, may be secretly copied to a single data tape. To make matters worse, once such information has been transferred, its electronic form makes it much easier to analyze.

Although achieving fail-safe protection against espionage is impossible, some measure of protection may be achieved by limiting access to information. Most applications, for example, allow passwords to be established so that users can only access data relevant to their assigned duties. Keeping such systems current, however, requires significant management commitment and oversight. Particularly critical in this regard is ensuring that a user's access rights are terminated when the individual quits or is fired.

Another way that managers can reduce the espionage threat is to ensure that users are properly trained in security procedures. Stolen passwords represent a particularly serious threat to security. But that threat can also be significantly reduced through user education (see Exhibit 19.8). Managers can also reduce the threat of compromised passwords by ensuring that users and system administrators periodically change passwords.

sabotage destruction of information by a perpetrator

VULNERABILITY TO SABOTAGE   Even more chilling to a manager than espionage, **sabotage** is the destruction of information by a perpetrator. Our reliance on information technology has increased our vulnerability to this threat by making information easier to destroy and by making it possible to destroy records without having physical access to those records. For example, the information architecture in many firms makes it possible for the saboteur to destroy data over the phone, without taking the risk of being physically present.

Exhibit 19.8
Protecting Passwords

> ➤ *Avoid writing a password down.* Never leave a written password anywhere near the system on which it is used, or write it down next to the user ID for the system.
> ➤ *Never type a password when someone is looking.* The easiest way to get someone's password is to watch it being typed.
> ➤ *Never use the same password on two systems.* On many systems, the system operator can read users' passwords. An unscrupulous system operator could use that information to access other user accounts with the same password.
> ➤ *Never use meaningful personal information for a password.* Using information such as birthdays, children's names, or your brand of car may make it possible for a persistent co-worker to get into your account.
> ➤ *Never use an actual word for a password.* The manner in which passwords are stored on many systems makes it possible for hackers, using a dictionary, to determine the password of any user who uses an actual word.

While motivation for sabotage can come from many sources, revenge (by disgruntled employees, for example), commercial gain (by competitors), and vandalism (by hackers who destroy systems for fun) are three of the most common perils. The nature of the sabotage itself can also vary. In some cases, it may consist of the simple erasure of data. In other cases, data may be substituted, as was the case when students in a California school electronically altered their transcripts to get better grades. The best protection against such threats is to employ the same security precautions used against espionage, and to back up the system on a regular basis. Such backups, which involve saving all the information on the system's hard disk to tapes or other removable storage media, ensure that lost or damaged data can be restored.

Norton Anti-Virus software, produced by Symantec, is one of the most sophisticated programs for fighting computer viruses.

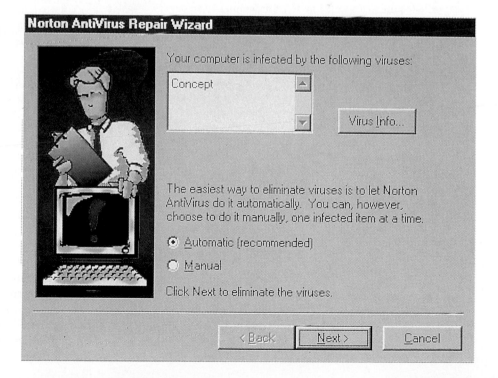

SPOTLIGHT ON TECHNOLOGY

The Future of the Internet

The global euphoria that has recently come to surround the Internet has, in some cases, caused managers to lose perspective on the actual strengths and weaknesses of the system. As we have already noted, the Internet seems to offer unparalleled opportunities for research, public relations, and communications. A number of characteristics of the Internet, however, are far less desirable from a business standpoint. Among the most serious of these are the following:

➤ *Lack of Central Authority:* Unlike other entities a manager deals with, the Internet is more of a community than an organization. Moreover, it is a community with no leader. As a result, managers who find themselves overly dependent on the Internet may find they have nowhere to go when parts of the system go down, as they routinely do.

➤ *Lack of Underlying Organization:* While tremendous amounts of information are present on the Internet, there is no obvious way to find any particular piece of information. Further, even when a piece of information is found, there is no way to ensure its accuracy.

➤ *Conflict of Purpose:* In the past, the generally accepted purpose of the Internet was to foster scholarly interaction between its users. As a way of encouraging new sites to connect to the Internet, red tape and accompanying security requirements were kept to a minimum. From a commercial perspective, consequences of how the Internet has evolved are far-reaching. There are no built-in security systems to facilitate financial transactions, such as wiring funds or using a credit card. While attempts have been made to rectify these problems, it is unclear how successful they will be. In addition, the rules of the Internet explicitly forbid its use as an advertising medium. As a result, it is not clear how welcome new commercial Internet sites will be, particularly those established explicitly to sell products. There is a significant risk that experienced Internet users, sometimes referred to as "old-timers," will actively harass new sites whose purposes appear to be inconsistent with existing Internet practices.

➤ *Network Performance:* Most managers find it disconcerting to have their business depend on a system whose performance changes from minute to minute, and which could go down at any time. Yet such performance variation is characteristic of the Internet and is largely unavoidable. A substantial fraction of the computers that make up the heart of the Internet, such as the university computers which route communications and messages, are also used for other purposes. Thus, keeping the local Internet connection functioning smoothly is not always the provider's top priority. Further, with the flood of new users and the invention of further ingenious uses for the Internet, there is a significant possibility, even likelihood, that performance will continue to degrade in the near future.

➤ *Individual Performance:* While universities and corporations generally have networks directly connected to the Internet, individuals usually access "the Net" using dial-up modems. Many of the most expressive features of the Net, including graphics, sound, and full-motion video, can take minutes or more to download. The presence of such delays is a major obstacle to companies wishing to promote their products.

Certainly, none of these weaknesses prevent a company from taking advantage of the Internet. But in the long run, they will have to be addressed before the Internet can evolve into the "information superhighway." Most experts believe that in the next ten to fifteen years, two important changes in the Internet will occur:

➤ High-speed connections to private homes, perhaps using cable TV wiring, will become commonplace.
➤ An increasing amount of Internet network traffic will be handled by private providers, such as MCI and AT&T. The results of privatization of the Internet are likely to be both improved performance and (in all likelihood) more fees for users.

Once these changes have occurred, the possible uses for the Internet will expand dramatically. The Internet will ultimately become a "necessity" for most firms, much like the phone system of today.

In addition, regular backups offer a measure of protection against environmental threats, such as earthquakes, tornados, hurricanes, and fires.

In recent years, a particularly common form of sabotage has become the **computer virus.** A virus is a program that attaches itself to other programs or computer disks, whenever the opportunity presents itself. Because of this replication, users who move programs or disks between machines can inadvertently cause a virus to spread. Viruses can also spread over networks if they are not properly protected.

computer virus program that attaches itself to other programs or computer disks

Viruses differ widely in the damage they occur. Some are relatively benign (for example, drawing peace signs, then disappearing). Others specifically attack the hard disk, erasing data and ultimately rendering the system worthless. Complicating detection, most viruses lie dormant on their host system for a significant period of time, so that careless users will give them opportunities to spread to other systems. In other words, a virus may be active on a system for months before actually making its presence known. Some confine their activities to specific days, such as the Michelangelo virus which destroys hard disks only on the artist's birthday (March 6th).

Unlike other forms of sabotage, routine backups do not provide effective virus protection. The problem is that in backing up the system, the virus is saved as well. Thus, restoring the system will also restore the virus. As a result, other forms of protection are usually required. The best is to follow the rules of proper virus hygiene, which include the following:

➤ Avoid all software that has not been acquired from known vendors.
➤ Keep floppy disks from unknown sources out of machines.
➤ Use **antivirus applications**, widely available programs that detect and remove viruses. These can be very effective against *known* viruses. Such programs are often marketed in subscription form, with regular updates that protect against new viruses.

antivirus applications programs that detect and remove viruses

By establishing and enforcing procedures that clearly state what software can and cannot be installed on company systems, and by ensuring that antivirus software is used routinely and kept up-to-date, managers play an important role in protecting their companies against computer viruses.

EMERGING TECHNOLOGIES AND THEIR IMPLICATIONS

4 **Identify emerging technologies and their implications.**

Just as information technologies transformed themselves over the past few decades, the decades to come will usher in entirely new uses for technologies. With these new uses will come new challenges for managers. Two of the most important emerging technology areas are the evolution of the worldwide network and the development of truly intelligent systems.

The Worldwide Network

Hardly a day goes by when the local newspaper does not carry an article on the Internet. As we have already noted, however, the Internet has a number of weaknesses when it comes to commercial uses. But what about the global networks of the future? At the present time, new communications infrastructures are being put in place. These infrastructures will ultimately change the ways in which we communicate and work.

bandwidth the amount of information a network can carry

INFRASTRUCTURE   The amount of information a network can carry is called its **bandwidth.** The bandwidth of a network, in turn, is determined by the physical components that make up the system. Today, a worldwide effort is being made to replace existing wiring with fiber optic cabling. A single optical fiber, the diameter of a human hair, can carry as much information as a cable the diameter of a rolling pin, containing thousands of wires. As a result, the potential bandwidth available for telecommunications will increase greatly. In practical terms, that means that information transfers that used to take hours will be possible in under a second.

IMPLICATIONS   For businesses, the impact of this change in infrastructure, which will not be fully realized until well into the next century, will be astounding. As local phone systems are upgraded or replaced, consumers will be able to connect directly into a global network that operates many times faster than today's Internet. The increased bandwidth will make it possible to offer far more goods and services electronically. Today, few people are willing to buy their clothing by computer. But in the future, consumers will be able to view photorealistic images of clothing in 3-D. **Virtual reality** display techniques, which combine computerized sights, sounds, and sensations to create a sense of actually "being there," may make it possible to simulate driving a new car, and may also allow the potential home buyer to simulate walking through a new home. While the services will not be free, they will likely be cheap enough to enable most consumers to be connected. Furthermore, as new services are offered over the network, so will opportunities to develop additional sources of revenue.

The high-speed connections between home and office will also have dramatic implications for how we work, manage, and are managed. Global "distances," already reduced by the telephone and air transportation, will shrink further as people from any part of the globe can meet face-to-face through their computers. **Video conferencing,** holding meetings between remote sites using sound and pictures transmitted over telecommunications links, today is limited mainly by the low bandwidth of existing telephone lines, making images grainy and jerky. Over the worldwide network, however, image quality will improve dramatically. The distinction between talking to images and talking face-to-face will blur. With such capabilities in place, what will become of the traditional workplace?

The effect of the worldwide network will be sweeping, and the managers who recognize its potential early enough will be the big winners. To recognize that potential, managers need to be willing to experiment with new technologies as they become available. Today's Internet, for all its weaknesses, affords managers precisely such an opportunity for experimentation, perhaps the single best justification for establishing a commercial Internet presence.

Truly Intelligent Systems

Since the 1950s, people have been attracted to, and horrified by, the notion of a truly intelligent computer. Initial efforts to make such a computer a reality led to the creation of the field of **artificial intelligence (AI).** The goal of AI has been to get computers to perform tasks traditionally associated with biological intelligence, such as logical reasoning, language, vision, and motor skills. Since its founding nearly forty years ago, the field has made some impressive strides (see Exhibit 19.9). The field has also made another important discovery: Tasks that are easy for humans are often extremely difficult for computers.

Researchers today are now concluding that many of the problems that AI has faced may stem from the fact that human brains and computers are organized very differently. A typical commercial computer has a single processor through which all information passes in a serial fashion, one piece of information at a time. The brain, however, is organized around hundreds of millions of neurons that operate in parallel. Although a single neuron is much slower than a computer CPU, the brain can still process information more than a million times faster than any computer. In pure information processing terms, today's supercomputers are probably less powerful than the brain of a housefly.

That situation will not last forever, however. Experimental computers with many CPUs that operate simultaneously, known as **massively parallel machines,** are

---

virtual reality display techniques, which combine computerized sights, sounds, and sensations to create a sense of actually "being there"

video conferencing holding meetings between remote sites using sound and pictures transmitted over telecommunications links

artificial intelligence (AI) initial efforts to get computers to perform tasks traditionally associated with biological intelligence, such as logical reasoning, language, vision, and motor skills

massively parallel machines experimental computers with many CPUs that operate simultaneously

Exhibit 19.9
Artificial Intelligence Examples

➤ *Robotics:* Today, some of the most productive factories in the world make extensive use of adaptive robots that originated from AI research.
➤ *Expert Systems:* These systems use sophisticated reasoning techniques, developed by AI, to accomplish difficult tasks, such as medical diagnosis. Companies such as Digital Equipment Corporation, Coopers and Lybrand, and American Express make routine use of expert systems, saving them tens of millions of dollars a year.
➤ *Natural Language Applications:* Computers with built-in voice recognition have become commonplace over the past five years, as have voice-driven phone systems. Both owe their existence to speech recognition research done in AI. Grammar checkers and translators depend heavily on natural language interpretation techniques pioneered in AI.
➤ *Object-Oriented Programming (OOP):* The OOP style, frequently employed in today's advanced systems, owes its existence to years of AI knowledge representation research.

already being constructed. If current trends in technology improvement continue (and they are expected to, at least for the next few decades), computers may well reach parity with the human brain around the middle of the next century. What will be the implications of these massively parallel machines for the work force? Even if these machines cannot be trained to think exactly like humans, how many jobs will be left that a computer cannot do? These questions are not purely academic. Today's college freshmen may still be in the work force when these systems become a reality.

BUSINESS DILEMMA

·COLLEGE·
HEALTH CLUB

Information Systems at College Health Club

Sue Kramer, president of College Health Club (CHC), considers some of the information that she would like to compile and use over time. First, she wants background information on the members so that she can determine their typical profiles. She initially recorded some background information for new members, but the information is on numerous index cards, making it difficult to determine profile characteristics of all members. Second, she wants to provide members with information about their progress (weight loss, endurance tests, and strength tests) from the time that they became members. She initially wrote this information on sheets of paper, and then attempted to update the information over time. However, she does not have time to continually ask the members for updates.

Dilemma

Sue's goal is to design a system in which she could more easily compile information.

Solution

Sue decides to use an information system in which the data are recorded on a computer file. She obtains information from new members when they pay for their membership, and inputs the information on computer. Each member's name is in the first column, age is in the second column, and other data are recorded as well. The computer can easily determine the average age for all members by computing the average of the numbers in the second column. The average for all other characteristics can be determined in the same manner.

Sue also decides to place a portable computer near the exercise area, where members can record their performance each day. Each member would have access to his or her own file with a code name. The members could input their weight on that day, the number of repetitions when lifting weights, the length of time that they did exercises, and so on. As the file is updated over time, it would indicate the progress to members. This type of information encourages members to continue their workouts (and therefore their memberships), because it indicates how they are improving from the time when they first joined CHC.

Additional Issues for Discussion

1 Explain the potential benefits of having a computer determine typical profiles of existing members.

2 Could Sue Kramer use computers for her business in any other ways?

3 Explain how an information system could help Sue send surveys to existing members so that she could obtain their feedback about her health club services.

SUMMARY

1 An electronic computer is a device capable of processing and storing vast quantities of information. The physical components of a computer are called hardware. Most computers are organized around four components: (a) central processing unit (CPU), (b) primary storage, (c) secondary storage, and (d) peripherals.

2 While there are many ways in which firms use computers, the most common uses are: (a) computational models, (b) data processing systems, (c) internal information systems, (d) end user productivity tools, and (e) interorganizational systems.

3 Some of the key challenges associated with managing today's information technologies are: (a) managing the firm's information system architecture, (b) acquiring software, (c) managing the development of information systems, (d) managing the implementation of information systems, and (e) managing the secrecy of information systems.

4 Two of the key emerging technology areas are the evolution of the worldwide network and the development of truly intelligent systems. The worldwide network has already allowed for high speed connections between home and office, and between firms and customers. Meanwhile, efforts are being applied to develop truly intelligent computer systems that can think and conduct tasks like humans.

KEY TERMS

active resistance
alpha testing
antivirus applications
application
artificial intelligence (AI)
bandwidth
beta testing
bugs
compact disks (CD-ROMs)
computer program
computer virus
database
decision support systems (DSS)
electronic computer
electronic data interchange (EDI)
espionage
file servers
floppy disks
gigabytes

hard disks
hardware
interorganizational systems (IOS)
local area network (LAN)
magnetic tapes
mainframe (multiuser) system
mainframes
massively parallel machines
megabytes
megahertz (MHz)
modems
network operating system
network system
optimization models
passive resistance
prototype
random access memory (RAM)
remote job entry systems
sabotage

software
software packages
spreadsheet
stand-alone system
statistical analysis
system architecture
systems development life cycle (SDLC)
terminals
turnkey system
video conferencing
virtual reality
"what-if" analysis
wide area network (WAN)
Winchester drives
word processor
work stations
workgroup software

REVIEW QUESTIONS

1 Discuss artificial intelligence and explain how it can be compared with human thought.

2 Define a computer and distinguish between hardware and software.

3 Distinguish the different forms of interorganizational systems (IOS).

4 Define a management information systems (MIS) program and discuss how it can be used to enhance decision making.

5 Explain the advantages of computer-based systems.

6 Discuss the security threat to a firm with respect to information technology.

7 Discuss the choice of application software confronting a manager. Why is it such a critical issue?

8 Identify the techniques for managing the development of an information system.

9 Identify the issues that managers must become familiar with regarding the management of information technology.

10 Explain the issues that should concern a manager in making a software applications decision.

DISCUSSION QUESTIONS

1 How do computers influence your everyday life?

2 Assume that a computer virus has affected your college or university. How may this virus affect your personal computer at home? What can be done to prevent this from occurring?

3 Designate the following computer features as either hardware or software applications: (a) keyboard, (b) WordPerfect 6.0, (c) output device, (d) artificial intelligence, (e) central processing unit, and (f) peripherals.

4 Assume that computers have been introduced into your department. Will your job change as a result? Will the benefits outweigh the costs?

5 Discuss the uses of computerized information systems implemented at your college.

RUNNING YOUR OWN BUSINESS

1 Explain how you would use information systems to monitor the operations within your business.
2 Explain how you might use the Internet to enhance the performance of your business.
3 What would you do to protect your system from sabotage, espionage, or computer viruses?

INVESTING IN THE STOCK OF A BUSINESS

Using the annual report of the firm in which you would like to invest, complete the following:

1 Does the annual report discuss how the firm uses information systems to monitor its operations?
2 Does the firm use information systems for internal distribution of information, or to provide information to external stakeholders (customers, suppliers, stockholders, distributors, and so on)? In what ways could these groups benefit from information systems?
3 Does the firm have its own web site on the Internet? Is the address listed in the annual report? If possible, visit this web site and describe the information that can be found there.

CASE 1 Applying Information Systems in Business

The major information systems (MIS) trends of the 1990s, downsizing, globalization, telecommuting, and rapidly expanding use of the Internet, have one thing in common. They have made life far more difficult for MIS managers.

The role of an MIS manager is changing significantly. The manager must ensure that the functions of the system have been communicated to users, allow potential users to participate in the system design and development process, and design systems that can achieve the firm's goals. This approach to MIS management has been nurtured and developed at the New York office of Credit Suisse, where Donald Gaffney is the manager of information technology.

Mr. Gaffney states that telecommuters are looking for advanced data services, such as the ability to instantaneously track global stock markets. The tools of telecommunications have improved upon the productivity of stock brokerage offices around the globe. Telecommunications include equipment such as computer networks, telephones, television, facsimile (fax) machines, and wireless communications. Telecommunications and computer networks are essential because they can link computers and allow them to share printers and data. Computer networks make it easier for people to obtain and share data, even if they are in remote locations. Credit Suisse has developed a telecommunications system using a videoconference link between their New York and London offices over Integrated Services Digital Network so that application developers sitting at their desktops can communicate. This telecommunication system at Credit Suisse replaces ordinary mail delivery. Information is shared within seconds. Information concerning a stock that has been recommended and is being purchased by investors in London is transmitted around the globe within seconds.

Questions
1 Define the role of an MIS manager.
2 Why is it important to have users participate in the design of information systems?
3 What do telecommunications include?
4 Why is rapid access to information so important to the employees of Credit Suisse?

CASE 2 Will Computers Replace Managers?

When it comes to information technology, you won't find greater enthusiasts than executives of United Parcel Service. The man with the plan, Chairman and Chief Executive Kent Nelson, says there's a good reason to be bullish on all this technology: "We realized that the leader in information management will be the leader in international package distribution—period."

It wasn't always like this. While UPS experimented

with every procedure imaginable, its manual package handling was so efficient that "every time we applied technology, it slowed us down," Nelson recalls.

UPS was not alone. At many companies, information technology became a source of frustration. A new breed of computer managers, known as chief information officers, emerged, which gave UPS a competitive edge on its closest rival.

UPS uses its personal computers, networks, fax machines, and other information tools to improve productivity and managerial decision making at UPS. Thanks largely to its new capabilities, revenue and profits are increasing at UPS.

Questions

1 Do you think computers can plan operations for business managers and make decisions for them?

2 From the customer's perspective, what would you expect the information system at UPS to deliver?

3 Why are information systems such an important element of the package delivery business?

VIDEO CASE Reliance on Computers For Success

When Hurricane Andrew tore into southern Florida in August, 1992, taking thirty lives and leaving 250,000 homeless, one of the casualties was Maria Elena Ibanez's business. Monster winds tore the roof off the building in Miami where International High Tech Marketing (IHTM) was located, causing expensive damage to office equipment, furniture, and inventory. IHTM's sales department was particularly hard-hit; it couldn't communicate with customers. Ibanez's personal office was gone.

Andrew killed off many enterprises. Would IHTM, a year-old marketer of computer hardware, software, and accessories in more than 85 countries, get back in business? If so, when?

Answers: (1) Yes, most definitely. (2) Two days.

Ibanez, whose home in the same section of Miami was destroyed by the storm, used her car as her personal office. A cable was run in at the home of one of her eighteen employees, and a computer network was set up with four computers functioning on batteries in case the power went off.

The employee's phone line was used for faxing, and Ibanez bought twelve cellular phones and gave them to her purchasing manager (in charge of purchasing supplies and materials) and salespeople. The salespeople began calling customers, and orders began coming in.

Ibanez rented warehouse space near Miami's airport from a friend, and as soon as the airport reopened after the storm, IHTM began shipping.

It took three months before the company's offices were restored, and for some of that time Ibanez and her staff used boxes as furniture. Yet, the year's sales rose by 700 percent. The key to the firm's performance was the use of technology and computers.

Questions

1 Explain why the computer information systems and the technology (such as the fax machine and cellular telephones) were so critical to the success of International High Tech Marketing (IHTM) just after the hurricane. That is, what problems would have occurred without the computer information systems and technology?

2 IHTM sells products to customers in more than eighty-five countries. Explain why computer information systems and technology are more crucial for communication between customers and salespeople than if the firm relied on just a few large local customers for most of its business.

3 What are some other ways in which the computer information systems can help IHTM's business operations, even in the absence of natural disasters such as hurricanes?

THE Coca-Cola COMPANY ANNUAL REPORT PROJECT

The following questions apply concepts in this chapter to The Coca-Cola Company. Review The Coca-Cola Company annual report when answering these questions.

1 Explain how accounting software would be beneficial for consolidating information at The Coca-Cola Company.

2 Offer one or more ways in which The Coca-Cola Company could use information systems to monitor its inventories.

3 Why would The Coca-Cola Company want to have a website page on the Internet? Use the Internet to find The Coca-Cola Company's website page (http://www.cocacola.com).

IN-TEXT STUDY GUIDE

Answers are in an appendix at the back of the book.

True or False

1 Many of the problems that artificial intelligence (AI) has faced may stem from the fact that human brains and computers are organized much the same way.

2 Management information systems (MIS) is the marketing function that oversees the adoption, use, and management of information technologies.

3 The physical components of a computer are collectively called hardware.

4 Sabotage is the destruction of information by a perpetrator.

5 An example of computer hardware is a spreadsheet that performs financial analysis in rows or columns to prepare financial statements.

6 Computer viruses are programs that attach themselves to other programs or computer disks, then replicate themselves on other programs and disks whenever the opportunity presents itself.

7 Remote job entry systems make doing business harder for the company but save the customer money.

8 Video conferencing is holding meetings in the same area using sound and pictures transmitted over telecommunications links.

9 A computer model using statistical analysis of data applies statistical principles to predict future behaviors.

10 The goal of artificial intelligence has been to get computers to perform tasks traditionally associated with simulated experiences.

Multiple Choice

11 A computer crime whereby information is gathered illegally is known as:
a) sabotage.
b) blackmail.
c) artificial intelligence.
d) expert system.
e) espionage.

12 The process that serves to enhance managerial decision making, which has opened the door to both improved revenue and reduced costs, is a:
a) spreadsheet.
b) database.
c) word processor.
d) decision support system.
e) computer.

13 A display technique that combines computerized sights, sounds, and sensations to create a sense of actually "being there" is:
a) computer programming
b) virtual reality.
c) spreadsheet analysis.
d) artificial intelligence.
e) management information systems.

14 The heart of the computer is the:
a) keyboard.
b) software application.
c) central processing unit (CPU).
d) hard drive.
e) random access memory (RAM)

15 A large computer used primarily to service an entire organization is a:
a) mainframe.
b) microcomputer.
c) minicomputer.
d) management information system (MIS).
e) computer program.

16 Once a fully functional version of the application software has been created, a wider group of users is given the software, in a process called:
a) alpha testing.
b) prototype.
c) software resistance.
d) active resistance.
e) beta testing.

17 Experimental computers with many central processing units (CPUs) that operate simultaneously are known as:
a) computer programs.
b) artificial intelligence.
c) management information systems.
d) massively parallel machines.
e) worldwide network.

18 The traditional approach to managing systems development, which involves decomposing a system into its functional components, is:
a) virtual reality.
b) video conferencing.
c) systems development life cycle.
d) information technology.
e) information systems.

19 A software program that may be used to generate reports from a company's client list is a:

a) computer network.
b) database.
c) spreadsheet.
d) video conference.
e) teleconference.

20 The process of transferring a managing system to its intended users is called:
a) implementation.
b) alpha testing.
c) prototypes.
d) beta testing.
e) video conferencing.

21 The amount of information a network can carry is called its:
a) alpha test.
b) computer program.
c) implementation.
d) artificial intelligence.
e) bandwidth.

22 Incremental development techniques involve the rapid creation of a working system with limited functionality, known as a(n):
a) alpha test.
b) video conference.
c) beta test.
d) prototype.
e) computer network.

23 A system that allows information to be shared across organizational boundaries is known as a(n):
a) computer program.
b) computer virus.
c) interorganizational system.
d) internal information system.
e) artificial intelligence.

24 The programs that determine the specific tasks a computer will perform at any given time are called:
a) hardware.
b) software.
c) mainframe.
d) virtual reality.
e) bugs.

25 In software application, errors in the code are commonly referred to as:
a) bugs.
b) computers.
c) gigabytes.
d) RAM.
e) megahertz.

26 An interorganizational system that allows the computers of two or more companies to communicate directly with each other without human intervention is called a(n):
a) remote job entry system.
b) internal information system.
c) decision support system.
d) executive information system.
e) electronic data interchange (EDI).

27 The amount of random access memory (RAM) installed on a particular system is measured in millions of characters called:
a) gigabytes.
b) megahertz.
c) bugs.
d) megabytes.
e) CD-ROM.

28 Programs that detect and remove viruses are known as:
a) computer crime.
b) virtual reality.
c) antivirus applications.
d) video conferencing.
e) telecommunicating.

29 Devices that combine the functions of a monitor and a keyboard are called:
a) file servers.
b) terminals.
c) work stations.
d) mainframe.
e) networks.

30 An internal system designed to allow many users to interact with the same pool of data at the same time is called a(n):
a) information system.
b) artificial intelligence.
c) electronic data system.
d) data processing system.
e) interorganizational system.

31 Saving all the information on the system's hard disk to tapes or other removable storage media to ensure that lost or damaged data can be restored is known as:
a) computer networks.
b) virtual reality.
c) information systems.
d) electronic data processing.
e) backing up the system.

32 The system architecture where all the networks are directly connected by cabling to the file server is called a:
a) program network.

b) wide area network (WAN).
c) global network.
d) local area network (LAN).
e) computer terminal.

33 Software written specifically to meet the needs of the organization or user is known as:
a) customized software.
b) WordPerfect.
c) Lotus 1-2-3.
d) database.
e) COBOL.

34 A software system that is ready for use upon delivery from the vendor is called a:
a) microcomputer concept.
b) turnkey system.
c) local area network.
d) telecommuting.
e) teleconference.

35 Computer users uncomfortable with a new system or new technology may resort to:
a) active resistance.
b) virtual reality.
c) passive resistance.
d) turnkey system.
e) local area networks.

Internet Resources on the World Wide Web

Throughout this text we have introduced many different web sites. We hope these sites have provided you with a useful introduction to the power of the Web. However, because the Web is managed by no one person and is unlimited in potential for new applications and sites, it is beneficial to have a resource that will link you to daily news on the Net. One such site is operated by CMP Publishing. Their daily news services provides commentary on the people, places, and tools of the Internet. At this site you can join on-line discussions of Internet related topics. Recent discussion groups have included choosing an Internet provider, buying goods and services online, and making the Net safe for family surfing.

Exhibit 19.10

CMP Publishing Web Site

http://techweb.cmp.com/

CHAPTER 20

Risk Management

Business risk represents the possibility that a firm's performance will be lower than expected because of its exposure to specific conditions. Risk can be related to a specific product or division, or the entire firm. It results from uncertainty about the future, as firms rarely forecast future revenue or costs with perfect accuracy. Firms can use risk management to stabilize their performance; this allows them to obtain funds at a lower cost (because there is less risk of failure) and can increase their value.

Consider the case of Black and Decker, which produces power tools and a variety of industrial and household products. What types of risk is Black and Decker exposed to when producing these products? What types of risk is it exposed to after the products are sold? How can Black and Decker protect against its exposure to these types of risk? This chapter provides a background on risk management, which can be used to address these questions.

The **Learning Goals** of this chapter are to:

1   Provide an overview of the tasks involved in risk management.

2   Identify the ways in which firms are exposed to the economic environment.

3   Identify a firm's exposure to firm-specific characteristics.

4   Explain a firm's exposure to potential lawsuits.

5   Explain the alternative remedies for firms that are failing.

TASKS INVOLVED IN MANAGING RISK

1 | **Provide an overview of the tasks involved in risk management.**

Risk management involves identifying a firm's exposure to risk and protecting against that exposure.

Identifying Exposure to Risk

A firm can identify its risk by reviewing its normal business operations. Firms that use more machinery would likely be more concerned with injuries that could result from the machinery. Firms that produce toys should be concerned about potential injuries to children who use the toys.

Protecting against Risk

Once the exposure to risk is identified, firms must assess the alternative methods that can be used to protect against the risk and decide which method is more appropriate. Common ways to protect against risk are to eliminate the risk, shift the risk, or assume the risk.

ELIMINATING RISK   Firms can eliminate risk by eliminating the operations that caused it. For example, firms could eliminate the risk of injury from machinery by discontinuing the use of the machinery. They could avoid the risk of product defects in their production of toys by eliminating toy production. While eliminating the operations that caused risk effectively removes particular risks, firms that prefer to continue their existing businesses need an alternative solution.

property insurance protects a firm against the risk associated with the ownership of property, such as buildings and other assets

casualty insurance insures the potential liability to a firm for harm to others as a result of product failure or accidents

SHIFTING RISK   Firms can shift some types of risk to insurance companies by purchasing insurance. **Property insurance** protects a firm against the risk associated with the ownership of property, such as buildings and other assets. Thus, it can provide insurance against property damage by fire or against theft. **Casualty insurance** insures the potential liability to a firm for harm to others as a result of product failure or accidents.

Property and casualty insurance companies provide insurance for firms. Firms pay a periodic insurance premium for this type of insurance; the amount of the premium is partially dependent on the types of assets insured. The higher the market value of insured assets, the higher the insurance premium paid, other things being equal. But not all assets are insured at the same rate. Because a building located in a high-crime area is more vulnerable to theft, the insurance fee will be higher. In addition, the manufacturing operations of some firms are more likely to result in personal injuries than those of other firms. The casualty insurance premium paid is affected by the likelihood of personal injuries.

Insurance companies recognize that the probability of some events occurring can change over time. Consequently, they will adjust their premiums to reflect the change in probability. For example, firms experienced an increase in liability lawsuits during the 1980s. Anticipating a higher level of payouts on liability lawsuits, insurance companies increased their premiums.

Exhibit 20.1
Insurance Offered by
the Government

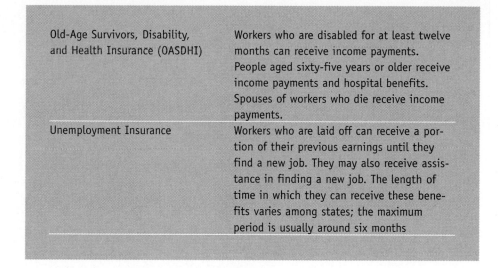

Old-Age Survivors, Disability, and Health Insurance (OASDHI)	Workers who are disabled for at least twelve months can receive income payments. People aged sixty-five years or older receive income payments and hospital benefits. Spouses of workers who die receive income payments.
Unemployment Insurance	Workers who are laid off can receive a portion of their previous earnings until they find a new job. They may also receive assistance in finding a new job. The length of time in which they can receive these benefits varies among states; the maximum period is usually around six months

actuaries employed by insurance companies to forecast the percentage of customers that will experience the particular event that is being insured

Actuaries are employed by insurance companies to forecast the percentage of customers that will experience the particular event that is being insured. This enables insurance companies to properly set the premium on that type of insurance.

The federal and state governments offer business-related insurance. Two popular types are summarized in Exhibit 20.1. Old-age survivors, disability, and health insurance (OASDHI) is funded by the social security taxes paid by employers and employees. Unemployment insurance is funded by unemployment taxes, which are usually paid by employers (although employees also incur an unemployment tax in some states). In general, the two types of insurance summarized in Exhibit 20.1 replace part of the income that is lost because of death, retirement, a layoff, or disability. While other forms of public insurance are available, they are more specifically directed toward particular types of businesses.

self-insurance a fund is created to cover any future claims

ASSUMING RISK   Some firms may be willing to assume their business risk with **self-insurance,** in which a fund is created to cover any future claims. Rather than pay insurance premiums, firms that self-insure contribute to their own insurance fund. Firms consider self-insurance when they believe the insurance premiums charged by insurance companies are higher than what they should need to cover any claims. However, firms that self-insure may be unable to create a fund large enough to cover some awards granted by the court system. Such firms may be forced into bankruptcy if they are judged to be responsible for damages to an employee or customer, especially when the damages determined by the court system are in millions of dollars.

COMPARISON OF METHODS TO PROTECT AGAINST RISK   The three methods used to protect against risk are compared for a firm that produces ladders in Exhibit 20.2. Trade-offs are involved when selecting the proper method. A firm is unlikely to eliminate the production of a product if it specializes in that product. Therefore, it would probably purchase insurance or self-insure. If the firm generates only a small amount of its total earnings from a product that creates substantial exposure to risk, it may eliminate the production of that product. The proper method for protecting against risk can be determined by estimating the costs of each method.

Exhibit 20.2
Illustration of How to
Protect against Risk

Firm's Operations	The firm produces ladders and other home repair equipment.
Exposure to Risk	Injuries to employees who produce ladders or to customers who purchase ladders.

Protecting Against Risk: Possible Solutions

1. *Eliminating Risk*	Discontinue the production and sale of ladders; focus on the production and sale of other home repair equipment that is less risky.
2. *Shifting Risk*	Purchase insurance to protect against possible injuries to employees who produce the ladders or customers who use the ladders.
3. *Assuming Risk*	Create a fund that can be used to self-insure against possible injuries to employees who produce the ladders or customers who use the ladders.

EXPOSURE TO THE ECONOMIC ENVIRONMENT

2

Identify the ways in which firms are exposed to the economic environment.

business risk the possibility that a firm's performance will be lower than expected because of its exposure to specific conditions

A firm's **business risk** is dependent on its exposure to the economic environment, including industry conditions, the national economy, and global economies.

Exposure to Industry Conditions

The performance of a firm is influenced by industry conditions, such as the degree of competition and industry regulations. A firm in a highly competitive industry is subject to a higher degree of business risk because its market share may be reduced. For example, many video stores went bankrupt after the industry became more competitive. A reduction in industry regulations may cause more competition in the industry. When the banking industry was deregulated in the 1980s, many banks failed because they could not compete effectively.

Exposure to Economic Conditions

The performance of a firm is also influenced by the national economy. The sensitivity of a firm's performance to economic conditions is dependent on the products or services sold by the firm. If the demand for the firm's products or services is very sensitive to the national economy, the firm has a high degree of business risk.

The performance levels of some firms are exposed to interest rate movements. In particular, firms whose products are purchased with borrowed funds may be affected by changes in interest rates. When interest rates rise, the demand for homes and automobiles may decline because the interest payments incurred by consumers who make purchases on credit would be too high. Therefore, firms such as homebuilders and automobile manufacturers can be affected by interest rate movements. Furthermore, any related firms such as suppliers of homebuilding parts or automobile parts are affected.

Firms that diversify their product mix may reduce their sensitivity to economic conditions (including interest rate movements), because some of the products may still be in demand even when economic conditions are poor.

Farmers, in particular, are exposed to the risks of weather in the form of too much or too little rain. Irrigation systems help farmers manage some of this risk. However, in a severe drought, such as the one that struck in 1996, the only protection a producer could have is drought insurance.

Exposure to Global Conditions

The sensitivity of a firm's performance to global economies is dependent on the firm's target markets and its competition. If the firm exports products to Europe, the demand for its products is influenced by the European economies. A firm that generates a large proportion of its sales in foreign countries can reduce its exposure to its national economy, but increases its exposure to specific foreign economies.

When firms conduct international business, their performance typically becomes more exposed to exchange rate movements. U.S. firms that rely heavily on exports may be severely affected by the depreciation of foreign currencies, because foreign demand for U.S. products declines when the values of foreign currencies decline. U.S. firms that rely heavily on imported materials for their production process may be severely affected by the appreciation of foreign currencies, because the cost of the imported materials increases when the values of foreign currencies increase. Firms that conduct international business may reduce their exposure to exchange rate movements by hedging with forward contracts.

Firms that conduct international business are also exposed to political events that could adversely affect their performance. For example, a foreign government may impose trade barriers or new tax rules that could reduce the earnings of U.S. firms that conduct business in that country. Such forms of so-called political risk can increase the firm's business risk. U.S. firms that conduct business in less-developed countries are more exposed to political risk than U.S. firms doing business in industrialized countries.

GLOBAL BUSINESS

Risk of Conducting Business in Less-Developed Countries

While less-developed countries offer numerous business opportunities, they also present various types of risk for U.S. firms. Consider the following examples:

1 When Eastman Kodak attempted to enter the Japanese market to sell film, the firms in Japan that distribute film to retail stores were unwilling to distribute Eastman Kodak film. These firms were already distributing film for Fuji, the largest producer of film in Japan.

2 Some U.S. firms made business agreements with Chinese government officials on conducting business in China. They later learned that those officials had no authority to make such business agreements.

3 Some U.S. firms that established businesses in the Soviet Republic have been exposed to massive corruption by suppliers and government officials.

While various types of insurance can reduce exposure to risks involved in international business, insurance cannot cover every possible type of risk in a foreign country. Firms can follow some general guidelines to reduce their exposure to risk. First, firms need to fully understand the country's rules regarding the taxes on earnings generated in that country. Second, they must determine whether there are any restrictions on sending funds back to the United States and whether any taxes would be imposed as a result. Third, firms should obtain approval for their business from the proper government officials. This may include city officials as well as central government officials. Fourth, firms should attempt to determine the characteristics of the industry in which they would compete in that foreign country. For example, some industries in foreign countries are controlled by organized crime. These general guidelines can help firms avoid specific countries that may present excessive risk. Alternatively, the guidelines may possibly enable firms to properly prepare for the types of risk that exist in some foreign countries.

Summary of Exposure to Economic Environment

Exhibit 20.3 summarizes the firm's exposure to the economic environment. The primary reason for the exposure is that the demand for the firm's product is affected by industry, economic, and global conditions. However, the firm's expenses may also be affected by these conditions.

Exhibit 20.3
Exposure to
Economic Environment

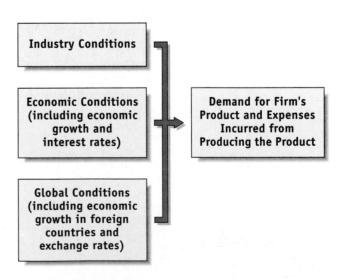

HEDGING RISK FROM ECONOMIC CONDITIONS

derivative instruments instruments whose values are derived from values of other securities, indexes, or interest rates

interest rate swap allows a firm to swap fixed interest payments for payments that adjust to movements in interest rates

Derivative instruments are instruments whose values are derived from values of other securities, indexes, or interest rates. Firms use many types of derivative instruments to hedge their risk resulting from economic conditions. To illustrate how a firm could use derivative instruments to reduce its risk, consider the following example. Assume a firm recognizes that it will be adversely affected by rising interest rates. It desires to take a position in a derivative instrument that will generate a gain if interest rates rise, which can offset the adverse effect on the firm. A popular derivative instrument known as an **interest rate swap** allows a firm to swap fixed interest payments for payments that adjust to movements in interest rates. Assume a firm that owes $100 million can negotiate an interest rate swap agreement in which it provides a fixed annual interest payment of $7 million per year over the next five years. In exchange, it will receive a payment based on the existing Treasury bill rate, as applied to $100 million. If interest rates are high at the end of each year, the firm will generate a gain on the interest rate swap. If the Treasury bill rate was 8 percent, the firm would receive 8 percent of $100 million, or $8 million ($1 million more than it pays out per year on the swap). If the Treasury bill rate was 9 percent, the firm would receive 9 percent of $100 million, or $9 million ($2 million more than it pays out per year on the swap). The higher the interest rates, the larger the gain, which can partially offset any adverse effects of the high interest rates on the firm's performance. Mobil Corporation commonly uses derivative instruments such as interest rate swaps to reduce potential adverse effects of interest rate movements.

In recent years, firms such as Gibson Greeting Cards, Dell Computer, and Procter and Gamble experienced large losses from their derivative positions. Consequently, firms began to ensure proper use of derivative instruments. Shortly after Procter and Gamble incurred a loss of about $100 million due to derivative instruments, it made a special effort to more closely monitor its derivative positions, as explained in a recent annual report:

Nick Leeson lost over $1 billion of Barings Bank money while trading derivative securities in Hong Kong. It is important for companies to carefully monitor high risk positions.

❚❚ *Our policy on derivatives is not to engage in speculative leveraged transactions.* ❚❚

❚❚ *The Company has taken steps to substantially increase the oversight of the Company's financial activities, including the formation of a Risk Management Council.* ❚❚

❚❚ *The Council's role is to insure that the policies and procedures approved by the Board of Directors are being followed within approved limits.* ❚❚

Derivative instruments can reduce risk when used properly. Numerous firms, including PepsiCo and DuPont, use derivative instruments to reduce risk.

EXPOSURE TO FIRM-SPECIFIC CHARACTERISTICS

3

Identify a firm's exposure to firm-specific characteristics.

A firm's business risk is also influenced by any unique characteristics of the firm that affect its ability to cover its expenses. In general, any characteristics that cause the firm to experience a sudden large loss tend to increase the firm's degree of business risk. Some of the more obvious firm-specific characteristics that influence business risk are identified next.

Limited Funding

Small firms tend to have less access to funding and therefore have less flexibility to cover their expenses. Limited funding results in more business risk. As firms grow, they expand their debt capacity and have more financial flexibility.

Reliance on One Product

Firms that rely on a single product to generate most of their revenue are susceptible to abrupt shifts in their performance, and therefore have a high degree of business risk. If the demand for the product declines for any reason, the firm's performance will be adversely affected. Firms that offer a diversified product mix are affected less by a reduction in the demand for a single product.

Reliance on One Customer

Firms that rely on a single customer for most of their business have a high degree of business risk, because their performance would decline substantially if the customer switches to a competitor. There are numerous cases in which firms rely heavily on one customer. For example, firms such as Boeing and Lockheed rely on some federal government orders for the products they produce. When the federal government reduces its spending, it orders fewer products from these firms. Whirlpool Corporation historically relied on Sears for much of its appliance sales. When Sears experienced a decline in appliance sales, it reduced its orders from Whirlpool. Firms can reduce their reliance on a single customer by spreading the sale of the product across markets.

Warren Buffet, the second richest man in America, has led Berkshire Hathaway to some of the greatest investment returns in U.S. history. Many are concerned about the future of the company if Buffet should fall into poor health or retire.

Reliance on One Supplier

Firms that rely on a single supplier for most of their supplies may be severely affected if that supplier does not fulfill its obligations. If that supplier suddenly goes out of business, the firm may experience a major shortage of supplies. Firms that use various suppliers are less exposed to the possibility of a single supplier going out of business, because they will still receive their supply orders from the other suppliers.

Reliance on a Key Employee

When a firm relies on a key employee for its business decisions, the death of that employee would have a severe impact on the performance of a firm. Consider a computer repair business that has only one employee who can perform the repairs. If the employee dies, this job may not be easily performed by other employees. Until the employee can be replaced, business performance may decline. Since a business cannot be managed as well following the death of a key employee, it may be less capable of covering its expenses.

HEDGING AGAINST LOSSES RESULTING FROM A KEY EMPLOYEE'S DEATH   Firms can hedge against losses resulting from a key employee's death by purchasing life insurance for their key employees. The firm would be identified as the beneficiary in the event that a key employee dies. This type of insurance provides the firm with compensation when a key employee dies, so that it may be able to offset the possible losses or reduced performance of the firm. The firm is cushioned from the loss of a key employee, and may be able to survive while attempting to hire a person to fulfill the key employee's responsibilities.

Consider an individual who runs a small business and applies for a business loan at a local bank. If the individual is killed in an accident, the business may deteriorate and the loan would not be paid off. A life insurance policy could designate creditors (such as a bank) as the beneficiaries to protect them against such a risk. Using this strategy, the business is more likely to be approved on a loan.

To illustrate the use of key employee insurance, consider the case of PRP, a research and development company located in Massachusetts. While PRP was developing a product to be used by cancer patients, the chief executive officer of PRP died. Consequently, investors were unwilling to invest in further development of the product because they were concerned that PRP would not survive without its chief executive officer. However, PRP had a $2.5 million life insurance policy on its chief executive officer, which provided sufficient funding when investors were unwilling to invest more funds in the firm.

whole-life insurance life insurance that exists until death or as long as premiums are promptly paid

From the perspective of the insured policyholder, **whole-life insurance** is life insurance that exists until death or as long as premiums are promptly paid. In addition to providing insurance, whole-life policies provide a form of savings to the policyholder. These policies build a cash value which the policyholder is entitled to even if the policy is canceled.

term insurance provides insurance for a policyholder only over a specified term and does not build a cash value for policyholders

Term insurance provides insurance for a policyholder only over a specified term and does not build a cash value for policyholders. The premiums paid by policyholders represent only insurance and not savings. While term insurance is only temporary and does not build a cash value, it is significantly less expensive than whole-life insurance. Policyholders must compare the cash value of whole-life insurance with their additional costs to determine whether it is preferable to term insurance.

decreasing term insurance provides insurance benefits to a beneficiary that decrease over time

To accommodate firms who need more insurance now than later, **decreasing term insurance** provides insurance benefits to a beneficiary that decrease over time.

This form of insurance may be used by a firm to cover a key employee. As time passes and the firm is more capable of surviving without the employee, less insurance would be needed in later years.

universal life insurance combines the features of term and whole-life insurance. It specifies a period of time over which the policy will exist, but builds a cash value for policyholders over time

Universal life insurance combines the features of term and whole-life insurance. It specifies a period of time over which the policy will exist, but builds a cash value for policyholders over time. Interest is accumulated from the cash value until the policyholder uses those funds. Universal life insurance allows flexibility on the size and timing of the premium. The growth in a policy's cash value is dependent on this pace. The premium payment is divided into two portions. The first portion is used to pay the death benefit identified in the policy and to cover any administrative expenses. The second portion is used for investments, and reflects savings for the policyholder. The Internal Revenue Service requires that the value of these savings cannot exceed the policy's death benefits.

HEDGING AGAINST THE ILLNESS OF A KEY EMPLOYEE   The illness of one or more key employees may adversely affect the performance of a firm. Many firms offer a program in which their employees obtain health insurance from health insurance companies. The insurance is generally cheaper when purchased through the firm.

Even if the firms have enabled employees to obtain health insurance through some type of health insurance plan, they may still be affected by the temporary absence of an employee. Firms can reduce the potential adverse effect of an employee illness by ensuring that more than one employee can perform each task.

Exposure to Property Losses

property losses financial losses resulting from damage to property

Property losses are financial losses resulting from damage to property. The damage may be caused by fire, theft, or weather conditions. The financial losses to the firm can result from payments that must be made to repair the damage. Alternatively, the losses can result from the interruption of the firm's operations. For example, if a fire in a factory forces the factory to be closed for one month, the financial loss is not just the cost of repair but also the forgone earnings resulting from closing the factory for one month.

HEDGING AGAINST PROPERTY LOSSES   Property losses may be avoided if the firm enforces policies that can prevent fire or theft. For example, firms that use flammable chemicals may attempt to ensure that all chemicals are not near any smoking areas. Firms can also use alarm systems to detect fire or theft. Furthermore, they can design their facilities in a way that protects against burglaries and poor weather conditions.

While firms can take many precautions to prevent property damage, they do not have complete control. Firms cannot completely safeguard against damage caused by fire, theft, or poor weather conditions. Therefore, they normally purchase insurance for protection. Insurance policies can vary in what they cover. Some firms may purchase insurance that covers the property in the event of a fire. Other firms may purchase insurance that covers the property under any conditions (including burglary and poor weather).

The annual premium paid for property insurance is dependent on the value of the assets that are to be insured. The annual premium charged to insure the property of a small factory is less than the premium charged for insuring a production plant of General Motors. Insurance companies that provide insurance assess the potential insurance claims that could occur, and set the insurance premiums accordingly.

Small businesses, such as a designer clothier, can be particularly vulnerable to property loss. A business such as By George (Austin, Texas) pictured here may lose all resources in a flood, fire, or robbery.

The annual premium paid for property insurance is also dependent on the probability of damage. The higher the probability, the higher the insurance premium. For example, the insurance premium for a factory that uses flammable chemicals will be higher than one of similar size that does not use flammable chemicals.

Exposure to Liability Losses

liability losses financial losses due to the firm's actions that cause damages to others or to their property

Liability losses to a firm are financial losses due to the firm's actions that cause damages to others or to their property. For example, the firm may be held responsible for an employee who is hurt on the job, or for a customer who is hurt because of a defective product produced by the firm.

HEDGING AGAINST LIABILITY LOSSES   Firms can hedge against liability losses by enforcing policies that ensure safety on the job and quality control of products produced. However, they cannot completely safeguard against liability losses with these policies. Consequently, most firms purchase insurance to cover liability damages. Some policies cover damages resulting from injuries to employees, while other policies cover damages resulting from product defects. Because of the large awards granted by the court system for various claims in recent years, liability insurance has become very expensive.

The annual premium paid for liability insurance is dependent on the probability of a liability claim and the size of the claim. Firms in the health-care industry are charged very high liability insurance premiums because the potential liability is so high. Also, firms that produce toys pay high liability insurance premiums because many liability claims result from injuries to children caused by playing with toys.

Exposure to Employee Compensation Claims

Firms must pay employee compensation (including all medical bills and lost wages) to employees who are injured at work. Proper risk management should assess exist-

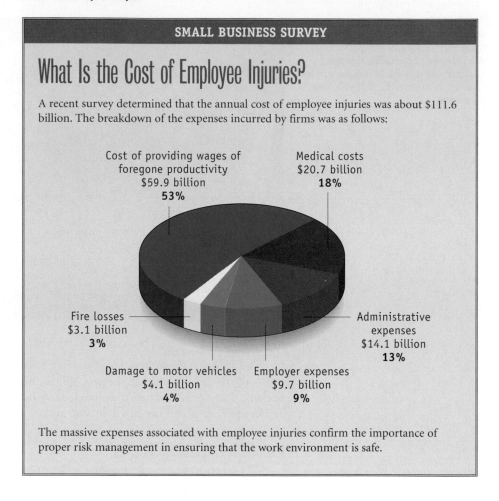

SMALL BUSINESS SURVEY

What Is the Cost of Employee Injuries?

A recent survey determined that the annual cost of employee injuries was about $111.6 billion. The breakdown of the expenses incurred by firms was as follows:

Cost of providing wages of foregone productivity
$59.9 billion
53%

Medical costs
$20.7 billion
18%

Fire losses
$3.1 billion
3%

Administrative expenses
$14.1 billion
13%

Damage to motor vehicles
$4.1 billion
4%

Employer expenses
$9.7 billion
9%

The massive expenses associated with employee injuries confirm the importance of proper risk management in ensuring that the work environment is safe.

ing business operations to ensure that all machinery and equipment is safe and that tasks are conducted in ways that will not cause injuries.

The Occupational Safety and Health Administration (OSHA) monitors firms to make sure that they use tools, machinery, and office facilities that are considered safe. In recent years, OSHA has focused on reducing the possibility of cumulative trauma disorders (CTD) that can affect a worker's wrists or hands. The use of computers, word processors, and other tasks that place pressure on the wrists has caused a major increase in compensation claims due to CTDs in recent years.

HEDGING AGAINST COMPENSATION CLAIMS   Firms can use effective risk management techniques to reduce their exposure to employee compensation claims. As an example, consider OshKosh B'gosh, a manufacturer of children's clothing which experienced a large number of compensation claims because of CTDs. An investigation found that many of the workers were affected by repetitious tasks that required force with the hands. Consequently, OshKosh B'gosh revised its operations to avoid the possible motions of employees that could have caused CTDs. It also rotated jobs among employees to alleviate stress over time on any particular part of the body. Finally, it provided job safety training to educate employees on how to perform tasks to avoid injuries. When firms use risk management techniques like those just described, they can improve employee morale and lower the expenses associated with workers' compensation.

Many companies now insist on workers wearing and using equipment that helps prevent personal injuries.

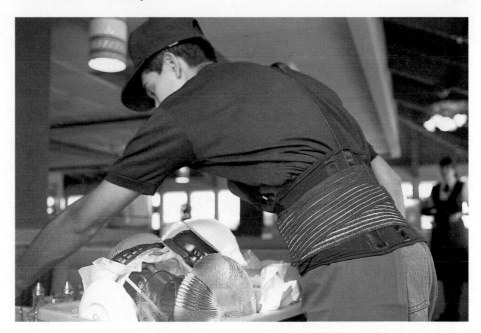

Some firms self-insure to establish a fund for covering employee compensation. Other firms purchase employee compensation insurance. The insurance premiums are dependent on the potential employee compensation that a firm may pay for on-the-job injuries.

Summary of Exposure to Firm-Specific Characteristics

Exhibit 20.4 summarizes the firm-specific characteristics to which a firm is exposed. The funding can be improved if the firm experiences strong performance. The risk of

Exhibit 20.4
Exposure to Firm-Specific Characteristics

Characteristic	How Firm Is Exposed
Limited Funding	Limited ability to cover expenses.
Reliance on One Product	Revenue will be reduced substantially if there is a large decline in the demand for a single product.
Reliance on One Customer	Revenue will decline substantially if the customer no longer purchases the firm's product.
Reliance on One Supplier	Potential shortages of supplies occur if supplier experiences problems.
Reliance on a Key Employee	Performance will decline if employee dies, becomes ill, or leaves the firm.
Property Losses	Expenses incurred from covering property losses.
Liability Losses	Expenses incurred from covering liability losses.
Employee Compensation Claims	Expenses incurred from covering compensation claims.

Exhibit 20.5
Other Types of Insurance

Business Interruption Insurance	Covers against losses due to a temporary closing of the business.
Credit Line Insurance	Covers debt payments owed to a creditor if a borrower dies.
Fidelity Bond	Covers against losses due to dishonesty by employees.
Marine Insurance	Covers against losses due to damage during transport.
Malpractice Insurance	Covers professionals from losses due to lawsuits by dissatisfied customers.
Surety Bond	Covers losses due to a contract not being fulfilled.
Umbrella Liability Insurance	Provides additional coverage beyond that provided by other existing insurance policies.
Employment Liability Insurance	Covers claims against wrongful termination and sexual harassment.

relying on a single product, customer, or supplier can be reduced by diversifying the firm's product line across many customers and by diversifying among suppliers. The risk of relying on a single employee can be reduced by diversifying job responsibilities or by purchasing insurance. The risk of property, casualty, or employee compensation losses can be covered by purchasing insurance or by self-insuring.

Other firm-specific characteristics may expose a firm to risk. Insurance may be purchased to cover these types of risk. A brief summary of other types of insurance that can be obtained is provided in Exhibit 20.5.

EXPOSURE TO LAWSUITS

4　Explain a firm's exposure to potential lawsuits.

In recent years, firms have been bombarded by lawsuits. To illustrate, consider the following statements from annual reports:

> *The company is a defendant in various suits, including environmental ones, and is subject to various claims which arise in the normal course of business.*
>
> —Motorola

> *The Corporation is involved in various lawsuits in the ordinary course of business. These lawsuits primarily involve claims for damages arising out of the use of the Corporation's products and allegations of patent and trademark infringement.*
>
> —Black and Decker

> **❚❚ *PepsiCo is subject to various claims and contingencies related to lawsuits, taxes, environmental and other matters arising out of the normal course of business. ❚❚***
>
> —PepsiCo

These examples are not the exception, but are typical for most large firms. It is not unusual for firms such as retailers or wholesalers to be sued for a product defect, even when they had nothing to do with the design or production of the product.

Assume you are a firm's risk manager who is responsible for ensuring that the firm's customers and employees are treated properly. Answer the following questions about whether the firm is subject to a possible lawsuit:

1 Your firm's product is tested by a government agency and found to be completely safe. Can your firm be sued by a customer for product defects?

2 Your firm has an employee who is consistently performing poorly at work and has consistently been given clear evaluations citing poor performance. If this employee is fired, can your firm be sued by that employee?

3 Your firm has an employee who not only performs poorly at work but also has begun to take illegal drugs at work. If this employee is fired, can your firm be sued?

4 Your firm recently promoted an employee who was selected as the most qualified for a new position. Can your firm be sued by other employees who are less qualified?

5 An employee recently walked into your office and other offices of the firm with a loaded gun. If this employee is fired, can your firm be sued by that fired employee? If this employee is not fired, can your firm be sued by other employees?

The answer to every one of these questions is a definite yes. Furthermore, you may be sued personally along with the firm. That is, the plaintiff may attempt to receive a court judgment on your individual assets as well as the firm's assets. The court system may prevent a plaintiff's efforts to sue other employees personally, but there is nothing to prevent the plaintiff from trying, regardless of the actual circumstances.

The court system may also rule in favor of a firm that has attempted to treat customers and employees properly. However, the firm incurs a large cost of defending against lawsuits. It may also experience a decline in business when the public is informed by the media about lawsuits. Plaintiffs' attorneys often spread the news of a lawsuit to the media, which pressures a firm to settle the lawsuit before the news does damage to its business. Furthermore, attorneys receive free advertising from the media when their names are mentioned in the paper. Many frivolous lawsuits have been settled because firms do not wish to use time or resources to defend against so-called nuisance lawsuits. Even in those cases in which a firm is willing to defend against a frivolous lawsuit and wins, it may take several years before a court judgment occurs.

In summary, risk managers may have some ability to prevent specific exposure to risk that can result in lawsuits and therefore in major expenses incurred by the firm. However, risk managers cannot prevent frivolous lawsuits that will be filed against the firm. They must simply recognize that such lawsuits may occur and should establish a budget that can be used to defend against them.

How the Threat of Lawsuits Can Affect Business Strategies

The size of the damages for compensating injured persons can vary among states. Consequently, the establishment or expansion of a firm in a specific location must

Potential Liability from Using Information Technology

With growing reliance on information technology, managers may find themselves subject to unfamiliar types of liability. Three categories of liability, in particular, are commonly associated with information technology: liability resulting from errors, liability resulting from failing to abide by licensing agreements, and liability resulting from inappropriate uses of technology.

➤ *Liability from Errors:* Although computers are not considered error prone, errors in hardware and software (known as bugs) do exist. At Citibank in the 1970s, for example, problems during the installation of financial exchange software led to a failure to deposit funds, which, in one night, cost the company tens of millions of dollars.

The severity of information technology errors is aggravated by the consistency with which they are made. In a manual accounting system, for example, errors tend to be sporadic, involving an occasional misplaced decimal or unbalanced journal entry. In a computer-based accounting system, a bug tends to produce systematic errors that can have major consequences. For example, the state of Florida recently uncovered errors in its human resources software that led to benefits being given recipients beyond their actual eligibility. These benefits were valued at over a hundred million dollars.

Companies that develop hardware and software are particularly vulnerable to errors. When Intel discovered an error in its Pentium processor logic, it cost the company millions to replace defective processors already installed in customer machines. Developers, in some circumstances, may also be held liable for the consequences of errors in their software. The potential for such liability needs to be considered before selling a software product. Companies that market financial and accounting products need to be particularly careful in this respect. A company such as Intuit, which markets the popular TurboTax tax preparation software package, could be wiped out if its product made a systematic error that caused its millions of customers to underpay or overpay their taxes.

➤ *Licensing Liability:* Another source of potential liability for firms stems from the failure to abide by application licensing aggreements. Piracy occurs when an individual or organization uses a copy of software that has not been paid for. Some companies, for example, buy one copy of an application, then put it on their network or on many individual work stations. In doing so they violate licensing agreements and, in the process, expose their companies to a significant, unnecessary risk. Software vendors, such as Microsoft, have a history of aggressively prosecuting such cases. The law allows them to collect three times the suggested list price of all pirated copies. Even worse, a vendor might decide to deny the company the right to use the software, a potential catastrophe when the software is critical to the business.

➤ *Inappropriate Uses of Technology:* A third form of potential liability associated with information systems stems from inappropriate or illegal uses of systems. For example, e-mail users have traditionally expressed themselves with a degree of candor ranging from the refreshing to the inappropriate to the downright illegal, as in cases where messages are used as a form of sexual harassment. Companies must ensure that their information technology is not used in such a fashion or be prepared to face disastrous consequences. To avoid these dangers, a clear policy stating how systems are to be used and how management intends to monitor them needs to be established and enforced.

consider the state laws. In California, large damages imposed by the court system have forced many firms into bankruptcy. Several other firms have moved out of California to reduce their exposure to the risk that a court will impose such damages.

Some products are more likely to result in lawsuits than others. A recent survey found that 47 percent of firms eliminated at least one of their product lines because of the threat of lawsuits, and 39 percent of firms withheld new products from the market because of the possible threat of lawsuits.

Concern about Arbitrary Judgements

Since laws cannot be explicitly written to cover every possible aspect of business, there will always be court cases whose judgments are dependent on the specific judges or juries involved. Consequently, attorneys attempt to position the court case so that it will involve judges or jurors who have a favorable bias. Plaintiffs tend to choose a court location in which the jury may be biased in favor of the plaintiff. Defendants may commonly prefer that the case be conducted in a different court.

To illustrate how positioning can determine the outcome of court cases, consider that in federal court cases from 1979 to 1991, plaintiffs won 73 percent of cases that were heard in the court in which they were originally filed. Conversely, when cases were transferred to other courts, plaintiffs won only 26 percent of the time.

The previous discussion suggests that positioning may be more relevant than the law itself. Because some laws are arbitrary, firms may be subject to major damages even if they make every effort to follow the law.

Conclusion for Risk Managers

Effective risk management can be used by a firm to prevent exposure to various types of risk that injure customers or employees. In this way, risk management can also enhance the firm's value by avoiding expenses that may result from compensating injured customers or employees, or other legal expenses that result from lawsuits.

In reality, risk managers must recognize that their firms may incur major legal expenses even if they properly conduct risk management. Yet, they can more accurately estimate their future expenses by anticipating that some lawsuits will be filed against them, regardless of their efforts to conduct business properly.

While firms cannot prevent arbitrary judgments, their risk management may be able to avoid unfavorable judgments by attempting to use procedures that are well documented and clearly demonstrate the firm's efforts to treat customers and employees properly.

REMEDIES FOR BUSINESS FAILURES

 5

Explain the alternative remedies for firms that are failing.

The extreme consequence of business risk is business failure, in which the firm's assets are sold to pay creditors part of what they are owed. In this case, a formal bankruptcy process is necessary. Yet, alternative informal remedies should be considered first, which could avoid some legal expenses. Common remedies are as follows:

➤ Extension
➤ Composition
➤ Private liquidation
➤ Formal remedies

Extension

extension provides additional time for the firm to generate the necessary cash to cover its payments

If a firm is having difficulty covering payments owed to creditors, these creditors may allow for an **extension,** which provides additional time for the firm to generate the necessary cash to cover its payments. An extension is feasible only if creditors believe that the firm's financial problems are temporary. If formal bankruptcy is inevitable, an extension may only delay the liquidation process and possibly reduce the liquidation value of the firm's assets.

If creditors allow an extension, they may require that the firm abide by various provisions. For example, they may prohibit the firm from making dividend payments until the firm retains enough funds to repay its loans. The firm may agree to any reasonable provisions required from an extension, since the extension gives the firm a chance to survive.

No creditor is forced to go along with an extension. Creditors who would prefer some alternative action must be paid off in full if an extension is to be allowed. If too many creditors disapprove of an extension, attempting one would not be feasible, as all disapproving creditors would first need to be paid what they are owed.

Composition

composition specifies that the firm will provide its creditors with a portion of what they are owed

If the failing firm and its creditors do not agree on an extension, they may attempt to negotiate a **composition** agreement, which specifies that the firm will provide its creditors with a portion of what they are owed. For example, the agreement may call for creditors to receive forty cents on every dollar owed to them. This partial repayment may be as much as or more than creditors would receive from formalized bankruptcy proceedings. In addition, the firm may be able to survive, since its future interest payments will be eliminated after paying off the creditors. As with an extension, creditors are not forced to go along with a composition agreement. Any dissenting creditors must be paid in full.

Private Liquidation

private liquidation creditors may informally request that the failing firm liquidate (sell) its assets and distribute the funds received from liquidation to them

If an extension or composition is not possible, the creditors may informally request that the failing firm liquidate (sell) its assets and distribute the funds received from liquidation to them. While this can be achieved through formalized bankruptcy proceedings, it can also be accomplished informally outside the court system. An informal agreement will typically be accomplished more quickly than formal bankruptcy proceedings, and is less expensive as it avoids excessive legal fees. All creditors must agree to this so-called **private liquidation,** or else an alternative remedy is necessary.

To enact a private liquidation, a law firm with expertise in liquidation will normally be hired to liquidate the debtor firm's assets. Once the assets are liquidated, the remaining funds are distributed to the creditors on a pro rata basis.

Formal Remedies

If creditors cannot agree to any of the informal remedies, the solution to the firm's financial problems will be worked out formally in the court system. The formal remedies are either reorganization or liquidation. Whether a firm should reorganize or liquidate depends on its estimated value under each alternative.

liquidation value amount of funds that would be received as a result of the liquidation of the firm

REORGANIZATION   Reorganization of a firm can include the termination of some of its businesses, an increased focus on its other businesses, revisions of the organizational structure, and downsizing. Consider a firm whose value as a "going concern" (a continuing business) would be $20 million after it reorganizes. Now consider the **liquidation value** of that firm, which is the amount of funds that would be received from liquidating all of the firm's assets. If the firm's liquidation value exceeds $20 million, it should be liquidated. The creditors would receive more funds from liquidation than what they would expect to receive if the firm was reorganized. Conversely, if its liquidation value is less than $20 million, the firm should be reorganized.

In the case of reorganization, the firm or the creditors must file a petition. The bankruptcy court then appoints a committee of creditors to work with the firm in restructuring its operations. The firm is protected against any legal action that would interrupt its operations. The firm may revise its capital structure by using less debt, so that it can reduce its periodic interest payments owed to creditors. Once the restructuring plan is completed, it is submitted to the court and must be approved by the creditors.

LIQUIDATION UNDER BANKRUPTCY   If the firm and its creditors cannot agree on some informal agreement, and if reorganization is not feasible, the firm will file for bankruptcy. A petition for bankruptcy must be filed by either the failing firm or the creditors.

The failing firm is obligated to file a list of creditors along with up-to-date financial statements. A law firm is appointed to sell off the existing assets and allocate the funds received to the creditors. Secured creditors are paid with the proceeds from selling off any assets serving as their collateral.

BUSINESS DILEMMA

Managing Risk at College Health Club

Sue Kramer, president of College Health Club (CHC) recognizes that CHC is exposed to various types of liability risk. Specifically, she knows that customers of the health club could possibly injure themselves when using the exercise or weight machines, or when doing aerobics exercises.

Dilemma

Sue wants to determine the alternative methods of dealing with this liability risk so that she could select the method that is most appropriate. What are the alternative methods for dealing with this risk? Which alternative would you recommend for CHC?

Solution

There are three alternative methods of dealing with the liability risk. One alternative is to eliminate the risk by eliminating the operations that cause the risk. Second, Sue could shift the risk to an insurance company by purchasing liability insurance. Third, Sue could assume the risk by setting up an insurance fund at CHC.

The first method is not feasible because it would require Sue to eliminate most of the services available to CHC members. The second method (purchasing insurance) can be expensive, but may even be necessary for CHC to borrow funds (lenders want to make sure that CHC is insured because if it is not, it would possibly be unable to repay its loans if it was liable for a customer's injury). The third method (self-insurance) can be a reasonable solution. However, most new firms tend to purchase insurance to avoid having to develop their own insurance fund. Firms that have been established for several years may consider self-insurance.

Additional Issues for Discussion

1 How can CHC possibly prevent injuries that result in liability claims?

2 Some firms are viewed as risky because they rely on one product (or service). Does CHC rely too heavily on one service? Is there any logical way in which CHC could reduce this risk?

3 CHC presently relies on Sue Kramer (the president) for all of its key business decisions. How could CHC hedge against losses that would occur if Sue became ill?

SUMMARY

1 Business risk represents the possibility that the firm's performance will be lower than expected because of its exposure to specific conditions. Risk management involves identifying the risk to which a business is exposed and protecting against that risk. The common ways to protect against risk are to:

➤ eliminate the risk (by eliminating the business operations that caused the risk),

➤ shift the risk (by purchasing insurance), or

➤ assume the risk (by creating self-insurance).

2 Firms are exposed to economic conditions, such as the national economy and interest rate movements. Firms can reduce their exposure to the economic environment by producing a variety of products that have different sensitivities to economic conditions.

3 Firms are exposed to risk because of limited funding; reliance on one product, customer, supplier, or key employee; and exposure to property, liability, and employee compensation losses. Firms that are exposed to risk because of reliance on a single supplier, customer, or key employee can reduce their risk by diversifying among suppliers and customers, and by diversifying the key managerial responsibilities among employees. Firms can protect against the risk of property or liability losses by purchasing insurance.

4 Firms are exposed to potential lawsuits by customers or employees. They can reduce this risk by ensuring that their products are safe and that working conditions are safe.

5 If a firm is unable to make its payment to creditors, it may consider three informal remedies. First, it can ask creditors to allow an extension, which provides additional time for the firm to cover its payments. Second, it could negotiate a composition agreement, in which it pays creditors a portion of what they are owed. Third, it could liquidate its assets and distribute the proceeds to its creditors.

In addition to these informal remedies, the firm may also consider formal remedies such as liquidation or reorganization through the court system.

KEY TERMS

actuaries
business risk
casualty insurance
composition
decreasing term insurance
derivative instruments

extension
interest rate swap
liability losses
liquidation value
private liquidation
property insurance

property losses
self-insurance
term insurance
universal life insurance
whole-life insurance

REVIEW QUESTIONS

1 Discuss the different types of life insurance a business can purchase for its key employees.

2 Compare the methods a firm could use to protect itself against risk.

3 Discuss how a firm can hedge against liability losses.

4 Define product liability for a firm that is attempting to compete in the marketplace. Can the firm hedge against this risk?

5 How can risk managers prevent "nuisance lawsuits" from being filed against their firms?

6 Discuss alternate informal remedies a business should consider before selling its assets to pay creditors and claiming formal bankruptcy.

7 Identify specific characteristics of a firm's operation to which it could be exposed.

8 Discuss a derivative instrument a firm could utilize when it is adversely affected by rising interest rates.

9 Discuss the advantages of an informal bankruptcy proceeding versus a formal proceeding.

10 For insurance purposes, why would a firm eliminate a product from its product line?

DISCUSSION QUESTIONS

1 Assume you are a financial manager and your firm is faced with possible bankruptcy. You are in charge of negotiating credit arrangements with your suppliers. Discuss what could be arranged.

2 Why would anyone consider life insurance for a business partner? After all, it is simply an expense. Defend your answer.

3 Is it possible to buy too much insurance for a business? If so, explain.

4 Assume you are an entrepreneur and that your business has only one customer, the federal government. What are the various types of business risks to which your firm is subjected?

5 Assume you are a business entrepreneur of a rollerblade manufacturing company. To what extent could you use risk elimination, risk shifting, and risk assumption in your risk management program?

RUNNING YOUR OWN BUSINESS

1 Describe how your business will reduce the risk of a loss due to a catastrophe such as a flood or fire.

2 Describe how your business will reduce the risk of a loss due to liability.

INVESTING IN THE STOCK OF A BUSINESS

Using the annual report of the firm in which you would like to invest, complete the following:

1 Is the firm highly exposed to economic or industry conditions? Has it used any strategies to reduce its exposure to that risk?

2 Is the firm highly exposed to liability risk, in which customers or employees may sue the firm? Has it used any strategies to reduce its exposure to that risk? Is it presently being sued by customers, employees, or the government? (Review the notes within the section called "Litigation" or "Contingent Liabilities" near the firm's financial statements.)

CASE 1 Selecting the Proper Insurance Coverage for a Business

A small specialty steel producer manufactures and distributes small consumer appliance tools, drills, and tips. This cutting tool manufacturer sells directly to distributors, which in turn sell directly to other retailers (Sears is a major account). This is a small-scale operation; the owner-manager, Joe Iezzi, works side by side with his ten-member crew.

Joe has many concerns about his company. He is concerned about defective drills, since he recently received a letter from an irate customer who lost two fingers using a drill produced by his company. He made an error in assuming he did not need insurance. In addition, Joe has a business risk because he does not have insurance in case any of his employees are hurt on the job and cannot work for a period of time. He wants to know if any type of insurance can be purchased to protect his employees while performing their jobs. Finally, Joe has expressed concern about what would happen to his company if it loses Sears as a customer. He has no risk insurance against this major account.

Joe has decided to develop a business insurance plan for his firm and wants to discuss the various types of risk involved in case something happens to his business. Joe has a business plan, foresees future business growth, and wants to insure that growth.

Questions

1 What type of insurance should Joe have obtained to cover his operation in case of defective products?

2 What type of insurance should Joe consider to protect his employees if an industrial accident occurs on the job?

3 Is there any form of insurance available for a single major account?

CASE 2   The Decision to Insure a Business

Bruce Leonard and David Mikan own and operate Master Lawncare, located in Cleveland, Ohio. The lawn care business has grown significantly over the years. An insurance agent has called on the partners to recommend an insurance plan. The partners want to protect their investment in case anything happens to either of them. They currently have no insurance on either partner or on the business operations. The partners viewed insurance as a cost of operations with very little benefit to the business. Also, they did not have adequate funds to purchase insurance.

This business concentrates on one major commercial account that keeps their crew busy all summer long in landscaping flower gardens, pruning shrubs and trees, and mowing grass. The operation has had few customer-related problems; however, some customers have complained recently about the quality of services being performed by employees in mowing and trimming lawns.

Another concern the partners have is with their employees. Several accidents have occurred in the handling of equipment, especially when mowing grass. David states, "We are going to get sued some day by our own employees, and the employees will own this company."

Questions

1   Is Master Lawncare subject to risk? If so, how can the risk be eliminated?

2   What are the business risks to which this partnership is exposed?

3   Recommend an insurance plan to Bruce and David. Be specific on the types of insurance you would recommend.

4   Should the partnership consider self-insuring its business, even if it needs its funds to support its growth?

VIDEO CASE   Protecting Against Property Damage

The Great Flood of '93 has left everyone at Mark Andy with much to be thankful for. Foremost is that the Chesterfield, Missouri, manufacturer of printing presses used in packaging for labels, tags, etc., survived.

The company, which is headed by Chairman Mark Andrews, Jr., had been advised on Friday, July 30, to take precautions at its headquarters office and plant. It did: Computers and files were moved to the second floor, although everyone was sure they would be restored to their proper places Monday.

They weren't. A Missouri River levee broke early Saturday, and the entire Chesterfield Valley was deluged. The plant was on a valley high spot, but water levels reached fifty-two inches inside.

Fortunately, Mark Andy Inc. had insurance to cover the expenses associated with the flood. The company was in good financial condition, which made it easier to deal with the flood.

However, quick action was necessary to keep from losing business to competitors. Managers weren't allowed access to the plant area for five days, but temporary office space was secured over the weekend, and all 275 employees were assured they would have plenty of work to do. A fifth of them assembled Monday morning and began contacting customers, advising them on orders. Vendors were told to deliver replacement parts as scheduled, and in two weeks parts were being shipped to customers at normal rates.

By the twelfth day the company had hired disaster cleanup specialists, and two hundred of its own employees, trained in reclamation safety and techniques, were cleaning the building in two twelve-hour shifts.

The company moved aggressively to regain market share lost in the first three months after the flood, and something as surprising as the extent of the flood happened: 1993 ended up one of Mark Andy's best years, financially. New equipment was bought, and the company went on a round-the-clock five-day workweek.

Questions

1   Mark Andy may not have recovered from the flood if it had not been backed by insurance. However, even with insurance, a flood can be devastating if the insurance payment is delayed. Explain why a firm in good financial condition (such as Mark Andy) can more easily survive a flood than another firm in weak financial condition, even if both firms are insured.

2   Some firms attempt to manage risk by creating their own insurance fund to protect against specific adverse events. Do you think a new firm should attempt to self-insure to protect against a flood?

3   The adverse effect of a flood on a business is not necessarily just the cost of replacing machinery. Describe some other adverse effects that may not even be covered by insurance.

THE 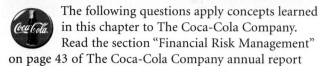 COMPANY ANNUAL REPORT PROJECT

The following questions apply concepts learned in this chapter to The Coca-Cola Company. Read the section "Financial Risk Management" on page 43 of The Coca-Cola Company annual report before answering these questions.

1 What type of insurance would protect the manufacturing facilities of The Coca-Cola Company? What other types of insurance might The Coca-Cola Company purchase to reduce its exposure to various types of risk?

2 Why does The Coca-Cola Company use derivative financial instruments?

3 What type of risk might The Coca-Cola Company expose itself to when it builds plants outside the U.S.? How might it reduce this risk?

IN-TEXT STUDY GUIDE

Answers are in an appendix at the back of the book.

True or False

1 From the perspective of the insured policyholder, term life insurance is in effect until death or as long as premiums are promptly paid.

2 Firms can use effective risk management techniques to reduce their exposure to employee compensation claims.

3 A reduction in industry regulations causes less competition in the industry.

4 Firms that do not offer a diversified product mix are affected less by a reduction in the demand for a single product.

5 Risk management involves identifying a firm's exposure to risk and protecting against that exposure.

6 Creditors may be willing to accept an extension rather than receive a portion of their loans back if the firm goes bankrupt and its assets are sold (liquidated).

7 If the firm and its creditors cannot agree on some informal agreement, and if reorganization is not feasible, the firm will file for deregulation.

8 The Internal Revenue Service requires that the value of the savings reflected on a universal life insurance policy cannot exceed the policy's death benefits.

9 Firms can completely safeguard against liability losses by enforcing policies that ensure safety on the job and quality control of products produced.

10 Self-insurance represents life insurance for one individual.

Multiple Choice

11 An agreement that specifies that the firm will provide its creditors with a portion of what they are owed is a(n):

a) business plan.
b) indemnity bond.
c) composition agreement.
d) surety bond.
e) interest swap.

12 Firms that rely on a single product to generate most of their revenue are susceptible to abrupt shifts in their performance and therefore have a high degree of:

a) business risk.
b) cash flow.
c) business certainty.
d) business diversity.
e) employee compensation claims.

13 A type of insurance that covers against losses due to dishonesty by employees is a(n):

a) employment liability insurance.
b) fidelity bond.
c) credit line insurance.
d) malpractice insurance.
e) surety bond.

14 A derivative instrument that allows a firm to swap fixed interest payments for payments that adjust to movements in interest rates is known as a(n):

a) debt equity swap.
b) income statement.
c) composition.
d) insurance contract.
e) interest rate swap.

15 A formal remedy for a failing firm is:

a) buy insurance.
b) interest rate swaps.
c) reorganization.
d) unemployment insurance.
e) workers' compensation.

16 Common ways that a firm can protect against risk are to eliminate the risk, assume the risk, or:
a) acquire risk.
b) purchase the risk.
c) discontinue the product.
d) sell insurance.
e) shift the risk.

17 A policy that insures the potential liability to a firm for harm to others as a result of product failure or accidents is:
a) casualty insurance.
b) property insurance.
c) life insurance.
d) universal insurance.
e) term insurance.

18 When firms believe the casualty insurance premiums charged by insurance companies are higher than what they need to cover any claims, an alternative to casualty insurance is:
a) interest rate swap.
b) self-insurance.
c) surety bonds.
d) marine insurance.
e) malpractice insurance.

19 _____ insurance is in effect until death or as long as premiums are promptly paid.
a) Term.
b) Decreasing term
c) Increasing term
d) Whole-life
e) Constant term

20 Financial losses due to the firm's actions that cause damages to others or to their property are:
a) revenue gains.
b) income gains.
c) health insurers.
d) product characteristics.
e) liability losses.

21 Common informal remedies for a failing firm are private liquidation, composition, and:
a) voluntary bankruptcy proceedings.
b) extension.
c) cease and desist orders by the court.
d) involuntary bankruptcy proceedings.
e) reorganization.

22 The two types of insurance offered by the government are:
a) OASDHI and unemployment insurance.
b) life and health insurance.
c) property and casualty insurance.
d) product and performance insurance.
e) term and group insurance.

23 A firm's business risk is also influenced by any unique characteristics of the firm that affect its ability to cover its:
a) term insurance.
b) life insurance.
c) health insurance.
d) revenue.
e) expenses.

24 A government agency that monitors firms to make sure that they use tools, machinery, and office facilities that are considered safe is the:
a) Federal Reserve Board.
b) Defense Department.
c) Department of Commerce.
d) Occupational Safety and Health Administration.
e) Department of the Interior.

25 Employment liability insurance covers claims against wrongful termination and:
a) diversification.
b) ecological concerns.
c) sexual harassment.
d) product liability.
e) death of a key employee.

26 To stabilize its performance, a firm may rely on:
a) a single customer base.
b) a single supplier.
c) a single employee.
d) risk management.
e) a single product.

27 Creditors are more willing to provide financing for low-risk ventures, since there is less chance of:
a) default on a loan.
b) revenues in the future.
c) uncertain economic conditions.
d) business success.
e) diversified businesses.

28 When a firm's products or services are very sensitive to the national economy, the firm is said to have a:
a) risk divergence.
b) composition.
c) high degree of business risk.
d) risk diversification.
e) risk assurance.

29 When U.S. firms conduct international business, their performance typically becomes more exposed to:
a) local conditions.
b) the U.S. economy.
c) reliance on one employee.
d) exchange rate movements.

e) reliance on one customer.

30 _____ are employed by insurance companies to forecast the percentage of customers that will experience the particular event that is being insured.
a) Self-insurance agents
b) Actuaries
c) Universal insurance agents
d) Property insurance agents
e) Casualty insurance agents

31 Firms can shift some types of risk to insurance companies by:
a) selling assets.
b) purchasing common stock.
c) acquiring liabilities.
d) purchasing insurance.
e) assuming risk.

32 Some firms may be willing to assume their business risk by creating a fund that is used to cover any claims, which is known as:
a) self-insurance.
b) term insurance.
c) group insurance.
d) health insurance.

e) pure risk.

33 A firm's business risk is dependent on its exposure to the economic environment, which includes industry conditions, the national economy, and:
a) actuaries.
b) insurance agents.
c) global economies.
d) casualty insurance agents.
e) universal insurance agents.

34 Firms can hedge against losses due to a key employee's death by purchasing life insurance for their:
a) equipment resources.
b) key employees.
c) economic resources.
d) future losses.
e) performance bond.

35 Universal life insurance combines the features of term and:
a) group insurance.
b) endowment insurance.
c) whole-life insurance.
d) cash-surrender value.
e) insurance savings.

Risk Management Information on the World Wide Web

The RISKWeb site (Exhibit 20.6) acts as a guide to risk management and insurance information on the Internet. It augments a risk management mailing list (RISKNet), an ongoing discussion group with participants that include risk managers from all over the world.

Exhibit 20.6
The RISKWeb WWW Server

http://www.riskweb.com/

CHAPTER 21

Synthesis of Business Functions

Managers of a firm commonly make management, marketing, and finance decisions. These managers must recognize how their decisions may affect a firm's revenue or expenses, and therefore its value.

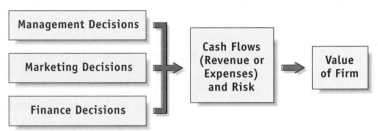

To illustrate how the management, marketing, and finance decisions affect the value of the business, consider the case of the Chicago Bulls organization. It carefully recruits its players (employees) and communicates each player's role and contribution in creating a service (entertainment). Consequently, the team has been very successful. The Bulls organization not only focuses on the development of its employees, but also its marketing and its financing. It uses marketing to promote its product (through clothing and other products that carry the Bulls name). It also uses financial management to determine how it should obtain the funds needed to pay its players. The marketing is dependent on the type of service (including the specific players) provided by the Bulls in a given year. The amount of financing needed by the Bulls organization is dependent on the cost (including player salaries) of providing its service.

The Bulls organization must make several business decisions that are related. How many employees are needed to run the Bulls organization? What methods should it use to motivate its employees (including its players)? What type of advertising should it use to promote its product? What other methods should it use beyond advertising to promote its product? How much money will be needed to finance the cost (including salaries) of producing its service? Will its retained earnings be sufficient to cover its expenses?

The first two questions relate to the management function, the next two questions to the marketing function, and the last two questions to the finance function. This chapter provides a synthesis of business functions, which will illustrate how business decisions are integrated. That is, the proper decision within one business function is dependent on the decisions within the other business functions.

The **Learning Goals** of this chapter are to:

1 Explain how a firm's value is determined.

2 Summarize the key business decisions and explain how they affect the firm's value.

3 Illustrate how one particular firm (IBM) recently made several key business decisions to increase its value.

VALUATION OF A BUSINESS

1   **Explain how a firm's value is determined.**

Recall that the value of a project is determined by estimating the present value of its expected future cash flows. A firm that assesses a new project is willing to invest in it if the present value of future cash flows exceeds the initial outlay that is needed to invest in the project. When investors consider investing in a firm, they can use the same logic. A firm's value is equal to the present value of its future cash flows. The firm's cash flow in any particular period is equal to its cash inflows minus the cash outflows

Most of the firm's cash inflows result from its sales. Most of its cash outflows typically result from payment of expenses or taxes. If a firm's payments received from sales and sent to cover expenses are made with cash, its cash flows normally reflect its earnings (after taxes). Thus the firm's value is highly influenced by its expected future earnings. The cash flows of a firm may also be affected by some other factors, but earnings are the typical driving force.

HOW BUSINESS DECISIONS AFFECT THE FIRM'S VALUE

2   **Summarize the key business decisions and explain how they affect the firm's value.**

Managers should manage the firm with the objective of maximizing its value. This objective is in the best interests of the owners who have invested their funds in the firm. Since the value of a firm is the present value of its future cash flows, managers should make decisions that increase these future cash flows.

Most business decisions that are intended to increase the firm's value can be classified as management, marketing, and finance functions. The main types of these decisions have been described throughout the text. When these decisions result in higher cash flows, they enhance the value of the firm. A summary of those decisions is provided next, with an emphasis on how each of those decisions can enhance the firm's value.

Management Decisions

Management is the means by which the firm uses employees and other resources (such as machinery). Some of the key management decisions are focused on strategic planning, determining the organizational structure, determining the production process, and motivating employees.

STRATEGIC PLANNING   Many decisions are based on the firm's strategic plan, which identifies the opportunities and direction of the firm's business. That is, the means by which a firm utilizes its employees and other resources are dependent on the opportunities that exist and the types of business projects that the firm implements. Proper planning can capitalize on opportunities that result in higher revenue or in lower production costs for the firm. Either result can improve earnings, which should increase the present value of the firm's future cash flows.

A firm that develops a more effective strategic plan has more potential to enhance its value. Consider two computer firms that were successful in the United States during the early 1990s, but have given up market share to new competitors in recent years. One of these firms may maintain its old strategic plan of simply trying to provide a specific type of computer to U.S. customers. The other firm may revise its strategic plan to revise the product it offers and the geographical market that it serves. It may offer a variety of computers to accommodate customers' various needs. It may also develop software packages to complement its computers. Furthermore, it may attempt to serve foreign markets as well. This revised strategic plan gives the firm more ways to maintain or increase its market share.

ORGANIZATIONAL STRUCTURE   An important management decision is the organizational structure, which identifies job descriptions for each job position and the relationships among those positions. Organizational structure is not a one-time decision, as it must be revised according to changes in the firm's strategic plan. A properly developed organizational structure can result in a low level of operating expenses. The organizational structure determines the manner by which human resources are allocated to complete various tasks.

In recent years, the organizational structures of many firms were revised to make more efficient use of human resources. Specifically, firms downsized their work force and delegated more responsibilities to those human resources whose job positions were not eliminated. The downsizing was commonly intended to achieve the same level of production at a lower cost. Consequently, firms were able to reduce their salary expenses, which enhanced their values and resulted in higher cash flows.

PRODUCTION PROCESS   A firm develops a production process to produce its products or services. The process defines how human resources are combined with other resources (such as the firm's plant and machinery) to produce the products or services.

Plant Site Decision   An important production decision is the selection of the plant site. This decision will determine the land cost. It will also determine the costs of hiring human resources and of transporting products.

Nineteenth century factories were always located near a source of water for an energy source, waste removal, or transportation of goods.

While managers want to select a plant site in an area that has low costs, they must also consider how revenue might be affected. If products can easily be transported, the optimal site may be based in a low-cost location, because the products could be sent to other locations where demand is strong. However, some locations that have a low land cost may not have an adequate supply of human resources.

Since the plant site decision can have a major impact on the firm's costs and possibly even its revenue, it can affect the firm's value. A large plant site can achieve a high production volume, but also results in high expenses. Plant site is not a one-time decision because it is reassessed whenever the firm experiences substantial growth or plans to produce new products.

Design and Layout Decisions   The design and layout decisions have a significant impact on production costs. The design represents the size and structure of the plant, while the layout is the manner by which the machinery and equipment are arranged within the plant. In recent years, many firms have begun to use flexible manufacturing, in which the layout is easily adjusted to accommodate a revision in the production process. Ideally, the layout can also be easily adjusted to accommodate a revision in the types of products produced. This allows the firms to revise their product line without incurring the costs of moving to a new site.

Another recent strategy by firms is to reduce their layout space in response to the downsizing of their work force. Consequently, these firms reduced not only their salary expenses but also their expenses resulting from renting or owning work space. This strategy reduced expenses further, resulting in larger cash flows and therefore higher firm values.

Quality Decision   The quality of the product that the firm produces is dependent on the production process used and the commitment of employees to quality. The higher the quality, the higher the level of customer satisfaction, which affects the product's reputation. Thus, the demand for a product is dependent on its quality and on the production process used. In an effort to increase the amount of referrals and repeat buyers, firms have recently begun to pay more attention to quality and customer satisfaction.

The emphasis on ensuring quality throughout the entire production process is referred to as total quality management (TQM). While TQM is used in various ways, it typically involves defining a desired quality level, developing a production process that can achieve that quality level, and controlling the quality level over time. TQM has been especially successful when employees have been allowed to help develop the production process intended to achieve the desired quality level. It has also been successful when assigning employee teams to monitor and control quality. Since higher quality can lead to higher customer satisfaction, it results in higher sales and therefore in higher cash flows to the firm.

Other Decisions Related to the Production Process   Firms may also improve the production process with the use of technology. They have automated many parts of the production process so that tasks are completed by machines without the help of human resources.

A final method of improving the production process is to produce in large volume so that economies of scale can be realized. Products that have a relatively high level of fixed costs can benefit from economies of scale.

MOTIVATING EMPLOYEES   Employees tend to be more satisfied with their jobs if they are provided (1) compensation that is aligned with their performance, (2) job

These Levi Strauss employees are happy because they have a casual and fun work environment.

security, (3) a flexible work schedule, and (4) employee involvement programs. Firms have been unable to offer job security, as they continually attempt to reduce their operating expenses by downsizing their work force. However, they have begun to offer compensation that is tied to employee performance, more flexible work schedules, and more employee involvement programs. To the extent that job satisfaction can motivate employees to improve their performance, firms may be able to achieve a higher production level by providing greater job satisfaction. Therefore, they may be able to increase cash flows (lower production costs per employee), and increase their value as a result of motivating human resources.

MANAGING EMPLOYEES   Beyond motivation, firms have some control over how well their employees perform. First, they have control at the hiring stage. Proper recruiting and screening can result in the selection of well-qualified employees. Firms can also control how well their employees perform by developing their skills. Specifically, firms focus on developing employees' technical, decision-making, customer service, safety, and human relations skills. Firms can also control employee performance by establishing proper procedures for evaluation. Employees should be informed about the criteria that are used to evaluate their performance and the weight assigned to each criterion. Proper management of human resources can help firms achieve a high level of production, which may enhance their value.

Marketing Decisions

Each firm uses a marketing mix, which represents the combination of its product, pricing, distribution, and promotion strategies used to sell products and services.

PRODUCT STRATEGIES   The success of a firm is highly influenced by the product that the firm is attempting to sell. Once a firm determines the product (or product line) that it will offer, it must identify its target market so that it can determine the profile of the customers that it must attract. As time passes, firms may attempt to revise their existing products so that they can differentiate their products from those of competitors. To create new products, they may also invest in research and development. In general, strategies to create or improve products can enhance the firm's revenue, which can result in higher cash flows and therefore in a higher firm value.

PRICING STRATEGIES   The revenue that a firm generates is directly related to the price charged for its product. The pricing decision can be influenced by the production cost and by competitor prices. Pricing a product too high can limit the quantity that consumers demand. However, pricing a product too low may not allow for sufficient profits. Proper pricing decisions can increase future cash flows (higher revenue) and can therefore increase the firm's value.

DISTRIBUTION STRATEGIES   The distribution channel determines the path of a product from the producer to the consumer. It determines the different locations where the product will be available. The firm's distribution strategies will influence the amount of customers that the product reaches. It may also affect the costs of delivering a product from the point of production to the consumer. Therefore, proper distribution strategies can enhance the firm's future cash flows.

Baseball card manufacturers such as Topps struggle with pricing, distribution, and promotion issues. Oversupply drives decreased demand from collectors and underproduction leads to lower revenues from sales.

SMALL BUSINESS SURVEY

What Are the Major Concerns of Small Businesses?

A survey of small businesses was conducted to determine their major concerns. The businesses were segmented into two groups: those with annual sales of less than $3 million and those with annual sales of more than $3 million. Various types of business problems are listed, along with the proportion of firms in each group that believes the problem poses a serious threat.

Problem	Firms with Less Than $3 Million in Sales	Firms with More Than $3 Million in Sales
Inadequate planning	58%	33%
Inadequate financing	48%	21%
Inadequate managerial skills of some employees in key positions	46%	23%
Not prepared for economic downturns	37%	26%
Inability to respond to market changes	30%	31%
Environmental regulations	29%	38%
Nonenvironmental regulations	18%	22%
Litigation (such as defending against lawsuits)	15%	21%
Employee theft or fraud	13%	11%
Foreign competition	11%	24%

Many of the major concerns detected by this survey were discussed in this text. Some of the concerns reflect exposure to economic conditions (economic downturns), industry conditions (regulations), and global conditions (foreign competition). Other concerns are focused on the firm's management (planning), marketing (response to market changes), and financing.

PROMOTION STRATEGIES   Firms use promotion strategies to increase the acceptance of products through special deals, advertising, and publicity. They commonly use promotions to supplement their product, pricing, and distribution strategies. New products are promoted to introduce them to potential customers. In addition, many popular products are promoted to protect their image and retain their market share. Effective promotion strategies enhance cash flows (by increasing revenue) and can therefore enhance the firm's value.

Finance Decisions

The finance function determines how the firm obtains and invests funds, as summarized next.

FINANCING STRATEGIES Firms use financing strategies to obtain the amount and type of financing desired. They may borrow from various financial institutions, such as commercial banks, finance companies, or savings institutions. Alternatively, they may issue bonds if they have a national reputation and need a large amount of funds.

If firms prefer to obtain equity financing instead of debt financing, they may attempt to obtain funds from a venture capital firm. Alternatively, they may issue stock if they need a large amount of funds. Proper financing strategies can enable the firm to obtain funds at a low cost and can therefore increase the firm's value.

BUSINESS INVESTMENT STRATEGIES Firms use investing strategies to allocate their funds across their business operations. They use capital budgeting to determine whether potential projects are feasible and should be implemented. For the project to be feasible, the present value of the project's cash flows must exceed its initial outlay. The discount rate used to discount future cash flows is based on the firm's cost of funds used to support the project. If the firm can obtain funds for the project at a relatively low cost, the project has a better chance of being considered feasible. Since many projects require substantial funding and are irreversible, capital budgeting decisions can have a major impact on the value of the firm.

Summary of Business Strategies

The most common types of business strategies are summarized in Exhibit 21.1. Notice from this exhibit that the primary impact of most management strategies is

Exhibit 21.1
Summary of Key Business Functions

Type of Management Strategy	Primary Impact of Strategy Decision Is on:	
	Cash Inflows	Cash Outflows
Planning	✓	✓
Organizational Structure		✓
Plant Site		✓
Production Design		✓
Production Layout		✓
Production Quality	✓	✓
Motivating Employees		✓
Managing Employees		✓
Type of Marketing Strategy		
Product Strategies	✓	
Pricing Strategies	✓	
Distribution Strategies	✓	
Promotion Strategies	✓	
Type of Finance Strategy		
Financing Strategies		✓
Investment Strategies	✓	

on the firm's cash outflows, since the strategies determine the cost of utilizing human resources and other resources. Conversely, the primary impact of most marketing strategies is on the firm's cash inflows, since the strategies determine the amount of revenue generated.

RELATIONSHIPS AMONG BUSINESS STRATEGIES

While the management, marketing, and finance decisions are distinctly different, they are all related. That is, the management decisions can be determined only after considering marketing information, while marketing decisions can be determined only after considering management information. Finance decisions are dependent on management and marketing information.

Relationship between Organizational Structure and Production

To illustrate how the management, marketing, and finance decisions are related, consider a firm that produces office desks and distributes them to various retail office furniture outlets. The organizational structure will be partially dependent on the product mix (a marketing decision). If the firm diversifies its product line to include office lamps, file cabinets, and bookcases, its organizational structure will have to specify who is assigned to produce and manage these other products. The selection of a plant site must be large enough, and the firm's design and layout must be flexible enough, to allow for the production of these other products.

Relationship between Pricing and Production Strategies

The firm's plant site, design, and layout decisions are also influenced by the pricing of the office furniture (another marketing decision). If the pricing strategy is to price the furniture high, the sales volume will be smaller. The firm's plant site, design, and layout should allow for sufficient (but not excessive) work space to achieve the relatively low production level needed to accommodate the expected sales volume.

If the firm prices its office furniture more competitively, it will anticipate a much larger sales volume. In this case, it would use a plant site, design, and layout to achieve a much larger level of production. Most firms choose the type of target market they wish to pursue and then implement a pricing strategy before deciding on the plant's site, design, and layout. That is, the pricing strategy dictates the level of production needed, which influences the plant site, design, and layout.

Relationship between Pricing and Distribution Strategies

The firm's pricing strategy also influences its distribution strategy. If the pricing strategy is intended to focus only on wealthy customers, the office furniture may be distributed exclusively to upscale outlets. However, if the prices are set lower to attract a wide variety of customers, the furniture will be distributed across many outlets to achieve broad coverage.

Relationship between Pricing and Promotion Strategies

The firm's promotion strategies will also be affected by the pricing strategy. If the pricing strategy is intended to focus only on wealthy customers, the promotions will be targeted exclusively toward those customers. However, if the prices are set lower to attract a wide variety of customers, the promotions will be targeted to cover a much broader group of potential customers.

The amount of funds spent on promotion will influence the firm's sales volume and therefore the production level. Consequently, the plant site, design, and layout decisions must consider the amount of promotion planned by the firm.

Relationship between Pricing and Financing Strategies

The firm's finance decisions will be dependent on its pricing decisions. If the firm is using a pricing strategy that will result in a relatively low level of sales (and therefore a low level of production), it will need a small amount of funds to support that production level. However, if the firm uses a pricing strategy that will result in a high level of sales (and therefore a high level of production), it will need a much larger amount of funds to support that production level. If the firm needs a relatively small amount of funds, it may decide to borrow from a commercial bank. However, if it needs a large amount of funds, it may issue bonds. It may also need to consider using some equity financing if the amount of funds needed would exceed its debt capacity.

GLOBAL BUSINESS

Integrating Business Functions on a Global Basis

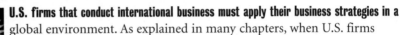 **U.S. firms that conduct international business must apply their business strategies in a** global environment. As explained in many chapters, when U.S. firms apply a particular business function (such as managing resources, marketing, or financing) to international business, they must consider the unique characteristics of the foreign country. The business functions that are applied to a particular foreign country are integrated. That is, the international management of resources is integrated with the international marketing strategies and financing strategies.

To recognize how these functions are integrated, consider the case of IBM, which generates more than 60 percent of its sales in foreign countries. IBM produces and sells a variety of computer products in numerous foreign countries. Its production decision of how much to produce in a particular country is influenced by input from the marketing function on the expected demand for each product in that area. The number of employees to be hired for production in a specific country is also dependent on the expected demand for IBM's products in that country. The demand for IBM's products within a particular country is partially affected by the degree to which the products are promoted there. The marketing function can consider this information when forecasting the demand for various products in a country. Because of the large demand for its products in Europe, IBM's European production facilities are massive. IBM's Latin American facilities are not as large because the demand for its products is much smaller than it is in Europe.

IBM's decisions regarding the design of various products are influenced by the marketing research that obtains feedback from customers who have purchased IBM's products or from surveys of prospective customers. The design of a product may be revised in a particular country if the marketing research determines that prospective customers in that country would prefer a revised design.

IBM's financing decisions for a particular country are based on the production and marketing decisions, which dictate the amount of funds that are needed to support the planned production volume and the marketing efforts. The larger IBM's

Software that Integrates Business Activities

Ten years ago, an important software category for today's businesses didn't even exist. Workgroup software packages are designed to help coordinate the various functions of a business, offering new means of communication and new methods of sharing work and information. In the mid-1990s, their popularity skyrocketed in the business world. Because Lotus Development Corporation held the premier position in this software category with its Lotus Notes package; it was acquired by IBM in 1995.

A workgroup software package typically runs on a computer network. Rather than having a single, well-defined function, workgroup packages offer a collection of features that help users share work. Among these features are the following:

➤ *Electronic Mail:* Workgroup packages offer sophisticated electronic mail capabilities, allowing users to exchange messages and files across the network. Advanced packages also offer gateways to other mail systems, such as the Internet. As a result, users throughout the world can communicate.

➤ *Time Management and Scheduling:* Packages provide the ability to create centralized company schedules and individual calendars, accessible by all who have the proper security.

➤ *Document Sharing Systems:* Packages allow users to create databases that contain or point to documents they are working on. Using these systems allows remote users to collaborate on the same document.

➤ *External Linkages:* Most packages provide users with the ability to call into the system and conduct activities remotely (for example, from a hotel room). Some packages also incorporate fax handling capability, allowing faxes to be sent, received, and routed automatically by the package.

➤ *Discussions and Conferencing:* Packages provide on-line discussion capability, allowing users to conduct conferences between remote sites and keeping a record of the proceedings.

➤ *Work Flow Processing:* Packages can be programmed to allow specific work flows, such as the process of creating and sending a bill, to be completely automated. Once a user initiates a specific job, the software keeps track of each step in the process and, once a given step has been completed, automatically routes it to the next step.

➤ *Security:* Packages allow users to designate security for documents, preventing unauthorized reading or editing.

Many managers believe that the real benefit of workgroup software is its use as a platform for further development. It is designed to be customized with add-on products, such as fax servers, video conferencing, project management software, and a host of industry-specific applications.

anticipated production and marketing expenses in a particular country, the more funds will be needed to cover these expenses. IBM obtains substantial financing for its operations in Europe because it needs a large amount of funds to support its substantial European operations. It requires a smaller amount of funds in Latin America because its operations are not as large.

Overall, this brief description of IBM illustrates how its management of resources, marketing, and financing decisions for any particular country are integrated, just as they are integrated when managing its operations in the United States.

Summary of Relationships among Business Strategies

Exhibit 21.2 shows the typical sequence of business functions. Many functions can be considered only after deciding on the type of product that will be produced and sold. The management and marketing decisions can be made after identifying the product (or product line). Once all management and marketing decisions are made, the amount of funds needed to support the business can be determined. The finance decision of how to finance the firm is dependent on how much funds are needed. All of these key business decisions will be periodically reassessed as the firm's business grows and its product line expands.

Exhibit 21.2
Common Sequence of
Business Functions

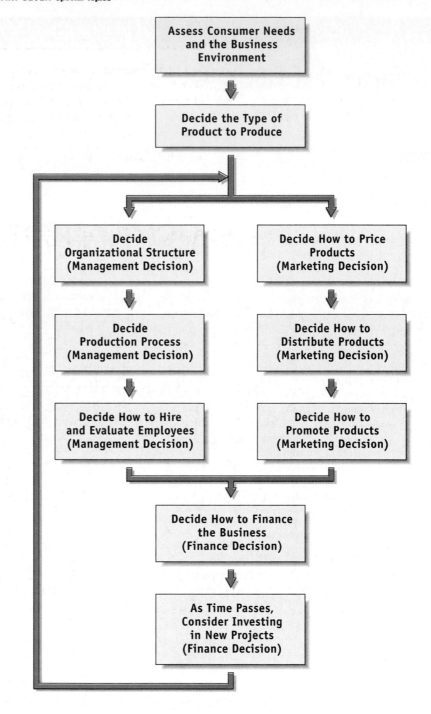

While accounting and information systems are not illustrated in this exhibit, they are needed to make proper business decisions. The accounting function is used to monitor the firm's financial condition and assess performance of previous management, marketing, and finance decisions. It can also be used to detect inefficient business operations so that they can be revised to reduce expenses.

Information systems are continually used to compile and analyze information about the firm's operations. The information can be used to help managers make proper management, marketing, and finance decisions.

BUSINESS STRATEGIES IMPLEMENTED BY IBM

3 Illustrate how one particular firm (IBM) recently made several key business decisions to increase its value.

To illustrate how a single firm must consider all the business strategies described throughout the text, recent strategies by IBM are summarized next. The various statements by IBM that follow were contained in IBM's annual report.

Mission and Strategic Plan of IBM

The primary mission of IBM is as follows:

> *We strive to lead in the creation, development, and manufacture of the industry's most advanced information technologies, including computer systems, software, networking systems, storage devices, and microelectronics.*

The mission for most firms is not changed very often, but the strategic plan is periodically revised in response to new business opportunities. IBM's recent strategic plan is as follows:

> *Setting strategies is our single-highest priority because they are critical to growth and building shareholder value. For more than a year now, we have been working on a dozen or so business and technology strategies.*

IBM's Social Responsibilities

IBM meets its social responsibilities by focusing on education and the environment, as explained next:

> *Our greatest focus . . . was a program known as Reinventing Education. Aimed at kindergarten through grade 12, this program calls upon local U.S. school districts to partner with IBM in a dramatic and deeply rooted restructuring of primary and secondary schools . . . . Technology will also play a vital role at the Education Village [created by North Carolina's school system next to IBM's Charlotte facilities]. Not only will it comprise part of the classroom curriculum and teacher training, but it will also connect schools to community centers and to students' homes.*

The expenditures by IBM not only demonstrate social responsibility but also may enable IBM to sell more computers to school systems.

IBM's Assessment of Its Industry

Since IBM is in the information technology industry, it closely monitors this industry and expects that its future performance will be influenced by industry trends:

▌▌ *Our industry, information technology—is a growth industry. In fact, it's just beginning to rev up . . . . Information technology will revolutionize every institution in our society— governments, schools, post offices, libraries, and of course, every form of commercial enterprise. Information technology will fundamentally alter the way individuals deal with these institutions and with each other . . . . We must provide products and services that improve customers' competitive position; that enhance their own customer service; that increase their productivity; that enrich their personal lives.* ▌▌

IBM's Penetration in Foreign Markets

IBM has penetrated numerous foreign markets where competition in the information technology industry is not as intense as in the United States:

▌▌ *We opened seven subsidiaries in Eastern Europe and Northern Asia . . . . We are on track to develop, within the next five years, billion-dollar operations in China, Eastern Europe, South Africa, and India.* ▌▌

IBM's Management Strategies

IBM's key management strategies include its organizational structure, the design and layout of its facilities, its production process, and its total quality management. Each of these strategies is discussed next.

IBM'S ORGANIZATIONAL STRUCTURE   IBM recently revised its organizational structure in two ways. First, it has downsized its work force:

▌▌ *The actions taken during the past two years to "right-size" the company have improved IBM's competitiveness in the rapidly changing market for information technology products and services. As a result, the company returned to profitability for the first time since 1990.* ▌▌

The downsizing by IBM helped reduce its operation expenses. In addition to downsizing, IBM also reorganized its employees who are responsible for selling PCs to customers:

▌▌ *Instead of being organized and managed by geography, today nearly all IBMers who call on customers belong to an industry group . . . . The logic behind the change is straightforward. Customers around the world told us they want to work with people who are familiar with the dynamics and challenges of their business.* ▌▌

IBM'S DESIGN AND LAYOUT Since IBM downsized its work force, it also revised its work space:

▌▌ *We consolidated work done by 89 data centers and now have 58—saving nearly $1 billion. By increasing our number of mobile employees and reducing work locations, we've eliminated 20 million square feet of office space worldwide. We're doing common-sense things too, like consolidating how we purchase goods and services across the company.* ▌▌

IBM'S PRODUCTION PROCESS IBM produces products in large volume to capitalize on economies of scale:

▌▌ *We are rapidly moving to common technology "building blocks" across IBM hardware units to take advantage of economies of scale.* ▌▌

A key task in planning the production process is to forecast demand for products so that the volume of products produced is adequate to accommodate the demand. This task can be extremely difficult, as illustrated by IBM's experience:

▌▌ *We didn't do well in forecasting demand for products. Demand outstripped supply in mainframes, storage devices, and certain PC models.* ▌▌

TOTAL QUALITY MANAGEMENT (TQM) Like most successful firms, IBM has increased its efforts to satisfy customers. Specifically, it has developed a variety of methods to enhance customer service:

▌▌ *Customers who need immediate help with an IBM product can call 24-hour-a-day operations, such as IBM's Help Center in the U.S.* ▌▌

IBM's Marketing Strategies

IBM's key marketing strategies include its products, pricing, and distribution. Each of these strategies is discussed next.

IBM'S PRODUCT STRATEGIES In the information technology industry, IBM and other firms continually assess their product strategies. Improvements in technology have resulted in numerous new products and revisions of existing products:

▌▌ *I [Louis Gerstner, chairman and CEO of IBM] have spent a good bit of time in our IBM labs, and I can tell you that right now, we see no limit to the pace of change for at least the next decade. And IBM will be a pacesetter. Last year we were No. 1 in the number of U.S. patents issued for the second year in a row, and our 1,298 patents last year were the most ever issued to any company in any year . . . . New products introduced in the past 12 to 18 months accounted for almost half our hardware revenues last year.*▐▌

IBM'S PRICING STRATEGIES   A review of IBM's main product lines suggests that its prices have been lowered in response to intense competition.

▐▌ *Overall, the company's hardware [product] offerings remain under price and competitive pressure . . . . It is also anticipated that the pressures on price and margin will remain for all hardware offerings . . . . Revenue from processors decreased . . . . resulting from continuing competitive pricing pressures.*▐▌

Given the intense competition throughout the industry, IBM's strategy to reduce prices may have been intended to simply maintain market share. To increase market share, it may need to capitalize on its technological advantages.

IBM'S DISTRIBUTION STRATEGIES   IBM delivers some products directly to the customer. It also distributes many of its products to retail computer stores worldwide:

▐▌ *Many customers, for example, like to simply pick up the phone and order products from us. Customers bought nearly $1 billion in products last year from our IBM Direct and PC Direct U.S. telesales operations . . . . Total PC Direct customers now number more than 100,000 . . . . Our presence in retail stores is also soaring. In Japan for example, IBM PC dealers doubled last year, from 500 to 1,000.*▐▌

IBM's Finance Strategies

IBM's key finance strategies include obtaining funds (financing) and investing funds in its businesses, as discussed next.

IBM'S FINANCING STRATEGIES   IBM recently attempted to reduce its amount of debt so that it could reduce its interest expenses:

▐▌ *Long-term debt declined $2.7 billion . . . due to the company's continuing focus on reduction of its outstanding debt obligations.*▐▌

While IBM reduced its debt, it increased its equity primarily by retaining a large amount of earnings. That is, IBM increased its use of equity financing while relying less on debt financing. As a result, Moody's Rating Service upgraded its credit rating on some of IBM's debt. Interest expenses declined by almost $700 million over a two-year period as a result of IBM's debt reduction.

IBM'S BUSINESS INVESTMENT STRATEGIES   IBM, like most firms, frequently invests in long-term projects as well as in short-term assets. While IBM reduced its work space in response to downsizing its work force, it still uses large amounts of funds on capital expenditures such as new plants and offices:

> ❚❚ *The company's capital expenditures for plant, rental machines, and other property were $3.1 billion for the year.* ❚❚

IBM also wanted to ensure that it had sufficient investment in short-term assets to maintain adequate liquidity:

> ❚❚ *Current assets increased $2.1 billion due to increases in cash . . . and marketable securities. . . . [C]urrent liabilities decreased $3.9 billion . . . with declines of $2.5 billion in short-term debt.* ❚❚

Conclusion about IBM's Strategies

Even with all the management, marketing, and finance decisions made to enhance shareholder wealth, IBM recognized that it must strive for continual improvement:

> ❚❚ *We, all of us at IBM, have a lot of work, a lot of change, a lot of rebuilding left to do if we are to complete our transformation.* ❚❚

To assess how IBM's strategies affected its performance, Exhibit 21.3 shows the income statement for 1992 (before these strategies were implemented) and in 1995

Exhibit 21.3
Income Statement for IBM Before and After Implementing Strategies

	Before Strategies Were Implemented (1992)	After Strategies Were Implemented (1995)
Revenue	$64,523	$71,940
Cost of Goods Sold	35,069	41,573
Gross Profit	29,454	30,367
Operating Expenses	37,693	21,829
Earnings Before Interest and Taxes	(8,239)	8,538
Interest	787	725
Earnings Before Taxes	(9,026)	7,813
Taxes	(2,161)	3,635
Earnings After Taxes	(6,865)	4,178

Note: Figures are in millions of dollars.

Exhibit 21.4
Change in IBM's Revenue, Expenses, and Earnings

Note: Figures are in millions of dollars.

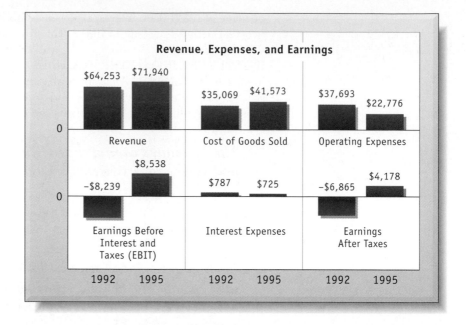

(after these strategies were implemented). The revenue was higher in 1995, while the operating expenses were about $15 billion less in 1995 than in 1992. Consequently, the earnings before interest and taxes were much better in 1995. Also, the interest expenses were reduced by 1995, which further improved IBM's earnings.

A comparison of some of the key income statement items for IBM between 1992 and 1995 is disclosed in Exhibit 21.4. The large decline in operating expenses was primarily attributed to downsizing the work force and the facilities.

Recall that ratio analysis is commonly used to assess a firm's liquidity, efficiency, and financial leverage. These financial characteristics are compared over time to show how IBM improved its financial condition as a result of implementing its strategies. Exhibit 21.5 shows that IBM was able to increase its liquidity, increase its efficiency, and reduce its degree of financial leverage.

BUSINESS DILEMMA

Integrating Business Decisions at College Health Club

Sue Kramer, president of College Health Club (CHC), is reconsidering the business plan she developed about one year ago when she established the health club. Her key decisions were as follows:

MANAGEMENT DECISIONS
1. Site of the facilities
2. Design and layout of facilities

MARKETING DECISIONS
1. Customer profile (target market)
2. Product (service) offered

Exhibit 21.5
Change in IBM's Liquidity, Efficiency, and Financial Leverage

Note: Figures are in millions of dollars.

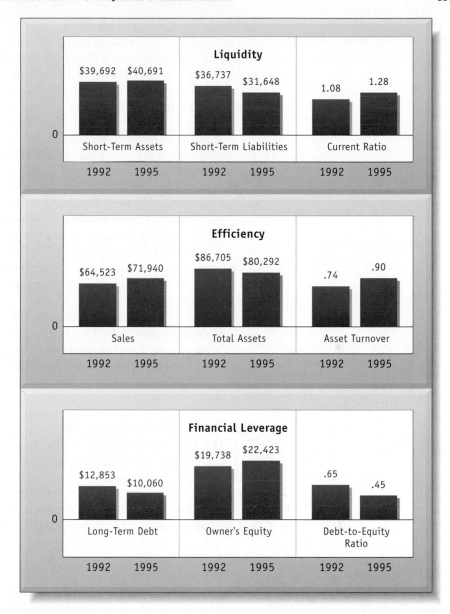

3 Pricing
4 Promotion

FINANCE DECISIONS
1 Financing (how much funding?)

Dilemma

Sue is considering the possibility of establishing another health club and needs to assess how these decisions are related. Offer your input on how the health club site, membership price, design and layout, and promotion strategies are influenced by the target market.

Solution

The first decision to be made is the product or service to be offered. Sue is planning to expand her existing service (health club) by purchasing another health club in a nearby college town. The health club would be primarily targeted toward the college students in that town. Since the target market is college students, Sue would select a site that is near the local college in that town.

The next decision is pricing or determining the annual membership fee. This decision affects many other decisions because it influences the size of the membership (and therefore the size of the facilities needed). If a low price is charged, the health club will attract more members, and larger facilities will be needed.

The design and layout of the facilities could be determined, based on the estimated number of customers (members) that may be using the health club at a given time. The design and layout should also allow for growth in membership over time. However, Sue does not want too much extra space, since she would incur higher expenses (whether leasing or purchasing facilities) for using extra space.

The promotion decisions will be intended to attract enough customers to fill up the facilities. The promotions would be targeted toward college students, who represent the target market.

While the pricing decision will affect the total revenue, the decisions about facilities and promotions will affect the total expenses. Sue can use her decisions to estimate the future cash flows resulting from a new healthclub and determine whether to establish a new health club. If she decides to invest in a new health club, she can assess the cash flows to determine how much funds she would need to borrow.

Additional Issues for Discussion

1 Can Sue copy her business plan that she used for CHC when developing a business plan for a new health club near a different college campus?

2 Why might the estimated expenses of the new health club be much different from the existing health club?

3 Assume that Sue decides to establish a second health club that focuses on executives instead of college students. What types of business decisions would be affected?

SUMMARY

1 A firm's value is equal to the present value of its expected future cash flows. The cash flows in any period are the difference between cash inflows (revenue) and cash outflows (expenses or taxes).

2 When management, marketing, and finance decisions are implemented in a manner that will increase cash flows, these decisions can enhance the firm's value. Management decisions focus on using human and other resources to produce products or services. Thus, these decisions typically affect cash outflows (expenses). Marketing decisions tend to focus on increasing revenue and therefore affect cash inflows. Finance decisions can affect interest expenses due to financing, and future cash flows due to the firm's business investments.

3 IBM applied several key business decisions to increase its value. Specifically, IBM used

➤ management decisions such as downsizing to reduce cash outflows,

➤ product and pricing decisions to increase (or at least maintain) cash inflows, and

➤ finance decisions to reduce its financial leverage.

REVIEW QUESTIONS

1 Discuss IBM's marketing strategy.

2 Discuss the relationship among business strategies used in management today.

3 Explain the stages during which a firm has control over its employees.

4 Explain how a firm can motivate employees to create job satisfaction.

5 Discuss how the firm's promotion strategy relates to its pricing strategy.

6 Explain why the financing that IBM obtains for its European operations is larger than that of its Latin American operations.

7 Discuss how IBM has revised its organizational structure.

8 How can a manager determine the value of a project?

9 Why is it important for a business to obtain funds at a low cost?

10 Discuss total quality management (TQM) as it relates to production.

DISCUSSION QUESTIONS

1 Assume you are a production manager. Why is TQM important for your firm to be competitive in your industry environment?

2 Assume you are the promotional manager of a well-known consumer products firm. You have been given the assignment of developing a promotional strategy for a new soap powder that is about to be introduced. Discuss.

3 Discuss why a target market should be selected before determining a pricing strategy or production capacity (or both).

4 Assume you are a marketing manager. How will your marketing decisions affect the value of the firm?

5 Assume you are a strategic planner for a computer manufacturer. Your mission is to develop a production strategy to move your organization into the twenty-first century. Discuss.

RUNNING YOUR OWN BUSINESS

1 Your business plan to make your business successful contains a set of management strategies (which includes production), marketing strategies, and finance strategies. If you have completed this "Running Your Own Business" exercise in the previous chapters, you already have addressed many important decisions on management, marketing, and finance. Provide a brief and general summary of the management (including production) plan for your business idea.

2 Provide a brief and general summary of the marketing plan for your business idea.

3 Provide a brief and general summary of the finance plan for your business idea.

4 Now that you have briefly summarized the management, marketing, and finance plans for your business idea, explain how the different plans are related. That is, explain how your plan for the facilities (within the management plan) is related to the type of product you plan to produce and the price you plan to charge (marketing plan). Also, explain how the financing decisions such as the amount of financing needed are dependent on your management and marketing plans.

INVESTING IN THE STOCK OF A BUSINESS

Using the annual report of the firm in which you would like to invest, complete the following:

1 Provide a brief summary of the firm's management strategies.

2 Provide a brief summary of the firm's marketing strategies.

3 Provide a brief summary of the firm's financing strategies.

4 Now that you have briefly summarized the firm's management, marketing, and finance strategies, explain how these strategies are related. For example, suggest how this firm's marketing decisions will affect its production decisions. Also, explain how the amount of financing is dependent on its marketing and production decisions.

CASE 1 Integrated Decisions at Chrysler

Bob Eaton, the CEO of Chrysler Corporation, can't find enough good people to expand as fast as he wants in global markets. Eaton laments: "For the first time in Chrysler's recent history, we have the capital available, but we don't have enough engineers and managers to grow any faster abroad than we are currently, which is about 20 percent a year."

A secondary concern at Chrysler is the need to improve upon productivity. Toyota is the world leader in productivity, requiring eighteen to twenty personnel hours to build an automobile, and is the quality leader in the industry. Chrysler requires twenty-eight personnel hours to build an automobile and is catching up to Toyota in quality.

Chrysler has become a market leader by introducing new products such as the four-door subcompact Neon, the Ram full-size pickup, and the hand-built Viper convertible. The value of Chrysler has increased dramatically because of the research and development of new products penetrating new markets in Europe and Asia.

Eaton credits Chrysler's comeback to the top to the management application of Chrysler's employees. The new management technique focuses on employee empowerment, especially in product decisions. When Chrysler sets out to create a new model or revamp an old one, it forms a team of about seven hundred people: from engineering, design, manufacturing, marketing, and finance, including specialists of all kinds. Although a vice-president chairs the group, all of the actual work is directed by leaders below that rank, and the group organizes itself as it sees fit. In essence, management works out a contract with the workgroup, setting objectives they hope to achieve, and then sets the team loose. The team does not come back unless a major problem arises.

When teams have power to create the car and responsibility to meet the budget, they do meet the budget. Because the teams are efficient and motivated to hold down costs, Chrysler is able to create a car from scratch for as little as $1.3 billion. It costs its U.S. competitors a lot more.

Questions

1 What is Chrysler's major problem?
2 How can Chrysler improve upon its efficiency?
3 How has Chrysler's management changed its planning strategy with regard to its employees?
4 How has Chrysler become a market leader?

CASE 2 Impact of Marketing Policies on Other Business Decisions

For the past few years, Wilson Foods Corporation, based in Oklahoma City, has been among the largest producers of processed pork products in the nation. One of the company's products is the Thomas E. Wilson Masterpiece ham, which was named after the company's founder. For several years now, Wilson has run a marketing sales promotion for this product each December. Customers who purchase one of these hams can send a coupon and proof of purchase to Wilson and receive a rebate of a few dollars. The total rebates paid by Wilson each year in connection with this promotional campaign amount to several million dollars.

Wilson's fiscal year ends on December 31, the same date that the Masterpiece ham promotional campaign ends. However, most of the coupons are not redeemed by customers until January. This creates a cash shortage and therefore affects the firm's financial planning at the end of the year. Janet, the controller of the company, estimates that $1.5 million of coupons will be redeemed after the end of the year.

She then notifies the sales manager of the product for which this promotional campaign was run that an additional $1.5 million of marketing expense must be recorded for that product as of December 31. The sales manager becomes upset. "We haven't even paid those coupons yet. They won't get paid until the next fiscal year. How can you justify making my division absorb a phantom expense like that? If you force us to take that 'hit,' my year-end bonus and the bonus of everyone in my division will be cut by 30 percent!"

Questions

1 Explain how the marketing (coupon) policy affects the firm's financial planning.
2 Is Janet correct that the promotional campaign will cost the firm an additional $1.5 million?
3 Is the $1.5 million expense a marketing expense or a production expense? How could a new coupon policy affect the firm's production decisions?
4 Assume that employees in the finance and production

departments are partially compensated according to the firm's earnings. Also assume that the firm's employees are upset about the coupon rebate expense at the end of the year, as they believe it reduces earnings and therefore their compensation. Do they have a legitimate complaint?

VIDEO CASE Integrated Solutions to a Firm's Problems

 When a California defense contractor, no longer in the Pentagon's good graces, abruptly had to stop buying parts it had contracted from Ace Company a dozen years ago, the small Boise, Idaho, manufacturer and machine shop was shellshocked.

Ace had invested heavily in the defense job, hiring and training people and buying equipment. Now it had to decide whether to liquidate its assets and pay off its creditors or borrow more money to continue. It stayed in business, knowing that the going would be rough. Henceforth it could borrow no more and must survive on cash flow alone. It relied on its suppliers to provide credit until it could make its payments. There were job cuts, and salaries of those who remained were frozen. President Raliegh Jensen took a pay cut.

He also took a hard look at company operations. A way of doing things eventually evolved, he says, that— relying on employees' help—narrowed down to honest commitment, on-time delivery, and quality parts.

Since they are thus associated with the customer, Jensen says, they have a heightened interest in the parts' quality. "Quality awareness is a characteristic that selected individuals instill in the rest of the group," he says, adding that a no-compromise attitude on quality has taken years to develop at his company and has required management dedication.

Ace has been split into groups, none containing more than twenty of its ninety employees, and each is a profit center with its own quarterly profit and loss statement. Groups share tools and machinery and form purchasing and marketing alliances. But they don't necessarily go to one another for work they don't do themselves. They are free to get it done on the outside.

The managers of the firm's different units were allowed to share the firm's profits as an incentive to make good decisions.

Employees, who are polled on their group managers' effectiveness, get bonuses on the basis of how well their groups do and for good individual attendance. As many as thirteen employees have missed no time for any reason in a whole year.

Jensen says Ace's structure "would probably not work for large corporations," but "we do not plan on being a large corporation." It has worked for Ace.

Sales have risen an average of 15.6 percent a year for a decade. The company has no complaints about profits.

Questions

1 What business strategy should Ace Company use so that it does not ever experience such a severe effect (like the effect twelve years ago) if one of its customers stops buying its parts?

2 Ace Company attempted to improve its cash flow by implementing policies to increase revenue and reduce expenses. What policy did Ace use to increase revenue? What policy did Ace use to reduce expenses?

3 How will the profit-sharing policy improve the firm's financial situation?

THE *Coca-Cola* COMPANY ANNUAL REPORT PROJECT

The following questions apply concepts learned in this chapter to The Coca-Cola Company. Review The Coca-Cola Company annual report when answering these questions.

1 How do you think The Coca-Cola Company's marketing and manufacturing of Coke soft drink are related?

2 How do you think The Coca-Cola Company's plans for future manufacturing are related to its financing decisions?

3 How do you think The Coca-Cola Company's marketing and financing tasks are related?

4 Based on what you have learned throughout this annual report project, discuss how The Coca-Cola Company integrates marketing, finance, and production to achieve the company's ultimate goal—maximizing shareholder value over time.

IN-TEXT STUDY GUIDE

Answers are in an appendix at the back of the book.

True or False

1 The means by which a firm uses its employees and other resources are independent of the opportunities that exist and the types of business projects that the firm implements.

2 In deciding plant location, land cost in some areas may be extremely high and may not have an adequate supply of human resources.

3 A firm's pricing strategy never influences its distribution strategy.

4 The firm's cash flow in any particular period is equal to its cash inflows minus the cash outflows.

5 Organizational structure is always a one-time decision and can never be revised.

6 Design and layout decisions have a significant impact on production costs.

7 Finance decisions are independent of management and marketing information.

8 When U.S. firms apply a particular business function (such as managing resources, marketing, or financing) to international business, they must consider the unique characteristics of the foreign country.

9 Beyond motivation, firms have some control over how well their employees perform.

10 A review of IBM's main product lines suggests that its prices have been raised in response to intense competition.

Multiple Choice

11 The combination of a firm's product, pricing, distribution, and promotion strategies used to sell products and services is a:

a) production schedule.
b) PERT diagram.
c) marketing mix.
d) GANTT chart.
e) promotional strategy.

12 The process that defines how human resources are combined with other resources to produce products or services is the:

a) financial process.
b) marketing process.
c) distribution channel.
d) net present value.
e) production process.

13 Products that have a relatively high level of fixed costs can normally benefit from:

a) economies of scale.
b) higher-priced strategies.
c) curtailing promotional strategies.
d) eliminating distribution channels.
e) more government regulations.

14 The path of a product from the producer to the consumer is determined by the:

a) GANTT chart.
b) PERT diagram.
c) production schedule.
d) distribution channel.
e) advertising campaign.

15 If small firms prefer to obtain equity financing instead of debt financing, they may most likely attempt to obtain funds from a(n):

a) Small Business Administration.
b) venture capital firm.
c) bank.
d) insurance company.

e) commercial finance company.

16 The primary impact of most marketing strategies is on the firm's:
a) social responsibilities.
b) GANTT chart.
c) PERT diagram.
d) net present value.
e) cash inflows.

17 Firms use _____ to determine whether potential projects are feasible and should be implemented.
a) production schedules
b) organizational charts
c) grapevine techniques
d) capital budgeting
e) competitive reactions

18 The typical driving force to enhance a firm's value is its:
a) earnings. b) debt.
c) liabilities. d) liquidity.
e) asset turnover.

19 The opportunities and direction of the firm's business are identified by their:
a) production schedule.
b) advertising plan.
c) strategic plan.
d) channels of distribution.
e) pricing strategy.

20 A structure that identifies job descriptions for each job position and the relationships among those positions is the:
a) leadership function.
b) organizational structure.
c) control process.
d) planning process.
e) mission statement.

21 The quality of the product produced by the firm is dependent on the production process used and the:
a) commitment of employees to quality.
b) grapevine techniques.
c) chain of command.
d) span of control.
e) organizational chart.

22 Employees tend to be more satisfied with their jobs if they are provided with the following, except for:
a) employee involvement programs.
b) job security.
c) isolation.
d) flexible work schedules.
e) compensation that is aligned with their performance.

23 Most business decisions that are intended to increase the firm's value can be classified as management, marketing, and _____ functions.
a) job sharing
b) competitive
c) union
d) finance
e) steering committee

24 The means by which employees and other resources (such as machinery) are used by the firm is:
a) unionism.
b) quality circles.
c) steering committees.
d) procedures.
e) management.

25 The selection of a plant site will determine the land cost, the cost of hiring human resources, and:
a) production layout.
b) the cost of transporting products.
c) process layout.
d) production control.
e) dispatching.

26 The emphasis on ensuring quality throughout the entire production process is referred to as:
a) quality circles.
b) logistics.
c) subcontracting.
d) outsourcing.
e) total quality management.

27 Firms use _____ strategies to increase the acceptance of products through special deals, advertising, and publicity.
a) pricing
b) product
c) promotion
d) distribution
e) strategic planning

28 The primary impact of most management strategies is on the firm's:
a) cash outflows.
b) social responsibilities.
c) trade credit.
d) leverage position.
e) competition.

29 The accounting function is used to assess performance of previous management, marketing, and finance decisions and to monitor the firm's:
a) site location.
b) financial condition.
c) layout decisions.

d) employee turnover.

e) safety record.

30 _____ are continually used to compile and analyze information about the firm's operations.

a) Leadership functions

b) Organizing functions

c) Information systems

d) Planning processes

e) Motivating functions

31 Some of the key management decisions are focused on the following, except for:

a) strategic planning.

b) wearing safety equipment.

c) determining the production process.

d) determining the organizational structure.

e) managing employees.

32 How funds are obtained and invested by the firm is determined by the:

a) finance function.

b) marketing function.

c) organizing function.

d) human resource plan.

e) advertising strategy.

33 The pricing decision is influenced mostly by the production cost and by:

a) size of the firm.

b) competitor prices.

c) social responsibility.

d) business ethics.

e) public relations.

34 U.S. firms that conduct international business must apply their business strategies in a:

a) global environment.

b) cartel arrangement.

c) noncompetitive spirit.

d) tariff country.

e) quota country.

35 Firms can control how well their employees perform by developing the following employee skills, except for:

a) technical skills.

b) decision-making skills.

c) customer service skills.

d) competitive instinct personalities.

e) safety skills.

Exhibit 21.6
Institute of Management and Administration (IOMA) Web site

http://starbase.ingress.com/ioma/

Directory of Business Information on the World Wide Web

A comprehensive directory of business information on the World Wide Web (WWW) is maintained by the Institute of Management and Administration (IOMA) (Exhibit 21.6). It features links to sources of business information, organized by business function, as well as links to up-to-date sources of business news.

I.O.M.A.
Institute of Management & Administration

Welcome to the Institute Of Management and Administration, *Information Services for Professionals* and your guide to business resources on the Internet. IOMA, a leading publisher of management and business information, is now offering sample articles from many of our newsletters, as well as 90-day trial subscriptions, to our Web visitors. Whether managing a law or accounting office, a defined contribution investment plan, or a computer network, professionals from virtually every industry can find invaluable, career-enhancing information in our newsletters.

We now feature all of IOMA's 27 newsletters which are updated every month.

IOMARATE **Up to the minute quarterly figures for IOMA's ratings of the most popular 401(k) investments!**

Please sign our guest book and help us update and improve our service.

The following is a directory of business-related Internet resources listed alphabetically by topic. You can scroll through the entire directory or jump from section to section using these links:

Competitive Intelligence and Strategy ● Corporate Finance and Investment
● Credit Management ● Design and Construction
● Financial Management, Accounting and Taxation ● Human Resources and Benefits
● Information Systems ● Insurance and Risk ● Internet Marketing
● Legal Resources ● Other Business Directories
● Purchasing,Inventory and Supplier Mgmt ● Sales and Marketing
● Small Business ● Usenet Newsgroups

How to Invest in Stocks

As a firm's business performance changes, so does its stock price. Since performance levels vary among firms, so do stock price movements. Investors who more effectively select the high-performing firms will typically earn higher returns on their investments. In the first eleven months of 1995, the stock price of Continental Airlines rose from $6.50 per share to $44.62 per share, or 686 percent. Thus, an investor who invested $10,000 in Continental stock at the beginning of this period would receive $78,600 by selling the stock eleven months later. Meanwhile the stock price of Tatham Offshore (an oil and gas exploration firm) declined from about $13.12 per share to $1.00 per share over that same period, which resulted in a loss of 92.35 percent. Thus, an investor who invested $10,000 in Tatham at the beginning of the period would have received just $765 by selling the stock eleven months later. Investors who understand how stock prices are affected by various factors may be more capable of selecting stocks that will generate high returns.

HOW THE FIRM'S STOCK PRICE AND VALUE ARE RELATED

A stock's price should represent the value of the firm on a per-share basis. For example, if a firm is valued at $600 million and has 20 million shares, its stock price would be:

$$\text{Stock Price} = \frac{\text{Value of Firm}}{\text{Number of Shares}}$$

$$= \frac{\$600,000,000}{20,000,000 \text{ Shares}}$$

$$= \$30 \text{ per Share}$$

As the performance of the firm increases, investors will increase their demand for the stock. Consequently, the stock price will rise.

A stock price by itself does not clearly indicate the firm's value. Consider Firms A and B, each of which has its stock priced at $40 per share. However, assume Firm A has 1 million shares outstanding and Firm B has 2 million shares. Thus, the value of Firm A is $40 million, while the value of Firm B is $80 million.

UNDERSTANDING STOCK QUOTATIONS

Stock quotations are provided by financial newspapers such as *The Wall Street Journal, Barrons,* and *Investors Business Daily.* They are also provided by *USA Today* and local newspapers. While the format of stock quotations varies among newspapers, most quotations provide similar information. Stock prices are always quoted on a per-share basis. Some of the more relevant characteristics that are quoted are summarized next. Use the stock quotations for IBM shown in Exhibit A.1 to supplement the following discussion.

Exhibit A.1
Example of a Stock Quotation

52-Week							Vol.				
Hi	Lo	Stock	Symbol	DIV	YLD	PE	in 100s	Hi	Lo	Close	Change
129	83	IBM	IBM	$1.40	1.2%	19	17,987	114½	113	113⅛	−1½

Note: These quotations are based on Sept. 6, 1996.

Fifty-Two Week Price Range

The stock's highest price and lowest price over the last fifty-two weeks is commonly quoted just to the left of the stock's name. The high and low prices indicate the range for the stock's price over the last year. Some investors use this range as an indicator of how much the stock fluctuates. Other investors compare this range with the prevailing stock price, as some investors purchase a stock only when its prevailing price is not at its fifty-two week high.

Notice that IBM's fifty-two week high price was $129 while its low price was $83 per share. The low price is about 36 percent below the high price, which suggests a wide difference over the last year. At the time IBM's stock price hit its fifty-two week low price, IBM's market value was about 36 percent less than its market value at the time its stock price reached its fifty-two week high.

Symbol

Each stock has a specific symbol that is used to identify the firm. This symbol may be used to communicate trade orders to brokers. Ticker tapes displayed in brokerage firms or on financial news television shows use the symbol to identify each firm. The symbol is normally placed just to the right of the firm's name if it is shown in the stock quotations. The symbol is usually composed of two or three letters for each firm. For example, IBM's symbol is IBM, Home Depot's is HD, and Motorola's is MOT.

Dividend

The annual dividend (DIV) is commonly disclosed just to the right of the firm's name and symbol. It represents the dividends distributed to stockholders over the last year on a per-share basis. For example, a dividend quotation of $4 suggests that annual dividends of $4 per share were distributed, which represents an average of $1 per share for each quarter. The annual dollar amount of dividends paid can be determined by multiplying the dividends per share times the number of shares outstanding. If the firm that provided dividends of $4 per share had 1 million shares of stock outstanding during the last year, it paid out annual dividends of $4 million.

Some stock quotation tables also show a dividend yield (YLD) next to the annual dividend, which represents the annual dividend per share as a percentage of the stock's prevailing price. For example, if the annual dividend is $4 per share and the stock's prevailing price is $80 per share, the stock's dividend yield is:

$$\text{Dividend Yield} = \frac{\text{Dividends Paid per Share}}{\text{Prevailing Stock Price}}$$

$$= \frac{\$4}{\$80}$$

$$= 5\%$$

Exhibit A.2
Dividend Yield Trends
for Two Firms

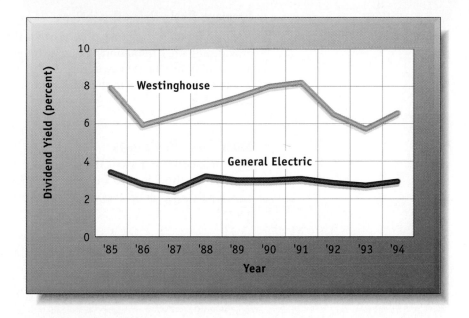

Some firms attempt to provide a somewhat stable dividend yield over time, while other firms do not. Notice from Exhibit A.2 how General Electric's dividend yield is stable, while the dividend yield of Westinghouse is very unstable.

Price-Earnings Ratio

Most stock quotations disclose the stock's price-earnings (PE) ratio, which represents the firm's prevailing stock price per share divided by the firm's earnings per share (earnings divided by number of existing shares of stock) generated over the last year. For example, if a stock is presently priced at $80 per share, and its earnings over the last year were $8 per share, the stock's price-earnings ratio is:

$$\text{Price-Earnings Ratio} = \frac{\text{Stock Price per Share}}{\text{Earnings per Share}}$$

$$= \frac{\$80}{\$10}$$

$$= 8.0$$

The price-earnings ratio is closely monitored by some investors who believe that a low PE ratio (relative to other firms in the same industry) signals that the prevailing price is too low based on its earnings. That is, the stock may be perceived as undervalued.

Volume

The volume (referred to as "Vol" or "Sales") of shares traded on the previous day is commonly provided within stock quotations. The volume is normally quoted in hundreds of shares. It is not unusual for 1 million shares of a large firm's stock to be traded on a single day. Some newspapers also show the percentage change in the volume of trading from the day before.

Previous Day's Price Quotations

The high price (Hi) and low price (Lo) for the previous trading day are normally provided by stock quotations, along with the closing price (Close) at the end of the day. In addition, the change in the price is also typically provided, and represents the increase or decrease in the stock price from the closing price on the previous trading day.

Stock Index Quotations

Most financial news reports the general performance of the stock market over a given day by citing how particular stock indexes changed. Each stock index represents a particular set of stocks. For example, the following indexes are commonly quoted:

Index	Description
Standard & Poor's (S&P) 500 Index	500 large firms
Dow Jones Industrial Average (DJIA)	30 large industrial firms
Standard & Poor's (S&P) 600 Small Cap	600 small publicly-traded firms
NASDAQ 100	100 firms traded on the NASDAQ

The two most commonly cited indexes are the S&P 500 Index and the Dow Jones Industrial Average, as they are monitored to assess general market performance for the previous day or a previous period. The firms that make up the Dow Jones Industrial Index are identified in Exhibit A.3. The S&P 500 and Dow Jones Industrial Average indexes are not proper indicators for specific industries or for smaller stocks.

MEASURING THE RETURN ON STOCKS

Stockholders can earn a return from a particular stock through a dividend or increase in the stock's price. Over a given period, the return to stockholders who invest in the stock can be measured as:

$$\text{Return} = \frac{(\text{Selling Price} - \text{Purchase Price}) + \text{Dividend}}{\text{Purchase Price}}$$

Notice that the numerator reflects a dollar amount composed of the difference between the sales price and purchase price, plus the dividend. This dollar amount is divided by the purchase price to measure the return.

For example, consider a stock that was purchased for $40 per share at the beginning of the year. Assume that a dividend of $2 per share was paid to the investor and that the stock was sold for $44 at the end of the year. The return on this stock over the year is:

$$\text{Return} = \frac{(\text{Selling Price} - \text{Purchase Price}) + \text{Dividend}}{\text{Purchase Price}}$$

$$= \frac{(\$44 - \$40) + \$2}{\$40}$$

$$= .15, \text{ or } 15\%$$

Exhibit A.3
Firms that Make Up the Dow
Jones Industrial Average Index

Firm	Recent Stock Prices	Market Value (in millions of $)
Allied Signal	45-1/8	$12,778
Aluminum Co. of America	52-1/2	9,371
American Express	44-1/8	21,521
AT&T	65-3/8	103,708
Bethlehem Steel	13-1/4	1,492
Boeing	73-3/4	25,255
Caterpillar	55-1/2	11,042
Chevron	50-1/8	32,684
Coca-Cola	75	94,589
Walt Disney	59-1/4	30,974
Dupont	64-1/2	35,795
Eastman Kodak	68-7/8	23,563
Exxon	79-3/8	98,565
General Electric	67	112,723
General Motors	46-7/8	35,035
Goodyear Tire & Rubber	40	6,094
IBM	95-1/8	54,099
International Paper	37-5/8	9,094
JP Morgan	77-1/2	14,561
McDonald's	44-1/4	30,709
Merck	59-5/8	73,666
Minnesota Mining & Mfg	64-1/4	26,998
Philip Morris	90-1/4	75,811
Procter & Gamble	89	61,138
Sears, Roebuck	39-3/8	15,294
Texaco	71	18,462
Union Carbide	37-3/4	5,123
United Technologies	90	10,981
Westinghouse Electric	15-7/8	5,702
Woolworth	15-3/8	2,045

Since the return on the stock is made up of dividends plus the increase in the stock's price, investors cannot just assess a stock's performance by its dividends. Some firms tend to pay out a higher proportion of their earnings as dividends. Yet, these firms have less ability to grow in the future, which may limit the potential increase in the stock price. Conversely, firms that retain (reinvest) most of their earnings pay low or no dividends, but are more capable of growing. Therefore, investors who are willing to invest in growth firms that do not pay dividends may benefit from larger increases in the stock price.

Return-Risk Trade-Off for Small Stocks

Some investors prefer to invest in stocks of small firms that have potential for a large increase in the stock price. They may attempt to invest before the firms have had much success, because they can purchase the stock at a relatively low price. If these

Exhibit A.4
Stock Price Trends of
Two Airline Firms

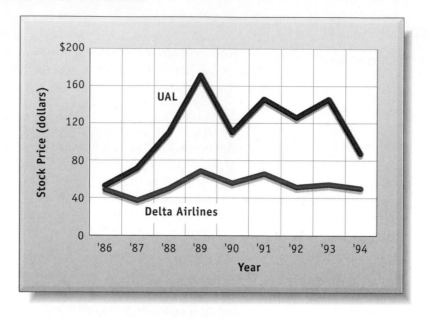

firms become successful, the share price should increase substantially. Many investors realize that if they had purchased shares of successful growing firms such as Microsoft or Compaq Computer when those firms went public, they would be millionaires now. However, for every huge success story, there are many other firms that have failed. Investors who invested in these other unsuccessful firms may have lost 100 percent of their investment.

Stocks of small firms tend to have potential for high return but also tend to have high risk. In addition, many stocks of small firms are not traded frequently, which means that investors who wish to sell their shares of these stocks are less capable of finding a buyer. This can force the investors to sell the stock at a lower price.

To illustrate how stock returns can vary among stocks, Exhibit A.4 shows returns for two different airline stocks, UAL (owner of United Airlines) and Delta Airlines. Notice how United Airlines increased substantially more than Delta during the 1987–91 period, but has declined in more recent years.

FACTORS THAT INFLUENCE STOCK PRICE MOVEMENTS

The perceived value of a firm (and therefore the stock's price) can change in response to several factors identified next.

Economic Effects

Any factor that enhances the expected performance of the firm can increase its value. For example, when economic conditions are expected to improve, the firm's performance may be expected to increase, and so should the firm's value.

Some firms are more sensitive to economic conditions, as a change in economic conditions affects the demand for some products more than others. A retail store such as Sears is more sensitive to economic conditions than a utility company. Therefore, the stock price of Sears should be more sensitive to economic conditions than the stock price of a utility company.

Market Effects

A stock's price can also be affected by general stock market conditions. Exhibit A.5 shows how the S&P 500 index (which is an index representing the stock prices of five hundred large U.S. firms) has moved over time. Notice how the market declined during some periods (such as from May 1990 to October 1990), but rose substantially during other periods (such as May 1994 to October 1995).

A stock's price may ride along with the general trend of the stock market. During some so-called **bullish** periods, stocks are heavily demanded because of investors' favorable expectations about the performance of firms. During other so-called **bearish** periods, investors are selling their stocks because of unfavorable expectations about the performance of firms. As an extreme example, the prices of stocks declined by about 22 percent when the stock market crashed on October 19, 1987. Most stocks declined by a large amount on that day. The crash illustrates how the general stock market momentum could even influence stocks of firms for which there was no new information regarding their future performance.

Industry Effects

The stock prices are also driven by industry factors. For example, expectations of future performance in the computer industry may be very favorable in a specific period, while expectations may be less favorable in the steel industry. During 1995, earnings in the aluminum industry and paper industry increased by more than 400 percent since the previous year. Meanwhile, earnings in the construction industry declined by 23 percent, while earnings in the tobacco industry declined 22 percent. Thus firms in the aluminum industry performed better than firms in the tobacco industry partially because of the industry conditions.

Characteristics of the Firm

In addition to market and industry effects, stock prices can also be affected by characteristics of the firm. For example, one firm may have better management than oth-

bullish periods in which stocks are heavily demanded because of investors' favorable expectations about the performance of firms

bearish periods in which investors are selling their stocks because of unfavorable expectations about the performance of firms

Exhibit A.5
Stock Market Trend (Based on the S&P 500 Index)

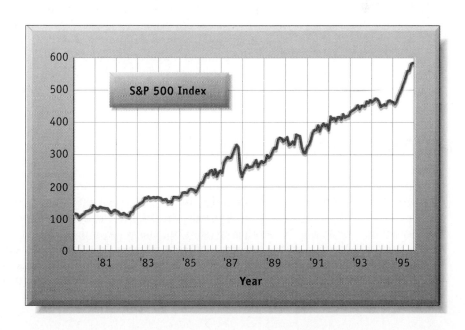

ers in the same industry, which could result in higher earnings and higher stock returns. Alternatively, a firm could experience a labor strike, which could cause its earnings and stock return to be lower than other firms in the industry. Stock price movements of firms in the same industry vary over time, even though these firms are affected by the same industry conditions.

A given firm may use many strategies that could cause its stock price return to be different from those of other firms in the industry. In general, any strategy that is likely to improve earnings will result in a higher stock price. For example, the stock price of Westinghouse rose after it had sold some businesses that were unrelated to its primary businesses. Investors may have expected that the management of Westinghouse would be more focused on what it does best. The stock price of IBM rose after IBM restructured its operations and eliminated thousands of jobs. Investors may have expected that operating expenses (such as salaries) would be reduced as a result of restructuring.

How Stock Prices Respond to New Information

The price of a stock adjusts in response to changes in the demand for the stock or in the supply of the stock for sale by investors. The price may change throughout the day. For example, Ben and Jerry's stock increased by about 21 percent on a single day in 1995 when it reported higher earnings. The new information caused investors to raise their expectations of future earnings, which reflects a higher value for the firm. This caused investors to increase the demand for the stock, which pushed the stock price up.

When Texas Instruments announced the creation of a new, powerful memory chip, its stock increased by 6 percent on a single day in 1995. The memory chip was expected to result in higher revenue and higher earnings.

The stock price of National Convenience Stores jumped 39 percent on a single day in 1995 in response to the announcement that its rival, Circle K, was attempting to acquire it. The stock price of a firm that is acquired by another firm tends to rise at the time of the acquisition, because of the strong demand for the firm's shares by the acquirer. When investors anticipate that a firm will be acquired, they purchase its shares prior to the acquisition attempt.

Just as stock prices may rise in response to favorable information, they may decline in response to unfavorable information. Italian Oven's stock price declined by 36 percent on a single day in 1996 when its chief executive officer resigned. Many investors took this information as a signal about future performance and sold their shares of Italian Oven. This caused downward pressure on the stock price.

IDENTIFYING UNDERVALUED FIRMS

Investors recognize that any new information about a firm's performance (especially its earnings) will affect its stock price. Yet, they would like to anticipate the information before all other investors so that they can take their investment position before other investors become aware of the information. For example, investors may attempt to forecast whether firms are implementing any major policies, such as acquisitions or layoffs. They use such forecasts to estimate future earnings. If their estimate of the firm's earnings is higher than that of most other investors, they may believe the firm is undervalued.

Exhibit A.6
Price-Earnings (PE) Trends for
Two Firms

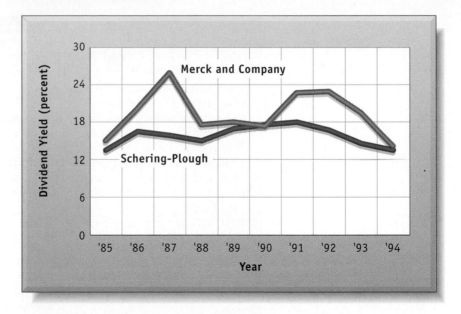

Some investors closely monitor the ratio of a firm's stock price to its earnings (called a PE ratio) to determine whether the firm's stock is undervalued. Consider Firm Z whose stock price is $20 per share and its recent annual earnings were $4 per share. This firm's PE ratio is 20/4, or 5. Assume that most firms in Firm Z's industry have a PE ratio of 9, which means that their stock prices are nine times their recent annual earnings, on average. Since Firm Z's stock price is only five times its recent earnings, some investors may believe that Firm Z's stock is undervalued. They may argue that its price should be nine times its annual earnings, or about $36. The PE ratios are shown in Exhibit A.6 for two firms over time. Notice how the PE ratio has been very stable for one firm but not the other. When the firm's PE ratio is unstable, it is not a reliable tool for determining whether the firm's stock is undervalued.

Stock Market Efficiency

stock market efficiency a term used to imply that stock prices reflect all publicly available information

Stock market efficiency is a term used to imply that stock prices reflect all publicly available information. That is, the prevailing prices have not ignored any publicly available information that could affect the firm's value. Consequently, stocks should not be overvalued or undervalued. The rationale for stock market efficiency is that there are numerous stock analysts who closely monitor stocks. If any stock was undervalued based on existing information, investors would purchase those stocks. The stock's price would be pushed higher in response to the strong demand by all the investors who recognized that the stock was undervalued. Conversely, investors holding overvalued stock would sell that stock once they recognized that it was overvalued. This action would place downward pressure on the stock's price, causing the stock price to move toward its proper level.

Even if the stock market is efficient, investors differ on how to interpret publicly available information. For example, investors may react differently to information that IBM's earnings increased by 20 percent over the last year. Some investors may view that information as old news, while others may believe it is a signal for continued high performance in the future. It is such a difference in interpretation that

SELF-SCORING EXERCISE

How Much Risk Can You Take?

Investing in the stock market isn't for those with queasy stomachs or short time horizons. The money you've earmarked for emergencies should be in liquid investments with relatively steady returns, such as money-market funds. But stocks are the backbone of a long-term portfolio for retirement or other goals that are at least ten to 15 years away.

This simple, self-scoring risk-tolerance test is designed to help you decide what percentage of your long-term money should go into stocks. As you (and your stomach) become more accustomed to the market's ups and downs, you might want to retake the test. Questions come from VALIC (The Variable Annuity Life Insurance Company) and other sources.

_____ 1. Which of the following would worry you the most?
   a) My portfolio may lose value in one of every three years.
   b) My investments won't stay even with inflation.
   c) I won't earn a premium over inflation on my long-term investments.

_____ 2. How would you react if your stock portfolio fell 30% in one year?
   a) I would sell some or all of it.
   b) I would stop investing money until it came back.
   c) I would stick with my investment plan and consider adding more to stocks.

_____ 3. You've just heard that the stock market fell by 10% today. Your reaction is to:
   a) Consider selling some stocks.
   b) Be concerned, but figure the market is likely to go up again eventually.
   c) Consider buying more stocks, because they are cheaper now.

_____ 4. You read numerous newspaper articles over several months quoting experts who predict stocks will lose money in the coming decade. Many argue that real estate is a better investment. You would:
   a) Consider reducing your stock investments and increasing your investment in real estate.
   b) Be concerned, but stick to your long-term investments in stocks.
   c) Consider the articles as evidence of unwarranted pessimism over the outlook for stocks.

_____ 5. Which of the following best describes your attitude about investing in bonds as compared with stocks?
   a) The high volatility of the stock market concerns me, so I prefer to invest in bonds.
   b) Bonds have less risk but they provide lower returns, so I have a hard time choosing between the two.
   c) The lower return potential of bonds leads me to prefer stocks.

_____ 6. Which of the following best describes how you evaluate the performance of your investments?
   a) My greatest concern is the previous year's performance.
   b) The previous two years are the most important to me.
   c) Performance over five or more years is most significant to me.

_____ 7. Which of the following scenarios would make you feel best about your investments?
   a) Being in a money-market fund saves you from losing half your money in a market downturn.
   b) You double your money in a stock fund in one year.
   c) Over the long term, your overall mix of investments protects you from loss and out-paces the rate of inflation.

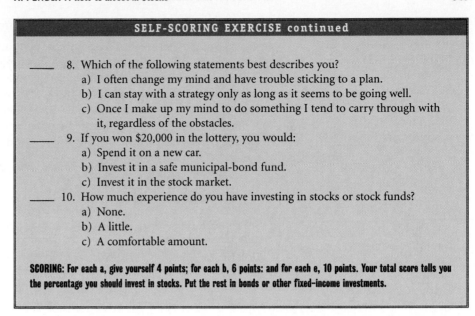

causes some investors to purchase a stock and others to sell that same stock, based on the same information.

STOCK TRANSACTIONS

stock broker facilitates the stock transactions desired

floor traders people on the trading floor of a stock exchange who execute transactions

Investors who wish to purchase stocks use a **stock broker** who facilitates the stock transactions desired. Brokers receive requests of trades from investors and then communicate these trades to people on the trading floor of a stock exchange (called **floor traders**) who execute transactions.

A typical stock transaction order specifies the name of the stock, whether the stock is to be bought or sold, the amount of shares to be traded, and the desired price by the investor. For example, one investor may call a broker and request: "Purchase one hundred shares of IBM; pay no more than $110 per share." A second investor who is holding IBM stock may call a different broker and request: "Sell one hundred shares of IBM at the highest price possible." Both brokers will send this information to the stock exchange. One floor trader will accommodate the buyer, while another floor trader will accommodate the seller. The two traders can agree on a transaction in which one hundred shares of IBM are sold for $110 per share.

Market Orders Versus Limit Orders

market order a transaction is requested for the best possible price

limit order a limit is placed on the price at which one would be willing to purchase or sell a stock

Investors can place a **market order,** which means a transaction is requested for the best possible price. They can also place a **limit order,** in which a limit is placed on the price at which one would be willing to purchase or sell a stock. Examples of a market order are: "(1) Purchase two-hundred shares of General Motors stock at the best [lowest] price available and (2) sell three-hundred shares of Eastman Kodak stock at the best [highest] price available." Examples of a limit order are: "(1) Purchase three-hundred shares of Disney; pay no more than $70 per share, and (2) sell one-hundred shares of PepsiCo; sell for no less than $40 per share."

Purchasing Stocks on Margin

on margin a portion of the funds needed to purchase a stock is borrowed

Investors can purchase stocks **on margin,** which means that a portion of the funds needed to purchase a stock is borrowed. Many brokerage firms provide loans to investors who wish to buy on margin. For example, an investor may place an order to purchase one-hundred shares of W. R. Grace stock at $50 per share. The transaction is priced at $5,000. An investor who has only $3,000 available may borrow the remaining $2,000 from the brokerage firm. There are limits on the funds that can be borrowed by investors. Normally, the amount borrowed cannot exceed 50 percent of the amount of the investment.

Types of Brokers

discount brokers ensure that a transaction desired by an investor is executed, but do not offer advice

full-service brokers provide advice to investors on stocks to purchase or sell, and also ensure that transactions desired by investors are executed

Different types of brokers provide services that investors need. **Discount brokers** ensure that a transaction desired by an investor is executed, but do not offer advice. Popular discount brokers include Olde, and Quick and Reilly. **Full-service brokers** provide advice to investors on stocks to purchase or sell, and also ensure that transactions desired by investors are executed. Popular full-service brokers include Merrill Lynch and Dean Witter.

Commissions on Stock Transactions

commission sales fee

Brokers charge a **commission,** or sales fee, to execute a stock transaction. The commissions charged by full-service brokers are typically higher than those charged by discount brokers. Commissions are sometimes set according to the number of shares traded. For example, a commission of $50 might be set for transactions involving one-hundred shares, $60 for transactions involving up to three-hundred shares, and $80 for transactions involving up to six-hundred shares. Some other discount and full-service brokers set their commissions according to the dollar value of the transaction. For example, some discount brokers may charge about 1 percent of the stock transaction value, while full-service brokers may charge about 3 to 8 percent of the stock transaction value.

round lots multiples of one hundred shares

odd lots less than one hundred shares

Investors typically purchase stocks in **round lots,** or multiples of one-hundred shares. They may also purchase stocks in **odd lots,** or less than one-hundred shares, but the transaction cost may be higher.

STOCK EXCHANGES

The main stock exchange in the United States is the New York Stock Exchange (NYSE). About 80 percent of the volume of all U.S. stock transactions are executed on the NYSE. The NYSE has a trading floor where traders exchange stocks. Many traders represent brokerage firms and execute the transactions that their customers desire. Other traders execute transactions for their own account. The trading resembles an auction, as traders selling a stock attempt to receive the highest possible price. Each trader may serve as a buyer for some transactions and a seller for others.

The largest firms in the United States (such as Exxon, IBM, and General Motors) have their stock listed on the NYSE. Firms that list their stock on this exchange must satisfy various requirements on their earnings, size, the number of shareholders who own their stock, and the number of their shares outstanding. They also must pay fees to list on the exchange. More than 200 million shares are sold per day on the NYSE.

Some firms list on other exchanges in the United States, such as the American Stock Exchange, the Midwest Stock Exchange, and the Pacific Stock Exchange. These exchanges also have a trading floor. The listing requirements to list a stock on these exchanges are not as restrictive. Consequently, many smaller firms that might not meet the NYSE requirements can list their stock on these stock exchanges.

Over-the-Counter Market

In addition to the exchanges just described, there is also an over-the-counter (OTC) market. The OTC market is most commonly used by smaller firms, some of which do not meet the size requirements to trade on the NYSE or American Stock Exchange. The stock transactions on the OTC are executed by traders through a telecommunications network rather than on a trading floor. There is a computerized network within the OTC for firms that meet specific size and capital requirements, called the **National Association of Security Dealers Automated Quotation (NASDAQ).** This system provides immediate stock price quotations. The network allows transactions to be executed without the need for a trading floor. Stocks of about five-thousand firms are traded on the NASDAQ.

National Association of Security Dealers Automated Quotation (NASDAQ) a computerized network within the OTC for firms that meet specific size and capital requirements

Regulation of Stock Exchanges

The Securities and Exchange Commission (SEC) was created in 1934 to regulate security markets such as the stock exchanges. It enforces specific trading guidelines to prevent unethical trading activities. For example, it attempts to prevent **insider trading,** or transactions initiated by people (such as employees) who have information about a firm that has not been disclosed to the public (called **insider information**). Consider an executive of an engineering firm that has just completed a contract to do work for the government that will generate a large amount of revenue for the firm. If the executive calls a broker to buy shares of the firm, this executive has an unfair advantage over other investors because of the inside information that has not yet been disclosed to the public.

insider trading transactions initiated by people (such as employees) who have information about a firm that has not been disclosed to the public

insider information information about a firm that has not been disclosed to the public

INVESTING IN FOREIGN STOCKS

Foreign stocks can also be purchased by U.S. investors. When foreign stocks are not listed on a U.S. exchange, the U.S. broker may need to call a broker at a foreign subsidiary, who communicates the desired transaction to the foreign stock exchange where the stock is traded. The commissions paid by U.S. investors for such transactions are higher than those paid for transactions on U.S. exchanges.

Many of the larger foreign stocks are listed on U.S. stock exchanges as **American depository receipts (ADRs).** An ADR is a certificate representing ownership of a stock issued by a non-U.S. firm. Some of the more popular ADRs are British Airways, Canon, EuroDisney, and Sony.

American depository receipts (ADRs) certificate representing ownership of a stock issued by a non-U.S. firm

INVESTING IN MUTUAL FUNDS

Mutual funds sell shares to individual investors and use the proceeds to invest in various securities. They are attractive to investors because they employ portfolio managers with expertise to make investment decisions. Thus, individual investors can place the responsibility of investment decisions with these portfolio managers. Second, individual investors with a small amount of money (such as $500 or $1,000) can invest in mutual funds. By investing in mutual funds, investors can be part owners of a widely diversified portfolio with a small amount of money.

The **net asset value (NAV)** of a mutual fund represents the market value of the fund's securities after subtracting any expenses incurred (such as portfolio manager salaries) by the fund, on a per-share basis. As the values of the securities contained in a mutual fund rise, so does the mutual fund's NAV.

net asset value (NAV) market value of the fund's securities after subtracting any expenses incurred

Types of Mutual Funds

Open-end mutual funds stand ready to repurchase the shares at the prevailing NAV if investors decide to sell the shares. Conversely, shares of **closed-end mutual funds** represent mutual funds that are sold on stock exchanges.

Most mutual funds tend to focus on particular types of securities so that they can attract investors who wish to invest in those securities. For example, **growth funds** invest in stocks of firms with high potential for growth. **Income funds** invest in stocks that provide large dividends, or in bonds that provide coupon payments. **International stock funds** invest in stocks of foreign firms. Each mutual fund has a prospectus that describes its investment objectives, its recent performance, the types of securities it purchases, and other relevant financial information.

open-end mutual funds stand ready to repurchase the shares at the prevailing NAV if investors decide to sell the shares

closed-end mutual funds represent mutual funds that are sold on stock exchanges

growth funds invest in stocks of firms with high potential for growth

income funds invest in stocks that provide large dividends, or in bonds that provide coupon payments

international stock funds invest in stocks of foreign firms

Load versus No-Load Mutual Funds

Open-end mutual funds that can be purchased only by calling a broker are referred to as **load mutual funds.** The term *load* refers to the transaction fees (commissions) charged for the transaction. Other open-end mutual funds that can be purchased without the services of a broker are referred to as **no-load funds.** These mutual funds are purchased by requesting a brief application from the mutual funds and sending it in with the investment.

All mutual funds incur expenses that result from hiring portfolio managers to select stocks, and from serving clients (mailing fees and so on). The **expense ratio** (defined as expenses divided by the assets) of each mutual fund can be assessed to determine the expenses incurred by each mutual fund per year. Some mutual funds have an expense ratio of less than .5 percent, while others have an expense ratio above 2 percent. The expense ratio is provided within the mutual funds prospectus. Since high expenses can cause lower returns, investors closely monitor the expense ratio.

load mutual funds open-end mutual funds that can be purchased only by calling a broker

no-load funds open-end mutual funds that can be purchased without the services of a broker

expense ratio expenses divided by the assets

KEY TERMS

American depository receipts (ADRs)
bearish
bullish
closed-end mutual funds
commission
discount brokers
expense ratio
floor traders
full-service brokers
growth funds

income funds
insider information
insider trading
international stock funds
limit order
load mutual funds
market order
National Association of Security
    Dealers Automated Quotation
    (NASDAQ)

net asset value (NAV)
no-load funds
odd lots
on margin
open-end mutual funds
round lots
stock broker
stock market efficiency

INVESTING IN THE STOCK OF A BUSINESS

Recall from Chapter 1 that you were asked to identify a firm that you would invest in if you had funds to invest. You were asked to record the price of the firm's stock at that time. Now, you should close out your position. That is, determine today's stock price and estimate your return on the stock as follows:

1 If the investment period is about three months, one dividend payment would have been made. Divide the annual dividend per share (which you recorded when you selected your stock) by 4 to determine the quarterly dividend per share (D).

2 Estimate the return (R), based on today's selling price (S), the purchase price (P) you paid at the beginning of the term, and the quarterly dividend (D):

$$R = \frac{S - P + D}{P}$$

This return is not annualized. If you wish to annualize your return, multiply R by ($12/n$), where n is the number of months in which you had your investment. Compare your results with those of other students.

To determine how well your stock performed in comparison with the stock market in general, determine the percentage change in the S&P 500 index over the term. This index represents a composite of stocks representing five-hundred large firms.

Offer explanations for the stock performance of your firm. Was the performance driven by the stock market performance in general? Was your firm's performance affected by recent economic conditions, industry conditions, and global conditions? How? Was its performance affected by specific strategies (such as restructuring or acquisitions) that it recently enacted? Discuss.

THE *Coca-Cola* COMPANY ANNUAL REPORT PROJECT

1 Using the shareholder information on page 75 of this annual report or the business section of a major newspaper, find the stock symbol for The Coca-Cola Company. What is The Coca-Cola Company's stock symbol?

2 On what stock exchanges is The Coca-Cola Company traded?

Stock Exchanges on the Internet

When considering personal investing, a good place to start browsing is the stock exchanges. The largest exchange is the New York Stock Exchange (NYSE) (Exhibit A.7). Its Internet address is http://www.nyse.com. The first two major U.S. exchanges to establish a presence on the World Wide Web (WWW) were the American Stock Exchange (AMEX) and the over-the-counter exchange National Association of Security Dealers Automated Quotation (NASDAQ) (Exhibit A.8).

Many brokerage firms such as Schwab, Fidelity, and Bull & Bear allow investors to obtain quotes, place orders, and sell stocks at a discount via the web (Exhibit A.9). Commissions can be as low as $19.95 per trade. An investor can get information from an on-line research service, place a trade, and receive confirmation of the transaction in minutes.

Exhibit A.7
New York Stock Exchange (NYSE)
Web Site

http://www.nyse.com

Exhibit A.8
NASDAQ Web Site

http://www.nasdaq.com

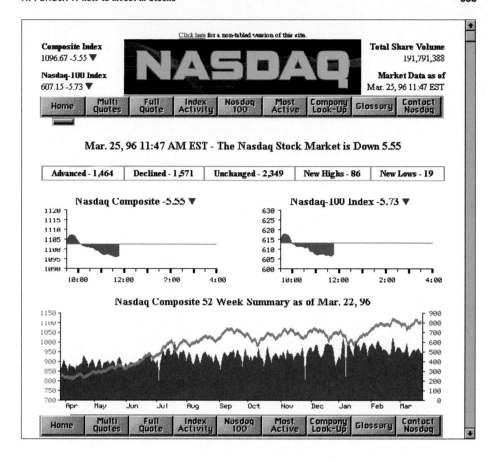

Exhibit A.9
Additional Sites with On-Line Trading Information

American Stock Exchange	http://www.amex.com
Fidelity Investors	http://www.fid_inv.com/brokerage/fidelity_plus_brokerage_acc.html
Savoy	http://www.savoystocks.con/
Stocks and Commodities—Onramp Access, Inc.	http://dgoats.onr.com/stocks/brokerage.html
Quick and Reilly	http://www.quick-reilly.com/
E Trade	http://www.etrade.com/
Charles Schwab	http://www.schwab.com/
Merrill Lynch	http://ml.com/
Aufhauser & Company	http://aufhauser.com/

Careers

This appendix suggests methods that can be used to make career decisions. Some of the more critical career decisions are (1) choosing a career, (2) the decision to pursue a career versus an additional degree, and (3) how to pursue a particular career.

CHOOSING A CAREER

Students who prefer to work for a firm rather than start their own business must decide the type of job and size of firm that would be ideal for them.

Type of Job
One's salary and level of job satisfaction is dependent on the type of job selected. This decision should be seriously considered by college students before they determine what subject to major in. Consequently, they can receive the educational background that is appropriate for the type of job they desire.

SALARIES While students should not necessarily choose the major that results in the highest salaries, they should at least be aware of salary differentials between majors before they select a major. This type of information is available at most large libraries.

The annual salaries paid for various jobs are disclosed in Exhibit B.1. The typical starting salary per job position is provided along with the average salary for the industry. This exhibit includes many jobs that are available only to people with a specialized education background and experience. Nevertheless, it shows how salaries can vary substantially among jobs. The actual salary of a specific job at a particular firm can vary from the numbers shown in Exhibit B.1, as salaries are also affected by the location and other characteristics unique to the firm.

JOB SATISFACTION Job satisfaction is another characteristic that must also be considered when choosing a career. The job satisfaction level for any given career varies among people. Thus, people may not know whether they like a particular type of job until after they have worked at it. This is a major dilemma because it is difficult to properly assess job satisfaction without on-the-job experience, which normally occurs after graduation.

Size of Firm
In addition to the type of job, people must determine whether they wish to work for a small or large firm. There are some obvious differences. Some commonly cited advantages of working for a large firm are more prestige, more training, and more opportunities for advancement.

Conversely, some advantages of working for a small firm are more attention from higher-level management and more diverse responsibilities. Also, fewer promotions are necessary to achieve a higher-level management position.

Exhibit B.1
Annual Salaries for
Various Job Positions

Job Position	Starting Salary	Average salary for the Industry
Accounting & Finance		
Public Accountant (Big Six firm)	$30,125	$38,625
Small firm	24,750	36,500
Corporate accountant		
Associate accountant	25,000	28,400
Senior auditor	37,200	42,500
Senior tax accountant	46,900	55,300
Controller	97,900	147,900
Treasurer	108,000	160,500
CFO	165,000	277,200
Advertising		
Advertising copywriter	30,000	50,000
Art director	27,500	47,500
Account executive	28,000	62,500
Creative director	150,000	300,000
Architecture		
Architect	27,000	35,000
Principal/partner	35,000	50,000
CEO	1,131,042	1,524,057
Consulting		
Strategic consultant	47,677	120,660
Human resources consultant	38,633	64,218
MIS consultant	39,120	81,569
Corporate Ethics		
Ethics Administrator	35,000	50,000
VP for ethics	95,000	140,000
Education		
University professor	39,050	49,490
Elementary teacher	25,693	36,357
Secondary teacher	26,077	37,764
Engineering		
Biomedical engineer	37,750	72,500
Chemical engineer	39,863	73,970
Civil engineer	30,690	62,000
Electrical engineer	33,000	65,876
Mechanical engineer	36,935	65,160
Industrial engineer	35,244	67,000
Financial Services		
Financial planner	27,000	50,000
Portfolio manager	40,000	100,000
Mortgage loan officer	27,200	54,600
Commercial loan officer	41,500	71,000
Actuary	25,382	36,914
Life insurance underwriter	23,500	37,564

Exhibit B.1 (continued)
Annual Salaries for
Various Job Positions

Group insurance underwriter	27,421	38,883
Government Jobs		
Economist	$21,486	$46,852
Budget analyst	21,486	38,885
Personnel manager	18,956	46,852
Health Care		
Family practice physician	86,300	123,700
HMO	96,700	123,300
Neurosurgeon	158,500	263,300
Cardiothoracic surgeon	175,900	312,300
Plastic surgeon	157,500	181,000
Registered nurse	34,600	39,800
Licensed physical therapist	35,500	45,500
High Technology		
Software engineer	33,702	54,470
Hardware engineer	33,592	54,704
CD-ROM Producer	35,000	60,000
Human Resources		
Employee training manager	49,500	59,000
Benefits manager	63,800	85,200
Human resources VP	118,100	188,700
Information Services		
Programming trainee	9,000	19,500
LAN/WAN specialist	27,900	41,000
Database specialist	33,229	45,193
Systems analyst	35,728	44,026
Applications programmer	25,992	49,000
MIS director	57,700	89,000
IRS agent		
Tax auditor	19,500	34,000
Revenue officer	19,500	34,000
Revenue agent	19,500	49,663
Law		
Associate in private practice	58,942	74,318
Partner in private practice	114,213	183,364
Public prosecutor	23,000	30,000
Public defender	20,000	28,900
Corporate lawyer	61,932	79,297
Chief legal officer	169,300	258,966
Paralegal	30,470	37,686
Lobbying		
Small trade group lobbyist	35,000	47,500
Large trade group lobbyist	100,000	300,000
Corporate lobbyist	36,000	60,000
Manufacturing		
Foreman	32,240	40,300
Purchasing agent	42,240	52,800
Warehouse manager	41,231	53,600

The advantages listed here do not apply to all large and small firms, as each firm has its own characteristics. Thus, it is strongly recommended that students apply for particular jobs at both small and large firms. The interviewing process may provide students with more insight on the differences between small and large firms.

CAREER VERSUS ADDITIONAL DEGREE

Students who receive their associates degree are faced with a decision of whether to pursue a bachelor's degree or a full-time career. Students who receive their bachelor's degree are also faced with a decision of whether to pursue a master's degree or a full-time career. Both decisions involve an additional degree versus a career. The following discussion relates to either one of these decisions.

While the appropriate decision varies among students, some general guidelines deserve consideration. Students should conduct a cost-benefit analysis of the decision to pursue an additional degree. Some of the more obvious costs are tuition, the forgone income that could have been earned by working instead of going to school, and the forgone on-the-job experience that could have been earned by working instead of going to school. Some possible benefits of pursing an additional degree are more marketability in the job market, a higher starting salary, and greater potential to be promoted.

The cost and benefits of attaining an additional degree can vary significantly among majors. In addition to the costs and benefits just identified, other factors also deserve to be considered. For example, some people may need a break from school and would prefer to begin their career right away. Others may perform best in school by continuing their education while the previous coursework is somewhat fresh in their minds.

A common suggestion is that one gets the most out of an additional degree by working full-time for a few years and then returning to school. The on-the-job experience may allow for a greater understanding and appreciation of coursework. However, the cost of such a strategy can be high. It is difficult for people to feel motivated on a job, knowing they will quit in a few years to pursue an additional degree.

Pursuing a Career and Degree

A popular compromise to the decision of a career versus an additional degree is to begin a career and pursue the degree part-time. Many firms will even pay the employee's tuition if the coursework could enhance the employee's performance on the job. This strategy allows people to obtain a degree without giving up the income and on-the-job experience that is forgone when pursuing a degree full-time. However, the disadvantage is that it may take five or more years to achieve the degree part-time. In addition, taking coursework at night after a long day on the job can cause fatigue and stress.

An extra degree does not automatically guarantee immediate success. The number of bachelor's and master's degrees have dramatically increased in recent years. Therefore, competition for existing jobs can be fierce even with additional education. However, an additional degree can be especially marketable when it complements existing skills. For example, many engineers have pursued master's degrees in business administration so that they could pursue management level positions at engineering firms.

Internships

Internship programs may allow students to gain on-the-job experience while pursuing a degree. Some internships provide a salary to the students, while others allow students to earn credit for the internship. An internship may also enable students to determine whether a particular type of job is desirable prior to selecting a major. It may even enhance the understanding of coursework. Yet, perhaps the largest benefit of the internship is the experience, which may increase the student's marketability upon graduation. Numerous firms frequently hire interns, including AT&T, Apple Computer, and Boeing. Yet, many more students apply for internships than the number of internships available.

Choosing a College

People who decide to pursue a college degree must also select the proper college or university. For these people who will be working while pursuing the degree, the choice of a college may be dictated by the location of the job. For others who have the flexibility to relocate, several criteria are worth considering. The first step is to identify the colleges that offer a degree in the main field of interest. College catalogs (available at many libraries) should be reviewed to compare the courses offered by each prospective college. Then, each college that offers a degree in that field can be more closely assessed to determine the course requirements, possible elective courses, and minor fields to choose from. Other factors such as tuition and location should also be considered. Several colleges offer a degree in any given field.

Some colleges are more prestigious than others, which can be important in attaining a good job. However, a college's reputation tends to vary. One college may have a strong program in one field but a weak program in others.

For people who plan to find a local job, the college would not need to have a national reputation. Yet, in many college towns, specialized jobs are scarce. Therefore, even if the college is not nationally recognized, it should be reputable from the perspective of potential employees who may hire its graduates.

PURSUING A CAREER

The key steps in pursuing a career are as follows:

➤ Applying for a position
➤ Creating a resume
➤ Interviewing
➤ Planning a career path

Each step is discussed in turn.

Applying for a Position

After determining the type of job desired, it is necessary to identify the prospective employers that may offer such a job in that field. The want ads in the local newspapers may identify firms in the local area that are trying to fill the position desired. However, local want-ads will not provide a complete listing of companies that wish to fill such a position. Some companies do not advertise openings, but simply select from their applicant file to fill positions. For this reason, a worthwhile step is to submit an application to any firms that may potentially hire for the position desired. Very little effort and expense is required to submit an application.

Exhibit B.2
How Firms Recruit Job Applicants

Recruiting Method	Percentage of Firms Surveyed that Used This Method
Help wanted ads	89%
Referrals from current employees	77%
Temporary help services	63%
Networking with associations	57%
Employment/recruiting firms	51%
College placement offices	48%
Job fairs	35%

Firms use a variety of methods to hire employees, as shown in Exhibit B.2. Based on this exhibit, people can improve their chances of being recruited by sending an application in response to an ad, asking friends with jobs to provide referrals, joining associations, and using the college placement service. They may even consider using employment recruiting firms, although these firms do not normally deal with entry-level positions.

Some people who are very interested in a particular job may revise their resume to fit that job. They could elaborate on any past work experience that is directly applicable to the job.

When students apply for a job, they should send a cover letter along with a resume. Exhibit B.3 provides an example of a cover letter that is used. While many formats can be used, the main purpose of the cover letter is to identify the job position and explain how one's qualifications fit the job position.

Students pursuing a career should contact the college placement center, which may invite firms to speak about careers. Firms also conduct interviews of students at many placement centers.

Many people are unable to identify the ideal job for which they are qualified. Yet, this does not prevent them from applying for jobs. The personnel department of each firm can determine whether the applicants are qualified for various positions.

Applying for a job is normally the easiest part of pursuing a career. Some people apply at one or two well-known firms and wait to be called. This can be a frustrating experience. People who are willing to consider several firms for employment are more likely to obtain a job. Even if a specific firm is most desirable, it is worthwhile to at least apply for a position at several firms.

Creating a Resume

The application process normally requires a resume to be included. Various resume formats are used, and no format is perfect for all situations. Most resumes for people pursuing entry-level positions are one page long. An example of a typical resume format is shown in Exhibit B.4. Whatever format is used, it should be designed to describe any characteristics that enhance job skills. The job objective states the desired job position, and can be tailored to fit the firm where the application is sent. The education and employment background should be listed in reverse chronological order (most recent experience listed first). Specific details that support job qualifications can be described in this section.

Exhibit B.3
Example of a Cover Letter

1022 N. Main Street
Tallahassee, FL 32306

June 9, 1996

Mr. Raymond Jones
President
Jones Manufacturing Co.
550 East 1st Street
Orlando, FL 32816

Dear Mr. Jones:

[State the specific job you are pursuing.]

I noticed that you have a job opening for a tax accountant. I just recently earned my accounting degree from Florida State University. I worked as an intern at Mega Accountants, Inc., in their tax department. Much of the intern work was focused on tax accounting for manufacturing firms. I believe that my educational and intern experience has prepared me for your tax accountant position. I have enclosed my resume, which provides more details about my education and intern background.

[Describe when you are available for work and how you can be reached.]

I am available for work immediately. Please call me at 999-555-1234 if you would like to interview me. I can be reached at that number during the morning on any day of the week. I look forward to hearing from you.

Sincerely,

Robert Smith

Interviewing

Firms conduct interviews to more thoroughly evaluate applicants. Various criteria cannot be evaluated from resumes alone, such as applicants' appearance and personality. Personal interviews allow firms to rate applicants according to these criteria. Many firms screen applications and resumes to identify a pool of qualified applicants. Then the qualified applicants are interviewed to determine the optimal applicant for the position. While strong qualifications on a resume enable an applicant to be interviewed, they do not guarantee a job. A person who interviews well may be preferable to one with a stronger resume who interviews poorly.

Firms design most interviews to provide the applicant with additional information about the position and to determine the following:

1 Is the applicant's appearance acceptable?
2 Would the applicant get along with customers?
3 Does the applicant have good communication skills?
4 Does the applicant have a genuine interest in the position?
5 Would the applicant work well with others?

Exhibit B.4
Example of a Resume

Resume

Robert Smith
1022 N. Main Street
Tallahassee, FL 32306

Job Objective: Entry-level accountant

Education: Florida State University, Sept. 1992–May 1996, B.S. in Accounting received May 1996;
                            Grade point average = 3.1 on a 4-point scale.

Work Experience: Intern at Mega Accountants, Inc., April 1995 to April 1996.

    ☐ Assisted tax accountants in compiling information submitted by clients that would be
used to file their tax returns.

    ☐ Researched previous tax court cases to provide information needed for determining
specific tax questions by clients.

    ☐ Met with prospective clients to explain the tax services offered by the firm.

Lantern Grocery Store, March 1991 to March 1994.

    ☐ Responsible for ordering stock, monitoring deliveries of stock, and placing stock on
shelves.

Professional Organizations: Treasurer of the Accounting Association at Florida State University, Member of
Business Club.

Extracurricular activities: Volunteer for Salvation Army, Intramural Sports (Baseball and Basketball).

References: Provided upon request.

Applicants cannot prepare for all possible questions that may be asked during an interview, but they should at least prepare for some of the more obvious types of questions that may be asked:

1 Why do you want to work for our company?
2 What do you know about our company?
3 Why do you plan to leave your present employer?
4 Why should our company hire you?
5 What are your strengths?
6 What are your weaknesses?
7 What are your salary requirements?
8 When would you be ready to begin this job?

Checklist for Building or Evaluating Your Resume

The following checklist can be used to create or evaluate your resume. Review your resume carefully, using the criteria listed. Then, for any area you rated "average" or "poor," revise your resume to make it "excellent." Alternatively, you may want to have a friend evaluate your resume using the checklist.

	Rating			
	Excellent	*Average*	*Poor*	Suggestions for Improvement
Does it stress accomplishments over skills and duties?				
Is the resume clear? Is it easy to get a picture of the writer's qualifications?				
Is irrelevant personal information left out?				
Does it avoid self-evaluation?				
Is the language clear and understandable?				
Does it emphasize benefits for a potential employer?				
Is it well printed on good, professional-looking stock?				
Does the layout invite attention? Do strong points stand out?				
Is the industry/product line of past employers clear?				
Do the sentences begin with action words?				
Does it sell the writer's problem-solving skills?				

While applicants cannot guarantee the outcome of the interview, a few simple but critical rules should be followed:

1 Dress properly.
2 Be on time.
3 Send a follow-up thank-you letter to the persons who interview you.

WHAT TO ASK IN AN INTERVIEW   A person who is being interviewed is normally allowed time to ask questions about the firm that is conducting the interview. These questions may be just as important as the applicant's answers in determining whether the job is offered. The questions show the applicant's interest in the firm and intelligence about the job. Some possible questions are listed here:

1 How much interaction is there between this position and related divisions?
2 How much responsibility is delegated by the supervisor of this position?
3 What is the typical educational background for this position?
4 Who is involved in the performance evaluation for this position?
5 To what extent does the position involve public relations or contact with customers?

A second set of questions would involve more details about the position, which could show the interviewee's competency in the area. While these questions would vary with the types of position, a few examples are provided:

1 What type of computer is used in the department?
2 Which companies are your key suppliers or customers?
3 What are your projections for sales within the division over the next year?

While asking questions can be valuable, the applicant must recognize the amount of time allocated for the interview so that the interviewer has sufficient time to ask questions.

Planning a Career Path

Even after a job is offered and accepted, career decisions must be made. On-the-job experience may affect the desired career path. Aspiring to achieve a position above the present position is natural. The planned career path to that position may involve either a series of promotions within the firm or switching to a different firm. While planning a career path is a useful motivator, the plans should be achievable. If everyone planned to be president of a company, most plans would not be achieved. This can cause frustration. A preferable career path would include short-term goals, since some ultimate goals may take twenty years or longer. The use of short-term goals can reinforce confidence as goals are achieved.

WHERE THE JOBS ARE

During the early and middle 1990s, massive downsizing took place, resulting in the elimination of many middle-management jobs. Yet, jobs were created in several industries, as shown in Exhibit B.5. The large increase in temporary and full-time work agencies is partially attributed to the downsizing, as firms are frequently hiring additional workers through these agencies over a short-term period.

Survey of Knowledge and Abilities Needed

Managers at several firms were surveyed to determine the type of knowledge and abilities that they believed were most critical for college students. Each type was rated by the respondent, and the average ratings were converted into a one-hundred-point scale. A higher score reflects a more critical need for that type of knowledge or ability. The results are summarized in Exhibit B.6. The survey results offer some gen-

Exhibit B.5
Industries in Which
New Jobs Were Created

	Number of Jobs Created from 1990 to June 1995
Temporary and full-time work agencies	899,000
Restaurants and bars	738,000
Local government administration	359,000
Hospitals	345,000
Recreation (health clubs, etc.)	344,000
Home health care	339,000
Nursing and personal care	310,000
Medical doctors' offices	290,000
Computer software	228,000
State government administration	255,000
Trucking and parcel delivery	222,000
Business services (drafting, etc.)	204,000
Residential care (rehab centers, etc.)	195,000
Management consulting and public relations	179,000
Social services	166,000
Offices of optometrists, podiatrists, etc.	144,000
Child day care	136,000
Grocery stores	136,000
Motion picture production	133,000
Elementary and secondary schools	106,000

eralizations about the knowledge and skills needed, but the results could vary among locations and may also change over time.

WORKING FOR A FIRM VERSUS OWNING A FIRM

During the course of a career, many people question whether to continue working for a firm or start their own business. Some people recognize the potential benefits of owning their own firm, such as being their own boss or the potential to earn a high level of income. However, the decision to start a business requires an idea for a product or service that will generate sufficient sales. A successful business also requires proper planning, production, marketing, and financing decisions, as explained throughout the text. Some general guidelines for developing a successful business, which apply to most firms, are listed here:

1 *Create a Product (or service) that the Market Wants.* A new business is typically created when the owner recognizes a product or service desired by customers that is not being offered by a sufficient number (or by any) existing firms.

2 *Prepare for Adverse Conditions.* An owner of a business should have enough financial backing to prepare for adverse conditions, such as a decline in economic growth or more intense competition. Even if the business is based on a good product (or service) idea, it may experience weak performance in some periods because of factors outside of its control.

Exhibit B.6
Critical Types of Knowledge
and Abilities

Critical Types of Knowledge	Score
Communications	91
Management	85
Information systems	83
Finance	72
Ethics	70
Marketing	67
Accounting	65
Quantitative methods	64
Economics	61
International issues	55
Environmental issues	52
Critical Abilities or Traits	**Score**
Planning	96
Organizing	96
Decision making	96
Acting ethically	92
Managing projects	91
Motivating	91
Analyzing carefully	90
Managing people	88
Loyalty	77
Willingness to work long hours	76

3 *Capitalize on New Opportunities.* A business should use a flexible strategic plan that adjusts in response to new business opportunities. Businesses that remain more flexible to change are more likely to capitalize on new opportunities.

4 *Ensure Customer Satisfaction.* The long-run success of many businesses is based on the quality of a product, which leads to customer satisfaction.

5 *Ensure Employee Satisfaction.* When owners of businesses create conditions that satisfy employees, they motivate employees to perform well and also avoid a high level of employee turnover.

6 *Promote the Product.* A good product will not sell unless the market is aware of it. Promotion may be necessary to ensure that the market is informed about the product.

Career Services on the World Wide Web

An important factor in managing employees is hiring the right people in the first place. During the past few years, the number of career placement services on the World Wide Web (WWW) has skyrocketed. A good example of such a site is the Internet's Online Career Center (Exhibit B.7), a web site sponsored by a nonprofit association of businesses. For other examples, see the table in Exhibit B.8.

Exhibit B.7
The Internet's Online Career
Center Web Site

http://www.occ.com/

The Internet's
Online Career Center
The Internet's first and most frequently accessed career center

Keyword Search All Jobs: [   ] **Search** Help
OCC is sponsored by a non-profit association of leading corporations
A, B, C, D, E, F, G, H, I, J, K, L, M, N, O, P, Q, R, S, T, U, V, W, X, Y, Z
OCC Member Jobs | By Industry | By State | By City | Search Firms

Submit Resumes |Submit Jobs

FAQ | Jobs | Resumes | Career Fairs and Events | Cultural Diversity
OCC | Recruiter's Office | Career Assistance | On Campus | Help

HEADLINES

New Feature! JWT SPECIALIZED COMMUNICATIONS INTRODUCES "HRLive"
A monthly digest of HR news, views, tips and trends.

New Feature! MEMBER COMPANIES MAY ENTER 'HTML' ADS INTO THE
DATABASE!

Exhibit B.8
Career Placement Services
on the World Wide Web

Magellan-Career	http://www.mckinley.com/browse_bd.csi?career
Career Mosaic	http://www.careermosaic.com/
Career.Com:	http://www.career.com/
America's Employers	http://www.americasemployers.com/
The Help Wanted Page	http://helpwantedpage.com/
Career Web	http://cweb.com/
Monster Board	http://monster.com/
Index-Definitive Guide to Internet Career Resource	http://www.phoenix.placement.oakland.edu/career/internet.htm
Job Trak	http://www.jobtrak.com
Student Center	http://www.studentcenter.com/
College Grad	http://www.collegegrad.com/

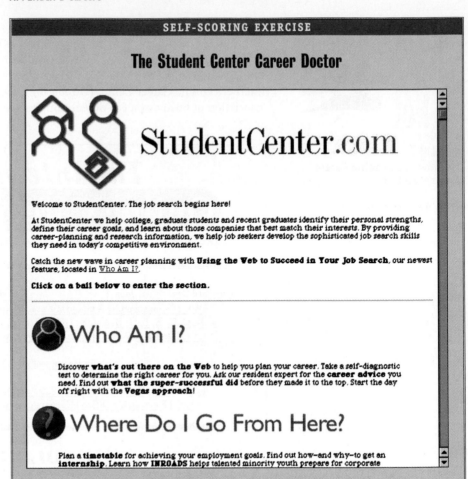

Another excellent source of career information on the web is the Student Center Career Doctor located at http://studentcenter.com. This site offers a self-diagnostic test to determine the right career for you. The self-scoring exercise shown above can only be done on-line.

Answers to In-Text Study Guide

Chapter 1

True/False

1. False
2. False
3. False
4. False
5. False
6. False
7. False
8. True
9. True
10. True

Multiple Choice

11. e
12. c
13. c
14. e
15. b
16. b
17. b
18. a
19. a
20. a
21. d
22. e
23. c
24. b
25. c
26. e
27. a
28. d
29. a
30. b
31. c
32. a
33. e
34. e
35. e

Chapter 2

True/False

1. False
2. False
3. True
4. True
5. True
6. False
7. True
8. False
9. True
10. False

Multiple Choice

11. a
12. c
13. c
14. e
15. d
16. b
17. d
18. a
19. a
20. c
21. d
22. c
23. c
24. b
25. a
26. b
27. d
28. a
29. b
30. b
31. b
32. a
33. c
34. a
35. d

Chapter 3

True/False

1. True
2. True
3. True
4. False
5. True
6. False
7. True
8. True
9. False
10. False

Multiple Choice

11. c
12. e
13. a
14. e
15. e
16. c
17. d
18. b
19. a
20. b
21. d
22. c
23. e
24. c
25. c
26. b
27. e
28. d
29. b
30. d
31. d
32. d
33. b
34. b
35. e

Chapter 4

True/False

1. False
2. True
3. False
4. True
5. False
6. False
7. True
8. True
9. False
10. True

Multiple Choice

11. a
12. b
13. c
14. d
15. a
16. c
17. c
18. d
19. a
20. b
21. e
22. c
23. d
24. c
25. e
26. c
27. a
28. c
29. e
30. a
31. b
32. d
33. a
34. e
35. b

Chapter 5

True/False

1. False
2. False
3. True
4. False
5. False
6. False
7. True
8. True
9. True
10. False

Multiple Choice

11. c
12. e
13. b
14. a
15. c
16. d
17. a
18. b
19. d
20. d
21. b

22. c
23. a
24. d
25. c
26. e
27. b
28. a
29. d
30. b
31. b
32. a
33. c
34. c
35. d

Chapter 6
True/False
1. False
2. False
3. True
4. True
5. True
6. False
7. True
8. False
9. False
10. True

Multiple Choice
11. a
12. c
13. b
14. e
15. a
16. d
17. a
18. c
19. a
20. c
21. a
22. b
23. a
24. d
25. a
26. e
27. b
28. c
29. a
30. e
31. c
32. c
33. b
34. a

35. d

Chapter 7
True/False
1. False
2. False
3. True
4. False
5. False
6. True
7. True
8. True
9. False
10. True

Multiple Choice
11. b
12. d
13. b
14. e
15. a
16. c
17. d
18. a
19. e
20. b
21. d
22. c
23. c
24. e
25. a
26. b
27. c
28. a
29. d
30. b
31. e
32. b
33. a
34. e
35. c

Chapter 8
True/False
1. True
2. True
3. False
4. False
5. False
6. True
7. False
8. True
9. False

10. True

Multiple Choice
11. e
12. a
13. d
14. e
15. b
16. a
17. e
18. a
19. c
20. a
21. b
22. b
23. b
24. a
25. c
26. c
27. d
28. e
29. a
30. b
31. c
32. d
33. a
34. c
35. b

Chapter 9
True/False
1. True
2. False
3. False
4. True
5. True
6. False
7. False
8. True
9. False
10. True

Multiple Choice
11. e
12. b
13. e
14. c
15. b
16. a
17. d
18. b
19. c
20. b

21. e
22. a
23. d
24. c
25. a
26. e
27. d
28. b
29. c
30. a
31. d
32. c
33. e
34. a
35. d

Chapter 10
True/False
1. True
2. True
3. True
4. True
5. False
6. True
7. False
8. True
9. False
10. False

Multiple Choice
11. a
12. c
13. b
14. a
15. e
16. d
17. a
18. e
19. c
20. b
21. d
22. e
23. b
24. c
25. a
26. d
27. e
28. a
29. b
30. c
31. d
32. b
33. c

34. e
35. a

Chapter 11

True/False

1. True
2. True
3. False
4. False
5. True
6. False
7. False
8. True
9. True
10. False

Multiple Choice

11. c
12. a
13. b
14. e
15. a
16. d
17. a
18. b
19. c
20. e
21. d
22. d
23. e
24. a
25. b
26. c
27. b
28. c
29. e
30. a
31. b
32. c
33. a
34. e
35. c

Chapter 12

True/False

1. False
2. True
3. False
4. True
5. True
6. True
7. False
8. True

9. True
10. True

Multiple Choice

11. c
12. a
13. e
14. b
15. d
16. a
17. d
18. c
19. b
20. c
21. b
22. a
23. c
24. e
25. a
26. c
27. e
28. d
29. b
30. b
31. c
32. e
33. a
34. e
35. d

Chapter 13

True/False

1. False
2. False
3. True
4. False
5. True
6. True
7. True
8. False
9. True
10. False

Multiple Choice

11. c
12. d
13. c
14. b
15. a
16. d
17. b
18. c
19. a

20. e
21. e
22. a
23. c
24. a
25. a
26. e
27. e
28. c
29. e
30. c
31. a
32. d
33. a
34. b
35. e

Chapter 14

True/False

1. True
2. False
3. True
4. False
5. False
6. True
7. True
8. False
9. True
10. False

Multiple Choice

11. d
12. a
13. e
14. a
15. b
16. c
17. a
18. b
19. e
20. c
21. b
22. c
23. d
24. a
25. b
26. c
27. d
28. e
29. b
30. a
31. a
32. b

33. c
34. b
35. a

Chapter 15

True/False

1. True
2. True
3. True
4. True
5. True
6. True
7. False
8. True
9. False
10. True

Multiple Choice

11. b
12. a
13. e
14. c
15. b
16. d
17. a
18. e
19. a
20. d
21. e
22. c
23. b
24. d
25. a
26. c
27. e
28. d
29. c
30. a
31. b
32. c
33. e
34. a
35. b

Chapter 16

True/False

1. True
2. True
3. False
4. False
5. True
6. True
7. False

8. False
9. True
10. True

Multiple Choice
11. b
12. d
13. a
14. c
15. e
16. c
17. d
18. a
19. b
20. e
21. b
22. e
23. a
24. d
25. e
26. c
27. e
28. b
29. c
30. d
31. b
32. c
33. e
34. a
35. d

Chapter 17
True/False
1. False
2. True
3. True
4. False
5. False
6. True
7. True
8. False
9. True
10. False

Multiple Choice
11. c
12. e
13. a
14. d
15. e
16. a
17. c

18. b
19. a
20. e
21. b
22. c
23. e
24. a
25. e
26. b
27. d
28. b
29. d
30. a
31. c
32. d
33. b
34. a
35. e

Chapter 18
True/False
1. False
2. True
3. False
4. True
5. False
6. False
7. False
8. True
9. True
10. False

Multiple Choice
11. e
12. d
13. b
14. c
15. a
16. e
17. d
18. c
19. b
20. a
21. e
22. d
23. c
24. b
25. a
26. e
27. d
28. c
29. b
30. a
31. e
32. d
33. a
34. b
35. c

30. c
31. a
32. c
33. e
34. b
35. d

Chapter 19
True/False
1. False
2. False
3. True
4. True
5. False
6. True
7. False
8. False
9. True
10. False

Multiple Choice
11. e
12. d
13. b
14. c
15. a
16. e
17. d
18. c
19. b
20. a
21. e
22. d
23. c
24. b
25. a
26. e
27. d
28. c
29. b
30. a
31. e
32. d
33. a
34. b
35. c

Chapter 20
True/False
1. False
2. True
3. False

4. False
5. True
6. True
7. False
8. True
9. False
10. False

Multiple Choice
11. c
12. a
13. b
14. e
15. c
16. e
17. a
18. b
19. d
20. e
21. b
22. a
23. e
24. d
25. c
26. d
27. a
28. c
29. d
30. b
31. d
32. a
33. c
34. b
35. c

Chapter 21
True/False
1. False
2. True
3. False
4. True
5. False
6. True
7. False
8. True
9. True
10. False

Multiple Choice
11. c
12. e
13. a

14. d	20. b	26. e	32. a
15. b	21. a	27. c	33. b
16. e	22. c	28. a	34. a
17. d	23. d	29. b	35. d
18. a	24. e	30. c	
19. c	25. b	31. b	

GLOSSARY

A

accounting summary and analysis of the firm's financial condition

accounts payable money owed by the firm for the purchase of materials

accounts receivable management sets the limits on credit available to customers, and the length of the period in which payment is due

across-the-board system all employees are allocated a similar raise

active resistance users type in bad data or repeatedly crash the system to make it unusable

actuaries employed by insurance companies to forecast the percentage of customers that will experience the particular event that is being insured

advertising a nonpersonal sales presentation communicated through media or nonmedia forms to influence a large number of consumers

affirmative action a set of activities intended to increase opportunities for minorities and women

agency problem when managers do not act as responsible agents for the shareholders who own the business

agents match buyers and sellers of products without becoming owners

aggregate expenditures the total amount of expenditures in the economy

alpha testing as the application approaches full functionality, it is often made available to a carefully selected subset of sophisticated users

antivirus applications programs that detect and remove viruses

application programs and data associated with performing a specific task

appreciates strengthens in value

artificial intelligence (AI) initial efforts to get computers to perform tasks traditionally associated with biological intelligence, such as logical reasoning, language, vision, and motor skills

assembly line consists of a sequence of work stations, in which each work station is designed

to cover specific phases of the production process

asset anything owned by a firm

auditing an assessment of the records that were used to prepare the firm's financial statements

autocratic leadership style that retains full authority for decision making

automated tasks are completed by machines without the use of employees

autonomy divisions can make their own decisions and act independently

B

balance of trade the level of exports minus the level of imports

balance sheet reports the book value of all assets, liabilities, and owner's equity of firms at a given point in time

bandwidth the amount of information a network can carry

basic accounting equation Assets = Liabilities + Owner's Equity

benchmarking a method of evaluating performance by comparison to some specified (benchmark) level, typically a level achieved by another company

best-efforts basis the investment bank does not guarantee a price to the issuing firm

beta testing once a fully functional version of the application has been created, a wider group of users is given the software

board of directors a set of executives that is responsible for monitoring the activities of the firm's president and other high-level managers

bond mutual funds investment companies that invest the funds received from investors in bonds

bonds long-term debt securities (IOUs) purchased by investors

bonus an extra one-time payment at the end of a period in which performance was measured

bookkeeping the recording of a firm's financial transactions

boycott refusing to purchase products and services

brand advertising a nonpersonal sales presentation about a specific brand

brand loyalty consumers become loyal to a specific brand over time

branding a method of identifying products and differentiating them from competitors

break-even point point at which total revenue equals total cost

break-even point the quantity of units sold at which total revenue equals total cost

bugs errors in the code

business ethics a set of principles that should be followed when conducting business

business plan a detailed description of the proposed business, including a description of the business, the types of customers it would attract, the competition, and the facilities needed for production

business risk the possibility that a firm's performance will be lower than expected because of its exposure to specific conditions

bylaws general guidelines for managing the firm

C

call feature provides the right for the issuing firm to repurchase the bonds before maturity

capital budget targeted amount of funds to be used for purchasing assets such as buildings, machinery, and equipment that are needed for long-term projects

capital budgeting comparison of the costs and benefits of a proposed project to determine whether it is feasible

capital gain the price received from the sale of stock minus the price paid for the stock

capital long-term funds

capital structure the composition of debt versus equity financing

capitalism an economic system which allows for private ownership of businesses

carrying costs costs of maintaining (carrying) inventories

casualty insurance insures the potential liability to a firm for harm to others as a result of product failure or accidents

centralization an effort to maintain most authority among the high-level managers

certified public accountants accountants that meet specific educational requirements and pass a national examination

chain has more than one outlet

chain of command identifies the job position to which each type of employee must report

chain-style business a firm that is allowed to use the trade name of a company and follows guidelines related to the pricing and sales of the product

charter a document to incorporate a business; the charter describes important aspects of the corporation

co-branding two noncompeting products are combined at a discounted price

commercial banks obtain deposits from individuals and primarily use the funds to provide business loans

commercial paper a short-term debt security normally issued by firms in good financial condition

commissions represent compensation for meeting specific sales objectives

common stock a security that represents partial ownership of a particular firm

communism an economic system which involves public ownership of businesses

compact disks (CD-ROMS) optical techniques

comparative advertising intended to demonstrate a brand's superiority by comparison with other competitive brands, which can persuade customers to purchase a specific product

compensation package represents the total monetary compensation and benefits offered to employees

competitive advantage an organization's unique qualities that allow it to compete successfully with other organizations offering similar products or services

composition specifies that the firm will provide its creditors with a portion of what they are owed

compressed work week compresses the work load into fewer days per week

computer program collection of step-by-step instructions to the processor

computer virus program that attaches itself to other programs or computer disks

conceptual skills the ability to understand the relationships between the various tasks of a firm

conglomerate merger combination of two firms in unrelated businesses

consumer markets exist for various consumer products and services (such as cameras, clothes, and household items)

consumerism the collective demand by consumers that businesses satisfy their needs

contingency planning alternative plans developed for various possible business conditions

contribution margin difference between price and variable cost per unit

controlling the monitoring and evaluation of tasks

convenience products widely available to consumers, are purchased frequently, and are easily accessible

corporate anorexia firms become so obsessed with eliminating their inefficient components that they downsize too much

corporation a state chartered entity that pays taxes and is legally distinct from its owners

cost of goods sold the cost of materials used to produce the goods that were sold

cost-based pricing estimating the per-unit cost of producing a product and then adding a markup

cost-push inflation higher prices charged by firms are caused by higher costs

coupons used in newspapers, magazines, and ads to encourage the purchase of a product

craft unions organized according to a specific craft (or trade), such as plumbing

creditors financial institutions or individuals who provide loans

critical path the path that takes the longest time to complete

current assets assets that will be converted into cash within one year

customer profile characteristics of the typical customer (based on gender, age, hobbies, and so on)

cyclical unemployment people who are unemployed because of poor economic conditions

D

database program is intended to generate reports from a firm's client list

debt financing the act of borrowing funds

decentralized authority is spread among several divisions or managers

decision support systems (DSS) computer models that are used to improve managerial decision making

decline phase the period in which sales of the product decline, either because of reduced consumer demand for that type of product or because competitors are gaining market share

decreasing term insurance provides insurance benefits to a beneficiary that decrease over time

defensive pricing the act of reducing product prices to defend (retain) market share

deintegration strategy of delegating some production tasks to suppliers

demand schedule a schedule that indicates the quantity of the product that would be demanded at each possible price

demand-pull inflation prices of products and services are pulled up because of strong consumer demand

demographics characteristics about the human population or specific segments of the population

departmentalize assign tasks and responsibilities to different departments

depreciates weakens in value

depreciation a reduction in the value of the assets to reflect deterioration in assets over time

derivative instruments instruments whose values are derived from values of other securities, indexes, or interest rates

design represents the size and structure of the plant or office

direct channel a producer of a product deals directly with a customer

direct foreign investment (DFI) means of acquiring or building subsidiaries in one or more foreign countries

distributorship a firm in which a dealer is allowed to sell a product produced by a manufacturer

divestiture the sale of an existing business by the firm

dividend policy decision regarding how much of the firm's quarterly earnings should be retained (reinvested in the firm), versus distributed as dividends to owners

dividends income that the firm provides to its owners

downsizing an attempt by a firm to cut expenses by eliminating job positions

downsizing the act of reducing the number of employees

E

earnings after taxes the earnings before taxes minus taxes

earnings before interest and taxes (EBIT) the earnings before interest and taxes minus interest expenses

economic growth the change in the general level of economic activity

economies of scale as the quantity produced increases, the cost per unit decreases

electronic computer a device capable of processing and storing vast quantities of information

electronic data interchange (EDI) allows the computers of two or more companies to communicate directly with each other

employee benefits additional privileges beyond compensation payments such as a paid vacation; health, life, or dental insurance; and pension programs

employment test a written test of each candidate's abilities

empowerment allows employees power to make more decisions

entrepreneurs people who organize, manage, and assume the risk of starting a business

equilibrium interest rate the interest rate at which the quantity of loanable funds supplied is equal to the quantity of loanable funds demanded

equilibrium price the price of a product at which the quantity of the product supplied by firms equals the quantity of the product demanded by customers

equity financing the act of receiving investment from owners (by issuing stock or retaining earnings)

equity the total investment by the firm's stockholders

equity theory compensation should be equitable, or in proportion to each employee's contribution

espionage process of illegally gathering information

esteem needs respect, prestige, and recognition

excise taxes imposed on the production of particular products by the federal government

exclusive distribution the use of only one or a few outlets

expectancy theory employee's efforts are influenced by the expected outcome (reward) for those efforts

exporting the sale of products or services (called exports) to purchasers residing in other countries

extension provides additional time for the firm to generate the necessary cash to cover its payments

external recruiting an effort to fill positions with applicants outside the firm

F

family branding branding of all or most products produced by a company

fashion obsolescence no longer in fashion

Federal Reserve System the central bank of the United States

federal budget deficit when the amount of federal government spending exceeds the amount of federal taxes and other revenue received by the federal government

file servers one or more machines that store and provide access to centralized data

finance companies typically obtain funds by issuing debt securities (IOUs) and lend most of their funds to firms

finance means by which firms obtain and use funds for their business operations

financial accounting accounting performed for reporting purposes

fiscal policy decisions on how the federal government should set tax rates and spend money

fixed assets assets that will be used by a firm for more than one year

fixed cost the cost of production that remains unchanged regardless of how many units are produced

fixed costs represent operating expenses that do not change in response to the number of products produced

fixed-position layout employees go to the position of the product, rather than waiting for the product to come to them

flexible manufacturing a production process

that can be easily adjusted to accommodate future revisions

flextime programs programs that allow for a more flexible work schedule

floppy disks removable secondary storage

flotation costs costs paid to investment banks for their advising, their efforts to sell the securities, printing expenses, and registration fees

forward contract states an exchange of currencies that will occur at a specified exchange rate at a future point in time

forward rate the exchange rate that the bank would be willing to offer at a future point in time

franchise arrangement whereby a business owner allows others to use its trademark, trade name or copyright, under specific conditions

franchisee firm that is allowed to use the trade name or copyright of a franchise

franchisor firm that allows others to use its trade name of copyright, under specified conditions

free-rein leadership style that delegates much authority to employees

frictional unemployment people who are between jobs

full-service retail store generally offers help in the purchase of products and provides servicing if necessary

G

Gantt chart illustrates the expected timing for each task within the production process

general partners partners who manage the business, receive a salary, share the profits or losses of the business, and have unlimited liability

general partnership all partners have unlimited liability

generic brand products not branded by the producer or the store

gigabytes billions of characters

going public the act of initially issuing stock to the public

gross domestic product (GDP) the total market value of all final products and services produced in the United States

gross profit is equal to net sales minus the cost of goods sold

growth phase the period in which sales of the product increase rapidly

H

hard disks sealed magnetic disks

hardware the physical components of a computer

hedge action taken to protect a firm against exchange rate movements

hierarchy of needs needs are ranked in five general categories. Once a given category of needs is achieved, people become motivated to reach the next category

horizontal merger combination of businesses that engage in the same types of business

hotelling (just-in-time office) firm provides an office with a desk, a computer, and a telephone for any employee who normally works at home but needs to use work space at the firm

human resource manager helps each specific department recruit candidates for its open positions

human resource planning the act of planning to satisfy a firm's needs for employees

hygiene factors work-related factors perceived to be inadequate

I

importing represents the purchase of foreign products or services

incentive plans provide employees with various forms of compensation if they meet specific performance goals

income statement indicates the revenue, costs, and earnings of firms over a period of time

indenture a legal document that explains the firm's obligations to bondholders

independent retail store has only one outlet

independent the decision of whether to adopt one project has no bearing on the adoption of other projects

individual branding assign a unique brand name to different products or groups of products

industrial markets exist for industrial products that are purchased by firms (such as plastic and steel)

industrial unions organized for a specific industry

industry advertising a nonpersonal sales presentation about a specific industry

industry demand total demand for the products in the industry

inflation the increase in the general level of prices of products and services over a specified period of time

infomercials commercials that are televised separately rather than within a show

informal organizational structure an informal communications network among a firm's employees

information systems include information technology, people, and procedures that work together to provide appropriate information to the firm's employees so they can make business decisions

initial public offering (IPO) the first issue of stock to the public

initiative the willingness to take action

injunction a court order to prevent the union from a particular activity such as picketing

inside board members board members who are also managers of the same firm

institutional advertising a nonpersonal sales presentation about a specific institution

institutional investors financial institutions that purchase large amounts of stock

insurance companies receive insurance premiums from selling insurance to customers, and invest the proceeds until the funds are needed to pay insurance claims

intensive distribution distribute the product across most or all possible outlets

interest rate swap allows a firm to swap fixed interest payments for payments that adjust to movements in interest rates

internal auditors specialize in evaluating various divisions of a business to ensure that they are operating efficiently

internal recruiting an effort to fill open positions with persons already employed by the firm

international licensing agreement type of alliance in which a firm allows a foreign company (called the "licensee") to produce its products according to specific instructions

international unions include members that work in other countries

interorganizational systems (IOS) employ computers and telecommunications technology to move information across the boundaries of the firm

interpersonal skills the skills necessary to communicate with customers and employees

intrapreneurship assignment of particular employees of a firm to create ideas, as if they were entrepreneurs who were running their own firms

introduction phase the initial period in which consumers are informed about the product

inventory control the process of managing inventory at a level that minimizes costs

inventory management determines the amount of inventory that is held

J

job analysis the analysis used to determine the tasks and the necessary credentials for a particular position

job description states the tasks and responsibilities of the job position

job enlargement program to expand (enlarge) the jobs assigned to employees

job rotation allows a set of employees to periodically rotate their job assignments

job satisfaction degree to which employees are satisfied with their jobs

job sharing two or more persons may share a particular work schedule

job specification states the credentials necessary to qualify for the job position

joint venture an agreement between two firms about a specific project

just-in-time (JIT) system that attempts to reduce materials inventories to a bare minimum by frequently ordering small amounts of materials

L

labor union established to represent the views, needs, and concerns of labor

Landrum-Griffin Act required labor unions to specify in their bylaws the membership eligibility requirements, dues, and collective bargaining procedures

layout represents the arrangement of the machinery and equipment within the factory or office

leading the process of influencing the habits of others to achieve a common goal

leasing renting the assets for a specified period of time

less-developed countries countries that have relatively low technology

leveraged buyout a purchase of a company (or the subsidiary of the company) by a group of investors with borrowed funds

liability anything owed by a firm

liability losses financial losses due to the firm's actions that cause damages to others or to their property

limited liability company (LLC) a firm that has all the favorable features of a typical general partnership but also offers limited liability for the partners

limited partners partners whose liability is limited

limited partnership a firm that has some limited partners

line of credit an agreement that allows access to borrowed funds upon demand over some specified period

line organization an organization chart that contains only line positions and no staff positions

line positions established to make decisions that achieve specific business goals

line-and-staff organization an organizational structure that includes line positions and staff positions and assigns authority from higher-level management to employees

liquid access to funds to pay bills when they come due

liquidation value amount of funds that would be received as a result of the liquidation of the firm

liquidity management means by which short-term assets and liabilities are managed to ensure adequate liquidity

liquidity the firm's ability to meet short-term obligations

local area network (LAN) individual work stations are directly connected by network cabling to the file server

local unions composed of members in a specified local area

lockout prevents employees from working until an agreement between management and labor is reached

macroeconomic conditions reflect the overall U.S. economy

magnetic tapes removable secondary storage

mainframe (multiuser) system uses a single central computer

mainframes large computers used primarily to service entire organizations

management by objectives (MBO) allows employees to participate in setting their goals and determining the manner by which they achieve their tasks

management means by which employees and other resources (such as machinery) are used by the firm

management the utilization of human resources (employees) and other resources (such as machinery) in a manner that best achieves the firm's plans and objectives

managerial accounting the type of accounting performed to provide information to help managers of the firm make decisions

managers employees who are responsible for managing job assignments of other employees and making key business decisions

manufacturing arrangement a firm that is allowed to manufacture a product using the formula provided by another company

market coverage degree of product distribution among outlets

market share a firm's sales as a proportion of the total market

marketing intermediaries firms that participate in moving the product toward the customer

marketing means by which products (or services) are developed, priced, distributed, and promoted to customers

marketing mix the combination of product, pricing, distribution, and promotion strategies used to sell products

marketing research accumulation and analysis of data in order to make a particular marketing decision

marketing the actions of firms to plan and execute the design, pricing, distribution, and promotion of products

massively parallel machines experimental computers with many CPUs that operate simultaneously

materials requirements planning (MRP) a process for ensuring that materials are available when needed

matrix organization the interaction among various parts of the firm to focus on specific projects

maturity phase the period in which competitive products have entered the market, and sales of the product level off because of competition

megabytes millions of characters

megahertz [MHz] millions of cycles per second

merchants become owners of the products and then resell them

merger two firms are merged (or combined) to become a single firm owned by the same owners (shareholders)

merit system allocates raises according to performance (merit)

microeconomic conditions are focused on the business or industry of concern

middle management often responsible for the short-term decisions

mission statement describes the firm's primary goal

modems devices that permit the digital signals inside computers to be transmitted over lines designed primarily for voice communication

monetary policy decisions on the money supply level in the United States

money supply demand deposits (checking accounts), currency held by the public, and travelers checks.

monopoly sole provider of goods or services

motivational factors work-related factors that please employees

mutual funds investment companies that receive funds from individual investors, which they pool and invest in securities

mutually exclusive only one of the projects can be accepted

N

national unions composed of members throughout the country

negative reinforcement motivates employees by encouraging them to behave in a manner that avoids unfavorable consequences

net present value equal to the present value of cash flows minus the initial outlay

net profit margin a measure of net income as a percentage of sales

net sales the total sales adjusted for any discounts

network operating system handles the communications between machines

network system connects individual microcomputers together in ways that allow them to share information

news release a brief written announcement about the firm provided by that firm to the media

Norris-LaGuardia Act allowed unions to publicize a labor dispute

notes payable short-term loans to the firm made by creditors such as banks

O

obsolete less useful than in the past

one-level channel involves one marketing intermediary between the producer and the customer

open-book management educates employees on their contribution to the firm and enables them to periodically assess their own performance levels

operating expenses composed of selling expense and general and administrative expenses

operational planning establishes the methods used for the near future (such as the next year) to achieve the tactical plans

optimization models used to represent situations that have many possible combinations of inputs and outputs

order costs costs involved in placing orders

organization chart a diagram that shows the interaction among employee responsibilities

organizational structures the structure within the firm that identifies responsibilities for each job position and the relationship among those positions

organizing the organization of employees and other resources in a manner that is consistent with the firm's goals

outside board members board members who are high-level managers of other firms

outsourcing act of purchasing parts from a supplier rather than producing the parts

owner's equity includes the par (or stated) value of all common stock issued, additional paid-in capital, and retained earnings

P

par value the amount that the bondholders receive at maturity

participative leadership style that allows the leaders to accept some employee input, but the leaders usually use their authority to make decisions

participative management employees are allowed to participate in various decisions to be made by their supervisors or others

partners co-owners of a business

partnership a business that is co-owned by two or more people

passive resistance users uncomfortable with a new system overstate difficulties associated with learning the tech-nology

patents allow exclusive rights to the production and sale of a specific product

penetration pricing if a firm wants to be sure that it can sell its product, it may set a lower price than those of competitive products to penetrate the market

pension funds receive employee and firm contributions toward pensions and invest the proceeds for the employees until the funds are needed

perquisites additional privileges beyond compensation payments and employee benefits

personal selling a personal sales presentation used to influence one or more consumers

physiological needs the more basic requirements for survival

picketing walking around near the employer's building with signs complaining of poor working conditions

planning represents the preparation of the firm for future business conditions

policies guidelines for how tasks should be completed

political risk the risk that the country's political actions can adversely affect a business

positive reinforcement motivates employees by providing rewards for high performance

predatory pricing firms lower their price to drive out new competitors

preferred stock a security that represents partial ownership of a particular firm and offers specific priorities over common stock

premium a gift or prize provided free to consumers who purchase a specific product

press conference an oral announcement about the firm provided by that firm to the media

prestige pricing firms may use a higher price if their product is intended to have a top-of-the-line image

price skimming the price of the product may initially be set high if no other competitive products are in the market yet

price-elastic the demand for a product is highly responsive to price changes

price-inelastic the demand for a product is not very responsive to price changes

prime rate the rate of interest typically charged on loans to the most creditworthy firms that borrow

private liquidation creditors may informally request that the failing firm liquidate (sell) its assets and distribute the funds received from liquidation to them

private placement the selling of securities to one or a few investors

privately held ownership is restricted to a small group of investors

privatization government-owned businesses sold to private investors

procedures steps necessary to implement a policy

producer brands represent the manufacturer of products

product differentiation effort of a firm to distinguish its product from competitive products in a manner that makes it more desirable

product layout positions the tasks in the sequence that they are assigned

product life cycle the typical set of phases that products experience over their life

product line a set of related products or services offered by a single firm

product mix the assortment of products offered by a firm

product physical goods as well as services that can satisfy consumer needs

production control involves purchasing materials, inventory control, routing, scheduling, quality control

production efficiency the ability to produce products at a low cost

production management (operations management) the management of a process in which resources (such as employees and machinery) are used to produce products and services

production process (conversion process) a series of tasks in which resources are used to produce a product or service

production schedule a plan for the timing and volume of production tasks

profit sharing a portion of the firm's profits that is provided to employees

program evaluation and review technique (PERT) schedules tasks in a manner that will minimize delays in the production process

promotion an assignment of a higher-level job with more responsibility and compensation

promotion budget the amount of funds that have been set aside to pay for all promotion methods over a specified period

promotion mix the combination of promotion methods that a firm uses to increase the acceptance of its products

promotion the act of informing or reminding consumers about a specific product or brand

property insurance protects a firm against the risk associated with the ownership of property, such as buildings and other assets

property losses financial losses resulting from damage to property

prospectus a document that discloses relevant financial information about the securities and financial information about the firm

protective covenants restrictions imposed on specific financial policies of the firm

prototype creation of a working system with limited functionality

public accountants provide accounting services for a variety of firms for a fee

public offering the selling of securities to the public

public relations represent actions taken with the goal of creating or maintaining a favorable public image

publicly held shares can be easily purchased or sold by investors

pull strategy firms direct their promotion directly at the target market, who in turn request the product from wholesalers or producers

push strategy producers direct their promotion of a product at wholesalers or retailers, who in turn promote it to consumers

Q

quality control a process of determining whether the quality of a product meets the desired quality level

quality control circle a group of employees who assess the quality of a product and offer suggestions for improvement

quota limits the amounts of specific products that can be imported

R

random access memory (RAM) space in which to temporarily store information

ratio analysis an evaluation of the relationship between financial statement variables

rebate a potential refund by the manufacturer to the consumer

reengineering the redesign of a firm's organizational structure and operations

reinforcement theory reinforcement can control behavior

reminder advertising intended to remind consumers of product's existence

remote job entry systems systems that allow the user to interact directly with a company's internal systems

restructuring the revision of the production process in an attempt to improve efficiency

return on assets (ROA) measures the net income of the firm as a percentage of the total amount of assets utilized by the firm

return on equity (ROE) earnings as a proportion of the equity

return on equity (ROE) measures the return to the common stockholders (net income) as a percentage of their investment in the firm

right-to-work allows states to prohibit union shops

risk the degree of uncertainty about the firm's future earnings

routing the sequence (or route) of tasks necessary to complete the production of a product

S

S-corporation a partnership that has thirty-five owners or less and satisfies other criteria. The earnings are distributed to the owners and taxed at the respective personal income tax rate of each owner

sabotage destruction of information by a perpetrator

safety needs job security and safe working conditions

salary (or **wages**) represents the dollars paid for a job over a specific period

sales manager individual who manages a group of sales representatives

sales promotion the set of activities that are intended to influence consumers

salvage value amount of money that a firm can receive from selling a project

sampling some of the products produced are randomly selected and tested to determine whether they satisfy the quality standards

sampling the act of offering free samples to encourage consumers to try a new brand or product

savings institutions obtain deposits from individuals and primarily use the deposited funds to provide mortgage loans

scheduling the act of setting time periods for each task in the production process

seasonal unemployment people whose services are needed only on a seasonal basis

secondary market a market where existing securities can be traded among investors

secured bonds bonds backed by collateral

segments subsets of the market that reflect a specific type of business and the perceived quality

selective distribution distribute the product among selected outlets

self-actualization the need to fully reach one's potential

self-insurance a fund is created to cover any future claims

self-service retail store does not provide sales assistance or service, and sells products that do not require much expertise

sexual harassment unwelcome comments or actions of a sexual nature

shareholder activism the active role that stockholders take to influence a firm's management policies

shopping products are not purchased frequently

shortage the quantity supplied by firms is less than the quantity demanded by customers

social needs need to be part of a group

social responsibility firm's recognition of how its business decisions can affect society

socialism an economic system that contains some features of both capitalism and communism

software packages applications purchased off the shelf

software programs that determine the specific tasks a computer will perform at any given time

sole proprietor the owner of a sole proprietorship

sole proprietorship a business owned by a single owner

span of control the number of employees managed by each manager

specialty products considered by specific consumers to be special, which means that these consumers would make a special effort to purchase them

specialty retail store specializes in a particular type of product

spot exchange rate the exchange rate quoted for immediate transactions

spreadsheet program is intended to perform financial analysis

staff positions established to support the efforts of line positions

stand-alone systems consists of one or more computers

statistical analysis applies statistical principles to understanding relationships between data elements and predicting future behaviors

stock certificates of ownership of a business

stock mutual funds investment companies that invest funds received from individual investors in stocks

stockholders investors who wish to become partial owners of firms

store brands represent the retail store where the product is being sold

strategic alliance a business agreement between firms whereby resources are shared to pursue mutual interests

strategic plan intended to identify the firm's main business focus over a long-term period, perhaps three to five years

stretch targets production efficiency targets (or goals) that cannot be achieved under the present conditions

strike discontinuation of employee services

structural unemployment people who are unemployed because they do not have adequate skills

supervisory (first-line) management usually highly involved with the employees who engage in the day-to-day production process

supply schedule a schedule that indicates the quantity of the product that would be supplied (produced) by firms at each possible price

surplus the quantity supplied by firms exceeds the quantity demanded by customers

system architecture the basic logical organization of computers

systems development life cycle (SDLC) involves decomposing a system into its functional components

T

tactical planning smaller scale plans (over one or two years) that are consistent with the firm's strategic (long-term) plan

Taft-Hartley Act an amendment to the Wagner Act, prohibited unions from pressuring employees to join

target market a group of individuals or organizations with similar traits who may purchase a particular product

target market market of customers that fit the customer profile

tariff tax on imported products

teamwork a group of employees with varied job positions are given the responsibility to achieve a specific goal

technological obsolescence inferior to new products

telemarketing the use of telephone for promoting and selling products

tender offer a direct bid by the acquiring firm for the shares of the target firm

term insurance provides insurance for a policyholder only over a specified term and does not build a cash value for policyholders

terminals devices that combine the functions of a monitor and a keyboard

time management the manner by which managers allocate their time when managing tasks

times interest earned ratio measures the ability of the firm to cover its interest payments

top (high-level) management includes positions such as president, chief executive officer, chief financial officer, and vice-president that make decisions regarding the firm's long-run objectives

total quality management (TQM) the act of monitoring and improving the quality of products and services produced

trade deficit amount by which imports exceed exports

trademark a brand whose form of identification is legally protected from use by other firms

Treasury bills short-term debt securities issued by the U.S. Treasury

turnkey system ready for use upon delivery from the vendor

two-level channel two marketing intermediaries are between the producer and the customer

U

underwriting syndicate a group of investment banks that share the obligations of underwriting the securities

underwritten the investment bank guarantees a price to the issuing firm, no matter what price the securities are sold for

universal life insurance combines the features of term and whole-life insurance. It specifies a period of time over which the policy will exist, but builds a cash value for policyholders over time

unlimited liability no limit on the debts for which the owner is liable

unsecured bonds bonds that are not backed by collateral

upward appraisals used to measure the managerial abilities of supervisors

V

variable costs costs that vary with the quantity produced

variable costs operating expenses that vary directly with the number of products produced

variety retail store offers numerous types of goods

venture capital firm composed of individuals who invest in small businesses

vertical channel integration two or more levels of distribution are managed by a single firm

vertical merger combination of a firm with a potential supplier or customer

video conferencing holding meetings between remote sites using sound and pictures transmitted over telecommunications links

virtual reality display techniques, which combine computerized sights, sounds, and sensations to create a sense of actually "being there"

W

Wagner Act prohibited firms from interfering with workers' efforts to organize or join unions

"what-if" analysis generating different potential business scenarios to answer questions

white knight a more suitable company that would be willing to acquire a firm and rescue it from the hostile takeover efforts of some other firm

whole-life insurance life insurance that exists until death or as long as premiums are promptly paid

wide area network (WAN) when telecommunications technologies are employed to connect pieces of the network

winchester drives sealed magnetic disks

word processor program is intended to create documents

work station an area in which one or more employees are assigned a specific task

work stations access the software and data on the file server

work-in-process inventories represent inventories of partially completed products

workgroup software provides a broad array of user-friendly features, such as electronic mail, document management systems, and work-sharing systems

working capital management the management of a firm's short-term assets and liabilities

Y

yellow-dog contract a contract requiring employees to refrain from joining a union as a condition of employment

COMPANY INDEX

Chapter 10 *284*: © Will van Overbeek; *286*: © Kim Newton/Woodfin Camp and Associates, Inc.; *287*: © Will van Overbeek; *290*: Courtesy of the Ford Motor Company; *293*: Courtesy of The Coca-Cola Company; *295*: Courtesy of Wood-Mizer; *296*: © Will van Overbeek; *310*: The Malcolm Baldridge National Quality Award photograph by Steuben.

Chapter 11 *311*: © Francis Li/The Gamma Liaison Network; *312*: Courtesy of Target Stores; *316*: © Doug Menuez/SABA; *317*: © Will van Overbeek; *320*: Al Bello/Allsport; *324*: AP/Wide World Photos. *The Dallas Morning News,* John F. Rhodes; *329*: © Will van Overbeek

Chapter 12 *340*: Courtesy of the Boeing Company; *344*: © Dirck Halstead/The Gamma Liaison Network; *352*: Courtesy of Marriott; *358*: Courtesy of the Dow Chemical Company; *371*: © Jim Graham/The Gamma Liaison Network; *373*: © Will van Overbeek; *374*: Francis Li/The Gamma Liaison Network

Chapter 13 *376*: Courtesy of Taco Bell Corporation; *379*: © Ed Thompson; *382*: Courtesy of Spalding; *390*: © Alex von Rosenberg; *391*: © Phil Matt/The Gamma Liaison Network; *399*: Courtesy of General Motors Corporation

Chapter 14 *410*: Courtesy of Union Pacific Corporation; *412*: © Will van Overbeek; *419*: © Will van Overbeek; *424*: Naoki Okamoto/The Stock Market

Chapter 15 *438*: ChromoSohm/Joe Sohm/Photo Researchers; *441*: Courtesy of Schott Glaswerke, Mainz, Germany; *448*: Courtesy of Wood-Mizer; *449*: Courtesy of Merck and Co., Inc.; *454*: Courtesy of Taco Bell Corp.; *456*: AP/Wide World Photos

Chapter 16 *469*: John Madere/The Stock Market; *470*: Culver Pictures, Inc.; *473*: Courtesy of the AICPA; *479*: © Sergio Dorantes/Sygma

Chapter 17 *494*: Courtesy of Lone Star Steakhouse and Saloon, Inc.; *497*: © Alex von Rosenberg; *499*: Courtesy of Chris Knapp; *503*: © Alex von Rosenberg; *512*: © Grandadam/Tony Stone Images, Inc.

Chapter 18 *522*: © The Gamma Liaison Network; *524*: © Will van Overbeek; *527*: Courtesy of Marriott; *535*: Courtesy of The Coca-Cola Company; *554*: John Madere/The Stock Market

Chapter 19 *555*: © Will van Overbeek; *556*: Courtesy of Roslyn Stendahl/Dapper Design; *559*: © Will van Overbeek; *561*: © Will van Overbeek; *563*: David Frazier/Photo Researchers, Inc.; *573*: Courtesy of Symantex Corporation

Chapter 20 *586*: Charles Gupton/Tony Stone Worldwide; *591*: © Will van Overbeek; *593*: © Miladinovic/Sygma; *595*: © Maiman/Sygma; *597*: © Will van Overbeek; *599*: © Will van Overbeek

Chapter 21 *612*: Courtesy of the Chicago Bulls; *615*: © James Randklev/Tony Stone Images; *617*: Courtesy of Levi Strauss and Co.; *618*: Richard Hutchings/Photo Researchers, Inc.

Feature and Exhibit Credits

Chapter 1   *Small Business Survey, page 12:* Opinion Research Corp. and *The Wall Street Journal,* 22 May 1995, p. R12; *Spotlight on Technology, page 16:* Lance Ulanoff, "Business Tools: The Manager's Toolkit," *PC Magazine* 13, no. 19(1994): 214–18.

Chapter 2   *Small Business Survey, page 47: Inc.,* May 1993, 42; *Exhibit 2.5, page 49: Entrepreneur Magazine* and *Sun Sentinel,* 29 May 1995, p. 7; *Exhibit 2.9, page 53:* Campbell Soup Company 1995 annual report; *Self-Scoring Exercise, page 54:* "Do You Have the Skills Necessary for Achievement" from Nelson and Quick, *Organizational Behavior* © West Publishing Company; *Case 2, page 60:* Andrew E. Serwer, "Trouble in Franchise Nation," *Fortune,* 6 March 1995, pp. 115–29; *Exhibit 2.13, page 65:* Copyright 1995. *USA TODAY.* Reprinted with permission.

Chapter 3   *Exhibit 3.3, page 72:* Bureau of Labor Statistics and *USA Today,* May 15 1995, 3B; *Exhibit 3.5, page 77: Business Week,* 22 April, 1996, 102; *Spotlight on Technology, page 82:* "Frontier Airlines, Inc. (A)" Harvard Business School Case 9-189-074; "A Note on Airline Reservation Systems," Harvard Business School Case 9-189-098; *Self-Scoring Exercise, page 83:* J. B. Cullen, B. Victor, and C. Stephens, "An Ethical Weather Report: Assessing the Organization's Ethical Climate." Reprinted with permission of publisher, from *Organizational Dynamics,* Autumn/1989, copyright 1989. American Management Association, New York. All rights reserved; *Self-Scoring Exercise, page 84:* Issues adapted from J. O. Cherrington and D. J. Cherrington, "A Menu of Moral Issues One Week in the Life of the *Wall Street Journal,*" *Journal of Business Ethics* 11(1992): 225–265. Reprinted by permission of Kluwer Academic Publishers; *Surfing the Net, page 87:* Richard Scoville, "Find It on the Net," *PC World,* January 1996, 125–130.

Chapter 4   *Exhibit 4.1,* page 105: Federal Reserve Bulletin; *Exhibit 4.2,* page 106: Federal Reserve Bulletin; *Spotlight on Technology, page 119:* T. Grandon Gill. *American Financial Network, Inc. (A).* Florida Atlantic University, DIS Department case study; *Case 2, page 125:* Gabriella Stern and Rebecca Blumenstein, "Out of Reverse," *The Wall Street Journal,* 15 January 1996.

Chapter 5   *Small Business Survey, page 141:* "The State of Small Business," *Inc.,* 1995, 78; *Exhibit 5.5, page 144: Business Week,* 14 August 1995; *Case 1, page 155:* Don Clark, "Software Makers Are Expected to Post Solid Profit Gains for December Quarter," *The Wall Street Journal,* January 1996.

Chapter 6   *Exhibit 6.2, page 165:* U.S. Department of Labor, Bureau of Labor Statistics, December 1994; *Exhibit 6.5, page 170:* Federal Reserve Bulletin; *Global Business, page 171:* Adapted from C. Barnum and N. Wolniansky, "Taking Cues from Body Language," *Management Review* 78 (1989): 59. Adapted by permission of publisher, from *Management Review,* June 1989, © 1989. American Management Association, New York. All rights reserved. And from E. Ferrieux, Le Point, *World Press Review,* July 1989. Used with permission; *Spotlight on Technology, page 180:* AUCNET: TV Auction Network System. Harvard Business School Case #9-190-001. 1990; *Case 2, page 189:* Rosanna Tamburri, "Washington, Ottawa Near Timber Pact That May Lift U.S. Home-Building Costs." *The Wall Street Journal,* December 1995.

Chapter 7   *Case 2, page 224:* Jeffrey Tannenbaum, "Planet Hollywood Founder Sees a World Full of Theme Cafes," *The Wall Street Journal,* 12 December 1995.

Chapter 8 *Self-Scoring Exercise, page 237:* Danny Miller and Cornelia Droge, "Psychological and Traditional Determinants of Structure" Figure Only, Vol. 31, No. 4 (December 1986), page 558, © *Administrative Science Quarterly; Case 2, page 251:* Jim Carlton, "Apple's CEO Says Problems Are Fixable," *The Wall Street Journal,* 20 February 1996.

Chapter 9 *Case 2, page 278:* Robert L. Rose, "A Productivity Push at Wabash National Puts Firm on a Roll," *The Wall Street Journal,* 7 September 1995.

Chapter 10 *Self-Scoring Exercise, page 291:* "Are You A Highly Satisfied Customer?" from Nelson and Quick, *Organizational Behavior,* © West Publishing Company; *Exhibit 10.4, page 301:* Challenger, Gray & Christmas Inc.; *Case 1, page 305:* Michael Barrier, "Who Should Get How Much—And Why?" *Nation's Business,* November 1995, 58–59; *Case 2, page 305:* Christina Del Valle, "Total Quality Management: Now, It's a Class Act," *Business Week,* October 1994.

Chapter 11 *Self-Scoring Exercise, page 327:* Survey-Feedback-Action (SFA) Federal Express Company, Memphis, TN; *Small Business Survey, page 328:* Survey by Richard Freeman (London School of Economics) and Joel Rogers (University of Wisconsin), 1995; *Case 2, page 335:* Bruce Tulgan, *Human Resources Focus,* November 1995.

Chapter 12 *Small Business Survey, page 348: Inc.,* January 1994, 96; *Small Business Survey, page 351:* Survey of Small Business CEOs, Executive Committee, San Diego, March 1993; *Spotlight on Technology, page 353:* T. Grandon Gill, "High Tech Hidebound: Case Studies of Information Technologies That Inhibited Organizational Learning," *Accounting Management and Information Technologies* 1, no. 5(1995): 41–60; *Exhibit 12.6, page 354:* Adapted from R. S. Schuler and S. E. Jackson, *Human Resource Management,* 6th ed. (St. Paul: West Publishing, 1996), 370; *Exhibit 12.7, page 355:* Adapted from R. S. Schuler and S. E. Jackson, *Human Resource Management,* 6th ed. (St. Paul: West Publishing, 1996), 412; *Case 2, page 362:* Michael Barrier, "Closing the Skills Gap," *Nation's Business,* March 1996, 26–28; *Self-Scoring Exercise, page 369:* Questionnaire developed by C. D. Spielberger. Appeared in W. Barnhill, "Early Warning," *The Washington Post,* August 11, 1992, B5. Reprinted from *The Washington Post* (Aug. 11, 1992) with the permission of Dr. Charles D. Spielberger.

Chapter 13 *Exhibit 13.3, page 382: The Wall Street Journal,* 29 March 1995, B1; *Small Business Survey, page 385: Inc.,* June 1995, 88; *Exhibit 13.4, page 386:* Standard & Poor's *Compustat* and *Business Week,* 3 July 1995, 79; *Case 2, page 404: Fortune,* 12 June 1995, © 1995 Time, Inc.

Chapter 14 *Small Business Survey, page 417: Inc.,* January 1995, 90; *Spotlight on Technology, page 428:* "The Gillette Company: Evolution of Electronic Data Interchange Strategy (A)," Harvard Business School Case 9-191-010; "A Note on Electronic Data Interchange," Harvard Business School Case 9-190-022; *Case 1, page 432:* Trisha Collopy "Comics Distributor, Publisher Knows Information Is Power," *Baltimore Business Journal,* 20 October 1995, sec. 1 Y13, N22; *Case 2, page 433:* © West 1996.

Chapter 15 *Exhibit 15.6, page 445:* McCann-Erickson and Standard and Poor's Industry Survey, April 1995, M15; *Small Business Survey, page 450: Inc.,* December 1992, 27; *Case 1, page 462: The Wall Street Journal,* January 1996; *Case 2, page 462: Forbes,* 24 April 1995.

Chapter 16   *Case 1, page 489:* Michael Knapp, *Financial Accounting: Focus on Decision Making* (St. Paul: West Publishing, 1996), 107; *Case 2, page 489:* Michael Knapp, *Financial Accounting: Focus on Decision Making* (St. Paul: West Publishing, 1996), 97.

Chapter 17   *Exhibit 17.10, page 513: Moody's Handbook of Common Stocks; Case 2, page 518:* Sidney Rutberg, David Moin, Valerie Seckler, and Stan Gellers, *Women's Wear Daily,* 7 March 1996, 12.

Chapter 18   *Exhibit 18.2, page 526:* PepsiCo 1994 Annual Report; *Spotlight on Technology, page 534:* "Texas Instruments Capital Investment Expert System," Harvard Business School Case 9-188-050; *Small Business Survey, page 541: Inc.,* April 1994, 114; *Case 1, page 545:* Steven Lipin, Jim Carlton, Douglas Lavin, David P. Hamilton, "Packard Bell to Receive Case Infusion in $650 Million Accord with Bull," NEC, *The Wall Street Journal,* 7 February 1996.

Chapter 19   *Case 1, page 580:* Neal Weinberg, "Telecom Managers Feel Squeeze," *Computerworld,* 20 November 1995; *Case 2, page 580:* Peter Coy, "The New Realism in Office Systems—Computers Can't Take the Place of Good Management—But They Can Help," *Business Week,* 15 June 1992.

Chapter 20   *Small Business Survey, page 598: Inc.,* April 1995, 112.

Chapter 21   *Small Business Survey, page 619:* "The State of Small Business," *Inc.,* 1995, 79; *Case 1, page 634:* Marshall Loeb, *Fortune,* 20 March 1995; *Case 2, page 634:* Michael Knapp, *Financial Accounting: Focus on Decision Making* (St. Paul: West Publishing, 1996), 62.

Appendix A   *Exhibit A.3, page 643: Forbes,* 18 December 1995, 302; *Self-Scoring Exercise, page 648:* VALIC (The Variable Annuity Life Insurance Company)®.

Appendix B   *Exhibit B.1, page 658: Fortune,* 26 June 1995, 82–84; *Exhibit B.2, page 662: The Wall Street Journal,* 27 February 1995, R7; *Self-Scoring Exercise, page 665:* T. Jackson, *Not Just Another Job: How to Invent a Career That Works for You* (New York Times Books, 1992), 194; *Exhibit B.5, page 667: Fortune,* 18 September 1995, 53; *Exhibit B.6, page 668: Business Education Forum,* April 1993, 23–26.